A DOCUMENTARY HISTORY OF

The Negro People in the United States

A DOCUMENTARY HISTORY

OF

The Negro People in the United States

1951–1959

Volume 6
From the Korean War to the
Emergence of Martin Luther King, Jr.

Edited by
HERBERT APTHEKER

Preface by
HENRY LOUIS GATES, JR.

A Citadel Press Book
Published by Carol Publishing Group

A Citadel Press Book
Published by Carol Publishing Group
Citadel Press is a registered trademark of Carol Communications, Inc.

Editorial Offices: 600 Madison Avenue, New York, N.Y. 10022
Sales & Distribution Offices: 120 Enterprise Avenue, Secaucus, N.J. 07094
In Canada: Canadian Manda Group, P.O. Box 920, Station U, Toronto,
    Ontario M8Z 5P9
Queries regarding rights and permissions should be addressed to
Carol Publishing Group, 600 Madison Avenue, New York, N.Y. 10022

Carol Publishing Group books are available at special discounts
for bulk purchases, for sales promotions, fund-raising, or
educational purposes. Special editions can be created to
specifications. For details contact: Special Sales Department,
Carol Publishing Group, 120 Enterprise Avenue, Secaucus, N.J. 07094

Manufactured in the United States of America

10 9 8 7 6 5 4 3 2 1

Library of Congress Cataloging-in-Publication Data

Aptheker, Herbert, 1915–
   A documentary history of the Negro people
in the United States.

   Vols.   have imprint : Secaucus, NJ : Carol
Pub. Group; also have statement : A Citadel
Press book.
   Contents : [1. 1661-1910]—[etc.]—v. 5
From the end of the Second World War to the
Korean War.—v. 6. From the Korean War to
the emergence of Martin Luther King, Jr.
   1. Afro-Americans—History—Sources.
I. Title.
E185.A58   973'.0496073   51-14828
ISBN 0-8065-1431-0

Contents

Preface

Herbert Aptheker was born in Brooklyn, New York, July 31, 1915. He received three degrees from Columbia University: a B.S. in 1936, an A.M. in 1937, and a Ph.D. in 1953. He has been awarded honorary degrees by Martin Luther King University and the University of Halle. He served in the U.S. Army from 1942 till 1946 and was discharged with the rank of major.

Dr. Aptheker has received awards from the Guggenheim Foundation, the Social Science Research Council, the Rabinowitz Foundation, and the American Council of Learned Societies. He has been editor of *Masses and Mainstream* and *Political Affairs*. He has been a visiting lecturer at University of California at Berkeley Law School, Bryn Mawr, Yale, and the University of Massachusetts. He served for many years as the director of the American Institute of Marxist Studies. He was one of W. E. B. Du Bois's closest friends and was chosen by Dr. Du Bois to be his literary executor.

Aptheker's published books and pamphlets include:

1938	*The Negro in the Civil War*
1939	*American Negro Slave Revolts*
1940	*The Negro in the American Revolution*
1941	*The Negro in the Abolitionist Movement*
1945	*Essays in the History of the American Negro*
1948	*To Be Free: Studies in American Negro History*
1951–1974	*Documentary History of the Negro People in the United States* (3 vols.)
1954	*Lauriats of Imperialism*
1955	*History and Reality*
1955	*Era of McCarthyism*
1956	*Toward Negro Freedom*
1957	*The Truth About Hungary*
1959–1960	*History of the American People* (2 vols.)

ix

1985   *Against Racism,* ed.

1987   *Racism, Imperialism, Peace*

1989   *The Literary Legacy of W. E. B. Du Bois,* ed.

1989   *Abolitionism, a Revolutionary Movement*

1992   *Antiracism in U.S. History*

I first encountered Herbert Aptheker's name in an undergraduate survey course in Afro-American history taught at Yale in the 1969–1970 academic year by William McFeely. I was a sophomore. We read Professor Aptheker's *American Negro Slave Revolts.* I was astonished to learn both that the slaves had resisted slavery, so consistently and so nobly, and that most other historians had completely ignored these acts of resistance.

As I matured as a student, I read more and more of Dr. Aptheker's considerable list of works, relying upon him increasingly as one of the principal commentators on the African experience in America. When his monumental complete edition of Du Bois's works was published, I managed to find the savings to purchase it, and I read it straight through.

Had he published these volumes alone, his reputation as a judicious scholar and as a meticulous editor would have been secure.

Shortly after the Du Bois editions appeared, Dr. Aptheker was the victim of a pernicious attempt by certain members of the History Department at Yale to block him from teaching a "college seminar" course there. Because they were unable to state publicly any sound reason for refusing to authorize the course, many of my fellow faculty members at Yale felt that Dr. Aptheker was being censored for ideological reasons. So we noisily protested the actions of the History Department and found an alternate sponsor, and the course was offered. When I became the chairman of the Department of Afro-American Studies at Harvard, one of the first scholars I invited to lecture here was Dr. Aptheker.

The Documentary History of the Negro People in the United States brings together most of the germinal pieces of writing created by Afro-Americans reflecting on their condition as Afro-Americans in a racist state. These volumes, now grown to six with the publication of *A Documentary History of the Negro People in the United States, 1945–1951, volume 5, From the End of World War II to the Korean War* and *A Documentary History of the Negro People in the United States, 1951–1959, volume 6, From the Korean War to the Emergence of Martin*

Luther King, Jr., are indispensable to a full understanding of African-American history. Dr. Aptheker's editorial apparatus is superb. These volumes are essential reading for all students and scholars of Afro-American Studies.

Henry Louis Gates, Jr.

Introduction

THE FIRST VOLUME of this *Documentary History* appeared in 1951; it ended with the founding of the National Association for the Advancement of Colored People (NAACP), in 1910. Other volumes brought the drama to the closing year of the Second World War (1945).

The present volume begins with that year. (One hopes that will be the last World War.) Its structure, like the predecessors, is chronological, but the first five documents cover several years prior to and after this volume. This is done in an effort to convey a sense of the sweep of the period.

As in the previous volumes, the words come from African-American people themselves, with rare exceptions whose need will appear to the reader. The only changes made were corrections in typographical errors.

The fifteen years preceding the explosion of the 1960s tend to be neglected in the available literature. They were, however, momentous, and the reader will see how they prepared the foundation for the 1960s.

In the preparation of this book, the aid offered by David Fathi and Katharine Gelles has been invaluable. As has been true for over fifty years, the critical assistance of my wife, Fay, has been crucial.

A DOCUMENTARY HISTORY OF

The Negro People in the United States

SUMMARY JUSTICE—THE NEGRO GI IN KOREA (1951)

by Thurgood Marshall

Thurgood Marshall, at this time NAACP special counsel, spent five weeks in January and February 1951 investigating conditions facing African-American soldiers in Korea.

Thirty-nine Negro American soldiers convicted and sentenced by courts-martial held in Korea asked the NAACP to represent them. All, beginning with Lt. Leon A. Gilbert, who received sentence of death on September 6, had pleaded "Not Guilty." When we examined records of the trials, we knew something was very wrong.

These soldiers were members of the 24th Infantry Regiment. This Regiment won the first notable United Nations' victory in retaking the rail and highway city of Yechon on July 28 after a bloody sixteen hour battle. At Bloody Peak, its Third Battalion fought its way up and down the mountain several times in the face of superior enemy fighting power, with whole companies being wiped out. Despite staggering casualties, these infantry-men fought on until they took Bloody Peak and held it.

And yet, we were faced with a large number of courts-martial cases involving Negroes, with conviction for cowardice, for desertion, for misbehavior in the presence of the enemy and other serious offenses. It seemed hard to believe that these men could change over from heroes to cowards, all within a few days, even under the violent pressures of warfare.

Letters from the men insisted they had been treated unfairly. In most cases there was no dispute between the prosecution and the defense on points of law, but versions of the facts given by witnesses varied widely.

We needed facts. It would do little good to submit appeals for review of these trials unless we found out everything we could about each individual case. And the place to get the facts was across the Pacific.

At first, General MacArthur refused permission for me to go to Tokyo, where the prisoners were. He sent a cable which read:

Not the slightest evidence exists here of discrimination as alleged. As I think you know in this command there is no slightest bias of its various members because of race, color or other distinguishing characteristics. Every soldier in this command is measured on a completely uniform basis with the sole criteria his efficiency and his character. Nevertheless, on receipt of your message I at once ordered the Inspector General to make thorough investigation of your charges and will be glad to have you forward here any evidence in your possession bearing upon the matter.

In any individual trial a soldier can obtain special counsel to defend him if he so desires. In such individual trial there would of course be no objection to Thurgood Marshall representing the accused and coming to this command for such purpose. You understand of course that courts martial are convened by the Major Subordinate Commander in Korea and the hearings are conducted there.

Decision No Help

This decision of MacArthur's was certainly no help to the men who had already been condemned, and we were continuing to receive requests from others who had been convicted under questionable circumstances. We did not hear of these trials until long after they took place, so the General's willingness to have me represent men who might be accused in the future was not encouraging. That same afternoon Walter White, executive secretary of the NAACP, sent another cable to MacArthur, urging reconsideration of its decision, and said:

Examination of courts martial records indicates many convicted under circumstances making impartial justice improbable.

He also forwarded a memorandum of twenty-three cases of individual soldiers, and requested a conference between General MacArthur, the Inspector General, and myself. On December 24, MacArthur cabled that there was "no objection" to such a conference.

Immediately after my arrival in Tokyo on January 14, General MacArthur ordered that I be given the fullest cooperation from everyone under his command. My work was to be carried on through the office of the Inspector General. The most complete cooperation possible was forthcoming throughout my stay.

I must emphasize that every consideration was shown me. But it helped reveal how little consideration had been given to men who had risked their lives for their country.

All the condemned men were confined in a stockade outside Tokyo. I was permitted to see every man I wanted to, as many times as I liked, and with complete privacy. Altogether, I saw about eighty men. I talked to Lt. Gilbert half a dozen times, and to some of the others several times. It was possible to get each man's story, as he wanted to tell it, asking him to explain any questionable or obscure details. All the information which had been lacking in the courts-martial records became available for checking—names of witnesses, dates, times of day, places—everything a defense lawyer should have when a man's life is at stake.

Further Investigation

Each day a list of all points which warranted further investigation was submitted to the Inspector General. Inquiry into these detailed points would begin that very day, so that this checking process moved along only a few days behind my questioning.

I then went back and did my own checking on stories that did not quite fit together. In this way it was possible to separate hearsay from facts. It helped distinguish exaggerated statements from the facts, and to document these facts whenever possible.

In many cases, charges were made or strengthened by officers whose statements in the records of the trials called for extremely careful checking. It wasn't possible for some of the things they said to be true. And yet, to find out where they now were required use of the Locator File in the huge six-story Dai Ichi building which was MacArthur's Far East Command headquarters. I hate to think how many times it turned out that the officer had been killed in action. Back in August, September, and October of 1950 the casualty rate was terribly high.

After three weeks of this process, I made a preliminary report to General MacArthur and General Hickey, his chief of staff. This was at a conference in the Dai Ichi building at night. I told them what had been found so far in my investigation, what I believed to be the cause of these courts-martial trials, and who, in my opinion, was to blame.

Went to Korea

Then I told General MacArthur I wanted to go to Korea, and they made arrangements for the same complete cooperation that had been given to me in Tokyo.

All through my inquiry in Korea I was allowed to see anybody I needed to see. From the beginning to the end of that part of my trip a Deputy Inspector General, Colonel D. D. Martin, accompanied me. With his authority and with my published orders from MacArthur, we could open any door. And we did. Whenever I could more easily get what was needed by myself, I would arrange to go alone. This was wholly satisfactory to Colonel Martin.

Since the 24th Infantry Regiment is part of the 25th Division, which is a part of the 8th Army, we first flew to the 8th Army headquarters in Korea. There I talked with officers at the top level and men in the lower echelons to get some further idea of what was going on.

Next we went to the 25th Division headquarters. A whole day was spent getting the stories of the officers who served as defense counsel in the courts-martial cases. Although it is obvious to any lawyer that the cases were prepared in extreme haste, not a single one of these men would admit he did not have sufficient time to prepare his cases properly.

Their legal abilities cannot be questioned. The letter of the military law was observed in nearly every instance.

What Happened

What actually happened in virtually every case was that a defendant would be confronted by two officers, who told him they were assigned to serve as his counsel. Then, observing the letter of military law, they would tell the prisoner, *"You are allowed to choose your own counsel if there is anyone you prefer."*

"Then I want Captain A," the accused man would say.

They'd be sorry, but Captain A was busy right now in a fire fight with North Korean forces on his Main Line of Resistance. His company needed him.

"What about Lieutenant B?" the prisoner would ask.

It was regrettable, but Lieutenant B was up on a ridge with his platoon and could not possibly be disturbed because the enemy was threatening to engulf the whole situation. While the accused man was assured of counsel of his choice, the court-assigned counsel advised him to choose them. The trial was going to begin very shortly. He's been charged with a serious offense, and he needed counsel. Captain A and Lieutenant B were away, and they—the two assigned-counsel—were right there. So was the trial.

In numerous instances the counsel spent no more than fifteen or twenty minutes with the men about to be tried. There were cases when a man was pulled out of his foxhole—told to get out of his blanket, get dressed and ride to Pusan. He'd arrive in Pusan in the middle of the night, be allowed to go to sleep for a while on the court-room floor, only to wake up for his trial to be held then and there.

Since these officers had no wish to endanger their careers, they certainly were not going to concede that there had been insufficient time to prepare the cases properly.

Main Question

The following day we rode by jeep to the rear headquarters of the 24th Infantry Regiment. Although this area was called "in the rear" you could hear our artillery firing way behind you. Later we went up to the forward headquarters, where you use a jeep without any springs so as not to mar the accuracy of the 35 and 50 caliber machine guns mounted on them. We were all issued weapons, since an estimated one thousand guerrillas were still at large in the country we went through. The cold air was raw and biting, but we used an uncovered jeep, because the officers with us preferred to be in the open, where they were more likely to see what they ran into on all sides.

It became apparent that we would have to consult the official records to prove what had actually happened to the regiment during those three months last summer and fall. The files we needed were kept at the 25th Division's rear. We hitchhiked a ride back to Pusan, far behind the lines, then took another jeep to———(place withheld, by military request). There we found the Division Judge Advocate's office.

In a single room were the investigation reports, military order, and complete files of courts-martial records. Anything connected with any case was available for scrutiny. Here was the precise information, available nowhere else on earth, affecting the condemned soldiers.

The 24th Infantry had been up in the front lines for 93 straight days. Two white regiments were also fighting as long, one of them for 95 days. During that time the ratio of troops of the entire 25th Division serving in Korea, by race, was one Negro to 3.6 white men.

Officers White

The 24th Regiment was the same kind of Negro regiment the Army had maintained since 1865. All enlisted men were Negroes, but for the most part the officers above the level of lieutenant were white. As was apparent from my visits to the Locator File in Tokyo, the casualty rate for these officers and their replacements were extremely high. Although many of these officers were dead, they and many of their successors were responsible for the facts revealed by a comparative table drawn up to show how differently Negro and white defendants were treated by courts-martial proceedings.

A court martial begins with a complaint—usually made by an officer. The commanding officer either arrests the man or allows him to go free. An investigation, by another designated officer, ascertains whether the official charges are well founded.

In the 25th Division, between the time of Lt. Gilbert's conviction on September 6 and my visit in late February, there was a total of 118 complaints filed for all types of offenses. Of these, 82 resulted in trials, the rest being either withdrawn or dropped.

Out of the 82 cases which resulted in general court-martial trials 54 were Negroes, 27 were white, and one was Japanese. In these 82 cases, 66 were investigated by white officers and 16 were investigated by Negro officers.

Most of the charges filed against Negroes—60 of them—were for violation of the 75th Article of War, misbehavior in the presence of the enemy. This means cowardice. In Army life there is no more serious charge.

In the files were complaints against white soldiers for sleeping on their posts during guard duty, up on the front lines within spitting distance of the enemy. But they were not charged with any violation of the 75th Article of War. They were charged with sleeping on their posts. White boys were charged with leaving a sentry post and sleeping on duty who did not even put up a defense, and they were acquitted. One man was found wrapped up in a blanket sound asleep. In this case, his commanding officer testified, "*I saw him there and he was sleeping.*" One witness testified he didn't *think* the man was asleep. Other witnesses took the stand all saying the boy was asleep. One sergeant testified, "*I was right there. I not only saw him, but I heard him. If he wasn't sleeping, he was snoring while wide awake.*"

This accused soldier was acquitted, found not guilty.

100 Percent White

Was it a coincidence that all the commanding officers who approved charges were white, that the entire staffs of the Inspector General's office, and of the trial Judge Advocate's office were 100 percent white? Was it also purely coincidental that one week before my visit to Korea a Negro was added to each of these two staffs?

Here is a summary of the actual results of courts-martial in Korea for alleged violation of the 75th Article of War:

	Negro	White
Charges withdrawn	23	2
Charges reduced to AWOL	1	0
Acquittals	4	4
Sentenced	32	2
	60	8

These are the sentences given to the defendants:

	Negro	White
Death	1	0
Natural Life	15	0
50 years	1	0
25 years	2	0
20 years	3	0
15 years	1	0
10 years	7	0
5 years	2	1
3 years	0	1
	32	2

The white defendant who got the worst sentence (five years) offered as his defense that he was a chronic drunkard, but this sentence has been since reduced to one year.

The investigation-reports, all kept as official records by the Army, revealed that no credence was ever given to the story each individual accused man would tell. The investigating officers totally ignored the statements of the men about to be charged with the worst offenses in the Army code. Scant effort was made to find out what was true and what was not. I had not only talked to these men, but had the benefit of the investigations made by the Judge Advocate's officers to check what stories could be proved.

The Men

And what actually happened? Who were the individuals condemned to serve out their lives in army prisons, or endure terms of 10, 15, 20, 25 and 50 years at hard labor for being cowards?

One boy convicted of cowardice had enlisted when he was fifteen. He remained in that bloody, frozen Korean fighting without telling anybody he was under age, knowing full well that he could at any time be returned to the United States as a hero. This coward remained in the front lines of his own free choice until he was confronted with court-martial charges. We checked, and found he told the truth. His 18th birthday occurred 11 days after his court martial convicted him of being a coward.

One unit of the 159th Field Artillery consisting of Negro enlisted men and white officers was in a river bed, where it was very peaceful and quiet. It was so quiet that the officers went back to town that evening. At fifteen minutes after midnight, enemy mortar shells dropped down on that unit in rapid succession. There was considerable confusion.

The captain in charge of the unit gave the command to Close Station and March Order. Artillery men do not expect to have enough time to spell out every word in such a situation. The specific order is given by the letters, CSMO. When an officer says CSMO, he means *Get Ready to Get Out*.

They coupled the guns to vehicles called prime movers, a kind of big truck. None of the court-martial testimony is disputed except the application of the CSMO order. The captain admitted he gave it, but says it was for only one gun crew to move out and not the other batteries. He further admitted that his commanding officer had instructed him over the field telephone, *"Don't issue any order. You stay there and fight."*

Even though the batteries were all coupled up to leave, the word was given to uncouple and get back to firing shells. One gun crew of fourteen Negroes, however, had heard the order CSMO and had moved out too fast to get the new order. Twelve men were back the very next morning, even though the battery had moved to a new position that night. The other two men reported to duty shortly afterward. Even with the emergency CSMO order they had all taken the trouble to learn the location of their new firing position.

Confusion Confounded

The commanding officer told them that there had been so much confusion and misunderstanding that nobody knew what was going on. They were to forget about the incident, to go back to work and fight the war. And so the fourteen men forgot about it and were back on duty as before. Nevertheless, even though every one of the fourteen men had returned, charges of misbehavior were made subsequently.

Two of the men were court martialed. Three others, who testified for the two soldiers on trial, were also court martialed. At the two trials the captain gave three distinctly different stories under oath as to what had happened.

It is safe to say that this captain did not know what happened. He was confused. I talked with him and he still does not know what happened. But he has been promoted to Major, while five Negroes are in prison. Three of them are serving twenty years at hard labor and two of them received life sentences for "misconduct in the presence of the enemy."

As General MacArthur indicated in his cable to Walter White, when he first vetoed my visit overseas, under any decent system a man is treated as an individual. The terrible thing about these trials was the hopeless feeling common to every individual defendant. They felt they had no chance. The files showed these trials were held without any respect for the rights of individuals. The courts-martial were carried out with efficient haste, almost as on an assembly line. As many as four cases in a single day were tried, running on through the night, with all concerned anxious to get them over with.

Quick Justice

In four cases the trials which sentenced men to life imprisonment ran 42 minutes, 44 minutes, and the other two for 50 minutes each. This included the entire process of hearing the charges read, swearing in witnesses, examining all the evidence presented, hearing arguments (if any), explaining to the men their rights under the manual of courts-martial, the recess periods, discussion by the court and pronouncing sentence. Other trials ran an hour or an hour and ten minutes. I have seen many miscarriages of justice in my capacity as head of the NAACP legal department. But even in Mississippi a Negro will get a trial longer than 42 minutes, if he is fortunate enough to be brought to trial.

The men in the stockade had a common feeling of hopelessness. Some men with air-tight defenses had not presented evidence clearly demonstrating their innocence of the charges. Time and again I would ask them, *"Why didn't you tell your lawyer what really happened? Why didn't you tell the court? Why didn't you tell somebody?"*

Even though each man is an individual in the eyes of God and under our Constitution, these individuals gave me the same answer. *"It wasn't worth trying. We knew when we went in there we were all going to come out the same way. Each one of us hoped and prayed we would only get life. They*

*gave that officer, Lt. Gilbert, death, only because he is a Negro. What did
you expect them to give a Negro enlisted man? We know what the score is."*

Such a spirit of hopelessness will strip away from any man the ability to
defend himself adequately. One particular sergeant imprisoned in the
stockade outside Tokyo was representative of the devotion we have come to
associate with our armed forces. Under fire in Korea three of his
commanding officers were killed in a period of two days. This man had
kept his company together. He did not lose a single wounded man in
ninety days. He brought every injured man out, sometimes on his own
back. He saw to it that his men received hot food, regularly, which he took
up to them at the remoter points along the firing line. One after another
he saw his friends killed, but refused to be relieved. Day in and day out,
he kept on fighting, several times in command of the entire company
because there weren't officers around.

Battle Fatigue

This sergeant is charged with willful disobedience of an order. When
he was charged, when he talked to his lawyer, when he went into the
courtroom, during the trial, and even after the sentence he never told any
of them that right in his pocket was a slip from a doctor, a medical corps
captain, certifying that this man was suffering from battle fatigue and
should be returned to the rear for treatment. He never told anyone about
this slip until he talked to me. I called the captain of the guard
immediately and asked to have the sergeant's belongings searched. In the
condemned man's wallet, taken away from him with the rest of his
personal effects upon his reception at the stockade, was the slip of paper.

"Why didn't you tell them?" I asked.

"It wasn't worth it," he said. *"It wouldn't help me. You saw what
happened to Sergeant B_____, didn't you, when you talked with him?
Sergeant B_____ put in as evidence the official record book kept by the
Army hospital showing he was there on the days they charged him with
being away from duty. The court didn't pay any attention to it. They are
not paying attention to anything we say."*

There were men who were punished more than once for the same
alleged offense. Four Negro soldiers were attached to a mess hall miles
behind the front lines. When they finished work one day, their sergeant
told them they could go off and do what they liked. They told me it was

customary to drive a jeep to a place where the showers had been set up. When they returned from their shower the sentry told them there was supposed to be no movement in that section, but they could drive around by the road to the back part of the mess-hall area.

These men were picked up on the road going to Pusan. They said they were lost. When these men were brought in by the M.P.'s, their commanding officer said, *"You fellows have had easy jobs behind the lines, but you haven't appreciated it. For your punishment, I am going to put you in the front lines."*

Perhaps this captain was right. He put two of these men in a heavy mortar outfit and two others with a machine-gun unit. They were in fierce front-line fighting for twenty-one days and twenty-one nights. Perhaps they deserved this, since other men had been on prolonged duty in battle without mess-hall duty behind the lines or shower baths after work.

Their record in battle was never questioned. But these four men were pulled out, brought back and court martialed for violation of the 75th Article of War because of the incident that had happened three weeks before, miles behind the lines. They were sentenced to twenty years each for misbehavior before the enemy. The only crime which they could conceivably have been charged with involved the use of a jeep, without permission, which has not yet been charged against them.

Officer Behavior

How could officers of our Army behave in such a way? The official records proved that they did, but the explanation for their behavior was still lacking. My last Sunday in Korea was spent at a very forward position of the 24th Infantry Regiment, where I talked to the key man in every company of the regiment and of the 159th Field Artillery battery. These men knew what was behind these courts-martial operations.

The Regiment's forward positions were then moved north of Seoul. They had just taken an airstrip six hours before we got there.

These soldiers were survivors of the action occurring prior to and during the three months of courts-martial. There was one man whose father had been in the regiment for twenty years, and he's been in it for nine. I talked to about seventy of these veterans, asking them to tell me what had been going on last summer and fall.

One after another, they all said the same thing. The regiment's morale had been at a disastrously low ebb. Their white officers were in many instances Southerners who had brought their prejudices with them when assigned to duty with the 24th Infantry.

Time and again these officers told the men whom they were going to order into battle, *"I despise nigger troops. I don't want to command you or any other niggers. This Division is no good, and you are lousy. You don't know how to fight."*

I cannot imagine a worse situation in combat, where a man does not care what happens to those serving under him. There is no way to make the soldiers care less what is going to happen to the outcome of the fighting, or to their officers.

Casualties High

The casualty rates among the enlisted men and officers was disproportionately high. And how could it help but be high, when you are following such leaders? This wasn't told about one officer, but about several, by fighting men who were not court martialed and certainly had no reason to tell anything but the truth.

This explained these courts-martial proceedings to me. I think the high rate of casualties among officers made it necessary to assign the blame. The answer was a wholesale conviction of Negro soldiers who had survived this prejudiced leadership.

When I talked to the men that Sunday, morale in the 24th Infantry was certainly high. They had a new commanding officer, Colonel John T. Corley. They were proud of his having earned more battlefield decorations than any officer in the active Army. He respects them, and every man with whom I talked admired him. They repeatedly told me how, instead of ordering them forward into action, Colonel Corley goes out himself and commands, "Come!"

There are still some other officers in the regiment whom the men do not respect, and have little reason to respect. So long as that sort of officer is in command of jim-crow troops, we may expect the same pattern of injustice in the future. These soldiers are fighting and dying for us, who should see to it that they are not subjected to the kind of leadership which despises them.

Made Report

I now had the information for a complete report to General MacArthur, with recommendations. According to Army procedure, MacArthur did not have official responsibility for the disposition of the individual courts-martial cases. After the trials were approved by the major general in command of the 25th Division, the records were forwarded for review to the Judge Advocate General's office in the Pentagon in Washington. There the NAACP has been representing the condemned men, and has already arranged for a number of the sentences to be reversed or reduced.

But in my report it was necessary to place the ultimate responsibility for these courts-martial squarely upon General Douglas MacArthur. He had both the authority and the responsibility for maintaining or ending racial segregation in the Army's Far East Command.

In the large headquarters staff of MacArthur's Far East Command at the time, in the Dai Ichi building, there were no Negroes except for three civilian clerks. This is but one of several buildings with thousands of army personnel; nowhere were there more than one out of four men fighting with the 25th Division in Korea is a Negro American. There was a handsome, elite honor guard of crack riflemen which used to guard headquarters and the person of MacArthur, but there was not a Negro among them. Headquarters had a football team, all white. There wasn't even a Negro in the headquarters band.

MacArthur Responsible

This was General MacArthur's responsibility. He was at the time the Supreme Commander of American and United Nations troops then engaged in battle with a Communist enemy which seeks to divide us from the rest of the world. The Communists preach and propagandize how Americans abuse colored people, and MacArthur had allowed discrimination in his own headquarters. Negro troops in Korea are not succumbing to the Communist propaganda any more than they believed the Germans in the last war. They see how the Communists are killing Negroes as thoroughly as they are killing others.

Major General Doyle O. Hickey, who was MacArthur's chief of staff, told me that the General was aware of these things and that a study was being made to find ways and means for correcting them. I told him that the United States Air Force took just one day to end segregation. They gave a single order, and the Air Force is now an integrated, American body of men using the best efficiency and skill each man can provide in his country's service.

Three blocks down Avenue A from the Dai Ichi building is the Far East Air Force headquarters. Negroes work alongside white soldiers there in the guard, in the offices, wherever they are capable of doing good work. The first time I went by the Air Force building there were two guards of the Air Police standing at attention. One happened to be white; the other was colored. And after the Dai Ichi building, it was a very pleasant experience to see the guard being checked by the Sergeant of the Guard, who on that day happened to be a Negro. The same policy is now in force in the U.S. Navy.

I told General MacArthur that if the Air Force and the Navy, both drawing men from the same forces as the Army, frequently from the same families, have done this without any disadvantageous results, there was no reason why the Army couldn't do it. The Army is eliminating segregation in other places, and the Far East Command has no special problems which would place it at an extra disadvantage. It is disgraceful to have the Japanese clerks in the canteens told to discriminate against Negro service men during their five day recreation rotation from Korea.

In every war in which this country has participated, Negro Americans have had to fight for the right to fight. At the start of each war, military leaders have questioned the Negro's abilities and finally accepted Negro participation under the pressure of necessity.

Although 920,000 Negroes served in the Army during the Second World War, the Army didn't take most of them until manpower shortages impelled their acceptance, using them for menial jobs wherever possible. These men were treated as inferiors in the southern training camps. The great majority were used for arduous, dirty work overseas, but they covered themselves with glory just the same.

To date, the Cold War has erupted into violent action in one area, the Far East. There we face the potential enmity of hundreds of millions of men whose skins are not white, who look with extreme care to see how white men feel about colored peoples.

The NAACP believes that the men and women in our Armed Services shall have first preference on our time and efforts. But we are not only a group of Americans seeking *correction* of vicious practices and for the survival of this country, we also work to prevent injustice. The best way to accomplish this in our Armed Services is to work to bring about complete abolition of segregation now.

To date the legal department of the NAACP has secured reduction of sentence for twenty of these soldiers, but we have just begun. The NAACP is working to secure the appropriate exoneration or abbreviation of sentence for every man treated unjustly because of his race or color.

Crisis, May 1951, vol. 58, pp. 297–304; 350–55.

2

ATHLETICS AND THE ARTS (1951)

by Sterling A. Brown

At a conference sponsored by the Division of Social Sciences of Howard University, May 3–4, 1951, Sterling Brown, poet, essayist, and professor of literature at Howard, contributed an extraordinary survey of two central areas of life.

This subject is a Goliath, and I am not sure that my slingshot can bring it down. The fields are numerous and their yield now at long last so abundant that thorough reckoning is out of the question. I should like to give something of the story of participation, some measure of the integration of the Negro athlete and of the Negro artist in the areas of music, the dance, the drama, moving pictures, the plastic and graphic arts, and literature. In some of the fields I have no business trespassing. I can plead only an active interest in all of them and in the general theme of integration.

The areas where integration is more solidly rooted are considered more fully; those where integration is only a promise are less considered. That, rather than the author's athletic and artistic preferences, is the factor governing the proportion of space devoted to each area. The respective stories of integration, however, have striking parallels, which should be pointed out. All of these stories are of significance to the student of American culture.

By integration I mean, in agreement with so many others at this conference, complete acceptance. I mean a parallel in the sports and the arts to what the political spokesmen call "first-class citizenship." The integration of the Negro athlete or artist means his acceptance as an individual to be judged on his own merits, with no favor granted, and no fault found, because of race. It means that, whether second-baseman or pugilist, jazz trumpeter or concert singer, poet or painter, the Negro will be judged evenly, neither over-rigorously nor over-gently, according to the standards of his calling. If his achievements warrant, he should receive the rewards as man, not as Negro; if they do not, he should be sent to the bush leagues (literal in the world of sports, figurative in the arts).

But the integrated man is a whole man, not a fractional. By integration in the arts I do not mean loss of artistic identity. The moot point of the Negro's distinctive gifts will of course be considered in this essay. While there is no Negro way to play shortstop, many believe that there is a distinctive Negro quality in the arts derived from the folk, such as jazz and the popular dance. Integration does not have to mean the loss of such distinctiveness; it does not have to mean, for instance, the dilution of the deep blues into bluing-tinted water. Integration should mean fundamental respect for genuine quality, whatever its source, and acceptance of it in its wholeness.

In the arts, integration of the material of Negro life, as worthy of serious treatment, often preceded the integration of the Negro artist. This type of integration, therefore, certainly calls for consideration.

Athletics

With the current success of Minoso with the Chicago White Sox; Jethroe with the Boston Braves; Suitcase Simpson, Doby, and Easter with the Cleveland Indians; Willie Mays and Monte Irvin with the New York Giants; Campanella, Newcombe, and Jackie Robinson with the Brooklyn Dodgers; and the ageless Satchel Paige with the St. Louis Browns, the integration of the Negro in baseball seems assured. But this integration, accepted easily now, was not achieved so easily. Many pressures were needed: the challenge of World War II and the postwar years that democracy should live up to its professions; the agitation for One World and for an FEPC; the Mayor's Anti-Discrimination Committee in New York City; continual insistence from fair-minded sports writers and fans, as well as from Negro organizations—all were needed before Jackie Robinson first donned a Montreal uniform to participate in our national game.

Only one other Negro before Robinson had broken into all-white professional baseball, and he had to pass as an Indian. A delegation of his racial fans, overproud of his achievement, waited upon him one day with flowers, gifts, and speeches, and cut short his major league career. This took place a half century ago. Within the last decade it became more and more apparent that there were good Negro ballplayers in the Negro leagues. The long lines at the turnstiles, the sell-out crowds gathered to see the great Satchel Paige or Josh Gibson, certainly had their effect on major league club-owners, particularly when their average attendance was low.

In any consideration of integration, the saga of Jackie Robinson is instructive. Branch Rickey, who is responsible for his entry into major league baseball, was aware of many hurdles. Rickey had been manager of the St. Louis Cardinals in whose park no Negro had been allowed to sit in the grandstand. He knew how large a proportion of ballplayers are from the South. Therefore, in addition to finding a Negro ballplayer who could "deliver on the line in major league competition," he also had to select for his brave experiment "a Negro who would be the right man on the field" and one who would be most easily accepted by his teammates.[2] Robinson filled the bill in many respects. In the first interview, Rickey gave Jackie what he considered the crucial test. He warned him of insults, of "beanballs"; he acted out, with great realism, the roles of hot-headed players who came in with spikes and tempers flying high. Puzzled at first, Jackie asked, "Do you want a ballplayer who's afraid to fight back?" Rickey replied, "I want a ballplayer with guts enough not to fight back." Finally, after Rickey pretended to be a maddened player in the World Series who punched Robinson "right in the cheek," Jackie came up with, "I've got two cheeks...that it?," an answer that Rickey considered correct.[3]

Jackie Robinson's phenomenal success, as fielder, base-stealer, and hitter, as the spark plug of one of the finest teams of the last few years; his popularity with teammates, other ballplayers, and fans; his exemplary conduct on field and off; and his remarkable restraint when faced by the insults and crises that Rickey prophesied are widely known. It was no easy

[1]"Folk" versions of this anecdote vary, but the most authenticated account seems to be in Roi Ottley's *Black Odyssey* (New York: Charles Scribner's Sons, 1948), p. 204.
[2]Arthur Mann, *The Jackie Robinson Story* (New York: F. J. Low Co., Inc., 1950), p. 6.
[3]*Ibid.*, p. 60.

triumph, and the strain upon Robinson must have been severe. But his great pioneering succeeded. Today he can be less circumspect; he can participate in "rhubarbs," can argue with umpires and tangle with over-aggressive rivals as any other player can, and without its becoming a racial issue. He is still subject to a certain specialized criticism: sports writers have accused him of "popping-off" because of his pointed criticism of umpires, and even this last year he has received threatening letters from crackpots. But he is less symbol now than second-baseman; has been accepted by fans, fellow ballplayers, and sports writers as a great infielder. The American public seems willing now to recognize that on the baseball diamond a Negro ballplayer may well be temperamentally closer to Ty Cobb than to George Washington Carver.

A sports writer prophesied that once Jackie established himself as a star, the fans would lose sight of his color. Established also as stars are Don Newcombe, selected as pitcher for the All-Star team; Campanella, Brooklyn's most valuable player of the year; Sam Jethroe, the leading base-stealer; Doby and Easter, Cleveland's sluggers; Mays and Minoso, two of the leading rookies of the year in their respective leagues; and Monte Irvin, the batting champion of the World Series.

Nevertheless, Walter White's belief that "within two years few persons thought of them as Negroes but only as good ballplayers,"[4] seems over-sanguine. It is hardly likely that the color of these players has been completely lost sight of. From exclusion to complete acceptance is not such a swift trip as all that. Certainly among Negroes the color of these stars is not forgotten. Negro ballplayers are nearer to integration than are Negro baseball fans; Robinson and Campanella are more integrated in the Ebbetts Field clubhouse than Negroes are in the borough of Brooklyn. Reminded constantly and forcibly of race, Negro fans indulge in race pride instead of race obliviousness. In the box scores and long lists of batting averages Negroes zealously hunt out the records of the few Negro players. If their home clubs use no Negroes, they crowd the parks when teams with Negro players come to town; they boo rather than cheer the home team; local pride takes a back seat to racial. A cartoon by Ollie Harrington runs somewhat in this way: an exasperated woman, just from the ball game, says, "And there was Campanella catching, and New-combe pitching, and Jackie playing second base, and up comes Sam

[4]Walter White, "Time for a Progress Report." *The Saturday Review of Literature*, September 22, 1951, p. 38.

Jethroe. And there was 35,000 white folks looking at me to see what I was going to do!"

I once attended a game at Ebbetts Field with Ralph Bunche, who has been given a permanent pass by the Brooklyn club. He took along a couple of United Nations officials whom he was introducing to the great American game. In the first inning, Jackie Robinson parked a two-run homer. Ralph jumped up, yelling as frenziedly as any of the Dodgers' fans; the officials who knew Dr. Bunche best as a wise mediator, of established impartiality, seemed amazed. It was a good night for Ralph Bunche; Don Newcombe won his game; Campanella and Robinson for the Dodgers, and Thompson and Irvin for the Giants played flawless ball, and after the game Dr. Bunche went to the dressing room to get Jackie's autograph on a baseball.

A Gallup poll would probably register as one of the closest approaches to racial unanimity the hope of Negroes last season that Cleveland and Brooklyn should play in the World Series with the Giants a third choice. When the Dodgers blew their chances and lost in the thrilling play-off, a stoical taxi driver philosophized thus to me: "Well, now we got television, it works out for the best. Campanella couldn't play nohow, and Newcombe couldn't pitch every day; but just think of all those million white folks looking in their screens and seeing three Negroes in the Giant outfield, left to right, right to left, all my folks." When Doby and Easter hit the long ball, when Jethroe steals a base (although one overly race-conscious lady deplores his stealing since it harks back to a stereotype), when Robinson and Campanella star and Newcombe hurls a fine game, Negro fans get a great lift. Even a racial bunt causes more noise than an Aryan homer (a poor thing but mine own). Therefore, for all of Robinson's Frank Merriwell home run in the last game of the season, there was no joy in Bronzeville when the Bums lost in the play-off. And the grief was compounded when the Giants lost the series.

But the Negro is in professional baseball to stay. Once the juke boxes had a record, "Did You See Jackie Robinson Hit That Ball?," and Jackie Robinson caps were the rage. But now Jackie has many allies in the majors; the minor leagues, including some Southern teams, are training Negroes; even the Washington Senators are flirting with the idea of hiring Negro players, and that is a real index of integration.

Once integration is begun in one area it seems to ease over into neighboring territory. The success of Negroes in baseball on the diamond and in the locker room, and their box-office appeal helped to break up the exclusion in professional football.

As amateurs, Negroes have for many years played on teams representing northern and western colleges, though the election of Levi Jackson and of Bob Evans to the captaincy of the Yale and the University of Pennsylvania elevens, respectively, were news events of national moment. Early professional football in the North and West made use of a few Negro stars like Duke Slater, Fritz Pollard, and Paul Robeson; but when the National Football League was organized Negroes were excluded. The maverick league, the American Conference, kicked over the traces, however, in several ways; and one of the most important was the use of Negro players. Here again, the city of Cleveland was one of the pioneers. Of recent years, northern and western cities like Cleveland, Detroit, Los Angeles, and New York have signed up such stars as Kenny Washington, Motley, Gillom, Willis, Buddy Young, Taliaferro, Ford, Tunnell, and Deacon Towles, the ground-gaining rookie of the year. In the 1951 championship play-off, the teams included ten Negro stars.

In basketball two highly successful all-Negro teams, the Renaissance Club and the Harlem Globe Trotters (who recently lived up to their name by conducting an international barnstorming tour against the Collegiate All Stars), have long acquainted the sports world with the prowess of Negroes. Negro collegiate teams have played a good brand of basketball; Negroes have increasingly made the teams of northern and western colleges. Though for a long time none played on the teams of the Big Ten of the Midwest, one of the busiest basketball centers, they have been numerous on the many collegiate teams of Metropolitan New York, another busy center. Some clubs of the professional leagues have Negro players on their rosters. The Washington Capitols Club was the first interracial team in the history of professional sports in the District of Columbia.

In professional football and basketball the competition for places on the comparatively few teams is fierce. It is likely, however, that outstanding Negro stars will continue to find places, particularly on the teams of northern cities. It is worth notice, moreover, that a Negro has played with the professional football team of Richmond, Virginia.

The integration in baseball, basketball, and football is significant as integration in team play. It is, of course, familiar that Negro athletes have long done well in sports involving individual against individual, such as boxing, and track and field athletics.

In the early nineteenth century a few Negroes—Tom Molineaux pre-eminently—were famed as pugilists, but they won their best purses in England. Since the turn of the century, when featherweight George Dixon, lightweight Joe Gans, and welterweight Joe Walcott (after whom the present heavyweight champion was named) held titles concurrently, Negro prizefighters have more than maintained their own. The roll call is impressive with champions, near champions, good-enough to be champions, and dangerous contenders. (And, of course, a due share of clubhouse "stumble-bums.") The supremacy of Negro fighters has at times irked white America. Jack Johnson was a great stylist defensively and offensively in the ring, but his behavior outside the ring, while little different from that of other prizefighters of his time, was considered unfitting for a Negro. A frenzied hunt for a "white hope" to displace the unpopular Johnson came up with Willard and then Dempsey. Negro heavyweights, especially Harry Wills, were given the run-around. Barred from championship stakes, great Negro boxers like Sam Langford, Joe Jeannette, and Sam McVey fought each other so often that it became a habit.

When Joe Louis came along, his conduct, both in the ring and out, made him a most popular champion; Louis accelerated the change that was already coming over the sports public. In addition to Louis, Henry Armstrong, the only man to hold three titles at one time, and Ray Robinson, called the greatest living fighter "pound for pound"—to name the most brilliant of a long line of champions—have done much for the popularity of Negro fighters, and of course for the appeal of the sport itself. At the writing, five of the six major weight divisions have Negro champions, and at least four have Negroes as the outstanding challengers. The two heavyweight champions to follow Joe Louis are Ezzard Charles and Jersey Joe Walcott; and the man to whom Ray Robinson lost his middleweight championship, only to regain it soon after, was Randy Turpin, an English Negro.

Even on the managerial side Negroes are entering the picture, though for a long time Negro managers of Negro prizefighters were frozen out as money-makers. Truman Gibson, a Negro attorney, is an important figure in the International Boxing Club, a controlling power in pugilism. All in all, Negroes are in the foreground of the boxing picture. Any other picture is inconceivable.

In track and field athletics, where again it is man against man, Negro athletes have long-standing national prestige. From the early days of

Howard Drew to the present, the record of Negro runners and jumpers has been brilliant. An incomplete listing would include such champions of the recent past as Jesse Owens, Eulace Peacock, Eddie Tolan, Ralph Metcalfe in the sprints; Ned Gourdin, Ed Gordon, DeHart Hubbard in the broad jump; Cornelius Johnson and Dave Albritton in the high jump; Johnny Woodruff in the middle-distance runs; and John Borican, decathlon champion; and present stars such as Ewell in the sprints; Dillard in the hurdles, Reggie Pearmon, Mal Whitfield, McKinley, LaBeach, and Rhoden in the distance events. Nine of the eleven girls representing the Unites States in the 1948 Olympics were Negroes. Only in pole vaulting and the mile- and two-mile run are Negroes presently missing from the ranks of leading contenders.

When Jesse Owens, aided by such stars as Metcalfe, Woodruff, Archie Williams, and Cornelius Johnson, assured the United States of a clear-cut victory in the Olympic Games in Berlin in 1936, Hitler left the stadium in a huff, refusing to shake Owens's hand, thereby violating a time-honored custom. The Nazi press discounted the American victory as being won by "its black auxiliary force."

"Actually," *Der Angriff* contended, "the Yankees,...had been the great disappointment of the Games, for without these members of the black race—their 'auxiliary helpers'—the Germans won."[5]

This charge can be properly discounted as another of the Nazi "big lies." But it contained one grain of truth, symbolized by the fact that, in spite of the outstanding achievement of Owens and his Negro teammates, they would not have been allowed, on their return to the United States, to race against white athletes in the nation's capital. This exclusion is now fortunately ended; Negroes participate in unsegregated track meets in the District of Columbia, and even, though still exceptionally, in the deeper South.

In such "leisure class" sports as tennis and golf, Negroes have had a much harder road. Almost all of the finest tennis players of the world can afford to play the game throughout the year. Many have received costly coaching. Promising young players who are not in the upper income brackets are in a measure subsidized by wealthy clubs and the National Tennis Association. Membership in the latter is restricted, and the tournaments under its auspices are open only to members of constituent clubs. Negroes founded the American Tennis Association, and sought unavailingly to have the bars lowered to the National Tennis Association.

[5]Roi Ottley, *op. cit.*, p. 270.

A few democratic individuals—Don Budge was one—played exhibition matches with Negroes. The first Negro to play in a "white" tournament was Reginald Weir, who had won the Negro national title several times. But no Negro has participated in the men's national tournament at Forest Hills. Through the courageous and determined sponsorship of former champion Alice Marble, Althea Gibson was invited to participate in the national tournaments at Forest Hills and the World's Championship at Wimbledon. The reigning champion of the Negro Association, Miss Gibson acquitted herself well. But tennis among Negroes—an after-work pastime—is of course less highly developed than among those whose wealth and leisure permit them to follow it as a vocation. Negroes lag behind the really great players just as whites who play the public courts lag behind the experts of the private clubs.

It is likely that integration of Negroes in tennis will take place, as it has started, in local open public court tournaments rather than in those of private clubs, which exclude on grounds additional to race. An interesting instance of integration, in reverse order, took place this summer at Wilberforce, where eleven white players from Dayton entered the Negro National Tournament. The American Tennis Association is, of course, without color bars.

The story repeats itself in golf. Many Negroes play the game well; it is a commonplace around many courses that Negro caddies shoot lower scores than the tired businessmen whose clubs they carry. A few public golf tournaments are "open" in the literal sense of the word, but most Negro golfers are segregated. Recently, Joe Louis, by threatening a suit, caused the Professional Golfers Association to loosen its ban on "nonwhites." As in tennis, Negroes have their own association and hold a Negro National Championship.

In swimming, the story is about the same, with some participation in northern schools and colleges. In a few prestige sports—polo, the "millionaire's game," and rowing (with the exception of Joe Trigg at Syracuse)—Negroes have yet to make their marks. A few Negroes play professional hockey in Canada, but the first Negro to play organized hockey in the United States is Art Dorrington, a Nova Scotian who has wandered down to the southern clime to play with the Washington Lions. Cricket and soccer, British games, find many stars among the American Negroes from the West Indies and Africa, and occasionally visiting British teams are interracial. The long-standing racial bar in bowling has been lowered. The new integration extends even to such a social game as bridge—a few whites have competed in the Negro national championship, and a referendum is under way to allow Negro players to join the American Contract Bridge League.[6] I am uncertain whether to consider wrestling a sport or play-acting. Whichever it is, wrestling, in contrast to boxing, has seen few professional Negro participants. In amateur wrestling, Negroes have made the teams of northern colleges. The Howard University team has had matches with Gallaudet College, one of the first instances of integrated intercollegiate athletics in the District. But in the parade of races and nationalities on the television screen, Negro wrestlers are missing. Perhaps this is further proof of E. Franklin Frazier's dictum that "the Negro is being integrated first into those areas involving secondary contacts as opposed to primary contacts."[7] Be that as it may, from my experience with television I would say that the integration of the Negro in wrestling is one gain that I can contemplate without frenzy.

The acceptance of Negroes in American sports is now taken for granted to such a degree that it has posed a nice dilemma for integrationists. A letter written by E. B. Henderson, the leading historian of the Negro in sports, and for many years a staunch fighter against segregation, illustrates this:

> Certain sections of the American press still designate the racial association of criminals but seldom identify by race those who add to our prestige or culture. Too many Americans are ignorant of the fact that dozens of our Olympic athletes are colored boys and girls.... It is interesting to note how sports announcers fail to identify the great galaxy of football players on college and pro teams during the fall season.... Is this due to network policy that does not want to disturb the theory of the racists that there are innately inferior and superior racial groups?[8]

Ideally, the integrationist wants Negroes accepted on equal terms with all other men, to be judged strictly in terms of ability, without attention being given to such incidentals as race. Nevertheless, integration has not yet been achieved so fully that race pride is lost. Actually, many integrationists believe that the report of the death of "racism" in America has been greatly exaggerated, that it is not even moribund. As a counter-offensive they insist on publicizing facts proving the Negro to be worthy of

---

[6]This information was given me by Allen Woolridge, an authority on bridge and its organizations.

[7]E. Franklin Frazier, *The Negro in the United States* (New York: The Macmillan Co., 1949), p. 693.

[8]E. B. Henderson, "Colored Boys in Sports," in "Letters to the *Star*," *The Washington Star*, December 6, 1948.

integration. This seems a necessary immediate strategy to bring about inclusion. Achieving the ultimate ideal of completely ignoring race, of never even mentioning it, seems at this point of race relations in America to be a dim, far-off event.

Jazz Music

As in American sports, so in the arts, integration has gone apace. In American popular music the integration of the Negro composer and performer has been longest and most solid. As far back as 1855, an Austrian named Kurnberger wrote *Der Amerika müde (He Who Is Tired of America)*. One of the chief reasons for his hero's furious repudiation is that in the United States, "music is always left to the Negroes."[9] Though Kurnberger had never visited America, he was correct in stating the strong influence of the Negro on New World music.

A century later, the great influence of that hybrid, Afro-American music, is even more pervasive, whether in folk music, jazz, or concert music. It has reached European composers as well. Marshall Stearns, a close student of American music, is convinced that

when the history of our folk and popular music is written, it will be found that— alongside the varying influence of every culture group in this country—an ever-increasing trend toward the incorporation of Negro musical characteristics in general and rhythm in particular has been taking place in our popular music.[10]

As far as jazz music is concerned, genuine integration of Negro material and of artists seems established. The recent histories of jazz have stressed the importance of the Negro idiom and musicians. The early accounts glorified Paul Whiteman, who usurped the title "King of Jazz" because of his semi-symphonic attempts to bring jazz closer to respectability. These books failed to mention the real king, Joe Oliver; the crown prince, Louis Armstrong; and the early, historically important bands of Fletcher Henderson and Duke Ellington. Present-day historians have toppled Whiteman from his throne as "King of Jazz," and look upon the "Whiteman Era" as a failure. They have traced jazz to its origins among

[9]H. E. Jacob, *Johann Strauss, Father and Son* (New York: The Greystone Press, 1940), p. 365.

[10]Marshall W. Stearns, "American Popular Music," paper read at the Conference on Music in Contemporary American Civilization held by the Committee on Musicology, American Council of Learned Societies, Library of Congress, December 13–14, 1950.

Negroes in the South, especially in New Orleans; they have stressed its derivations from Negro folk music, sacred and secular, from ragtime and brass band marches; they have told how it emerged as collective poly-rhythmic and polyphonic improvisation, a new kind of music that swept over America in the first decades of the century. Negro musicians Buddy Bolden, Bunk Johnson, King Oliver, Louis Armstrong, Sidney Bechet, Johnny Dodds, Jimmy Noone, Kid Ory, and Jelly Roll Morton—all from New Orleans—play prominent roles in the history. Negro composers Scott Joplin, W. C. Handy, Clarence Williams, and Spencer Williams were also important, and behind these a host of anonymous composers of blues and stomps that had become traditional.

Therefore, though a white band from New Orleans, the Original Dixieland Jass (sic) Band, was the first to make the new music commercially successful, the jazz musicians knew where the genuine source of the idiom and the best performers were to be found. Such prestige helped the Negro musician to integration. He might not be wanted or even allowed in the better-paying places, but he earned the respect, sometimes begrudged, of white fellow musicians who recognized his skill. Bix Beiderbecke, the brilliant young white cornetist, listened for hours to Bessie Smith, both in person and on records, rapt by her voice and delivery as she moaned the blues. The white musicians who form what is called the Chicago school have told the story of how they haunted the Southside to listen to Oliver and Armstrong and other Negro stars. Most came to worship, a few, alas! to steal; one Negro trumpet player, Freddie Keppard, refused to record lest his secrets of style be revealed, and another, King Oliver, regretted, in his declining years, the way the "educated cats" had stolen his stuff. Mezz Mezzrow, in his autobiography, *Really the Blues*, has revealed the fervent admiration shared by young Chicagoans for the great Negro jazz pioneers.

This respect for individual performers helped breach the wall of segregation. First instances of Negroes and whites playing together, except for private jam sessions, took place in recording studios. There was something of subterfuge in this: in those early days the companies did not list the personnel; the public did not have to know what went on inside the studio walls; and in order to make good records, good men on their instruments were sought, regardless of their color. So in the early years of recording, Fats Waller played piano for Ted Lewis, and Jelly Roll Morton for the New Orleans Rhythm Kings; and to switch around, Jack Teagarden and Joe Sullivan played with one of the bands Louis Armstrong picked up for a recording session. But these early instances involved single outstanding personalities. In the thirties the practice broadened: a notable free-and-easy come-and-go existed between the men in Teddy Wilson's and Benny Goodman's bands, and Lionel Hampton recorded many hits with thoroughly mingled groups.

Benny Goodman, who has done so much toward integrating Negro musicians, believes "one of the most important things that has happened musically in the last few years is the number of times good musicians have gotten together and played in mixed bands on records—something they don't get a chance to do in public."[11] Goodman points out that the first time that white and colored musicians played together for a paying audience in America was in 1936 when he and Gene Krupa sat in with Fletcher Henderson's orchestra at the Grand Terrace in Chicago.[12]

In the thirties, John Hammond planned to take to Europe an all-star band, "the first mixed band in jazz history." The interest of Europeans in jazz was then ardent, as it has remained, and the acceptance of a mixed band would be, of course, much easier than in America. The fine plan collapsed, however, probably because of labor difficulties in England. In the meanwhile, Goodman and Krupa had recorded with Teddy Wilson; the charming performances of this trio had won many enthusiasts around the country who wished to hear the group in person. A successful concert gave rise to "the thought of a white and colored group playing in a hotel room... pretty revolutionary at the time."[13] At first Wilson played intermission piano while the band was off the stand, "and the trio was made a part of the floor show, spotted separately."[14] After a few days' trial, it was apparent that the thing was a natural from every standpoint.

After the trio and the quartette, with Lionel Hampton added, there was progress to Goodman's sextette, and soon Negroes were regular sidemen with the band. Other mixed bands were organized by Goodman's fellow Chicagoans, Joe Sullivan and Mezz Mezzrow. Such name band leaders as Tommy Dorsey, Artie Shaw, Harry James, and Gene Krupa made use of talented Negro stars, and a few white sidemen have played with Negro bands. But these bands are still exceptional; travelling and living accommodations still pose problems; and so integration in the large

[11]Benny Goodman and Irving Kolodin, *The Kingdom of Swing* (New York: Stackpole Sons, 1939), pp. 129–130.
[12]*Ibid.*, p. 210.
[13]*Ibid.*, p. 214.
[14]*Ibid.*

commercial bands remains token and not real. Negro bands, for all of their prestige in the jazz world, are still denied the most lucrative spots in hotel, theater, and radio work. Many of the famous Negro bands have broken up because of the current financial stress in band business.

In private jam sessions where fellow artists meet for relaxation on a basis of mutual respect—where a man is esteemed by his skill on trumpet, piano, trombone, or guitar—there integration is at its highest. In public jam sessions, in concerts such as the Jazz at the Philharmonic, there is complete acceptance. In the world of commercial jazz, however, integration is still unusual. The musicians may share mutual respect; but the magnates of commercial jazz seem to believe that the American public is not ready to see Negro and white musicians side by side.

Regardless of exclusions from the best-paying jobs both past and present, it is incontestable that Negroes have played an integral part in the history of jazz. The inventiveness of individual Negro artists, whether the "classic" blues stylists, Bessie Smith, Ma Rainey, and Lonnie Johnson; or the early New Orleans pioneers like Jelly Roll Morton, Oliver, and Bechet; or virtuosos on their instruments like Earl Hines and Coleman Hawkins; and of orchestra leaders such as Fletcher Henderson and Count Basie who were unique in their styles of swing music, and Duke Ellington, who introduced a new tone coloring, is fundamental in jazz history. Wherever a new type of jazz becomes popular—whether boogie-woogie, which came from tenement flats of Chicago and Kansas City and swept America until there is now hill-billy and cowboy boogie-woogie; or be-bop, of which cult Dizzy Gillespie and Charlie Parker are high priests—Negro performers will be found as originators. White bands pay Negro bands the flattery of imitation, the influence of Lunceford, Basie, and Ellington being easily apparent. Negro songstresses like Ivy Anderson, Ella Fitzgerald, Lena Horne, Billie Holiday, and Sarah Vaughan have set very definite singing styles and are widely imitated. Bing Crosby and other popular singers praise the singing of Louis Armstrong as influential in their formative years. The "jump" style of spiritual singing, widely popularized by the Golden Gates, has now influenced even the Grand Ole Opry in Nashville, the hill-billy musical capital. The give-and-take among barber shop quartettes has of course been strong; the jazz fillip added by the Mills Brothers helped to found a style. A logical outcome of the reciprocity is the Mariners, a quartette of two Negroes and two whites who learned integration in the Coast Guard and whom Arthur Godfrey uses on his programs, to the horror of Governor Herman Talmadge of

Georgia, who suggests legislative action and economic boycott as a means to stop the new-fangled integration.

Despite the Negro's undoubted formative influence, jazz does not belong to the Negro. It is not an African music, though some analysts like Rudi Blesh stress the African survivals. It was never completely the American Negro's, or if so only briefly. Music rises over even the high walls of separation. As already pointed out, the first bands to popularize the new jazz were white bands out of New Orleans. In the dispersion and popularization white bands were of importance; in the preservation of the spirit of the older jazz when threatened by commercialism, the white musicians known as the Chicagoans (including Muggsy Spanier, Joe Sullivan, Jess Stacy, George Brunies, Pee Wee Russell, Wild Bill Davidson, Jack Teagarden, and Bud Freeman) struggled devotedly to keep the music from straying too far from its original qualities. In any type of contemporary jazz from New Orleans revival to be-bop, white musicians are among the best. One of the interesting aspects of jazz history is that young white bands are doing most now to keep alive the parent tradition of Oliver, Armstrong, and Jelly Roll Morton, whereas young Negro musicians, in revolt against the past, have gone in for the novelties of be-bop. To go further into that phenomenon would exceed the limits of this essay.

Concert Music

The progress toward integration in serious music has been slower. In 1870, the ethnologist Dr. Van Evrie declared dogmatically: "Music is to the Negro an impossible art, and therefore such a thing as a Negro singer is unknown."[15] His statement was patently absurd even then when such a singer as Elizabeth Greenfield, "The Black Swan," had won acclaim in both the free states and England, and the Fisk Jubilee Singers were just about ready to make their triumphant musical tour. Yet even though the egregious belief might be disowned, America by and large held out no great welcome to the serious Negro musician.

Even before the Civil War, and of course increasingly after, many Negroes seriously studied classical music. Though the first concert artists were too often considered by the rest of America as curiosities, the desire to perform concert music was strong. Negro singers, violinists, pianists, and concert orchestras of outstanding ability and advanced training

[15]C. J. Van Evrie, *White Supremacy and Negro Subordination* (New York: Van Evrie, Horton & Co., 1870), p. 102.

emerged, but they performed largely for their own. Many barriers had to be breached before the Negro was accepted as a concert artist. Despite international recognition, Roland Hayes was unrecorded by major phonograph companies for many years. Hayes's undaunted will, however, had much to do with weakening the barriers, and his success on the concert stage and on phonograph records together with that of Marian Anderson, Dorothy Maynor, Paul Robeson, Todd Duncan, Carol Brice and others proves that the individual concert singer has arrived. Yet, as Howard Taubman has pointed out:

> You cannot name more than a handful who have reached the top in the field of serious music....It is because they do not have the educational opportunities. If they have the chance to study, they have even less chance of using their talents in public. A Negro must have an exceptional gift to crash through to distinction....There are no Negroes in symphony or opera orchestras....Nor are there any in theater pit orchestras, radio house bands, hotels, or on sustaining or commercial radio programs....The situation is grim. It is not peculiar to music and the remedy will come only when the entire nation begins to live up to the letter and spirit of the thirteenth, fourteenth, and fifteenth amendments of our Constitution as well as the dictates of an enlightened humanity.[16]

Mr. Taubman wrote this over a decade ago. In the meanwhile it seems that the "dictates of an enlightened humanity" have not appreciably strengthened. But a few swallows point to the looked-for summer. Whereas Madam Evanti sang her operatic roles only in Europe and South America, Camilla Williams, Todd Duncan, and Larry Winters have appeared with the New York City Center Opera Company; and the dancer, Janet Collins, has joined the Metropolitan Opera Company. Adele Addison, a promising young soprano, the featured soloist at the Berkshire Music Festival of 1951, has sung two seasons with the New England Opera Company. The early "native opera" *Deep River* by Harling and Stallings and the experimental *Four Saints in Three Acts*, starring Edward Matthews, acquainted Americans with the rich potentialities of the Negro in musical drama. The "folk-opera" *Porgy and Bess*; the various swing Mikados; *Carmen Jones*, whose book was Harlemized by Oscar Hammerstein, but whose score remained Bizet's; and the more recent *Lost in the Stars* and *The Barrier*, an interracial venture uniting the talents of Langston Hughes, Jan Meyerowitz, Muriel Rahn, and Lawrence Tibbett, all bore witness to training, precision in a more sophisticated art-form,

---

[16]Howard Taubman, *Music as a Profession* (New York: Charles Scribner's Sons, 1939), pp. 143–144.

and dramatic ability that in all likelihood will pave the way for genuine integration. Excluded from grand opera for so long, Negroes formed their own local opera groups. But they were training themselves for inclusion. Mary Cardwell Dawson, director of the ten-year-old National Negro Opera Company, states, "By its repeated successes...the company has gained the respect and recognition of other races, and doors are now being opened to colored artists which have never before been open."[17]

The Hall Johnson, Eva Jessye, and other choruses have served not only as first-rate singing groups but also as training and proving grounds. To this group must be added Leonard de Paur's Infantry Chorus, which according to Virgil Thomson "could, without half trying, raise the whole level of our current taste in semi-popular music."[18] Using a wide range of material from Palestrina to contemporary American composers, Conductor de Paur clarifies his aims:

> When we sing a Cossack song, we're as near to being Cossacks as we can get; when we sing the Jewish chant Eli Eli, we're as close to being Jews with their whole history of oppression and religious faith as is possible for us.[19]

More and more Negro singers and instrumentalists are being accepted as American, as world artists, without limitation upon repertoires. A few Negroes, Louis Vaughn Jones, the violinist, for instance, have played in local symphonic orchestras, and Dean Dixon is widely known as a symphonic conductor. Negro composers, notably William Grant Still and Howard Swanson, whose *Short Symphony* the New York Critics Circle called the best new orchestral work of the last season, have won national acceptance. A worthy instance of integration is interracial choral singing, directed by Werner Lawson and others.

By and large, however, the truth remains: individual Negro concert singers are warmly acclaimed, but in operatic and symphonic music the Negro musician is far from integrated. The tabu on Negro artists at Constitution Hall, though its stringency has recently been released, is still uncomfortably symbolic.

Dance

The story of the dance repeats that of music, to which it is so closely related. The material, the idiom of the Negro dance, has been assimilated

[17]*The Washington Afro-American*, December 25, 1950, p. 6.
[18]*Time*, January 12, 1948, LI, No. 2, p. 38.
[19]*Ibid*.

into American dancing, especially of the ballroom and theatrical varieties. As James Weldon Johnson often quipped, "Where music and dancing are concerned, Americans are always doing their best to pass for colored." The influence on America's ballroom dancing of the folk dancing of the American Negro, of dances with such names as the Turkey Trot, the Fox Trot, the Bunny Hug, and the Grizzly Bear, is indisputable. Vernon and Irene Castle, who taught a generation of American dancers to break away from the old European waltzes, polkas, and schottisches, really took the dances out of the barnyards, out of denims and ginghams, and put them in ballrooms in tuxedos and evening gowns. An important guide to the Castles was James Reese Europe, their favored band leader, whose music was grounded on the traditional Negro idiom. The later dances—the Big Apple, trucking, the boogie, the Susie Que, the various types of jitterbugging—all stem from the same folk sources. Like the earlier dances, these later dances

... will be toned down and formalized by the dancing masters when [they reach] the pupils. There will be nothing left of the uncouth jive jamming, but all the basic steps will be there, carefully lifted out of the groove, analyzed and arranged in neat routines guaranteed to disturb nobody but your Aunt Caroline who still clings to the cotillion. That is the way this particular clash between propriety and freedom of the dance has been ending for the past five hundred years.[20]

From Latin America, and chiefly of Negro origin, have come the tango, the conga, the rhumba, the samba, and the latest mamba. The inventiveness of such famous dance teachers as Billy Pierce, of such masters as Bill Bojangles Robinson, Eddie Rector, and the Nicholas Brothers, has influenced current tap dancing. According to John Martin again:

The Negro has certainly given us at least the basis for all our popular dances.... His dance brings a certain vitality... to what would otherwise be a distinctly anemic field. The Negro, indeed, has discovered for himself a rich and admirable recreational dance and his contribution to [American] development along these lines has far greater potentialities than have been realized.[21]

Admirable study into the roots of American Negro dancing has been made by Katherine Dunham, stressing the West Indian backgrounds, and

---

[20]John Martin, "From Minuet to Jitterbug," *The New York Times Magazine*, November 7, 1943, p. 17.
[21]John Martin, *Introduction to the Dance* (New York: W. W. Norton, 1939), p. 163.

Pearl Primus, stressing the African. Together with Belle Rosette and Josephine Premice, who dance in the Caribbean tradition, these are accepted as American dancers and choreographers of significant achievement and promise. Haitian, West Indian, and African dance groups (especially that of Asadata Dafora) have met with high esteem. As far as integration goes, however, the building on these origins, the folding of these styles into major American choreography, is still in the future. Tamiris has founded dances on Negro spirituals and set a group work, "How Long Brethren," to Negro songs of protest. Occasionally a bold producer has sponsored a chorus of white and Negro dancers, but this remains an exception. Janet Collins's inclusion with the Metropolitan Opera is certainly a striking step to integration. John Martin has written:

A development that is destined to have great significance in the postwar dance world is the emergence of a number of highly gifted Negro artists. As a direct result of the old minstrel tradition, the Negro has heretofore been confined almost exclusively to the inertias of the entertainment field, but with the advent of the modern dance, in which he has found a medium for expressing himself in forms of his own devising, he has begun to find his rightful place in the creative arts and to do so with impressive results.... Eventually, no doubt, the purely objective racial approach to the art will give place to a more universal attitude in which the artist dances simply as an individual human being, allowing his racial heritage to voice itself freely through him but not to limit his range of subject and content.[22]

Art

Important in the culture of Africa and the West Indies, dancing could thrive as a folk-art in American slavery, since all that was needed was the voice to sing and the hands and feet to beat out the vigorous rhythms. For the similarly important plastic arts of Africa, there could be no such survival. Alain Locke has written:

We will never know and cannot estimate how much technical African skill was blotted out in America. The hardships of cotton and rice-field labor, the crudities of the hoe, the ax, and the plow reduced the typical Negro hand to a gnarled stump, incapable of fine craftsmanship even if materials, patterns and artistic incentives had been available.[23]

[22]John Martin, *The Dance* (New York: Tudor Publishing Co., 1946), p. 145.
[23]Alain Locke, *Negro Art, Past and Present* (Washington, D.C.: Associates in Negro Folk Education, 1936), pp. 2–3.

The story of the Negro artist in America runs parallel to the stories already told in this essay. Historians have recorded earlier Negro painters, even in Colonial days, but the first really noteworthy Negro artist is Henry O. Tanner. Like Roland Hayes and Marian Anderson, Tanner received his first great recognition from Europe. Tanner found it difficult to obey the injunction of his teacher, Thomas Eakins, to remain in America.[24] An expatriate like so many artists of his generation, he sought refuge and inspiration in France from an America disdainful of artists in general, and of a Negro artist in particular. There he remained, seeking finer artistic training and criticism, painting Biblical subjects chiefly in Europeanized style. The New Negro movement, sharing in the awakened interest in African art, was more congenial to aspiring artists than Tanner's time was to him. Many of the younger artists discovered the African tradition, stimulated by the vogue among advance guard artists and critics in Europe and America. But the tradition was a discovery, not an old land revisited.

From the time of the New Negro movement, Negro artists have increased in numbers and ability. Several artists have achieved strikingly. But there is no single school, no dominant stylist; eclecticism, as might be expected, marks their work, as it does that of other American artists. Painters as various as Aaron Douglas, Archibald Motley, Hale Woodruff, James Porter, J. Lesesne Wells, Lois Jones, Charles Alston, Horace Pippin, Jacob Lawrence, Romare Bearden, Elton Fax, and Charles Sebree and the sculptors Sargent Johnson, Augusta Savage, and Richmond Barthé range the gamut of styles from realism to abstractionism. These artists are not confined to racial themes; some find rich inspiration in Negro experience, and some do not. A sculptor like Richmond Barthé is equally at home in his carving of a Harlem dancer or of a bust of Katherine Cornell. Jacob Lawrence is drawn to stirring epochs in the life of his people; Lois Jones is drawn to the landscape of her deeply loved France; both are exercising an artistic right. Certainly the plastic and graphic artist's freedom has been so hardly won that he should not be constrained within racial bonds. The quality of the painting or sculpture is what matters.

In black-and-white, and cartooning generally, Charles Alston, Ollie Harrington, and E. Simms Campbell rank with America's most popular artists. Campbell has been one of the steadiest cartoonists for *Esquire*

---

[24]Oliver W. Larkin, *Art and Life in America* (New York: Rinehart & Co., Inc., 1949), p. 279.

since its start, and his bevy of harem beauties is more widely known than his hilarious cartoons of Negro life.

The controversy over the use of subject matter from Negro life has become less of a pressing issue: like all American artists, Negro artists now join opposing sides in such controversies as regionalism versus internationalism. In a recent debate, Thomas Benton rephrased his old objections to "Parisian esthetics which was more and more turning art away from the living world of active men and women into an academic world of empty pattern..."[25] and took his stand by "meaningful subject matter—in our cases specifically American subject matter."[26] James Thrall Soby believes that American art must "find its way into the international mainstream where it...must now take an upright, strong course," and while not ruling out regionalism, takes his stand that form, "whether abstract or realistic, remains a central part of [the artist's] business."[27]

What James Porter wrote in 1943 has even more support today:

> The future of the Negro painter is promising. No longer does he find himself handicapped by poor facilities for study. Moreover, the public attitude toward the Negro painter is changing rapidly from indifference to active encouragement."[28]

An instance in point is the recent award of prizes in the Corcoran Art Show to Richard Dempsey. No fanfare was made of his being a Negro; race was incidental or unmentioned in accounts of his achievement; he was an artist living in Washington whose paintings were judged as prize worthy.

As far as the treatment of Negro life and character by white artists goes, the caricature and the overstress of the sentimental or the exotic belong to the past. The advent of realists at the turn of the century has made for a recognition of the artistic possibilities of Negro life and character, worthy of sincere and dignified presentation.

Drama

This recognition also marks the recent history of the drama. Negro oldtimers of the theatre remember ruefully the old cry, "Never let a nigger

---

[25]Thomas Hart Benton, "What's Holding Back American Art," *The Saturday Review of Literature*, December 15, 1951, p. 9.
[26]*Ibid.*
[27]James Thrall Soby, "A Reply to Mr. Benton," *loc. cit*, p. 14.
[28]James A. Porter, *Modern Negro Art* (New York: The Dryden Press, 1943), p. 133.

speak a line," i.e., confine him to singing and dancing roles. It was only after a quarter century of fabulous success for *Uncle Tom's Cabin* that a genuine Negro played the title role; even as late as the 1930's, a revival of *Uncle Tom's Cabin* called *Sweet River* had a white girl in the role of Eliza, pronouncing the "disses" and "dats" with the precision of elocution school. In black-face minstrelsy, Negro performers were not accepted for half a century; in serious drama the actor Ira Aldridge, like the painter Tanner, had to go to Europe to make his reputation.

The segregated Negro theatre became chiefly a theatre of vaudeville comedy and song and dance. Such star performers as Bert Williams, George Walker, Flo Mills, Josephine Baker, Ethel Waters, and Bojangles Robinson were noted for drollery, pantomime, or singing and dancing ability. It was only at the end of his career that the acting ability of Richard Harrison was discovered; the same story is true of Rose McLendon. Ethel Waters had a long apprenticeship as singer and dancer in honkytonks and cabarets and in musical shows before Broadway discovered her potentialities as actress in *Mamba's Daughters*.

Before Eugene O'Neill, the Negro character in drama was minor, most often a servant for comic relief. Whenever serious attention was given to him, he was a pawn to be battled over, or a "tragic mulatto" waking up to discover the woe of being a Negro, as in Sheldon's *The Nigger*. But in the 1920's and 30's *The Emperor Jones, All God's Chillun Got Shoes, Porgy and Bess, In Abraham's Bosom, The Green Pastures, Run, Little Chillun*, and *Stevedore* brought more revelatory material to the stage. Negro actors, whether trained in Negro vaudeville in such rare companies as the Lafayette Players, or in college dramatic and little theatre groups, were found ready to step into the roles.

Negro actors came into their first large opportunities in these dramas of social realism, concerned with the tragic aspects of Negro life in America. With the Federal Theatre's *Haitian Macbeth*, a trend of adapting famous plays and operas to a "Negro" (or Harlemized) style began. Louis Armstrong's trumpet was called upon to aid Shakespeare in *A Midsummer Night's Dream; Carmen* became *Carmen Jones* of Harlem; *The Mikado* was presented in two versions, one "Hot" and one "Swing"; even *Lysistrata* introduced a kind of swing into ancient Athens.

This fusion of unlike traditions, of Negro song and dance with theatrical masterpieces, often leaves unsatisfied not only the devotees of each tradition but also the fewer admirers of both. But it seems to please

Broadway impresarios more than the experiment of having Negroes play the masterpieces straight.

A few brave experiments have cast individual Negro performers in the famous dramas of the past. Reversing the historical procedure, Canada Lee, with the aid of white make-up, acted the role of Bosola in Webster's *The Duchess of Malfi*; he also acted Caliban in *The Tempest*. Mr. Lee, in all likelihood, owed his selection to his acting verve, but the roles—of villain and of grotesque brute—smacked of earlier casting practices. More to be cheered was the casting of Paul Robeson as Othello, the first instance of a Negro in the role in a professional Broadway production. This did not take place, however, until Robeson's Othello had been most favorably received in England; after glowing reports, Broadway was finally prepared to see a real Negro playing opposite a white Desdemona. The tremendous box-office success on Broadway and the road is indicative of a great change in audience and critical response. In 1924, against *All God's Chillun Got Wings*, Eugene O'Neill's drama of an interracial marriage, there were dire threats of violence, especially when it was learned that the white wife was called upon to kiss the hand of her husband (played by Paul Robeson). But this *Othello*, with Robeson, Uta Hagen, and Jose Ferrer in the leading roles, ran consecutively longer than any Shakespearian drama has done. A different kind of achievement, still a prime instance of integration, was the Scandinavian tour of the Howard Players, whose presentation of *The Wild Duck* interested the Norwegian ambassador so much that he had the government of Norway invite the troupe to play before Ibsen's countrymen.

Instances of individual Negro stars in dramas not based on Negro life are the stellar appearances in Menotti's *The Medium* of Leo Coleman, throughout the long run, and of Zelda Duke George in the leading role. Integration of whites and Negroes in choruses of musical shows was featured in the Federal Theatre *Sing for Your Supper* (1939), *Call Me Mister* (1946), *Bloomer Girl* (1944), and especially *Finian's Rainbow*, a fine spoof of racism, where Negroes shared major and minor roles. *Beggar's Holiday*, an adaptation of *Gay's Beggar's Opera*, united the talents of two Negroes—the composer Duke Ellington and the co-producer and designer Perry Watkins—with those of two whites—lyric writer John LaTouche and co-producer John R. Sheppard; and the cast was thoroughly interracial.

The all-Negro musical comedies, *Cabin in the Sky* by Lynn Root,

Vernon Duke, and John LaTouche; and *St. Louis Woman*, with book by two Negroes, Arna Bontemps and Countee Cullen, with music by the white song writers, Harold Arlen and Johnny Mercer, and directed by Rouben Mamoulian, were star-studded extravaganzas, but they did not create the furor on Broadway caused by those high-hearted shows of the twenties, such as *Shuffle Along* and *Running Wild*. Revivals of the earlier musical shows also did not last long, nor did the revival of *The Green Pastures*; the theatrical fashion has changed.

Most fundamental in integration have been such realistic plays of the last decade as *Native Son, Strange Fruit, Deep Are the Roots, Jeb,* and *On Whitman Avenue*, which set forth with honesty and insight certain tragic aspects of race relations in America. The success of *Anna Lucasta* is significant: written originally about Polish life, it was adapted to a Harlem setting, and thereby revealed that the fundamental humanity was the same. The play also demonstrated the good work that was being done by the American Negro Theatre, and introduced Broadway to some promising young actors. Though commercially unsuccessful, Theodore Ward's *Our Lan'* and Paul Peter's *Nat Turner* have interpreted the Negro's militant role in American history in new fashion. At present, however, no realistic plays of Negro life are on Broadway.

The Negro playwright is still missing from the picture. As one of the signposts to integration, Langston Hughes wrote the lyrics for *Street Scene*, collaborating with Elmer Rice and Kurt Weill in an able production; he also prepared an operatic version, *The Barrier* from his play *Mulatto*. Richard Wright collaborated with Paul Green on *Native Son*. Theodore Ward's *Our Lan'* was the first play by a Negro to be sponsored by the Theatre Guild. But Negro playwrights still have little chance to serve the apprenticeship *in the theatre* so necessary for learning the exacting, technical craft.

Integration of the Negro playwright is therefore far behind that of the material and that of the actor. Edith J.R. Isaacs sees Broadway as "too hurried and harried and too expensive" to offer much to any playwrights. Where, then, is the hope for Negro playwrights? The answer, she states, is simple, and has little to do with race. "The answer will apply if playwrights—all playwrights—will learn to take their time; if they will stop looking with over-eager eyes at the fortunes rolled up by half-a-dozen hit plays a year, and count the money and time and the talents and the courage that are squandered every year on Broadway failures...."[29] She

[29]Edith J. R. Isaacs, *The Negro in the American Theatre* (New York: Theatre Arts, Inc., 1947), p. 134.

concludes that Negro dramatists must, like any other dramatists, learn their craft *before* they head for Broadway. "Among the Negro actors who have made good, those that were well trained have had the best results and ... they got their training before they met the tough professional competition of Broadway."[30]

The tributary theatre, then, is still the Negro playwright's best hope. Even there the outlook is dubious, for Randolph Edmonds, one of the sturdiest workers in that field, writes ruefully that if anybody knows where to locate good scripts of Negro life "he knows more than the writer who is going into his twenty-fifth year in the educational theatre."[31]

Moving Pictures

The lag of the moving pictures behind legitimate drama is nowhere more apparent than in the treatment of Negro life. The earlier story is familiar: in lighter pictures Negroes were inevitably shown as pop-eyed, quaking, terror-stricken at ghosts, or as slow-drawling, indolent nitwits; in "serious" pictures such as *The Birth of the Nation* they were shown as threatening beasts, if they were not slaphappy slaves and buffoons. Hollywood's most successful *Gone With the Wind* merely perpetuated these stereotypes. All-Negro shows like *Hallelujah* and *Hearts of Dixie* did little more than add a kind of local color and exotic quaintness. *Imitation of Life* was sentimental, without understanding. Only an occasional bit character, like the Negro doctor in *Arrowsmith* came anywhere close to authenticity and sincerity. The filming of such dramatic successes as *The Emperor Jones* and *The Green Pastures* were high-water marks in the period before World War II, but neither was based on the common experience of Negro life in America.

During and after World War II, efforts to bring the treatment of Negro life close to reality came to a head. Negro and trade union organizations, film writers and artists, such political figures as Walter White and Wendell Willkie brought promises from Eric Johnston and other powers in Hollywood that better and truer roles would be forthcoming. The first ventures, however, were merely such superior musical shows as *Stormy Weather* and *Cabin in the Sky*. These were lavishly produced in the tradition of Hollywood extravaganza; there was an abundance—perhaps a superabundance—of song and dance talent; artists like Lena Horne,

---

[30]*Ibid.*, p. 138.
[31]S. Randolph Edmonds, "The NAACP Program and Negro Theatrical and Musical Artists," *The Pittsburgh Courier*, November 3, 1951.

Katherine Dunham, and Ethel Waters and musicians like Fats Waller, Duke Ellington, and Cab Calloway got fuller opportunities on the screen. Occasionally Negro performers were given better spots in films not concerned primarily with Negro life, but even some of these newer pictures were *verboten* in certain areas of the South, where shots of Negro and white actors sharing the scene had to be cut out by orders of the local censors.

Serious social commentary was still missing. One of the oddities of the history of moving pictures in America was that for a long time the best treatment of convict labor, of sharecropping, and of lynching were to be found respectively in *I Was a Fugitive From a Georgia Chain-Gang*, *The Grapes of Wrath*, and *They Won't Forget*. In each of these the central character was white, and the injustices, certainly marked in the experience of American Negroes, were in all cases directed against whites. In *They Won't Forget*, a film depicting the lynching of a white Northerner, a Negro janitor has a minor role. A historian of the moving pictures calls his portrayal "one of the few instances in American films in which the fear and oppression that fill the life of the Negro is strikingly told."[32]

In the last few years serious realism has strengthened in Hollywood. The causes of the franker recognition of social ills are several. One is the present need for national unity and for counteracting divisive forces. More than ever Americans feel that the moral leadership of world democracy, which they have assumed, must be firmly grounded. The Negro's determined struggle for full citizenship is slowly gaining in Hollywood as elsewhere. Authors are growing more aware of the Negro's status in, and importance to America: and audiences have a maturity of outlook, which, if not recently developed, is only recently being taken into consideration by Hollywood moguls.

Of the pictures in the new trend, *Intruder in the Dust* showed a Negro of stiff-necked pride, shrewdness, and courage set against the vicious mob spirit of the South. *Lost Boundaries* showed a more genteel but still searing race prejudice in a small New Hampshire town when a family's Negro blood is discovered. *Pinky* showed the dilemma, familiar in fiction but not in moving pictures, of the very fair Negro torn between service to "her" people and an interracial marriage (service and marriage being mutually exclusive according to this version). *Home of the Brave* stressed the fundamental sameness of Negro and white troops. *No Way Out* dealt

[32]Lewis Jacobs, *The Rise of the American Film* (New York: Harcourt, Brace and Co., 1939), p. 486.

with the pathological roots of race hatred and the difficulties confronting a young Negro doctor, against which he pitted great doggedness. *The Quiet One* is a powerful documentary on the impoverished lives of Negro children.[33]

All of these were marked by sympathy and sincerity; all presented serious aspects of Negro life in America. From the young GI in *Home of the Brave*, the young doctor in *No Way Out*, and Lucas Beauchamp in *Intruder in the Dust*, the reach is very far back to Stepin Fetchit and Amos and Andy. One can be grateful for these favors, which are by no means small, yet feel it a critical duty to point out that the pictures contained grave weaknesses.

Two of the pictures handle the book-worn theme of "passing" and the "woebegone mulatto," with little insight and too many clichés. That the doctor in *Lost Boundaries* was "forced" to buy a white practice in a New England town because he was too light to join the staff of a Negro hospital in the South, is certainly news to the Negro medical profession, or to anybody else with 20/200 vision. The Inferno of Harlem in contrast to the Paradise of the New England small town is too pat for credence. The solution in *Pinky*, brought about by the largesse of an old aristocratic lady who rose above the crass prejudices of her area, is as unconvincing as the initial dilemma of the heroine. The attack on prejudice in *No Way Out* was two-fisted, but also wild-swinging in places; the psychotic villain showed his race-hatred so violently that the audience might be forgiven for overlooking its own less violent but no less sinister prejudices. *Home of the Brave*, taken from a play in which the central figure is Jewish, stressed the theme that Negroes and whites are not different, psychologically, but underplayed the acutely different social factors. The close of *Home of the Brave* with the one-armed white veteran and the chastened Negro going off to start an interracial restaurant reminds one of Dickens's London more than of Harlem or Southside Chicago or Cicero, Illinois.

Ralph Ellison sees a danger in these films:

For the temptation toward self-congratulation which comes from seeing these films and sharing in their emotional release is apt to blind us to the true nature of what is unfolding—or failing to unfold—before our eyes. As an antidote to the sentimentality of these films, I suggest that they be seen in predominantly Negro audiences. For here, when the action goes phony, one will hear derisive laughter, not sobs. Seriously, *Intruder in the Dust* is the only film that could be shown in

---

[33]Later pictures, especially *The Well*, continue this social realism, but the writer has not yet seen them.

Harlem without arousing unintended laughter. For it is the only one of four in which Negroes can make complete identification with their screen image. Interestingly, the factors that make this identification possible lie in its depiction not of racial, but of human, qualities.[34]

Nevertheless the treatment of the Negro in these films goes far beyond what might have been envisioned a decade ago. The integration of material, and even of actors is certainly far ahead of the integration of technicians, authors, and directors in Hollywood. Here there is still almost complete exclusion. This is not solely a matter of integration of employment. Before Negroes will be integrated fully in Hollywood they must be allowed to enter into the manifold processes that go into the making of pictures. Before films of Negro life can reach truthfulness and significance and revelation, Negro authors and consultants must be integrated into the industry.

Literature

In American literature, Negro life and character have been considered worthy material for well over a century. Concerned with what differentiated the American experience from the European, early novelists turned to the Negro in America as a fertile source. Less wary than when writing about the Indian, these authors delivered *obiter dicta* on the basis of brief and superficial acquaintance. The slavery controversy produced stereotypes; proslavery authors concentrated on contented and comical slaves; antislavery authors on victims—either submissive like Uncle Tom, or militant like George Harris, or the tragic octoroon like Eliza. True to the prevailing literary fashion, both sides shrouded reality with sentimental idealization. To buttress social policy in the Reconstruction and after, authors created the stereotype of the brute Negro, insulting and swaggering (and incidentally wanting to vote). The "tragic mulatto" stereotype was further developed, in order to dramatize the evils of miscegenation.

It was only with the development of realism that characterization of the Negro broke some of the shackles of stereotyping. It was only then that genuine integration of the material began. Before this, treatment of Negro life and character was set apart in an alcove of special pleading. Paul Laurence Dunbar, part of the local color movement, and Charles Waddell Chesnutt, both a local colorist and a problem novelist, presented Negro

---

[34]Ralph Ellison, "The Shadow and the Act," *The Reporter* (December 6, 1949), I, 19. *No Way Out* was not included in his review.

characters who were more than walking arguments or exotic oddities. W. E. B. Du Bois in *The Souls of Black Folk* revealed the depth of Negro experience rather than the surface. Like the writers of the Irish Renaissance, these authors were beginning to uncover the essential dignity of their material.

The Negro author, however, was less integrated than the material of Negro life. Though highly praised by the leading critic, William Dean Howells, Dunbar expressed resentment at the groove to which his audience relegated him. Chesnutt's racial identification was concealed by his publishers, who feared that knowledge that he was a Negro would injure his reception in a market where there was a high premium on books *about* Negroes but not by Negroes.

In the 1920s, interest in Negro life reached a new high. It was stimulated by southern white authors like Stribling, Du Bose Heyward, Julia Peterkin, E. C. L. Adams, Roark Bradford, and Howard Odum, all of whom had studied Negro folk life carefully; and by Carl Van Vechten, who took Harlem for his province. Coincidentally, the New Negro movement, centered in Harlem but drawing recruits from many sections, began reporting Negro life from the inside. Influential mentors of this "Renaissance" were Alain Locke and Charles S. Johnson, then editor of *Opportunity*. In both theory and practice, James Weldon Johnson taught younger Negro authors to respect the material of Negro life.

The poets Claude McKay, Countee Cullen, and Langston Hughes and the fiction writers Jean Toomer, Rudolph Fisher, and Eric Walrond, won nationwide recognition. Walter White and Jessie Fauset wrote of the hitherto neglected Negro middle class. Though there was exploitation as well as exploration of Negro life, the New Negro movement turned out a body of intrinsically sound work, and most definitely opened publishers' offices to Negro authors. Previously, a Negro appearing in a publishers' office was likely to be considered (rightly) as a messenger with a package.

From the New Deal '30's to the present, the deepening regionalism and the social awareness in American fiction have naturally influenced novels and poetry of Negro life. Novelists such as Arna Bontemps, Zora Hurston, Richard Wright, Chester Himes, and Ann Petry joined with such white novelists as Erskine Caldwell, William Faulkner, Lillian Smith, and Bucklin Moon in presenting Negro life with a new fullness and depth. Negro life in the back country, in small southern towns, in industrial cities, and in Harlem, lodestone of so many novelists, received a fairly thorough coverage. Negro personalities of many types are now in the picture: illiterate farm hands, frustrated intellectuals, the long-suffering accommodator, the bad Negro run amok, the hat-in-hand race leader, the militant returning veteran, the run-of-the-mill "little man" wanting happiness and no trouble—the list is very long.

As far as representation of Negro life is concerned, then, there has been increasing integration in American literature. Though plays of Negro life are now scarce, novels and biographies of Negro life, by both white and Negro authors, appear steadily. A few of these books become best-sellers; many are good-sellers. That the pocket-size reprint editions include many books of Negro life is warrant that canny publishers find the material to have the requisite vitality to reach a large public. This, in turn, is part guarantee of integration into the economics of literature, an important matter since professional Negro authors, i.e., those making a living from their writings, are still few.

The amazing career of Frank Yerby in the field of the historical romance, where he has turned out novel after novel, all best-sellers; the high esteem of Willard Motley, among both the critical and the wider reading public, for his novel of an Italian gangster in Chicago; the experiments of such authors as Zora Neale Hurston, Ann Petry, and William Gardner Smith who have turned from writing chiefly of Negroes to writing of whites; all of these have caused many literary commentators to speak of the integration of the Negro author as something near at hand. The majority of the critics in the valuable *Phylon* Symposium of the Negro in Literature (Fourth Quarter, 1950) are of this opinion.

What is meant by the integration of the author is not always made clear, however. To some it seems to mean "the making of cake and Cadillac money by free lancing for the pulps." The opening of the larger magazines to Negro authors is another sign, one of undue optimism from where I sit, for I can see only a few swallows to indicate *that* summer. Others seem to equate integration with avoidance of Negro life; the thesis seems to run that writers, in order to escape the personal perplexities and the artistic distractions of race, should turn from writing about American Negroes to writing about American whites. Those exploiting this thesis the farthest make integration into a literary "passing for white." A young artist once told me plaintively, "I don't want to paint Negroes; I want to paint human beings." I should have thought his ambition estimable, if I had not learned that for him the groups were mutually exclusive.

The freedom of the Negro author has long been a debated subject. Dunbar ruefully believed that his audience turned from his "deeper" poetry to praise "a jingle in a broken tongue." Cullen rightfully insisted on being considered poet, rather than "Negro poet":

What shepherd heart would keep its fill
For only the darker lamb?

From Fisk University recently a group of young writers issued a brave manifesto, in opposition to chauvinism, special pleading, and

...to having our work viewed, as the custom is, entirely in the light of sociology and politics, to having it overpraised on the one hand by those with an axe to grind or with a conscience to salve...to having it misinterpreted on the other hand by coterie editors, reviewers, anthologists...because we deal with realities we find it neither possible nor desirable to ignore....[35]

Hugh Gloster deplores "the limiting and crippling effects of racial hypersensitivity and Jim-Crow esthetics."[36] And J. Saunders Redding has spoken a valedictory, *On Being Negro in America*:

I hope this piece will stand as the epilogue to whatever contribution I have made to the "literature of race." I want to get on to other things....The obligations imposed by race on the average educated or talented Negro (if this sounds immodest, it must) are vast and become at last onerous. I am tired of giving up my creative initiative to these demands.[37]

White critics have also noticed the limitations forced upon Negro writers. Bucklin Moon, a novelist and publishing editor, believes that "the whole of Negro life has a richness, in spite of second-degree citizenship, which seems made to order for the writer."[38] The Negro writer, however, "under the existing American mores, ... is always, in essence, telling the same story."[39]

Our racial mores are changing, but so slowly that it seems unlikely that any immediate solution of this creative frustration is likely to come from that direction....There will always be a place for the Negro protest novel, but until it

[35]Robert Hayden, Myron O'Higgins, *et al., Counterpoise* (Nashville [Tenn.]: 1948).
[36]Hugh Gloster, "Race and the Negro Writer," *Phylon* (Fourth Quarter, 1950), XI, 4, p. 369.
[37]J. Saunders Redding, *On Being Negro in America* (Indianapolis: The Bobbs-Merrill Co., 1951), p. 26.
[38]Bucklin Moon, "A Literature of Protest," *The Reporter*, I, 17 (December 6, 1949), p. 36.
[39]*Ibid.*

becomes the exception, rather than the rule, American literature will suffer along with the Negro artist.[40]

Jean Paul Sartre believes that, faced with disfranchisement and other evils, the Negro writer cannot "pass his life in the contemplation of the eternal True, Good, and Beautiful." "Thus, if an American Negro finds that he has a vocation as a writer, he discovers his subject at the same time." Whether "pamphleteer, blues writer, or the Jeremiah of the Southern Negroes," the Negro writer "sees the whites from the outside, assimilates the white culture from the outside," and will show the alienation of the black race within American society, "not objectively, like the realists, but passionately."[41] Unlike Bucklin Moon, Sartre sees this absorption, an instance of the "engagement" of the author, as a good thing.

Bernard Wolfe sees the Negro as similar to the pariah in a caste society; and "interplay of image, reflex, and masquerade" goes on constantly; the Negro artist for long has been passively enslaved by the "white man's tyrant image." Now, however, the caste system is "losing its hold on the Negro's inner life." and here and there something new is being added: "a rebellion against both reflex and false face, a disowning of the white man's image entirely."[42]

According to Cedric Dover, his fellow Eurasian writers and colored writers generally exist in an arid and lonely atmosphere, with an audience small and "poorly schooled, priest-ridden, socially and intellectually imitative, limited in its attitudes."[43]

We have allowed our creativeness to be crushed not only by oppression and exploitation, but by our own sycophancy, bigotry, Uncle Tomism, and desire to equal and excel our masters in the culture they have allowed us to sniff.[44]

From a position on the extreme left, Lloyd Brown argues that the Negro writer is still in a Jim-Crow ghetto, excluded from general avenues of expression; but he adds that the Negro writer, far from being preoccupied

---

[40]*Ibid.*, p. 37.

[41]Jean Paul Sartre, *What Is Literature?* (New York: Philosophical Library, 1949), pp. 77–78.

[42]Bernard Wolfe, "Ecstatic in Blackface," *The Modern Review*, III (January, 1950), pp. 201ff.

[43]Cedric Dover, *Feathers in the Arrow* (Bombay: Padma Publications, Ltd., 1947), p. 17.

[44]*Ibid.*, p. 21.

with Negro material, "has not been Negro enough—that is, has not fully reflected the real life and character of the people."[45]

Diametrically opposite, a swing of the pendulum from the usual protest against the publishers' unwillingness to take forthright work about Negro life, Richard Gibson tells of liberal publishers who rejected a novel because it did not deal topically with a race theme. He also attacks the Professional Liberal as a bane to the Negro writer:

> The Professional Liberal will not fail to remind him that he cannot possibly know anything else but Jim Crow, sharecropping, slum-ghettos, Georgia crackers, and the sting of his humiliation, his unending ordeal, his blackness.[46]

And so the war rages. Several of the battlers are "either-or" extremists. Echoes resound of battles long ago: propaganda versus pure art; the ivory tower versus the arena of action; the sociological versus the belle-lettristic; the radical versus the conservative; the conscious avoidance of racial material versus the exclusive use. But these extreme positions confuse, it seems to me, the real battle line.

Even if the status of Negroes in America did not make the propaganda novel a natural expectancy, such mentors as Zola, Dreiser, Steinbeck, and Farrell in uncovering the lower depths would certainly have been potent influences. It cannot be gainsaid, however, that concentration on the problem has narrowed and hardened creative writing among Negroes. True to the tactics of pressure groups, characters have too often been villains or victims. Mob violence and lynching have become the hackneyed climaxes to dramatize the Negro's wrong; apparently easy, apparently sure-fire "big scenes," they are often ineptly handled artistically and miss fire. But all of this is not the fault of "race material"; it is rather bad characterization, weak dramatization of the theme, and often fails just because the writer is not being true to the type of Negro life that he feels and has absorbed most deeply. An example of different use of "race material" is such a novel as Owen Dodson's *Boy in the Window*. Its achievement is the sensitive, painstaking account of a Negro boy's growing up in Brooklyn and Washington, obviously set firmly in the author's experience. Race impinges on the plot, but fundamentally the novel gives the picture of childhood. It cannot be said that the boy's being

---

[45]Lloyd Brown, "Which Way for the Negro Writer?," *Masses and Mainstream*, 4 (April, 1951), p. 54.

[46]Richard Gibson, "Is the Negro Writer Free?," reprinted from *The Kenyon Review*, Spring, 1951, in *The Negro Digest*, XX, 11 (September, 1951), pp. 43ff.

a Negro is incidental; in most of the experience it is central. But the novel sets out to solve no problem, to denounce no wrongs, only to reveal personality and a way of life, which it does with great skill. And critics generally have considered it an American, not a Negro, novel, revealing a significant American, not Negro, talent.

That way, it seems to me, true integration lies. It does not lie in default, in letting the treatment of Negro life go by forfeit. On examination, what most of the sponsors of the exodus from Negro materials really are attacking is not race material, but its treatment. The real *bête noire* is not so much the Negro as it is the Negro Problem, handled in crude, ungainly fashion.

There is nothing new in the belief that Negro artists can only be free when they write about white people. Dunbar, believing that "we must write like the white men...our life is now the same,"[47] concentrated on white characters in three of his four novels, and the results were negligible. Before the present vogue, Chesnutt, Arna Bontemps, and William Attaway wrote fiction about white characters, but their fiction about Negroes is superior.

The best-selling successes of Yerby and Motley are pointed to as signs of an artistic maturity and emancipation, refuting the theory that the artist writes best about what he knows best. But such instances do not really refute. As far as Yerby is concerned, escapist romance we always have with us, and the industrious novelist can find historical material galore to deck out in glamour and excitement; his success does not depend upon how deeply he has absorbed his material and how significantly he communicates it. Yerby's canny skill as a plot contriver, not his illumination of history, has built up his immense following. Motley's success in an opposite direction, that of social protest on a naturalistic base, is an exception proving the rule. Granted Motley's undoubted talents, there is no reason why a Negro brought up in a polyglot, fringe community should not render its life vividly and movingly.

But Negro writers, by and large, do not have similar experience to levy upon; too often, in the words of Sartre, they see "the whites from the outside." Ann Petry, making use of her experience as the daughter of a druggist in a Connecticut small town, writes a novel about whites in such a community; Zora Hurston, from her copious knowledge of folklore, writes a novel about crackers in the Florida scrub. To a degree they are

[47]Benjamin Brawley, *Paul Laurence Dunbar* (Chapel Hill, North Carolina: University of North Carolina Press, 1936), p. 77.

drawing from experience, but this is not what they *fully* know, only what they *half* know. As a consequence, Miss Petry's *Country Place* does not measure up to her earlier *The Street*, and Miss Hurston's *Seraph on the Suwanee* falls far below her *Mules and Men* and *Their Eyes Were Watching God.*

The new freedom (if it is new) is good, in that freedom is better than forced confinement (if it was forced). But the proof must be in the caliber of the work produced, instead of in the fact that Negroes are no longer writing about Negroes. Much of the hostility to the treatment of Negro life in art is summed up in James Weldon Johnson's phrase, "second generation respectability." "A man climbing a steep hill does not like to stop and look back down," a friend once said to me. Many Negroes to whom integration in America can be symbolized by fish-tail Cadillacs and mink coats (which are certainly *one* kind of Americanization) are hurt to the quick by such characters as Porgy and Bigger Thomas; their ears are jarred by even God's trombones. They do not want art to deal with Negro life, whether truly or falsely, with revelation or caricature; they just want out. All of the critics counseling flight, of course, are not afflicted by this anti-Negro feeling, which is as pronounced in many Negroes as anti-Semitism is in many Jews. Some readers and critics, with greater literary pretensions, are just offended by modern realism, whether of Oakies or Shanty Irish or Ghetto Jews or Tobacco Road Anglo-Saxons or Reservation Navahos. But whether anti-Negro or anti-realistic, or both, such readers and critics hail as the only integration the fact that a few Negroes, with varying success, have written novels about white characters.

But Phillis Wheatley, writing her heroic couplets in the manner of Pope for the matter of Puritan Boston, is less integrated in American culture than Frederick Douglass, writing *My Bondage and My Freedom* and treading the anti-slavery platforms, a peer among peers, with Wendell Phillips and Theodore Parker. W. E. B. Du Bois's *Souls of Black Folk* is more integrally American literature than Dunbar's novels about white people. Countee Cullen's poems on Keats are no more integrated in American poetry than his "Shroud of Color," and Cullen, who disliked the term "Negro poet," is no more and no less an American poet than Langston Hughes. Braithwaite's biography of the Bronte sisters stands no better chance of integration, merely because of the stature of the subjects, than his autobiography, *House Under Arcturus*. Frank Yerby's romances of the Old South are no more integrated in American historical fiction than Arna Bontemps's *Black Thunder*, which is about a slave insurrection.

James Weldon Johnson's *Along This Way* and short stories by Jean Toomer, Eric Walrond, and Rudolph Fisher are as integral to American literature as the new, "emancipated" fiction is, even though new types of publishers' promotion have raised this fiction to best-selling prestige.

What [asks David Daiches] is a great work of fiction?... We shall probably find that the greatest works are those which, while fulfilling all the formal requirements, most adequately reflect the civilization of which they are a product. This does not conflict with the traditional view that great art presents the universal through the particular.... [48]

For the most serious and important modern fiction, it is a truism that the artist must have fullest comprehension of his material in order to achieve the "solidity of specification" that is basic. Before he can attain to the universal he must have absorbed those particulars which come from his deepest experience, those that he understands best and to which his imagination is most responsive.

Though telling of Irish writers, Sean O'Faolain says good things for Negro writers, or those of any minority, to heed:

The Irish writer was a provincial while he imitated slavishly and tried to write beyond his talents; he ceased to be a provincial when he wrote of what he knew and could describe better than anybody else.... It was an entirely new thing for men to realize the full and complete dignity of the simplest life of the simplest people. Once they had acknowledged that, then they were free to do anything they liked with it in literature—treat it naturalistically, fantastically, romantically, see it in any light they chose. They had conquered their material by accepting it. [49]

Two historians of American poetry praise the elder generation of Dunbar, Johnson, and Braithwaite, who "not without wisdom... saw the figure of the Russian poet, Alexander Pushkin, as a distant end in view for their accomplishment." [50] The careers of Alexander Dumas, *pere* and *fils*, in nineteenth century drama and fiction are also held up by many as beacons to the American Negro writer. But these men were accepted to a degree almost unknown by American Negroes even today. For the elder Dumas, at home on Parisian boulevards and in the salons; for the younger, equally at home in the Parisian theatre world; and for Pushkin, the brilliant courtier and poet of St. Petersburg, race was unquestionably meaningless. For resemblances to such social situations, one must go to

[48]David Daiches, *The Novel and the Modern World* (Chicago: The University of Chicago Press, 1939), p. 219.

[49]Sean O'Faolain, *The Irish* (New York: The Devin-Adair Co., 1942), pp. 162ff.

certain Latin-American countries (Cuba and Brazil, for instance) and even here the situations are not parallel. To envisage the future of the Negro writer in the United States in terms of the acceptance and achievement of Alexander Dumas and Alexander Pushkin seems to overlook too many complicating factors.

It is easy to agree with Charles Glicksberg that contemporary Negro authors suffer from "psychological repression and cultural frustration," and that an "exacerbated racial motif" results. But, as he points out, that does not end the story. The motif is justified and fruitful:

> The Negro writers in the United States know what they are about. Their ultimate goal is not to accentuate differences of color and race, not to deepen the cleavage and render inevitable the sense of cultural alienation. Their objective is nothing less than complete assimilation, not in the sense of discarding whatever belongs properly to him as a man and as a member of his group, but in the sense of being an integral part of the life of the nation.[51]

Signs of integration are heart-warming. On one—certainly not negligible—level, the reissue in the cheap editions of books by Negro authors and by white authors on Negro life is a good sign. On a higher level are the Book-of-the-Month selections of Richard Wright and the Pulitzer Prize award in poetry to Gwendolyn Brooks. A few anthologies and textbooks include a sprinkling of Negro names and works. More and more frequently literary fellowships are won by Negroes; literary groups receive Negroes on the basis of equality; Negro authors share the hospitality and stimulation of Yaddo and summer schools of writing. Another good sign is the Negro author's surrender of his missionary fervor, the conscious struggle to overcome his alienation, to secure as much objectivity as possible, to see and render not whites and Negroes, but men (which is not the same as "conscious avoidance of race"). There are also good signs that an audience is increasing in America and abroad, and that the Negro audience is losing some of its hypersensitivity, and learning something of the respect due to its artistic interpreters. Most important of all, are the signs that the Negro writer is gaining in craftsmanship and understanding.

When Negro authors emerge worthy to tell the story, the stories, of the Negro in America, they will write with authenticity and power, not

[50]Horace Gregory and Marya Zaturenska, *A History of American Poetry* (New York: Harcourt, Brace and Co., 1946), p. 397.

[51]Charles I. Glicksberg, "Eurasian Racialism," *Phylon*, XII (First Quarter, 1951), p. 18.

because of any racial *mystique*, but because they have lived the story so fully, brooded upon it so deeply, and fashioned it with loving and informed care. And that will mean not only that the Negro author is integrated into American literature, but even more that he will be given passport to enter the Republic of Letters of the world.

But that is the dim hope for the far-off time. The present fact weighs heavily: that, despite all the multiplied signs of integration, the Negro author, like the Negro athlete and the Negro artist in any field, is not likely to achieve full integration in American culture until American Negroes, by and large, are themselves integrated into all the rights and responsibilities of full American citizenship.

E. Franklin Frazier, ed., *The Integration of the Negro into American Society, Papers Contributed to the Fourteenth Annual Conference of the Division of Social Sciences* (Washington: Howard University Press, 1951), pp. 117–47. Footnotes in original.

3

CHANGES IN LEGAL STATUS OF THE NEGRO

by William R. Ming, Jr.

On the same occasion that produced Sterling A. Brown's study of "Athletics and Arts" came that of the African-American's legal status in mid-twentieth century. From this essay, by a leading Illinois attorney, is extracted that section touching on changing legal status—one that anticipates the explosion of the *Brown* decisions in 1954 and 1955.

What I can say is that there have been some important decisions, particularly by the Supreme Court of the United States, which, under the doctrine of *stare decisis*, should be followed in similar cases. If they are, especially in the lower courts, some major changes in the legal status of Negroes will result. Perhaps, even more important, some seeds of legal theory have been planted in opinions. If they germinate and grow, radical changes may result. In addition, there have been a few, but only a few, statutory changes which are relevant here.

Let us examine, though not in detail, some of these decisions and statutes. I have endeavored to classify them to reflect, in some measure, my opinion of their importance so far as the legal status of Negroes generally is concerned.

To begin with, therefore, since law is an instrument of government, let us look at those changes in the law, if there are any, with respect to participation of Negroes in the affairs of government. Such changes will inevitably result in other changes in legal status as Negroes participate in government.

It is now an accepted principle of American political organization that, while we do not have universal suffrage, every adult, sane, fairly literate person who has not been convicted of a felony is entitled to participate equally in the selection of officers in government. Only thus can representative government be achieved and maintained. Thirty years ago it would have been only a slight exaggeration to say that no Negroes could vote south of the Mason-Dixon Line, where the great bulk of Negroes still live. Despite the 14th and 15th Amendments, this condition was maintained by a series of statutory limitations, including the "grandfather clause," which, though it was outlawed as early as 1915, persisted in various forms till 1939, the poll tax, and the exclusion of Negroes from the Democratic primaries. In addition, there was the hooded, but not veiled, threat of the Ku Klux Klan and similar groups to prevent participation by Negroes in the selection of government officers.

Despite the temporary set-back of an adverse decision in *Grovey v. Townsend*, Negroes in Texas fought stubbornly against their exclusion from the Democratic primaries, which are determinative of the elections in their State as in other southern states. Finally in 1944 in *Smith v. Allwright*, the Supreme Court of the United States held that it was a violation of the Constitution of the United States for even the Democratic Party to exclude Negro voters, otherwise qualified, from the Democratic primaries in that State. Similar decisions followed in the federal courts with respect to the primaries in South Carolina. Equally significant was the decision outlawing the infamous "Boswell Amendment" to the Constitution of Alabama, which literally authorized local registrars to exclude any voter from registration thus barring him from all elections, general as well as primary, if he failed to "understand and explain" a section of the Federal Constitution to the satisfaction of the registrar. You can imagine how that worked in Alabama.

The poll tax, of course, remains in seven states and the federal courts have steadfastly refused to recognize that its purpose is not to raise revenue for those states, but to provide the means by which both Negroes and poor whites can be kept from voting. Nevertheless, the outlawing of the "white primaries" has opened the polls to hundreds of thousands of

Negro voters. Authoritative evidence as to the extent to which Negroes in the South have availed themselves of the opportunities to vote is not available. Conservative estimates, however, at various places in Texas, South Carolina, Florida, Alabama, and Georgia indicate an ever-increasing number of Negro voters moving to the polls despite threats, intimidations, floggings, lynchings, and destruction of property. If one looks at the 15th Amendment, it cannot be said that these decisions represent any change in the formal legal status of Negroes. But if one looks at the facts as to the exclusion of Negroes from the polls, it can rightfully be asserted that these decisions mark a major change in their status as voters. What is even more important, as Negroes participate in government, it may reasonably be expected that their legal status will tend to become what they require their officers of government to provide for them.

To move on, in a country, one of whose prime characteristics is the institution of private property, an important aspect of legal status is the extent to which the law provides enforcement for, and protection of, property rights. In the Anglo-American legal system, traditionally, major emphasis has been placed for centuries on the protection of the rights of individuals to real property and particularly to that on which they resided. This protection, however, has, until recently, been provided for Negroes only if their residences were located in an area where the majority of the community was willing to allow them to live. Essentially, of course, these ghettos are an urban phenomenon. But that is only because restrictions on living space involve more people in cities than they do in rural communities. Put another way, in rural areas the principle of racial segregation is as strictly enforced as it is in Chicago, Los Angeles, New York, Washington, or Birmingham. Somewhat surprisingly, the Supreme Court of the United States had held more than thirty years ago that city and state governments were prohibited by the 14th Amendment from requiring racial residential segregation. Ingenious property lawyers, however, relying upon doctrines developed by the Anglo-American legal institutions to permit urban property owners to protect light and air for urban residents, devised agreements between property owners whereby they contracted not to sell or rent their property to Negroes, Jews, and other minority groups. In some cities the acreage covered by these restrictive covenants was fantastically high. In practically every American city there was 100 per cent coverage by such agreements of the areas immediately adjacent to Negro ghettos. A long and determined fight against these restrictions was finally successful. In 1948 the Supreme Court of the United States in a series of decisions, *Shelley v. Kramer, Sipes v. McGhee*, and *Hurd v. Hodge*, held that neither state nor federal courts had the power to enforce such agreements.

In effect what the court held was that no owner of real property was barred from selling or renting that property to a Negro simply because the owner had previously agreed that he would not do so. This limited character of the Restrictive Covenant decisions is important to notice. The court did not hold that any Negro had a right to buy property wherever he chose. It did not hold that Negroes could not arbitrarily be excluded from the market for any particular real estate. It simply held that an owner of real estate was not prohibited from renting or selling to a Negro by any agreement with respect to the matter which the owner might have made in the past.

This decision was important in view of the widespread use of restrictive covenants and in view of the fact that their enforcement prevented Negroes from using their own economic resources as a means of solution of their individual housing problems. The decision, however, did not solve the housing problem for Negroes, though it did enable many Negroes to buy and rent more and better housing.

Nevertheless the decision offers the possibility of a major change in the legal status of Negroes because of the legal theory upon which the court relied in order to justify its decision.

To demonstrate the importance of the decision in this regard it is necessary briefly to refer to some earlier constructions of the 14th Amendment. In 1883, after the northern army had withdrawn from the southern states and the radical abolitionist Republicans had lost their political power in the national government, a majority of the Supreme Court of the United States deliberately construed the 14th Amendment in a fashion well calculated to reduce its effectiveness. You will remember that as a part of the abolitionist legislative program which produced the 14th and 15th Amendments, the Congress had also adopted a Civil Rights Act which, broadly speaking, made it a federal offense to deny to any person on account of his race or color, access to any place of public accommodation. In the Civil Rights cases the Supreme Court held that this statute exceeded the powers of Congress because, they said, the 14th Amendment applied only to governmental action by the states and that therefore, though Congress was given power to enforce the amendment by appropriate legislation, it could not regulate the conduct of private persons to carry out the purposes of that amendment. To date there has been no contrary judicial expression.

The major significance of the Restrictive Covenant cases, therefore, is found in the fact that, while purporting to adhere to this limitation on the power of the federal government, the court nevertheless denied to private persons the assistance of the state and federal courts in carrying out private discriminatory agreements. To do otherwise, said the court, would be to deny the equal protection of the laws to Negroes since, restrictive covenant or not, a white person similarly situated would not be the object of such judicial action. Indeed, the court expressly said that the federal law did not prevent private persons from making restrictive covenants; it only prevented state and federal courts from enforcing them.

The decision thus appears to open a host of possibilities. To begin with, all of the "jim-crow" statutes would appear to be invalidated. If the "equal protection" clause of the 14th Amendment prohibits a state court from enforcing even a private agreement with a discriminatory result, then certainly no state legislation to the same end could be enforced by a court. To the skeptics who would grumble that a Negro's "property" interest was involved in the Restrictive Covenant cases, let me point out that on the basis of precedents a similar property interest in schools and carriers can be established. Besides, the real basis for the court's decision here was its conclusion that race was not a proper basis for determining what the governmental action should be. One state court, in California, has already adopted this view in holding unconstitutional that state's prohibition of mixed marriages.

Other possibilities suggest themselves. If the owner of a public place refuses to serve a Negro would-be patron, and calls a police officer to require the Negro to leave or be arrested, it would appear to be a violation of the "equal protection" clause for the officer who would be exercising state power to take any action he would not take if the would-be patron were a white man. Similarly, if the owner of a hotel refuses to furnish accommodations to a Negro and the latter brings an action for damages, it would appear that if the court refuses those damages to the plaintiff, it has denied him the equal protection of the laws, since such an action would lie if the would-be patron were a non-Negro. Innumerable analogous situations can be imagined. If this line is followed the end of governmentally enforced segregation is in view. That indeed would be a radical change in the legal status of Negroes in the United States.

I have suggested this aspect of the Restrictive Covenant decisions in an article on those cases. This argument was made in the *Sweatt* and *McLaurin* cases which I will come to in a moment. The court neither accepted nor rejected it. Shortly after the publication of my article on this subject, however, a former clerk of one of the justices who had participated in the Restrictive Covenant decisions hotly denied that the court had any intention of going so far. Without regard to the judicial intention, however, if it is a denial of equal protection of the laws and thus a contravention of the 14th Amendment for a state court to enforce an agreement between private persons which applies only to Negroes, it appears to follow inevitably that the state courts are forbidden to enforce any relationships between individuals which differ on the basis of the race of the individuals involved.

Judicial treatment or residential segregation since the Restrictive Covenant cases furnishes an illustration of the difficulties involved in making generalizations about the legal status of Negroes. It will be remembered that all three of these cases arose from the efforts of adjacent property owners to secure injunctions restraining Negro purchasers of property from occupying that property. Seizing on that fact, the Missouri Supreme Court in *Weiss v. Leaon* affirmed the decision of a Missouri trial court which had dismissed a similar action against a Negro property owner, but which had upheld the right of adjacent property owners to maintain an action for money damages against the white seller of the property to the Negro purchaser.

On the theory announced by the Chief Justice of the United States in the Restrictive Covenant cases that the equal protection clause prohibited the use of the states' judicial power to limit the right of Negroes to occupy property, this result seems impossible to justify. In effect, of course, what the Missouri court did was to provide a sanction against the owners of property who sign restrictive covenants. This seems likely to prevent them from selling the property to Negroes even though the same court concedes that it would have no power under the decision in *Shelley v. Kramer* to enjoin the Negro purchaser's use and occupancy of the property. The Missouri decision, if followed, would mean that the market price to a Negro purchaser of any given piece of property covered by a restrictive covenant would be the market price of such property plus the amount the seller estimated he might be forced to pay in damages. Thus, the Missouri court would approve a price differential on specific property based solely on the race of the purchaser of such property.

Unfortunately, because of organizational and professional difficulties too involved to warrant consideration here, no petition for *certiorari* in the Supreme Court of the United States was filed in the *Weiss* case. Thus the decision stands as the law of Missouri and invites other state courts to commit the same error. It seems likely, however, that faced with such a case the Supreme Court of the United States would reach the opposite result because the judicial remedy of money damages is indistinguishable as "state action" from the grant of an injunction.

From the foregoing it must not be inferred that racial segregation has lost its legal sanctions yet. Indeed in the public education cases the court thus far has clung to its pernicious "separate but equal" doctrine. This, despite the fact that it has been demonstrated to them that the doctrine was invented by a court which was engaged in sabotaging the 14th Amendment as it was told by one of its own members, Mr. Justice Harlan, a great stalwart in the fight for liberty of an oppressed people, now all but forgotten save by those lawyers who seek to undo the damage he could not prevent. But the fight for equal educational opportunities for black children goes on. You know the celebrated cases, *Gaines, Sipuel, Sweatt, McLaurin*, and the equal teachers' salary cases, headed by *Alston v. School Board of Norfolk*. At the same time, however, other graduate and professional schools as in Arkansas, of all places, Kentucky, Louisiana, and others, have opened their doors to qualified young Negroes, some even without litigation.

The court's refusal to outlaw segregation as such has imposed a monumental, back-breaking task on a people determined to improve the opportunities for their children. It means that as we move from the top-level to the grade schools innumerable cases must be brought. Many have already been tried, successfully, particularly in Virginia, but more will be necessary as long as the courts refuse to recognize that people cannot be separately educated to live together.

In these cases, particularly, there has been a splendid cooperation and contribution of the social scientists. In fact, Howard's Dean Thompson has testified in so many that he now gives legal advice as well as his opinion on educational matters, though he probably reached the peak of his forensic career when he gravely advised one court that a Negro boy or girl would have access to more books if he went to jail in that state rather than to its Negro school since their prison library had substantially more books than their Negro college did! Other men from this institution, and other scholars from other schools from California to Harvard have given their time and skills in this fight.

I regret to admit that, even in my own state of Illinois where the *state* law prohibits it, segregated schools are sanctioned by law in a large part of the State. But the fight goes on. It can be said, I think, that the legal status of separate schools is in flux as at the end of this month a trial involving rural South Carolina elementary schools begins in Charleston in federal court, Governor Byrnes notwithstanding.

A vital area in which our legal status has made little progress is in that of job opportunities. Led by Charles H. Houston, that deeply-mourned champion of the rights of his people, Negro railroad workers have in recent years wrested from the brotherhoods the right to work in that industry. As an illustration of the problems in this area, those craft unions had utilized powers conferred on them by a federal statute to assure them the right to bargain collectively with the railroads, for the purpose of ousting Negro employees from their jobs while simultaneously excluding them from membership in the unions. In the *Tunstall* and *Steele* cases the Supreme Court recognized the obligation of equality that such a labor monopoly must accept if it is to exercise that vast power conferred by the Railway Labor Act and held the brotherhoods responsible in damages to the Negro workers they had ousted.

Similarly, eight states, New York, New Jersey, Massachusetts, Connecticut, Rhode Island, New Mexico, Oregon, and Washington, have enacted fair employment statutes. Two other states, Indiana and Wisconsin, have adopted measures which are little more than exhortations to employees to stop job discrimination. Several northern cities have FEPC ordinances. Meantime, the federal wartime FEPC has come and gone.

Little objective data are available as to the effectiveness of these measures. Some critics have been caustic as to their shortcomings. Other observers have been enthusiastic. In any event we are a long way from a legal status of equal job opportunity. No court has ever wholly recognized the right to work as one which is judicially enforceable. The conflict with the interests of employers is obvious. Meanwhile, even in periods of "full employment," thousands of Negroes are on relief, as in Illinois, where nearly 80 per cent of all persons on relief in the State are Negroes, though we are less than 8 per cent of the total population.

Here is a great weakness in our status. Job discrimination condemns thousands of black workers to poverty or to a marginal existence which blights the workers and denies all opportunities to their children. To this problem our best efforts must be directed. So far only FEPC and industrial unions have appeared as remedies. Even the latter failed, however, in its southern organizing drive, "Operation Dixie." We must develop other remedies.

Another area which has attracted considerable public attention over the years is that of segregation in public conveyances. You will remember that it was with respect to a public conveyance that the Supreme Court first enunciated the "separate but equal" doctrine in upholding a Louisiana "jim-crow" statute in 1896. No such statute has ever been declared invalid, though in the *Morgan* case in 1946 the Virginia "jim-crow" statute was held invalid as applied to an interstate carrier. The court based the result on orthodox notions of the limitations of state authority. Interestingly, however, in the *Bob-lo* case in the next year those same limitations were held not to prevent requiring a small steamer plying between Detroit and a pleasure island on the *Canadian* side of the river from being forced to obey the Michigan civil rights statute. Most recently, following the line it had taken earlier in the *Mitchell* case with respect to Pullman facilities in 1940, the court held in the *Henderson* case that an interstate carrier which denied dining car facilities to a Negro passenger had violated the Federal Transportation Act, and that the carrier's obligation to render service to its passengers without discrimination was not satisfied by providing a segregated table for its Negro passengers.

The equal legal status of Negro interstate travelers on public conveyances thus seems assured, though some railroads still persist in their practices even in northern terminals. The symbolic importance of this issue cannot be ignored. Like all other segregation, its legal sanctions must be destroyed and probably will be shortly.

The last major area which I shall attempt to discuss is that of criminal trials. As I have said, entirely satisfactory data are lacking as to whether the operation of criminal law enforcement is to any great extent affected by the race of the defendant. Many of us believe that it is. Some legal remedies to prevent this have been won but the over-all picture seems far from satisfactory. For example, ever since 1880 it has been held that systematic exclusion of Negroes from grand or trial juries violated the 14th Amendment and would be a ground for setting aside a conviction of a Negro defendant. It has never been entirely clear whether it was to protect the defendant or to preserve the right of Negroes to serve on juries. Some of us who have represented Negro defendants before juries which included one or more staid, middle-class, middle-aged, "respectable" Negroes have concluded that class, environment, habits, religion, and temperament are more important in jurors to a defendant than race. But innumerable convictions of Negroes by state courts have been set aside on this ground in the past seventy years.

Similarly, after a false start, the Supreme Court held in *Brown v. Mississippi* that a conviction was invalid if returned by a court under mob domination. Likewise, the protection of all defendants from the "third degree" has been freely extended to Negroes, at least in the federal courts, and several convictions have been set aside on this ground in cases like *Chambers v. Florida* where peace officers freely admitted beating confessions out of helpless defendants.

Only last month the court came close to the heart of the real problem in *Shepherd v. Florida* but set aside the conviction on the "jury" ground. This was much to the disgust of Justices Jackson and Frankfurter, who concurred but pointed out that the newspapers in the county had adjudged the defendants guilty and demanded their execution before the trial in news stories and editorials aimed at inflaming local prejudices so that a fair trial was impossible.

But this same problem exists in many jurisdictions in both the South and North. How are latent racial animosities and prejudices to be overcome so as to assure Negro defendants a fair trial? Few cases satisfy the test of "mob domination," but the injury to the particular defendant is just as real. Frequently, waiver of a jury and trial before a judge alone is helpful in communities where judges are elected and Negroes vote. But this is not sufficient. Some means are necessary to protect hapless, and often penniless, Negro defendants from the racial prejudice which often is the sole basis for conviction.

Conclusion

Other topics could be discussed. Among them would be the status of the Negro in the armed forces. Lagging far behind its sister services, the Navy and Air Forces, the Army persists in maintaining segregated units. As mobilization moves on apace, no satisfactory legal remedies have been found to assure Negro inductees of that equality of status to which their assumption of obligation entitles them. Another interesting legal development which warrants exploration is the prohibition of group defamation. Only recently, following a New Jersey opinion to the contrary, the Illinois

Supreme Court has upheld such a statute. But an exhaustive description of the legal status of Negroes on the changes which are occurring is not possible here.

Following the leadership of the NAACP and its Special Counsel, Thurgood Marshall, lawyers both black and white in many places throughout the country are, sometimes with a bright flash, more often with a steady stroke, carving out a new legal status for Negroes. They are supported by an ever-growing host of Americans of all races, creeds, and colors who recognize the legal status of Negroes as the barometer of freedom of all Americans. Before those true Americans is the rest of the world torn by conflicting ideologies struggling for the support of peoples of every race and color. Rightly the world's peoples judge American democracy by its results for America's largest minority. In such a milieu law and legal status is ever-changing. A body of law which sanctions only full integration may be a long way ahead, but chattel slavery is even farther behind.

E. Franklin Frazier. *op. cit.*, pp. 204–212.

4

CALL TO A CONFERENCE (1951)

by Ruth Jett

Among the papers in the editor's possession is a "Call to a Conference on Radio, Television and the Negro People." This was issued in 1951. The most active person in this effort was Ruth Jett, who, in 1951, produced Alice Childress's *Just a Little Simple* and *A Medal for Willie* by William Branch. Both had considerable runs at the Club Baron in Harlem. The Call, in mimeographed form, follows. The conference itself was held in November 1951; more on this will appear in subsequent pages.

THE FACTS:

THE AMERICAN people spend more time listening to the radio than they do at any other activity except sleeping and working. Radio is one of the most potent forces shaping America's thinking.

In name, if not in fact, radio belongs to the people. No license for radio station operation can be granted or renewed unless evidence is given to the FCC that the broadcast emanating from that station will serve the convenience, interest, and necessity of the Public.

Four major networks originate programs 14 hours a day. 1200 stations pulse out network and local programs 18 hours a day.

This means:

—72 fifteen minute broadcast periods for each station each day.
—504 fifteen minute broadcast periods for each station each week.
—604,800 fifteen minute broadcast periods each week for all stations.

There are 604,800 fifteen minute broadcasting periods each week,

BUT—

—Not one, not a single one, is produced by a Negro.
—Not one, not a single one, is directed by a Negro.
—Not one, not a single one, employs a Negro commentator.
—Not one, not a single one, concerns itself with Negro news.
—Not one, not a single one, employs a Negro sound effects man.
—In all those 604,800 broadcast periods there is only an occasional Negro singer or musician and two or three Negro orchestras.
—6 Negro engineers are employed in all radio.
—6 Negro writers are employed in all radio, and only one is employed full time.
—6 Negro announcers are employed in all radio.
—A few Negro actors work for radio when they can get work.

And of all the 604,800 fifteen minute broadcast periods per week, there are not more than 12 such periods which give any portrayal of Negro life whatever. And the portrayal of Negro life they do depict is a slander upon the Negro people.

The truth about Negro Americans is not held a fit subject for radio. The Negro is isolated and misunderstood and not allowed to communicate. Radio today has posed for each of us the question: Is the greatness and humanity of Negro America—of Crispus Attucks, Frederick Douglass, Marion Anderson, Paul Robeson, Jackie Robinson—to be presented over the radio channels forever in terms of "Amos 'n Andy" & "Beulah"?

In keeping the truth about Negroes from the airwaves, in presenting and perpetuating the stereotype, American radio caters to lynch mentality. Radio is ever mindful of offending "The South." Radio is ever mindful of the feelings of the lyncher, while it violates the rights of the lynched! We know that the first step in the creation of a lynch atmosphere is to deprive the individual in danger of lynching of human dignity.

And what is true of radio is becoming true, also, of Television.

　—Action must be taken to end this situation within radio, so long tolerated even by liberals and honest-thinking persons. There has been much talk in the past, but little action.

　—Action must be taken now to tear down the Iron Curtain which keeps the truth about Negroes from America.

　—Action must be taken now to make a permanent place in radio for Negro actors, writers, singers, directors, producers, engineers, sound effects men, clerks, secretaries and all other types of personnel.

　—Action must be taken now to provide a means of expression and communication, an outlet for the cultural riches of the Negro people.

　—Action must be taken now to guarantee that Television does not emerge ridden with the same distortions and attacks upon the Negro people, the same lily-white "purity" in employment.

THIS IS A CALL FOR A CONFERENCE
TO INITIATE SUCH ACTION.

5

UNCLE TOM IS DEAD! (1951)

by William R. Hood

Efforts to resist the reactionary wave, fed by the Cold War, included significant organizing movements by African-American working men and women. One such, with high promise—alas thwarted by McCarthyism—was the creation of the National Negro Labor Council. Its first convention was held in Cincinnati on October 17, 1951; its keynote speech was delivered by William R. Hood (born in Georgia in 1910), who had been a worker in the auto industry beginning in 1942. At this time, Hood was secretary of Local 600, in Detroit, of the United Auto Workers.

BROTHERS AND SISTERS: This is a historic day. On his day we, the delegated representatives of thousands of workers, black and white, dedicate ourselves to the search for a new North Star, the same star that Sojourner Truth, Nat Turner and John Brown saw rise over the city of Cincinnati over a century ago.

We come conscious of the new stage in the Negro people's surge toward freedom. We come to announce to all America and to the world, that Uncle Tom is dead. "Old Massa" lies in the cold, cold grave. Something new is cooking on the Freedom Train.

We come here today because we are conscious at this hour of a confronting world crisis. We are here because many of our liberties are disappearing in the face of a powerful war economy and grave economic problems face working men and women everywhere. No meeting held anywhere in America at this mid-century point in world history can be more important nor hold more promise for the bright future toward which humanity strives than this convention of our National Negro Labor Council. For here we have gathered the basic forces of human progress; the proud black sons and daughters of labor and our democratic white brothers and sisters whose increasing concern for democracy, equality and peace is America's bright hope for tomorrow.

We, the Negro working sons and daughters, have come here to Cincinnati to keep faith with our forefathers and mothers who landed right here from the banks of the Ohio River in their dash for freedom from chattel slavery through the Underground Railroad. We come here to pledge ourselves that the fight for economic, political and social freedom which they began shall not have been in vain.

Yes, we are here as proud black American working men and women; proud of the right to live, not humiliated anymore. We are proud, too, because of our democratic white brothers and sisters who have come here; proud because these staunch allies are not afraid to stand shoulder to shoulder with us to fight for that which is right.

The Negro Labor Council is our symbol, the medium of expression of our aims and aspirations. It is the expression of our desire and determination to bring to bear our full weight to help win first-class citizenship for every black man, woman and child in America. We say that these are legitimate aims. We say that these aspirations burn fiercely in the breast of every Negro in America. And we further say that millions of white workers echo our demands for freedom. These white workers recognize in their struggle for Negro rights, the prerequisites of their own aspirations for a full life and a guarantee that the rising tide of fascism will not engulf America.

And we say that those whites who call the National Negro Labor Council "subversive" have an ulterior motive. We know them for what they are—the common oppressors of both people, Negro and white. We charge that their false cry of "subversive" is calculated to maintain and extend that condition of common oppression. We say to those whites: "You have never seen your mothers, sisters and daughters turned away from thousands of factory gates, from the air lines, the offices, stores and other places of desirable employment, insulted and driven into the streets many times when they tried to eat in public places—simply because of their color. You have never been terrorized by the mob, shot in cold blood by the police; you have never had your home burned when you moved out of the ghetto into another neighborhood—simply because you were black. You are not denied the franchise; you are not denied credit in banks, denied insurance, jobs and upgrading—because of the pigmentation of your skin. You are not denied union membership and representation; you do not die ten years before most of the people because of these many denials of basic rights.

"Therefore, you who call this National Negro Labor Council 'subversive' cannot understand the burning anger of the Negro people, our desire to share the good things our labor has produced for America. You do not understand this. So you sit like Walter Winchell, one of our attackers, in the Stork Club in New York and see that great Negro woman artist, Josephine Baker, humiliated and not raise a finger.

"The Negro Labor Council is dedicated to the proposition that these evils shall end and end soon. The world must understand that we intend to build a stronger bond of unity between black and white workers everywhere to strengthen American democracy for all. If this be subversion—make the most of it!"

A most significant event took place in Chicago in June of 1950. Over nine hundred delegates, Negro and white, gathered there to chart a course in the fight for Negro rights. They came from the mines, mills, farms and factories of America. Many of them were leaders in the organized-labor movement: seasoned, militant fighters. They voiced the complaints of Negro America.

The delegates were told that as you looked throughout the land you could see Negro men and women standing in long lines before the gates of the industrial plants for jobs, only to be told that no help was wanted—while at the same time white workers were hired. Negro women are denied the right to work in the basic section of American industry, on the airlines, in the stores and other places. Those who were hired into industry during World War II have for the most part been systematically driven out—often in violation of union contracts. Vast unemployment since the war has struck the Negro community a severe blow.

In thousands of factories throughout the land Negroes were denied upgrading and better job opportunities. Too often the unions did not defend or fight for the right of the Negro workers to be upgraded.

We heard there in Chicago that Negro workers were denied any opportunity to participate in the great number of apprenticeship-training programs either in industry or in government, in such fields as the building trades, machine tools, printing and engraving, and other skilled fields.

We found out there that thousands of lily-white shops exist throughout the land, where no Negro has ever worked.

We discovered that federal, state and city governments maintain a severe policy of Jim Crow discrimination, beginning with the White House and moving on down to the lowest level of municipal government.

Our black brothers and sisters from the South told of unemployment, low wages, wage differentials, Jim Crow unions, peonage, sharecrop robbery and miserable destitution. They described the perpetuation of conditions in twentieth-century America that are cruelly reminiscent of slavery.

Black firemen and brakemen came to tell of the collusive agreements between railroads and the railroad brotherhoods to throw Negroes out of the railroad industry after a hundred years or more, and of the denial of union membership in these unions and no representation. A number of A.F. of L. unions were singled out for their policy of exclusion and job "monkey business" as regards black workers. We also learned that the C.I.O. had joined the war crowd of colonial oppression and exploitation and was running fast from its early position of the thirties, when with John L. Lewis at its head it really fought for Negro rights.

Many of the delegates were stunned to hear of the thousands of denials of civil rights in public places in every state in the union. We were saddened and angered when we heard about the frameups of the Martinsville Seven, Willie McGee, the Trenton Six, and countless other

Negroes because they were black and for no other reason. We were horrified to hear of the many police killings of Negroes from New York City to Birmingham, Alabama.

Negro families were still hemmed into the ghettos, charged higher rents, chained by restrictive covenants, mob terror and finally even bombed if they were not lucky or able to move out in time. The rats are given ample opportunity to wreak their damage upon human beings, their destruction through disease and death.

Our delegates made it clear in that 1950 convention that inferior Jim Crow schools are still the policy in the South and Jim Crow quotas in the colleges of the North. The desire of black children for education and a full, useful life is yet a dream unrealized.

Is there any wonder then that this great Chicago gathering of the black working sons and daughters of our land said that this oppression can no longer exist in our America? Or is it any wonder that we received the full support of these stalwart democratic white workers present there who truly love democracy and recognize our common, basic unity of interests? So it was that they, in all righteous indignation, gave unto us, the continuators' organization, a mandate. They said to us: "Go out and build strong the Negro Labor Councils throughout the land. Build them into instruments of democracy, equality and unity."

They gave unto us the main task of fighting on that front which we knew best—the economic front for jobs, upgrading, for an end to the lily-white shops, for apprenticeship training, government jobs, local and state fair-employment-practices legislation, the nondiscrimination clause in union contracts and finally, with emphasis, the right of Negro women to work anywhere and everywhere.

They gave unto us the mandate to build an organization composed in the main of Negro workers, united and determined to wage an uncompromising struggle against Jim Crow—to build an organization which can unite with white workers who are willing to accept and support our program—to exclude no freedom fighter!

That mandate commissioned us to cooperate with those existing organizations, community and trade-union, which have undertaken genuine campaigns for the full citizenship of the Negro people.

We were directed to build a new type of organization—not an organization to compete with those existing organizations of the Negro people already at work on many civil rights struggles. The delegates who met at Chicago demanded an organization of Negro workers from a wide variety of industries, organized and unorganized, from the great industrial centers of the North, the urban communities of the South and the farm workers from the great rural areas. Such an organization will encourage Negroes to join unions and urge unions to organize Negroes. It will call upon the entire Negro people to support labor's fight....

During the course of our Council building there has been opposition from some of the trade-union leaders, particularly to this convention. They have accused us of attempting dual unionism, and some of them have gone so far as to advise Negro workers not to participate in this convention. To them we say: "Look at the Bill of Particulars, then tell us if it is not true that we are second-class citizens in this land. Negroes are still barred from many trade-unions in this country, denied apprenticeship training, upgrading, and refused jobs in many, many places."

We are not represented in the policy-making bodies of most international unions. We say when the mobs came to Emerald Street in Chicago and to Cicero, Illinois, we did not see the great trade-unions move. Yet, the basic right to live in Cicero was denied, not only to the family of Harvey Clark, but to the Negro people as a whole. We say that we will no longer permit the denial of these basic rights in our country, and are pooling our strength for that purpose. We intend to do it on the basis of cooperation and unity, wherever possible, with the organized labor movement.

We wish to say further that the day has ended when white trade-union leaders or white leaders in any organization may presume to tell Negroes on what basis they shall come together to fight for their rights. Three hundred years has been enough of that. We ask for your cooperation—but we do not ask your permission!

We believe it to be the solemn duty of trade-unions everywhere, as a matter of vital self-interest, to support the Negro workers in their efforts to unite and to play a more powerful role in the fight of the Negro people for first-class citizenship based upon economic, political and social equality. We believe, further, that it is the trade-unions' duty and right to encourage the white workers to join with and support their Negro brothers and sisters in the achievement of these objectives....

Brothers and sisters! Eloquence is a mighty weapon in the struggle for our just demands. But what is more eloquent than the struggle itself? The big white bosses, the men in Washington, will move far more rapidly when they see millions of us in struggle than when they hear speeches alone.

The Negro Labor Councils are, above all, organizations of struggle. We stand for the unity of all Negro workers, irrespective of union affiliation, organized and unorganized; for the unity of Negro and white workers together; for the unity of Negro workers with the whole Negro people in the common fight for Negro liberation; and for the alliance of the whole Negro people with the organized labor movement—the keystone combination for any kind of democratic progress in our country....

We face a number of grave tasks. We are called upon to chart a course that will win thousands of new job opportunities for Negro men and women, that will convince the organized-labor movement to complete the organization of the South on the basis of equality and nonsegregation, that will help bring the franchise to all the peoples in the South.

We are on the high road to a more democratic America. We are on the way toward breaking the grip of the Dixiecrats and the Northern reactionaries on our national life. I know that as you hammer out a program in these two days you will speed up the Freedom Train; you will give greater spirit and meaning to the Negro Labor Councils; you will adopt the battle cry of the great Frederick Douglass—"Without struggle there is no progress."

We move on, united—and neither man nor beast will turn us back. We will achieve, in our time, for ourselves and for our children, a world of no Jim Crow, of no more "white men's jobs" and "colored only" schools, a world of freedom, full equality, security and peace. Our task is clearly set forth. Brother and sisters, we move on to struggle and to victory!

P. S. Foner, *op. cit.*, pp. 843–49.

6

RECENT ADVANCES TOWARD ELIMINATION OF SEGREGATION IN U.S. ARMY (1951)

by Revella L. Clay

If there is such a thing as a thoroughly pleasant result of a global war which cost this nation alone the loss of 948,574 lives, Executive Order 9981 issued by President Truman on July 26, 1948 is that. Issued as a direct result of the cataclysmic repercussions of World War II which established the United States as the supreme protector of the "Free World" and which forced a new international and internal examination of America's pretensions of being the democratic ideal, this order is one of the most momentous acts of modern American history. For it rescinded this nation's official recognition of the tradition of non-democratic use of Negro manpower in its defense mechanism, replaced that tradition with a policy of democratic use of Negro manpower, and formed the foundation for the significant though still incomplete advances which are being made towards the elimination of segregation from the United States Army.

As a statement of policy, Executive Order 9981 was revolutionary. In it, Harry S. Truman, stated, among other things, that: "It is hereby declared to be the policy of the President that there shall be equality of treatment and opportunity for all persons in the armed services without regard to race, color, religion or national origin. This policy shall be put into effect as rapidly as possible, having due regard to the time required to effectuate any necessary changes without impairing efficiency or morale." This "equal treatment regardless of race" edict contrasted sharply with the tradition of "non-equality based upon race" which had been in effect until its issuance.

At the very outset of the acceptance of Negroes in the regular army in 1866 when Congress by statute created two infantry and two calvary regiments of colored soldiers, treating Negro soldiers as unequals was inherent in army policy. In all this nation's mobilization plans through World War II, an unalterable two-point tradition rigidly determined the selection and utilization of Negro manpower: (1) that Negro troops must be used in separate units; and (2) that Negro troop strength must not exceed the Negro proportion in the civilian population. Courageous service of Negroes in the Spanish-American War during which colored soldiers won Medals of Honor, this nation's highest valor award, failed to alter this policy. Negroes served in larger numbers, performed a wider range of duties in World War I, rendered commendable though frequently trouble-ridden service—but they always served in separate units. As early as 1922 this policy was attacked when a Southern general warned futilely that utilization of Negroes in large separate units "wasted manpower and fomented trouble." Again at the outbreak of hostilities leading to this nation's entry in World War II, the army was counseled to change its policy. But as late as 1940 the inherent "tradition" was in effect, and received the sanction of the White House when the late President F. D. Roosevelt decreed that the policy of not intermingling the races in the armed services "has proven satisfactory over a long period of years" and recommended its continuance.

Not until the spotlight of world attention was focused upon this nation during the last world war was the "tradition" seriously questioned. Fighting for the principle of "keeping the world safe for democracy," the United States, with armies divided by race, was especially vulnerable for the first time. Spearheaded by militant organizations like the National Association for the Advancement of Colored People and by the Negro press, "Eliminate Jim Crow from the Armed Forces" became the hue and cry on the homefront while Negroes, selected by a one-tenth quota and segregated by color, performed World War II duties. The fact that the mentalities and abilities of Negroes serving in the last world war were far superior to the army's estimate of them complicated matters. There was no doubt that Negro manpower was being wasted: Negro men were prepared for special skills. The army's position was uncomfortable. Finally in 1945 the Gillem board was appointed to study the "problem." This board sat for three and a half months. Finally it went on record as recognizing the fact that Negroes merited greater opportunities than the army policy gave them; but still clinging to the non-equality "tradition," that much prized hangover of early American slave domination attitudes, the board recommended the continuance of segregation. So it remained for Executive Order 9981 to revolutionize army policy.

While the order revolutionized policy, it failed to revolutionize "over-night" the un-democratic practices of the conservative army. The president's order, it developed, was both a whipping post and a crutch. Its clause giving "time to effectuate changes" became a crutch for the army to limp along with the business of turning-over from segregation to non-segregation. As a matter of fact, the army, largest branch of defense with a present manpower strength of 1,500,000, was the last of the three branches to comply with Executive Order 9981. With the smallest number of Negroes, the navy was the first to outline a program for putting into effect President Truman's armed forces edict, issuing its non-segregation order in May, 1949. The air force, which is credited with having done the best all-around job in implementing non-segregation, followed the navy in June, 1949. It was not until January 16, 1950, that the army, prodded by the President's Committee on Equality of Treatment and Opportunity in the Armed Services, established by his executive order, issued its non-segregation credo. Its order included these statements: "All manpower will be utilized to obtain maximum efficiency in the Army ... Army school quotas will make no reference to race or color...Selection of personnel to attend Army schools will be made without regard to race or color...Military occupational specialities will be opened to qualified enlisted personnel without regard to race or color...In furtherance of the policy of the President, it is the objective of the Department of the Army that Negro manpower possessing appropriate skills and qualifications will be utilized in accordance with such skills and qualifications." In a March 27, 1950, amendment to this order the army ordered that "effective with the month of April all enlistments in the Army within over-all recruiting quotas will be open to qualified applicants without regard to race or color."

In the wake of this action, a variety of advances has been reported in the utilization of Negro manpower in the army. Some of these advances are summarized here:

ENLISTMENTS, RE-ENLISTMENTS: Qualified Negroes may now enlist in the regular army under requirements equally applicable to all races without restrictive quota limitations. Individuals satisfactorily completing a period of enlistment may re-enlist under procedures applicable to all eligible personnel regardless of race.

OPPORTUNITIES FOR PROMOTION: Negro enlisted men now hold a percentage of non-commissioned officers ranks which compares favorably with the over-all grade spread of army command enlisted personnel. Among Negro personnel as of December 31, 1950, 1.8 per cent were master sergeants, 3 per cent were sergeants, first class, 8.1 per cent were sergeants, and 19.2 per cent were corporals. The selection of regular and non-regular army officers for promotion has operated without racial consideration. Prior to June, 1950, there was only one Negro colonel in the army. Today there are four. In addition, 17.5 per cent of all Negro majors and 10.5 per cent of all Negro captains on active duty have been selected for promotion to the next higher grade since September, 1950.

SCHOOLS: The army has gradually begun to open up every segment of its military schooling system to Negroes. It has abolished racial quotas for school selection and prescribed selection of qualified personnel without regard to race or color. Today of all enlisted students receiving military schooling, Negroes represent approximately 8 per cent, as compared with 3.4 per cent of a year ago. Enrollment of Negro officers in schools, too, has steadily increased. For example, Negro enrollment in comparison with total enrollments was 1.9 per cent in 1947; 2.26 per cent in 1948; 3 per cent in 1949; and approximately 4 per cent in 1950.

TRAINING DIVISIONS: Some of the most needed and practical advances have been made in the assignment of Negro enlistees in training divisions. In 1949 Negro enlistees were assigned to segregated units at Fort Dix, New Jersey, and at Fort Knox, Kentucky. Now this picture has changed to the effect that training divisions located at Fort Jackson, South Carolina, Camp Breckinridge, Kentucky, Fort Riley, Kansas, Fort Ord, California, Camp Chaffee, Arkansas, and Camp Roberts, California, are operated on an integrated basis. At these camps, Negro personnel work, eat and are quartered together with white personnel. The training divisions at Fort Dix and Fort Knox are now in the process of changeover from partial segregation to non-segregation.

Advancements have been made in the use of recreational facilities, including clubs and messes, post exchanges and theatres; in transportation; and in the training, housing and messing of all enlisted and officer personnel in attendance at army schools.

Despite these advances, however, there has been mounting proof that the army's old "inherent tradition" of inequality is dying "hard and slowly." While the army has stated its policy in concrete terms ordering non-segregation, Negro press writers have disclosed that in many instances this policy is not being carried out by army personnel. Recently, for example, Collins C. George, correspondent, of the Pittsburgh *Courier* in a tour of army installations throughout the country, discovered that integration is in various stages of development. He has found that Fort Dix, New Jersey, has changed "from a camp with one of the rottenest racial policies to a post with one of the best," and that Camp Rucker in Alabama is the "heartwarming story of the 'new Army' that is out to make soldiers of men, not Negro soldiers or white soldiers." But at Fort Bragg, North Carolina, Mr. George discovered glaring racial segregation. Writing in the May 12 issue of the *Courier*, the correspondent said: "Integration is a farce at Fort Bragg... by and large a complete mockery is made at Fort Bragg of the president's executive order supposedly ending segregation and discrimination in military establishments... Full separation of the races is still the rule at Bragg, with scarcely the slightest attempt made to give equal accommodations to the segregated Negro personnel of the post." Similar stories have been reported within the past few months by other writers of the Negro press—stories which indicate that integration in the armed forces, and in the army in particular, has not been accomplished.

The sincerity and effectiveness of the army in complying with the president's order, however, have met the greatest and most challenging test in the present Korean conflict. Once again, the army story is not good. Thurgood Marshall, special NAACP counsel, for example, while investigating courts martial of Negroes in Korea, found that excessive and unfair courts martial of Negroes were the direct result of their having fought in segregated units. Negro correspondents covering the front have reported that segregation is the rule, not the exception, in combat units serving in the Far East. As a matter of known fact, the famed Twenty-Fourth Infantry Regiment, which scored the first decisive victory in the Korean campaign for the United Nations forces, entered the conflict as a segregated unit of the Twenty-Fifth Infantry Division! These repeated stories of Jim Crow fighting units created controversy. But the defense authorities here in the Pentagon "sat pat," while the public came to the conclusion that segregation existed in the Far East because General Douglas MacArthur permitted it.

The lid was explosively blown off this theory, however, last spring when the Pittsburgh *Courier's* Washington Bureau Chief, Stanley Roberts, interviewed MacArthur following the General's recall to the United States. Mr. Roberts interviewed MacArthur relative to the General's racial views, and asked him pointedly if he had been responsible for the existence of "Jim Crow" units in his command. The Roberts query elicited this significant remark from MacArthur: "They (segregated units) were created in Washington and sent to me as already organized Jim Crow units. I did not ask for men by race. I did not ask for Negro nor for white men. . . . In my commands, if segregation exists . . . it exists as it may have been dictated from Washington." Congressional questioning of Pentagon defense officials has proved the MacArthur statements no distortion of the truth. Confidential correspondence between two United States senators and former Defense Secretary George Marshall has proved the army had not done its fullest in eliminating segregation. As a matter of fact new integration orders were sent out from the Pentagon as a result of the Roberts exposé as told by General MacArthur. As a direct result of the Roberts interview, it has been revealed that "the Far East Command has been directed to inactivate the Negro 24th Infantry Regiment and to replace it with an integrated infantry regiment." Further, "general integration has been ordered in the Eighth Army in Korea and in units in Japan of both combat and service type, excepting only the 40th and 45th

Infantry Divisions." This integration was to have been phased over a three-month period with a target date of September 30 for completion. General Matthew Ridgway was told to give the order his full support.

That the army is making advances toward the elimination of segregation cannot now be challenged; but how long it will take for complete integration to be effected is a moot question. It took this nation three wars and the loss of 3,392,660 lives in World Wars I and II alone to decide to treat the Negro men who served and died in this country's defense as "equals." Authorities are optimistic that it will not take so long for non-segregation in the army to be effected. Significantly, the die for democratic treatment of Negro soldiers was cast when Executive Order 9981 was issued. With that foundation laid the army can now continue to advance, as it has within the past three years, towards the total elimination of segregation.

Negro History Bulletin, October 1951, pp. 20–22; 24.

7

THE ACCUSERS' NAMES NOBODY WILL REMEMBER, BUT HISTORY RECORDS DU BOIS (1951)

by Langston Hughes

The Peace Information Center, headed by Du Bois, functioned from April 3 to October 12, 1950. Secretary of State Dean Acheson attacked it in a public statement on July 12, 1950, and the State Department demanded, in August 1950, that the officers and staff of the center register as "agents of a foreign power." From August to November 1950, Du Bois campaigned on the American Labor party ticket for the office of U.S. senator (and received over 200,000 votes). On February 9, 1951, he and others at the center were indicted as unregistered foreign agents. Du Bois was arraigned on this charge on February 16, 1951—during Negro History Week and one week prior to his eighty-third birthday. After several delays, the trial began on November 8, 1951. The government completed its case on November 19; the judge directed an acquittal on November 20, 1951.

The persecution of Du Bois aroused worldwide alarm and protest. It required courage, in that time, for Langston Hughes to write the column that follows:

If W. E. B. DU BOIS goes to jail a wave of wonder will sweep around the world. Europe will wonder and Africa will wonder and Asia will wonder, and no judge or jury will be able to answer the questions behind their wonder. The banner of American democracy will be lowered another notch, particularly in the eyes of the darker peoples of the earth. The hearts of millions will be angered and perturbed, steeled and strengthened.

They will not believe that it is right, for Dr. Du Bois is more than a man. He is all that he has stood for over eighty years of life. The things that he has stood for are what millions of people of good will the world around desire, too—a world of decency, of no nation over another nation, of no color line, no more colonies, no more poverty, of education for all, of freedom and love and friendship and peace among men. For as long as I can remember, Dr.Du Bois has been writing and speaking and working for these things. He began way before I was born to put reason above passion, tolerance above prejudice, well-being above poverty, wisdom above ignorance, cooperation above strife, equality above Jim Crow, and peace above the bomb.

Today the books of W. E. B. Du Bois are on the shelves of thousands of libraries around the world, translated into many languages, known and read by scholars everywhere. The work of his youth, his monumental "Study of The African Slave Trade" is still the authoritative book on that nefarious traffic. His "Souls of Black Folk," "Dark Water," and "The Quest of the Silver Fleece" are among the most beautiful and stirring of volumes about democracy's color problems ever written. Through those books in the first decades of this century the consciences of many young Americans were awakened.

As co-founder of the National Association for the Advancement of Colored People, Dr. Du Bois gave America one of its greatest liberalizing organizations whose contributions to democracy through legal test cases and mass unity, history will list as invaluable. As the founder of the Pan-African Congress, he linked the hand of black America with Africa and Asia. As a teacher and lecturer in the colleges and forums of the nation, he has had an immeasurable influence for good upon young minds. As editor of "The Crisis" for many years, he developed the first distinguished, lasting journal of Negro opinion in the Western World. Dr. Du Bois is the dean of Negro scholars. But not only is he a great Negro, he is a great American, and one of the leading men of our century.At the age of eighty-three he is still a wellspring of knowledge, a fountain of courage, and a skyrocket for the great dreams of all mankind.

Somebody in Washington wants to put Dr. Du Bois in jail. Somebody in France wanted to put Voltaire in jail. Somebody in Franco's Spain sent Lorca, their greatest poet, to death before a firing squad. Somebody in Germany under Hitler burned the books, drove Thomas Mann into exile, and led their leading Jewish scholars to the gas chamber. Somebody in Greece long ago gave Socrates the hemlock to drink. Somebody at Golgotha erected a cross and somebody drove the nails into the hands of Christ. Somebody spat upon His garments. No one remembers their names.

Chicago Defender, October 6, 1951. A full account of this case is in Du Bois's *In Battle for Peace*. Reprint. (Millwood, N.Y.: Kraus-Thomson, 1975).

8

WHITE CHAUVINISM AND THE STRUGGLE FOR PEACE (1951)

by Pettis Perry

Pettis Perry was one of the national leaders of the Communist party. At the time of writing, in the fall of 1951, he was under indictment by the federal government for violation of the Smith Act.

Every interest and aspiration of the Negro people is directly contrary to the reactionary policy of U.S. imperialism.

Accordingly, the peace forces, unless and until they face up to this question, will never win the Negro masses—the broad sections of the Negro workers, the sharecroppers, the Negro farmers, in the fight for peace. And without this, the peace movement can never be an effective movement in the United States.

Needless to say, it is not incumbent on the peace movement to support the entire program for Negro national liberation. Indeed, none of the Negro organizations has such a program. But it is imperative that some of the basic questions in relation to the Negro people's struggle be tackled by the peace movement; and the Left-progressive forces—first of all, the Communists—have a duty and responsibility, through patient teaching and persuasion, to bring the understanding of this position to broad sections of the whites. For example, the peace camp in general, and the Left forces in particular, should begin to raise in a new way the question of the fight against Jim Crow in the armed forces. It is insufficient to say that we are against Jim Crow in the armed forces. The time has come to speak in concrete terms: The abolition of Jim Crow in the army means among other things, the complete merging of Negro and white in every branch of the service without exception; the army should have Negro officers of every rank, including generals; Negro officers should not be limited to the command of Negro troops, and they are not simply to serve as advisers to white officers on how to handle Negroes, but they are to be officers in the full sense of the word, commanding officers of units and camps, in the North and South. Nothing short of this represents abolition of Jim Crow in the army....

Every district needs to give immediate consideration to the question of Negro representation as a mass political demand which would be most effective for the 1952 elections. This, quite aside from the question of just putting up a Negro candidate from time to time. Think of the irony of the situation: of the forty-eight states not one has a Negro on its highest court. Yet the Republicans and Democrats meet every two years in convention and adopt resolutions on anti-lynching and anti-poll tax bills, etc., as bait to the Negro people, without any real challenge from the Left and progressive forces on such matters as the persistent failure to appoint Negroes to high judicial office and influential administrative positions. It is high time to demand that Negroes be appointed to all the courts in the country. Every time there is such a vacancy the demand must be raised that state and Federal governments appoint Negroes.

The subject of redistricting is another aspect of the question of Negro representation. This should be taken up immediately and the demand raised that areas like New York, for instance, be so redistricted that the Bronx, Brooklyn and Queens will have the opportunity of electing Negro congressmen, state senators, etc. Not even in Harlem's own borough of Manhattan is there a Negro state senator. For the New York elections in 1952 this should become a key demand. In developing these movements on a state-wide scale we must see them as helping to promote a national movement that would energetically take up the question of Negro representation at all levels in the South and the actual enforcement of the Fourteenth and Fifteenth Amendments. This immediately raises as something of prime importance the question of reviving the campaign for the immediate passage of an anti-poll tax bill at this session of Congress, so as to facilitate the whole process of achieving Negro representation on all levels in the South.

Finally, the central problem confronting the Negro people is the fight for peace and for civil and democratic rights. The war economy has produced little or no increase of employment so far as the Negro people are concerned. And Negro women, who were driven from industry right after the Second World War, have never regained any mass base in industry anywhere in the country. With regard to Negro youth, the prospect for jobs is dismal indeed. Thus, the question of jobs and job discrimination is a fundamental one confronting the Negro people, and it is here that the labor movement is weakest.

There are only two or three unions in the whole country that in the last year have boldly tackled this question. First, there is the Marine Cooks and Stewards, which is the only union threatening to strike on this issue, in this case in connection with efforts to prevent a Negro woman from becoming a stewardess on one of the steamship lines. The second is District 2 of the International Woodworkers of America, which is in the State of Washington. In the early spring that District took steps to guarantee that Negroes be brought into the industry, hitherto entirely white. This was done, and the process of employment and integration of Negroes already began in the early part of this spring. What is more, in April, the leaders of the union went before their convention and explained why this policy had been adopted. The convention went on record, not only approving it, but calling upon all locals to engage in a vigorous campaign against the Jim Crowism that barred Negroes from living in many of the towns in the area. Consider the fact that this District is part of a Right-led International, and yet such a far reaching step can take place in a period like the present.

Within the labor movement generally, however, the fight for Negro rights and the struggle against white chauvinism remain extremely weak, a condition that must be changed if we are going to make the headway that we should.

Originally published in *Political Affairs*, October 1951; reprinted as a pamphlet by New Century Publishers (New York, February 1952), pp. 11–12; 20–21.

9

FIGHT ON JIM CROW
COSTS JOB, HOME (1951)

This was the headline of a brief account by a black correspondent of the treatment accorded the Reverend Joseph Albert Delaine, a leader among South Carolina black people seeking egalitarian education facilities. This Clarendon County case was one that eventuated in the 1954 *Brown* decision.

Columbia, S.C., Dec. 25—Because he served as chairman of a Negro parents' committee which initiated a court challenge of the segregated school system in Clarendon County, the Rev. J. A. Delaine has:

1. Seen his home burned to the ground.
2. Been fired from his job as a school teacher.
3. Been forced to leave the town of Summerton and the church of which he was pastor.
4. Been subjected to a $4,500 judgment for "slander" and a second law suit which would tie up his property.
5. Heard his life threatened.
6. Seen members of his family, his friends, and fellow members of the parents' committee fired from their jobs.

Delaine was fired from his school job by white officials two days after his committee filed its suit challenging Jim Crow in the schools. His wife, two sisters and a niece were among 11 other Negroes fired from their jobs right after filing of the suit.

Next, the white officials of the Clarendon County School Board against whom the suit was filed, in turn sued Delaine for slander. A local court found him guilty and placed a judgment for $4,500 against him.

Finally, in October, someone set fire to Delaine's home. Summerton firemen looked on without taking any steps to save the house. It burned to the ground.

The Sheriff, asked why he failed to investigate the arson, said: "Nobody asked me to."

Compass (N.Y.), December 25, 1951; on the Reverend Delaine, see Richard Kluger, *Simple Justice* (New York: 1976), *passim.*

10

"WHAT TURNS ME COLD" (1952)

by W. E. B. Du Bois

Dr. Du Bois's acquittal of the charge of being an "unregistered foreign agent" occurred in November 1951. In 1952, *In Battle for Peace* was published, a stirring account of the indictment, the international defense effort, the trial and the directed acquittal—one of the earliest victories over McCarthyism. In that book Dr. Du Bois penned an especially vivid passage on the class and racist nature of so-called justice in the United States:

What turns me cold in all this experience is the certainty that thousands of innocent victims are in jail today because they had neither money, experience nor friends to help them. The eyes of the world were on our trial despite the desperate effort of press and radio to suppress the facts and cloud the real issues; the courage and money of friends and of strangers who dared stand for a principle freed me; but God only knows how many who were as innocent as I and my colleagues are today in hell. They daily stagger out of prison doors embittered, vengeful, hopeless, ruined. And of this army of the wronged, the proportion of Negroes is frightful. We protect and defend sensational cases where Negroes are involved. But the great mass of arrested or accused black folk have no defense. There is desperate need of nation-wide organizations to oppose this national racket of railroading to jails and chain-gangs the poor, friendless and black.

W. E. B. Du Bois, *In Battle for Peace* (New York: Mainstream, 1952); reprinted by Kraus Thomson (Millwood, New York, 1978), p. 153.

11

THE NEGRO ARTIST LOOKS AHEAD (1951)

by Paul Robeson

The *Call*, published in preceding pages, led to the opening session of the Conference for Equal Rights for Negroes in the Arts, Sciences and Professions, held in New York City on November 5, 1951. This effort to break the severely racist practice in the areas mentioned continued and produced significant achievements in the ensuing years.

We are here today to work out ways and means of finding jobs for colored actors and colored musicians, to see that the pictures and statues made by colored painters and sculptors are sold, to see that the creations of Negro writers are made available to the vast American public. We are here to see that colored scientists and professionals are placed in leading schools and universities, to open up opportunities for Negro technicians, to see that the way is open for colored lawyers to advance to judgeships—yes, to the Supreme Court of these United States, if you please.

It is not just a question of jobs, of positions, of commercial sales. No— the questions at hand cannot be resolved without the resolution of deeper problems involved here. We are dealing with the position in this society of a great people—of fifteen million closely-bound human beings, of whom ten millions in the cotton and agricultural belt of the South form a kind of nation based upon common oppression, upon a magnificent common heritage, upon unified aspiration for full freedom and full equality in the larger democratic society.

The Negro people today are saying all up and down this nation (when you get on the streets, into the churches, into the bars to talk to them): "We will not suffer the genocide that might be visited upon us. We are prepared to fight to the death for our rights."

One great creation, modern popular music, whether it be in theatre, film, radio, records—wherever it may be—is almost completely based upon the Negro idiom. There is no leading American singer, performer of popular songs, whether it be a Crosby, a Sinatra, a Shore, a Judy Garland, an Ella Logan, who has not listened (and learned) by the hour to Holiday, Waters, Florence Mills, to Bert Williams, to Fitzgerald, and to the greatest of all, Bessie Smith. Without these models, who would ever have heard of a Tucker, a Jolson, a Cantor?

Go into the field of the dance. Where could there have come an Astaire, an Eleanor Powell and a James Barton without a Bill Robinson, a Bert Williams, an Eddie Rector, a Florence Mills? How could Artie Shaw and Bennie Goodman have appeared but for a Teddy Wilson, Turner Latan, Johnny Dunn, Hall Johnson, Will Marion Cook? Whence stems even Gershwin? From the music of Negro America joined with the ancient Hebrew idiom. Go and listen to some of the great melodies. Here again is a great American composer, deeply rooted, whether he knew it or not, in an African tradition, a tradition very close to his own heritage.

I speak very particularly of this popular form. This is very important to the Negro artists, because billions, literally billions of dollars, have been earned and are being earned from their creation, and the Negro people have received almost nothing.

At another stage of the arts there is no question, as one goes about the world, of the contribution of the Negro folk songs, of the music that sprang from my forefathers in their struggle for freedom—not songs of contentment—but songs like "Go Down, Moses" that inspired Harriet Tubman, John Brown, and Sojourner Truth to the fight for emancipation.

I think of Larry Brown who went abroad, heard Moussorgsky, heard the great folk music of other lands and dedicated himself, as did Harry Burleigh before him, to showing that this was a great music, not just "plantation songs."

One perhaps forgets my own career, and that for five years I would sing nothing but the music of my people. Later, when it was established as a fine folk music, I began to learn of the folk music of other peoples. This has been one of the bonds that have drawn me so close to the peoples of the world, bonds through this likeness in music that made me understand the political growth of many peoples, the struggles of màny peoples, and brought me back to you to fight here in this land, as I shall continue to do. . . .

So we are dealing with a people who come from great roots. There is no need to quote the names of an Anderson or a Hayes and many more; or of the great scientists—of a Julian, of a Carver. No need today for the

Negro people to prove any more that they have a right to full equality. They have proven it again and again.

The roots of this great outpouring we are talking about today in the cultural expression of my people, is a great culture from a vast continent. If these origins are somewhat blurred in this America of ours, they are clear in Brazil where Villa-Lobos joins Bach with African rhythms and melodies; in Cuba and Haiti a whole culture, musical and poetic, is very deep in the Africa of its origins—an African culture quite comparable to the ancient culture of the Chinese—similar in religious concepts, in language, in poetry, in its sculpture, in its whole esthetic—a culture which has deeply influenced the great artists of our time—a Picasso, a Modigliani, a Brancusi, an Epstein, a deFalla, a Milhaud.

As I have said, in spite of all these contributions to our culture, the fruits have been taken from us. Think of Handy, one of the creators of the Blues; think of Count Basie, playing to half-filled houses at the Apollo; colored arrangers receiving a pittance while white bands reap harvests. What heartbreak for every Negro composer! Publishing houses taking his songs for nothing and making fortunes. Theatres in the heart of the Negro communities dictating to Negro performers what they shall act, arrogantly telling Negro audiences what they shall see....

Let us touch for a moment on radio and television. We all know the difficulties—no major hours with Negro talent, an occasional guest appearance eagerly awaited by the Negro audience. Why this discrimination? Well, these mass media are based on advertising, commercialism at its worst, and the final answer is very simple. It goes to the root of all that has been said. The final answer is: "The South won't take it."

Now, I had a program myself in the '40s, all set up by one of the biggest advertising agencies, a very fine program, a dignified program in which I would have been doing Othello and many other things. One morning they said, "We made some inquiries and the South just won't have it. You can come on once in a while and sing with Mr. Voorhees, and so forth, but no possibility of a Negro artist having his own program." Not *that* dignity. And so we have allowed the South with its patterns to determine for all America how, when and where the Negro will be denied an opportunity.

I think that public opinion could be aroused on this issue. This is a matter of national protest, of national pressure. These media happen to be under the control of Federal Communications. We are dealing here with matters as serious as the passage of an Anti-Lynch Bill, Anti-Poll Tax and Free Voting Legislation, of F.E.P.C., of the whole issue of Federal and States rights. We can demand a change in the public interest in the pursuance of democratic procedures. Added to this, of course, can be pressure on the advertisers who wax fat today from the purchases of Negro customers. These latter, plus their allies, could have very decisive influence.

The films today are of vast significance and influence. Here, too, the South determines the attempts to camouflage, to pass off so-called progressive films, to find new approaches to the treatment of the Negro. They have been very thoroughly analyzed and exposed for what they are by V.J. Jerome in his exhaustive pamphlet on "The Negro in Hollywood Films." Here, too, the mounting of the right kind of campaign could shake Hollywood to its foundations, and help would be forthcoming from all over the world. Their markets everywhere in the world could be seriously affected, if the lead came from here.

The struggle on this front could have been waged with some real measure of success at any time, but today conditions insure the careful heeding of the collective wrath of the Negro people and their allies. For today, in the struggle extending all over the world, all pronouncements of our wonderful democracy ring hollow and clearly false as soon as one points the finger at the oppression of fifteen million second- and third-class citizens of this land....

The Government can be pressured in this time and it certainly can be pressured on this issue. Most important for us here is the recognition of the Negro's rights to all kinds of jobs in the arts, not only the rights of the artists, but technical jobs for engineers, all sorts of opportunities in production, in scenic design, at all levels. I am very much interested in that: I've got a son, Paul, who studied engineering at Cornell, majored in Communications. I'd like to see him get a good job in television.

And so in the case of Actors Equity—we who are members of Equity must fight not only for the rights of Negro actors, we must see that the stage-hands are there. We must fight within the AFL, Equity's parent organization, for the right of Negroes to work in *every* field. And so in the American Guild of Musical Artists and in the American Federation of Radio Artists—they are shouting an awful lot these days about how democratic and American they are: Let them show it!

The final problem concerns new ways, new opportunities based upon a deep sense of responsibility in approaching the problem of the Negro people in its totality. There are despoilers abroad in our land, akin to these who attempted to throttle our Republic at its birth. Despoilers who would have kept my beloved people in unending serfdom, a powerful few who blessed Hitler as he destroyed a large segment of a great people.…

And let us learn how to bring to the great masses of the American people *our* culture and *our* art. For in the end, what are we talking about when we talk about American culture today? We are talking about a culture that is restricted to the very, very few. How many workers ever get to the theatre? I was in concerts for 20 years, subscription concerts, the two thousands seats gone before any Negro in the community, any worker, could even hear about a seat. Even then, the price was $12.00 for six concerts. How could working people ever hear these concerts? Only by my going into the trade unions and singing on the streets and on the picket lines and in the struggles for the freedom of our people—only in this way could the workers of this land hear me.

We are talking about a culture which as yet has no relationship to the great masses of the American people. I remember an experience in England. I sang not only in Albert Hall, the concert halls, but also in the picture theatres, and one night I came out and a young woman was standing there with her mother, an aged lady. "My grandmother wants to thank you very much. She always wanted to hear you in person. She heard you tonight and she's going home. She just had sixpence above her bus fare." So she was able to hear me. Later, that was so in the Unity Theatre in London—now a theatre which has stretched all over England. Here in America, in 1948 in the Deep South, I remember standing singing to white workers in Memphis, workers who had come out on strike that Negro workers might get equal wages.

In the theatre I felt this years ago and it would interest you to know that the opening night of *Othello* in New York, in Chicago, in San Francisco (I never told this to the Guild), I told Langner he could have just one-third of the house for the elite. I played the opening night of *Othello* to the workers from Fur, from Maritime, from Local 65.

Just the other night I sang at the Rockland Palace in the Bronx, to this people's audience. We speak to them every night. To thousands. Somewhere, with the impetus coming from the arts, sciences and professions, there are literally millions of people in America who would come to hear us, the Negro artists. This can be very important. Marion Anderson,

Roland Hayes, all of us started in the Baptist Churches. I'm going right back there very soon. If you want to talk about audiences, I defy any opera singer to take those ball parks like Sister Tharpe or Mahalia Jackson. . . .

Haydn with his folk songs—the people made it up in the first place. The language of Shakespeare—this was the creation of the English-speaking people; the language of Pushkin, the creation of the Russian people, of the Russian peasants. That is where it came from—a little dressed up with some big words now and then which can be broken down into very simple images.

So, in the end, the culture with which we deal comes from the people. We have an obligation to take it back to the people, to make them understand that in fighting for their cultural heritage they fight for peace. They fight for their own rights, for the rights of the Negro people, for the rights of all in this great land. All of this is dependent so much upon our understanding the power of this people, the power of the Negro people, the power of the masses of America, of a world where we can all walk in complete dignity.

Masses and Mainstream, January 1952, pp. 7–14; published in part.

12

THE NEGRO PEOPLE
VERSUS
The Smith Act (1951)

by Richard E. Westbrooks and Earl B. Dickerson

As the Cold War intensified, efforts at the illegalization of the Communist party were pressed forward. On the federal level, the Smith Act and later the McCarran Act were main devices. Under the former, several leaders of the party were jailed; this included African-Americans, notably Henry Winston, Benjamin J. Davis, Jr., and Claudia Jones. Two black attorneys from Illinois, Richard E. Westbrooks and Earl B. Dickerson, submitted, on September 27, 1951, the following brief for a rehearing by the U.S. Supreme Court.

Petition

We, the undersigned Negro citizens, each a member of the bar of the State of Illinois and also of this Court, respectfully request leave to submit the following memorandum as *Amici Curiae* in support of the pending application for rehearing in this cause.

Memorandum

The decision of this Court (*Dennis, et al. v. United States of America*) rendered on June 4, 1951, with two justices dissenting, sustained the constitutionality of the teaching and advocacy provision of the Smith Act and upheld the conviction of the petitioners for the offense of agreeing to teach and advocate the violent overthrow of the government in violation of that Act.

This memorandum is not concerned with the factual issue of whether or not petitioners did engage or did agree to engage in such advocacy. We assume that the jury's verdict is conclusive on this point in this Court. The majority of this Court, however, in sustaining the convictions and upholding the constitutionality of the Smith Act, has so narrowed the permissible area of freedom of advocacy as to give cause for justifiable concern to every citizen who cherishes the guarantees of the First Agreement.

Negro citizens, constituting as they do a specially persecuted minority group in our body politic, see in the opinion of the Court's majority the enunciation of at least two legal concepts which are at variance with the prior decisions of this Court and which, if allowed to stand, are bound to have a disastrous impact upon the century-old struggle of the Negro people for complete emancipation.

I. The Limitation on the Right to Protest

The most important right which the citizens of a democracy enjoy is the right to political expression, the right to advocate changes with respect to the basic issues of their society. It is in this way that government is made responsive to the will of the people.

Negro citizens are vitally concerned over the Court's decision, both because they regard the right of political expression as a basic democratic right and because history has taught them that liberty is indivisible. The constitutional rights of the Negroes under the Thirteenth, Fourteenth and Fifteenth Amendments cannot be divorced from the free enjoyment by all our people of the protections of the Bill of Rights. The decision in weakening a basic liberty places in jeopardy the special rights written into the Constitution to assure democratic protections of Negroes.

Moreover, Negro citizens have a special and vital interest in the right of free expression. The most precious right which a minority can enjoy under any form of government is the right to protest; the right to voice its complaints and to request, urge, demand and advocate governmental redress. The democratic principle can only work if every minority group is assured and, indeed, guaranteed access to all of the means of protecting itself against discrimination and unfair treatment.

The Negro people are peculiarly dependent upon the exercise of the fundamental rights involved in political expression in order to achieve its legitimate goals in a democracy. Discrimination against the Negro people is deeply embedded in the fabric of government—particularly the governments in the Southern states. Efforts to remove inequalities inevitably involve basic attacks upon governmental attitudes and conduct.

It is inevitable that the decision will inhibit and impair legitimate efforts to extend democratic protections to the Negro people. This is so for two reasons:

In the first place, advocacy of fundamental changes in government so as to extend democratic protections to the Negro might well be equated, under the broad terms of the Court's decision, with advocacy of the violent overthrow of the government. In the second place, as Justice Black's dissenting opinion points out, the decision imposes a prior restraint upon political expression. If the present decision is permitted to stand, few, whether Negro or non-Negro, will undertake to challenge the "Black Codes" of the South or to condemn the governmental policy of supporting Jimcrow laws or poll-tax restrictions on the right to vote. Only individuals with great courage will vigorously condemn the failure to apprehend and prosecute those who engage in mob violence against Negroes. In short, the decision casts a chilling shadow of fear even over those areas which it does not literally reach.

The inevitable effect of the decision is to undermine, if not destroy, effective protest with respect to government practices and policies inimical to the welfare of Negroes.

II. Clear and Present Danger

Prior to the decision in this case, right of protest would have been protected by the First Amendment, notwithstanding the "clear and present danger" formula's limitation upon the otherwise absolute prohibition which the literal terms of that Amemdment impose upon governmental action in the realm of speech. For, until this decision, at least two safeguards remained: the first of these was this Court's clear distinction between advocacy and conduct as crystallized in its opinion in *A.C.A. v. Douds*, 339 U.S. 392; and the second was the assurance, based upon *Whitney v. California*, 274 U.S. 357, and *Pierce v. United States*, 252 U.S. 239, that in no event could mere speech, regardless how intemperate, be successfully prosecuted unless and until a jury of one's peers should find that it *clearly and presently* threatened an evil within the competency of the government to prevent. The decision of the majority in this case appears to destroy both of these safeguards.

The majority opinion, while seeming to retain the "clear and present danger" formula as interpreted in *Douds*, appears to us to completely negate that formula by regarding as "conduct" what was charged in the indictment and found by the jury to be "advocacy." Thus, the "clear and present danger" formula originally devised by Justices Brandeis and Holmes as a compromise by means of which actionable words which are tantamount to an "attempt" or an "incitement" could be punished while preserving the constitutional protection against the prohibition of speech as such (*Schenck v. United States*, 249 U.S. 47; *Abrams v. United States*, 250 U.S. 616; *Schaefer v. United States*, 251 U.S. 466, and *Whitney v. California, supra*) is set at naught; and those of us whose eventual complete emancipation is dependent upon changing the status quo are again in that twilight zone which characterized this Court's First Amendment decisions prior to the *Schenck* case. See Chafee's "Freedom of Speech" (1920).

What speech or writing is or is not actionable in the future will depend not upon the clarity and immediacy of the danger to the public welfare, but rather upon whether the judiciary believes that what is said or written represents a sane, sober, safe and orthodox view. As Mr. Justice Jackson's concurring opinion shows, henceforth the "clear and present danger" formula is to be reserved for the protection of the speech or writing that does not matter—"the hot-headed speech on a street corner, or circulation of a few incendiary pamphlets...."

The abandonment of the "clear and present danger" principle creates special concern for those familiar with the techniques which have historically been employed to retard and to crush the struggle for the achievement of Negro rights. From the very beginning the movement for the liberation of the Negro people was falsely attacked as a movement committed to force and violence. Every attempt to better the lot of the Negro people was attacked and slandered as an effort to incite insurrection. The abandonment of long-established constitutional tests will inevitably invite the revival of these techniques of repression and subjugation.

Deeply disquieting also is the revival in the decision of the conspiracy concept as a means of justifying the abandonment of the traditional constitutional protections. Long ago Negroes, like trade unionists, recognized that only through group action could effective inroads be made upon prejudice and discrimination. Historically, these collective efforts were attacked and slandered as "conspiracies." Even today efforts of the Negro people through unincorporated associations or groups bound together by consciousness of common interests to achieve democratic liberties are denounced and attacked as sinister "conspiracies."

The majority opinion in the present case also repudiates the whole history of the Sixth Amendment with its guarantee of a jury trial of the basic issues in all criminal sedition cases. The struggle of the English people to wrest from the province of a crown-appointed judiciary the right to determine in such cases whether alleged seditious utterances tended to cause disrespect or contempt for the authority of the crown was not lost from the minds of those who fashioned our Bill of Rights.

The successful fight of those English barristers like Lord Erskine, which culminated in Fox's Libel Act of 1792, and the courageous defense by the lawyers in the *Peter Zenger* case in this country were fresh in the thoughts of those who wrote the guarantee of the Sixth Amendment into our Constitution. It was the means devised by them to insure that the direct representation of the people—the jury, as distinct from the appointee of the State, the judge—should assess the criminality of every utterance claimed to be seditious.

The Brandeis-Holmes formula of "clear and present danger," as the dissenting opinion of Mr. Justice Douglas makes clear, had the distinction of preserving this modicum of protection by leaving it to the jury in each jury-trial case to determine the evil tendency of the utterance. For this Court to now hold, as it does in the present case, that the jury's function is limited to ascertaining whether or not the utterance was in fact made and that it then becomes the sole function of the judge to determine whether such an utterance presents a clear and present danger is to reverse not merely *Pierce v. United States, supra,* and *Whitney v. California, supra,* but two centuries of struggle by English-speaking peoples to commit to the ultimate protection of a jury of their peers the issue of the extent to which they might criticize their government with impunity.

Here again the adverse decision of this Court on this issue has peculiar significance for the members of a persecuted minority whose history has been one of continuous struggle for the right to have the guilt or innocence of one of their members in the ordinary criminal case assessed by a democratically selected jury of their peers. For this Court to hold now, as it does in the present decision, that a Negro accused of seditious utterances against a State or the Federal government is not entitled to a jury but is relegated to the opinion of a single judge whose views on social, economic or political issues is bound to be conditioned by his own background, is in effect to relegate the whole movement of the Negro people toward full equality in American life to a status which differs only in theory from that suffered by Negroes prior to the Civil War.

Conclusion

For the reasons herein set forth we urge upon this Court a reconsideration and reversal of its present decision in this case.

Masses and Mainstream, February 1952, Vol. 5, pp. 52–56.

13

THE KILLING OF HARRY T. MOORE
AND HARRIET MOORE (1952)

by Paul Robeson

On Christmas evening, 1951, a bomb exploded beneath the home of Mr. and Mrs. Moore in Mims, Florida. Mr. Moore died at once; Mrs. Moore died on January 3, 1952. Mr. Moore was a leader of the Florida NAACP and founder of the Progressive Voters League, seeking to encourage African-American voting. In

June 1952, the NAACP awarded Harry T. Moore, the Spingarn Medal. The killers of the Moores were never apprehended.

Paul Robeson's response to the murders follows:

Harry T. Moore died the death of a hero. He is a martyr in the age-long struggles of the Negro people for full dignity and equality. His name must never be forgotten and his courageous deeds must ever be enshrined in our memories. His death must be avenged!

The bomb which took the life of this fearless fighter for freedom, made a shambles of his home at Mims, Fla., and placed his wife at death's door in a hospital 40 miles away, has shaken the peace and tranquility of every Negro household in the United States.

There can be no mistaking the meaning of this event. The murder of Harry Moore was a lynching of a special kind. It was a political assassination.

Its aim was to short-circuit the growing clamor for votes and justice in the South by beheading those who are brave enough to demand their rights or strong enough to lead the organized mass movement.

In 1948 Maceo Snipes and Isaiah Nixon both gave their lives to Georgia mobs because they sought to exercise the right to vote.

In South Carolina, Albert Hinton, NAACP state president, was kidnapped, and John McCray, head of the Progressive Democratic Party, was framed on a trumped-up libel charge—because of their leadership in the voting movement.

Only last month in Opelousas, La., John L. Mitchell was shot in cold blood by a deputized bandit because he had dared sue for his right to be registered as a voter.

Now the dastardly assassination of Moore comes as a threat to every Negro man and woman in the land:

Give up your efforts to be full citizens! Despair in your hopes to vote and hold office in the South! Remain a people apart, inferior in status, despised and trampled upon—or we will blow you all to Kingdom come!

Shall we accept this verdict of Klansmen? Shall we permit the ferocious attack of these 20th century barbarians to blunt the edge of our common strivings?

No, we cannot! We should not be true to ourselves, our forefathers, or the memory of Harry Moore if we did!

The need of the hour is for thousands of Harry Moores to rise and take the place of the fallen one. From the colleges and schools of the South, from the plantations and country districts, from the mines, mills and factories, new fighters for full freedom must take our brother's death as the signal for their unending dedication to their people's needs.

The need of the hour is for resistance to the lynchers, an end to the spilling of our precious blood!

The need is for a demand that will ring out in every home in the United States and resound around the world:

Death to the assassins of Harry Moore and to the lyncher-sheriff McCall who killed Samuel Shepard in cold blood!

Ban the Ku Klux Klan and smash this odious conglomeration of un-American bandits to smithereens!

Indemnify the bereaved families of the lynch victims!

Impeach Fuller Warren, whose conduct as governor is hostile to the interests and liberties of a majority of the people of Florida!

Guarantee, through the exercise of federal power, the unrestricted enjoyment of every constitutional privilege by all Negro people in every part of the United States!

Has the time not come for an unequivocal declaration of unremitting war against Jim Crow by the Negro people joined together in an all-embracing unity?

To be sure, it has. We shall not be forever turned from our duty by the slanderous characterizations of our common foe or by real political differences among ourselves.

What better time than now to plan for a great convocation of the leaders of the Negro people on February 14, the birthday of the immortal Frederick Douglass, to be held in the nation's capital or in a major Southern city?

There, the bishops and ministers of our churches, leaders of our fraternal life, spokesmen for women and youth, labor leaders and political figures could plan a common action for freedom.

Setting politics aside, inseparably bound by what so urgently unites us—our common peril—we could give needed hope and inspiration to the rising masses of our people, guidance to our next tasks, and pause to the enemy within the gates.

This, to me, is the first lesson of the murder of Harry T. Moore. It is a challenge to all Negro leadership. The masses look to see who will be the first to answer.

Freedom, February 1952; in Foner, *op. cit.*, pp. 305–7.

14

A PETITION TO THE PRESIDENT OF THE UNITED STATES AND THE U.S. DELEGATION TO THE UNITED NATIONS (1952)

Early in 1952, forty-seven distinguished African-American men and women made public the following petition, aiming especially at the pro-colonialist foreign policy of Washington. Noteworthy is the fact that signers came not only from the North and West, but also from border states like Maryland and Kentucky and the southern states of Louisiana, Virginia, Texas, Arkansas, and Georgia. The author is not known to the editor, but the style and content are reflective of Du Bois—one of the signers.

As human beings we share the world-wide concern for finding the way to peace. As Americans we share the common concern of our fellow citizens as to our country's foreign policy and where it is leading us. As Negroes we have deep bonds of sympathy, growing out of a common experience of suffering and struggle, with the two-thirds of the world that is called colored and which has been or still remains under the domination of the United States, Great Britain, France and other countries in what is called the Western World.

We address this petition to you, Mr. President, and to this government's Delegation to the United Nations, because we believe that the policy our government is pursuing with respect to these hundreds of millions of subject peoples in Africa, Asia, the Pacific and the Caribbean—a policy reflected in the status of this country's own Negro citizens—will decisively determine the issue of world war or world peace.

This petition is motivated by what in our view is the indefensible position on several important questions taken by the United States Delegation to the United Nations General Assembly meeting in Paris, and also by certain recent Presidential pronouncements.

First, we deplore the fact that the United States Delegation has again, as in previous sessions of the U.N. General Assembly, refused to support the forthright condemnation of the vicious system of racial discrimination practiced by the government of the Union of South Africa. While the majority of the U.N. members assailed South Africa's "apartheid" policy, exemplified in the Group Areas Act, and urged suspension of that law pending settlement of the South African-Indian dispute, the United States Delegation abstained.

Again, the United States, having previously joined with Great Britain and South Africa in trying to prevent Rev. Michael Scott, delegated spokesman for the Africans of Southwest Africa, from speaking before the Trusteeship Committee of the U.N. General Assembly, abstained from the majority-supported resolution expressing "admiration and gratitude" to Rev. Scott and regret that the tribal chiefs of Southwest Africa had been prevented by the South African government from appearing at the Paris U.N. meeting. It is especially noteworthy that all but two of the nine abstaining votes on this resolution came from colony-holding powers of the Western World.

Does the United States Delegation's stand on these matters perhaps arise from fear of U.N. exposure and criticism of discriminatory practices in the United States? Or is it because of the close financial ties between this country and South Africa? Dr. Malan's government, a fascist government, has lately been the beneficiary of substantial United States loans from New York banks and through the International Bank for Reconstruction and Development. And were it not for the gold which the United States takes from South Africa—not to mention manganese, uranium ore, copper and other minerals and raw materials—and were it not for the large investments of American corporations in that country, it is generally agreed that South Africa's slave-labor economy would quickly collapse.

Secondly, we deplore the major role played by the United States Delegation to the Paris U.N. General Assembly meeting in forcing through the decision of that body not to take up consideration of the Moroccan charges brought against France. According to the *N.Y. Times* (Dec. 4, 1951), Sir Mohammed Zafrullah Khan, Pakistani Prime Minister, told the U.N. delegates that the United States representative would have to bear responsibility for the further shedding of Moroccan blood.

The Western powers, he observed, always supported the general principle of freedom for colonial peoples but almost invariably voted against specific implementation of the principle; whereas the Eastern

European countries had won the gratitude of the Asian countries by always supporting such implementation.

Did not this American support of the French on the Moroccan question result from the fact that it was with the French government, and without consultation with or the consent of the Moroccan people, that the United States government negotiated for the construction of a network of U.S. air bases in Morocco estimated to cost a half billion dollars? The *London Economist* (March 10, 1951) traced the outbreak of violence in Morocco and other Moslem areas to General Juin's efforts to liquidate the central national independence party of Morocco (Istiqulal) and purge the country of dissident elements "before American soldiers arrived to begin construction work on new air bases."

As in Morocco so in other areas United States political policy has been dictated by United States military objectives—to the detriment of the interests of the inhabitants. The *N.Y. Times* (Nov. 26, 1948) reported that "Considerations of military strategy... have determined the attitude that the U.S. Delegation has adopted on the question of the Italian colonies." And the *Manchester Guardian* (Nov. 14, 1949) observed that the Anglo-American solution of this question represented "a rather sorry example of the subordination... of native interests to Great Power interests." The U.N. grant of "independence" to Libya was in effect bought with agreements for the long-term maintenance by the United States of its Wheelus Air Base in Tripoli and for continued occupation of the territory by U.S.-British-French military forces.

Third, we are deeply disturbed, Mr. President, by the communique of January 9, 1952, on your talks with Mr. Churchill, with its reference to "a complete identity of aims between us" with regard to the Middle East, and to your agreement to "continue to work out together agreed policies to give effect to this aim." We ask whether this can mean anything except the continued application of pressure by every possible means, including the use of military force as in Egypt, in order to maintain Anglo-American influence and economic and military dominance in Iran, Egypt, and other Middle Eastern countries now striving for national independence.

"Some United States Middle Eastern experts," says *Business Week* (Oct. 27, 1951),"feel that the only policy that would have a chance of success now would be a barefaced return to old-fashioned gunboat imperialism—sugar-coated with a lot of economic assistance." Is this the agreed-upon Anglo-American policy, Mr. President?

A leading Negro newspaper, the *Afro-American* (Nov. 3, 1951), commenting editorially on our government's support of Britain in Iran and Egypt, states: "It appears that neither England nor the United States seems to be interested in the fundamental right of these darker nations to be supreme in their own territories and compel all foreigners to leave, if that is their desire."

The present state of affairs in North Africa, the Middle East, and Southeast Asia points up the urgent importance of the declaration by India's representative, Mrs. Vijaya Lakshmi Pandit, to the U.N. General Assembly on October 25, 1946: "The use of troops against the national aspirations of people for the protection of imperial vested interests, and virtually as armies of occupation threatening both weaker peoples and the world peace as a whole, calls for unreserved condemnation by the United Nations, and for the demand that all such troops shall be withdrawn." Such action by the United Nations is now imperative. Will the United States support it?

Fourth, we object to the continued alliance of the United States with Britain, France, and other colonial powers in the Trusteeship Committee at the Paris U.N. Assembly meeting in opposing, as at previous sessions, various proposals for the advancement of the interests of colonial peoples. The *N.Y. Times* (Jan. 16, 1952) reports that a "unique" development of the Paris meeting was the fact that "the small nations took the initiative and carried a series of resolutions on dependencies that at best are unwelcome to the Western Powers."

Among the colonial resolutions opposed or not supported by the United States Delegation was one asking the nations administering U.N. trust territories to set deadlines for the independence of those areas. This has been repeatedly demanded ever since the establishment of the trusteeship system, and repeatedly opposed and defeated by the colony-holding powers. Here is one instance of what Sir Zafrullah referred to as the readiness of the Western Powers to endorse the general principle of colonial liberation while consistently opposing action on specific issues toward that end.

Fifth, we regard it as a deplorable backward step that the United States at the Paris U.N. meeting won its fight by the narrow margin of 30 to 24 votes, to exclude economic and social rights from the proposed U.N. Covenant of Human Rights, to be left for inclusion in a separate and later covenant. The United States Delegation argued that to include economic, social and cultural rights in the same covenant with political rights would prevent some countries from ratifying the instrument because state-guaranteed economic rights tended in the direction of the welfare state.

This seems to us to be an evident effort to appease the Dixiecrat and other reactionary elements in our government who have for so long blocked enactment of effective Fair Employment Practices legislation. We believe with the opponents of the United States position that political freedom is impaired if not negated unless it is accompanied by effective guarantees of economic and social freedom. The Negro people in the United States certainly know this.

Another instance of apparent appeasement of the anti-democratic forces in the United States is the insistence of the American Delegation upon inserting a qualifying provision in the Covenant of Human Rights virtually relieving federal governments, such as the United States, of responsibility for violations of the Covenant in the component units of the federal government—for example, in the state of Florida or Mississippi.

We cannot review here the numerous weaknesses, attributable mainly to the United States Delegation and relating especially to discrimination and the rights of colonial peoples, which have been incorporated in the Declaration and Covenant of Human Rights. This circumstance led U.N. Assistant Secretary General Henri Laugier in April, 1950, to charge openly that delegates in the Commission on Human Rights were favoring a limited and weak Covenant of Human Rights.

The Negro people of the United States are deeply concerned with the achievement of effective international safe-guards for human rights—for themselves and for darker peoples throughout the world who are the victims of the racist doctrine of white supremacy. From this racism stems the failure of our government to protect the lives and rights of its Negro citizens—in Cicero, Illinois; in Groveland and Mims, Florida; and from it stems also the inhuman repression of non-white peoples in Asia and Africa by the Western powers. Those non-white peoples most assuredly want none of the "American way of life" experienced by 15 million Negro Americans. Nor can the continued rule of racism in the United States be ended as long as the enslavement of darker peoples throughout the world continues.

In your recent State of the Union Message, Mr. President, you declared, "The peoples of Asia want to be free to follow their own way of life." We agree wholeheartedly, and we would add that the peoples of Africa, the Caribbean, Latin America and other lands want the same. However, the quoted sentence in its context actually meant that the peoples of Asia must be "free" to remain within the Western sphere of influence. It seems to us truly extraordinary that in both your State of the Union and Budget Messages to Congress you could deal with the subject of the hunger and need of the Asian and other peoples without once even mentioning the root cause of their miserable condition—namely, their long-suffering subjection to Western economic and colonial overlords.

In the above-mentioned Messages to Congress you placed great emphasis, Mr. President, upon the aid programs which the United States can provide for economically backward peoples. But, as is well known, these same peoples have a deep suspicion of this aid; long before Point Four was conceived they had a popular saying that their overlords were willing to do most anything for them except get off their backs. These peoples realize that in order to use economic or other assistance for its *own* benefit, a nation must first of all be free to determine its *own* economic and social goals. As an African leader has recently said, "Self-government and independence must be the initial capital to be invested in the non-self-governing territories."

We submit, Sir, that though it may be possible for the Western Powers to find and bribe puppet-spokesmen among oppressed nations, it is impossible either to bribe or coerce whole peoples whose national consciousness and will to freedom have become articulate. This is the inescapable meaning of national revolts today sweeping Asia, the Middle East, and Africa.

If America's name is not to be hated throughout the world wherever people struggle for liberty, our government must completely revise its foreign policy and give concrete evidence, through its conduct in the United Nations and in all areas of international economic, political and military relations, of its genuine and unequivocal support of the principle of national self-determination.

The policy now being pursued, the policy of bribery and coercion to make the American or Western way of life prevail, can lead only to national and international disaster. This policy if continued, we believe, will surely lead only to more Koreas. Peace cannot be won with either guns or dollars. The only conceivable world of lasting peace is a world of free peoples living together in mutual cooperation, equality, and respect.

WE PETITION YOU to work to build such a world. We urge:

1. that our government go on record condemning, as a flagrant violation of human rights and serious threat to world peace, the racist program of the government of the Union of South Africa exemplified in the Group Areas Act, and that it use its full influence to press for the South African government's adherence to the recommendations of the United Nations respecting South West Africa and the grievances of Indians in South Africa.
2. that our government seek the fullest and speediest implementation of the Charter provisions and recommendations of the United Nations relating to the advancement of the welfare and freedom of colonial peoples;
3. that our government strive for the creation and adoption of a U.N. Covenant of Human Rights which will provide truly effective protection of the economic, social, civil and political rights of all peoples in all countries;
4. that our government lend its full support to fulfillment of the demands for national self-determination voiced by subject peoples in Africa and all other areas of the world, and that it withhold assistance of any kind from any government engaged in suppressing such demands;
5. that our government and all other governments withdraw their military forces and installations from all foreign territories where their presence is not authorized by agreement of all the major powers;
6. that our government, together with the other major powers, undertake sincere and serious efforts toward reaching a general agreement so that the world of lasting peace which we seek may become a glorious reality.

INITIATING SPONSORS

(Partial List)

REV. STACY ADAMS
Dallas, Texas
MRS. ROBERTA HENNOIX ALLEN
Louisville, Ky.
BISHOP C. C. ALLEYNE
Philadelphia, Pa.
REV. E. R. ARTIST
Brooklyn, N.Y.
MRS. CHARLOTTA A. BASS
New York City
MRS. MAUDELLE B. BOUSFIELD
Chicago, Ill.
DR. PHILIPS BROOKS
Brooklyn, N.Y.

DR. LUCIEN BROWN
New York City
MRS. ADAH S. BUTCHER
Washington, D.C.
DR. H. A. CALLIS
Washington, D.C.
DR. JOHN E. T. CAMPER
Baltimore, Md.
FELIX A. CUMMINGS
New York City
W. P. DABNEY
Cincinnati, O.
RAYMOND DENNIS
Chicago, Ill.

EARL DICKERSON
Chicago, Ill.
DR. W. E. B. DU BOIS
New York City
REV. CHARLES C. S. ENGLAND
Brooklyn, N.Y.
REV. G. LINWOOD FAUNTLEROY
Oakland, Calif.
ARTHUR HUFF FAUSET
Philadelphia, Pa.
DR. CARLTON B. GOODLETT
San Francisco, Ill.
EWART GUINIER
New York City
REV. CHARLES A. HILL
Detroit, Mich.
REV. D. B. KYLE
Little Rock, Ark.
MRS. SENORA B. LAWSON
Richmond, Va.
DR. CATHERINE D. LEALTAD
New York City
SAMUEL J. LITTLE
Savannah, Ga.
LARKIN MARSHALL
Macon, Ga.
REV. PAUL L. McCLURE
Las Vegas, Nev.
CARLTON MOSS
Hollywood, Calif.
REV. JACOB C. OGLESBY
Detroit, Mich.
OLIVER T. PALMER
Washington, D.C.

SAM PARKS
Chicago, Ill.
ONSLOW PARRISH
Detroit, Mich.
SIDNEY POITIER
New York City
WILLARD B. RANSOM
Indianapolis, Ind.
DR. FREDERICK RHODES
New Orleans, La.
PAUL ROBESON
New York City
DR. R. A. SIMMONS
Boston, Mass.
MRS. PAULINE TAYLOR
Youngstown, Ohio
MRS. MARY CHURCH TERRELL
Washington, D.C.
MRS. MARGAULTA TIMMS
Philadelphia, Pa.
A. M. TRUDEAU
New Orleans, La.
REV. WILLIAM D. TURNER
Philadelphia, Pa.
HARCOURT A. TYNES
White Plains, N.Y.
ELDER J. W. WARNER
Richmond, Va.
DR. FORREST ORAN WIGGINS
Univ. of Minnesota
COLEMAN A. YOUNG
Detroit, Mich.

The document is in the editor's possession.

15

I ACCEPT THIS CALL (1952)

by Charlotta Bass

The Progressive party, in its April 1952 convention, selected Charlotta Bass to be its vice presidential candidate. The nominee, in this unprecedented action, had been a leader of the Republican party and in 1940 was western regional director of Wendell Wilkie's presidential campaign. In 1948 she broke with the Republican party over the peace and civil rights issues and helped found the Progressive party. In 1950 she was a congressional candidate for that party. For forty years, Charlotta Bass was editor of the *California Eagle*, published in Los Angeles.

For the first time in the history of this nation a political party has chosen a Negro woman for the second highest office in the land.

It is a great honor to be chosen as a pioneer, and a great responsibility....

I shall tell you how I came to stand here. I am a Negro woman. My people came before the Mayflower. I am more concerned with what is happening to my people in my country than war. We have lived through two wars and seen their promises turn to bitter ashes.

For forty years I have been a working editor and publisher of the oldest Negro newspaper in the West. During those forty years I stood on a watch tower watching the tide of racial hatred and bigotry rising against my people and against all people who believe the Constitution is something more than a piece of yellowed paper to be shut off in a glass cage in the archives.

I have stood watch over a home to protect a Negro family against the outrages of the Ku Klux Klan. And I have fought the brazen attempts to drive Negroes from their home under restrictive covenants. I have challenged the great corporations which extort huge profits from my people, and forced them to employ Negroes in their plants. I have stormed city councils and state legislatures and the halls of Congress demanding real representation for my people....

I cannot help but hark back to the thirty years I spent in the Republican party as an active member... As a member of the great elephant party, I could not see the light of hope shining in the distance, until one day the news flashed across the nation that a new party was born.

Here in this party was the political home for me and for my people. Here no one handed me a ready-made program from the back door. Here I could sit at the head of the table as a founding member, write my own program, a program for me and my people, that came from us. In that great founding convention in Philadelphia in 1948 we had crossed the Jordan.... Now perhaps I could retire.... I looked forward to a rest after forty years of struggle.

But could I retire when I saw that slavery had been abolished but not destroyed; that democracy had been won in World War I, but not for my people; that fascism had been wiped out in World War II, only to take roots in my own country where it blossomed and bloomed and sent forth its fruits to poison the land my people had fought to preserve!

...Where were the leaders of my nation—yes, my nation, for God knows my whole ambition is to see and make my nation the best in the world—where were these great leaders when these things happened?

To retire meant to leave this world to these people who carried oppression to Africa, to Asia, who made profits from oppression in my own land. To retire meant to leave the field to evil.

This is what we fight against. We fight to live. We want the $65 billion that goes for death to go to build a new life. Those billions could lift the wages of my people, give them jobs, give education and training and new hope to our youth, free our sharecroppers, build new hospitals and medical centers. The $8 billion being spent to rearm Europe and crush Asia could rehouse all my people living in the ghettos of Chicago and New York and every large city in the nation.

We fight that all people shall live. We fight to spend our money to end colonialism for the colored peoples of the world, not to perpetuate it in Malan's South Africa, Churchill's Malaya, French Indo-China and the Middle East.

Can you conceive of the party of Taft and Eisenhower and MacArthur and the big corporations calling a Negro woman to lead the good fight in 1952? Can you see the party of Truman, of Russell of Georgia, of Rankin of Mississippi, of Byrnes of South Carolina, of Acheson, naming a Negro woman to lead the fight against enslavement?

I am stirred by the responsibility that you have put upon me. I am proud that I am the choice of the leaders of my own people and leaders of all those who understand how deeply the fight for peace is one and indivisible with the fight for Negro equality.

And I am impelled to accept this call, for it is the call of all my people and call to my people. Frederick Douglass would rejoice, for he fought not only slavery but the oppression of women.

I make this pledge to my people, the dead and the living—to all Americans, black and white. I will not retire nor will I retreat, not one inch, so long as God gives me vision to see what is happening and strength to fight for the things I know are right.For I know that my kingdom, my people's kingdom, and the kingdom of all the peoples of the world, is not beyond the skies, the moon and the stars, but right here at our feet.

I accept this great honor. I give you as my slogan in this campaign— "Let my people go."

Gerda Lerner, ed., *Black Women in White America: A Documentary History* (New York: Pantheon, 1972), pp. 342–45; originally in *National Guardian*, April 2, 1952.

16

THE NEGRO VOTER AND THE 1952 ELECTIONS

by W. E. B. Du Bois

A characteristically analytical examination of the 1952 election, especially from the vantage point of the African-American, was presented in a column by Dr. Du Bois.

If you should ask the average Negro voter, representing the intelligent "middle-class" artisan, professional man, business man and white collar worker, how he is going to vote next November, he would tell you frankly, if he replied at all, that he really did not know.

He stands today quite flabbergasted. Between the Democrats and Republicans there is no difference so far as his chief interests are concerned: Peace, Civil Rights, FEPC, Suffrage, Education, Taxes. Both parties are pledged to war and cry peace; both are pledged to civil rights and neither will implement that pledge; their reactionary elements will unite against their liberal wings to kill any proposition which looks toward real civil liberty for Negroes.

At the same time President Truman will talk as loudly for a real FEPC as Republican Senator Ives, and neither will act accordingly. Sparkman, who if the Democrats win will preside over the Senate and might even become President said clearly in Mobile, Ala., on April 17, 1950, that he was one of the Southern Senators

banded together and pledged to use every parliamentary device possible to defeat civil rights legislation.

Nixon, who will be in a similar position if the Republicans win, has supported the filibuster, opposed FEPC and is a McCarthy red baiter. As presiding officer of the Senate or as President, Nixon would act exactly as Sparkman would.

The candidates for the Presidency will do some slick doubletalk to Negroes during the next two months. Both, after having pacified the South with opposition to a national FEPC with teeth and refusal to enact anti-lynching or anti-poll-tax legislation, will express to Negro delegations their deep interest in Negro progress and pious determination to do everything they can for this race. It will be a stout-hearted doubter who will come from the hospitality of such interviews without being convinced that Eisenhower-Stevenson is not his man.

War and Jim Crow

On the matter of Peace, the Negro feels strongly but says little. Our armed forces are still in the main "jim-crowed," and every Negro knows Eisenhower has defended and Stevenson never opposed this policy. There can be no doubt of the heavy incidence of federal war taxation on groups like Negroes who are hard-put to maintaining a decent standard of living on deliberately lowered income.

Moreover, this nation is fighting colored peoples by arms and money in Asia and Africa, and Negroes know this and are ashamed and resentful. They want to get out of all participation in this attempt to reduce colored folk the world over to subordination. This is why they knew that Paul Robeson voiced their thought in Paris in 1949. Last July a South African court sentenced four of the most promising Negro and Indian leaders to hard labor in jail under the "Suppression of Communism" Act because

... it is common knowledge that one of the aims of communism is to break down race barriers and strive for equal rights for all sections of the people, and to do so without any discrimination of race, color or creed.

In the same way, U.S. Negroes who complain of discrimination and injustice are accused of "communism," while our government loans South Africa $80 million dollars and arranges to furnish them arms and U.S. banks invest a million dollars in its industry. Our consul-general said in 1950 that South Africa "has a greater future than almost any young country in the world."

Now this is an impasse and the intelligent Negro voter is completely stymied. The difference between the Democratic and Republican parties so far as his interests are concerned is exactly the difference between tweedledum and tweedledee. On the other hand, as never before the Negro holds the balance of power between the two old parties, and he knows it. He was not deaf nor blind when, in the Democratic convention, the Confederate flag commemorating the War between the Slave States and the Free was openly waved between rebel yells and "Dixie." He saw that the urge toward human slavery was not yet dead in this Free Democracy of the West.

The Republican convention tried desperately to soft-pedal the Negro question. The number of Negro delegates reached a new low by reason of disfranchisement within the party based on disfranchisement in the states, and Negro speakers and even preachers were ignored—a far cry from the day when the Republican convention of 1884 was opened by a black temporary chairman.

The Negro Has the Power

Yet the facts about the Negro vote in 1952 are so clear that despite desperate effort the situation is forcing itself to the front pages of the *New York Times*. Of the 150 million persons in the U.S. in 1950, some 97 million will be 21 years of age in 1952; of the nearly 15 million Negroes, over 8½ million will be prospective voters. But this possible voting population of white and black is systematically and deliberately reduced so that few more than half the possible voters appear at the polls. Our voting list is small because we want it small and try to keep it small by law and custom; not only by registration hindrances, poll taxes in six states, and other devices, but because women and Negroes for the most part do not vote.

In 12 former slave states the total population in 1950 was 38,868,000, yet the total vote in 1948 was 5,831,000. In the North and West 40% of the total population actually voted. In the slave South it is only 15%. If we take individual states our democratic methods as interpreted by race hate and caste are even clearer:

	% POPULATION VOTING	Distinguished Citizens
Alabama	7%	Sen. Sparkman
Georgia	12%	Rep. Wood, chairman, Un-American Comm., and Gov. Talmadge
Louisiana	15%	Sen. Long
S. Carolina	6%	Gov. Byrnes
Texas	14%	Martin Dies, originator of witch-hunting
Virginia	12%	Sen. Bryd

There are today 4½ million Negroes in the North, 9½ million in the South and a little less than a million in the West. In the North, perhaps 2,750,000 Negroes will vote, mostly in the large cities of Michigan, Illinois, Indiana, Ohio, New York, Pennsylvania, Connecticut, New Jersey, Delaware, Maryland and California. These 11 states cast nearly half the electoral votes for President. The difference in the voting strength of the two major parties in these states varies from zero to four per cent, while the Negro population ranges from three to 16 per cent. Thus the Negro vote here can decide whether Eisenhower or Stevenson will be our next President.

This the Democrats and Republicans know right well. And they are arranging their campaign accordingly—which involves considerable sums of money to influence Negro opinion; to organize clubs and speaking bureaus; indirectly advise advertisers, influence preachers and to put pressure on employees in federal state and city service. All this, in these days of hysteria and witch-hunting, will add up. Then there is the political patronage; offices and promises play a large role; today the promise of judicial or foreign service positions is being waved before colored men of prominence.

These influences, by no means confined to Negroes, play a larger part in a group like theirs whose economic foundation is less secure than that of the white population. For such reasons, fears and temptations, a considerable number of Negroes will line up with one or the other of the two main parties, in accordance with their clear personal interests.

In the South there will be a peculiar situation. The number of Negroes voting will increase:

	TOTAL 1948 VOTE	NEGROES PROBABLY ELIGIBLE 1952
Arkansas	242,000	75,000
Alabama	215,000	45,000
Florida	577,000	121,000
Georgia	418,000	125,000
Louisiana	419,000	95,000
N. Carolina	791,000	95,000
Oklahoma	721,000	60,000
Texas	1,147,000	175,000
Tennessee	550,000	150,000
S. Carolina	143,000	100,000
Virginia	419,000	71,000

The Negro vote in the South, however, will be for the most part registered in the Democratic primary and will go to the Democratic party.

It will thus have no influence on the Presidential vote unless Dixiecrats again play a part. Democracy in the South will eventually depend on the Negro vote, but not in this election.

"Show What Democracy Is"

For all these reasons a large element of the Negroes will vote "straight." But there will be left a large core of Negro voters: unconcerned, unpledged and unafraid; young men with ideals, thoughtful men and women who see in this election a chance to make history; to show the civilized world that the American Negro knows what democratic government is and how to make it function, to help change this nation from being the leading warmonger of the world into a nation of freedom, without color caste, willing to live in friendship with the world.

Moreover, the Negro voter, just as the white voter, is not confined to a choice between two political parties as the allied and associated Republican and Democratic parties are striving to make true today. It is the concerted effort of those who control public opinion through the press, periodicals, broadcasts and public platforms, to make the public believe that the very existence of the Progressive Party is un-American and subversive; that a party which stands for Negro rights, broader social control of wealth, and world peace, does not deserve support.

When the Progressive Party welcomes the support of all persons of every race and belief, including Catholics, Protestants and Jews; Negroes, Japanese and Mexicans; Republicans, Communists and Democrats; because of this, the party is labeled "subversive" and every effort is made to keep Americans even from having a chance to hear its appeal or to vote for its platform. Yet this platform is the most enlightened one before the electorate this year, and particularly it is a test of the degree to which American Negroes believe in themselves and their rights as citizens.

The Negro must realize what third party movements mean in a democracy. He knows that third party movement freed the slaves. The Republicans as a third party won the election of 1860 because the pro-slavery Dixiecrats of that day took 845,000 votes from the Democrats and elected Lincoln a minority president. Another third party in 1892 made possible the election of a northern Democrat, winning over the Republicans because the Populist, Weaver, polled a million votes. Many of these came from Negroes and more might have been attracted, but the Populist Movement from 1890 to 1900 not only failed to support Negro suffrage, but finally opposed Negro civil rights.

40 Years of Political Struggle

It was in the election of 1912 that the Negro tried to reach political maturity. The situation was difficult. The Negro voter had become the football of politics, the most exploited worker, and a social outcast despite his desperate and notable struggle upward. Theodore Roosevelt had tried at first to defend Negro rights, but his luncheon with Booker Washington raised such a blind fury in the South that he abandoned hope of the future role of this race in politics. His chosen successor, Taft, therefore cast the Negro quite out of consideration, promising the white South in his inaugural to appoint no Negroes to office without white approval.

When later, Roosevelt founded the Bull Moose Party, I was sure that here was a chance for the Negro voter. But Roosevelt turned his back on me and my plank and threw his influence behind Alton B. Parker and the "lily-whites" of Louisiana; and although he rolled up a vote of four million, he only succeeded in making Woodrow Wilson President.

Many Negroes saw in this election a new opportunity. The Taft Republicans had no use for us. The liberals who followed Roosevelt sympathized, but did not think our support worth alienating the white South. Thereupon a number of Negroes, including a few politicians, a few preachers like Bishop Alexander Walters, and many young radicals like Monroe Trotter and myself, threw ourselves on the mercies of Woodrow Wilson and tried to induce him to make some gesture to show that the Democratic Party would appreciate our support; that the Republicans no longer owned us body and soul. Instead then of following the third party, a large group of us tried to make Negroes vote the Democratic ticket.

It was tough job. To most Negroes of the older generation, desertion of the party of Lincoln was sacrilege, while support of the "jimcrowing," lynching, disfranchising South was sheer insanity. But we secured from Wilson a written pledge to treat Negroes with justice, "and not mere grudging justice." It was a chance, but many Negroes took it, and perhaps 100,000 Negro votes helped make Wilson President, although he hardly needed them to win.

We lost our gamble. The Wilson administration brought increased discrimination and an extraordinary amount of proposed anti-Negro legislation.

In 1916 Negroes were politically homeless. Hughes would take no stand, and Wilson was silent. In 1920 Negroes rushed to support Harding, not only because of the rumor of his Negro descent, but because of his promise to free Haiti. In 1924 a few Negroes voted for La Follette as I did, but not many. The campaign of 1928 brought such concerted vilification of Negroes, as an echo of the anti-Catholic propaganda and complete surrender of Hoover to the white South, that Negroes of all shades of opinion united in an unprecedented appeal for political justice in "this astonishing campaign of public insult toward one tenth of the nation."

Then came industrial depression and the reign of Roosevelt from 1933 to 1945. The Negro vote swung completely over to the New Deal. They did not get complete justice but they got economic help in their dire distress, a share in effective administration, and unprecedented recognition not only in politics but in the FEPC and in the trade union movement. Landon got no Negro support and Willkie only small.

And then, in 1948, came Truman. The Progressive Party appealed strongly to Negroes, but Truman took their civil rights program and promised more than he ever meant to fulfill or ever really tried. The bulk of the Negro vote supported him, and, with Dixiecrat opposition, he squeezed through to become a minority President.

The "Dilemma" of 1952

Now comes 1952—and the Negro voter is faced by the greatest dilemma in his political life. Truman is going to repeat his vaudeville act for Negroes and believes that they are fools enough to fall for him a second time. They are not that dumb, but they ask, what else? The Republicans are ready with money, appointments, and flattering publicity, but also with Nixon, war, and no civil rights.

The first answer to this is, don't vote, stay away from the polls—or confine your vote to local offices. This is silly. It is precisely what every professional politician earnestly prays for. Give the public such small choice that they will not vote, and thus let us nail down our hold on power!

What venal politics and selfish political control fears is the Protest Vote. That spells danger with a big D. If a Third Party in the campaign of 1952 could roll up a minority vote of three or even two million votes, the doom of War and Big Business in power politics would in calculable time be certain. When, then, President Truman weeps crocodile tears over 20 or 30 millions who neglect to vote, he knows perfectly well that they do not vote because they think voting is useless. Nothing would please the anti-Negro forces more than to have the Negro vote stay home next November.

Vote, then, but for whom? In 1928 Negro voters could choose only between the devil of Hoover and the deep sea of Tammany and the South. So today comes the second proposal to Negro voters: "the lesser evil." Vote for Truman, he tried. (Did he?) Vote for Stevenson, he may try. (Will he?) You can't get what you want, therefore settle for what you can get. That is exactly what American prejudice would love to have you do—what it has advised for 75 years. If you follow this path, the Negro American will never reach freedom. He'll always settle for something less.

Can Negro Voters Fail?

Today there is no such necessity. There is the Progressive Party, offering Negroes everything they ask. Reaction, North and South, is scared stiff lest the Negro will have sense enough to accept this offer.

The Progressive Party is pledged to a complete program of civil and economic rights; is headed by a defender of the rights of working people and a Negro woman. At first blush one would say: How can a single Negro voter fail to vote for this party, if only to serve notice on all future parties that if they fail to meet the legitimate demands of Negroes they lose three million votes in the North and West, and eventually five million more in the South when this land becomes a free democracy instead of a fraudulent imitation in 12 states?

Thus for a Negro with ordinary common sense there is no real dilemma in this election. Vote, and vote for the only party which support your just demands. If your position is such that it would be too risky for you publicly to announce your political choice, say nothing and vote secretly, as is your right. You need tell nobody what your choice is. As my dead friend, Henry Hunt, used to say: "I can keep silent in seven different languages."

Moreover, do not stop with your vote for President. See that a Progressive like Marcantonio is returned to Congress. Where there is no Progressive candidate, scan the record of other Congressmen on issues touching you. Grant that the Democrat, Adam Powell, votes right when he votes—but know that most of the time he is not in his seat in Congress, and does not vote at all on anything. Out of 100 chances to vote in 1952 he was present only 44—the worst record of any of the 24 New York congressmen, if not of all members of Congress.

Learn the records of your county, city and local officials; and if a pledged Progressive is not available, do not let a reactionary war-monger and big businessman slip into office over your careless inaction. This year, as never before, the American Negro has opportunity to show the world his political maturity, unafraid of threats even of being called "communist."

National Guardian, September 11, 1952; in H. Aptheker, ed., *Newspaper Columns* by W. E. B. Du Bois, 2 vols. (White Plains, N.Y.: Kraus-Thomson, 1986) 895–900.

17

WITH A VOICE FULL OF FURY (1953)

by Yvonne Gregory

One of the Trenton Six, Collis English, died in prison late in 1952. Here is an account of his funeral, written by a young African-American poet.

Sunbeams the color of dusty lemons sift through a stained glass window marked "given by the Deaconesses." Lemon color dusts across lilies, across gladioli, over chrysanthemums, asters and roses that stand huddled together in bunches and baskets, wreaths and wired floral designs in a semi-circle directly beneath the church pulpit. Sifted through the bright stains of glass and petals, the dusty sunbeams touch lemon light soft and gentle along the slender still form of a young black man. He lies natty and correct in Navy blues against crushed white funeral satin. And white stars on a navy blue ground wink from the American flag folded beside his still black head in the formal folds of ceremonial honor.

Collis English lies in his coffin. Collis English, 26, veteran of World War II, is being buried with honor by his government. Collis English, one of the Trenton Six, lived six years behind prison bars, and now he lies among the stars and the roses and the satin and the sunbeams. Finished and snuffed and stiff with death; dead of heartache; dead of heartstrain and heartpain, of heart sickness and heartbreak. Dead, so dead, of the heart disease. His heart burst before the bars would burst. And now he is dead and this is his funeral.

In choir loft and balcony, filling up the pews, are some 800 mourners. Black and white they settle down in the church, settle down with pain and anger. Which is more present here, pain or anger, when the black family shrouded and banded with black grief comes to take its place in the front pews, and eyes are forced to center on two figures in the procession? Is anger more painful or pain more angry when eyes and ears are crowded with the immense grief of the mother and sister of the dead man? Who of the 800 can endure the sight of Mrs. Bessie Mitchell moving heavily and uncertainly, her head bowed in sorrow and her mobile, sensitive brown face quivering with agony? Can the 800 persons encompass even among their number the vastness of the awesome small, stooped delicacy of Mrs. English? The presence of their sorrow here, the reason for their sorrow, is too big for the church's four walls. It is larger than the town of Trenton, New Jersey; wider than the distance from Maine to Texas; deeper than the Mississippi River; older than the Constitution of these United States; taller than the Empire State building, and swifter to span distances than the newest jet plane. It is sorrow with a voice full of fury.

Bessie Mitchell's voice is sorrow-rough and fury-sharp as it tears the thin web of sound stretched out through the church by the congregation, singing a Hymn of Solace. Bessie Mitchell's voice and the timidly proffered hymn make a strange pattern of point and counter point. The congregation sings:

> Come ye disconsolate, where e'er ye languish
> Come to the mercy seat, fervently kneel.
> Here bring your wounded hearts
> Here tell your anguish.
> Earth has no sorrow
> That heaven cannot heal...

And Bessie Mitchell shouts: "They *murdered* him! O people, people! The law murdered my brother! I tell you, it *was* murder!"

The funeral rites proceed over, under and around the agony of Mrs. Mitchell the sister and Mrs. English the mother. Sometimes the two of them are quiet and spent against the high wood backs of the pews. Other women hover over them constantly, with small bottles, soft clothes and steady, compassionate hands. Sometimes their grief is audible like the low, running sound of a river moaning to itself at night. Sometimes the voice of Mrs. English calls out a wordless loss. And sometimes and often, the furious sorrow of Bessie Mitchell, the fighter, spouts up like a geyser. In those moments it seems she must surely be heard and understood and answered by the rage of women in Africa and Alabama and Asia who know the exact measure of her pain.

A church reporter speaks. Two trade union leaders, black and white, speak with the voices of thousands of union members, black and white. NAACP leaders speak and a young Negro woman poet reads messages of condolence. When another young Negro woman sings tenderly and passionately... "To you, beloved comrade, we make this solemn vow, the fight will still go on..." Bessie Mitchell half rises from her seat, stretches out her arms to the figure in the Navy uniform stiffened out against the stiffly folded, stiffly starry-flag, and cries:

"He *was* my comrade, my brother! He was a fighter and they *murdered* him! O it was murder, Collis. Tell everybody they *murdered* you!"

A man reads the obituary and the 800 bow their heads through the hideously brief moments it takes to tell the story of Collis English's life. ...He was born, reads the man. He grew through childhood, into adolescence, finished high school. He was known as a fine lad in his community. Then he answered the call of his country, and in the service of his country he contracted the rheumatic fever which finally and fatally affected his heart. He was discharged from the Navy after three years' service. He served six years in prison and in prison he died.... The obituary is finished.

From behind the muffling fall of her black mourner's veil the voice of Bessie Mitchell is heard. It sounds far away and sad and amazed as she says:

"So young, so young, he never *even* had a girl friend. They didn't *even* let him have time to be in love, my poor little brother...."

The Negro doctor who diagnosed the heart condition of Collis English for the state of New Jersey speaks. Because he told the truth about that heart, the doctor himself is now under indictment for perjury. He stands above the body of the former prisoner and says with slow, bitter comprehension: "I told the truth about his heart and it seems he had to die to prove my diagnosis was correct."

The national executive secretary of the Civil Rights Congress speaks. Quietly, through tight lips, William L. Patterson says: "We say that you were murdered, Collis English. We know who murdered you, and we promise you that they will be punished for their murder." His brief speech is punctuated by repeated choruses of "amen" and "that's true" from the congregation.

Many ministers speak and offer solace of various kinds to the bereaved family. Some offer memories of the Collis English they knew. Some recount the ways in which they helped to fight for his freedom. Some urge more action and some urge more prayer.

Bessie Mitchell leans on the shoulder of William Patterson and sobs: "O Collis, we've got to let the people know about your murder."

The funeral program is done. Now the undertakers in their striped grey pants and their decorous black coats and their air of properly arranged and modest mournfulness take charge. They are nimble and authoritative at their task of directing the congregation into two lines which file past the casket to take their last (and for some, their first and last) look at Collis English.

Negro and white, men, women, young people and children are tense with the anger of sorrow and the sorrow of anger. A teen-aged Negro girl wearing a kerchief on her head stops in front of the coffin. A moment before, when she had glimpsed the neat pleats of the smart Navy uniform, she turned to a friend behind her in the line and said: "He looks real nice." Now her soft little face is startled out of contour by fearful confrontation of death's finality, death that is so dead and can *never* look nice. As she stares wide-eyed, tears spurt up from a well deep in her heart she had never known was there. The line goes on.

And among those who view the body of Collis English are:

Mrs. Josephine Grayson, widow of Francis Grayson, one of the Martinsville Seven, murdered by the State of Virginia; Mrs. Rosalie McGee, widow of Willie McGee, murdered by the State of Mississippi; Mrs. Amy Mallard and Doris Mallard, widow and daughter of Robert Mallard, murdered by the Klan of Georgia.

When these women face the still, slim form of Collis English, most of the other mourners must turn their own faces away. But Doris Mallard returns to the casket a second time. The second time she holds the tiny hand of her six-year-old brother, Johnny. When her turn comes again, Doris Mallard lifts Johnny fiercely, and holds his tiny wriggling body for a terrible moment above the stone-stillness of Collis English.

The last member of the congregation to stand beside the coffin is a Negro man about 25 years old. He walks gravely to the bier, bends toward the face for a suspended second, straightens up lightly and swiftly, touches the folded finality of Collis English's hands with one of his own. Then he turns and swings away up the church aisle with his head high. To those who saw the gesture and recognized it as a common form of greeting or farewell among Negro young people, usually accompanied by the phrase: "Give me some skin," it was a gesture almost too poignant to have witnessed. It said: "Everything is *rough* out here, man, but we'll make it on through somehow. You played your part, man. I appreciate it, daddy. Thanks, man. Here's some skin."

The pallbearers move up to the casket now. Among them are men who made up four of the Trenton Six. These four were freed after five years in prison. One still remains behind bars. The four look hard at the rigidity which is all that is left of the man who suffered and hoped and fought for freedom by their sides for half a decade. Their faces are almost as closed and silent as the face in the coffin.

The time has come for the immediate family to take their last look at their son and brother. But neither Mrs. English nor Mrs. Mitchell can move from their seats and so the agile undertakers obligingly wheel the casket up to the two of them. Bessie Mitchell makes a hoarse, ragged sound and falls speechless toward the coffin.

Fragile and bent, Mrs. Emma English, unyielding mother of two unyielding children, walks softly past her daughter to her son. Gently and tenderly her work-gnarled black hands lift the white silk at the foot of the casket. Slowly, gently, and tenderly, she covers the face of her dead child. In the curve of her slight black figure at this instant, there is all delicacy and all resiliency. In her gesture there is mountain strength and flower beauty; earth patience and warm sun-love; rain fierceness and rain tenderness; tall forest dignity and never-ending river-rushing faith in life. In this instant, with this gesture, the mother of Collis English becomes all the world's oppressed women, all the world's robbed mothers.

But when Mrs. English has completed her task, something occurs which seems to have been deliberately contrived to mock the grief of mother and sister; to mock the angry sorrow of the funeral. First, the casket is closed with the funeral ritual.

Then, over the burst heart, the sealed mouth, the rigid limbs, the dreadful death of Collis English is draped the flag of the United States of America. It had been forgotten, or not clearly known by most of the mourners that this was to be a burial with full military honor. The colors of his country shroud the coffin, the casket, the bier, the body, the death and the life of Collis English.

Now flag, casket, flowers, pall-bearers, ministers, speakers, family and mourners leave the church, are gathered into a 60-car procession, ride through the town of Trenton, capital of the state of New Jersey, and enter the Greenwood Cemetery. And there in the hushed burial place the mockery that had been barely a slight smirk in the church broadens into a loose-lipped, leering grin.

Lined up in formation, white gloved hands resting on their up-barrelled guns, are some ten white soldiers with white scarves wound around their necks and white helmets slanting across their faces. They stand as though on guard. On guard of what?

In the tent erected over the open grave, the coffin has been lowered. The pall-bearers clutch edges of the American flag, now stretched taut above Collis English's last and final resting place in or on his country's earth. In the few chairs the family sits, and those of the mourners who can find room pack the rest of the small space. A minister consigns ashes to ashes and dust to dust and then there is a sudden splitting, outrageous explosion of sound. The soldiers are firing their guns. The government of the United States salutes Collis English in his grave with three heavy blasts from ten or more guns fired by ten or more white soldiers from the Jim Crow ranks of the United States Army.

In the howling shock of silence that follows the blast, two of the soldiers enter the tent and stand on either end of the grave. They remove the flag from the hands of the pall-bearers. Then, in silence that is like sound, they begin a strange, precise, intricate, ritualistic folding of the bright striped and starred material. When they have folded it according to their formula, one brings the bundled flag over to Mrs. English. (Now the grin of mockery takes on even new dimensions and becomes the reckless, heedless cackle of a madman who thinks he is clever.) On top of the bundle are three shiny empty bullet shells. The white soldier bows low before the black mother, presents the bundle of cloth and spent metal to her and speaks rapidly and briefly. The only words he says which can be distinguished are:

"... your country honors you ... son, who fought honorably in the service of ... "

The funeral of Collis English is over. As people drift away from the tent down the rows of graves, Bessie Mitchell stops a group of Negro and white women and asks painfully, through lips cracked with sobbing:

"You all are going to Washington tomorrow, aren't you?"

Shocked by the morning's contrasts, and still sorrowing in spirit beside the grave of Collis English, one of the women replies, wonderingly:

"To Washington? Why, Bessie?"

Bessie Mitchell's eyes, swollen with pain, stare in bewildered surprise.

"Why? To be in the demonstration to free the Rosenbergs, that's why," she says.

Masses and Mainstream, February 1953, Vol. 6, pp. 2–7. An account of this case was offered in the printed *Brief of the National Lawyers Guild, Amicus Curiae* submitted to the New Jersey Supreme Court (Docket No. 180). This is in the editor's possession.

18

IN DEFENSE OF NEGRO LEADERSHIP (1953)

by Rev. Edward D. McGowan

Sen. Joseph McCarthy and FBI director J. Edgar Hoover were profoundly racist. The reactionary terror associated with their names fell with special force upon African-Americans. A result was the creation in 1953 of the Committee to Defend Negro Leadership. This was chaired by the Reverend Edward D. McGowan, for many years minister of the Epworth Methodist Church in the Bronx, New York. At the time of the delivery of this speech, he was pastor of the Asbury Methodist Church in Frederick, Maryland.

The speech was delivered on April 30, 1953, at the meeting in Detroit of the National Fraternal Council of Churches, U.S.A. The council represented twelve denominations with 7 million members.

On behalf of the Committee to Defend Negro Leadership, I want to thank you for permitting me, its chairman, to present the urgent cause of that Committee to such a distinguished assembly—yes, to you who are the core of leadership as well as the makers of leaders for the Negro people. There are some among you who have been the victims of the forces of reaction and oppression. Attempts have been made to discredit your distinguished leadership by name-calling and other smear tactics—your abilities to think and to arrive at decisions and courses of action that result in a better way of life for your people have been slandered by such false accusations that other individuals or groups do your thinking for you—

that you who are leaders because you do have these abilities are so weak that you can be easily "used" to "front" for other individuals or groups.

Halt Enemies of Negro Freedom

These attacks by the forces of reaction and enemies of the freedom of the Negro people have reached such alarming proportions that you and I must rise up in some concerted action to call a halt to these forces who would dictate to fifteen million American citizens who their leaders must be, how they must think and what they may speak.

I stand here this evening—a representative and a product of three movements in religion that were champions of the rights of the individual to freedom of thought, speech and action.

Nearly 2,000 years ago the founder of the Christian Community gave his life for the right to think, to speak and to believe according to the dictates of his own conscience rather than be told by a religious hierarchy what he must think, speak, believe.

He believed that his sacrifice would vouchsafe that same freedom to generations following.

I would be a traitor to him and to thousands of martyrs and saints— traitor to a movement whose influence has made crooked lives straight— whose power has caused the blind to see and the lame to walk, made bad men good, made somebodies out of nobodies—a traitor indeed if I remained silent in my generation when these freedoms of the spirit were in jeopardy.

If at this crucial moment in history his ways are too hard for me I mus renounce my claim to be a part of his movement.

I am also a Protestant—a movement whose leader, Martin Luther. nearly four centuries ago made a bold stroke for the right of the individual Christian to freedom of conscience, thought, and speech, in the area of religion, rather than to be dictated to by a religious hierarchy.

As a good Protestant I must protest every act that threatens the gains made by a movement whose followers in these nearly 400 years have "wrought righteousness, quenched the violence of fire, escaped the edge of the sword, and out of weakness were made strong."

I am a Methodist—a movement whose leader, John Wesley, exercised his freedom to think, speak and believe according to the dictates of his own conscience, rather than conform to the decadent religious atmosphere of his age.

As a representative and a product of three great religious movements that have championed freedom of conscience, thought and speech I must be vigilant lest these hard won gains of these 2,000 years be lost to this and succeeding generations.

I must with every ounce of my being vouchsafe these same freedoms to every individual and group in society. Even to those with whom I disagree—I must oppose every instrument that threatens these freedoms to *any group* because I know that that same instrument in the hands of those who disagree with me will deprive me of the freedoms which have nourished and sustained me these 38 years.

Racism at Home and Abroad

And so I must protest the attempt of the Un-American Activities Committee to impugn the leadership of Bishop W. J. Walls by calling this great leader of a great denomination a "subversive,"

—The insult and abuse to which Rev. Charles A. Hill of this city (Detroit) was subjected by this same committee,

—The attempt of the U.S. State Department to deny passport rights to the Rev. James H. Robinson of New York City because he insisted on voicing the Negro and colonial peoples' demands against racism as practiced at home and exported abroad.

The refusal of the neo-fascist Malan government in South Africa to permit Bishop Frederick Jordan and Bishop Primm to administer the work of the A.M.E. Church in South Africa. The reasons for this denial being that the A.M.E. Church has cooperated in the resistance of the African people to the unjust laws.

Drums of Freedom in Africa

The accusation against the A.M.E. Church is correct because the A.M.E. Church has been preaching the gospel—a gospel that emphasizes the dignity of the human personality and wherever the gospel is preached, men rise up to walk in freedom and in dignity.

The drums of freedom have begun to sound across Africa and it is the rhythm of justice, equal opportunity and a decent life for its millions who have known this land as home for many centuries. The rhythm of those drums will not be silenced.

And so, I too must protest—yes, find ways in which to make effective protest against the persecution of those leaders in South and East Africa—

Dr. Dadoo, Dr. Z.K. Matthews, Jomo Kenyatta and the five other leaders who were sentenced to seven years hard labor—because they oppose the exclusion of the African people from the political and economic life in a country which belongs to them.

I refuse to be engulfed by the hysteria and fear of our times because I firmly believe that given a chance Democracy will stem the tide of this and every age. Only those who daily by their deeds try to retard the full flowering of the democratic way of life become hysterical in the face of the world situation.

I know too that every denial of freedom weakens democracy.

I say these things in the face of the fact that I too am a victim of attack in another form though for similar reasons. You and I must be alert for the more subtle forms of attack that would silence those who speak and act for a more abundant life for the people.

Though my voice is not especially loud or strong, it seems that when I have spoken in behalf of PEACE and first class status for fifteen million American citizens too many people could hear me (possibly the FBI also) when I would speak in New York. And so my superiors possibly feel that not so many people will hear me and it will be much safer down in Maryland to which I am being transferred as of May 24th.

If in hysteria and fear we continue the course we are on, we will awake on tomorrow to discover that the house of Democracy has fallen—not because of the attack of some enemy without—rather it will have fallen because of weakening from within by the denial of freedom.

—Freedom to *print and publish the truth* as was true of John H. McCray, Negro editor of the *Lighthouse* and *Informer* who was sentenced to sixty days on the chain gang because he championed the right of Negroes to vote in South Carolina.

—Freedom to *speak the truth* as in the case of Dr. J. Minor Sullivan who was indicted and is out on $1,000 bail because he dared give testimony in court showing that defendants in the Trenton Six case were drugged at the time of their so-called confessions.

Dignity and Full Citizenship

Negro Americans believe in our democratic way of life and their fight for first class status is motivated by the belief that when they really become first class citizens, democracy will be impregnable against every foe. They know also that the longer these rights and freedoms are delayed the weaker becomes the house of democracy—the greater becomes the despair and the hopelessness of millions who await some sure word of hope.

And so they are insisting that NOW is the time. *This* is the hour, not tomorrow or the day after. They are saying to America, "Let us *this* day make this a government *of* the people, *by* the people, *for* the people. With liberty and justice, not only for whites, Democrats, Republicans, Socialists—but liberty and justice for *all* the people.

The attack against the leaders of the Negro people by the forces of reaction is an attempt to curb the mounting struggle of our people for dignity and full citizenship.

And so we must, by concerted action, foil the attempt of all those forces that would discredit the real leaders of the Negro people and substitute those who dare speak only as their masters please.

What could be more fitting than that I should be given the opportunity of presenting the cause of the Committee to Defend Negro Leadership to the National Fraternal Council of Churches. Bishop [A.W.]Womack— when you speak you represent four million Negroes and some thirteen denominations. *We* made you our leader. We did not ask anyone whether or not we *could* make you our leader. We made you our leader because we saw in you qualities that we liked. We believed that you would represent the aspirations of our people for dignity and first class status. And as the leader of the National Fraternal Council of Churches when you speak you not only represent four million church members but fifteen million Negro Americans. And we will protest with every ounce of our being any attempt by the forces of reaction to silence you.

Hopes and Aspirations

Dr. [W.H.] Jernigan, though there are thousands who do not know you personally, whenever your name is called a feeling of pride wells up in the breast of our people because we recognize you as our leader. We are grateful for the tremendous contribution which you have made in the interest of the Negro people and to the cuase of religion in your 88 years. *We* have made you our leader and we did not consult anyone to find out if we *could* or *could not* make you our leader. And we will protest any effort to silence you when you speak in our interest. The Negro Church had its beginning at this point of the right of the individual to dignity and first class status. Believing that all men are equal at the foot of the cross, the Negro established a church in which he could worship God in dignity and with a healthy sense of self-respect and not as a servant. We remembered that Jesus said, "I have not called you servant but friend."

And to the Negro church has been entrusted the responsibility of translating the hopes and aspirations of the Negro for dignity and freedom into reality. When my grandparents sang the spiritual, "I am Going to Eat at the Welcome Table One of These Days," it is true that they meant eternity. But they also meant that they were looking forward to a day in time when they would no longer have to eat in the kitchen of white folks but would eat at a table of their own in their own dining room at which they could sit in freedom and with dignity.

Now and again you and I are privileged to catch a glimpse of eternity. We are privileged to see "the Lord, high and lifted up" and to hear the beautiful harmonies of the Cherubim and the Seraphim as they chant, "Holy, Holy, Holy, Lord God Almighty, Heaven and Earth are full of Thy glory." This Christ of God disturbs us. He will not let us be at ease until the music of the Cherubims and Seraphims gets translated from eternity to the lips of the men and women in the towns and cities where we serve.

Or again we are taken to some island of Patmos, where in the spirit on the Lord's day we catch a vision of a new heaven and a new earth coming down from God out of heaven to dwell among men. And this Christ of God disturbs us—will not let us be at ease until in Mississippi, Alabama, Detroit, Texas or New York there is at least some concrete or asphalt on which our people can walk.

In Defense of Negro Leadership

The Church must continue to translate into time the visions of eternity—must continue to translate into reality the hopes and aspirations of our people.

The Committee to Defend Leadership which represents such outstanding leaders of the Negro people as Bishop C. Alleyne, Bishop R. C. Ransom, Mrs. Mary Church Terrell, Rev. Charles A. Hill and Mr. Coleman A. Young of Detroit, Rev. Joseph Evans of Chicago, Mrs. Andrew W. Simkins of S.C., invites your cooperation and participation in its efforts in this direction.

We are convinced that we must come to the defense of all Negro leaders who are attacked. We will not succumb to the enemies of the Negro people who would divide us by name calling and smear tactics. For we know that a better life for our people will not be achieved by a divided people. And so I must defend a Paul Robeson, the greatest artist of this century. Paul Robeson has interpreted the classics for me in a way that no other person could. When he sings I am thrilled as no other person can thrill me. I know Paul Robeson personally and he has talked to me from the depths of his heart and I will come to my own conclusions about Paul Robeson—no one else can tell me what I must think or believe about this great leader of the Negro people.

"In the Shouting Out Times"

And so I must defend Dr. W. E. B. Du Bois, who when he speaks reveals a vast knowledge—a knowledge of the universe. Dr. Du Bois is the greatest scholar of this century; yet he has placed his vast knowledge and his skill as a scholar at the service of his people. He has spent more than 50 years in fighting for the dignity and first class status of 15 million Negro citizens and because of this the Negro people have made him their leader.

I must defend a Ben Davis. There are some who tell me that he is a Communist. In New York City more than 75,000 Negroes and whites elected him to the City Council on two occasions. They did not seem to question his politics. They knew that he was fighting for a better way of life for the Negro people and so they made him their leader. They did not ask permission as to whether they *could* or *could not* make him their leader.

In the struggle for full citizenship rights many different kinds of forces must unite for victory.

> In the shouting out times
> In the stand up and be counted days
> When the roll is called
> Where will you be?
> In the shouting out times
> In the stand up and be counted days
> Do you close your eyes?
> Do you turn your head?
> Are you afraid?

Pamphlet published by National Committee to Defend Negro Leadership located in Brooklyn, New York. Its treasurer was Owen Middleton. In editor's possession.

19

SEGREGATION MEANS INEQUALITY (1953)

by NAACP Defense Fund

The NAACP Legal Defense and Education Fund, Inc., was established in 1939 as a tax-exempt organization. Its main purpose was to conduct the mounting legal work of the NAACP. It was this Legal Defense Fund that was responsible for arguing the cases eventuating, in May 1954, in the unanimous Supreme Court decision holding segregated education to be unconstitutional.

Published below is the "Summary of Argument" of the brief presented by the fund to the October 1953 term of the Supreme Court. Observe that the brief argues against delay in the implementation of desegregation; for the wisdom of that advice see the essay by Kenneth B. Clark, published hereafter. Alas, the Court, in its 1955 decision, suggested implementing desegregation "with all deliberate speed," which meant much deliberation and little speed. (Published in part.)

These cases consolidated for argument before this Court present in different factual contexts essentially the same ultimate legal questions.

The substantive question common to all is whether a state can, consistently with the Constitution, exclude children, solely on the ground that they are Negroes, from public schools which otherwise they would be qualified to attend. It is the thesis of this brief, submitted on behalf of the excluded children, that the answer to the question is in the negative: the Fourteenth Amendment prevents states from according differential treatment to American children on the basis of their color or race. Both the legal precedents and the judicial theories, discussed in Part I hereof, and the evidence concerning the intent of the framers of the Fourteenth Amendment and the understanding of the Congress and the ratifying states, developed in Part II hereof, support this proposition.

Denying this thesis, the school authorities, relying in part on language originating in this Court's opinion in *Plessy v. Ferguson*, 163 U.S. 537, urge that exclusion of Negroes, *qua* Negroes, from designated public schools is permissible when the excluded children are afforded admittance to other schools especially reserved for Negroes, *qua* Negroes, if such schools are equal.

The procedural question common to all the cases is the role to be played, and the time-table to be followed, by this Court and the lower courts in directing an end to the challenged exclusion, in the event that this Court determines, with respect to the substantive question, that exclusion of Negroes, *qua* Negroes, from public schools contravenes the Constitution.

The importance to our American democracy of the substantive question can hardly be overstated. The question is whether a nation founded on the proposition that "all men are created equal" is honoring its commitments to grant "due process of law" and "the equal protection of the laws" to all within its borders when it, or one of its constituent states, confers or denies benefits on the basis of color or race.

1. Distinctions drawn by state authorities on the basis of color or race violate the Fourteenth Amendment. *Shelley v. Kraemer*, 334 U.S. 1; *Buchanan v. Warley*, 245 U.S. 60. This has been held to be true even as to the conduct of public educational institutions. *Sweatt v. Painter*, 339 U.S. 629; *McLaurin v. Oklahoma State Regents*, 339 U.S. 637. Whatever other purposes the Fourteenth Amendment may have had, it is indisputable that its primary purpose was to complete the emancipation provided by the Thirteenth Amendment by ensuring to the Negro equality before the law. The *Slaughter House Cases*, 16 Wall. 36; *Strauder v. West Virginia*, 100 U.S. 303.

2. Even if the Fourteenth Amendment did not *per se* invalidate racial distinctions as a matter of law, the racial segregation challenged in the instant cases would run afoul of the conventional test established for application of the equal protection clause because the racial classifications here have no reasonable relation to any valid legislative purpose. See *Quaker City Cab Co. v. Pennsylvania*, 277 U.S. 389; *Truax v. Raich*, 239 U.S. 33; *Smith v. Cahoon*, 283 U.S. 553; *Mayflower Farms v. Ten Eyck*, 297 U.S. 266; *Skinner v. Oklahoma*, 316 U.S. 535. See also *Tunstall v. Brotherhood of Locomotive Firemen*, 323 U.S. 210; *Steele v. Louisville & Nashville R.R.Co.*, 323 U.S. 192.

3. Appraisal of the facts requires rejection of the contention of the school authorities. The educational detriment involved in racially constricting a student's associations has already been recognized by this Court. *Sweatt v. Painter*, 339 U.S. 629; *McLaurin v. Oklahoma State Regents*, 339 U.S. 637.

4. The argument that the requirements of the Fourteenth Amendment are met by providing alternative schools rests, finally, on reiteration of the separate but equal doctrine enunciated in *Plessy v. Ferguson*.

Were these ordinary cases, it might be enough to say that the *Plessy* case can be distinguished—that it involved only segregation in transportation. But these are not ordinary cases, and in deference to their importance it seems more fitting to meet the *Plessy* doctrine head-on and to declare that doctrine erroneous.

Candor requires recognition that the plain purpose and effect of segregated education is to perpetuate an inferior status for Negroes which is America's sorry heritage from slavery. But the primary purpose of the Fourteenth Amendment was to deprive the states of *all* power to perpetuate such a caste system.

5. The first and second of the five questions propounded by this Court requested enlightenment as to whether the Congress which submitted, and the state legislatures and conventions which ratified, the Fourteenth Amendment contemplated or understood that it would prohibit segregation in public schools, either of its own force or through subsequent legislative or judicial action. The evidence, both in Congress and in the legislatures of the ratifying states, reflects the substantial intent of the Amendment's proponents and the substantial understanding of its opponents that the Fourteenth Amendment would, of its own force, proscribe all forms of state-imposed racial distinctions, thus necessarily including all racial segregation in public education.

The Fourteenth Amendment was actually the culmination of the determined efforts of the Radical Republican majority in Congress to incorporate into our fundamental law the well-defined equalitarian principle of complete equality for all without regard to race or color. The debates in the 39th Congress and succeeding Congresses clearly reveal the intention that the Fourteenth Amendment would work a revolutionary change in our state-federal relationship by denying to the states the power to distinguish on the basis of race.

The Civil Rights Bill of 1866, as originally proposed, possessed scope sufficiently broad in the opinion of many Congressmen to entirely destroy all state legislation based on race. A great majority of the Republican Radicals—who later formulated the Fourteenth Amendment—understood and intended that the Bill would prohibit segregated schools. Opponents of the measure shared this understanding. The scope of this legislation was narrowed because it was known that the Fourteenth Amendment was in process of preparation and would itself have scope exceeding that of the original draft of the Civil Rights Bill.

6. The evidence makes clear that it was the intent of the proponents of the Fourteenth Amendment, and the substantial understanding of its opponents, that it would, of its own force, prohibit all state action predicated upon race or color. The intention of the framers with respect to any specific example of caste state action—in the instant cases, segregated education—cannot be determined solely on the basis of a tabulation of contemporaneous statements mentioning the specific practice. The framers were formulating a constitutional provision setting broad standards for determination of the relationship of the state to the individual. In the nature of things they could not list all the specific categories of existing and prospective state activity which were to come within the constitutional prohibitions. The broad general purpose of the Amendment—obliteration of race and color distinctions—is clearly established by the evidence. So far as there was consideration existing, both proponents and opponents of the Amendment understood that it would proscribe all racial segregation in public education.

7. While the Amendment conferred upon Congress the power to enforce its prohibitions, members of the 39th Congress and those of subsequent Congresses made it clear that the framers understood and intended that the Fourteenth Amendment was self-executing and particularly pointed out that the federal judiciary had authority to enforce its prohibitions without Congressional implementation.

8. The evidence as to the understanding of the states is equally convincing. Each of the eleven states that had seceded from the Union ratified the Amendment, and concurrently eliminated racial distinctions from its laws, and adopted a constitution free of requirement or specific authorization of segregated schools. Many rejected proposals for segregated schools, and none enacted a school segregation law until after readmission. The significance of these facts is manifest from the consideration that ten of these states, which were required, as a condition of readmission, to ratify the Amendment and to modify their constitutions and laws in conformity therewith, considered that the Amendment required them to remove all racial distinctions from their existing and prospective laws, including those pertaining to public education.

Twenty-two of the twenty-six Union states also ratified the Amendment. Although unfettered by Congressional surveillance, the overwhelming majority of the Union states acted with an understanding that it prohibited racially segregated schools and necessitated conformity of their school laws to secure consistency with that understanding.

9. In short, the historical evidence fully sustains this Court's conclusion in the *Slaughter House Cases*, 16 Wall. 36, 81, that the Fourteenth Amendment was designed to take from the states all power to enforce caste or class distinctions.

10. The Court in its fourth and fifth questions assumes that segregation is declared unconstitutional and inquires as to whether relief should be granted immediately or gradually. Appellants, recognizing the possibility of delay of a purely administrative character, do not ask for the impossible. No cogent reasons justifying further exercise of equitable discretion, however, have as yet been produced.

It has been indirectly suggested in the briefs and oral argument of appellees that some such reasons exist. Two plans were suggested by the United States in its Brief as *Amicus Curiae*. We have analyzed each of these plans as well as appellees' briefs and oral argument and find nothing there of sufficient merit on which this Court, in the exercise of its equity power, could predicate a decree permitting an effective gradual adjustment from segregated to non-segregated school systems. Nor have we been able to find any other reasons or plans sufficient to warrant the exercise of such equitable discretion in these cases. Therefore, in the present posture of these cases, appellants are unable to suggest any compelling reasons for this Court to postpone relief.

In Thomas R. Frazier, ed., *African-American History: Primary Sources* (New York: Harcourt Brace, 1970), pp. 368–72.

20

DESEGREGATION: AN APPRAISAL OF THE EVIDENCE (1953)

by Kenneth B. Clark

A key role in producing the desegregation ruling by the Supreme Court in 1954 was played by historian John Hope Franklin and psychologist Kenneth B. Clark. The latter was the author of a special issue of the *Journal of Social Issues* (Vol. 9, no. 4, 1953) whose title is given above. From that study is abstracted the section called "Findings" (pp. 13–64); the reference section is omitted.

I. A trend toward desegregation is found in many areas of community life and involves various social institutions. While the majority of these examples of desegregation come from Northern, Border, Midwestern and Southwestern states, there are examples of successful desegregation in Southern states.

Areas of Recent Change from Racially Segregated to Nonsegregated Patterns

The following instances of desegregation in various institutions and areas of American life are not necessarily a complete listing of all of the instances of desegregation which have taken place within the past ten years. This list presents merely those areas and instances of racial desegregation which have come to our attention during the course of this survey. In a few instances, the desegregation may have occurred earlier than ten years ago. Such instances, however, are included in the listing if they are a part of an area which has been increasing in rate and extent of desegregation during the past ten years.

1. The Church

Protestant Churches
Individual parishes
University of the South, other theological schools and church supported colleges and universities in southern states

Catholic Churches
Individual parishes, e.g., Newton Grove, N.C.
Parochial schools:
St.Louis, Mo.
Wilmington, Del.
Washington, D.C.
Church supported colleges, universities, hospitals.

2. The Armed Forces

Army
Camps, schools on camps in southern states, housing, personnel
Navy
Ships, personnel, navy yards in southern states

Air Force
Personnel, bases

Marine Corps

3. Housing

Interracial housing in northern and border states

Non-segregation in residential areas in southern states

A cursory glance at the cities in which integration in public housing has been accomplished indicates that it is possible in a wide variety of socio-political climates. It exists in some form in such diversified communities as New York, Honolulu, T. H., Cheyenne, Claypool (Ariz.), Berkeley, Seattle, Philadelphia, Modesto (Calif.), Newark, Youngstown, San Diego, Chicago, Hartford, Portland (Ore.), Boston, Vancouver, Chambersburg (Pa.), Lima (Ohio), Bloomfield (N.J.), Sausalito, Princeton, Yonkers. These are communities large and small, East and West (and Midwest), Republican and Democrat, urban and suburban, wealthy and not-so-wealthy, with a large melting pot population, and with a relative homogeneous population, with a large Negro population and with a small Negro population.... Integration... is not found in any of the southern or border states.

4. Interstate Transportation

Railroads—Pullman, dining cars, coaches
Buses
Airplanes—airports in southern states

5. Hospitals and Health Services

Interracial hospitals in southern states
Admission of Negroes to medical societies
Use of Negro personnel on hospital staffs

6. Public Accommodations and Recreational Facilities

Hotels, restaurants and theaters, moving picture houses in Washington, D.C. and other border states

Public facilities—southern and border states:
  Playgrounds, public parks, swimming pools
Private recreation facilities

7. Organized Sports

Baseball
  Big league teams
  Minor league teams in the South
Tennis, bowling, etc.
  Intercollegiate competition between
  northern and southern colleges in the South

8. Labor Unions and Industrial Employment

Unions in the South

George S. Mitchell of the Southern Regional Council has stated that within the last dozen years, "not only has trade unionism found rather general acceptance in the South, but mixed trade unionism, with Negroes and whites in the same local together, has become a Southern institution no longer much resisted. Of the estimated 2,750,000 trade unionists in the South, probably as many as 700,000 are Negroes."

Expansion of employment opportunities in the South

Bibbs Company	Columbus, Georgia
Chrysler Corp.	New Orleans
Glenn Martin	Baltimore, Maryland
Flintkote Company	New Orleans
Happy Day Laundry	Nashville, Tennessee
Higgins, Inc.	New Orleans
Ingalls Shipbuilding	Brunswick, Georgia
International Harvester	New Orleans; Memphis; Louisville, Kentucky, Evansville, Indiana
Norfolk Navy Yard	Norfolk, Virginia
Rheems Manufacturing Co.	New Orleans
Swift and Company	New Orleans

Other industries

Bell Telephone Company (10 companies)	National Smelting
Curtiss Wright	RCA
Douglas Aircraft	Sperry Gyroscope
General Cable	Western Electric
	Winchester Arms

9. Politics and Government

Negroes voting in Democratic primaries in southern states
Election of Negroes to public offices in southern communities

That Negroes are becoming an increasingly important factor in southern and national politics is indicated by the estimate that there were 1,200,000 registered Negro voters in 12 southern states in 1952. It is noteworthy that predictions of violence and excessive social unrest were made when these voting cases were before the courts. These predictions have not come true. Instead the following partial list of Negro public office holders and elected officials in the South demonstrates that the court's granting to the Negro the right to participate in the Democratic primaries in southern states has had, to date, beneficial effects for the Negro and no detrimental consequences for the society as a whole:

Harold Trigg, a Negro, has been a member of the North Carolina State School Board for three years. Raleigh, North Carolina, has or has had lately Negro school board members.

Newport News, Virginia, appointed C. W. Scott, a Negro, to its school board April 1953.

Richmond, Virginia, appointed Booker T. Bradshow, a Negro, to its school board.

Nashville, Tennessee, appointed Coyness L. Ennix, a Negro, to its school board, January 1952.

Darlington, South Carolina, appointed G. Perry Gandy, a Negro, to its school board, January 1951.

Maryland appointed Dwight O. W. Holmes, a Negro, to its State Board of Education, June 1951.

Kentucky has had Negro representation on its school board since 1944.

Atlanta, Georgia, elected Rufus E. Clement, a Negro, to its city school board, May, 1953.

Augusta, Georgia, elected W. C. Ervin, a Negro, to its city school board, November 1952.

The following towns have elected Negroes to the City Council or Board of Aldermen:

Richmond, Virginia, had a Negro City Counselor for one term about 1951–52.

Atlanta, Georgia, in May 1953 elected A. T. Walden and Miles G. Amos to serve on the Executive Committee of the Democratic party for the City.

Winston Salem, North Carolina, also elected Mrs. Sarah Marash, a Negro, to serve on its City party Executive Committee, April 1953.

The number of southern states that have a poll tax has gone down from eleven to five within the past ten years. The Negro vote in the South which was estimated at 250,000 in 1940 is now estimated at over 1,000,000. George Mitchell states:

> Two, at least, of Southern School Boards include Negro members. We know of five or six local school boards which have or have lately had Negro members.... [In]Richmond...Greensboro...Winston-Salem...Nashville... Negroes have won their way to places on the City Council. In twenty North Carolina cities Negroes are currently candidates for elective municipal offices. Sixteen major Southern cities employ nearly 65,000 Negro persons, and 468 of these are engaged in managerial or professional tasks.

10. Higher Education

As of September, 1953, some Negro students were enrolled on the undergraduate, graduate, or professional levels in the following publicly supported or private colleges and universities in southern or border states.

State supported graduate level or professional schools

Arkansas A and M College, Monticello, Ark.
Arkansas Polytechnic Institute, Russellville, Ark.
Arkansas State Teachers College, Conway, Ark.
Arkansas State College, Jonesboro, Ark.
Arkansas University
North Carolina State College, Raleigh, N.C.
Oklahoma University
Oklahoma A & M College
Southern State College, Magnolia, Ark.
Tennessee University
Texas University
Virginia Medical College

Delaware University
Henderson State Teachers College, Arkadelphia, Ark.
Kentucky University
Louisiana State University
Maryland University
Missouri University (including 5 state supported colleges)
North Carolina University
Virginia University
Virginia Polytechnic Institute
William and Mary College (including Richmond Professional Institute and the Norfolk Division of W & M—VPI)
West Virginia University

State and municipal, undergraduate level

Amarillo Junior College, Amarillo, Texas
Cincinnati College of Music
Delaware University
Del Mar Junior College, Corpus Christi, Texas
Hardin Junior College, Wichita Falls, Texas

Howard County Junior College, Big Springs, Texas
Louisville University, Louisville
Louisiana State University, Baton Rouge, La.
Paducah Junior College, Paducah
Virginia Polytechnic Institute

Private

Alderson-Broaddus College,
    Philippi, W. Va.
American University,
    Washington, D.C.
Austin Theological Seminary,
    Austin, Tex.
Bellarmine College, Louisville,
    Ky.
Berea College, Berea, Ky.
Black Mountain College, Black
    Mountain, N.C.
Catholic University of America,
    Washington, D.C.
Columbia Theological Seminary,
    Decatur, Ga.
Cumberland (Presbyterian)
    Seminary, Decatur, Ga.
Dumbarton College of Holy
    Cross, Washington, D.C.
Georgetown University,
    Washington, D.C.
Georgetown Visitation Convent
    (Junior College), Washington,
    D.C.
Imaculata Junior College,
    Washington, D.C.
Incarnate Word College, San
    Antonio, Tex.
Johns Hopkins University,
    Baltimore, Md.
Louisville Theological Seminary,
    Louisville, Ky.
Loyola College, Baltimore, Md.
Loyola University, New Orleans,
    La.
Mt. St. Mary's College,
    Emmitsburg, Md.
Nazareth College, Louisville, Ky.

New Orleans Baptist Theological
    Seminary, New Orleans, La.
Notre Dame Seminary, New
    Orleans, La.
Our Lady of the Lake College,
    San Antonio, Tex.
Park College, St. Louis, Mo.
St. Johns College, Annapolis,
    Md.
St. Louis University, St. Louis,
    Mo.
St. Mary's University, San
    Antonio, Tex.
Scarritt College, Nashville, Tenn.
Southern Baptist Theological
    Seminary, Louisville, Ky.
Southern (Lutheran) Seminary,
    Columbus, S.C.
Southern Methodist University,
    Dallas, Tex.
Southwestern Baptist Seminary,
    Fort Worth, Tex.
Trinity College, Washington,
    D.C.
Union Theological Seminary,
    Richmond, Va.
University of the South School of
    Theology, Sewanee, Tenn.
Ursuline College, Louisville, Ky.
Vanderbilt School of Religion,
    Nashville, Tenn.
Virginia Episcopal Seminary,
    Alexandria, Va.
Washington University, St. Louis,
    Mo.
Wayland College, Plainview,
    Texas
West Virginia Wesleyan,
    Buckhannon, W. Va.
Webster College, Webster
    Groves, Mo.

Southern Negro colleges with white students

Interracial contacts on the graduate or undergraduate level among
students in the South are not limited to the admission of Negro students to

previously all white southern colleges. Some Negro colleges in the South and border states have developed a program which makes it possible for them to admit white students on the graduate or undergraduate level, or provide contact with white college students through a student exchange program with a northern interracial college...

11. Preparatory Schools

A systematic program to place qualified Negro students in outstanding preparatory schools has been developed within the past four years by the National Scholarship Service and Fund for Negro Students. This development may be of significance in illustrating the changes in racial practices of educational institutions. It must of course be noted that (1) the issue, rather than pertaining to deliberate segregation, was one of exclusion or non-application of Negroes in terms of social and economic class factors; (2) the schools listed are all in the northern or New England states; and (3) the proportion of Negro students involved is small.

When asked to evaluate the success of this program and the adjustment of the Negro students at these preparatory schools, Richard L. Plaut, Director of the National Scholarship Service and Fund for Negro Students stated: (letter July 28, 1953)

> What happened in all of these situations from our direct knowledge (and I don't mean to be glib about it) is exactly *nothing*. The students were enrolled and, from all the information we have gathered in keeping track of them, they were easily adjusted, took an active part in student life, and turned out to be either outstanding or average members of the community; as they would have been in any community.

Support for this positive evaluation is found in a statement by George P. Milmine, Assistant Headmaster, Hotchkiss School. In describing the adjustment of the first Negro student admitted to Hotchkiss, Milmine states:

> His presence at school has raised no difficulties—socially or otherwise. Possibly a few people have been critical of the school's policy, but there is abundant evidence that boys, parents, and alumni have generally approved. Certainly this boy's status as a member of the school has been excellent, and the record he has made will make it easier and pleasanter for other Negro boys to enter Hotchkiss, with a general feeling of good will and expectation of happy and successful accomplishment.

The following preparatory schools have offered scholarships to and accepted Negro students:

Abbott Academy
Buxton Academy

Groton School
The Gunnery

Lawrence Academy
Loomis School
Lenox School for Boys
Monson Academy
Northfield School for Girls
Perkiomen School
Phillips Academy at Andover
Phillips Exeter Academy
Putney School

Riverdale Country Day School
Slovak Girls Academy
Taft School
Westminister School
Westover School for Girls
Westtown School
Williston Academy
Windsor Mountain School

12. Elementary and Secondary Public Schools That Have Desegregated Within the Past Five to Ten Years*

Arizona
  Phoenix (elementary and
    secondary schools)
  Tucson (elementary schools)
California
  Imperial Valley
Delaware
  Arden (elementary school)
  Claymount (elementary and
  secondary schools)
  Hockessin (elementary school)
Kansas
  Merriman (elementary school)
  Topeka (elementary schools)
  Wichita (elementary and
  secondary schools)
Illinois
  Alton (grade and Junior High
    schools)
  Cairo (elementary and
    secondary schools)
  East Moline (elementary
    school)
  Bordentown (elementary
    schools)
  Burlington (elementary
    schools)
  Camden (elementary schools)
  Fair Haven (elementary
    schools)
  Florence (elementary schools)
  Freehold (elementary schools)

Long Branch (elementary
  schools)
Montclair (elementary schools)
Mount Laurel (elementary
  schools)
Palmyra (elementary schools)
Pine Branch (elementary
  schools)
Princeton (elementary schools)
Riverside (elementary schools)
Salem (elementary schools)
Trenton (elementary and
  secondary schools)

New Mexico
  Carlsbad
  Las Cruces

East St. Louis (elementary and
  secondary schools)
Edwardsville (elementary and
  secondary schools)
Golconda (elementary school)
Harrisburg (elementary
  schools)
Madison (secondary school)
Metropolis (elementary and
  secondary schools)
Sparta (one classroom, high
  school)
Ullin (secondary school)
Tamms (secondary schools)

*From the files of the Field Staff of the Legal Division of the NAACP. This list is not considered to be complete.

Indiana
  Elkhart
  Evansville
  Indianapolis
  Gary
  South Bend
Maryland
  Baltimore (Technical High
    School)
New Jersey
  Asbury Park (elementary
    schools)
New York
  Hillburn (elementary schools)
  Hempstead (elementary
    schools)
  New Rochelle (elementary
    schools)

Ohio
  Chagrin Falls
  Cincinnati (swimming classes,
    secondary schools)
  Hamilton
  Glendale
  Marion
  Wilmington
  Xenia
Pennsylvania
  Carlisle (elementary schools)
  Harrisburg (elementary and
    secondary schools)
  Nether Providence Township
  West Chester (elementary
    schools)
  Upper Providence Township

Desegregation Resulting from Population Changes

As an example of a previously white church in an area of transition, [S. Garry] Oniki describes the adjustment problems and process of St. John's Lutheran Church located in the Bronx, New York City. This church was built in 1860 by German immigrants. Gradually, middle and upper class Americans of European background displaced the German speaking low income congregation. In the 1940's Negroes began moving into the area surrounding the church and by 1947 the community was almost entirely Negro. Rather than selling the church or excluding Negroes, the minister, with approval of the Church Board, decided to attempt to integrate Negroes into the church in a cautious gradual manner.

A first step was the integration of Negro children into the Sunday School. A number of qualified Negroes were encouraged to teach the racially mixed classes in the church school. A part-time professional Negro worker was then engaged to supervise the children's educational program and to assist in the meeting of Negro parents. Some Negroes decided to join the church. At the present time, Negroes constitute fifteen per cent of the congregation and ten per cent of the church membership.

The relatively small proportion of Negro membership may be accounted for by the fact that there was resistance to the racially inclusive policy on the part of some of the white parishioners. Many of these people who overtly objected to Negroes joining the church withdrew from the church when the new policy went into effect. Several families voiced their objections, but were willing to go along with the decision to integrate. Oniki states further that even at the present time "although the church has opened its door to Negroes, the congregation as a whole would object to a large number of Negroes joining the church. The white members would leave St. John's and take with them much of the financial support which is necessary to maintain the present program."

The Warren Avenue Congregational Church of Chicago, on the other hand, is an example of a church which has conscientiously and successfully integrated individuals without regard to race and color in its congregation. This church was also located originally in a fashionable area which went through a transition in racial population. Thirty churches in this community moved away. However, the Warren Avenue Church decided to remain as an integrated church and to open its doors directly and immediately to people of all races. Today the church consists of members of nine different races. It has also developed an extensive and successful community program.

Desegregation Through Voluntary Public Opinion and Citizens' Activity

After continued protest against extensive discrimination and segregation of racial and religious minority groups, a committee composed of representatives of leading community groups and city officials in Minneapolis conducted a comprehensive community self survey of community institutions, including educational, medical, housing, employment, public and private facilities, and other areas, in order to determine the facts. While professional persons were consulted, local citizens assisted extensively in making the survey.

At the conclusion of the self survey, a larger committee of the same groups was formed to present the survey findings to the community and to sponsor a community educational program in order to mobilize public opinion and secure support for nondiscriminatory policies. Smaller committees worked with the policy making persons to encourage the adoption of nondiscriminatory policies. In some cases this was done quietly "behind the scenes" and in other instances there was publicity. As a result of this cooperative community survey and educational program, extensive changes from segregated to nonsegregated policies were effected without difficulties.

A similar effort, on a more limited scale, was carried out by the Committee on Civil Rights in East Manhattan (New York City). This group, composed of representatives of twenty-three organizations, worked entirely on a volunteer basis with advice from social scientists. In June, 1950, CCREM tested the racial practices of sixty-two restaurants in a small section of New York City by sending matched Negro and white couples to dine in them. Although no Negro team was refused service, in 42 per cent of the restaurants the Negroes were given clearly less desirable tables or markedly inferior service to that given the white testers. Without publicity CCREM presented its findings to all of the organizations in the restaurant field in New York City—both management groups and labor unions—and secured from each of them a resolution of equal treatment for all patrons. At this point a news release and other publicity were issued, stressing not only the existence of discrimination but the industry's promised cooperation to end it. During the next year four letters were sent to the owners or managers of all the restaurants within the survey area urging them to sign individual nondiscrimination pledges. One third of them did so. Individual conferences were held with the managers of restaurants in which discrimination had been encountered. A resurvey in the spring of 1952 covering ninety-two restaurants found discrimination in only 16 per cent.

It is not clear, of course, whether all of this decrease could be attributed to CCREM's efforts. This was a period of change in the civil rights field; more specifically, just before the survey the State Civil Rights Law had been amended to provide more effective enforcement of provisions with respect to public accommodations. Although the new law had not yet gone into effect, it is possible that the discussion attending its passage influenced restaurant practices.

Desegregation Through Referendum

Webster Groves is a suburb of St. Louis, Missouri. A publicly owned pool was built and opened in 1949. It operated in 1949 and 1950 under a policy of excluding Negroes. The pool was closed in the summer of 1951, after Circuit Judge John A. Williams ruled that Negroes would have to be admitted at all times or a separate pool built for their use. The pool remained closed for two years, 1951 and 1952.

During this period an Independent Citizens Committee sought to have the municipally owned swimming pool opened on a nonsegregated basis.

This committee canvassed about 4000 homes in Webster Groves and raised $6800 in cash to help finance the operation of the pool. The citizens group appealed directly to the Mayor and the City Council in a letter to the Mayor in which it asked for a survey of opinion of Webster Grove residents. The letter stated, "If the results of the poll warrant it, we would like to have you open the pool immediately." The letter further stated:

We believe that the majority of Webster citizens do not want a $190,000 investment on which we are paying interest and principal to stand idle, if some of our citizens want to use it and will be able to guarantee its financially sound operation on the only basis which is compatible with the laws and court decisions of the United States.... If you are afraid of race riots, gentlemen, you do not have much faith in the citizens of Webster Groves or in your police department.

The Mayor and City Council rejected these requests and insisted that the pool would remain closed. The reasons stated were that the money raised would be insufficient to operate the pool and that the official bodies "are unanimous in our belief that the Independent Citizens Committee represent a minority point of view in the community on this matter." They maintained that opposition to nonsegregated swimming was at least "three times as great" as sentiment for it. They insisted: "We believe that citizens, as a whole, would prefer to keep the pool closed than open it to limited use by those who might be expected to patronize it on a mixed swimming basis." The City Council and the Parks Committee suggested, however, that "it would probably be desirable to put the question to the test of a ballot or impartial survey at the earliest appropriate time."

At the next municipal election, reported as "hotly contested," Webster Groves voted out of office its resistant incumbent city official and also voted to open its swimming pool to Negroes. The vote for opening the swimming pool "to all citizens of Webster Groves on a nonsegregated basis regardless of race" was 4223 to 3572. In spite of the fact that this vote was only advisory in nature, it was understood that the successful candidates favored the opening of the pool on a nonsegregated basis. It may be of interest to note that of the 4200 residents who voted to open the pool on a nonsegregated basis, only 190 were Negroes. It is clear from these figures that the Negro vote was too small to have any decisive effect. The pool reopened on May 30, 1953. There were about 300 people in attendance of which approximately 30 were Negroes. There was no racial incident or friction. There was ample police coverage but "it really didn't seem necessary."

The Webster Groves Swimming Pool incident is one of the rare cases in which desegregation in a public accommodation took place because of the expressed opinions of a majority of whites who were opposed by public officials who sought to maintain the segregation. Generally in cases of desegregation it appears that it is necessary for a strong authority—a public official with prestige and status—to buck the majority of whites who appear to desire continued segregation. In Webster Groves the pattern was reversed and the opinion of the majority prevailed. The obstructing public officials were voted out of office.

It appears that the people were unwilling to permit a public facility to remain unused and stand merely as a symbol of racial segregation. When they were presented with a choice of racial desegregation or no publicly supported facilities, the majority of them in this border state community chose nonsegregation in spite of the adamant resistance of their public officials. In this case, the strength of economic considerations and self interest was greater than the traditional racial segregation pattern. It should also be noted that in spite of the fact that the initial impetus to desegregate this swimming pool came from a court order, the desegregation occurred without the aid or intervention of the usual race relations or social action organizations.

Desegregation Through Threat of Publicity

Before 1951, public swimming pools were not open to Negroes in Tucson, Arizona. A member of the NAACP attempted to get the local branch of that organization to take on the project of seeing that the pools were desegregated. He was unable to arouse any interest since the group felt that "jobs are more important." He decided to go ahead on his own with the aid of a few friends who formed themselves into an informal committee. They went to see the City Recreation Director and discussed with him the matter of the racial policy of the pools. The director who was a former Texan with a reputation for fairness stated that he could not control the discriminatory behavior of lifeguards and other employees. He suggested it would be better for the group to consult with the City Council on this matter.

The leader of the informal committee assured the director that his group wanted to avoid publicity on this matter, *but if it were necessary they would have to give the city of Tucson unfavorable national publicity.* This would be necessary unless a clear statement of a nondiscriminatory racial policy at the pools was made by some responsible city official. The director then agreed to speak to the City Council and the Mayor on this matter. Three or four weeks later the City Council ruled that all city parks and swimming pools were to be opened to everyone. Park and pool personnel were told of the new policy before opening day. It was agreed that there would be no newspaper publicity. The leader and members of the committee communicated this to the Negro community through schools and churches. On opening day, Negroes attended the various pools throughout the city. Everyone agrees that things are "going well" under the new policy of desegregation.

It was suggested that one of the factors responsible for the ease and effectiveness of this specific desegregation was the "possibility in the minds of city officials that schools might soon be integrated—hence, other city owned facilities should follow suit."

Desegregation Through Moral Argument

Until six years ago, Wayland Baptist College in Plainview, Texas, like other white private colleges in the South, had never enrolled a Negro student or any student who was not a white "Anglo-Saxon." At that time, a new president was hired. He outlined to the Board of Trustees his plan to admit to the college students from the Orient, Latin America, and Europe. When these students began to arrive there was some objection and resentment by the students and by some of the pastors who were interested in the school. One pastor "preached a dogmatic sermon on the 'sin against God' in mixing up the races." This opposition decreased to the point where the whole area began to talk proudly about "Wayland's international friendship project."

The president of the college describes the circumstances surrounding the admission of the first Negro student to that college as follows:

Occasionally an Oriental or Latin American would ask an American roommate why there were no Negroes at Wayland. A few of these questions were passed on to me by white students. At last small groups of students would come with the same question. I countered with the question, "Would a Negro student be welcome here? Really welcome?"

Such questions brought about several informal polls. The result of each poll was increasingly encouraging. And finally when the first Negro made application our faculty voted one hundred per cent for admission. Only eight students opposed and none of these were strong in their opposition.

But what about the Board of Trustees? Some would give vigorous opposition, I feared. At a called meeting of the Board, I presented the application from the Negro and said in effect, "I know what our customs and traditions dictate but surely to us there are stronger voices—the voice of democracy and the voice of Christianity." By an overwhelming majority the Negro was admitted, but not until nearly every member told of his prejudice and of his internal battle. Fortunately, nearly every member had had several of our international students as house guests.

Now, the next question. How would the Negro be admitted? On a segregated basis? No, thanks be unto God. The door to the dining hall was thrown wide open and so were all other doors.

Desegregation Through Activity of Community Action Agencies

The Pittsburgh experience with racial conflict at a public swimming pool illustrates the role of community action agencies. Two large outdoor pools in Highland Park are used by thousands of swimmers each day of the summer. Negroes had never used these pools, it being generally accepted that they went to the Kline Pool on Washington Boulevard, a shabby inadequate pool located on the edge of the park. Because of proximity to the East Liberty neighborhood, there is a high percentage of Italian-American patronage of the Highland Park pools. In the summer of 1948, two interracial groups attempting to swim in the pool aroused considerable public attention, some violence, and a number of arrests.

In June, 1951, A.J. Allen, Executive Director of the Urban League, and a friend went to the Highland Park pool to swim and were given rough treatment by some young fellows. This incident was ignored by police and the Negroes were advised to stay away. The NAACP threatened a suit. The Mayor's Civic Unity Council set up a committee to look into the matter and a citizen's group including representatives from labor, the clergy, and businessmen was formed. Study of the facts pointed to extreme tensions between youths of Italian-American background and Negroes. Gangs traveled around the neighborhood in cars and responded to calls from some of their members who were at the Park whenever Negroes appeared. Upon the urging of the Citizens Committee and the Mayor's Civic Unity Council, the NAACP withdrew the threat of legal action. As a result of many meetings the following recommendations were made:

A. A clear statement of nondiscriminatory policy of the city to be posted in many places about the park, and near the pool.

B. Police to be given special instructions about their functions with reference to nondiscriminatory use of public facilities.
C. Steps to be taken to engage interracial personnel, particularly several Negro lifeguards.
D. Certain protective awnings to be arranged at one end of the park where outsiders may not reach bathers to heckle or hurt them.
E. Kline Pool to be abandoned permanently.
F. Steps to be taken to set up a schedule to assure Negro patronage of the pool by Sunday School groups, clubs, etc. to give mutual encouragement and also a constant assurance of Negro use, until popular acceptance is general.

During the winter of 1951–52, all preliminary steps were taken with reference to police, personnel, and signs, and public education in the neighborhood was undertaken through the churches, schools and other social institutions. In the summer of 1952, under the direction of a Negro minister, groups of Negro youths, men, and women swam every day in the pool, and by the end of the summer the record showed that 5,000 Negroes had enjoyed its use. During the summer of 1953, the Negroes shared freely in the pool with no trouble at all.

Early in 1952, trouble was experienced at a small neighborhood pool in the Paulson school district, not far from Highland Park Pool. Threats were heard that the neighbors of Paulson Pool would not permit the intrusion of Negro swimmers even though they "must put up with them at Highland Park Pool." The same steps were followed in this case, although a more personal form of education and persuasion was needed since the pool was specifically of local interest. Hiring of a Negro lifeguard and a planned schedule of use by Negroes has brought about acceptance and peace.

Desegregation Through Decision of Responsible Authority

A number of examples of systematic racial desegregation are found within the Catholic Church. The case described below is significant in that it involves a situation in a southern state and it illustrates clearly the role of a responsible authority in an act of desegregation.

In June of 1953, Bishop Waters decided to merge two Catholic parishes—Holy Redeemer, a white parish, and the Negro parish of St. Benedict which was 200 yards away—in Newton Grove, North Carolina. There was wide speculation on whether this decision would be accepted by the white parishioners and the community. Many of the white parishioners objected strenuously and attempted to prevent other whites from attending the services of the merged parish. This overt objection decreased, however, and an increasing number of white and Negro Catholics are now attending the same church in Newton Grove, N.C.

In order to clarify this specific situation and state the general policy of the Catholic Church as interpreted in this diocese, Bishop Waters discussed the matter of racial integration in a pastoral letter which was read in every church throughout his diocese. This diocese includes nearly all of North Carolina. The essence of this letter was widely published in the daily press throughout the country. It received "considerable editorial comment—all favorable." The following quotation presents the essence of this declaration:

> So that in the future there can be no misunderstanding on the part of anyone, let me state here as emphatically as I can: There is no segregation of races to be tolerated in any Catholic Church in the Diocese of Raleigh. The pastors are charged with the carrying out of this teaching and shall tolerate nothing to the contrary. Otherwise, all special churches for Negroes will be abolished immediately as lending weight to the false notion that the Catholic Church, the Mystical Body of Christ, is divided. Equal rights are accorded, therefore, to every race and every nationality as is proper in any Catholic Church and within the church building itself everyone is given the privilege to sit or kneel wherever he desires and to approach the Sacrament without any regard to race or nationality. This doctrine is to be fully explained to each convert who enters the Church from henceforth in the Diocese of Raleigh.

Bishop Waters left no doubt concerning his willingness to assume the full personal responsibility for the fact and consequences of desegregation:

> As Pastor of your souls, I am happy to take the responsibility for any evil which might result from different races worshipping God together, but I would be unwilling to take the responsibility of those who refuse to worship God with a person of another race. May the example of American soldiers who died to stamp out the philosophy of "The Master Race" in a war with Hitler in Germany prevent us from following a similar course.

Desegregation Through Non-Judicial Governmental Action

On June 19, 1950, the City of Philadelphia, the Philadelphia Board of Education, and the Philadelphia Housing Authority entered a formal agreement for the construction of new housing developments which would have a clause prohibiting discrimination or segregation in any housing projects on the basis of race or color. Early in 1951, the Housing Authority appointed an Advisory Committee which included represent-atives of leading community organizations, to review the current policies and practices for the purpose of making recommendations. Later, the committee recommended that the original agreement be instituted as soon as possible. In May, 1952, the Housing Authority passed a resolution incorporating the formal agreement made in 1950, including a statement that, effective immediately, all housing units would be rented on the basis of need without regard to race or color.

After the passage of this resolution, the Executive Director of the Housing Authority held a first meeting with the full staff, interpreting the new policy and insisting on complete compliance with it. A series of meetings for the education and training of the staff were held. Managers made visits to several recently desegregated housing projects for observa-tions. After a statement of policy was sent to all tenants, a statement was issued to the press for the first time. On June 9, 1952, the first of a series of meetings was held with representatives of community organizations to plan for the implementation of the new policy. This program included close cooperation with city officials and law enforcement officers and surveying the communities adjacent to the projects for positive and negative forces, "trouble spots," and tension areas. Professional con-sultants on human relations advised on these programs. In addition, the Housing Authority adopted a nondiscriminatory employment policy on all staff levels and deliberately placed Negro and white workers throughout the projects and in the central office. Applications of prospective tenants were carefully screened.Managers carefully selected projects in terms of location, general residential areas, and specific units within a project for the placement of the first Negro families who moved into a formerly all white project.

On July 19, 1952, approximately seven weeks after the public announcement of a nonsegregation policy, the first Negro family was housed in a formerly all white development. Police cars in contact with city officials patrolled the area. No incidents were reported. Subse-quently, additional Negro families were placed in formerly all white projects, and vice versa, without difficulty.

In August 1952, some racial incidents occurred. After additional police were alerted, these incidents stopped. "When those who disapproved the program saw or became aware of the forthright attitude of the Authority Board and staff, gradual acceptance of integration resulted."

Desegregation Through Legislative Action

In 1945, a Fair Employment Practices Bill created and authorized a New Jersey State Committee Against Discrimination as a subordinate division of the State Department of Education. The function of this committee is to administer this law as it related to education, and to establish regional councils of representative citizens throughout the state to study and make recommendations regarding segregation and discrimination. These councils conducted an extensive state wide educational program.

During 1946, five such councils were organized in counties maintaining segregated public schools. Several council committees approached local boards of education about change in the policy of segregation to one of nonsegregation. As a result of these visits, the school boards of Long Branch and Salem made a start toward eliminating segregated public schools in the years 1947–48. Other school boards were stimulated to develop similar programs. "It was surprising to note how many of these board members agreed that it was wrong to segregate children."

During this same period, two state studies on segregated public schools were made. The first study was a report by the Urban Colored Population Commission of the State of New Jersey which officially called attention of the state legislature to the extent of segregated schools. The second survey was made by the New Jersey State Conference of NAACP Branches, under the direction of a National Office representative, to determine the extent of segregation and discrimination in New Jersey public schools. The following findings were reported: (1) extensive segregated public schools due primarily to the gerrymandering of school district lines or the absence of such lines; (2) unequal physical facilities and curricular in the all Negro schools; (3) Negro teachers employed only in the all Negro schools; (4) the teaching load in the all Negro schools was three times that of all white schools.

In June 1947, state NAACP representatives were invited to repor findings of the survey to the State Commissioner of Education and the State Division Against Discrimination. The Commissioner of Education agreed that during the 1947–48 year, he would cooperate in the conduct of an official survey concerning the extent of segregated public schools. Subsequently, members of the State Division urged that segregated public schools be prohibited in the proposed state constitution.

Article 1, Section 5, of the new state constitution, adopted September 10, 1947 and ratified November 4, 1947, states: "No persons shall be... segregated... in the public schools because of religious scruples, race, color, ancestry or national origin." In January, 1948, immediately following the induction of the legislature under the new constitution, the Governor let it be known to all state departments that the new constitution was to be strictly enforced. The Commissioner of Education assigned the jurisdiction of the antisegregation school clause to the Division Against Discrimination.

"There was only one county, Gloucester, which did not vote to adopt the new constitution. In this county, one finds most of the few examples of apparent resistance to the law. Here some school districts have [taken] and are taking a rather long time to integrate their schools." Negro parents in one of the noncooperating school districts sent their children to the all white schools, thus forcing the school board to desegregate the schools. Subsequently, the other districts followed suit.

As a result of the New Jersey law against discrimination and the activities of the State Commissioner of Education, 43 school districts in New Jersey desegregated their elementary public schools. The New Jersey desegregation program has been accomplished with an increase in the number of Negro teachers employed in the state public school system. The State Commissioner reports that in 1945–46 a total of 479 Negro teachers were employed as compared with 645 Negro teachers employed in 1952.

The overall picture is good. In spite of the opposition to integration in many communities, the consensus of testimony of school officials and teachers has been to the effect that the anticipated difficulties did not occur. Teachers and pupils of both races are working together in harmony. These smooth transitions have been effected regardless of the procedures used to integrate the systems. One common element in them was the decision to refuse exceptions to any parents. Some officials mixed the pupils and staffs without recourse to any particular scheme. Others put all of the colored teachers in a particular grade. Some assigned pupils by pulling names out of a hat. One system asked for a year to educate the citizens for the change. Important is the fact that all of these methods have now been abandoned.

Earlier experiences demonstrated that education alone had not been able to bring about these changes (desegregated public schools, nondiscriminatory employment practices). But legislation accompanied by educational techniques designed to influence the attitudes of men has achieved results without the friction or riots predicted by those who fear change in controversial areas.

The contribution from these various sources combined to produce a climate of opinion which would be favorable to such changes as resulted from the civil rights clause in the new constitution. In addition to the desegregation which took place in the southern counties and the increased integration in the northern counties (which had mixed schools except in instances of segregation because of residential restriction or loose policies of transfers whereby white pupils could be transferred out of predominantly Negro areas), there was an increase of elections and appointment of Negroes to local boards of education.

Several social agencies have engaged in programs of integration on their own and minority group members are being employed in greater numbers in positions previously denied to them or which were open in only rare instances.

Desegregation Through Threat of Court Action

Until 1952, the school system of Tamms, Illinois, included one all white and one all Negro elementary school and one all white high school. Negro high school students living in the Tamms district, which included several smaller communities, were required to attend the nearest all Negro high school, either in Cairo, Illinois, or in an adjacent county. Free bus transportation was provided.

In September 1952, several Negro parents and an NAACP National Office representative met with the school board to request a change of admission policy. They stated that if Negro students were refused admission to the all white high school, a suit would be filed to withhold state aid funds. Several days after the board refused to change their policy, twelve Negro students applied and were refused admittance to the all white high school. On the same day, when it was clearly realized that a suit to withhold state aid funds would actually be filed, school officials notified each parent individually to send their children back to the school the following morning. The following morning, the students were admitted without any incident. There was no newspaper publicity concerning this change of policy. The high school principal told several Negro parents that because of inadequate physical facilities, no additional students, white or colored, would be admitted that semester.

In September 1953, several days before the 1953–54 school term started, the Board of Education notified the Negro parents living in the high school district that bus transportation to the all Negro high schools would be discontinued and that all Negro students were to attend the Tamms High School. Despite objections from some Negro and white parents, the board refused to change the policy, and on the opening day of school, all students in the district, Negro and white, attended the high school without incident. The new policy was not announced publicly through the newspapers either prior to or subsequent to the change.

Negro students are participating in most school activities without any friction. In the fall of 1952, after a Negro student who excelled in baseball was refused permission to participate on the baseball team, the white members of the team quit in protest. Subsequently, the Negro students were allowed to participate on the team and played all "home" games but were refused permission to play in any game scheduled at another school. The all white baseball team at the nonsegregated Cairo High School was required to cancel the game when it was learned that a Negro student was on the Tamms team.

Desegregation in Face of Pending Court Action

After the Board of Education of East St. Louis, Illinois, repeatedly refused to change their policy of maintaining segregated public schools and after Negro students were refused admission to the all white schools nearest their homes, a suit was filed in the Circuit Court of St. Clair County in May 1949 on behalf of those Negro students who had been refused admittance and all others similarly situated. In dismissing the suit on technical grounds, Circuit Judge R. W. Griffith stated that Illinois law definitely prohibits segregation and that " . . . the members of a Board of Education have a duty imposed upon them by virtue of their office, not to exclude from such schools, directly or indirectly, any such child on account of its color." In addition, the Court interpreted the school statutes to state that school state aid funds, amounting to $677,989 would be withheld from the Board of Education if it should be determined that the district was segregating students on the basis of race.

Faced with the prospect of immediate additional court action and the subsequent probability of losing state aid funds, on December 20, 1949, the Board of Education unanimously passed a resolution ending the policy of segregation in public schools on the first day of the spring school semester, January 30, 1950. Announcing the new policy publicly, the Board President stated that "the statement (of the Circuit Court) takes the matter out of the hands of the Board of Education."

Desegregation Through Court Action

As a result of the decision in the *Sweatt* case—and other related cases—by the United States Supreme Court, Negroes are enrolled in the graduate and undergraduate levels in at least 33 state or municipally supported institutions of higher education in the South.... In addition to these institutions directly affected by the United States Supreme Court decisions, at least 42 private colleges and universities in the South and border states have changed their policy and now also admit Negroes.

II A. Desegregation which resulted from litigation and judicial decision is just as effective as desegregation resulting from other causes.

The effectiveness of judicial decision in bringing about either desegregation or significant changes in the status of minority groups is supported by the facts that as a result of the Supreme Court White Primary decisions there are now over 1,000,000 registered Negro voters in the southern states; Negroes are served in dining cars and Pullman accommodations in interstate railroad transportation; and over 2,000 Negroes have been admitted to previously all white state-supported graduate and professional schools in southern states.

The following cases of a court-determined desegregation of the public schools in Trenton, N.J., and a nonjudicial "voluntary" desegregation of a private church-sponsored theological college in Tennessee are presented not because they are directly comparable but to make clear by example that court-determined desegregation is as effective, if not more so, than desegregation due to other causes. In fact, desegregation resulting from the decision of Federal Courts has more extensive effects than voluntary desegregation of a given unit of a social institution.

Desegregation Resulting from Litigation and Judicial Decision

Prior to 1944, the Board of Education of Trenton, New Jersey, maintained segregated Junior High Schools. All Negro students were assigned to one junior high school, regardless of place of residence, and all white students were assigned to the white junior high school nearest their home. The all Negro junior high school also included approximately 2,000 elementary students and an all Negro faculty. When the school board refused to change its policy of segregating students, a suit was filed asking that Negro students be admitted to schools without regard to race or color. In 1944, the New Jersey Supreme Court ordered the Trenton Board of Education to cease segregating junior high school students on the basis of race or color. This court order was given in spite of the fact that the junior high school for Negroes was found to have equal academic standing.

As a result of the New Jersey teacher tenure law, which includes a seniority clause, the integration of teachers as well as the desegregation of students had to be considered. After extensive study, the Board of Education made public a resolution to integrate the entire school system to include both teachers and students. School district lines were redrawn, without regard to race or color. A community education program was planned to interpret the new policy.

Desegregation was effected as planned, without incident and without an exception. Students were assigned to and attended the school in their district. All teachers were reassigned throughout the school system without regard to race or color. The successful desegregation program in Trenton was one of the stimulants for the subsequent statewide public schools desegregation program.

Desegregation Determined by Internal Organizational Pressures

The issue of a racially exclusive student admission policy of the School of Theology of the University of the South (Sewanee) was raised by a resolution passed by the Fourth Provincial Synod of the Episcopal Church in October, 1951, calling for the admission of students of all races in Episcopal seminaries in the South. The Board of Trustees of the School of Theology rejected the request of this resolution at its regular meeting in June, 1952, by a vote of 45 to 12. When presented with this action of their board, the dean and eight members of the faculty of the school requested the trustees to reconsider their action. Only one full-time faculty member did not join the rest of the staff in reinforcing this request with the promise to resign if the board did not rescind its policy of racial exclusion. On October 6, 1952, the protesting members of the faculty submitted their joint resignations to become effective at the end of the year, 1952–53. These resignations were accepted by the Vice Chancellor of the University of the South, Edward R. McCrady.

In November 1952, thirteen bishops of the dioceses of the Fourth Province met in Atlanta and adopted a resolution requesting the Chancellor of the University to call a meeting during the first week of February, 1953, to discuss the issue. The University of the South is wholly owned and operated by twenty-two Episcopal dioceses governing all of the southern states. Its Chancellor is Bishop Mitchell of Arkansas.

At the June 4, 1953, meeting of the Board of Trustees a resolution was passed "instructing the Vice Chancellor and the Committee on Admissions to consider all applications for admission to the School of Theology on the same basis regardless of race." The new dean of the School of Theology, Bishop Edmund P. Dandridge of Tennessee, expressed his gratification at this resolution and the overwhelming majority by which it passed. He stated, "It has opened the doors of the Theology School to men of all races and has done so in a manner that links this action with the history and traditions of Sewanee."

The day following the trustees' action, a Negro Protestant Episcopal minister applied for admission to the five week summer graduate study class of the School of Theology. The university authorities declared that his application would be considered "in the same way in which other applications are and in the light of the resolution adopted by the trustees yesterday—'regardless of race'." This student was admitted and attended the summer session without incident.

III. There have been many methods used in the desegregating process. These vary from many types of "gradual" desegregation to the many types of "immediate" desegregation.

III A. Types of "gradual" desegregation involve one or more of the following methods:

1. *(deadline) Specified time for desegregation process.*
2. *(time for preparation) Type of preparation specified and time for completion of preparation before or during desegregation.*
3. *(segmental progressive desegregation) Plan for progressive desegregation in limited units of organized structure.*
4. *(quota desegregation) Limit on the number of Negroes to be introduced in a given unit at any one time.*

Gradual Desegregation

In 1949, the Indiana State Legislature repealed the school statute permitting segregation and prohibited segregation of public schools on the basis of race or color and discrimination in the employment of public school teachers. This statute provides that at the beginning of the September, 1949, school year and thereafter, school officials shall discontinue enrollment on the basis of race or color of students entering public kindergarten, the first grades of elementary schools, and the first year of junior and senior high schools by assigning kindergarten and elementary students to the schools within their district and by permitting junior and senior high school students to attend the school of their choice within the limitations applicable alike to all students regardless of race or color. The statute further provided that where equipment and facilities were not available for enrollment and integration of first year students in September, 1948, the period for enrollment may be extended as follows: September, 1950, for kindergarten and grade schools; September, 1951, for junior high schools; September, 1954, for senior high schools. After these dates, all public school students shall be admitted and enrolled in the schools in their district without regard to race or color. (*House Enrolled Act No. 242*)

On August 27, 1946, the Board of Education of Gary, Indiana, adopted a resolution prohibiting segregated public schools, to be implemented no later than September, 1947. During the year that elapsed between the adoption of the resolution and its implementation, school officials, in cooperation with community groups, conducted an extensive and intensive community educational program in an attempt to secure support for the nondiscriminatory policy. Schools were rezoned without regard to race or color. Desegregation was to be effected as follows: In September 1947, all Negro kindergarten and elementary school students were to be admitted to the schools in their district. An additional grade was to be integrated each year by the same procedure. In addition, the school curriculum was revised to meet the nonsegregated situation.

Time for preparation was also provided in the case of the schools of Indianapolis, Indiana. After enactment of the 1949 statute prohibiting segregated public schools, the following plan of desegregation was adopted: In September, 1949, students in the first grades of the elementary schools and first year junior and senior high school students were required to attend nonsegregated schools within their district. For each of the following three years, successive year students were admitted to these nonsegregated schools. Integration at all grade levels was achieved at the close of the 1952–53 school year.

Desegregation in the parochial schools in Washington, D.C. illustrates the operation of another type of gradual process. Instead of a direct and immediate order to desegregate all parochial schools, the Rev. Patrick A. O'Boyle, Archbishop of Washington, merely talked to his clergy and school officials individually. His approach was one of tactful, patient, persistent persuasion. Throughout the period of desegregation, starting during 1948, there was no publicity. Every effort was made to avoid antagonizing the opponents of desegregation and mobilizing their opposition. It has been pointed out, however, that from the moment the decision was taken to desegregate the Catholic school system, Archbishop O'Boyle was positive and unwavering. The policy was clear and unambiguous. There was no hesitancy, compromise, or postponement.

In view of the fact that the Archbishop did not order or command integration but sought to win the cooperation of individual pastors and school officials, the pace of integration varied from school to school. An essentially gradualist policy was adopted: Negroes were first introduced in the lowest grades of the primary schools and the first year of high schools. It was assumed that through this process Negroes would eventually be included in every grade. In spite of this gradual approach, some opposition to the desegregation process was expected. This opposition took the form of circulation of rumors to the effect that "Negroes are taking over our school system." Groups of irate white parents waited on their pastors, and some parents withdrew their children from the schools or migrated from Washington to the nearby Maryland and Virginia suburbs. The response to these forms of opposition was always a firm and courteous restatement of the fact that the desegregation policy had been established by the Archbishop and that "It was the Catholic thing to do."

When the new Archdiocesan John Carroll High School for boys was opened in September, 1951, Negroes entered its first class without any public discussion or debate on the issue. The general acceptance of this fact and the absence of any racial incident at the John Carroll High School is believed to have accelerated integration in other schools in this Archdiocese.

After about five years of the gradual persuasive approach to desegregation of the parochial schools in Washington, D.C., there are some schools which continue to be predominantly or exclusively white schools, some which are exclusively Negro schools and some which have had an increased proportion of Negro students as the racial composition of the neighborhood has changed. School desegregation has been more rapid in the city of Washington than in the nearby counties of Maryland that are also a part of the same Archdiocese.

The consequences of school desegregation in this area have been conceded to be positive. There has been a steady increase in the number of Negro students accepted in the Archdiocesan school system. People have begun to accept this desegregation as a matter of course and, with some exceptions, are not alarmed about it. "The vast majority of Catholics in the Archdiocese are now willing to concede that, on the race issue, 'our Archbishop was right'."

The above cases, particularly the Gary and Indianapolis examples, indicate that the approaches to "gradual" school desegregation singled out in Principle III A are not independent of one another. It is clear from these cases that the statement of an arbitrary time, beyond a period of one year, for the completion of desegregation is accompanied by an elaborate preparatory program and, more significantly, by a plan of segmentalized progressive desegregation.

An example of "gradual" desegregation illustrating the fourth category (quota desegregation) is found in the procedure adopted by the United States Navy. Desegregation in the Navy could be described as "gradual." The percentage of Negroes assigned to a ship was restricted. Within a period of five years a general policy of nonsegregation was in full operation.

III B. Types of "immediate" desegregation were found to use one of the following approaches:

1. *Abolishing segregated Negro facility and admission of Negro into previously white facility.*
2. *Opening of all facilities without regard to race or color.*
3. *Ruling that white facility cannot exclude Negroes—but leaving option to Negroes whether they will seek admission to white facility or continue in all Negro one.*
4. *A combination of 1 or 2 above with recognition or specification of the time which might be required for the necessary administrative adjustment in order to effect the desegregation.*
5. *Nonsegregation policy instituted at founding of institution.*

Abolition of Segregated Negro Facility

The Edwardsville, Illinois, Board of Education closed the all Negro elementary school and transferred Negro students to the formerly all white elementary school.

The experiences of the U.S. Air Force at its largest installation, the Lackland Base at San Antonio, Texas, with 26,000 persons, also illustrate the fact that direct desegregation, the abolition of the Negro facilities, and the inclusion of Negroes in the general facilities, can take place without major difficulties.

The following dispatch by B.K. Thorne appeared in the *N.Y. Times* on September 18, 1949:

The first ten weeks of the integration of the white and Negro Air Force enlistees taking their initial training has been completed in thorough harmony, it was stated today by Maj. Gen. Charles W. Lawrence, Commanding General of the indoctrination division of the Air Force Training Command.

All the recruits at vast Lackland Air Force Base here, the largest installation in the whole Air Force, live, eat and study as a body and the grouping together of Negro and white personnel has not caused any incidents.

"The integration of the base was accomplished with complete harmony," General Lawrence stated: "Orders went through to completely end segregation among trainees on a certain date and when that date arrived the segregation was ended. No unpleasant incidents resulted and the white boys and the Negro boys in the training are getting along well together. And of course the same applies to the WAFS (members of the Women's Air Force)."

There is no discrimination in picking the leaders and Negroes often lead the mixed flights.

Opening of All Facilities Without Regard to Race or Color

In St. Louis the process of desegregation was accomplished by a direct order from Archbishop Ritter. He refused to be swayed by the open opposition of over 700 Catholic parents and quieted further action on their part by the threat of excommunication. A few of these parents withdrew their children from the parochial schools and sent them elsewhere. However, six months after the new policy went into effect an Archdiocesan official stated that they had "received not one report of friction among white and Negro pupils since the new policy of Archbishop Joseph E. Ritter was put into effect."

The pattern of desegregation of the parochial schools in Wilmington, Delaware, combined the direct methods used in the Diocese of St. Louis with the persuasive methods of Washington, D.C., diocese. Private Catholic academies such as Salesianum School for Boys and Ursuline Academy for Girls had opened their doors to Negro students about two years prior to the statement of a desegregation policy applicable to the parochial schools of the entire Archdiocese. The Rector of the Salesianum School for Boys, Rev. Thomas A. Lawless, OSFS, describes the process of desegregation at this school as follows:

There are no *mechanics* about it. We merely register these young men (Negroes) just the same as other students—we assign them to the class for which they are qualified—and that's all.

Opposition from some parents and threats to remove their boys from the school was met by the "calm, but very firm" explanation: "All right, if you want to take your boy away from our school, that's your privilege." Not one of these threats was carried out. There has never been a racial incident among the students in spite of the fact that the desegregation was not a limited one, but rather approaches the point of integration. Negro students participate in the Senior Prom which is held in the Gold Ballroom of the Dupont Hotel in Wilmington.

Partly as a result of the successful racial desegregation at Salesianum School, two things happened: (1) All of the *private* schools in the Wilmington area immediately declared a policy of desegregation; and (2) all Catholic schools in the area were *immediately* opened to Negroes. Archbishop Fitzmaurice sent a directive in 1952 to the heads of all parishes within his diocese announcing the new policy. This change in policy was not made a public issue. There was no mobilized public opposition. The policy was clear, firm and put into immediate operation. At the present time, *all* of the parochial schools of Wilmington, Delaware, admit students without regard to race or color.

Option to Use of Nonsegregated Facility Left to Negroes

In December 1949, the East St. Louis, Illinois, Board of Education passed a resolution to end segregation in the public schools, effective January 30, 1950, the beginning of the spring semester, and "...publicly agreed to begin to transfer Negro school children upon their application to schools from where they had formerly been excluded." In the absence of any school zone lines, students had the choice of continuing in the all white or all Negro schools or transferring, by choice, to the school nearest their home, regardless of race or color.

A similar pattern was followed in the desegregation of public accommodations in Washington, D.C. John O'Connor writing in the *Interracial*

Review states that when the Supreme Court of the United States handed down a decision preventing discrimination in restaurants in Washington, D.C., "all restaurants supported the verdict and no incident of any kind was reported." Contrary to expectations in some quarters, the Negro population did not rush into all formerly white restaurants in huge numbers. The city's three legitimate theaters now admit all citizens without regard to race. This is also true of four downtown movie houses. Negroes may attend banquets and other functions in several of the large hotels, and hotel accommodations are available to them in several of the largest ones. Two of these, the Wardman Park and the Carlton Hotel, which recently came under new management, will now also accept individuals without regard to race or color.

In discussing the role of the Justice Department in helping to end segregation in Washington restaurants by carrying a test case to the Supreme Court, Attorney General Brownell stated:

I am happy to say that the citizens of Washington have accepted the responsibilities of citizenship. There has not been a bit of trouble. (New York *Times*—U.P. Dispatch, August 17, 1953)

Immediate Desegregation with Time for Adjustment

On June 3, 1953, the National Capitol Housing Authority announced the adoption of a nondiscriminatory policy, effective June 1, 1953, in those projects designated as being located in areas that offered public housing to both Negroes and whites. In four particular projects meeting these requirements, the policy was to be effected September 1, 1953. This date was purposely selected in order to "...permit a period of staff preparation of management personnel, tenants, and neighborhood residents." The Indiana schools described in III A above are also illustrations of this type of "immediate" desegregation.

Nonsegregation Policy Instituted at Founding of Institution

An example of a social institution begun on an interracial basis is the Church for the Fellowship of All Peoples in San Francisco. This church started in 1943 as a small neighborhood experiment in interracial meetings held in the Negro district. Initially, financial support was provided by the Presbyterian Board of National Missions. This church has had an interracial ministry since its inception. Dr. Howard Thurman, a Negro and formerly co-pastor, broadened the base of the congregation of the church so that it now serves the total San Francisco community "and to some extent the nation itself." The racial composition of the present membership of 300 is 60 per cent white and 40 per cent Negro, Latin American, and Oriental. The church at present has no denominational ties and has constructed its new building in a white neighborhood in order to avoid the community problems which might retard its integrative program if it remained in a Negro neighborhood or a transitional tension area. Fellowship Church considers its prime purpose that of maintaining its interracial character so that it might serve as an example to American Protestantiam.

An example of this approach in the area of employment is found in the policy which was initiated when three large scale industrial plants of the International Harvester Company were opened in Memphis, Tennessee; Louisville, Kentucky; and Evansville, Indiana. These plants were opened with an announced nondiscriminatory, nonsegregated policy.

III C. Approaches to desegregation were found that combined "gradual" and "immediate" features.

An examination of actual cases of desegregation reveals that the terms "gradual" and "immediate" do not define independent and necessarily different processes. In a given case of desegregation these two processes may overlap and become practically indistinguishable. Desegregation in the Armed Forces may be used as one of the best examples of the difficulty in classifying the desegregation process in these convenient terms. The fact is that every act of desegregation which took place necessarily had to be "immediate" as far as a given unit of the Army, Air Force or Navel Ship was concerned. On the other hand, the desegregation of the entire Army, or Navy, or Air Force required a longer time to be accomplished—was "gradual." The process of desegregation in the Armed Forces as seen in the following descriptions illustrates this point among others.

The Appendix to Appellants' Brief—The Effects of Segregation and the Consequences of Desegregation: A Social Science Statement concluded, with appropriate documentation:

Extensive desegregation has taken place without major incidents in the Armed Services in both Northern and Southern installations and involving officers and enlisted men from all parts of the country, including the South.

Since the publication of this statement, there has been evidence that the process of desegregation has been continuing in the same direction, including more and more units of the Armed Services and at an increasing pace.

James P. Mitchell, Assistant Secretary of the Army, reported that the Army's program of wiping out racial segregation is ahead of schedule and that "at least 90 per cent of the Negroes in the Army are serving in nonsegregated units." According to Mitchell, "The Army policy is one of complete integration and it is to be accomplished as soon as possible." He stated further that the program was highly successful. "This success is seen not only in the small number of remaining nonsegregated units but in the acceptance of Negro officers by white soldiers.... There is no apparent recognition of color."

An evaluation of the nonsegregation policy of the Army was made for the general public by Ernest Leiser. Leiser states the opinion that the "matter-of-factness" of the Army staff planners in introducing non-segregation has been a major factor in the success of this program. In describing the desegregation process as it was executed in the European Command beginning in early 1952, Leiser quotes a battalion commander from the deep South, as follows: "We got the order. We got detailed instructions for carrying it out and a time limit to do it in. And that was it." In spite of the continuation of some friction between whites and Negroes, whites and whites, Negroes and Negroes, "thus far there has not been a single major incident traceable to integration. And in fact... the frictions and antagonisms which lay behind race conflicts in the past have been substantially reduced."

In the Navy, the process of desegregation dates back to World War II and was begun under the leadership of the then Secretary of the Navy Forrestal, and his special aide, Lester Granger. Prior to this time, the pattern of racial segregation in the Navy was among the most rigid to be found in the armed services. Negroes were assigned exclusively to the steward and mess branch of the service. As a result of the activities of Forrestal and Granger, the Navy embarked on an extensive program of desegregation which is still in process. Desegregation in the Navy could be described as "gradual." The percentage of Negroes assigned to a ship was restricted. Within a period of five years a general policy of nonsegregation was in full operation.

There was general concern among officers that desegregation would lead to racial friction. However, commanding officers, petty officers, and lower grades, both white and Negro, agreed that there was no friction and that desegregation worked smoothly. It was agreed also that desegregation increased the general efficiency of the Navy. "The Navy has found that integration is by far the most practicable, economical, democratic and ethical solution of the race problem."

Evidence concerning the success of the desegregation program of the Navy has come from many sources. One of the best examples of personal observation which supports the judgment of the success of this policy is presented by Captain William Gallery of the United States Navy. Captain Gallery describes the difficulty which he faced with the Negro sailors who were assigned to the Officers' Mess and the Ward Room early in World War II when the Navy still had a policy of rigid racial segregation.He states that he had more trouble with these ten colored men than with all the rest of the men on the ship. Since that time, the Navy has changed its policy and assigned men to different jobs on the ship without regard to their color. Under the new policy, this commanding officer now states:

> The colored boys got in no more trouble than their white companions. The fact that the Navy ignored their color in assigning them to a job and a place to sleep and eat was obviously accepted by the white members of the crew. . . . In the light of my previous experience with colored boys aboard ship, I was astonished to see that the policy of nonsegregation worked out so well.

In spite of the success of the Navy's policy in opening other branches of the service to Negroes, the steward branch has remained composed of Negroes and a few Filipinos. Robert B. Anderson, Secretary of the Navy, has started a movement to integrate this remaining segregated branch. Mr. Anderson was quoted as saying that he had asked Vice Admiral James L. Halloway, Jr., Chief of Naval Personnel, to develop plans which would bring about an integrated stewards branch. Mr. Anderson stated:

> I would consider it one of the rewarding accomplishments of my administration if I could eliminate all barriers to complete integration without reflection on those of any race in the Navy.

There are indications, without adequate documentation at hand, that the process of desegregation is proceeding at the same pace in the Marine Corps. There have been no reports of racial friction or impairment of military efficiency as a result of the change to nonsegregation in this department of the armed services.

Within a year after the Air Force gave the directive to desegregate,

18,489 out of 25,891 Negroes were in nonsegregated units. According to Kenworthy, "almost without exception, commanding (white) officers stated frankly that although they had recognized the merits of the new Air Force racial policy... they had been apprehensive. Without any exception, they added that their fears had been completely groundless, and that they were amazed at the ease with which the new policy had been effected and the absence of trouble." Nonsegregation extends to officers and non-com's clubs, swimming pools, and social affairs on the base in southern states.

John A. Hannah, Assistant Secretary of Defense for Manpower and Personnel, summarized the situation in a recent interview.

Q. Have you solved the problem of segregation in the Army?

A. I think remarkable progress has been made. The Air Force and the Navy are completely integrated. The Army is about 95 per cent integrated.

Q. What does that mean?

A. That means that there are no colored men in the Navy or Air Force who are serving in "colored" units. They are all serving in integrated units. And that is true of 95 per cent of the colored men in the Army. We still have a few colored units, but they are being done away with rapidly. In eight months there will be no nonintegrated units in the Army. Universally the answer from our commanders is that it is desirable and works out very well in spite of all contrary predictions—it works very well.

IV. Compared with the varieties of "immediate" desegregation, the various types of "gradual" desegregation do not necessarily insure "effectiveness" of the desegregation process or increase its chances of acceptance by those who are opposed to desegregation.

IV A. Time, itself, does not seem to be related to the "effectiveness" of the desegregation process.

There is evidence that a school district can be effectively desegregated within the following intervals: December of one year to January of the next year; the spring of one school year to the fall of the next school year; a period of two or more school years.

IV B. Opportunity and time for preparation of public for change is not necessarily related to "effectiveness" and "smoothness" of change.

An interval of time for change not only may be used for positive preparation, but may also be used as opportunity to mobilize overt resistance to change.

Further Examples of "Immediate" Desegregation vs. Time for Preparation

The decision of the East St. Louis, Illinois, Board of Education to desegregate the schools was made in December, 1949, and was put into effect on January 30, 1950. During this interval of *one month* all necessary preparations were made. "Termination of racial segregation at the start of the new semester was effected smoothly, with no demonstration and no reports of mass truancy," it was reported by Assistant Superintendent L.G. Osborn. The St. Louis *Post Dispatch* pointed out that it took 85 years to decide to do away with segregated public schools. "What had long seemed impossible suddenly became possible. Not only that, the end of racial segregation produced no demonstration or mass truancy. It was decisive, but peaceful."

In April, 1948, the Board of a New Jersey suburban community issued a public statement adopting a policy of nonsegregated public schools, effective September, 1948. In September, 1948, desegregation was effected as planned, without difficulty.

In the New Jersey public schools, the Commissioner of Education stated in June, 1948, that twenty-two school districts had completed and publicly announced plans for complete integration of pupils and teachers in their schools at the opening of school in the fall. During the summer of 1948, eight additional school boards announced that in September, 1948, the public schools would open on a nonsegregated basis. Desegregation was accomplished without major difficulties.

On the other hand there is the example of a New Jersey community which planned a *two-year* desegregation program as follows: desegregation of seventh and eighth grade students the first year; desegregation of elementary school students and faculties the second year. "Whether this helped or whether it [desegregation] could have been done just as well a year earlier is a moot question."

An example of speedy accomplishment of desegregation of Army units is contained in Leiser's description in the *Saturday Evening Post*, December 13, 1952, which states:

The Army's directive to begin the integration program was called from Washington to the European Command—EUCOM—headquarters, then in Heidelberg, last March. The program was inaugurated officially the first of April. Barely a month later, a score of major all-Negro units had already been broken up and several thousand Negro officers and soldiers had been spread out in all the white combat divisions and supporting arms of the United States 7th Army, which mans our front line in Europe.

Longer time periods for preparation may be accompanied by greater rather than lesser difficulties. On August 27, 1946, the Board of Education of Gary, Indiana, adopted a resolution providing for nonsegregated elementary and secondary public schools to be effected no later than September, 1947. During the one year period between the adoption and the implementation of this policy, school authorities in consultation with professional intercultural education experts conducted an extensive and intensive community-faculty-student educational program in an attempt to obtain support for the new policy.

At the recommendation of an official school agency, composed of professional and lay persons, school district lines were redrawn without regard to race or color and a gradual program was planned, as follows: In September, 1947, all Negro kindergarten and elementary school students (grade 1–6) were to be admitted to the schools in their district without regard to race or color; each year thereafter an additional grade was to be integrated by the same procedure.

In spite of these preparations and careful planning, there were repeated rumors during the summer of 1947 of a student strike if the non-segregation policy was effected. School officials in cooperation with faculty members and city authorities intensified their efforts to prevent any such strike. On September 3, 1947, when 38 Negro elementary school students were admitted to a formerly all white elementary and high school, the high school students began a strike which lasted approximately nine days....

IV C. Segementalized "gradual" desegregation not only does not insure the "effectiveness" of desegregation, but has been found to increase the chances of resistance and resentment of those whites immediately involved in the desegregation.

This point is clearly established by the sequence of events surrounding the plan for desegregation of the public schools in Gary, Indiana. (See IV above). The experience of the Bronx Lutheran church in a transitional neighborhood which attempted desegregation through a "segmentalized gradual" approach is also an example of the noneffectiveness of this approach. The experience of the private Minneapolis hospital which formerly assigned Negroes to private rooms and then attempted to move them to wards with white patients, again demonstrates that opposition is not necessarily decreased by this "segmentalized gradual" approach to desegregation.

Segmentalized Desegregation vs. Uniform Application of Policy

In 1949, partly as a result of the stimulation from intergroup agencies in the District of Columbia, the Washington, D.C. Recreation Board adopted a policy and program of progressive elimination of segregated playgrounds and other public recreational facilities. As a consequence of this new program, the city-wide Division of Recreation, which was originally divided into a white division and a separate Negro division, was integrated into a unified structure as far as the personnel responsible for the adult recreational program was concerned. The youth program continues to be administered under separate Negro and white division heads.

At the present time, 35 of the 130 recreational units have been opened for use of both whites and Negroes on a nonsegregated basis. The other 95 units continue on a segregated basis, with about a third for Negroes and the remaining two-thirds reserved for whites only. In some cases, the "open" units are supervised by white and Negro recreation staff personnel.

According to the information obtained from the headquarters staff, there have been no incidents of any significance resulting from the policy of having Negroes and whites working together. There has been no resistance or lack of cooperation on the part of the staff in working in a nonsegregated playground when they are so assigned. Sixty per cent of the 250 Recreation Department employees are white and forty per cent are Negro. The supervisors of the Recreation Department report, however,that whenever a playground is opened on a nonsegregated basis, there is a tendency for white children to withdraw from active participation in the recreational activities of the unit and it becomes predominantly Negro in attendance. Under these circumstances, attempts by local playground leaders to stimulate and sustain neighborhood interracial playground activities have met with little success.

This is one of the clearest examples of the ineffectiveness of the segmentalized progressive approach to desegregation. As a given unit is desegregated or is made "open" while the majority of units remain segregated or "restricted," the desegregated "open" units lose status in the eyes of the whites and they continue to behave in terms of the traditional pattern of racial attitudes by leaving the "open" units and migrating to the all white units. This can be dealt with effectively only by desegregating all units at a given time.

Quite other results have been reported where a firm policy has been uniformly employed:

> One housing authority, credited with a "model" operation for states where nonsegregation laws have recently been enacted, expressed conviction that objectivity and decisiveness can be achieved only by uniform application of an open-occupancy policy throughout the entire program.... The managers advocated introducing racial integration into all of the projects under the program at approximately the same time. Positively, this was to establish the unqualified assumption of responsibility for complying with a law which granted no exceptions. Practically, it also eliminated any dangers of implicit favoritism in applying the policy. Tenants in no one project could claim that their project was being singled out while others retained racial homogenity. Project managers also would not feel that some of them were expected to comply with the law while others were to be immune. The decision to apply the policy throughout the program is largely credited with the intensive earnestness of all the project managers, none of whom chose to be a failure in a management operation in which others were successful.

V. The various types of "immediate" desegregation are no more likely to lead to nonviolent resistance or violence than are the varieties of "gradual" methods of desegregation. There is some evidence which suggests that a directive requiring the abolishing of the Negro facility and the admission of Negroes into the previously "all white" facility is an especially effective method of desegregation. It results in the following:

1. accomplishes the fact of desegregation in a shorter period of time;

2. involves a larger number of the concerned whites and Negroes;

3. and is accepted in a shorter time by the community with little overt resistance or controversy.

It is reported that in September 1951, the Board of Education of Metropolis, Illinois, announced that the all Negro high school would be closed and that Negro students would be transferred to the formerly all white high school. The change was made with little publicity, almost no opposition, and without incident. In the spring of 1952, the Board of Education announced that, effective September 1952, the all Negro elementary school would be closed and Negro students transferred to the formerly all white school. Desegregation was effected with little publicity or opposition and without incident....

*VI. The likelihood of desegregation being accompanied by active resist-
ance or violence is not directly dependent upon the degree of expressed
racial prejudice among the whites prior to the desegregation. Prejudiced
whites accommodate as well to a changed social situation as do less
prejudiced whites. There is also some evidence that a change in the social
situation brought about by desegregation tends to decrease the intensity of
expressed racial prejudice.*

The evidence gathered by the Cornell University Studies of Intergroup
Relations in twenty American communities reveals that "segregation and
discrimination are not closely related to the intensity of prejudice in the
individual." Analyzing these results further, the authors conclude "that
within wide limits prejudiced persons will accept and participate in a
thoroughly mixed and integrated setting if integrated patterns are
established and accepted as appropriate by other participants in that
situation."

A systematic study of specific cases of desegregation tends to confirm
the statistical research findings of the Cornell studies. The successful
desegregation of the Armed Services certainly *must have involved many
whites who were initially prejudiced*—and some who continued their
prejudices—against Negroes. The existence of these prejudices did not
impair the effectiveness of the desegregation process in the Armed
Services. A number of empirical studies in such fields as housing, Armed
Services, etc., show that the ability of whites to accommodate to a
desegregated situation cannot be reliably predicted from the intensity of
their anti-Negro prejudices. Indeed the housing studies show that initially
unfavorable attitudes may be changed to more favorable attitudes with
certain types of interracial contact.

Other observers have come to similar conclusions:

...The personal attitudes of the people in any community with respect to
segregation as measured by a public opinion poll are not likely to be a good
indicator of the effective strength of the opposition or support for local authority
policy.

Insofar as attitudes are concerned, studies in the field show that the experience
of living in open occupancy projects in itself contributes toward modification of
overt prejudices. Even those who express objections to racial and religious
minorities often do not reflect these feelings in their actions.

Preliminary research findings indicate that those prospective tenants without actual biracial housing experience are more likely to prefer segregated housing and to expect conflicts between the races in nonsegregated housing.

The Cornell studies present statistics which show that whereas the racial attitudes of all whites are likely to be favorably influenced by contact with Negroes, the most prejudiced or bigoted whites "are most likely of all groups to have their prejudices affected favorably by contact with Negroes."

Independence of Attitudes and Behavior in Cases of Desegregation

The following cases clearly and specifically illustrate the discrepancy between expressed negative attitudes and adjustment to a concrete social situation.

Until recently, the private hospitals of Minneapolis had the policy of assigning Negroes to private rooms in order to keep them from coming in contact with white patients in the wards. As a reaction to the pressure from many community sources, the Minneapolis Hospital Council held a series of meetings in an attempt to help these hospitals change this awkward pattern. The first attempt to change this pattern used the method of asking the white patients who were admitted to the hospital if they would mind sharing accommodations with a Negro patient. This approach did not work since the objection from the whites "was almost universal." The hospitals were then forced to assign accommodations to patients without regard to race. When this definite step was taken, it was accepted as a matter of course by all concerned. There have been only *three* complaints in the year and a half since this new policy has been in operation. In these three cases, the complaints were answered by the admitting office with the simple explanation that the policy of the hospital was one of racial nondiscrimination. The considered judgment of a hospital administrator, who was at first skeptical of the wisdom of the new non-segregation policy, is that "the situation is working very smoothly."

In Tucson, Arizona, the elementary schools were maintained on a segregated basis prior to 1951. Students attended the school nearest their homes on the basis of race; the high school was nonsegregated. Approximately eleven years ago, the Superintendent of Public Schools, soon after his appointment, integrated elementary school extracurricular sport and music programs. About six years later, the Superintendent attempted to accustom school officials, administrators, and parent-teacher groups to the idea of an eventually integrated school system.

In the spring of 1950, a public statement made by the Superintendent supporting the pending state permissive segregation school statute and nonsegregated elementary schools in Tucson initiated a wave of unorganized negative public reaction which included threatening letters, phone calls, charges of mishandling school affairs. No overt incidents were reported, however. Subsequently, influential community leaders and organizations publicly supported the superintendent's position. Although local opposition gradually decreased, the permissive segregation referendum was overwhelmingly defeated in Pima County, which includes Tucson.

One year later, in March, 1951, when it became apparent that the state legislature would pass a permissive school segregation statute, the superintendent stated at a meeting of the school board that if the bill were enacted, the board should desegregate the schools, effective no later than September, 1951. Initially hesitant, the board finally agreed to a policy of nonsegregation.

The superintendent immediately put into effect an educational program in the school and community utilizing intercultural techniques. The actual method of desegregation was planned in consultation with parents, teachers and Negro leaders. School zone lines were redrawn to allow for an increasing school population and to distribute Negro students in schools nearest their homes. All students, regardless of race or color, were required to attend the school in their zone. No exceptions were granted. Negro and white teachers were reassigned to various schools. More Negro than white teachers were assigned to those schools which had a predominant number of Negro students and vice versa. As long as several Negro students attended a school, at least one Negro teacher was assigned to that school. Additional Negro teachers were employed through the school system. As a result of this plan, Negro students and teachers were to be assigned to five of the six junior high schools. The Negro principal of the formerly all Negro junior high school was retained in that position. Desegregation was finally effected as planned without any difficulty or incident. When the change actually took place, there was little opposition to the new policy....

VI A. There is always some degree of opposition to desegregation.

All of the cases analyzed for this report are illustrative of this principle.

VI B. A small minority may precipitate overt resistance or violent opposition to desegregation in spite of general acceptance or accommodation by the majority.

Violence by a Minority

There is evidence that the conflict resulting from the attempted desegregation of the St. Louis, Missouri swimming pool reflected primarily inept handling of this tense situation by police and public officials. Suggestive evidence that this conflict was not due to the desegregation order *per se* is found in the fact that two other pools in St. Louis were operating on a pattern of desegregation without any racial conflict on the same day that the riot took place at the third pool. There is further evidence that the violent disturbance was precipitated by a group of adolescent boys from the underprivileged neighborhood in which the pool is located.

VI C. Incidents of overt violent resistance to desegregation have been quite rare.

Of all of the cases of actual desegregation in the many institutions, with the exception of private housing, examined for this survey, there were only four cases in which violent opposition to the desegregation process occurred. Of the 59 communities included in this survey which have desegregated their schools within the past five years, only one incident of violence accompanied the change. This violent incident occurred in Cairo, Illinois. Nonviolent overt resistance to the desegregation of a school was found also in one case—Gary, Indiana.

It has been generally recognized that violence does not inevitably accompany desegregation. In a detailed survey of the consequences of desegregation, *Time* magazine, (August 31, 1953, p. 40) presented the following information:

In answer to the question, What will Georgia do if the U.S. Supreme Court outlaws segregation in the schools?, Governor H. Talmadge states... Georgia... might well turn "the public schools over to a private system. It is the only thing we can do.... If we don't do this, I have not got enough National Guardsmen and the Federal Government enough troops to prevent strife. Blood will flow in the rivers." ...But last week, in communities and on campuses all over the U.S., there was ample evidence to prove one thing: wherever segregation has been abolished, no blood has flowed.

In East St. Louis, scene of the race riot of 1917, the police were out in force on the day that Negro children entered the white schools: several principals had received anonymous letters from white adults threatening to burn down the buildings. But, says Chief George Dowling, "there were no demonstrations. Before some of the hotheads knew it, the whole thing was over, and everybody just settled down to live quietly."

The incidence of violence in the area of public and private housing desegregation has been uncommonly frequent. The factors responsible for this are not completely understood at the present, and this area should clearly be subjected to further intensive study. There are, however, some suggestive clues.

The greater incidence of violence associated with the attempts of Negroes to obtain private housing in "white" communities both in the North and the South seems to be a pattern which reflects among other factors the racial attitudes of real estate interests and the lack of adequate police protection. "A consistent pattern that characterizes these outbreaks has been the disinclination of local police to intervene effectively. At times this has extended to active connivance by the police with the rioters."

In spite of continued racial restrictions in private housing in northern states and some incidents in regard to public housing in northern and some border regions, violent opposition to desegregation is quite rare. The prediction of such violence, however, is frequent. Violence was specifically predicted by the attorney generals of the seventeen states in a brief *amicus curiae* which they filed with the Supreme court in the *Sweatt* case:

The Southern states trust this Court will not strike down their power to keep peace, order, and support of their public schools from maintaining equal separate facilities. If the states are shorn of this police power and a physical conflict takes place, as in the St. Louis and Washington swimming pools, the states are left with no alternative but to close their schools and prevent violence....

Briefly summarized, the Southern states know that intimate social contact in the same schools will lead to withdrawal of public support of the schools, to physical and social conflict, and to discontent and unhappiness for both races.

In spite of this plea and these predictions, the United States Supreme Court decided that Negroes had to be admitted to state supported graduate and professional schools if there were no other equal facilities available to them. As the above list indicates, not only did Negroes attend the state supported universities in the South but as a result of these decisions many private southern colleges who were not involved in the litigation or affected by the decision voluntarily opened their doors to Negro students. These predictions of violence have been proven to be unfounded.

VI D. Desegregation has been accomplished in instances where there is initially strong opposition as well as in instances where there has been minor opposition.

In Cairo, Illinois, during the week following overt violent resistance to the prospect of nonsegregated public schools, several Negro students were transferred to formerly all white elementary and secondary schools without incident. Three weeks after the first Negro student had been transferred, a total of approximately twenty-one Negro students were attending formerly all white schools without incident. The following school semester, "... in the fall of 1952, colored children were admitted to formerly all white schools without a single incident."

Time magazine, August 31, 1953, comments:

When the NAACP went into action in Cairo, in southern Illinois, in the winter of '52 to fight segregation in the schools, some citizens decided to take the law into their own hands. One band of whites lit a cross on the levee, another fired a shotgun at the house of a Negro dentist, and still another tossed a dynamite bomb into a Negro physician's backyard. But, in spite of such hooliganism, Negro children began enrolling in the white schools. In the last year there have been a few fist fights, but gradually Cairo is learning to take some kind of desegregation in its stride. For the first time, Negroes have even begun to appear at meetings of the P.T.A.

In East St. Louis, Illinois, a Negro student had been refused admission to an all white elementary school and some white pupils went on strike against the prospect of Negroes in "their" classrooms. A suit was filed in the Circuit Court of St. Clair County to prohibit segregated schools. A little more than a year later the eighty-five year old segregation policy ended without any of the outbreaks which had been anticipated. More than a hundred colored pupils enrolled in six schools which had previously been white schools and two white pupils began attending a school which had formerly been reserved for colored children. The police did not report a single racial disturbance.

The smooth adjustment to the enforced nonsegregation policy of the Gary, Indiana, children who had gone out on strike for ten days against the enrollment of Negro children in "their" school is another illustration of the fact that initial hostility to desegregation does not in itself block permanently its accomplishment.

An example from the field of employment is found in the policy of the International Harvester plants. The industrial relations managers at the Memphis, Tennessee, and the Louisville, Kentucky, plants of this company reported that wildcat stoppages and protests are necessary "growing pains." They believe that by firm judicious handling of the tension which develops in whites when they are first required to work with Negroes, the white workers emerge from each crisis with a wider acceptance of the policy and that the number and intensity of incidents continue to decline.

VI E. Opposition and overt resistance to desegregation are decreased, if not eliminated, when the alternative for the whites is the complete loss of a desired public facility or the imposition of a direct economic burden or some other important stigma.

VII. Active resistance, and sometimes violence, though rare, are associated with desegregation under the following conditions:
A. Ambiguous or inconsistent policy;
B. Ineffective policy action;
C. Conflict between competing governmental authority or officials....

Ineffective police action has accompanied the use of organized nonviolent and violent opposition both in the North and South to prevent the initiation or the expansion of nonsegregated private housing. One of the most recent such instances of violence occurred in Cicero, Illinois, in July, 1951. Similar forms of opposition have occurred in St. Louis, Missouri; Detroit, Michigan; Atlanta, Georgia; East St. Louis, and Chicago, Illinois; Birmingham, Alabama; Spokane, Washington, and Miami, Florida. It has been stated: "A constant pattern that characterizes these outbreaks has been the disinclination of local police to intervene effectively. At times this has extended to active connivance by the police with the rioters."

Evidence is available to indicate that the violence which was associated with the attempt to desegregate the swimming pool in Washington, D.C., was not only a result of interracial hostility but also reflected an undercurrent competition between two governmental groups for the control of the recreational facilities in the city. The Department of Interior had a basic policy of nonsegregation and sought to make the public pools available to all citizens without regard to racial distinctions. The District of Columbia's Recreation Board, supported by some southern Congressmen, on the other hand, attempted to capture control of all recreational facilities and enforce a segregation policy.

VIII. The accomplishment of efficient desegregation with a minimum of social disturbance depends upon:
 A. A clear and unequivocal statement of policy by leaders with prestige and other authorities;
 B. Firm enforcement of the changed policy by authorities and persistence in the execution of this policy in the face of initial resistance;
 C. A willingness to deal with violations, attempted violations, and incitement to violations by a resort to the law and strong enforcement action;
 D. A refusal of the authorities to resort to, engage in or tolerate subterfuges, gerrymandering or other devices for evading the principles and the fact of desegregation;
 E. An appeal to the individuals concerned in terms of their religious principles of brotherhood and their acceptance of the American traditions of fair play and equal justice. . . .

The Important Role of Authorities

The importance of the role of authorities, almost independent of other factors, in determining whether a situation is to be segregated or not is illustrated by Rutherford B. Stevens' findings about the interracial practices that prevail in mental hospitals. This study was conducted for the Committee on Social Issues of the Group for the Advancement of Psychiatry. Information was obtained from a questionnaire sent to the superintendents of 253 public and 191 private mental hospitals and sanitariums. Two hundred ninety six responses were received from the 444 institutions to whom questionnaires were sent. The results indicated that a wide variety of interracial practices existed in mental institutions. Most public institutions and some private sanitaria reported a racially mixed staff or patients or both. Public institutions in the South segregated Negro patients—at times placing them in separate buildings. A pattern of segregation was also generally found in the border states. However, interracial practices varied considerably among the institutions within a given state. The following quotations from two administrators of state hospitals in a border state illustrate this point:

Separate wards. As far as possible we feel it is best for them to be by themselves. (34% Negro patients)

Random placement. No reason to regard Negro differently than white. (16.7% Negro patients)

Stevens comments:

These divergent practices are particularly interesting in view of the fact that many administrators explained their discriminatory policies as in accordance with community traditions.... Within the same state, segregation is not practiced when the proportion of Negroes is higher.... *The subjective factor of administrative policy is more important than the objective factor of proportion.* [Italics K.B.C.]

Among those institutions that did not practice segregation of their Negro patients, the administrators indicated that the mixing of races proved to be a satisfactory and effective arrangement. Among the methods reported used in handling the complaints of white patients are the following:

We have on two occasions told white patients that they have to leave the sanitarium if they make another discriminating remark.... On one occasion, we have typed a little note—"We are all created equal"—and have placed it on the table where the patient was seated....

Patients ordinarily do not object to the lack of segregation. If in rare instances objection is raised, correction of the attitude is attempted; if unsuccessful, the objection is disregarded. In fact, I believe some corrective pressure is brought to bear by more intelligent patients.

Stevens mentions the fact that many of the administrators described their personal experiences during World War II in nonsegregated military hospitals in the South. In these hospitals there was none of the anticipated racial difficulty. "It is known, also, that numerous white and Negro mentally ill patients from regions of marked racial discrimination and segregation have been successfully treated in nondiscriminatory hospital environments.... This experience is very common in hospitals located in border states with a large out-of-state population, such as the Winter Veterans Hospital in Topeka, Kansas."

Refusal to Compromise Principle

The material presented under the principle of Uniform Application of Desegregation Policy (IV-C) is also relevant to the support of this principle.

In the spring of 1948, the board of education of a large industrial New Jersey community voted to eliminate segregation in the public schools, effective September, 1948. Subsequently, the board refused to accept the recommendations of a special committee which had been appointed to study methods of desegregation and instead merely passed a resolution which included a declaration of its intent to end segregation, rezoned the school boundaries, and revised its regulations concerning school attendance in the new districts. One observer believed that had the resolution been terminated at that point, the integration of schools in the city would have been accomplished with a minimum of administrative difficulty.

The original resolution stated essentially that all pupils and new entrants in the elementary schools must enroll and subsequently attend the school designated for their particular district under the newly revised elementary school boundaries. However, an additional section of the resolution permitted students, upon application, to continue in the school they had been attending until they completed the grades scheduled in that particular school.

It appeared as obvious to everyone interested in the successful integration of this school system, that the Board had provided an out for any white parent who did not wish his child to attend any of the former all colored schools. [Although the school board later agreed to implement the original resolution in September 1948], the end result of this vacillation on the part of the school board was that only partial desegregation was accomplished by September 1948.

Marion T. Wright points out that the common element in an effective and smooth transition from a segregated to nonsegregated public school is "the decision to refuse exceptions to any parents."

Cases are not difficult to find in which desegregation has been negated by subterfuge. Within the past few years, the United States Supreme Court has handed down a series of decisions which have stated that segregation in interstate transportation, in Pullman accommodations, dining cars, railroad coaches and buses, is illegal. The practical consequences of these decisions vary according to the level and type of transportation accommodations. The court decisions have largely eliminated segregation or discrimination in Pullman accommodations and in the dining cars in the South.

The decisions have not been equally effective as far as railroad coaches and buses are concerned. Negroes are still for the most part shunted to Jimcrow cars and in the rear of buses in interstate travel. A Negro must be quite aggressive to obtain his constitutional rights in these areas of transportation. The reasons for the lag in the practical desegregation of coaches and buses seem to be due to: (1) lack of desire on the part of large numbers of Negroes to demand their legal rights in these specific instances; (2) lack of desire on the part of the policy makers and their subordinates in these carriers to take a firm and positive stand enforcing the court's decision; (3) lack of adequate follow-up, leading to strong enforcement, by responsible social agencies; and (4) lack of adequate publicity to the effect that the court's decisions are being ignored.

Moral and Religious Appeals

The issue of the admission of Negro students at St. Louis University was precipitated by a sermon which was preached in the university chapel by Father Claude Heithaus, S.J. The University yielded to the pressure resulting from this sermon. The decision to admit Negro students met with favorable editorial comment in the St. Louis press. The first Negro students were admitted within a year after the sermon was preached. A problem arose around social affairs and the feeling of the university authorities that if Negroes were to attend the formal proms, a dangerous situation might develop. Again, Father Heithaus took a firm positive stand with the result that four Negro couples attended this dance during their first year. No incidents or friction developed.

For additional examples of the effectiveness of moral and religious appeals in certain areas of desegregation see Wayland Baptist College (II), and Desegregation in Parochial Schools.

On the basis of their extensive survey of various communities in the nation, the Cornell group concludes:

Examination of an extensive store of research reports suggests that leaders who control the operating practices of an institution or social environment can establish the policies for that environment within a wide range of community customs. These new policies then become the established practices and customs to which participants conform.

After five years of research on the problem of intergroup relations involving field investigations into hundreds of practical problems, these investigators present as the outcome of their reflection and judgment a number of tentative recommendations related to the actual process of school desegregation. Among these recommendations are the following:

Work with appropriate law enforcement officials to help ensure the quick and effective application of police sanctions wherever tension spots or overt conflict threatens to arise.

Announce clearly and explicitly the policy governing desegregation, the reasons for it, the expectation of compliance by the administration, and the firm intention to achieve a fair and impartial enforcement.

IX. Wherever desegregation has occurred under the above conditions, it has been consistently evaluated as socially beneficial or otherwise successful.

All of the examples examined and cited in this report, except those rare instances of overt violence which blocked the desegregation process and cases of progressive and segmentalized desegregation, support the principle that when desegregation takes place it is generally evaluated, even by those who were initially skeptical, as successful and is seen as increasing rather than decreasing social stability. . . .

IX A. The scale of the institution—its largeness or smallness or the number of people involved—does not necessarily determine the success or failure of desegregation. There is some suggestive evidence that the larger the scale of the desegregation the greater the likelihood of general acceptance or the lack of overt resistance. . . .

IX B. There is evidence that effective desegregation in one institution of a community or in one area of American life tends to facilitate desegregation in other institutions and areas.

In every case of successful desegregation, an independent evaluation of its social consequences was positive. Some of these expressed judgments specifically asserted that desegregation in this area led to or was expected to lead to desegregation in other areas of the community. . . .

IX C. On the other hand there is evidence that effective desegregation in one area or institution of a community does not necessarily bring about a desegregated pattern in other areas or institutions of that community.

The following case study of an interracial hospital in Phoenix, Arizona, illustrates the fact that a successful nonsegregated institution in a community does not always reflect the absence of desegregation in other areas and institutions of that community. One may speculate, however, concerning the degree to which the prior existence of this nonsegregated hospital in Phoenix precipitated or facilitated the movement toward general desegregation which has since included the desegregation of the Phoenix School System. The fact nevertheless remains that this hospital operated successfully on a nonsegregated basis for many years in a community which was characterized by racial segregation in almost every other area of community life.

In 1951 when Arizona was described as "almost as southern as Louisiana," when there was compulsory segregation in the school system, compulsory segregation or exclusion of Negroes in all theatres, hotels and restaurants, there existed in Phoenix probably one of the most interracial hospitals in the United States. Negroes are employed in all branches of the hospital staff. Some Negroes are in supervisory positions, responsible for white and Negro workers. The training school for practical nurses and the school for registered nurses have been interracial since their beginning in October, 1944. The white and Negro students in the school for registered nurses live together in the nurses' home, eat together and have their social life together. There has never been an incident of racial discord. Both the colored and white girls come from all regions of the United States. Some of the white nurses have come from the South. White interns have come to the hospital from Duke, Tulane, Arkansas, Mississippi and other southern universities and medical schools. Not one of these individuals has ever objected to working side by side with Negro doctors and nurses.

The evidence indicates that this interracial hospital in an essentially southern situation has been professionally as well as socially successful.

After seven years of operation, Memorial is now Arizona's busiest general hospital, with 232 beds that are full most of the time. . . . The superintendent, not satisfied with his own observations and opinions, secured the services of Southwest Opinion Research, an independent polling organization, to determine patients' attitudes toward being served by nurses of mixed races. Almost always the reaction was favorable—even glowing.

There is no evidence to indicate that at present the majority of whites in the South who work on the same job with Negro workers, who belong to the same unions, who attend the same Catholic Church, or who attend the same graduate and professional schools necessarily extend their areas of contacts with Negroes beyond these specific desegregated situations. If the social pattern requires segregated transportation, they conform to this in the same way that they conform to the requirements of the desegregated work, church or school situation.

The Cornell Social Science Research Center's memorandum states:

A man who accepts quite naturally the participation of Jews in his service club or as neighbors, may object strongly to having Jews belong to his golf club. Workers who accept and vote for Negroes as officers in their union may strongly oppose having a Negro family move into their neighborhood. But we have observed cases in which a white family moves into a neighborhood and finds that a "nice respectable" Negro family is living down the block from them and that the other white neighbors accept the family and are even seen to be neighborly with them, and the typical outcome is that the new residents come to take for granted the fact that they have a Negro neighbor who is accepted.

This report also states: "Association in the school does not result in attitudes which are generalized to *all* social situations."

X. The conditions which lead to successful desegregation seem to be as effective when used in the South as they are in other regions of the country. Specific social institutions in the southern states have been effectively desegregated.

Most convincing evidence of the possibility of desegregation in a specific social institution in a southern state is found in the interracial activities of some of the Catholic Dioceses in the South. The effect of the widely publicized policy pronouncement of the presiding Bishop Waters of the Diocese of North Carolina is a clear example of this fact.

Another example of the possibility of desegregation within the Catholic Church in the southern states is found in the state of Louisiana. In 1953, Archbishop Joseph F. Rummel of the Diocese of New Orleans, Louisiana, sent a letter to the parishes of his diocese forbidding segregation in his churches, "just as there will be no segregation in heaven." This letter was read in all of the pulpits of his archdiocese. As a concrete demonstration of the meaning of his letter, Bishop Rummel's celebration of his silver jubilee as a Bishop was marked by complete racial integration. Whites and Negroes were seated side by side at the pontifical mass held in the Cathedral and at the civic reception given for the Archbishop in the McAlister auditorium of Tulane University.

An increasing number of Negro physicians are being accepted on the staffs of hospitals in southern states. Of the 167 hospitals which have appointed Negro physicians to their staffs, 12 of these are in the following southern and border states:

Washington, D.C.	Arkansas
Maryland	Arizona
Virginia	Florida
Missouri	Georgia

Some southern hospitals are beginning to use Negro nurses on a nonsegregated basis. There has been a continuous integration of Negro nurses in Catholic hospitals in the United States. An example of such integration in a southern state is the use of Negro nurses in Wheeling Hospital in West Virginia. This hospital is conducted by the sisters of St. Joseph.

The acceptance of Negroes on the major league baseball teams is not a phenomenon restricted to the north since these teams play exhibition spring training games in the South and since there are also Negro players on some minor league southern teams.

The following United Press dispatch reflects the fact that Negroes have been accepted as players in organized baseball in some southern states. It further indicates the degree to which this fact in itself has made necessary some modification of the existing mores and restrictive racial laws:

ANOTHER BLOW TO JIMCROW. Dallas, Tex., Sept. 18 (UP).The annual Dixie Series between the nation's two Class AA baseball leagues, the Southern Association and Texas League, today was expected to be played without incident with the promise that a segregation law will be amended. Negroes have never played in the Southern Assn., but the two Texas League finalists in the Shaughnessy playoffs, Dallas and Tulsa, both have Negro players. Birmingham, Ala., which is playing Nashville in the final round of the Southern playoffs, has a city ordinance prohibiting Negroes from playing against whites. But Birmingham Mayor, James W. Morgan, said yesterday the City Commissioner would amend the City Code.

Documented data illustrating the increasing pattern of racial desegregation in various aspects of life in the southern states have already been presented in this report. Among the areas in which this process is most marked are Army camps and schools run by the Army, Air Force bases, Naval installations, higher education, industrial employment, and politics.

X A. There is evidence to suggest that there can be effective desegregation of elementary and secondary schools in the southern states.

One could state that the above evidence showing in detail successful cases of desegregation and nonsegregation in many areas of life in southern states suggests that nonsegregated schools are also possible in this region of the country. It is not necessary to establish this point by analogy only, however. There is some tentative suggestive evidence that the fact of nonsegregated schools is not a completely novel experience for the contemporary South.

There are persistent rumors to the effect that white and Negro children attended or are attending the same elementary schools in some rural communities in the South. George Mitchell states:

In two or three known instances, private or parochial schools in southern locations are open to children of both races, and whispers continue to be heard of public schools in remote counties which have admitted their handful of Negro children rather than go to the expense of building and maintaining for so few a defensibly equal school.

In a letter (September 30, 1953) Mitchell also states:

It is rumored that in some other Ozark mountain county in Arkansas, one or more Negro children are attending public, otherwise white schools, but I have no means of verifying the rumor.

Virginius Dabney writing in the *Saturday Evening Post* states:

One place where such conditions [Negro and white children going to the same school] exist is in the border state of West Virginia. In a half dozen counties there the few Negro children have been attending overwhelmingly white schools for a good many years, although the segregation pattern prevails, in general, throughout the state. There has been no trouble. The whites in these mountains come from substantially the same stock as the mountaineers in the neighboring states of the Upper South.

21

LILY WHITE TRADITIONS TUMBLING (1954)

by Augusta Strong

Very important breakthroughs against Jim Crow were emerging in the weeks prior to the momentous *Brown* decision. Some are described by an African-American woman. The first report (a) is from Birmingham, Alabama; the second (b) gives no point of origin; the third (c) was filed from the all-black city Mound Bayou, Mississippi, on May 12, 1954.

[a]

A Negro attorney has entered the Democratic primary here...as a candidate for a seat in the state legislature. Arthur D. Shores, a former vice-president of the National Association for the Advancement of Colored People, is running for one of seven seats in the House of Representatives from Jefferson County. He is one of 27 candidates in the primary which will be held May 4, followed by a run-off election the first of June.

Though the proportion of Negro voters to whites is still small in this area, Negroes comprise about one third of the population and over the last two decades, especially, have organized a strong movement to win the right to vote.

Shores has participated actively in this movement. In 1944 when the white primaries were being challenged before the Supreme Court, he attempted to file as a candidate in the Jefferson County primaries.

His application was thrown out, however, when Democratic party officials found out that he was a Negro. Though the Supreme Court has since outlawed the white primary, the Alabama Democratic machine today uses as its symbol a white rooster with the slogan "White Supremacy."

The symbol still has meaning in the state. Alabama is one of six Southern states which retains the poll tax. The Alabama Board of

Registrars still has absolute power to determine "educational" and "character" qualifications for voters. In the Birmingham area, white voters are estimated to outnumber the Negroes 15 to 1, though Negroes comprise more than one third of the population.

Election gains were made by Negro voters in two other areas of the South during April, again indicating results won from the wide right-to-vote movement of recent years.

The first Negro city councilman took his seat in the Joplin, Missouri Council April 13, after an election won with the support of large numbers of white voters. M. W. Dial, principal of the Lincoln School, was elected as one of five councilmen-at-large, running fifth in a field of 26 candidates, in which he was the only Negro.

In Opelousas, Louisiana, local leaders proudly reported that for the first time in a city election, 2,000 registered Negro voters turned out for the mayoralty election.

The weight of their votes—there are 5,000 registered voters in the city—carried the election of candidate Percy Ledoux.

Negro leaders were elated over their success in defeating Mayor T. W. Huntington, who had held office for 13 years. They attributed the victory to the fact that white workers, for the first time had united their voting strength with Negroes, for the good of both groups. They hailed the end of the atmosphere of terror that had kept Negroes from the polls previously.

Mayor-elect Ledoux, in a postelection speech promised the appointment of Negro police and juvenile officers.

Daily Worker, April 25, 1954.

[b]

Recent and forthcoming electoral contests thorughout the nation include a growing number of Negro candidates running for local offices, sometimes with the endorsement of major parties, often as independents. Many of the contests, even for minor offices, are of more than ordinary significance since they occur, in many instances, in areas where Negroes have only recently overcome voting barriers or have only recently won the fight for public office.

EAST ST. LOUIS, Ill.—Dr. Arthur M. Jackson was elected last week to the hitherto lily-white School Board in a popular election. In this city, which maintained segregated schools until four years ago, he ran second in a field of 12 candidates, with 8,856 votes.

CROWLEY, La.—The election of two Negro candidates to City Council in this city of 15,000 is being hailed here as an accepted fact, upon the withdrawal of two white candidates for the post.

Both were unopposed in the Democratic primary. David L. May, high school principal and Joseph A. Pette, barber shop operator, will break the jimcrow barriers here for the first time when they are installed in the Council in July. Both men were supported by the winning mayoralty candidate, chief of police, and many white voters.

The victory for May, a World War II vet, came after many defeats, since he first sought public office 10 years ago. Pette, also a veteran, had been a leader in the fight to win admission of Negroes to state supported universities equally with white students.

TUSKEGEE, Ala.—Mrs. Jessie Guzman, editor of the Negro Yearbook, an educator for 33 years, is opposing a white attorney for the position of the Macon County School Board—for the first time in this Black Belt county.

An all-white school board presides over the 25,771 Negroes and 4,777 whites in Macon County. Mrs. Guzman is campaigning on a platform of "democratic distribution of public school funds" and seeking the "welfare of all children regardless of race."

OTHER ALABAMA contests in which candidates are pioneering for the May 4 primaries are in Birmingham and Mobile. In Jefferson County, Dr. Arthur D. Shores has qualified to run in the Democratic primary for state legislature; he is president of the Alabama Progressive Democratic Association....

In Mobile County which has more than 5,000 registered Negro voters, three are running for posts on the County Democratic Committee. Two thousand Negro voters have registered since Dec. 15 when poll tax laws were modified. E. D. Nixon of Montgomery, a leader of the National Association for the Advancement of Colored People, has filed for a similar post at Montgomery.

ST. PETERSBURG, Fla.—The Rev. W. R. Johnson is a candidate for the School Board of Pinellas County. Active in clerical circles and in civic groups, he says of his bid for election: "My reason for entering the race...is that I feel it is high time for the Negroes of Pinellas County to have a share of the responsibility of operating the schools of our county."

NEWARK, N.J.—Three Negroes are running for seats in the City Council in May 11 elections. Despite a Negro population of 76,000, there are and have been no representatives in the Council. Irving Turner is supported by the Voters Independent Council; Harry Hazelwood has CIO endorsement; Roger Yancey has the support of many Negro civic leaders.

Daily Worker, May 2, 1954

[c]

A freedom rally in this all-Negro town last week drew 5,000 participants, who adopted a resolution to raise a defense fund of $100,000 for civil rights and cheered speakers calling for "first-class citizenship in Mississippi."

The gathering marked the third annual meeting of the Regional Council of Negro Leadership, headed by Dr. T. R. M. Howard, a Mississippi physician, who founded the statewide organization.

Dr. Howard told the crowd assembled in a huge tent, "We are on a great crusade in Mississippi and it will not end until the humblest sharecropper has received full citizenship rights.

"Most of the things you hear about Mississippi are true, but we are not going to ask God to fight our battles. Instead, we are going to use dollars and fight until we are free."

Thurgood Marshall, NAACP counsel, was the main speaker. Marshall had been invited, with leading Negro lawyers and leaders from Georgia, Alabama, Louisiana, Texas, Arkansas and Tennessee, to discuss a new approach to problems if the Supreme Court outlaws segregated schools in the South.

Marshall emphasized the NAACP campaign for full freedom by 1963:

"Come hell or high water. We'll be free by 1963," he declared. "The question of civil rights and the question of the treatment of Negroes in the U.S. is no longer a question on the local or national level.

"It has become an international question, one that is watched closely by all other nations, especially Russia."

Placards bearing the slogan "Liberty and Justice for all" were carried in the parade preceding the meeting. Mayor B. R. Green of Mound Bayou delivered the welcome address.

The meeting was widely featured in the Negro press, with the Atlanta Daily World urging all Georgia leaders to follow the example of

Mississippi and set up similar organizations for funds to be used "in the struggle for first class citizenship and the holding of gains that might come to us."

The Mound Bayou fund is specifically being raised to file suits against sheriffs and circuit clerks in county offices who deny Negroes the right to register as voters.

Daily Worker, May 13, 1954.

22

WHAT NEGROES WANT NOW (1954)

by Walter White

The above was the title given by *U.S. News and World Report* to an interview it held with Walter White very soon after the Supreme Court decision of May 17, 1954. The magazine was racist in its orientation; the above title and the drift of some of the questioning reflect that.

Q *What is the next move to be made in the long fight to end segregation, Mr. White? Now that you've won in education, what comes next?*

A Of course, our next task is that of seeing to it that there is full implementation of the Supreme Court decision.

Q *But won't the effects of the decision reach beyond the schools?*

A Now that the 58-year-old decision in Plessy vs. Ferguson [in which the Court held that separate facilities for Negroes are legal if equal] has been overruled, the new decision will apply not only directly to education, but indirectly also to other phases of human living.

Our next job is in the field of housing, in the field of employment, and in the expansion of the Negro's voting strength. Now let me make clear here that we do not favor bloc voting. But through no choice of his own, on issues like this, the Negro, whatever his economic status, has an understandable concern about human rights and civil rights and equal opportunities, and that Negro vote, both in the South and in the North, will continue to be interested in the job of completing the abolition of segregation.

Q *Do you think this school decision will contribute to breaking down other barriers between the races—social barriers?*

A Well, I don't want to be misunderstood on that. I'd like to make my position very clear, that I believe that friendship between two human beings is a matter which concerns those two individuals and nobody else. If, for example, as is unquestionably true, Governor Byrnes does not want to invite me to be his guest in the Governor's Mansion of South Carolina, certainly no law exists, and no law should ever exist, that requires him to do that. I might also feel that same way about inviting Governor Byrnes into my house, here in New York. But when you say "social barriers," I assume that you mean living as normal human beings in an enlightened society, and certainly I think it's going to have an effect.

Q *Do you think that the association of pupils in public schools could possibly lead to an increase in intermarriage between the races?*

A That could be true. When human beings get to know each other and to respect each other, friendships develop and some of those friendships develop into love and into marriage. But there has been no noticeable increase in such friendships in the States where there has been no segregation. I think it will not materially increase the number of such instances.

Q *Does the NAACP plan any legal challenges of some State laws which bar interracial marriages?*

A We've always opposed such laws on the basic ground that they do great harm to both races; they deny the women of a so-called minority group protection of their person, and it also is an improper and immoral thing to do. It really places a premium on extramarital relationships on both sides of the racial fence. If two people wish to live together, it is most un-Christian to say that they must live together in sin instead of holy wedlock.

Q *Do you then plan any further or immediate contests of this issue as a result of this ruling?*

A No, we have no such plans.

Violence? Short-Lived—

Q *You don't anticipate any serious trouble as a result of this decision?*

A I won't go quite that far. Unfortunately, some Southerners—and particularly men like Governor Herman Talmadge of Georgia—have said repeatedly that "blood will flow in the streets like rivers" should the

Supreme Court outlaw segregation. Frankly, I don't believe it. Now, there may be some instances of friction that will be deliberately fomented by people who want to stop this growth toward an integrated society, but I believe that the authorities, both federal and State, will step in and nip in the bud any significant fomented violence that may be attempted.

Q *You do think that there might be violence?*

A There may be some, but I think it will be short-lived, and I don't think the instances will be numerous. Now, there may be some scraps between the youngsters, but even now there is friction among white children attending all-white schools and between Negro children attending all-Negro schools. I don't think there will be any measurable amount of friction, above what normally exists among healthy children. Today there are more than 2,000 young Negroes attending professional and graduate schools in Southern States. All except five States now admit Negroes. About four times that number attend summer schools, and there's never been a single bit of trouble.

Q *Won't there be some communities where Negroes themselves will voluntarily go along with continued segregation and raise no protest or legal issue?*

A I don't think so for a variety of reasons. Negroes themselves have long realized that their children are being denied equal education. This is true not only in the North and the cities of the South, but in the rural areas. What will be done is a continued campaign to wipe out every vestige of segregation not only in schools but in housing, which is equally important, in the matter of jobs, in the right to vote.

Power of 2 Million Votes—

Q *On the question of voting, Mr. White, how strong is the Negro vote?*

A That brings me to one very important factor in this whole question which has been overlooked, namely, that the Negro today in the South is becoming an increasingly important political factor.

In the primary election in Alabama a few days ago, it was the Negro vote which re-elected John Sparkman as United States Senator. Now, Mr. Sparkman is an able, a sincere, a good man, but he has been very timorous on this issue of civil rights, and he has repeatedly made the statement that he favors the Southern position of continued segregation. But the record of his opponent, Congressman Laurie Battle, was so much worse than that of Senator Sparkman that between 50,000 and 60,000

Negroes in Alabama voted straight down the line for John Sparkman, if only as the lesser of two evils.

Today in the South there are close to 2 million registered Negro voters. When we won, after many, many years of litigation and attempted legislation, in 1944, the case of Smith vs. Allwright—in which the Supreme Court outlawed the barring of Negroes from the so-called White Democratic primaries in the South—there were less than 200,000 registered Negro voters in the South. By 1948 the number had increased to 750,000. In 1952 the number had jumped to 1,300,000.

And a quiet but steady campaign is now going on with the objective of 3 million registered Negro voters in the South by 1956. As a result, in many of the Southern States, as in the case cited in Alabama, the Negro vote holds the potential balance of power in a reasonably close election.

Q *Has this change been brought about entirely by the Negroes' own efforts?*

A It isn't the Negro alone who is doing this. The South has grown much more than most people realize. For example, no longer is it the No. 1 economic problem of the nation. It no longer depends on the one-crop system of cotton. There's been a tremendous industrial invasion in the South. They do not want to see this new prosperity shucked off. You have more young people, intelligent people, young men, for example, who fought in nonsegregated units in Korea.

There's also the factor of the efforts of the churches in the South, the labor unions, and other groups who now are beginning to realize that the Achilles heel of American foreign policy, as well as in the domestic policy, as was pointed out recently in Washington by Ambassador Henry Cabot Lodge, is the question of color in the United States.

These economic, these moral, these ethical, these international pressures are leading to a greatly changed psychology in the South. No longer can politicians be elected to office simply on a platform of "Keep the Negro down."

Q *You feel, then, that public opinion now is ready for this change?*

A Well, let me cite you the example of the Southern press. Long before this decision was handed down by the Supreme Court, virtually every newspaper in the South had already written editorials saying that the Court has ruled as it has, we must accept it because we believe in constitutional government; we're not going to give the Communists or other enemies of America any excuse for further deriding America and lowering American prestige in other parts of the world; let's be calm about it, let's be intelligent, and let's arrive at a peaceful, intelligent conclusion and program of action.

In Effect Late in 1955—

Q *What is going to be the direct effect of this Supreme Court decision? Does this mean now that beginning next year there will be no more segregation in schools? Or will the change take years?*

A In a number of instances, in Delaware and Kansas, for example, they have already taken steps to eliminate segregation, and I think that will be true in many places in the South as well. But it won't take place generally next September, because in the decision handed down on May 17, the Supreme Court ordered arguments for the fall term in Court to determine what shall be the nature of the decree for implementation of the decision. So that those arguments will be held in the fall, and the decrees will be handed down probably sometime next winter, and it won't become effective until the school term beginning in the fall of 1955.

What States Will Do—

Q *Do you think that the Southern States that have made threats of defiance will actually resist the Court's decision?*

A I think that there will be some States which will attempt to use various tactics of delay. In South Carolina, for example, Governor Byrnes has asked and secured authorization in an election to abolish the public-school system rather than obey the Supreme Court—which is rather shocking coming from a man who has had so distinguished a career as Governor Byrnes has had, as a former Justice of the Supreme Court, a former Secretary of State, a former Assistant President, a man of very great distinction. But I don't think Mr. Byrnes really believes that he is going to be able to abolish the public-school system.

In the first place, a good many millions of dollars have been invested in education in South Carolina and in other Southern States. The people are not going to have that turned over to private individuals, private organizations, as he has suggested. Certainly they will not ask for the total abolition of education for whites as well as Negroes. Both white and Negro South Carolinians will certainly rise up in effective protest against it.

As for turning it over to private individuals, that is one of the most harebrained proposals of current times. Because if they did turn education over to private individuals, with hundreds of millions of dollars' worth of public property, that would invite educational racketeers to debase standards, and you would see such corruption and such inefficiency that it would be unbearable. Then if the States should step in and take action to protect its children and its investment, it would come within the purview of the Supreme Court. So that I am sure that that is wholly a tactic of delay that is being attempted.

Q *Do you think any State actually will do away with public schools?*
A No.

Q *Will it be possible for some States or districts simply to ignore the decision and carry on, in effect, segregation in their own community?*

A They will attempt it. But I think public opinion has grown, if I may be immodest for a moment, in the 45-year effort of the National Association for the Advancement of Colored People not only to secure legal decisions within the framework of the democratic process, but also to educate the public on the nature of the extent and injustice of discrimination which grows out of segregation. And certainly we shall continue to take every legal action which is necessary to insure complete compliance with the Supreme Court's decision.

No Action? Court Order—

Q *How will that decision be enforced? Who will police it?*
A If they attempt to evade the decision of the Court, then what we will do is to take such school officials into the federal district court, the circuit court of appeals, and eventually to the Supreme Court, probably on a show-cause order, to have them show cause to the federal court that they are complying with the decision.

Q *In carrying out this school desegregation order, what kind of decree will the NAACP seek from the Court?*

A We will ask the Court to issue a decree ordering the abolition forthwith of segregation. A great deal of time has been allowed by the Court already—there has been 91 years since the Emancipation Proclamation was signed by Abraham Lincoln—and we think that it is about time that the guarantees of the Emancipation Proclamation and the Fourteenth and Fifteenth amendments should be implemented. The South is more ready for the change from segregation to integration than professional politicians believe it to be.

Q *You think the change could be made quickly?*

A I think it could be made much more quickly than people think.

Q *Do you think that the end of segregation could come within a year; that is, within a year from next autumn?*

A It can come, and I believe that in most instances it will come. There will be attempts at delays, but we do not believe they are going to be successful. And we shall oppose them.

Housing: A Complication—

Q *Suppose we take the specific case of some Southern town about half Negro and half white, the races living in separate parts of the town, with Negro schools in one part and white schools in the other: How will desegregation be accomplished in a town like that?*

A If there continues to be rigid housing segregation there won't be as rapid or as material alteration of the pattern of segregation at the grammar-school level.

Q *It is possible, then, that almost entirely Negro schools could continue in such a town automatically because of the housing division?*

A For the time being, yes.

Q *That would be a natural consequence, rather than an artificial one?*

A Yes. And the important factor in that connection is that one of the most enlightened of all social programs of the past 20 years has been federal, State and other aid to housing. Virtually every large American city, North as well as South, is ringed about with new housing developments, which have been constructed either with the aid of FHA [Federal Housing Administration] mortgage insurance, or through the Veterans' Administration or the HHFA [Housing and Home Finance Agency]. Many of those developments bar not only Negroes but members of other minorities. The Negro is getting a little better housing, but not to the extent of other Americans.

He is getting hand-me-down, secondhand housing in many instances, as the whites migrate out to the more modern suburbs—which, incidentally, is going to affect profoundly the political composition of the major American cities. Jews and Catholics have a tradition of remaining near their synagogues and churches. Negroes are still hemmed in by housing segregation, so that more and more so-called minorities are going to become increasingly powerful, so far as political control of the major American cities is concerned. I mean, for example, last year, Hulan Jack, a Negro businessman, was elected Borough President of Manhattan, and that was a logical development, because one third of the votes cast in the borough of Manhattan in the last election were cast by Negroes.

Q *Do you think that the school ruling will contribute to the ending of housing segregation—in other words, that mixed schools will lead to mixed residential areas?*

A I think that it will affect not only housing but every department of American life.

Better Education—

Q *Will the end of segregation really help Negro children get a better education?*

A There is no doubt that that is true. Where you have had vast disparity in school equipment, in length of school terms, in the quality and quantity of education, it causes the Negro child to start out as an adult human being with at least one strike against him. The abolition of segregation is going to mean that to a greater extent than ever before in the history of the Negro in America he is going to have the basic training which is necessary to compete in an increasingly competitive world.

Q *Could the end of separate schools possibly result in lowering the general level of education in any way?*

A Experience has demonstrated just the opposite. It has meant higher standards, less money wasted on perpetuating a dual system of education. It has resulted in more education and better education for both whites and for Negroes.

Q *It is anticipated, I suppose, that Negro teachers will now teach both white and Negro students, and vice versa?*

A Yes.

Q *Do you think that there is any danger that local boards will have a tendency to favor white teachers when it comes to employment?*

A There will be attempts of that sort—in fact, we had one instance of it in Topeka, Kans., where, after the cases had been argued, six Negro teachers were notified that they would not be re-employed. But the NAACP sent one of its attorneys there, and the matter was discussed and taken up, and then the school board found that public opinion in the community did not favor this attempt to penalize the Negro teachers, and they were rehired.

Q *Probably you've been in contact since the Supreme Court school ruling with many Negro leaders—how do they feel about it?*

A There is great jubilation.

Q *Do you consider this as a major victory in your campaign for full equality?*

A I think unquestionably it is the major victory to date. We haven't solved the problem yet. We still have a good many odds and ends, but I want to say this, that one somewhat overconfident individual telephoned me right after the Court handed down its decision, and he said, "The NAACP is on its way out of business." I said, "I would be delighted to see the NAACP go out of existence because it was no longer necessary for such an organization to exist."

U.S. News and World Report, May 28, 1954, pp. 54, 57–59. David Lawrence, publisher of the magazine, "was one of Hoover's favorites," as Kenneth O'Reilly stated in *Racial Matters: The F.B.I.'s Secret File on Black America* (New York: Free Press, 1989), p. 209. This magazine played a leading role in publicizing the "scientific racism" of the 1950s.

23

NEW EMANCIPATION (1954)

by Henry Lee Moon

Immediately after the *Brown* decision, the NAACP called for a meeting of its southern leadership to plan strategy for the future. This was held in Atlanta on May 22–23, 1954. Under the optimistic title given above, Henry Lee Moon described that meeting.

While Governor Herman Talmadge was shouting defiance of the Supreme Court and threatening armed resistance to its edict against segregation in the public schools, Negro leaders from seventeen Southern and border states and the District of Columbia were soberly formulating a program of action "to meet the vital and urgent issues" raised by the order. Meeting in Atlanta May 22–23, on call of the National Association for the Advancement of Colored People, the leaders of the association's Southern units were neither fearful nor gloating. They were assured but not vaunting; reasonable but not compromising. They hailed "this memorable decision as a victory not for Negroes alone but for the whole American people and as a vindication of America's leadership of the free world."

The tone of the conference was set by a message from Dr. Channing H. Tobias, chairman of the N.A.A.C.P. board of directors, who expressed the opinion that "the entire South will meet the test of the Supreme Court decision in the spirit of loyal, law-abiding citizens." Further, Dr. Tobias urged: "It is important that calm reasonableness prevail, that the difficulties of adjustment be realized, and that without any sacrifice of basic principle the spirit of give and take characterize the discussions. Let it not be said of us that we took advantage of a sweeping victory to drive hard bargains or impose unnecessary hardships upon those responsible for working out the details of adjustment."

The eighty men and women who gathered in the capital of the South have borne the brunt of the battle to end segregation in their respective states. They are recognized spokesmen of the Negro race in their communities. Most of them are professional or small business men— lawyers, doctors, clergymen, teachers, real-estate operators, insurance agents, and shopkeepers. They chose as their chairman, James M. Hinton, the clergyman and business man who is president of the N.A.A.C.P. in South Carolina, the group which sponsored the first of the five cases decided by the Supreme Court on May 17.

Although the publicity given to the conference was largely focused upon such national leaders as Walter White, executive secretary of the N.A.A.C.P., and Thurgood Marshall, its chief counsel, the formulation of policy was the work of the delegates, as the responsibility for effectuating it at the local level will be theirs. The Atlanta Declaration which they drafted will undoubtedly eclipse the famous speech of Booker T. Washington in the same city as a milestone of Negro progress in America. Washington's address, delivered at the opening of the Atlanta Exposition on September 18, 1895, anticipated by eight months the court's *Plessy v. Ferguson* decision establishing the "separate but equal" doctrine. Sometimes called the "Atlanta compromise," it counseled separation "in all things that are purely social," which was interpreted to mean acceptance of the South's segregation policies.

Like the sage of Tuskegee fifty-nine years ago, the N.A.A.C.P. delegates offered cooperation with Southern whites, but with this significant difference: they made the offer as equals, not as suppliants. The fallacious and humiliating doctrine of "separate but equal" having been set aside by the new ruling, they expressed a readiness "to work with other law-abiding citizens who are anxious to translate this decision into a program of action to eradicate racial segregation in public education as speedily as possible." To this end, they directed the units of the association "in every affected area to petition their local school boards to abolish segregation without delay and to assist these agencies in working out ways and means." They pledged the "total resources of the N.A.A.C.P.... to facilitate this great project of ending the artificial separation of America's children on the irrelevant basis of race and color."

The Declaration recognized "that school officials will have certain administrative problems in transferring from a segregated to a non-segregated system," but made it clear that the N.A.A.C.P. would "resist the use of tactics contrived for the sole purpose of delaying desegregation." Further, the N.A.A.C.P. leaders promised to "accelerate our community-action program to win public acceptance of the court's de-segregation order from all segments of the population."

Advocates of segregation have tried to frighten Negro teachers into silence, if not acceptance of Jim Crow, by asserting that only white persons would be permitted to teach mixed classes. Presenting the case for segregation before the Supreme Court in the first argument in December, 1952, J. Lindsay Almond, Jr., Virginia's Attorney General, flatly stated that "Negroes would not be employed to teach white children in a tax-supported school system in Virginia." All over the South there has developed a sudden and lachrymose concern about the fate of the Negro teacher.

The delegates to the Atlanta conference described this as a false issue in view of the shortage of teachers. As one pointed out, the abolition of segregation in the schools did not mean the abolition of children. Moreover, in many instances Negro teachers are better qualified than their white colleagues, since the best-trained white persons can often get higher-paid positions in private employment. However, in recognition of this propaganda tactic, the Declaration called for "integration at all levels, including the assignment of teacher personnel on a non-discriminatory basis," and gave assurance that "the fullest resources of the association, including the legal staff, the research staff, and educational specialists on the staff, will be utilized to insure that there will be no discrimination against teachers as a result of integration."

Concern was expressed about the financial problem involved in the development of an integrated school system in the region. "We are aware," the delegates affirmed, "that our region has been overburdened in its efforts to provide education for all children—in part because of the dual system—and, accordingly, we strongly support federal aid to assist our states in the building of new schools and the expansion of educational facilities for all our children, provided any such legislation contains the necessary safeguards to insure the distribution of funds in accordance with the... court's decision."

It was reported that some local school boards were trying to get Negroes to accept continuance of segregation on a "voluntary" basis. Such a plan, Mr. Marshall pointed out, would be unlawful. The rights conferred by the Constitution are personal and individual and cannot be bargained away by any group.

The conference ended on a note of hope and anticipation. New impetus has been given to the N.A.A.C.P. drive to complete emancipation by the 100th anniversary of Lincoln's Proclamation of January 1, 1863.

Hopes were heightened when on May 24, the day after the conference closed, the Supreme Court cleared its docket of pending segregation and discrimination cases and handed down decisions extending its May 17 ruling to public housing and publicly supported colleges and universities and presaging its extension to municipally owned golf courses and other tax-supported recreational facilities. These cases involved the University of Florida, Louisiana State University, Hardin Junior College at Wichita Falls, Texas, a municipal golf course at Houston, and an open-air amphitheater in Louisville, Kentucky.

Emancipation seems nearer than ever before.

Nation, June 5, 1954, pp. 484–85.

24

ALAIN LOCKE (1954)

by W. E. B. Du Bois

Alain Locke, born in Philadelphia in 1885, died in New York City on June 9, 1954. He was among the most influential forces in cultural and intellectual matters for much of his life. At the funeral services, two days later, Channing Tobias presided. Among those who spoke was Du Bois:

Alain Locke was a man who deliberately chose the intellectual life; not as a desirable relief from reality, but as a vocation compared with which all else was of little account. In a land like America and among a group as inexperienced as American Negroes this was simply not understandable. That a man in the midst of money-making or gambling should at intervals devote some time to thought itself or to the bases of human reasons, is in our day possible if not profitable. But to give a life to thinking and its meaning, that is to most Americans quite inexplicable. So that to many this lonely figure, who spoke quietly and smiled with restraint, became often an object of pity if not evil gossip and ridicule.

Yet in truth Alain Locke stood singular in a stupid land as a rare soul who pursued for nearly half a century, steadily and unemotionally, the only end of man which justifies his living and differentiates him from the beast and bird; and that is the inquiry as to what the universe is and why; how it exists and how it may change. The paths pointed out by Socrates and Aristotle, Bacon and Descartes, Kant and Hegel, Marx and Darwin, were the ones Locke followed and which inevitably made him unknown and unknowable to a time steeped in the lore of Micky Spillane. And yet in Locke's life lay a certain fine triumph. He knew life's greater things: pictures and poetry, music and drama, conversation which was not filth, laughter not clownish, and appetites which never fell to cheap lust. His severe logic, his penetrating analysis, his wide reading gave him a world within, sparsely peopled to be sure, but finely furnished and unforgettable in breadth and depth. It built a man not fit for war, but nobly courageous and simply consistent, who could bear pain and disappointment and yet live and work. For his dark companions he had faith and fellowship; for their smaller problems advice and guidance. But for himself he had only truth.

His quest for truth and logic was no easy task. It was often contradictory and disappointing. It either appealed in vain to understanding or found no understanding to which it could appeal. It was a thankless task to those who see life as money, notoriety or dirt. And yet its faithful pursuit is more than living. It is more than death.

We may mourn that his latter days of hard-earned leisure could not have lasted longer. But perhaps he would say if he spoke now, that life is not length of days nor plethora of pleasure but satisfaction of work attempted, and that surely he had.

Phylon, Third Quarter, Vol. 15 (1954) XV: 251–52. There is no book-length biography of Locke, but see the account by Michael R. Winston in DANB, pp. 398–404; see also R. J. Linnemann, ed., *Alain Locke: Reflections on a Modern Renaissance Man* (Baton Rouge, La.: Louisiana State University Press, 1982).

25

THE MISSISSIPPI NEGRO'S STAND ON SEGREGATION IN ITS PUBLIC SCHOOLS (1954)

by T. R. M. Howard, M.D.

Mississippi's governor, Hugh White, held a conference on July 30, 1954, to consider the *Brown* decision. He invited an African-American to present his views. A group of black leaders unanimously elected Dr. Howard as spokesperson. He said:

GOVERNOR WHITE, STATE OFFICIALS, MEMBERS OF THE STUDY COMMITTEE, LADIES AND GENTLEMEN:

I wish to express my personal thanks to the Governor for finally calling in a group of Negroes to discuss one of the most vital issues of our age. A question as vital as the question which is before us today cannot be settled by decree, nor by a committee of one group going behind closed doors— bringing the solution of the problem to the other group on a "take it or leave it" proposition.

This grave problem can and will be settled in our great State by men of good will of both races sitting down at the conference table, with mutual respect for each other's God-given American rights, and working out the problem. There has never been any problem too great for Mississippians to solve and we are going to solve this problem together.

We, the Negro citizens of Mississippi, realize that this segregation issue strikes at every issue for which the South has stood ever since there has been a South. The thinking Negro knows that no people give up their vital traditions without a struggle.

During the 164-year history of our Supreme Court, there have been momentous decisions which have dealt with race relations in these United States of America. The first was Taney's Dred Scott Decision in 1857, and the second was the unanimous decision of the Supreme Court outlawing segregation in the public schools of the United States of America on Monday, May 17, 1954.

A noted journalist, Mr. Kenneth Toler, writing in the Sunday, July 18, 1954, *Commercial Appeal* about the meeting today, comparing it with the meeting of the constitutional convention of 1890, states, and I quote, "In 1890 the purpose was to work out a plan for segregation of the races; the 1954 meeting has that same objective." The Negroes who have come here today have not come to help work out any trick or plan to circumvent the decision of the Supreme Court outlawing segregation in the public schools. We believe that the decision is a just and humane decision and our beloved South should have known that it was the only decision that could have been given in the light of America's position in the world today.

We have come to help chart the way for mutual understanding so that the public school in Mississippi may be saved within the spirit of the Supreme Court's decision. We fully realize the tremendous responsibility that is ours in attempting to make any suggestions for the solution of so grave a social problem as segregation. In making any suggestion for the operation of our public schools in Mississippi, we believe that the leaders of both racial groups must be willing to confer and deliberate with each other, always on a high level of mutual discussion and always devoid of suspicion, fear or intimidation. In this connection, we believe that the Governor should accept a 25-man Negro committee, the names of which should be submitted by the Negro leaders here assembled, to work jointly and together with a 25-member white committee to work out the details of our future public school program in Mississippi. We realize that the Supreme Court has only said that segregation is unconstitutional. It has not said yet when and how it is to end. We are not going to try today to get in front of the Supreme Court on the "when and how."

Governor, we believe that the pressure for the recent Supreme Court's decision was brought about largely because of the so-called "Separate but Equal" school theory. You know, as well as we know, that we have had the *Separate* all right but in very few cases have we had the *Equal*. You have had a school equalization law here in Mississippi since 1890 but you forgot about this law until you began to feel the sharp lash of the Supreme Court of the United States of America, and today you wish to bargain with us. You will give us schools, if we give you our freedom. Fundamentally, there is no such thing as separate but equal in a matter as vital as the education of our children. The Mississippi Negro public school system has been so lacking in buildings and facilities that the Negro children have developed a complex which has caused them to want to go to the white school in their community, not for social reasons; but because the white school was the best school in the community. No wonder Chief Justice Warren said in his historic decision, "To separate children from others of similar age and qualifications solely because of their race generates a feeling of inferiority as to their status in the community that may affect their hearts and minds in a way unlikely ever to be undone."

We believe that it is practical and logical to build our schools in communities where the people live, not on the basis of race but for the convenience of the children. We believe that buildings and equipment should not be labeled for white or colored but schools built to all standard specifications for the children of Mississippi. We can all agree to start this type of a building program immediately. We should have assurance, however, by appropriate legislative approval, that this school building program will be on the basis of need and not because the Negroes of the State have agreed to any type of segregation in our schools. We should like to have the assurance that competent biracial committees will serve on this school building program. Governor, you have a tremendous wealth of Negro "know how" in Mississippi that you have never called upon to help work out any mutual problems.

We believe that it is morally and legally wrong for those who have sworn to uphold the laws of our land to talk about abolishing the public school system, in order to evade the laws of our land. For Mississippi to abolish her public school system would be an unthinkable catastrophe, especially for the white children of the State, because you have for them a good public school system. For the average Negro child today, you certainly do not have much to offer in the way of public schools; and if you abolish them today, you will lose more than the Negro.

In the light of my foregoing statements, I wish to offer the following suggestions for the operation of a system of public schools for all the children in the State of Mississippi:

I. As the Supreme Court Decision has done away with the laws dealing with our schools in Mississippi, we petition the Mississippi State Legislature to write a new school law for the State of Mississippi without mentioning race, creed or color. A law which in substance will say, "Mississippi shall provide school buildings and school facilities for all of her children."

We endorse the Governor's plan to call a special session of the State Legislature to consider among the other things, a new school law, and appropriating enough money to build new schools and buy new equipment to bring all of our schools up to an arbitrary standard, which can best be fixed by our experts in the field of education.

II. We seriously recommend that competent Negroes be appointed to all policy-making boards affecting both races on a state and local level. The day is past and forever gone when one race can work out all the problems affecting another group and bring it to them as a "take it or leave it" proposition. We are demanding a chance to help shape our own destiny. We have seen too many costly blunders made in Negro school buildings and in other matters affecting the Negro simply because the Negro was not consulted. You may think you understand our problem, but you have got to be a Negro in Mississippi at least 24 hours in order to understand what it means to be a Negro in this State.

III. We recommend that an independent biracial commission be appointed to look into the three institutions of higher learning which are today serving the Negro people of the State—as to location of these schools; as to the need for three separate schools of this nature; as to faculty qualifications; as to enrollment; as to physical plant; as to equipment; as to operation appropriation—in absolute comparison at all levels with similar institutions of higher learning in the State of Mississippi. Here, as in the elementary and high schools, we have had the separate but in no case the equal.

IV. We recommend that because of the tremendous cost to the State of the elementary and high school building program and because it would cost added millions in building, equipment and faculty employment to bring any one of the three state colleges which today serve Negroes up to the recognized level of doing graduate work and professional work, that the higher institutions of learning in the State of Mississippi which are already doing graduate and professional work open their doors immediately and admit all students who qualify for graduate and professional work, regardless to race, creed or color. (I wish to remind you that this is being done in every state in the Union except Florida, South Carolina, Georgia, Alabama and Mississippi. The thinking Negroes would like for this to be done without taking the matter to the Supreme Court. You and I know what the answer will be if the issue goes to the Supreme Court.)

A brilliant young man in my town made application to the law department of our state university over six months ago and until this day he has not received an answer. Right here in Jackson, white nurses and Negro nurses sit in the same classes together. They are doing it in Arkansas, Louisiana and Texas. It can be done without racial trouble at the University of Mississippi.

Your big fear, of course, is social equality. There is not a thinking Negro in Mississippi today that bothers about social equality, but we are mighty concerned about equality of educational opportunity.

V. We recommend that instead of the term "voluntary segregation" we use and follow the path of voluntary integration, until the Supreme Court says "when and how." No child would be forced to attend any particular school and on the other hand, no child would be denied the right to attend a particular school, solely because of race, creed or color. We are willing to leave the details of a final plan to a fifty-man biracial committee.

With all the injustices that you have heaped upon the Negro in Mississippi, with all the inequalities which have been ours in the field of public education; with all the suffering which has been ours at your hands simply because the great God of the Ages made us black—with all that you have done, we have never let you down. We helped you drive out the wild beast, we cleared the wilderness, we have tilled your soil and made it the richest soil on earth. We have gone to the ends of the earth to fight, bleed and die for Democracy that even today we do not know anything about in Mississippi. We have never failed you or let you down. Through 250 years of slavery and 91 years of physical freedom you have taught us that the Constitution of the United States is the greatest document on earth. You have taught us to uphold and obey the laws of the land. During your present administration, Governor White, you have asked the Negro of Mississippi to accept the responsibility of citizenship. So today, when the eyes of the Democratic forces of the world are focused upon America, let us not reduce the Constitution to a mere scrap of paper by asking Negroes to help you evade the law of the land. A chain is no stronger than its weakest link. If Mississippi is a weak link in the chain of American Democracy—America is Weak.

Several months ago, I saw a painting in one of the colored schools in the state which was done by a teen-age plantation boy. It was the picture of an old Negro man sitting in a rocking chair. There were deep-bitten wrinkles in his dark face. His kinky, woolly hair had turned to a snowy white and there was a faraway expression in his age-dimmed eyes. At the old man's side stood a woolly-headed Negro boy who was looking up into the old man's face, with his little mouth opened. Under the picture these words were written, "Grandpa, what was slavery?"

Governor, every Negro before you today is looking forward to the day when right here in Mississippi our grandchildren will look into our faces and ask of us, "Grandpa, what was segregation and discrimination in a Democracy such as ours?"

Journal of Human Relations (a quarterly published by Central State College, Wilberforce, Ohio) 3: 104–7. (Autumn 1954)

26

MISSISSIPPI NEGROES TURN DOWN GOVERNOR'S "VOLUNTARY SEGREGATION PLAN" (1954)

The Mississippi governor, at the July 30, 1954, meeting, responded to Dr. Howard's remarks with proposals that, in effect, would retain segregation but in the guise of a "voluntary" agreement from the assembled black leadership. That leadership responded, the same day, with a statement issued "by Negro leaders from every area of the State of Mississippi." It warned of "the Kremlin's" interest and asked that "our state leaders and agencies will not ask us to do those things which will destroy our influence with our own people." The full text of the response to the governor follows.

The Jackson Declaration

The spotlight of our nation and of the world of free democratic peoples is upon the state of Mississippi today. They are looking to see what we are going to do. Even the Kremlin enemies of democracy are watching for an opportunity to catch us in a moment of weakness and to ridicule our institutions. Facing such a challenge we pray to God that we may not fail in our duty toward our state, toward democracy and toward our people. In this hour of destiny and for the sake of our posterity we cannot do otherwise than take our stand for the ideals of our America and the whole free world—for justice, human brotherhood and equality of opportunity for all.

I. Respect for law is the foundation of a free democratic society. Therefore, because of the obligations of citizenship and because any effort to circumvent the law would be in derogation of the paramount allegiance of the citizens of the state to the government of the United States, and therefore, in violation of Article 3, Section 7, of the Constitution of the State of Mississippi, we can do no other than to endorse and abide by the decision of May 17, 1954, of the Supreme Court of the United States.

II. We call to the attention of all citizens of Mississippi the urgent need to provide at once the additional desperately needed classrooms for the education of the children of the state. We invite all citizens to join hands to work for the common goal of more and better schools for every child in Mississippi.

III. As an aid to preparation and to help create that spiritual climate of understanding and mutual respect so necessary to the helpful achievement of these goals we propose the following considered action: That Negroes be appointed on all policy making Boards and Committees at all levels in matters of human relations.

IV. As a representative committee we respectfully request that our state leaders and agencies will not ask us to do those things which will destroy our influence with our own people. It is our declared aim to continue to do all in our power to preserve the present good relationship between the races that we have in Mississippi and to be worthy of the respect of citizens of both races.

V. Let us, therefore, rally to one standard—to remove as soon as possible from the lives of our children, both Negro and white, those severe penalties which they now suffer because of an inadequate and segregated system of education. The time has come to strike our tents of apathy, fear and reaction and to move forward together toward a bright future of greater opportunity for all. This we can do if we face this issue in the light of Christian vision and with faith in our fellow men.

VI. The satisfactory solution of the school problem is the keystone for the solution of many of the other vital problems in the State of Mississippi. The only solution to the school problem that Mississippi can morally and financially afford, and at the same time will meet the approval of the United States Supreme Court, is to consolidate and integrate the present schools on all levels and then equalize and expand within the framework of consolidation and integration. After these schools have become consolidated and integrated, equalization can then take place rapidly throughout the state and within the ability of the state to pay. The principal requirement under the consolidated and integrated program is that each child must attend the school nearest his or her home. In a state where the population of the two principal racial groups is approximately equal, it is not commendable but nevertheless true, that even under a consolidated and integrated program in Mississippi, the attendance in the schools will be largely white or largely colored, for the present at least, inasmuch as the residential areas are largely segregated. The end results of equalization within the framework of consolidation and integration will be a more enlightened, courageous and economically secure populace and thereby a better State, Country and World.

Journal of Human Relations, cited work, pp. 108–10.

27

RACISM IS SACRILEGIOUS (1954)

by Benjamin E. Mays

Benjamin E. Mays was president of Morehouse College in Atlanta for twenty-seven years; he had served as dean of religion at Howard University (1934–40) and in his final years was president of the Atlanta Board of Education.

Dr. Mays was an organizer, in 1948, of the World Council of Churches; as a member of the council's central committee he delivered a major address at its meeting at Northwestern University in August 1954. The concluding section, with its title supplied by the editor, follows:

My distinguished colleague, B. J. Marais, sought the thinking of the fourteen leading theologians of Europe on this subject, including Emil Brunner and Karl Barth. They all agree that we can find no justification in the Bible for a segregated church based on race or ethnic origin. This universalism in the gospel is climaxed and attested to by the fact that Christ died for all mankind. So if there are those among us who seek support in the Bible for segregated churches based on color, race, caste, or ethnic origin, they must turn elsewhere for support.

Your Commission has gone further. We have delved into church history: ancient, medieval, and modern. We have sought to find out what the churches have practiced through the centuries in their worship and fellowship. New Testament scholars and church historians all agree that since its inception the Christian church has had in its membership people of different nations, races, and even colors. Nowhere in the early church do we find distinctions drawn on the basis of country or race. James (2:1-6) condemns the separation of cultural and social groups in the local church. The fact that the early church drew no distinctions based on race or color, and that Christians were often described as a "new people" or a "third race," drawn from many racial or ethnic groups, is attested by

Tertullian, Origen, Ignatius, Hermas, Barnabas, Clement, and others. Their position is sustained by later scholars: Harnack and Ramsay, Cadoux and Moffatt, Griffith and Latourette. We seek in vain for signs of segregation based on race and color in the church of the first centuries of the Christian era.

What was true of the early church was true of the church of the Middle Ages. In both the ancient and the medieval church, the basis of membership was faith in Jesus Christ, our Lord. The basis of membership was faith, not race; Christ, not color; creedal acceptance, and not nationality. The creeds of Christendom have always been formulated and enforced in terms of certain beliefs about God, Jesus, man, sin, and salvation; never on theories about race or ethnic groups. In summarizing this fact, Marais says: "In the extensive literature of the history of the Church till after the Reformation, we look in vain for any sign of a racial basis for admission to the congregation." If color, race, or cultural background was a condition of membership in the local congregation of the early church or the local church of the Middle Ages, our survey does not reveal it.

It seems clear, then, that the color or racial bar in the church is a modern thing. It was not, in fact, until the seventeenth century that the outlines of the modern race problem began to emerge. It is the modern church that again crucifies the body of Christ on a racial cross. Race and color did not count in the early existence of the Protestant Church. It was when modern Western imperialism began to explore and exploit the colored peoples of Africa, Asia, and America, that the beginning of segregation and discrimination based on color and race was initiated. It was then that color was associated with "inferiority," and whiteness with "superiority." Our Commission writes: "The broad pattern of major racial group tensions which trouble the world today had its historical origins in the period of European overseas exploration and expansion into America, Asia, and Africa. The resulting exploitation of one group by another, involving groups differing in race, varied in the three countries. But the same general relation of asserted superiority and inferiority developed between the white world and the colored world. Color became first the symbol, and then the accepted characteristic of the intergroup tensions."

Your Commission concludes, therefore, that the modern church can find no support for this practice of segregation based on race, color, or ethnic origin in the Bible, no basis for it in the ancient and medieval churches, and none for it in the various theologists of the Catholic and Protestant churches.

Your Commission has probed beyond the church and the Bible. We have sought to find out what support modern science gives for segregation and discrimination. We could quote scientist after scientist on the question of whether there is or is not an inherent superiority which one race possesses over another. Forty or fifty years ago, scientists were divided on the subject. Also, men argued that some groups were biologically superior to others. Hundreds of volumes were written to justify a denial of equal opportunity to some peoples on the ground that they were inferior and that God had made them that way. But now there is no disagreement among the top scientists of the earth. As a recent UNESCO publication points out, "In matters of race, the only characteristics which anthropologists have so far been able to use effectively as a basis for classification are physical (anatomical and physiological). Available scientific knowledge provides no basis for believing that the groups of mankind differ in their innate capacity for intellectual and emotional development. Some biological differences between human beings within a single race may be as great or greater than the same biological differences between races." In another connection, the United Nations publication speaks for modern science on race: "All of us believe that the biological differences found amongst human racial groups can in no case justify the views of racial inequality which have been based on ignorance and prejudice, and that all of the differences which we know can well be disregarded for all ethical human purposes." At long last, science has caught up with religion, for it was Paul who declared, on Mars Hill nineteen centuries ago, that God made of one blood all nations of men.

If the church can find no support in science for ethnic and racial tension, none in the Bible for segregation based on race or color, none in the practices of the ancient and medieval churches, and none in Christian theologies, the questions naturally arise: How can segregation and discrimination in the church be justified? What can the churches do to put themselves in line with the gospel, the practices of the ancient and medieval churches, and in line with the findings of modern science? If the modern churches cannot practice full Christian fellowship in worship and membership, how can they preach the prophetic word to secular organizations that discriminate on grounds of race, color, and caste? To answer these questions is our task at Evanston. It is to these problems that the

Commission on the Church Amidst Ethnic and Racial Tensions will address itself.

There is one aspect of this subject which we often overlook. Usually the question is, what does discrimination or segregation do to the person segregated, to the disadvantaged person? It is conceded that segregation and discrimination hurt the pride of the person discriminated against, that they retard his mental, moral, and physical development, and that they rob society of what the disadvantaged group might contribute to enrich humanity. We agree that imposed separateness breeds ill-will and hatred, and that it develops in the segregated a feeling of inferiority to the extent that he never knows what his capabilities are. His mind is never free to develop unrestricted. The ceiling and not the sky becomes the limit of his striving.

But we seldom realize what discrimination does to the person who practices it. When we build fences to keep others out, erect barriers to keep others down, deny to them the freedom which we ourselves enjoy and cherish most, we keep ourselves in, hold ourselves down, and the barriers we erect against others become prison bars to our own souls. We cannot grow to the mental and moral stature of free men if we view life with prejudiced eyes, for thereby we shut our minds to truth and reality, which are essential to spiritual, mental, and moral growth. The time we should spend in creative activity we waste on small things which dwarf the mind and stultify the soul. It is both economically and psychologically wasteful. So it is not clear who is damaged more—the person who inflicts the discrimination or the person who suffers it, the man who is held down or the man who holds him down, the segregated or the segregator. Your Commission and the Assembly will wrestle with this problem.

The churches are called upon to recognize the urgency of the present situation. Even if we laid no claim to a belief in democracy, if the whole world were at peace internationally, if atheistic Communism had never developed, if Fascism had never been born and Nazism were wholly unknown, a nonsegregated church and social and economic justice for all men are urgent because we preach a universal gospel that demands that our deeds reflect our theory. To proclaim one thing and act another is sheer hypocrisy. It weakens the influence of the church, not only in its own fellowship but throughout the world. It hampers our efforts to evangelize Africa and Asia. It is not Communism, not Fascism, not the struggle between East and West, but the gospel itself which demands interracial justice and an unsegregated church. We should move inter-racially in the church, not from fear of Communism but from our "concern for our brother for whom Christ died." It has always been the responsibility of the church and the gospel to plow new ground, smash traditions, break the mores, and make new creatures. Such was the role of the Hebrew prophets, of Jesus and Paul, of the early church, of Savonarola and Martin Luther, of Livingston and Albert Schweitzer.

In the Commission we will wrestle with the ever present question, "To what extent is the church to be governed by expediency?" Is it wise to live up to the gospel we preach, or is it wiser to conform to the mandates of a secular society? Shall the church obey the laws of the state when they violate the laws of love, or the law of God which commands us to love one another? What should be the attitude of the churches toward laws that are obviously unjust and discriminatory? Obey them? Seek to change them? Violate them?

Finally, the task before the Commission and the Assembly is to show how the theme of the Assembly, *Christian Hope,* is related to racial and ethnic tensions, not only in the past days but in the present days. The major problem will not be to demonstrate from the Bible and from church history that it is only in modern times that race has become a basis for church membership. The task will be to show how the gospel of Christ can be presented and lived so as to make new creatures of men and women in the area of race, and bring hope and abundant life to all men—not only beyond history but in history. We refuse to believe that God is limited in history and that we must wait until the end of history before his mighty works can be performed.

We have known for centuries what the Bible says about race. We have known for a long time that the early church and the church of the Middle Ages did not segregate on the basis of race and ethnic origin. We know that there is no scientific basis for our treating one group as inferior to another. The gospel on race has been proclaimed for nineteen centuries. One world conference after another has condemned racial separation in the church. Yet segregation remains the great scandal in the church, especially in the United States and South Africa. The local churches permit secular bodies such as the state and federal courts, the United Nations, big league baseball, professional boxing, colleges and univer-sities, the public schools, and theaters to initiate social change in the area of race. But even when secular bodies initiate the change, local churches,

Negro and white, follow slowly or not at all. It will be a sad commentary on our life and time if future historians can write that the last bulwark of segregation based on race and color in the United States and South Africa was God's church.

We have plenty of light on the subject, but like Pilate of old we lack the will and moral courage to act on the light we have and the knowledge we possess. Clearly, knowledge is not enough. Paul knew this centuries ago when he said in essence, "I find myself doing that which I know I ought not to do and I find myself failing to do that which I know I ought to do." We quote Tennyson:

> Let knowledge grow from more to more,
> > But more of reverence in us dwell;
> > That mind and soul, according well,
> May make one music as before,
> But vaster...

Drinkwater likewise deserves to be used in this context when he profoundly wrote:

> Knowledge we ask not—knowledge Thou has lent,
> But, Lord, the will—there lies our bitter need,
> Give us to build above the deep intent
> > The deed, the deed.

Here at Evanston the church will want to know how to deal with race within its own membership, the local congregation. The question will be: How can the local church so exemplify the spirit of Christ in Christian fellowship that the world will be compelled to follow its example?

At this Assembly, the people will want to know whether the church has any responsibility as an organized group for the alleviation of racial injustice in social, political, and economic life. What is the church's responsibility as an organized group? What is the responsibility of the individual Christian? What is the church's duty toward assisting the individual to fulfill his Christian task in his daily vocation? Above all, we should ask ourselves the question: Can there be a Pentecost in 1954?

If there can be a Pentecost in 1954, the individual Christian will be responsive to the gospel and he will act on his Christian convictions. There is no dichotomy between what we believe and what we do. We do what we believe. If an atheistic Communist can act on his belief, a

Christian can act on his. If a Communist is willing to suffer for his convictions, go to jail and die for them, surely the followers of Christ's God can suffer for theirs. The true believer, like Peter, Paul, and Jesus, is not a slave to his environment. He can rise above it and transform it. He will testify to the unity in Christ by his daily deeds.

If there is to be a modern Pentecost, the church must do likewise in its worship and membership. It must also encourage its members to exemplify in their vocations this supra-racial unity in Christ. Being thus convinced, all Christians here in Evanston will take appropriate steps in their respective congregations to make it possible for the will of God to operate, to the end that all church doors will be opened in membership and worship to all who serve and love the Lord. For the church is God's creation, not man's, and it belongs to God. And in God's domain, all men are equal.

Benjamin E. Mays *Born To Rebel: An Autobiography,* (New York: Scribners, 1971), pp. 352–56.

28

A TEACHER LOOKS AT INTEGRATION (1954)

by Nick Aaron Ford

The widespread optimism with which much of the African-American population greeted the *Brown* decision, is a striking feature of the essay by a professor in the English department at Morgan State College in Baltimore. That it appeared in a publication of Atlanta University emphasizes this original sense of hopefulness.

On the afternoon of May 17, 1954, a few hours after the Supreme Court of the United States rendered its momentous decision against segregation in the public schools, I heard a white woman say, without anger or bitterness, "I don't understand why the Court wants to make Americans do things that are uncomfortable for both races."

She was speaking on a hastily prepared television program that was presenting samples of "on the spot" reactions to the big news that had announced the end of an eighty-year era. I was greatly impressed by the restraint and sincerity of this spokesman who undoubtedly expressed the feelings of a large segment of our national population. I was pleased with the kindly glow of her countenance and the absence of visible signs of rancor. I could sympathize with her bewilderment, for I could understand the basis of it.

As I sat before my television, I began to wonder what answer could be given to this genuine complaint. Probably a glance backward into history might help. The almost incredible hardships endured by the founding fathers as they struggled to establish a settlement in the new world were certainly not comfortable. But they neither hesitated nor complained, for they believed that the challenge of freedom and righteousness was more important than comfort. A roll call of all the great advances made by the benefactors of our civilization assures us that there was little comfort for the pioneers. We know that comfort is neither sought nor found on bloody battlefields, in stuffy laboratories, or in the deep caverns of excavations. Little men and little nations seek comfort; great men and great nations ask only for vision to see and know the right.

But despite the haste with which our bewildered lady was required to form her opinion of this legal revolution, she did not make the mistake, often made by the less thoughtful, of suggesting that most of the discomfort would fall upon the shoulders of the white race. Although the great majority of Negroes have been working and praying and fighting for many years to bring about this victory, the price for them has been and will continue to be high. Let us enumerate some of the losses Negroes will sustain.

First, unprepared Negro teachers who are now holding classes in dilapidated buildings in many rural areas of the South will not be able to move into an integrated system. While visiting a Negro college last summer in the deep South, I met one of these submarginal teachers who had come to take some summer courses. She occupied the chair beside me in the cafeteria and instigated the following exchange of conversation:

"Are you from these parts?" she asked.

"No," I answered, "I am from Baltimore."

"Where's that?" she inquired, puzzled.

"In Maryland," I said.

"Where's Maryland?" she continued, more puzzled.

"Above Washington, D.C.," I explained.

"That's a new one on me," she admitted, after shaking her head in apparent disbelief. "I ain't never heard of that state before."

After I had satisfied her that Maryland was somewhere in the United States, she wanted to know whether or not I thought Negro teachers would lose their jobs because of the Supreme Court decision. She said her county superintendent of education had told her that all colored teachers in the South would be fired if segregation should be abolished. She said she would like to see segregation end, but she would hate to lose her job. Her husband was dead and she had two young children to support. I told her that most likely she could find another kind of job and that she should be glad that her children would have a better chance than she had had to get a good education.

As I talked to her, my mind wandered to other situations where poorly prepared white teachers would lose too in competition with better prepared Negro teachers. I thought particularly of a large city in a border state where twenty percent of the white teachers who are not on permanent tenure do not have degrees, while all of the Negro teachers (plus a long list of applicants) have college degrees. Certainly, there will be losses for both races, but there will be gains that will outweigh the losses.

For Negroes, however, there will be another loss less tangible and more far-reaching than the one I have cited above. There will be the loss of the psychological wall of "racial defense" which has served to excuse the shortcomings of lazy, dishonest, unambitious Negroes for the past eighty years. No longer will a Negro's illiteracy be excused on the basis of lack of educational opportunity. No longer will certain unskilled jobs be "saved" for the Negro alone out of sympathy for his inability to compete on equal terms for jobs that require a reasonable degree of intelligence and education. No longer will cooks and maids in white people's employment be excused for using illiterate language and uncouth manners. When they are trained in the same schools and under the same wholesome conditions as people of all other races they will be expected to maintain the same standards of manners and conduct. To the lazy, shiftless, unambitious Negro, this will be a great loss indeed, and one for which he will find no compensation.

A third loss will occur in the area of racial leadership. During the past eighty years high qualities of leadership have been developed in countless Negroes in thousands of communities throughout the nation, for the grave problems that arose as a result of educational segregation demanded such leadership. Officers of Negro P.T.A.'s alone form a considerable number of men and women who but for such urgent need would probably have never developed their inherent powers to lead. In addition, numerous other organizations and associations were established to fight for better school facilities, to elect local school officials pledged to improve minority schools, and to supplement county and state aid to poorly supported schools. With no further need for such racial pressures, a large proportion of potential Negro leadership will be lost forever. But the leadership that develops through integration will be more skillful, more enlightened, and more effective, for it will emerge through wider and stronger competition.

On the other hand, the gains which will result from genuine integration will be tremendous. On the international political level it will give America a new opportunity to gain much lost respect and leadership among the darker peoples of the world, who represent approximately three-fourths of our global population. To the darker peoples, the policy of segregation in the southern part of our country could never be satisfactorily explained. A nation which seeks to lead the world in the ways of democracy must itself maintain a national policy of equality for all of its citizens. If a democratic nation does not exercise the power to maintain democracy within its own borders, how can it convince foreigners that it has the will to implant, to nurture, and to protect a democratic way of life in alien lands?

On the national political level a policy of integration will remove from the demagogue and the professional hypocrite the platforms of racial salvation and damnation upon which many state and national officeholders have climbed to power. Qualification for political office will no longer be based on the force or lack of force with which a candidate can propound his theories of race relations, but rather upon his competent training in the science and art of public service and his genuine interest in the common welfare of all the people. In the national Congress it will mean the virtual end of the filibuster, since this device has been used mainly to block legislation favorable to the safeguarding of the rights of the Negro minority.

In the field of medicine great impetus will be given to the Negro doctor to make a larger contribution to the health of the nation. Because of the denial of admission to practice in the great hospitals of the country, many skilled Negro surgeons are forced to bury their talents in the ill-equipped laboratories and operation rooms of second-class institutions. Who knows how many Charles Drews (the Negro doctor who first discovered how to preserve blood plasma) have been "forced to blush unseen and waste their fragrance upon the desert air." With the proper use of the full resources of Negro doctors and nurses, the health status of the nation will be improved immensely.

In industry a considerable rise in efficiency will result from the full integration of the Negro worker. With equal educational opportunities, the Negro will be prepared for numerous positions requiring special skills now denied him. The increased competition for skilled positions will result not only in more highly selected personnel, but also in the maintenance of a higher level of efficiency as an insurance against replacement. Furthermore, increased efficiency in unskilled jobs will be insured by the knowledge that all jobs will be filled on the basis of merit and not race. Many lazy, inefficient Negroes are now holding menial jobs in industry because those jobs are understood to be "Negro jobs." Consequently competition is only among unambitious, untrained members of one race. The removal of racial restrictions from top positions will be but a prelude to a similar treatment of all positions. Free competition on all levels of industry is bound to increase efficiency proportionately.

But, above all, the greatest gain from integration will be moral and spiritual. No longer will the white man be encouraged by custom and legal sanction to teach his children the outworn doctrine of racial superiority. To inflict upon one's children the false assumption of superiority on the basis of race is to tie a moral and spiritual millstone around the necks of those one loves. The countless stories of conversion (and the tortuous guilt complex that has followed) of those liberated souls who in their maturity have managed to break the stranglehold of such a doctrine are warnings which loving parents cannot afford to ignore. Before May 17 many patriotic, law-abiding white parents felt obligated to pass on the southern tradition of race relations to their children. The Supreme Court decision has now relieved them of that responsibility. They can hereafter be honest with themselves and their children without secretly feeling that they have betrayed a trust. In fact, unless they now refrain from such indoctrination they will find it difficult to reconcile their respect for law and order with their refusal to obey the law of the land as unanimously interpreted by the highest court in the land.

It is not my purpose here to minimize the struggle that many well-intentioned white southerners are now undergoing in the privacy of their own households and the secrecy of their own hearts as they valiantly attempt to conform to the precedent-shattering decision of the Supreme Court. Many of them have grave fears as to the desirability or workability of integration in the deep South. Let us examine some of these fears.

On the same television program with the bewildered lady previously described was another woman who represented another element of popular opinion. She was bitter. She was defiant. She had already made up her mind. "I'm against it!" she said. "It'll set back the education of white children fifty years. Our children will be saying 'dem there' and 'dis here' and all such broken language like that. Negro children will drag our children down to their level."

It is clear that this lady was afraid of the educational influence of Negro children upon the majority race. We must admit that many Negro children do come from homes in which illiterate language is used. But is the Negro race so superior that a few children who have not yet learned how to speak correct English can contaminate the many white children who do speak acceptably? Does it not seem more reasonable to expect that the Negro children, being members of the minority race, will be anxious to discard the dialect of the ghetto and to conform in every way possible to the majority pattern? In fact, one of the important arguments for integration is that it will hasten the conformity of the minority.

If the logic of our defiant lady were sound, it would be most unwise for white people to employ uneducated Negro women, or women of foreign extraction who cannot speak the English language correctly, to nurse their young children who are passing through the most impressionable stages. Does the illiterate language of a Negro nurse or cook or maid whom the children greatly admire warp the children's language out of its natural setting? All evidence proves the contrary. Then why should the language of a few Negro children for whom there is no special attachment be so much more powerful than that of the parents and intimate playmates?

Secondly, there is the fear that educational integration will lead to intermarriage. If children of various races are permitted to attend school together they will soon learn to disregard color as a measure of merit or worth or friendship and may even learn to like one another so well that romantic love might result. This, of course, to many white people is sufficient reason alone to forbid integration. In order not to prolong the discussion let us ignore the "rightness" or "wrongness" of such a result and comment only on the likelihood of its occurrence.

In such northern states as Pennsylvania, New Jersey, and New York there has always been educational integration, yet cases of intermarriage in those states are almost negligible. Strangely enough, a considerable number of those that do occur is made up of couples (the bride and the groom) who were born and reared in the South and educated in separate schools.

Thirdly, there is a fear that mixed schools in the South will lead to violence. This fear is completely contradicted by numerous experiences on other levels. Integration of adult civilians in defense plants in the South was effected without violence or bitterness. Integration of soldiers in southern training camps has been perfected without any untoward incidents. It is a common sight to see in such states as Georgia and South Carolina the finest kind of camaraderie between white and colored soldiers (both natives of those states) in the barracks, in the recreation rooms, and in groups hitchhiking on the highways. It is common knowledge that children have far less prejudice than adults. When the superintendent of education of a southern city was asked to express his opinion of the workability of integration in his city, he replied, "At least, we will have no trouble from the children."

In the light of the above discussion, it seems reasonable to expect, provided there is good will and good faith on the part of educational and political leaders as well as on the part of patriotic and law-abiding citizens, that integration in the schools will become an accomplished fact everywhere in America within the next two or three years.

Phylon, third quarter, 1954, vol. 15, pp. 261–66.

29

DEATH FOR THE 'MISERABLES' (1954)

by John H. McCray

Among the black leaders victimized by the repression described by the Reverend Edward D. McGowan, in an earlier selection, was John H. McCray, editor of a black newspaper in Columbia, South Carolina. He contributed a column fairly regularly in the 1950s to the influential *Afro-American* (Baltimore). Here is an example:

Unless Gov. James F. Byrnes commutes their sentences, two teenage boys will die in South Carolina's electric chair early on the morning of Oct. 15.

The youths are Frank Wilson, 16, and his brother, Charlie, 18.

Both were convicted of slaying a 15-year-old white youth, Glenn Farmer, who surprised them the night they let themselves into the fish market where Frank worked with a key he had evidently taken. The Lee County jury failed to recommend mercy and the death sentence was mandatory.

Many pleas and prayers that their lives will be spared are heard and read; and offering most of these are white citizens, churchfolk and women who head organizations and who are engaged in community services.

And the depths to which some of these citizens are moved indicates that underneath what may sometime seem to have been a calloused skin, beats a heart that is both warm and human.

One of these, a white Baptist minister, pleads that the state law which makes murder during a robbery a capital offense is mis-applied in their case. The law, he says, was intended for use when such a crime occurred in a residence.

If Frank and Charlie are electrocuted they will be numbers nine and ten of teenagers the chair has claimed since 1944—and everyone of them colored. Youngest among the eight electrocuted was George Stinney Jr., convicted when he was just 13 of "attempted criminal assault" on two white girls, eight and five years, respectively.

Accounts of his electrocution were ominous; the cap kept slipping and flopping about his small head as if in protest of its application.

Omitting discussion of the pros and cons of capital punishment, leaving out the declaration by a member of the S.C. Legislature 11 or 12 years ago that the electric chairs in his state were primarily "protection" for white people; ignoring even the technical and maybe conjectural points around the application of the state law in the Wilsons' case there is something else from which we cannot escape wrapped up in their plight, and other teenagers who've had to pay the supreme price.

Frank and Charlie, like too many others for whom now we fight, never had a fair chance in Bishopville. There are no recreation centers, no playgrounds—not anything for them and their kind.

Cotton fields and cheap farm pay, inadequate and grossly inferior schools, and an economically prostrate family, were some of the things they waded their way through.

They were too young to vote, too young to pay poll taxes; they were too young to join the Army and too young to make legal contracts.

But, by paradox perhaps, they are not too young to die under ramifications of laws imposed upon them by the same state.

Whatever their failings, their limitations, these were ground into them by their state and community. And there is something deeper, and meaningful aside from the obvious utter resignment and grief expressed in the terse words of their mother's letter of rejection of their bodies to penitentiary officials.

"You can keep Charlie's and Frank's bodies. Thank you," she wrote. Yes, keep the bodies of the "miserables" you have made.

Afro-American, October 16, 1954.

30

"TO KEEP FROM BEING INSULTED" (1954)

by Jo Ann Robinson

Four days after the May 17, 1954, *Brown* decision of the Supreme Court, African-American women of Montgomery, Alabama, sent a letter to the mayor that projected what became, within a year, the historic Montgomery bus boycott movement. The letter was signed by Jo Ann Robinson, president of the city's Women's Political Council. It was dated May 21, 1954, but the city's receipt stamp, for unclear reasons, is July 26, 1954. Here is a copy of this letter:

Honorable Mayor W. J. Gayle
City Hall
Montgomery, Alabama

Dear Sir:

The Women's Political Council is very grateful to you and the City Commissioners for the hearing you allowed our representatives during the month of March, 1954, when the "city-bus-fare-increase case" was being reviewed.

There were several things the Council asked for:

1. A city law that would make it possible for Negroes to sit from back toward front, and whites from front toward back until all the seats are taken:

2. That Negroes not be asked or forced to pay fare at front and go to the rear of the bus to enter:

3. That busses stop at every corner in residential sections occupied by Negroes as they do in communities where whites reside.

We are happy to report that busses have begun stopping at more corners now in some sections where Negroes live than previously. However, the same practices seating and boarding the bus continue.

Mayor Gayle, three-fourths of the riders of these public conveyances are Negroes. If Negroes did not patronize them, they could not possibly operate.

More and more of our people are already arranging with neighbors and friends to ride to keep from being insulted and humiliated by bus drivers.

There has been talk from twenty-five or more local organizations of planning a city-wide boycott of busses. We, sir, do not feel that forceful measures are necessary in bargaining for a convenience which is right for all bus passengers. We, the Council, believe that when this matter has been put before you and the Commissioners, that agreeable terms can be met in a quiet and sensible manner to the satisfaction of all concerned.

Many of our Southern cities in neighboring states have practiced the policies we seek without incident whatsoever. Atlanta, Macon and Savannah in Georgia have done this for years. Even Mobile, in our own state, does this and all the passengers are satisfied.

Please consider this plea, and if possible, act favorably upon it, for even now plans are being made to ride less, or not at all, on our busses. We do not want this.

Respectfully yours,

The Women's Political Council

Jo Ann Robinson, President

David J. Garrow, ed., *The Montgomery Bus Boycott and the Women Who Made It: The Memoir of Jo Ann Gibson Robinson* (Knoxville: Univ. of Tennessee Press, 1987).

31

HISTORY IN THE MAKING: MONTGOMERY, ALABAMA

The preface to Mrs. Robinson's *Memoir* sets the stage for the boycott that shook the nation:

Montgomery, Alabama!
Third largest city in the state, and once the capital of the Confederacy of

the eleven southern states that waged the Civil War against the rest of the United States. The home of Big Jim Folsom, once-powerful governor of Alabama, and also of controversial Governor George Wallace, who suffered the bullet of a would-be assassin that left him a cripple and virtually an invalid.

Montgomery, whose state capital buildings sit high on a hill, overlooking the beautiful southern city below, pierced by its main artery, Dexter Avenue. Dexter audaciously and conspicuously provides space for the Dexter Avenue Baptist Church for black people, where Dr. Martin Luther King, Jr., leader of the 1955–1956 Montgomery Bus Boycott, served as pastor.

Dr. King and I often discussed the probability that Montgomery was the only city that a boycott could have thrived in. For Montgomery was a college town. Alabama State College was an institution of which the black masses took advantage. It did not take in all the masses, but the so-called "upper crust" graduated from college with degrees. They were well read. Parents worked days and went to college nights. Children went to college because the college was there. The effect on attitudes was amazing: few inferiority complexes, no fear of "whitey," great faith in self, in families, and in people. A college town develops attitudes of defiance against discrimination, and people there are less prone to succumb to force. It also cultivates desires for learning and generates some philosophic depth.

Even so, in Montgomery, before December 5, 1955, thousands of black citizens gave every impression of being willing to go on enduring discrimination on buses, suffering humiliation and embarrassment, for the sake of peace. In the words of the poet Paul Laurence Dunbar, they wore "the mask that grins and lies" to hide their hurt feelings. Many white people thought blacks were a "happy-go-lucky" people. Although blacks felt they were being deprived of their rights, they endured nevertheless, complacent and tolerant, though dreading every ocassion on which they had to accept the treatment they received on buses. They complained and grumbled among themselves but kept on enduring, riding the monsters for the sake of peace.

The bus boycott originated in the demeaning, wretched, intolerable impositions and conditions that black citizens experienced in a caste system commonly called segregation. The segregated bus system had existed for over half a century. Although from the beginning protests had been registered repeatedly, black people had had no choice. The system confined them, but it could not obliterate their bitterness, humiliation, and anger. They were determined to get an education, to become financially secure, so that when the time came they would be prepared to walk away from the system. And on December 5, 1955, fifty thousand people—the generally estimated black population—walked off public city buses in defiance of existing conditions which were demeaning, humiliating, and too intolerable to endure.

For thirteen months they refused to ride those carriers, until conditions had been changed to meet their approval. And in December 1956, thirteen long months after the bus boycott began, the federal courts ordered the buses integrated, and buses began operating without segregation or discrimination.

David Garrow, ed., cited work, pp. 7–8.

32

THE VOLCANO ERUPTS (1954)

by Jo Ann Robinson

On March 2, 1955, a young black woman, Claudette Colvin, after refusing to vacate her seat on a city bus, was brutally removed and arrested. Preliminary defense efforts by organized African-American groups led their members to believe Ms. Colvin would not be convicted, but, at most, reprimanded. But:

Claudette Colvin's case came up, but instead of being tried under the city law, under which she was arrested and booked, she was tried under state law. (While the city ordinance provided that no one could be convicted of failing to vacate a seat unless another seat was available for that person, the state law contained no such requirement, and simply gave drivers the legal authority to assign seats as they chose.)

Instead of being exonerated as we anticipated, Claudette Colvin was found guilty and released on indefinite probation in her parents' care. She had remained calm all during the days of her waiting period and during the trial, but when she was found guilty, Claudette's agonized sobs penetrated the atmosphere of the courthouse. Many people brushed away their own tears.

The verdict was a bombshell! Blacks were as near a breaking point as they had ever been. Resentment, rebellion, and unrest were evident in all Negro circles. For a few days, large numbers refused to use the buses, but as they cooled off somewhat, they gradually drifted back. Cold weather and rain, too, encouraged a return to the buses. But there was much discontented grumbling; complaints streamed in from everywhere to attest to people's resentment.

The public reaction was sympathetic to Claudette. Many black and white people contributed money to help with her case, which was appealed to a higher court. White people as far away as California and Oregon sent money to help pay legal fees. Hundreds of expressions of support from people throughout the country encouraged her and boosted her morale....

In October 1955, Mary Louise Smith, an eighteen-year-old black girl, was arrested and fined for refusing to move to the rear of the bus. Her case was unpublicized and no one knew about it until after her arrest and conviction. She, too, was found guilty; she paid her fine and kept on riding the bus.

Intermittently, twenty to twenty-five thousand black people in Montgomery rode city buses, and I would estimate that, up until the boycott of December 5, 1955, about three out of five had suffered some unhappy experience on the public transit lines. But the straw that broke the camel's back came on Thursday, December 1, 1955, when an incident occurred which was almost a repeat performance of the Claudette Colvin case.

In the afternoon of Thursday, December 1, a prominent black woman named Mrs. Rosa Parks was arrested for refusing to vacate her seat for a white man. Mrs. Parks was a medium-sized, cultured mulatto woman; a civic and religious worker; quiet, unassuming, and pleasant in manner and appearance; dignified and reserved; of high morals and a strong character. She was—and still is, for she lives to tell the story—respected in all black circles. By trade she was a seamstress, adept and competent in her work.

Tired from work, Mrs. Parks boarded a bus. The "reserved seats" were partially filled, but the seats just behind the reserved section were vacant, and Mrs. Parks sat down in one. It was during the busy evening rush hour. More black and white passengers boarded the bus, and soon all the reserved seats were occupied. The driver demanded that Mrs. Parks get up and surrender her seat to a white man, but she was tired from her work.

Besides, she was a woman, and the person waiting was a man. She remained seated. In a few minutes, police summoned by the driver appeared, placed Mrs. Parks under arrest, and took her to jail.

It was the first time the soft-spoken, middle-aged woman had been arrested. She maintained decorum and poise, and the word of her arrest spread. Mr. E.D. Nixon, a longtime stalwart of our NAACP branch, along with liberal white attorney Clifford Durr and his wife Virginia, went to jail and obtained Mrs. Parks's release on bond. Her trial was scheduled for Monday, December 5, 1955.

The news traveled like wildfire into every black home. Telephones jangled; people congregated on street corners and in homes and talked. But nothing was done. A numbing helplessness seemed to paralyze everyone. Very few stayed off the buses the rest of that day or the next. There was fear, discontent, and uncertainty. Everyone seemed to wait for someone to *do* something, but nobody made a move. For that day and a half, black Americans rode the buses as before, as if nothing had happened. They were sullen and uncommunicative, but they rode the buses. There was a silent, tension-filled waiting. For blacks were not talking loudly in public places—they were quiet, sullen, waiting. Just waiting!

Thursday evening came and went. Thursday night was far spent, when, at about 11:30 P.M., I sat alone in my peaceful single-family dwelling on a quiet street. I was thinking about the situation. Lost in thought, I was startled by the telephone's ring. Black attorney Fred Gray, who had been out of town all day, had just gotten back and was returning the phone message I had left for him about Mrs. Parks's arrest. Attorney Gray, though a very young man, had been one of my most active colleagues in our previous meetings with bus company officials and Commissioner Birmingham. A Montgomery native who had attended Alabama State and been one of my students, Fred Gray had gone on to law school in Ohio before returning to his home town to open a practice with the only other black lawyer in Montgomery, Charles Langford.

Fred Gray and his wife Bernice were good friends of mine, and we talked often. In addition to being a lawyer, Gray was a trained, ordained minister of the gospel, actively serving as assistant pastor of Holt Street Church of Christ.

Tonight his voice on the phone was very short and to the point. Fred was shocked by the news of Mrs. Parks's arrest. I informed him that I already was thinking that the WPC should distribute thousands of notices calling for all bus riders to stay off the buses on Monday, the day of Mrs. Parks's trial. "Are you ready?" he asked. Without hesitation, I assured him that we were. With that he hung up, and I went to work.

I made some notes on the back of an envelope: "The Women's Political Council will not wait for Mrs. Parks's consent to call for a boycott of city buses. On Friday, December 2, 1955, the women of Montgomery will call for a boycott to take place on Monday, December 5."

Some of the WPC officers previously had discussed plans for distributing thousands of notices announcing a bus boycott. Now the time had come for me to write just such a notice. I sat down and quickly drafted a message and then called a good friend and colleague, John Cannon, chairman of the business department at the college, who had access to the college's mimeograph equipment. When I told him that the WPC was staging a boycott and needed to run off the notices, he told me that he too had suffered embarrassment on the city buses. Like myself, he had been hurt and angry. He said that he would happily assist me. Along with two of my most trusted senior students, we quickly agreed to meet almost immediately, in the middle of the night, at the college's duplicating room. We were able to get three messages to a page, greatly reducing the number of pages that had to be mimeographed in order to produce the tens of thousands of leaflets we knew would be needed. By 4 A.M. Friday, the sheets had been duplicated, cut in thirds, and bundled. Each leaflet read:

Another Negro woman has been arrested and thrown in jail because she refused to get up out of her seat on the bus for a white person to sit down. It is the second time since the Claudette Colvin case that a Negro woman has been arrested for the same thing. This has to be stopped. Negroes have rights, too, for if Negroes did not ride the buses, they could not operate. Three-fourths of the riders are Negroes, yet we are arrested, or have to stand over empty seats. If we do not do something to stop these arrests, they will continue. The next time it may be you, or your daughter, or mother. This woman's case will come up on Monday. We are, therefore, asking every Negro to stay off the buses Monday in protest of the arrest and trial. Don't ride the buses to work, to town, to school, or anywhere on Monday. You can afford to stay out of school for one day if you have no other way to go except by bus. You can also afford to stay out of town for one day. If you work, take a cab, or walk. But please, children and grown-ups, don't ride the bus at all on Monday. Please stay off of all buses Monday.

Between 4 and 7 A.M., the two students and I mapped out distribution routes for the notices. Some of the WPC officers previously had discussed how and where to deliver thousands of leaflets announcing a boyott, and those plans now stood me in good stead. We outlined our routes, arranged the bundles in sequences, stacked them in our cars, and arrived at my 8 A.M. class, in which both young men were enrolled, with several minutes to spare. We weren't even tired or hungry. Just like me, the two students felt a tremendous sense of satisfaction at being able to contribute to the cause of justice.

After class my two students and I quickly finalized our plans for distributing the thousands of leaflets so that one would reach every black home in Montgomery. I took out the WPC membership roster and called the former president, Dr. Mary Fair Burks, then the Pierces, the Glasses, Mrs. Mary Cross, Mrs. Elizabeth Arrington, Mrs. Josie Lawrence, Mrs. Geraldine Nesbitt, Mrs. H. Councill Trenholm, Mrs. Catherine N. Johnson, and a dozen or more others. I alerted all of them to the forthcoming distribution of the leaflets, and enlisted their aid in speeding and organizing the distribution network. Each would have one person waiting at a certain place to take a package of notices as soon as my car stopped and the young men could hand them a bundle of leaflets.

Then I and my two student helpers set out. Throughout the late morning and early afternoon hours we dropped off tens of thousands of leaflets. Some of our bundles were dropped off at schools, where both students and staff members helped distribute them further and spread the word for people to read the notices and then pass them on to neighbors. Leaflets were also dropped off at business places, storefronts, beauty parlors, beer halls, factories, barber shops, and every other available place. Workers would pass along notices both to other employees as well as to customers.

During those hours of crucial work, nothing went wrong. Suspicion was never raised. The action of all involved was so casual, so unconcerned, so nonchalant, that suspicion was never raised, and neither the city nor its people ever suspected a thing! We never missed a spot. And no one missed a class, a job, or a normal routine. Everything was done by the plan, with perfect timing. By 2 o'clock, thousands of the mimeographed handbills had changed hands many times. Practically every black man, woman, and child in Montgomery knew the plan and was passing the word along. No one knew where the notices had come from or who had arranged for their circulation, and no one cared. Those who passed them on did so efficiently, quietly, and without comment. But deep within the heart of every black person was a joy he or she dared not reveal....

Before Monday was half gone, Negroes had made history. Never before had they united in such a manner. There was open respect and admiration in the eyes of many whites who had looked on before, dubious and amused. Even clerks in dime stores, all white, were more cordial. They were heard to add, after a purchase by a black customer, "Y'all come back to see us," which was a very unusual occurrence. The black customers held their heads higher. They felt reborn, important for the first time. A greater degree of race pride was exhibited. Many were themselves surprised at the response of the masses, and could not explain, if they had wanted to, what had changed them overnight into fearless, courageous, proud people, standing together for human dignity, civil rights, and, yes, self-respect! There was a stick-togetherness that drew them like a magnet. They showed a genuine fondness for one another. They were really free— free inside! They felt it! Acted it! Manifested it in their entire beings! They took great pride in being black.

The Monday Night Meeting at Holt Street Church

Six thousand black people, along with local reporters, packed Holt Street Baptist Church that night, December 5, 1955, for the first mass meeting of the bus boycott. In the main auditorium, the balcony, the basement, the aisles, steps, the front, side, and back yards, and for three blocks up and down Holt Street, people crowded near to hear what was said. Loud-speakers were set up so that crowds who sat in parked cars two blocks away could hear. Police cars patrolling the area warned those inside the church to turn down the volume, which was disturbing the people outside, but no one paid any attention. The volume stayed loud.

White journalists from Montgomery and other nearby places were on hand to report the news of the boycott. Cameras flashed repeatedly, taking pictures of the thousands gathered in the church. So intent were the people on what was being said that the photographers went unnoticed.

The pulpit was jammed with Baptist, Methodist, Congregational, Catholic, and other ministers, and with organization officials. They conducted a spirited devotion of prayer and hymns. Prayers were offered for "endurance, tolerance, faith in God." There were prayers for the city commissioners; for "misguided whites"; for the weak; and for all races and nations. People felt the spirit. Their enthusiasm inundated them, and they overflowed with "powerful emotion."

Reverend Ralph Abernathy, presiding, said the boycott was not a one-man show, nor a preacher's show, but the show of 45,000 black

Montgomerians. It was also a show of black Americans all over America and all over the world and of freedom-loving people everywhere. When one ministerial spokesman after another told of the tremendous success of the one-day boycott, cries of joy and thunderous applause pealed forth and "ascended the heavens to God Almighty," as one present was heard to say.

The leaders reiterated that the protest had been and would be kept Christian, non-violent, legal. Even Joe Azbell, city editor of the *Montgomery Advertiser*, seemed impressed, for in his article on Wednesday, December 7, he confessed that "there was discipline among Negroes which whites were not aware of."

When the question was posed as to whether the people would end the one-day bus boycott, thousands of voices shouted the same word, "No! No!" One lone voice cried out in clear tones, "This is just the beginning!" Thunderous applause was the response.

Those on the podium agreed, without one dissenting vote, that the protest must continue. Ministers pledged themselves and their congregations to remain off the buses until legal steps were taken that would insure fair, unbiased, equal treatment of all bus passengers. Mr. E.D. Nixon received an ovation when he observed that "Negroes stopped riding the bus because they were arrested, and now they are being arrested for not riding them."

As the *Alabama Journal* reported the next day, the Negroes passed a four-part resolution urging:

1. All citizens of Montgomery "regardless of race, color, or creed" to refrain from riding buses owned and operated by the City Lines Bus Company "until some arrangement has been worked out between said citizens and the bus company."
2. That every person owning or who has access to automobiles will use them in assisting other persons to get to work "without charge."
3. That employers of persons who live a great distance from their work, "as much as possible" provide transportation for them.
4. That the Negro citizens of Montgomery are ready and willing to send a delegation to the bus company to discuss their grievances and to work out a solution for the same.

At these times, after almost two months had passed and with no end in sight, groups of widely-read pedestrians, picked up along the way and carried home, would get into deep conversations when their faith wavered in the balance. Indeed, one must wonder about the peculiar turns that things take sometimes, and about the controlling force that may compel them. Call it fate, destiny, a trick of nature, or the will of God, there is an inexplicable something, a force or power that seems to direct men's lives and twist them into some particular shape. Sometimes that shape is good, sometimes not so good.

During such periods of intense suffering—and people did suffer, mentally, spiritually, and financially—there were those weary souls who began to question God's presence, to wonder where God was and if God was really with the whites on segregation. Even the white man's religion, some said, seemed to be based to a great extent on segregation and white supremacy. Then some mused, "Is God white?"

So they would reason as we drove along, going home from a hard day's work. "Whites were born into, and have lived a lifetime enjoying the role of the superior, feasting their egos on the belief in racial supremacy. To these people, blacks are not equal."

"Yes, those folks don't believe in racial equality, and because of that belief, they think that black people can exist on less than the whites can."

"Separate but equal is right, but it's this separate but unequal that is killing us."

"In the separate schools, libraries, recreational parks, types of employment, salaries, waiting rooms, drinking fountains—no matter what—there has not been equality."

Many of these people had become disillusioned with life itself and wondered at the hypocrisy of it all. How could one set of human beings be so cruel and inhuman to another set, just because of the color of their skin and the texture of their hair? Was it because the side in control *was* superior? Or were whites afraid that, if the other side was given a chance, *it* would prove superior? Was the white man really afraid of the black man?

Most of the drivers who picked up pedestrians as they walked along, tired and hungry, would find a way to bring them out of such moods. We would tell a joke on "whitey" that showed him in a less exalted position than someone had just pictured him in, and everybody would laugh. In no time they would have forgotten the ugly mood they were in and begin all over again. . . .

The Last Mile

Almost four months had passed since December 5, 1955. Every plan the City Fathers had proposed to end the boycott had failed. Most of

Montgomery's buses stood dusty and empty where they had been parked at Christmas. The MIA had developed its own free transportation service. There was a general belief that the situation could and would go on indefinitely.

The MIA continued to receive funds from all parts of the U.S. and many places abroad. People from across the world still came to see and write about the situation.

Each Monday night thousands of people attended the weekly mass meetings. Collections were always taken, and every person who could contributed religiously and generously of her or his earnings to operate the transportation services. All of us who had steady jobs continued to give a percentage of our earnings each week, as we had since the beginning of the boycott. Drivers were paid regularly and were satisfied with their salaries. The station wagons had to be kept in good repair; fuel bills were enormous. The more money we needed, the more people, locally and elsewhere, seemed to give. The giving, the sharing, the serving continued on throughout the spring, summer, and fall of 1956. By April it was clear that the bus company and Montgomery's City Fathers had realized that black Americans meant it when they said they would never return to the buses except on an integrated basis, for all other efforts to get city buses rolling again had failed. Then our case in the federal courts began to move forward.

On May 11, a three-judge federal court, sitting in the federal courthouse in downtown Montgomery, heard arguments in the MIA'S suit seeking a declaration that racially segregated seating on city buses violated the 14th Amendment's guarantee of equal government treatment of all citizens, irrespective of race, as the Supreme Court already had ruled on with regard to schools in its 1954 landmark opinion in *Brown v. Board of Education of Topeka*.

Several weeks later, on June 5, the judges announced that they had voted two to one against the constitutionality of segregated seating on Montgomery's city buses. Relegating black riders to the rear of city buses, or forcing them to stand over empty seats reserved for whites, or making them surrender seats to white passengers, were all unconstitutional practices.

Judge Richard T. Rives wrote the 2-to-1 majority decision. U.S. District Court Judge Frank M. Johnson joined him in the majority opinion. Their opinion struck down as unconstitutional the statutes requiring racially segregated seating on city buses.

After their opinion, the two judges were deluged for months with hate mail, abusive telephone calls, and threats from segregationists for the stand they took and the opinion they gave that helped to wipe out segregation. Old friends no longer spoke to them. Black Montgomerians, however, will never forget either Rives or Johnson.

Montgomery city officials, though, did not celebrate or welcome Rives' and Johnson's ruling. Instead, they announced they would appeal the decision to the U.S. Supreme Court. Five months passed without any resolution of the matter. The city's buses remained segregated, and the MIA's transportation system continued to function most effectively. Then, in mid-November, just as the City Commission, under prodding from local segregationists, moved in state court to enjoin the operation of our carpool system, the U.S. Supreme Court issued a brief but decisive order, upholding Rives' and Johnson's ruling that Montgomery's buses had to be integrated. We thought at first that the change would take effect immediately, but then learned, to our dismay, that the order would be effective only when formally served on Montgomery officials. The City Commission, however, seeking to postpone as long as possible the arrival of that order, petitioned the Supreme Court to reconsider its ruling. The court rejected that request, but the legal maneuvering delayed matters for several weeks, and it was not until Thursday, December 20, that U.S. marshals formally served the Supreme Court order on city officials. That night the MIA held two mass meetings, and the next morning Montgomery City Lines resumed full service on all routes. Among its first passengers of the day were Mrs. Parks, Dr. King, and Reverend Abernathy, who boarded an early morning bus and took seats in what had once been the reserved, whites-only section as news photographers snapped pictures of the historic event. . . .

After some time had passed, between 1958 and 1960, news spread that some of the teachers of Alabama State College, who supposedly had been supporters of the boycott, were being investigated by a special state committee. I was still teaching at Alabama State College when this took place. These tensions were heightened in the spring of 1960, when some of our students "sat in" at the Montgomery County courthouse's segregated snack bar and were arrested. As the political pressures on the college increased, I resigned in the summer of 1960 and accepted a teaching position elsewhere.

The first professor affected was the chairman of the history department, Dr. Lawrence D. Reddick. A scholar interested in preserving historical documents for future generations, he had attended many sessions of the boycott movement on Monday nights, recording data for a biography of Dr. King, *Crusader Without Violence* that was published in 1959. Reddick was tried in absentia, without a hearing, we were informed, and was never given the opportunity to defend himself or to ascertain why he was being terminated. Instead, he was ordered by state officials to "leave the campus of Alabama State College and the City of Montgomery!"

Also in trouble was the brilliant English teacher, founder and staunch supporter of the WPC, Dr. Mary Fair Burks. Her crime was that she manifested interest in making conditions better for people to live creatively and prosperously, by becoming involved and helping to improve conditions. Like me, she also chose to resign in 1960.

During those years the power of the presidency was taken from Dr. Trenholm by white state officials, although he remained the president in name. All of us teachers at the college began having evaluators from the state's education department visit our classrooms. They sat taking notes all during the class periods. This went on for some time, though nothing explicitly came of it, as far as I know. Teachers did not seem to mind, however, though all knew that the move was one of intimidation. The teachers' records, which had been requested earlier, must have been satisfactory, for after 1960 no more teachers were dismissed, no students were expelled, and the college family breathed a sigh of relief when the ordeal was over.

However, the boycott had affected everyone at Alabama State. There had been mental strain on the administration, the faculty, and the student body. Dr. Trenholm had suffered as a result of the boycott, though he had not been directly involved. Many of the teachers, including myself, were weary. We had been loyal to the institution, to Dr. Trenholm, to our profession. We were not subversive. We had just gotten tired of being second-class citizens!

In 1960, on the last day of the spring semester, a large number of faculty members, some of whom had taught at Alabama State for thirty years (I had been there for eleven), resigned. Oddly enough, not one of us knew that the others were resigning. Time hadn't permitted us to talk to each other. None of us had other jobs in hand at the time. But we felt that insecurity was better than these jobs, which were proving a constant threat to our peace of mind. We knew, too, that we were well-trained, experienced, with excellent records, and that we could get other jobs.

Garrow, cited work, pp. 42–47; 61–63; 112–13; 161–63; 168–69.

33

MISSISSIPPI AND FREEDOM (1955)

by Paul Robeson

Foretelling the historic upsurge of the late 1950s were developments in Mississippi, where the fiercest repression existed. The 1954 dispatch from Mound Bayou, printed in earlier pages, is background for the column by Paul Robeson that appeared early in 1955; an extract follows:

It is one thing to sit in New York, Chicago, Detroit and Los Angeles and say what Negroes in Mississippi should do or should have done, but it is another to live one's life out in the face of the most rabid of racists, armed with the power of the state and the actual support or hypocritical "neutrality" of the federal government, and still survive and make progress.

But that's what the valiant Negroes of Mississippi have done. They have, as it were, for the past 80 years been preparing for major battles— husbanding their strength, preparing their leaders, mastering the tactics of popular democratic struggle. They have sent their young men and women away to schools which provide greater opportunities than those afforded in the state and many, though not enough, have returned to take up front positions in the movement for equality.

Now, after all these years, the battle has been joined on a new and higher level. The NAACP, which for years had only negligible strength in Mississippi, can now boast a considerable and growing organization. Dr. T.R.M. Howard, militant surgeon of Mound Bayou, leader of the important fraternal order, the Knights and Daughters of Mount Tabor, has emerged along with others as an energetic and resourceful leader. The libertarian currents abroad in the world have stimulated the freedom-yearnings of Negroes and many veterans of World War II are impatient for the realization of the "promissory note" of equality in the name of which that great anti-Hitler conflict was waged.

So, today, Negroes of Mississippi, as of the whole South, are demanding implementation of the Supreme Court decision on segregation in education.

And as might be expected, the Dixiecrats have responded with howls of anguish and threats of retaliation. They have done this, of course, all over the South. But in Mississippi their retaliation has gone well beyond the point of threats.

The planters have organized a new Ku Klux Klan. They have laundered it a bit, given it a face-lifting, and called it White Citizens Councils. But no Negro in Mississippi will be fooled. He knows the Klan when he sees it, by whatever name it's called.

The misnamed Councils have begun to exert economic pressure on the leaders and membership of the NAACP. Are you a grocer, funeral director, physician, small farmer? Then the likelihood is that you could not function without credit. But the credit is in the hands of the banks and mortgage companies, dominated by the planters and big Wall Street concerns.

So, say the Citizen Councils, since we control the credit, we'll control the Negroes! We'll starve their leaders out. We'll draw up a new kind of blacklist, and any Negro who supports NAACP or calls for equality in education will have to find his living outside of Mississippi.

But the planters have reckoned without their hosts! When Governor Hugh White called what he thought were 100 "hand-picked" Negroes to his office to euchre them into endorsing a statement opposing the Supreme Court decision, they voted 99 to one for integration of education. In Mississippi, that takes courage!

And the response to the economic boycott of the Citizens Councils has been just as dramatic. Within three weeks, under the leadership of the NAACP national office, organizations and individuals from all parts of the country have deposited $143,000 in the Negro-owned Tri-State Bank of Memphis to provide lending capital for Negro businessmen, professionals and farmers who are being foreclosed by the "free enterprise" Dixiecrats of Mississippi.

All decent Americans are called upon to rally to the heroic Negro people of Mississippi. I should like to see the great organizations of labor deposit large sums in the Tri-State bank to help in this fight. The

Brotherhood of Sleeping Car Porters has already deposited $10,000. Other groups may deposit smaller, or larger, sums.

We must support the demand that President Eisenhower intervene and prosecute those who are violating federal law and regulations by deliberately withholding economic loans for political reasons.

Messages of moral support and solidarity should pour in to Dr. T.R.M. Howard at Mound Bayou, Mississippi.

Eventually as the struggle deepens, as it must, new forms of battle will be needed and found. At the moment we must use those at hand to sustain the brave Negro people of Mississippi.

We must support their movement for the right to vote so that with political power they may be armed with the guarantees of implementation of legislative enactments and judicial decrees. We must focus the attention of the entire nation on this critical front in the battle for democracy. This is Negro history in the making.

Freedom, February 1955; in P. S. Foner, *Paul Robeson Speaks*, 394–96.

34

THE MEANING OF BANDUNG (1955)

by W. Alphaeus Hunton

Dr. Hunton taught at Howard University for seventeen years; in 1943 he became educational director and then executive secretary of the Council of African Affairs, a position he held until McCarthyite pressures caused its demise in 1955. Dr. Du Bois, in his foreword to the book from which the following extract is taken, wrote, "I know of no one today who has a more thorough knowledge and understanding" of Africa.

At the Asian-African Conference held at Bandung, Indonesia, April, 1955, the voices of the peoples of the two continents were heard in a united declaration of their determination to submit no longer to the dictation of others, but to chart their own path of progress, freedom and peace; to accept no longer an inferior status among nations, but to assert their right to cooperate as equals in the advancement of all mankind. The Bandung Conference, attended by the official representatives of 29 countries embracing nearly a billion and a half inhabitants, marked a turning point. It represented the end of an historical era in which only white nations, with very few exceptions, could lay claim to the exercise of sovereign rights.

Bandung was a living demonstration of the practicability of coexistence. The delegates present represented practically every existing religious creed, political principle, and economic system; there were Christians and Shintoists, democrats and monarchists, communists and capitalists. Despite sharp exchanges of differences on some issues, they agreed unanimously on the final all-embracing Joint Communique. Said China's Premier Chou En-lai:

> The course which we peoples of the Asian and African countries have taken in striving for freedom and independence may vary, but our will to win and to preserve our freedom and independence is the same. However different the specific conditions in each of our countries may be, it is equally necessary for most of us to eliminate the state of backwardness caused by the rule of colonialism. We need to develop our countries independently with no outside interference and in accordance with the will of the people. The people of Asia and Africa... know that new threats of war will not only endanger the independent development of their countries, but also intensify their enslavement by colonialism. That is why the Asian and African peoples all the more hold dear world peace and national independence.

Such was the general common denominator of agreement. Said Indonesia's President Soekarno:

> What can we do? We can do much! We can inject the voice of reason into world affairs and mobilize all the spiritual, all the moral, and the political strength of Asia and Africa, on the side of peace.... We can demonstrate to the minority of the world, which lives on other continents, that we, the majority, are for peace, not for war.

Bandung signalized the fact that in the traditional continental strongholds of colonialism, and particularly Asia, the anti-imperialist forces had advanced to the state of taking in the whole world and not simply the boundaries of their respective countries as the province of their responsibility. It was the culmination of various Pan-African and Pan-Asian movements that first emerged after World War I, but which could not achieve full stature and unified form until solid gains had been made in the struggle for national liberation. It was at the same time the answer to an urgent need. Years before Bandung it was being said in South Africa, for example:

Our nationalism must transcend the barriers of nationality and geography and discover in the peoples of Africa brothers in a common struggle to assert the dignity of Africa.... [It] is suicidal for us to think along different lines when the European powers and settlers are coordinating their thinking and their planning, and as far as possible pooling their resources.[1]

African nationalists, still on the lower rungs of liberation's ladder, have eagerly grasped the outstretched hand of their Asian brothers. The Africans' horizon has widened. The struggle of Indians for the freedom of Goa becomes a reminder to West Africans that they too face a coming fight to break Portugal's hold on her colonies in Africa, and they say, "The bonds of friendship between Asia and Africa since Bandung must therefore grow even tighter still. With the one great vision which unites us, the colored people, hand in hand with other races, must fight for a world free from such sporadic outbursts of imperialist violence and repression be they in Goa or Morocco, South Africa or elsewhere."[2]

"Freedom and peace are interdependent. The right of self determination must be enjoyed by all peoples," the representatives at Bandung declared with one voice. In striking contrast was the strong opposition of the colonial powers to the inclusion of the right of national self-determination in the draft covenants of the United Nations on human rights. After protracted delays and debates a vote was finally taken at the 1955 General Assembly on a draft article which specifically included colonial and trusteeship territories and which stated in part,

All peoples have the right of self-determination. By virtue of this right they freely determine their political status and freely pursue their economic, social and cultural development. The peoples may, for their own ends, freely dispose of their natural wealth and resources.... In no case may a people be deprived of its own means of subsistence.

The vote was 33 in favor, 12 against, with 13 abstentions. Those in opposition were the United States, the United Kingdom, France, Belgium, Netherlands, Canada, Australia, New Zealand, Norway, Sweden, Turkey and Luxembourg. Shall we call these countries (adding South Africa, whose representatives were absent from the vote) the anti-Bandung minority of the world? Recent history has demonstrated that the more the Western powers seek to shore up their own economic and

[1]John K. Mgubane in *Inkundla Ya Bantu*, August 6, 1949.
[2]*Ghana Evening News*, September 15, 1955.

strategic interests at the expense of the "uncommitted" and so-called neutralist countries in Africa and Asia, the faster will their reputation and influence in those continents dwindle.

The term "neutralist," usually pronounced with a sneer by Cold War partisans, is not liked by leaders of the countries so designated because it implies simply a negative policy, one of noninvolvement or aloofness. Yet President Eisenhower among others recalls that "We were a young country once" and for 150 years found such a policy of neutrality and non-involvement in European power conflicts necessary. Instead of calling it "neutralism," Prime Minister Nehru defines India's position as "the positive independent policy of a country trying to make friends with all and not hostile to any country." The critics of "neutralism," he says, are suffering from a hangover from old ways of thinking; they have not got rid of the old conception of Europe or America declaring what policy other countries should follow.[3]

And President Nasser's view of the matter is similar. "What's a neutral policy? Neutrality is a term to use only in war. We adopt an independent policy, a policy of active coexistence. One-third of our trade is with the Western bloc, one-third with the Eastern bloc and one-third with the rest of the world. If our trade had all been with the West, we would be in a very critical position today. Thank God we had this policy."[4]

The Suez crisis that erupted in the summer of 1956 was the first head-on clash between Big Power domination and Asian-African self-determination following Bandung. That the issues could not be summarily resolved in the old ways of Western coercion and force, even though attempted, is proof of the existence of a new equation of world power. The abortive Anglo-French attack on Egypt indicated once again how desperate and degenerate the waning European imperialists are. It was a "preventive police action" to forestall Soviet aims and plans in the area, the aggressors said as a sort of after-thought. Does this foreshadow the shape of things to come? If the West's ideological and economic weapons cannot keep the African obedient to its dictation, will deadlier weapons be used, bombs such as fell on Port Said—all in the name of saving Africa from Communism?

Let us remember that the masses of Africans are not concerned with East-West differences and rivalries, that they *are* deeply concerned with

[3]*Indragram*, July 18, 1956.
[4]*Time*, August 27, 1956, p. 21.

winning their freedom, and that it is the continuance of Western domination in its various forms standing in the way of that freedom which will bring greater conflict and more war in Africa. The one alternative is the speedy grant of national self-determination, political and economic—freedom with no strings attached—to the continent's indigenous peoples.

W. A. Hunton, *Decision in Africa* (New York: International, 1957), pp. 226–29.

35

CAMPUS STIRRINGS (1955)

by Paul Robeson

Like many on the Left whose travels abroad were prevented and whose views faced censorship and distortion at home, Robeson nevertheless managed to visit some college campuses where both his unique artistry and his particular outlook were welcomed. As a result, Robeson was able to discern the beginnings of the rumblings on U.S. campuses—black and white—that were to contribute significantly to the storms of the late 1950s and 1960s. Here is the text of his account of a visit early in 1955 to Swarthmore College in Pennsylvania:

It is good, these days, to get out to the college campuses and see the stirring of new life among the students. The Ivy Curtain of conformity, which for a decade has shut them off from the sunlight of independent thinking, is beginning to wilt. The fresh breeze of free expression is beginning to filter into the stale atmosphere of the cold-war classrooms.

This changing scene, noted by various progressive writers and lecturers who have visited the colleges in recent months, is renewing for me the bonds which have always connected me closely with this area of American life.

So it is a real pleasure, nowadays, to receive from student groups a growing number of invitations to appear at various universities—Northwestern, Kansas, Wisconsin, Chicago, UCLA and others. Some of these requests are for concerts such as was held here at New York's City College a few months ago, in support of my right to function as an artist; and others are for lectures sponsored by campus supporters of academic freedom.

Last month at Swarthmore College it was my privilege to appear both as artist and citizen, and this is always most gratifying because for me these roles are one and inseparable. Swarthmore, to which I had been invited by the Forum for Free Speech, has an enrollment of 900; but an overflow audience of 1,000 attended. Students came from other schools in that part of Pennsylvania—from Lincoln, including some of the African students there, and from Bryn Mawr.

It was a moving experience, warm with memories of my youth in nearby Princeton, and the days when I had come to play baseball against Swarthmore with the Rutgers teams. Memories of my father who was a Lincoln graduate and of my brother Bill who studied there and took me around the school. Memories, too, of my mother, for Swarthmore is a Quaker college and she was one of the Bustill family with a Quaker tradition going back to colonial days.

The first part of the program consisted of songs and a scene from *Othello,* and there were piano solos by Alan Booth, the distinguished artist who accompanied me.

The muscial phase of the evening was in celebration of the 30th anniversary of my concert career as a singer, but it also served as the text for my talk which followed; and with song I illustrated the root idea of my stand as a citizen for equal rights for human dignity and fulfillment, for peace among the nations.

I sought to explain to these eager young listeners how my viewpoint— which many of them thought too radical—was the natural outgrowth of my development as a Negro artist. I recalled how love for the songs of my people, the only songs for my first five years as a singer, widened to include the songs of other peoples as I grew to know them and found in them a kindred soul, a kindred beauty. I recalled how that knowledge led to an interest in other peoples, in their history and cultures, and in their lives today.

And so the talk, like the songs, seemed to move around the world, noting the epochal social changes of our times, urging an understanding of that reality, stressing the all-important need for peaceful coexistence. But inevitably the talk returned to the starting point—to the struggle and aspirations of the Negro in America.

Many questions were asked in the general discussion which followed and here, too, the focus came to bear on the outlook for Negro advancement.

There was give-and-take on various matters, and everyone seemed to enjoy the exercise of free speech on this occasion. Indeed, as many of the students told me, the important thing for them was the chance to hear another viewpoint.

Yes, a ferment is growing among America's students, both Negro and white. Many are beginning to see that if a concern for future jobs has dictated conformity, a concern for their very lives requires that they think for themselves.

Freedom, May–June 1955; in Foner, ed., cited work, 403–05.

36

BEHIND THE LYNCHING OF EMMETT LOUIS TILL (1955)

by Louis E. Burnham

In August 1955, a fourteen-year-old lad from Chicago, visiting family in Mississippi, was lynched—allegedly for whistling at a white woman. The meaning of this act was analyzed in a pamphlet by Louis E. Burnham.

Burnham died at the age of forty-two, while lecturing in Harlem, in June 1960. He had been a youth leader and union organizer in the South in the 1930s and, though little known today, was one of the very important individuals plowing the ground for the resurgence of the freedom movement in the late 1950s and in the 1960s.

In all the foul record of human oppression, few crimes have matched in unbridled savagery the kidnap-murder of Emmett Louis Till. The discovery of the fiendishly mutilated body of this 14-year-old Chicago boy in Mississippi's Tallahatchie River on August 28, 1955, revealed more than the handiwork of a pair of hate-crazed "white supremacists."

It also reminded the nation that:

1. 11 million Negroes in the South, 92 years after the Emancipation Proclamation, are denied the commonest rights of humanity, to say nothing of their constitutional rights as citizens; and that
2. the entire South is ruled by a political clique so reactionary that it invites

comparison with the Dark Ages in mankind's upward climb from barbarism.

Let us look at the record.

A $1.00 Loaf of Bread

On May 7 in Belzoni, Mississippi, the left side of Rev. George W. Lee's face was blown away by a shotgun blast. The day before he had said: *"If God gives me grace and I'm living on the second day of August, I'm going to march boldly to the courthouse and register."* To this date no one has been indicted for the murder of Rev. Lee.

On August 13, Lamar Smith was shot down in broad daylight on the courthouse lawn in Brookhaven, Mississippi. He also was a leader in the voter registration campaign among Negroes. Though 30 to 40 citizens witnessed the shooting, not one would say what he saw and a grand jury failed to return an indictment.

Neither has anyone been brought to trial for the near-fatal shooting of Gus Courts, 65-year old Negro storekeeper of the same town of Belzoni, and a leader, together with Rev. Lee, of the right-to-vote movement. Both men had paid their poll taxes and been permitted to register—but not to vote.

Then, on December 4, 33-year old Clinton Melton, father of five young children, was shot and killed by Elmer Kimbell, barely twenty miles from the spot where Emmett Till's body was found. The killer, a local white businessman, claimed Melton, employed in a gas station, had put more gas into his tank than he had ordered.

A Yazoo City, Mississippi, plumber was charged a dollar for a loaf of bread. A veteran in the same town discovered that no store or business would cash his disability check. Both these men had signed a petition calling upon the school board to desegregate schools in line with the U.S. Supreme Court decision.

These examples could be multiplied a hundred fold in Mississippi. Yet, the terror is not confined to this one state.

Churches pastored by the Rev. J. A. Delaine were burned three times because of his leadership in the fight for the integration of schools in Clarendon County, South Carolina. The wife of this courageous pastor reported: *"I can't tell you how many times I've been spit at, cursed and called dirty names by little children and older folks alike, as I've walked down the streets of Lake City."*

In the Tidewater section of Virginia, near Heathsville, 23-year old Howard Bromley was shot to death by Ira D. Hinton, a wealthy storekeeper because the Negro dared put his arm on the white man's shoulder. *An all-white jury freed Hinton in 21 minutes.*

Union Meeting Attacked

In Umatilla, Florida, on October 19, white vandals unloosed shotgun blasts into the Masonic Hall, wounding 12 of 26 Negro citrus workers who had gathered for a union meeting.

From one end of the South to the other, law and order have broken down. A public climate has been created in which a Negro's life is worth no more than a white man's whim. Dr. T.R.M. Howard, intrepid leader of Mississippi Negroes, reports that in his state, "white people . . . get longer terms in jail for killing a deer out of season than for killing a colored man in the 18 Delta counties."

While the murder of young Till reveals the degradation heaped upon Negroes, the failure to punish his lynchers and kidnappers exposes the despoiling of the court system, the betrayal of the Constitution and the contempt for the American people's sense of justice prevailing among the Southern white ruling class.

The fight to avenge the murder of Emmett Louis Till has become a symbol of the Negro people's bitter struggle for first-class citizenship. Everywhere, they echo the determination of Mrs. Mamie Bradley, mother of the slain boy: *"I have invested a son in freedom and I'm determined that his death [shall not be] in vain."*

Not Just a "Case" but a "System"

It is worth noting that if Emmett Till had been a Mississippi farm boy instead of a Chicago lad on vacation in Mississippi, the world probably would never have known his fate.

Further, if all the rivers, swamps and woodlands of the Southern countryside could recount the tales of the tens of thousands of Negro bodies thrust into watery graves, strung up on unoffending trees, tortured and murdered by church-going, Democrat-voting defenders of the "American way of life," their story would be too horrible for decent humanity to bear.

Clearly, then, we are dealing not merely with a single "case" or even a number of "cases" of intimidation and murder. Roy Wilkins, executive secretary of the National Association for the Advancement of Colored People, provided the clue when he stated: *"We are dealing with a system!"*

What is this system whose most graphic and revolting feature is the organized brutality of lynchers? How does it work and what are its aims? Who profits from it and who are its victims? How firm are its foundations? How deep are its roots?

First, it must be clear that the system is not exclusively a Mississippi system. Mississippi is but the rawest manifestation of the plantation system which survives in one degree or another in the whole South.

The Plantation Economy

The plantation system is derived from and is a crude adaptation of slavery, which was abolished by decree in 1863. It is based on the bitter exploitation of masses of toiling, landless farmers. Seventy percent of these sharecroppers, tenant farmers and day laborers in the South are Negroes. Their lot, from cradle to grave, is abject poverty, enforced illiteracy and social abuse. They are the objects of racist ostracism, humiliation and brutality.

In 1947, the amount spent for food by Negro farm laborers in Mississippi was $136 for the year, or 37 cents per day. *It is practically the same today.*

Two years ago, the average annual *family* income for Negroes in 11 delta counties which make up the 3rd Congressional district of Mississippi—the area in which Emmett Till was killed—ranged from $399 in Sharkey county to a high of $741 in Coahoma. Almost half the Negro families in the district subsisted on less than $500 a year.

Significantly, the average per capita income for *all* Mississippians in 1953 was only $834, as compared with $1361 in Virginia, $1184 in Georgia, and $2258 in New York.

Though Negroes make up practically half of the population of Mississippi, they own only 17 percent as much land as white Mississippi farmers. The extent of the super-exploitation of Negroes is seen in the fact that only one Negro farmer in Washington county owns a mechanical cotton picker, as compared with 900 white farmers. Yet, Negroes make up 70 per cent of the total population of 70,504 in the county!

The homes of the Negro rural masses are usually no more than hovels, little changed from the cabins occupied three generations ago by their slave ancestors. Eight out of every 10 homes in the Mississippi delta have outside toilets. Only four per cent have telephones. More than half are without running water.

Whites Are Victims, Too

While the all-sided oppression of Negroes is the foundation of the plantation system, its horrors do not end with the Negro people. The low level of wages and working conditions on the plantations becomes the floor toward which employers constantly seek to force down the wage spread and working conditions among all workers, white as well as Negro, industrial as well as agricultural. The plantation system casts its shadow over the whole South and to a considerable extent over the rest of the country.

In Mississippi, for example, the requirements of this outmoded system of agricultural production dominate the economy so completely that there is no such thing as a state department of labor. In most Southern states such commonly-accepted protections as child labor laws, workingmen's compensation, minimum wage and maximum hours laws, either do not exist or are woefully inadequate.

The result is that the major regional industries of the South, textile and lumber, are among the lowest paid and least organized in the country. Among 250,000 sawmill workers in the South, most of whom are Negroes, there is practically no union organization and the average hourly wage of 80 cents is little more than half the average for sawmill workers in the Northwestern states. In textile, the lower wages and abominable working conditions which 300,000 Southerners, mostly white, endure are a constant threat to the maintenance of union conditions in New England mills.

The "Upper Classes" and the Mob

It is easy to see who profits from this system of economic exploitation—obviously the plantation landlords, millowners and industrialists.

Two generations ago Frederick Douglass, the great Negro leader, wrote: *"With a few noble exceptions, just enough to prove the rule, the upper classes of the South seem to be in full sympathy with the mob and its deeds. There are but few earnest words uttered against either. Press, platform and pulpit are generally either silent or they openly apologize for the mob and its deeds."*

In this respect the upper classes of the South have not changed. Indeed, today they are the open instigators of the anti-Negro terror. In Mississippi, the leading organizer of the pro-feudal camp is the plantation owner, Robert B. Patterson, and its leading ideologist is circuit judge Tom P. Brady. In South Carolina, a newspaper ad urging defiance of the law on integration was signed by 52 top leaders of industry, commerce, education and religion, including B. M. Edwards, president of the South Carolina National Bank.

When an effort is made to purchase an NAACP membership list in South Carolina for $10,000, in order to widen the area of victimization of Negro militants, it is clear we are confronted with an important center of wealth and power in the state.

A New Secession Movement

The white ruling class of the South is in open rebellion against the U.S. Constitution and the authority of the federal government. Since May 17, 1954, acts of nullification have crowded each other out of the headlines. An organized criminal conspiracy, led by the so-called White Citizens Councils and involving elected and appointed officials of government, has arisen in Mississippi, Alabama, North and South Carolina, Louisiana, Georgia, Florida and Virginia.

Increasingly, murder and other forms of force and violence are its weapons. Everywhere, it resorts to "economic pressure" to starve and persecute into submission all Negroes who dare stand up for their rights and support the NAACP.

A reporter for the Associated Negro Press reports from South Carolina: *"Vicious behavior, not the least unlike anything that might have been unleashed in similar situations in Hitler Germany, is evident on all sides.... The rebellion, now covering nearly a half of the State, is approaching in vigor and fervor the Secession movement of a century ago...."*

It is most alarming to the Negro people that, faced with this rebellion, the federal government assumes a posture of abject helplessness. The

Federal Bureau of Investigation fails to gather sufficent facts to guarantee conviction of a single lyncher. Its agents hastily intervene when white babies are reported missing, but pointedly refuse to budge when a Negro child is kidnapped. It refuses to protect the voting rights of Negroes in the South, while hounding Negro radicals all over the country.

This failure to "do duty" where Negroes are involved strengthens the widespread belief that the Department of Justice and the FBI are honeycombed from top to bottom with anti-Negro racists. Most important, these agencies are the arms of an administration dedicated to carrying out the policies of Big Business and the plantation owners. And the aim of those policies clearly is not Negro, or human, rights—but *profits*. Big Business thrives on Jim Crow. It is estimated that the annual "take" in super-profits of the industrial monopolies, based on the Negro-white wage differential, is more than four billion dollars.

The Silence of Guilt

This wage differential is directly traceable to the initial oppression of the Negro farming masses of the plantation areas. In addition, Big Business has increasingly assumed direct control over a large segment of the plantation economy. For example, 40 per cent of Mississippi's cotton production is absentee-owned. To an unsuspected extent, great food chains and insurance companies have bought up huge acreages of Southern farmland and have become the direct beneficiaries of the plantation system.

Perhaps this explains why the topmost leaders of the Democratic and Republican parties have been so conspicuously silent on the wave of terror against Negroes. Big Business and the Dixiecrats still wield dominant influence in *both* parties. The $4 billion in extra profits wrung out of the oppression of the Negro people has a great silencing influence among the political opportunists who control both legislative and executive branches of government.

In fact, the judiciary is not exempt from the political pressures of the times. It is generally recognized that the Supreme Court decrees of May 31, 1955, on segregation in education, *encouraged nullification of its original decision* by placing implementation in the hands of its most inveterate enemies, the Southern racist politicians, with no specific time-limit for compliance.

Southern Politics: Minority Rule

The murder of young Till and the freeing of his killers was made possible by the absolute and long-standing rape of political democracy in Mississippi. That's why the fight for equal rights in the South must include an attack on the political as well as the economic roots of oppression.

The plantation system provides the economic base of Dixiecratism and an unfailing bastion of support for all the forces of political reaction and fascism in the country.

In Mississippi's cotton-rich Third Congressional District, 70 per cent of the population are Negroes. Yet, the Negro vote in the district is negligible. Of the remaining 30 per cent of whites, only a small minority vote. The fundamental responsibility for government is monopolized by the plantation owners, their straw-bosses and hangers-on and a venal crew of professional politicians who serve their interests.

In most Southern states, there are two to five Congressional districts like Mississippi's Third. Roughly, 40 of the South's 122-member delegation in the House of Representatives hold their seats because of the unlawful usurpation of the most elementary political rights of the Negro people. So it is that in a House of Representatives of 534 members, there are but three Negroes rather than an approximate 50; and neither of these three is from a major center of Negro population in the cotton belt of the South.

This picture of lily-white legislative power is absolute on a state level in the South. Among 1,795 state legislators in 11 ex-slave states, not a single Negro can be found. Is there any wonder, then, that following the Supreme Court anti-segregation ruling of May 17, 1954, Southern legislatures got busy concocting illegal schemes to get around the decision? They have threatened to make the public schools "private" to keep Negroes out; to jail anybody advocating integration; to abrogate the First Amendment by prohibiting the right to petition for mixed schools; and to illegalize the NAACP. In Louisiana, the legislature has appropriated $100,000 of the public money (collected from Negro as well as white taxpayers) to hire lawyers to keep Negro children out of public schools with white children!

Dr. T.R.M. Howard reports that the racists *are fearful that, as the colored citizens have been aroused during the past three or four years, they must tighten restrictions on voting lest Mississippi might be sending a colored representative to Congress.*

In state after state the forward surge of the Negro people is the most distinctive and progressive feature of Southern politics. Negroes are tired of being governed by laws they have no part in making and by officials in whose choice they have no voice. Their demands echo back through the decades to the Boston Common, to Lexington and Concord, to the little hall in Philadelphia where a band of zealous revolutionaries drafted the first legal paper of this government, a Declaration of Independence stating that government "derives its just powers from the consent of the governed."

It must give the American people pause that slavery persisted in the presence of this great document for nearly 100 years, and that today, 180 years after its drafting, the Negro people of the South are being murdered for resisting taxation without representation.

Freedom Will Come

Despite the agonizing struggles of the past, despite the bloodstained path along which Negroes have inched their way toward equality in our land, freedom will come. It will come, first, because the mood of militancy of 17 million Negroes will not be denied.

Dr. Howard gave accurate voice to this mood when he told a great audience in Baltimore: *"We are tired of dying for something on Heartbreak Ridge, in Korea, that we can't vote for in Belzoni, Mississippi."*

This sentiment is not confined to city folks or to Northerners, to intellectuals or to working men and women. It embraces *all* groups or classes of Negroes. Most important, it is surging in the hearts of the most oppressed—the rural masses. Dr. Howard reports:

"I wish that you could go with me back in the swamps, in the plantations of Mississippi and see these eager young colored people who come forward and shake a hand and say, 'Dr. Howard, I'm with you; I'm with you.' You can hear that from plantation to plantation, people saying, 'I'm with you; I'm with you.'"

Yes, freedom will come because the Negro people, in the face of the severest trials, have made up their minds not to run.

Given an appraisal of its own strength, a growing alliance with labor, and a true estimate of its friends and enemies at home and on a world scale, what are the next steps for the Negro freedom movement? First is the fight for political democracy, majority rule, in the South. This fight encompasses the demands for: abolition of the poll tax, federal protection of the right to register and vote, passage of an anti-lynching bill, and reduction of Congressional representation of States which deliberately disfranchise Negroes, in accordance with Section II, Amendment 14 of the Constitution.

Program of Land Reform

In addition, organizations serious about the fight for equality must increasingly address themselves to a program to really change the conditions of the masses of rural poor. Such a program should include: a federal program to provide land for the landless, aimed at breaking up the plantation system; an effective program of long-term loans at low interest rates for purchase of provisions and implements; written contracts and federal regulation of crop shares so that tenants and sharecroppers receive a minimum of 70 per cent of their production; placement of agricultural employment under minimum wages, maximum hours and child labor laws; the right of the rural masses to organize and bargain collectively to improve their conditions.

The third major element in a popular program must be the demand for immediate enforcement of the Supreme Court rulings which void segregation in education and in the use of public parks, playgrounds, recreational and travel facilities.

Both Republicans and Democrats would like to avoid these issues in 1956. They must not be permitted to do so. Congress should be confronted with a massive, demonstrative demand for some such people's program for Negro rights. With every passing day, this demand of an aroused population must increase in intensity until it becomes irresistible.

This is the way to strengthen American democracy and to right the horrible wrongs committed against Emmett Till, the entire Negro people and the great American tradition of equality.

Louis Burnham, *Behind the Lynching of Emmett Louis Till* (New York: Freedom Associates, 1955). Fifteen-page pamphlet, copy obtained through the courtesy of the Niebyl-Proctor Library, Berkeley, California. See Stephen J. Whitfield, *A Death in the Delta: The Story of Emmett Till* (Baltimore: Johns Hopkins University Press, 1988).

37

THE CONSPIRACY TO DENY EQUALITY (1955)

by Roy Wilkins

The 46th Annual Convention of the NAACP, coming after the second *Brown* decision on May 31, 1955, sought to expedite the Court's directive that the desegregation ordered by the 1954 decision was to be implemented "with all deliberate speed"—a phrase subject to varied interpretations. The executive secretary of the NAACP entitled his report to the convention as above. This indicated his realization of the heavy task that impended.

With the May 31 opinion, it has become apparent that we have entered a new era, an era where racial discrimination and segregation are to be not merely morally wrong but contrary to the law and the Constitution....

...Our great Association which has carried the fight thus far is faced with new challenges, new responsibilities, new and more pressing calls to duty, to devotion, intelligence and skill. Each and every officer and member, wherever he may be, shares the heavy burden of the transition. None may shirk his duty, for that would be to betray the ones who come after. Let no one in tomorrow's world be able to say that in the years of decision, when destiny was in our hands, we failed to measure up. The people of 1903 had no such challenge and opportunity; nor did those of 1923, or 1943. This great day is ours. Upon us depend the speed, the order and the completeness of the victory.

We have emerged from more than a half-century of the doctrine of "separate but equal" set forth in the now-famous *Plessy v. Ferguson* case of 1896. We Negroes always knew the Plessy doctrine to be wrong and we fervently believed it to be unconstitutional. But it was not until our attorneys carried to the highest court the challenge to its legality that we finally shook off the shackles that had hobbled our progress since the turn of the century.

What did the Plessy era hold for us? To what kind of life were we committed by it? Discrimination and segregation was our lot....

...We have been subject to the whims and fancies of white persons, individually and collectively. We went to back doors and were forced to live in hollows and alleys and back streets. We stepped off sidewalks and removed our hats and said "Sir" to all and sundry, if they were white. If schools were provided, our children went to shanties and whites to schools. We rode in the rear seats of buses and trolleys and in the dirty, dangerous front end coaches of the trains. We could not vote. Our health and our recreation were of little or no concern to the responsible officials of government. In time of war we were called to serve, but were insulted, degraded and mistreated even as we fought to defend the flag that flew over every American. We were beaten, shot, lynched and burned and no man was punished for what he did to us.

Slowly in this fifty-eight years, we have lifted ourselves by our own bootstraps. Step by halting step, we have beaten our way back. It has been a long and tortuous road since the Dred Scott decision of 1857 which branded us as non-citizens and which, by the Plessy decision, gave the states and the nation as a whole the green light to treat us as they pleased....

We need only recall, not recount the victories along the way. We wiped out lynching. We knocked out the strongest barriers to voting, as well as the widely-used restrictive covenants on housing. We have clothed our fighting men with dignity. Travel is no longer an ordeal of both the body and the spirit. The courts, in the South as well as in the North, are becoming places where color-blind justice is dispensed. Our men and women are working at more and better jobs and at better and better wages.

Now, our children, at long last, are to have equality in education. They are to have a chance in the race of life without being penalized before they are born.

Truly, we are at the beginning of a new era. But just as the old order did not pass without prayer and struggle and sacrifice—even unto death—so the new order will not come into being unless we accomplish it by our own efforts. This is the beginning, not the end. This is a time for action, not for resting. Some have complained that they thought May 17 settled everything and that now they could retire and enjoy. Freedom never came to any people in that fashion.

We cannot be complacent as we see before our eyes the outlines of a conspiracy to deny, in 1955, the equality we have won for ourselves. For this school decision heralds the death of all inequality in citizenship based upon race. The Richmond, Virginia, editor, Virginius Dabney, correctly stated in 1953 that public schools segregation was the keystone in the arch of segregation. It has been knocked out and the arch will fall.

The conspirators know this, hence the desperation of their tactics. To us who have known the refined as well as the brutal methods of persecution, the emerging pattern is not new.

First they are organizing. Here and there, dotting the South, organizations have sprung up overnight, some with fancy names like Virginia's Defenders of State Sovereignty and Individual Liberty and others like the White Citizens' Councils in Mississippi which frankly declare their anti-Negro purpose.

Terror and intimidation are the weapons being used. The Mississippi Councils—now spreading to Alabama—seek to freeze Negroes economically and frighten them bodily.

"We intend," said one organizer, "to see that no Negro who believes in equality has a job, gets credit, or is able to exist in our communities."

"Is able to exist"—that means agree and knuckle under, or flee, or die.

It is not strange that in such an atmosphere, Rev. George W. Lee was murdered by a shotgun blast on May 7 in his home town of Belzoni, Miss. Rev. Lee's "crime" was that he was the first Negro to register to vote in his county and he had refused orders from whites to remove his name from the voting list. The state headquarters of the White Citizens' Councils is a scant sixty miles from Belzoni, in Winona, Miss.

But naked terror alone will not do the job. Even murder will not guarantee victory to the conspirators.

They have a well-oiled system, rooted in politics, by which they hope to stave off defeat. All these years the system has worked. Today they are trying to use it still.

At the local and state levels they have enforced disfranchisement of Negroes which in turn has permitted the election of local and state officers wholly indifferent to the plight, wishes and demands of our citizens. No better illustration of the effectiveness of this technique at this level can be found than the actions of the South Carolina, Georgia, Louisiana and Mississippi legislators during the past year in passing legislation frankly and brazenly labelled as efforts to deny the Negro equality and to prevent him from voting.

This same disfranchisement has permitted the election of congressmen and senators to Washington who are pledged to block any executive or legislative moves which recognize the needs of Negroes as citizens. These southern congressmen and senators have used their committee posts to smother legislation and, in the Senate, the filibuster to kill legislation.

While ham-stringing Presidents and choking off legislation they have not had as much success in hampering the courts, although they have done their best through their power to confirm judicial appointees. With but few exceptions they are now in full cry against the courts and especially the Supreme Court. If they had a ghost of a chance they would emulate South Africa in making Supreme Court decrees subject to ratification by the Congress.

Thus we have had a two-pronged political operation, one prong bottling up the Negro vote in the South at the ballot box level, and the other nullifying the Negro vote in the North by the use of blackjack tactics in both Houses of the Congress.

This system has worked through the decades whether a Democratic or Republican president has been in office. The only Chief Executive to buck it was Harry S. Truman who split his party rather than keep silent on his recommendations as to civil rights for Negro Americans.

The system has been aided by northern Democrats who seek "party unity" as they play poker politics with the civil rights of Negroes as the joker card.

The system is aided also by the Republicans who seek support for their program and who also continue to hope that they will be able to build a permanent party structure in the South. It might be added here that if they continue to talk like Dixiecrats, act like Dixiecrats, and vote like Dixiecrats, they will not have to infiltrate the South; it will have taken them over.

One of our principal objectives as an Association is the smashing of this iniquitous network of political strangulation which has its base in the choking off of Negro citizenship rights at the precinct or county level through denial of the ballot. During the past year we have stimulated increased registration by Negro citizens in many southern states. Intensive campaigns have been underway in Virginia, Alabama, North Carolina, and South Carolina. We expect to increase this activity in these and other states between now and the 1956 election.

Along with the effort to broaden the voting base in the South will go a campaign to use the northern Negro's voting strength to break the hold of the Dixiecrat system. Northern Democratic office holders may continue to receive Negro votes on the basis of their individual records, and many, like Senator Herbert Lehman of New York, have most excellent records. But increasingly, Negro voters—as far as the Democratic party is concerned—are demanding less unity with the system that disfranchises, insults, terrorizes, and generally creates an atmosphere in which violence can flourish. They want no unity with the White Councils of Mississippi; no unity with areas that murder men as Rev. Lee was murdered, for wanting to vote; no unity with the forces of slander, as exemplified by a nationwide radio talk of Senator Allen J. Ellender of Louisiana branding Negroes as ignorant, diseased, and crime-ridden; no unity with those who defy the law of the land as laid down by the Supreme Court, as exemplified by the recent television broadcast of Senator James O. Eastland of Mississippi.

On the other hand, the Republicans who hope and hope cannot expect substantial support as long as they "play footsie" with southern Democrats on civil rights. They wonder why the Negro vote does not return to the GOP fold. Well, thousands want to return because they are not comfortable in the party of Herman Talmadge, but they cannot see any percentage in changing as long as the Republicans play ball with the Dixiecrats.

These conspirators about whom I have been talking—the conscious as well as the unconscious ones—went so far as to enlist the prestige of the White House in their demands to maintain segregation and circumvent the national policy of no discrimination in the armed services. On June 8 the President in his press conference lashed out at those who seek anti-segregation amendments to pending legislation including the military reserves bill.

We who seek such amendments were accused of placing our special desires above the security of the nation. We want to say here plainly and unmistakably that it is not we who seek our own way at the expense of the country. It is the southern Democratic bloc which openly threatened to kill the military reserves bill unless it contained their provision for segregation. The President has every right to demand the legislation he deems necessary for the welfare of the nation, but in all fairness the blame for the delay on that legislation should be placed at the doorstep of those who are guilty.

We love our country. We have fought for it in the past and we will fight for it in the future, but we do not relish our patriotism being called into question because we demand our rights as American citizens.

We feel the same way about the anti-segregation amendment to the housing bill and to the bill which would provide aid to the states for the construction of public schools. We do not believe that housing which is provided out of the funds or the credit of all the people of the United States should be denied to any citizen because of his race or color. We do not believe that the tax funds of all the people of the United States should be given to any state or locality for the purpose of subsidizing these in defying the Supreme Court ruling on segregated schools.

Our legislative goals, of course, are not limited to amendments to pending bills. Although the President expressed the opinion in 1953 that the states should pass fair employment practice bills, only the states with Democratic administrations have so far complied, the latest being Minnesota and Michigan. Two state governments of the President's own party—Illinois and Pennsylvania—have defeated FEPC. Neither the 83rd or the 84th Congress has done anything on FEPC, nor has the President made any recommendation on this or any other civil rights bill.

Our Department of Justice will remain almost impotent in prosecuting civil rights crimes, such as the murders of Mr. and Mrs. Harry T. Moore of Florida, and Rev. Lee of Mississippi, until Congress passes a bill to strengthen the civil rights laws.

These and other bills to make secure the rights of all our citizens form the continuing objective of our members who will make their likes and dislikes known in the polling booths.

Yes, in fashioning the new era we shall use all the weapons at our disposal. Thurgood Marshall, our general counsel, has outlined how we will use the courts. We shall continue to use education and persuasion and moral pressure. Heartened by the support of millions of our white fellow citizens in all sections of the country, we welcome their participation in the crusade which is one not alone for us, but for our nation as a whole. And we shall use all the political power we can muster, for this is the most vital ingredient in a government of, by and for the people, not the white people; but all the people....

We shall go upright. We shall go in faith, without hatred of any man, but with determination in the righteousness of our cause, armed with the weapons provided for us. We shall not—we cannot—fail. We shall, we will, be free men.

Published by the NAACP (New York, 1955); given in part in Meier and Rudwick, *Negro Protest Thought in 20th Century,* pp. 256–62.

38

LIKE ONE OF THE FAMILY (1956)

by Alice Childress

Just as Langston Hughes's Simple fittingly opens the 1950s, so does Marge's friend convey the feeling that was to shake the heavens in the mid 1950s and crash into the revolutionary 1960s. Alice Childress, playwright and novelist, published Marge's wisdom through the aegis of an obscure publisher—itself reflective of the McCarthyite scourge.

Ridin' The Bus

I sure am glad we got a seat near the window, I'm that tired.... What do you mean by you thought I'd never stop walkin'? I like to sit in the back of the bus.... I certainly do, for many good reasons.... Well, the back is always less crowded, the air is better, it is also nearer to the exit door.... Why do I sound strange to you?... Marge, there is no way that you can compare ridin' in the back because you want to with ridin' there because you have to!... No indeed, I'll argue you down on that!... I've ridden both ways a whole lot so I can tell you the difference.

Well, for one thing when I walked to the back of this bus nobody was freezin' me up with stares. Have you forgotten what it feels like? All of them eyes that always have to follow you to your seat lookin' at you real mockin' like. Well, nobody pays us any mind and we didn't have to die a little on the inside because there was nothin' to this except findin' a seat. The next difference was the fact that when we took this seat it simply showed which one we had picked out and not which one was picked for us. Why don't you look around you and see who else is sittin' back here?... That's right, there's plenty of white folks too. Now, if they are from the South, it's probably the first time in their lives that *they* have had the opportunity to sit where *they* want!

... Why sure, they *can't* sit in the back down home and it seems that a lot of 'em think that's the best place to be.... No, I don't think of it in that way. Good, better or best, it's only the individual that can say which they like. Another thing, I get annoyed ridin' Jim Crow because you get a little more than just *separate seatin'*. You get rudeness, meanness and less for your money in every other way. There's been many a time when I was down home when the driver wouldn't stop when I pulled the cord, that is if I was the only one who wanted to get off, or if it was any other colored for that matter. I'd be so mad when he wouldn't let me off 'til we was four or five blocks past my stop. There's been many a time I've been left standin' with my hand held up to stop the bus and the driver would go whizzin' right on past. There's been other times when them drivers would go out of the way to splash a mud puddle on you.... Well, you know they was bein' upheld in everything they did! But the most miserable thing of all was when the back of the bus was full and the front almost empty. Yes, you'd just stand there and get madder and madder, especially when you'd be standin' by a colored mother holdin' her baby in her arms and look toward the front and see four or five white men and women ridin' along with about twenty seats between. I can tell you that although we knew it was the law, it didn't make anybody feel good to notice how the folks sittin' in the front would just go on readin' their newspapers and never even look up or feel the least bit self-conscious about us.... Oh yes, there are some places down South where the passengers are supposed to fill up from the front and the back as they come in, but I never liked that too much because if there were more colored we'd have to move back when the whites came on, and of course that was worse than bein' in the back in the first place.

... You are right, Marge, some people still think we want to sit with white people when they hear us talkin' about that Jim Crow ridin' and what they seem to forget is that there was never nothin' *equal* about those *separate* seats even though they were all on the same bus.

Watch where this white man sits when he gets back here. Well now, did you see that? He sat next to a colored man.... No, I don't think he especially wanted to or didn't want to. See how he's busy readin' his magazine? It is good to note also that the colored man never noticed him sitting beside him and went right on lookin' for his street. That's the way things *should* be—nice and easy like with no fuss or bother one way or the other. Sure, and when I feel like bein' exclusive, I take a *cab!*

"The Pocketbook Game"

Marge... day's work is an education! Well, I mean workin' in different homes you learn much more than if you was steady in one place.... I tell you, it really keeps your mind sharp tryin' to watch for what folks will put over on you.

What?...No, Marge, I do not want to help shell no beans, but I'd be more than glad to stay and have supper with you, and I'll wash the dishes after. Is that all right?...

Who put anything over on who?...Oh, yes! It's like this....I been working for Mrs. E....one day a week for several months and I notice that she has some peculiar ways. Well, there was only one thing that really bothered me and that was her pocketbook habit....No, not those little novels....I mean her purse—her handbag.

Marge, she's got a big old pocketbook with two long straps on it...and whenever I'd go there, she'd be propped up in a chair with her handbag double wrapped tight around her wrist, and from room to room she'd roam with that purse hugged to her bosom....Yes, girl! This happens every time! No, there's *nobody* there but me and her....Marge, I couldn't say nothin' to her! It's her purse, ain't it? She can hold onto it if she wants to!

I held my peace for months, tryin' to figure out how I'd make my point....Well, bless Bess! *Today was the day!* ...Please, Marge, keep shellin' the beans so we can eat! I know you're listenin', but you listen with your ears, not your hands....Well, anyway, I was almost ready to go home when she steps in the room hangin' onto her bag as usual and says, "Mildred will you ask the super to come up and fix the kitchen faucet?" "Yes, Mrs. E...," I says, "as soon as I leave." "Oh, no," she says, "he may be gone by then. Please go now." "All right," I says, and out the door I went, still wearin' my Hoover apron.

I just went down the hall and stood there a few minutes...and then I rushed back to the door and knocked on it as hard and frantic as I could. She flung open the door sayin', "What's the matter? Did you see the super?"...."No," I says, gaspin' hard for breath. "I was almost downstairs when I remembered...*I left my pocketbook!*"

With that I dashed in, grabbed my purse and then went down to get the super! Later, when I was leavin' she says real timid-like, "Mildred, I hope that you don't think I distrust you because..." I cut her off real quick...."That's all right, Mrs. E...I understand. 'Cause if I paid anybody as little as you pay me, I'd hold my pocketbook too!"

Marge, you fool...lookout!...You gonna drop the beans on the floor!

Story Tellin' Time

Marge, the folks I work for can get some worried about me. Like for example when I went in to the job this mornin' and put my newspaper on the hall table. In no time flat Mrs. B. picked up my paper and began to go through it. "Oh," says she, "it's so seldom that I see a colored paper, do you mind if I read it, Mildred?" "No," I says, "just you go on and help yourself." I went on and changed my clothes and after a while she got up and came in the bedroom where I was makin' up her bed. "Mildred," she says, "I see here where Paul Robeson is giving a concert somewhere. You wouldn't go to anything like that, would you?"

What did I say?. . . Almost nothin'. I just finished smoothin' the spread and started for the kitchen to do the dishes. Oh, yes, I did say, "Have you ever seen such a lovely bright sunshiny day?" In a little while she drifts into the kitchen and starts nibblin' on the subject again. "I know you wouldn't go to a concert like that.". . . No, Marge, I didn't bite on the bait. All I said was, "Where did you get these gorgeous orange juice glasses?" Honey, she wasn't thinkin' of lettin' up, and she keeps pursuin' the subject. "Mildred, Paul Robeson is the kind of man who gets his people in trouble. You don't want to get in trouble, do you?" Then I said, "No, indeed, I do not want to get in trouble." Now that would have been enough for anybody but you know who. "Mildred," she says, "the only reason I ask you these things is because I feel a concern for you and I'd also like you to *know* all about the kind of people that will make trouble. I'm sure that you've heard a lot about. . ." I cut her off then. "Mrs. B.," I says, "do you mind if I tell you a story?" Her face lit up like a flashlight. "I'd be simply delighted!" Then I dried my hands and told her this story.

Once upon a time there was an old slavemaster and he owned a slave named Jim, and hardly a day went by that old Master didn't say, "Jim, you got to have a whippin'," and he'd have Jim tied down and then he'd lay on the lashes hard and fast. Old Master never gave Jim enough to eat, just weevily meal and rancid salt meat and garbage scraps. And although Jim worked fourteen and fifteen hours a day, he didn't own a pair of shoes and the only thing he had to wear was cast off rags; in fact the only thing he got regular and on time was whippin's. . . and I say that to say this: Master was mean!

Fast as Jim and his wife had children, old Master sold them so's he could send his only son, little Master, to a big fancy college to get cultured and refined. And he sold Jim's wife so that he could give his only daughter, little Mistress, harp lessons and piano lessons and embroidery lessons so's she could grow up and be a cultured, genteel and refined Miss Lady.

When the Civil War broke out and was fought and won, it worried old

Master to death that he had to turn his slaves out in a cold, unfriendly world, and he stood on the big veranda that Jim had built and wept as he waved goodbye: "Who's gonna take care of you now?"

After old Master got over his cryin' spell, he formed the Ku Klux and went out shootin' down some of Jim's relatives just to let Jim know that old Master wasn't dead yet, or even dyin' for that matter. And then he put Jim to work on his land on a share plan....Jim sharin' all the work and Master's share bein' all the profit.

And Master used some of his profits to build special things for Jim's relatives like special schools, railroad waitin' rooms and county jails. He also spent some of his profits to pass laws makin' it illegal for Jim to eat in certain restaurants or go in theatres or even to marry whom he pleased or walk the streets after eleven o'clock at night. Master also told the hospitals not to admit Jim or his relatives and many of them died right at the hospital door.

In fact, old Master went so far as to pass laws against Jim's people socializin' with white folks who didn't agree with Master's plans. Old Master warned Jim that white folks who would live in the same buildin' with colored folks and laugh and talk with colored...well, folks like that were rabble-rousin', common, low-flung trash that were out to create trouble between Jim and old Master.

And old Master lynched thousands of Jim's kinfolks, and of course as time went by it was worth Jim's life to try and get to the polls to vote. And such misery old Master brought about...'til World War I.

And then old Master calls Jim and says, "Jim, boy, we all got our faults, you got yours and I got mine. Let's shake hands and go off and fight for Democracy so's we can live in peace." And Jim tried him one time and went, but when he got back old Master started the same old burnin' and killin'.

Time went by and one day old Master called Jim and he says, "Jim, you got your faults and I got mine, but let's shake hands and go off and fight one more war for Democracy, and this time I swear on the foundations of my plantation that this is it!"

I don't know whether Jim believed him or not, but he went on and said, "All right, we'll try it one more time."

Soon as Jim got back old Master was awful annoyed because Jim was walkin' around with a uniform full of medals and raisin' merry Ned about votin'. And old Master had veterans' eyes gouged out and the killin's started all over again.

Jim fought old Master all the way down the line until one day old Master called him again and said, "I'm not goin' to ask you to go to war any more, Jim, but I got a little 'police action' I'd like you to go and see about." Yes, Jim tried one more time and when he got back he went straight on up to the Supreme Court in order to get his children in the schools. Old Master got mad as the devil and said "I'll fight you with my last breath, blood will run in the streets and I'll spend my remainin' days seein' that your children don't get into the schools!"

Then, Marge, I looked full at Mrs. B. and said, "That is all to the story but the object of this tale is simply this: *I know who makes trouble for me!*"

... Yes, she said something after that. I'll bet you can't guess what it was. She said, "Yes, it sure is a nice sunshiny day, and I hope it doesn't rain."

On Leavin' Notes!

Good evenin', Marge. I just stopped by to say "Hey"... No thank you darlin', I do not care for any turkey hash, and I don't like turkey soup or creamed turkey either. Child, there's nothin' as sickenin' as a "hangin' around" turkey.

Well girl, I done come up with my New Year's resolution. . . . That's right, I made just one, and that is this: NOBODY THAT I DO DAYSWORK FOR SHALL LEAVE ME ANY NOTES. . . You know what I mean. Whenever these women are going to be out when you come to work, they will leave you a note tellin' you about a few extra things to do. They ask you things in them notes that they wouldn't dast ask you to your face.

When I opened the door this morning I found a note from Mrs. R . . . It was neatly pinned to three cotton housecoats. "Dear Mildred," it read, "please take these home, wash and iron them, and bring them in tomorrow. Here is an extra dollar for you. . . . " And at the bottom of the note a dollar was pinned.

Now Marge, there is a laundry right up on her corner and they charges seventy-five cents for housecoats. . . . Wait a minute, honey, just let me tell it now. . . . I hung around until she got home . . . Oh, but I did! And she was most surprised to see the housecoats and me still there. "Mildred," says she, "did you see my note?"

"Yes," I replied, "and I cannot do those housecoats for no dollar."

"Why," she says, "how much do you want?"

I give her a sparing smile and says, "Seventy-five cents apiece, the same as the laundry."

"Oh," she says, "well it looks as though I can't use you...."

"Indeed you can't," I say, "'cause furthermore I am not going to let you."

"Let's not get upset," she adds. "I only meant I won't need you for the laundry."

"I am not upset, Mrs. R...," I says, "but in the future, please don't leave me any notes making requests outside of our agreement...." And you know, THAT was THAT....No, Marge...I did not pop my fingers at her when I said it. There's no need to overdo the thing!

The "Many Others" in History

Good evenin', Marge. I am sorry I woke you up.... Yes, I know it's 12 o'clock.... Well, I got to work tomorrow too but I just have to tell you about your friend Mildred....

Honey, I went to a Negro History meetin' tonight. It was held on account of this is either Negro History week or somethin'.... Why, of course it should be a year-round thing, but a week or a month is better than a "no time," ain't it?

Marge, I really "fell in" at that meeting! Let's admit it—I look good, don't I?

Well, they had several speakers. There was one pretty young colored girl who was a little nervous but she came through fine and gave a nice talk about Harriet Tubman, Sojourner Truth and *many others*...and a distinguish lookin' man who was kinda grey at the temples spoke about Frederick Douglass, Nat Turner and *many others*....Then a middle age white woman delivered a rousin' speech about John Brown, Frances Harper and *many others*.

I noticed that everybody would name a couple of folk and then add "and many others." Well, when the talkin' was over they asked the people to speak up and express themselves.... Why of course I did! I got up and said, "This has been a delightful evenin' and I'm glad to be here but you folks kept talkin' about 'many others.'... But you didn't tell much about them.

"Now I can't think about the *many others* without thinkin' of my grandmother because that's who you are talkin' about....My grandpapa worked in a phosphate mill in South Carolina. He was a foreman and made eight dollars a week. He and grandma had seven children and paid eight dollars a month rent. It cost ten cent a week for each child to go to school, ten cent apiece for the nine in the family to belong to the burial society...and the pickings were lean. Each child had to have a penny a week for Sunday School and grandma put in two dimes a week for the church.

"Once in a while she squeezed out seven nickels so's the children could go see lantern slides. Them kids wanted at least one picnic during the summer. They ate up one can of condensed milk a day...a tablespoon in a glass of water...that's how they got their milk.

"Christmas and Easter was a terrible time of trouble and worry to my grandma...with seven kids lookin' for somethin' new....Toys? Grandma used to take a shoe box and cut windows in the sides, then she'd cover the windows with tissue paper, put a candle in the box, light it, cover it, cut a hole in the top, tie a string on the box so it could be dragged along and that was called a 'twilight trolley.'

"She'd pull up a clump of grass, tie it in the middle to make a 'waist line' and then comb the dirt out of the roots so she could braid them in two pigtails...and that would be a 'grass doll' with 'root hair.'...She'd get seashells and they would be 'play dishes'...and the boys got barrel wires for hoops and pebbles and a ball for 'jacks.'

"Every minute of grandma's life was a struggle. She never had a doctor except for 'sickness unto death' and neighbor women helped bring her seven into this world. Sometimes she'd get down to the 'nitty gritty' and have her back to the wall...all the trouble lined up facing her. What to do! What to do about...food...coats...shoes...sickness...death...underwear...sheets...towels...toothaches...childbirth...curtains...dishtowels...kerosene oil...lamp chimneys...coal for the stove...diapers ...mittens...soap and hunger?

"Next thing, Grandma would get cross at the children and she'd begin to grieve and cry if they'd make noise....Then she knew it was time to 'rally.' After the kids was off to bed she'd sit in her rockin' chair in the dark kitchen...and that old chair would weep sawdust tears as she rocked back and forth.

"She'd start off singing real low-like.... 'I'm so glad trouble don' las' always,' and switch off in the middle and pick up with... 'Saviour, Saviour, hear my humble cry'...and she'd keep jumpin' from tune to tune.... 'I'm gonna tell God all of my troubles when I get home'... 'Come out the wilderness leaning on the Lord'... 'When I've done the best I can'... and her voice would grow stronger as she'd go into 'It's not my mother but it's me oh Lord'... and she'd pat her feet as she rocked and rassled with death, Jim Crow and starvation.

"And all of a sudden the rockin' would stop and she'd jump up, smack her hands together and say, 'Atcha dratcha!'... and she'd come back revived and refreshed and ready to go at them drat troubles...."

That's what I told 'em, Marge.... *You know, it's amazing that we're all here today!*... Well, the way they took it you could tell that I was talkin' about their grandmas too.... So I told 'em, "I bet Miss Tubman and Miss Truth would like us to remember and give some time to the *many others*...."

I'm going upstairs and get some sleep now.... Stop that, Marge.... If I'd known you would cry, I wouldn't of told it.

Alice Childress, *Like One of the Family* (Brooklyn, New York: Independence Publisher, 1956), pp. 13–15; 26–27; 119–22; 154–55; 156–58.

39

MURDER CONTINUES:
WILL THE GOVERNMENT ACT? (1956)

by the Editors of the Crisis

Without significant federal intervention, unpunished terror and murder followed the Court decisions against segregation. There follows an editorial from the *Crisis* conveying the universal demands of the African-American population:

Civil Rights

So far Congress has done nothing on the vital issue of civil rights. Nor have the two most articulate Democratic presidential aspirants, Estes Kefauver and Adlai Stevenson, committed themselves—they have, so far, not even given lip service. But civil rights are so vital to Negroes that NAACP Executive Secretary Roy Wilkins has urged President Eisenhower to call upon Congress in his State of the Union message "to take favorable action on pending civil rights bills, especially those protecting the security of the person and the right to vote freely."

In his letter to the President, Mr. Wilkins cited the "series of murders and the wave of economic terror" in Mississippi and elsewhere in the South, and he asked Mr. Eisenhower to "recognize and denounce" these conditions in his message to be delivered at the opening of the second session of the 84th Congress.

As things are now, either technicalities in the federal civil rights laws are being construed so as to leave Negro citizens in the Deep South open to murder and economic reprisal or the present laws need to be amended and strengthened by congressional action. The Department of Justice must be given additional authority and administrative machinery to handle the increasing number of civil rights violations in the Deep South.

The George W. Lee and Lamar Smith assassinations in Mississippi, and the shooting of Gus Courts, were politically inspired, inasmuch as these men had registered to vote and had urged other Negroes to do likewise despite pressures and threats designed to keep them from voting.

In addition to murder and physical violence, the despicable weapon of economic pressure is now being used to prevent Negro citizens from exercising or attempting to exercise their citizenship rights.

In parts of Mississippi, Alabama, and South Carolina, according to verified reports, Negroes are being fired or denied credit on their homes, businesses and farms simply because they have asked for their rights as American citizens, including the right to vote. Negroes ask through the orderly process of petition for non-segregated public schools as ordered by the United States Supreme Court and the whites treat them with contempt, accuse them of being subversive, and retaliate with firings and boycotts. This is the way some white Americans are treating their fellow Americans in this great democratic nation.

This campaign of intimidation has even been extended to those white people who have hesitated to use the drastic and reprehensible tactic of forcing their Negro employees to choose between second-class citizenship and loss of livelihood.

Not even religion has escaped this terrorization. A Negro minister who gave leadership to efforts in South Carolina in behalf of civil rights had his church burned and he had to flee to New York City for safety. A white minister in South Carolina, whose parishioners include the Governor and a federal judge, had to resign his pulpit because he differed with the

Governor on the segregation issue. In Louisiana, a Negro priest assigned to a parish by his bishop was "persuaded" by local law enforcement officers not to say a mass at a church which included white parishioners.

In the light of these conditions Negroes are dismayed and bewildered at the silence and the apparent impotence of their Federal Government in the face of what is, to all intents and purposes, a rebellion against the United States Constitution and its guarantees to American citizens. The rebellion is in the open. The defiance is vocal and overt. The methods—murder and economic intimidation—are beneath decent and honorable combatants in any controversy short of actual war.

When the state governments fail to protect the people, they turn naturally to their Federal Government. Where else can they turn when their states, counties, and towns "let them down"? Are foreigners within our borders to receive more protection from the Federal Government than native-born citizens? Is the Federal Government going to continue to have more concern with civil rights in the Russian satellite countries than in our own South? Congress must pass civil rights legislation with teeth. The voters cannot be fooled with amendments to current legislation, lip service, and slogans.

Crisis, January 1956, pp. 35–36.

40

NEGRO VOTERS FACE 1956

by W. E. B. Du Bois

The dean of African-American scholars offered this view of the impending elections in 1956:

The most spectacular occurrence during the Eisenhower administration has been the school anti-segregation opinion of the Supreme Court. This was hardly a Republican measure, since seven of the justices were appointed by Democratic presidents and only two by Republican. Indeed it is doubtful if Eisenhower with his Southern birth and political ties to the South welcomed this unexpected decision. He has never hailed the decision and his administration has done nothing to carry it out.

The Eisenhower administration has allied itself with the South in doing nothing to enforce rights for Negroes and little to force a Fair Employment program except Nixon's phony meeting. The Attorney General and FBI have made no effective move in the outrageous Till murder, on Mississippi lawlessness, or on the open threats of nullification of federal law by demagogues like Eastland. The Department of Justice has hounded organizations like the Council on African Affairs out of existence, has driven West Indian Negroes out of the country when possible.

Eisenhower has made two major Negro appointments to office, but also has dismissed [Frank] Horne from his position of power in federal housing. Eisenhower has pleased Negroes by entertaining socially three Negro heads of governments; but Dulles, with the President's acquiescence, has been contemptuous of colored peoples like the Chinese; has let Henry Cabot Lodge Jr. ignore dark Krishna Menon, and has ruined our ties with Nehru and India. Segregation of Negroes in the army has lessened under Eisenhower, but slowly and with many bad results. Moreover, the high taxation of the Eisenhower administration falls with crushing force on Negroes, nearly a quarter of whose families get less than a thousand dollars a year.

Finally, the American attitude toward Russia smarts. There are few Negro Communists and not many more Socialists. Only a few Negro scholars and labor leaders realize the surge of socialism and most of these dare not risk their jobs by talking frankly. Negroes by and large have been firmly grounded in individual initiative and private profit. That was the meaning of Booker Washington and his crusade, and the powerful white forces behind him. But Negroes who hear of the lack of color prejudice in the Soviet Union are deeply impressed. Few whites in America realize that the thing which daily hurts in Negro experience more than disfranchisement or exclusion from social clubs is the hundred daily insults which a dark skin brings on the innocent and unassuming on the streets of every American city from New Orleans to Boston.

I remember once hearing a brown girl—a college graduate—say of Paris: "The thing I like here is going out in the morning without having to plan where I'll be able to get lunch!" Common decency on the street is what the Negro craves and he cannot think that the nation which grants this without question is such a threat to civilization. Negroes are tired of hearing their bribed emissaries testify abroad that the race problem in America is "settled"! One black American who tried that fairy tale in

India, where plenty of dark folk have had personal experience in the United States, was nearly mobbed. Frankly, Negroes are tired of fighting for "their country." They do not willingly sing, "My country, 'tis of thee!" Increasing numbers are beginning to question if there may not be more to socialism and communism than the newspapers print.

For these reasons and unless the very busy Attorney General and the liars hired by the FBI can find some way to punish murder in Mississippi, the Negro voter will not be attracted to Republicans in 1956.

But if he does not vote for Eisenhower, Tricky Dick, or Chiang Kai Knowland, for whom can he vote? Stevenson unfortunately has learned nothing about the race problem since the day of his grandfather. The pictures of him and Georgia's Talmadge do not attract Negroes. Kefauver is coy, and Harriman much too eager. There is no third party. The ADA can protest everything except the things which hurt fifteen million black folk. There is one thing which both the black and white voter can do next November, and that is to stay at home, just as forty million Americans usually do.

But the day must come, if not in 1956, then some time in 1960 or 1964, when the American people get tired of spending most of their government funds on war and insist on education and homes; when they will refuse to be stampeded by fear into crime and insanity, and choose the rule of a third party instead of supporting one party with two faces which are exactly alike.

Extracted from *American Socialist*, February 1956, vol. 3, p. 11.

41

THE SOUTHERN NEGRO STIRS (1956)

by Conrad Lynn

A courageous and militant African-American attorney, who personally participated in antiracist demonstrations in the South, offers a penetrating examination of the developing uprising in the South.

The most inspiring area in the United States today is the old South. The rest of the country exclaims in horror at the Till mutilation-murder and the sickening whitewash of its perpetrators. The cowardly Belzoni shootings, the bullwhip and shotgun reigns of a Sheriff McCall in Florida, or a Byrd, or Strider of Mississippi, expose the hideous visage of race dictatorship for all the world to see. Who can blame other Americans for decrying the hanging out of such dirty linen? But they view the scene from only one angle of vision. While the masses of Negroes accepted an economically depressed, socially inferior status, it was seldom necessary for the ruling class openly to employ such brutal tactics. Lynching was the prerogative of the poor white and the petty shopkeeper. It served the function of keeping the Negro in his place while the upper class remained carefully off stage. Now, such aloofness can no longer be pretended. A social structure is being shaken and the Southern aristocrat may soon have his back against the wall.

The Southern "way of life" was constructed around the turn of the century after the Negro had enjoyed a shortlived emancipation. The Southern pattern was less of a crazy quilt than the more hypocritical Northern accommodation. A tiny Negro business and professional class was permitted to exist but in a strictly segregated locale. It was reasoned, with some justification, that pressure from below could thus be siphoned off and the educated Negro could be given a stake as a minor partner of Jim Crow.

But two world wars have loosened the grip of the traditional ruling classes everywhere and at last the semi-feudal rulers of the South are confronted with the handwriting on the wall. The cotton-picking machine has chased the poor white from the fields as tenant farmer or overseer, and he has found employment in the Texas oilfields or in the many new industries that find his labor cheaper than in the unionized North. He is even painfully learning in the sugar refinery strikes in Louisiana and in the longshore struggles of the Gulf ports that he has a fundamental identity of interest with the despised blacks. The lesson is being learned slowly but inescapably.

Is it any wonder, then, that the ruling class in the South has openly assumed the helm in the savage struggle to smash the Negro back? The amalgamation of the White Citizens Councils into the Federation for Constitutional Government finds a score of ex-Governors and ex-Senators lined up with such active politicians as Talmadge, Eastland, Fielding Wright, Griffin and Strom Thurmond. Appropriately, a major industrialist, John U. Barr, is its chairman. One of its first acts was to put out feelers for alliance with Rumely and Mervin K. Hart. Thus, a special brand of American fascism appears on the scene.

Numberless anonymous little Negroes who trudged to the polls to vote, who dared to challenge Jim Crow on buses, who petitioned for non-segregated schools, are compelling a polarization of forces. In most instances these actions have been without the sanction of their major spokesman, the National Association for the Advancement of Colored People. Winfred Lynn was denied support when he refused to submit to induction in a segregated Army. Irene Morgan did not have official approval for sitting in the "white" section of a bus in 1946. The national office of the NAACP hesitates to endorse the fight of Andrew Wade and his white friends, the Bradens, for a home in an unsegregated neighborhood of Louisville.

What is true of the national body, however, is not true of the branches of this organization. When the writer was jailed in Petersburg, Va., in 1947, for refusing to move to the "colored" section of a bus, the local branch of the NAACP was quick to come to his aid. Local Negro leaders of the battle for equality in the South almost uniformly come from indigenous chapters in the various states. McCoy and Howard of Mississippi, the youthful Carl Gray of Montgomery, Ala., Simkins of Columbia, S.C., Calhoun of Georgia, to mention only a few, are all active NAACP members.

Until the recent past the NAACP has been dominated by its Northern constituents. The Northern middle-class Negro has accepted a second-class status which is for the most part not as galling as that suffered by his Southern brother. At the same time, influential in his councils, are liberal whites like Mrs. Eleanor Roosevelt and H. B. Lewis, whose hearts bleed for the Negro but who are anxious that the Negro not be too ready to bleed for himself. Inevitably the influence of this faction must wane as the struggle in the South intensifies.

Why is it that among the most prosperous Negroes in the South we find many of the most militant fighters for social emancipation? A glance at Morocco, the Gold Coast, or Indochina, affords a clue to the answer. In many respects the situation of the Negro in the South is analogous to that of oppressed colonials. Regardless of his economic station, he is barred in many crucial areas from participation in the national life. From this circumstance, however, we need not adopt the Communist deduction of "self-determination for the Black Belt." As much as any non-accepted group, the Negro in America seeks integration into the general body politic.

While the leadership of the current struggle has come from the educated middle-class Negro, as the fight deepens, the Moses Wrights among the downtrodden masses come to the fore. This is a sure sign that this campaign differs fundamentally from all that have preceded it. Every previous upsurge of the Negro has resulted in a compromise with his inferior status consolidated at a slightly higher level than that which existed before. Now his fight coincides with the stirring of that vast world of color in Asia and Africa, awakening from a millenium of apathy. The lowliest Negro veteran remembers his experiences in Asia and Europe. The impact of a changing economic organization arouses obscure impulses for more participation in society's benefits. "The Negro in America is the great proletarian. The white worker can dream of rising to middle-class status but the Negro is a worker in uniform, so to speak, a uniform he cannot take off: his skin. When such a group, deliberately kept for generations at the bottom of the social structure, begins to stir and raise its head, the whole edifice feels the shock." (D. MacDonald, *Politics,* February 1944.)

In the South, the Negro knows that his battle admits of no further compromise. The basis of the decision of the United States Supreme Court that segregation, *per se,* is discrimination, makes this implicit. That decision was itself only a recognition of the world struggle for men's allegiances. Any doubt that the final contest for integration has been joined can be resolved by a visit to a Southern Negro church, such as the one in Lake City, South Carolina, which was burned to the ground by the blind and desperate mob. In this cultural center of the Negro one is likely to hear on any occasion the singing of "O Freedom":

> *And before I'll be a slave*
> *I'll be buried in my grave*
> *And go home to my Lord*
> *And be free.*

The conflict assumes innumerable forms. In Augusta, Ga., the Negroes win the right to vote and throw out of office a reactionary Board of Education wedded to segregation. In Montgomery, Ala., a young Negro woman refuses to heed an order of a bus driver to give up her seat to a white woman. Three policemen drag her in chains to jail. Three days later

Carl Gray leads a boycott of 40,000 Negroes who walk as much as five miles to work rather than submit any longer to Jim Crow on buses. The Negro taxi-drivers cut their fare for their brothers to ten cents and even some white employers, in grudging admiration, call for their Negro servants in their own cars.

In Orangeburg, S. C., the White Citizens Council decrees the firing from jobs of Negroes who sign a petition for an unsegregated school system. The Negroes, who are in the majority there, place a selective boycott on the leaders of the Council. Economic ruin stares these worthies in the face. The Godchaux refinery in Louisiana hires armed thugs to break up the strike of Negro and white workers. The union quietly provides all its members with the weapons of self-defense.

In Louisville, Ky., a white man, [Carl] Braden, sells a home to a Negro friend, Andrew Wade, in an unsegregated neighborhood. Hoodlums stirred up by the real estate interests fire shots into the house. Friends of Wade, Negro and white, volunteer to move into his house with guns to protect home and family. In the dead of night a bomb is thrown under the home, partially destroying it. Wade sends his wife and baby away and grimly stays on with his rifle.

In Milford, Del., young white toughs set out to beat up Negroes in the black ghetto. They are thrown back and punished so severely by the erstwhile lowly blacks that the police have to rescue them. In Mississippi a bloody showdown impends as the whites and blacks sweep the hardware stores bare of guns and ammunition and the white banking authorities announce that they will no longer extend credit on the crops of the Negroes this spring.

Nor does the Negro stand alone in the area of the fight. Small groups of dedicated whites all over the South risk everything to stand by his side, foreshadowing the ultimate reawakening of the disadvantaged whites. The history of Populism and of native socialism in this region is ample testimony to the revolutionary potential of the Southern masses. Don West in Dalton, Ga., the Bradens in Louisville, Charlie Jones in Chapel Hill, Minter, Cox and Editor Hazel Smith of Mississippi, have but taken up the cause of their forebears.

Finally, the remainder of the country is profoundly affected by the course of this crucial struggle. For the first time, any obscure region in the South knows that the acts of the hooded mob in the dead of night may be exposed by a Murray Kempton, or a Desmond, or even an anonymous field hand in Mississippi who writes to a Chicago paper of the terror in his neighborhood. Unquestionably the Negro will experience attacks of mounting intensity as native fascism plays its last cards. But who can doubt the eventual outcome?

American Socialist, February 1956, vol. 3, pp. 7–9.

42

FIGHTING RACISM: A GRASS ROOTS ACCOUNT (1956)

by John Hope II

Rare are detailed accounts of consciously organized efforts to combat racism. One such was prepared by John Hope II when he was director of Industrial Relations in the Race Relations Department at Fisk University. The study was of the United Packinghouse Workers of America (UPWA) during the first half of the 1950s. Following are sections of the "Summary of Survey Findings" as to the implementation of the union's antidiscrimination program.

It is essential that the architects of the new A-D program have a clear image of the present pattern with all of the important elements standing in bold relief in order to whittle the problem down to its more workable component parts. Only by this means can adequate and well adapted tools be fashioned to cope with the many aspects of discrimination as a whole. Union leaders and other social engineers concerned with achieving equality of employment opportunity cannot safely eschew these details.

This chapter summarizes the findings in non-technical and nonstatistical terms for lay-readers and students who are concerned only with a panoramic view of intergroup relations in UPWA at mid-century. The assessment of the situation within the local union, the plant, and the community are discussed in turn from the points of view of local officials and rank and file members.

Relative Importance of Various Regions. The heart of the union is found in that large central area of the United States. Here almost six out of ten of its locals and three out of four of all members in the United States are located. This area is dominated by meat packing plants and is characterized by relatively large locals. Second in importance is the relatively new and expanding South where slightly more than one of each five locals and one out of each ten UPWA members are located. . . . It is characterized by small locals, many of which represent vegetable oil, sugar, and other vegetable processing as well as meat processing workers.

With regard to minority-majority community relations within these two great central regions, the area from the Gulf of Mexico to Canada embodies the most restrictive and stable "southern" patterns crystallized into law, the restrictive but less stable patterns of the border states, and the less restrictive and more tenuous "northern" pattern.

Westward within these two regions, the area changes from one with a bi-racial population with a high percentage of Negroes to one that includes an increasing number of Mexican-Americans as well. The West Coast region is numerically the least important UPWA section but it has significance for the study of minority problems because it is characterized by a multi-minority situation in which, unlike the Southwest, Mexican-Americans are employed in numbers closely approaching the size of the Negro group and where oriental groups also are present in small numbers. Here one finds the supreme challenge of the future in human relations—that of successfully unifying persons of different cultural, racial, national origin, and perhaps religious backgrounds within a single local capable of maintaining an efficient, stable, democratic organization of workers.

Industry Groups. Of the UPWA locals in the United States, approximately three-fifths have jurisdiction in meat packing plants; almost one-fifth in non-packing operations, including sugar refining, oil milling and refining, and fertilizer making while the remaining one-fourth represent a miscellaneous group.

Minority-Majority Mixture. Though the majority of the UPWA membership is white, Negroes constitute a large and growing numerical minority and Mexican-Americans a small but growing group. Out of each one hundred members in the United States, fifty-nine are white, thirty-four are Negro and seven are Mexican-American. Between 1943 and the end of 1948, there was a slight increase in the percentage of Negroes and Mexican-Americans and a compensating decrease in that of white members.

THE LOCAL UNION

Rank and File Participation. At a regular meeting of a UPWA local, white members are likely to be in the majority while the remainder of those present will include a large minority of Negroes and a small group of Mexican-Americans. However, in proportion to their respective total memberships, the number of Mexican-Americans attending will represent a larger turnout of their group than that represented by the Negroes present. As compared with the percentage of the total membership attending, Negro attendance is somewhat below normal while Mexican-American attendance is about normal.

By 1948, a larger percentage of the total membership appeared to be attending the local union meetings than during 1943. This tendency applied to minorities and majority alike. However, greater progress in this regard was apparent among white members than among the minorities. The percentage of white members present at meetings increased from 58% to 64% even though their percentage in total membership decreased from 65% to 59%.

Leadership Participation. The minorities appear to be well represented among the leadership positions in local unions. A substantial majority of the locals have Negro representation among each of five selected official positions. This situation prevailed in 1943 as well as in 1948. . . . Both Negroes and Mexican-Americans are found most frequently in the position of shop steward. The second most frequently held position for Negroes is membership on the grievance committee while this position is the least important among Mexican-Americans.

Quality as Union Members. The great majority of the local leadership consider both Negroes and Mexican-Americans to be good union members in normal times and under strike conditions. . . .

Mixed Participation—Business and Social Activities. Mixed participation of all members in the business activities of the local seems to prevail generally, but a noticeably smaller proportion of the locals sponsor mixed sports and social activities in which Negroes participate. This difference between business and social activities does not apply to Mexican-American participation. . . .

The full and unqualified acceptance of Negro members by the majority as equal participants in their local union affairs does not appear to depend solely upon their performance and quality as members. Despite their potential political importance, the extent of their rank and file and leadership participation, the high quality rating given them as union members by local officials and their effective contribution under strike conditions, they do not participate in mixed union-sponsored sports and social affairs as fully as they do in business activities. They seem less acceptable than Mexican-Americans in sports and social affairs.

THE PLANT

Extent of Utilization and Exclusion of Minorities. The customary and conscious exclusion of minorities from certain departments and job classifications remains an important practice in plants under the jurisdiction of UPWA though progress is being made in decreasing such unfair practices. Minorities are rather widely scattered among the departments, though not proportionately so; they are less widely diffused among a representative list of job classifications under the jurisdiction of UPWA but are conspicuously absent from the highly skilled mechanical jobs.

Difficulties in use of Minorities. Of the locals that report difficulties in the use of minorities, more of them observe opposition to initial hiring than to promotion or transfer of minorities already employed. For both of these types of difficulties, the opposition to Negroes appears more widespread than that to Mexican-Americans....

Recruitment Control. Directly or indirectly controlled methods dominate the initial employment facilities from which the majority of UPWA's members and potential members get their jobs. Such control applies to all groups and is exercised through the company employment office and by the recruitment of friends and relatives of present employees.

Upgrading and Segregated Plant Facilities. UPWA locals have not as yet eliminated restrictions upon the normal upgrading of qualified and eligible members because of their minority status, nor have segregated facilities completely disappeared from plants in which they are the bargaining agents. However, substantial progress appears evident in both. Restrictions on upgrading and segregated plant facilities are felt more widely by Negroes than by Mexican-Americans. One-third of the locals report that segregated facilities of some kind for use by Negro employees are present in their plants. Such separation of Mexican-Americans is almost non-existent.

Desirability on the Job. Virtually all locals feel that both Negro and Mexican-American members are desirable workers. Almost all of them also consider both minorities as *average* or *above average* in efficiency on the job....

THE COMMUNITY

Use of Public Facilities. Restrictions in the use of public facilities on equal terms by members of minority groups are widespread both in the immediate vicinity of the plants where they work and in the communities where they live. Such obstacles appear to be more intense in the latter than in the former and apply more generally to Negroes than to Mexican-Americans....

Protection of Benefits of Citizenship. The majority of local union officials believe that the minorities receive equal benefits of citizenship in their respective communities. However, abridgements of these benefits seem considerably more widespread as applied to Negroes than to Mexican-Americans. Of five selected standards, both minorities consider lack of equal protection by police and against brutality from the police the most serious threat to full benefits of citizenship. In descending order of importance to both, justice in the courts, protection against mob rule, and equal chance to vote are enumerated as significant....

Interest in Problems of Minorities. The overwhelming majority of locals report an active interest in both national and local issues of peculiar concern to minorities. Some of them co-operate with minority protective organizations in their communities, but there is much room for the improvement of minority-majority relations.

KNOWLEDGE AND ACCEPTANCE OF AN ANTI-DISCRIMINATION PROGRAM

The International appears to have a clear mandate from the local leadership to expand its anti-discrimination program. The leadership of virtually all locals knows that the International has a nondiscrimination program and most of them feel that this program has not gone far enough. The remaining group is content with the program to date. None express the opinion that it has gone too far. The majority of the locals are attempting to eliminate discrimination through education and persuasion.

FINDINGS OF RANK AND FILE STUDIES IN SELECTED CASES

KNOWLEDGE AND ACCEPTANCE OF THE NON-DISCRIMINATION POLICY

Is There a Non-Discrimination Policy? In two of the selected cities two-thirds or more of the members know that their International has a non-discrimination policy, while in the remaining cities about one-half are aware of this. However, there is a large group that is uncertain about the existence of such a policy. Apparently there is no important difference between the views of majority and minority groups. Local union officials are much better informed than the rank and file. Ninety-nine per cent of those reporting know of the policy. However, no more than two-thirds of the membership cognizant of it in any of the cities can accurately describe it. In some of these cities the minority group understands the program better than the majority.

While most of the members feel that their locals are following the International minorities policy, some state that their local approach is different and others do not know whether it differs or not. Here again the opinions of whites and Negroes are not conspicuously conflicting.

Is the Policy Working Well? A majority of the members feel that the International policy is working well in all but one community. Generally, a somewhat smaller percentage of Negro than white respondents think this, and the remaining members are uncertain.

Value of the Non-Discrimination Policy to Union and to Individual Member. In most of the cities a large majority of the members consider the non-discrimination policy helpful to the union, while a minority does not know whether it helps or not; very few believe that it hurts the union. The percentage of Negroes judging this policy as beneficial to the union is considerably larger than that of whites. This more widespread conviction of the minority group may arise from the fact that they feel a personal need for such protection. From 5 to 7 out of 10 Negroes state that they "did not get a fair deal as a worker in the packing industry because of their race, religion, or where they come from," while hardly any whites feel similarly.

Approval of Non-Discrimination Policy. Despite this difference in opinion as to the personal need for such a policy, a large majority of all members state that they approve of it. The proportion of Negroes endorsing it is larger than that of whites; moreover, the proportion of members favorable in the North is somewhat larger than that in the South.

Willingness to Participate in Education-General Worker and Anti-Discrimination. In all communities except one, a large majority of all members express willingness to attend after-hour union-sponsored classes and also to attend a union program including a discussion of discrimination. A larger proportion of Negro than of white members desires each of these union services. It would appear that the desire for this type of education is greater below than above the Mason and Dixon's line. Significantly, despite the differences in the customs and mores of North and South as to race relations, there is no apparent sectional difference in the willingness of white and colored members to participate in union programs that include discussion of discrimination. Further, with one exception, the proportions of both white and colored members willing to take part in such discussions are larger than those willing to attend after-hour general worker education classes in each of the cities studied. There is a sufficiently large number of both groups "on the fence" regarding general union education and anti-discrimination education to draw an even larger proportion of the membership into such programs through the use of effective promotional techniques.

FEELINGS, ATTITUDES, OPINIONS, AND PREFERENCES AFFECTING THE APPLICATION OF THE POLICY

Motivation of the Individual and Its Prospects. The minority group can always be more readily and easily motivated to destroy the roots of discrimination because this segment of the population is apt to feel the disadvantage and pain of prejudice more or less continuously in some form. The minority, therefore, tends to think about the problem much more than the majority.

Opinions as to What Local Unions Do About Discrimination. The majority of the members, white and Negro, feel that their locals have taken some action in cases of discrimination. However, more Negroes than whites disagree with this opinion. Impressive proportions of white and colored workers feel that more *could* and *should* be done.

Treatment of Minorities in Local Unions. The standard for the treatment of minorities varies widely from local to local. Certainly the studies show that this changes from geographical section to section and from one type of union activity to another. The large majority of white members state that Negroes in their local are treated the same as others but a somewhat smaller proportion of the Negroes share this opinion. On the more specific question, "Do Negroes participate freely and together with white members in union business affairs and in official entertainment?" there is much less of a consensus from city to city and between white and colored respondents. Standards of equal treatment are less apparent in the South than North and are less pronounced in official social entertainment than in business affairs both North and South.

Ability of Negroes to Get Along with Others. Almost none of the white members state that Negroes working in their department or other work unit get along unsatisfactorily with white workers.

Willingness to Work with Qualified Negroes. A large proportion of the white workers object to working with qualified Negroes on terms of equality despite the apparent harmony in a mixed work relationship. The objection to working with a qualified Negro where the latter's competence places him in the same or higher job status than his white associate is much more pronounced in the South than in the North.

PREVAILING PRACTICES—IN THE UNION, PLANT, AND COMMUNITY

Participation in Union and Community Leadership. Only a small minority of the members have ever held office in the local or membership on a union committee while both whites and Negroes have participated as officers and committeemen in all of the cities studied. In each the proportion of Negroes so engaged is smaller than that of white members. Likewise UPWA members are active in various community organizations, but in contrast to the union situation, the proportion of Negroes in leadership roles is significantly larger than that of the whites.

Rank and File Participation in Union and Community Organizations. While only a small minority of the local union membership has ever participated in its leadership, both white and colored members have taken a part in all cities studied though a somewhat larger proportion of the white than colored has so participated. On the other hand, on basis of rank and file interest as evidenced by attendance, the colored members appear to have been more active than the whites. Likewise, there seems to be some carry-over to participation in community organizations by UPWA members. A larger percentage of Negro than white members takes part both in the leadership and rank and file attendance at meetings of these organizations.

Patterns of Upgrading Negroes. At least one-fifth of the membership in all cities believe that Negroes are not upgraded as fast as other workers. A larger percentage of Negro than white members feels that there are restrictions to the upgrading of Negroes, and there is no significant geographical difference in this respect.

Use of Plant Facilities and Services. The use of plant facilities clearly and sharply reflects the prevailing community patterns of the geographical sections where the respective plants are located. All of those replying in the North report no separate facilities for Negroes while almost all in the South do have segregated facilities in the plants. Those most frequently cited are toilets and dressing rooms.

Community Patterns of Minority Access to Public Facilities and Services. Whether Negro and other minority members of UPWA have access to essential community services and the terms under which they can use such facilities constitute a legitimate and vital concern to the union—local and International. By the same token, the extent to which they enjoy the rights and protection of citizenship is a concern to the union. When these services are provided on a discriminatory basis, the resulting influence on the thinking and action of members and their immediate families will tend to undermine constantly the equalitarian objectives of the union in local and plant activities.

With regard to community services and facilities surrounding the plants, white and colored opinions as to whether or not such services are provided on a segregated basis are quite similar. However, there is a wide divergence between these groups as to whether those services are offered on a *separate but equal* or a *separate and unequal basis*. The preponderant Negro opinion is that they are unequal; most whites believe, or claim to believe, just the opposite. The opinions as to what conditions of use *should* prevail are even more divergent. A large majority of the Negroes feel that such services should be available *without segregation* while an even larger majority of white members in southern communities contend that they should be *separate but equal*. Very few white members and virtually no Negroes favor either *segregated and unequal* facilities or refusal to serve Negroes at all.

CONCLUSION

The findings of the Rank and File Survey clearly show the influence of the local environment upon the thinking and feeling of the individual member and upon the racial practices prevailing in those segments of the local community about which UPWA has a strong and justified concern— the local UPWA union; the plants where it has bargaining rights; and the communities of which its members are citizens.

The attitudes of the minority regarding race relations differ from those of the majority and the range of difference widens from those concerned primarily with internal union practices to those concerned with work relationship and opportunity, and finally, to those concerned with relationships as citizens and consumers of services in the communities. Furthermore, differences in the patterns of community race relations between North and South are clearly reflected in the attitudes and practices prevalent in these respective sections. The action and attitudes of white members tend to violate the southern pattern more distinctly in matters related to internal local activities and, in lesser measure, to plant practices than in those involving the communities where they live.

The minority group has a somewhat better understanding of the non-discrimination policy than the majority group, a greater sense of dissatisfaction about prevailing conditions, and a stronger incentive to change them. However, there is a sizable nucleus of white members who clearly comprehend this policy, recognize its importance for the maintenance of a strong union, and are ready to take a firm stand for its full application wherever the membership is concerned.

The New Anti-Discrimination Program

After the completion of the first report, the union began an anti-discrimination program in the winter of 1950. Shortly thereafter, on the basis of the second report, the first intensive city-wide action program was initiated in Kansas City. By convention resolution, a national A-D Department was set up under the direction of a vice president and with a small full-time staff.

The program was based on two assumptions: first, such a program must be administered primarily through the normal union channels at the district and local union levels with the guidance and assistance but not dominance of the Anti-Discrimination staff. Secondly, in choosing the specific problems to be attacked, priority should be given to internal and in-plant problems.

The development of such a program required the full and unwavering support of the policy-making leadership of the union—its president and International Executive Board. The presidential initiative and continuing concern for the success of this program provided an indispensable dynamic element. This executive support, in turn, could not have been sustained without the firm and continued backing of the legislative body of UPWA—the Constitutional Convention. The evolving process of implementing this A-D policy resulted in structural and functional changes at various points in the administrative organization.

In this chapter, three major types of developments will be discussed: Convention resolutions, frequently submitted by the International Executive Board, affecting the program; internal innovations that were necessary to implement the Union's anti-discrimination policy; and changes in human relations practices within the Union's sphere of influence, i.e., in-plant practices and those of the surrounding community.

ACTION OF THE UPWA CONVENTIONS

It will be recalled that the UPWA Constitution contains a strong A-D policy and that the concern of the union in such matters has been specifically extended to the community by its Constitutional Conventions.

Under this authority the president took the initiative in the fall of 1948 by seeking appropriate means to revitalize the Union's A-D program. His first step, authorized by the International Executive Board, was to undertake the UPWA Self-Survey of Human Relations. This action was sustained by the Sixth Constitutional Convention which also gave specific directives to locals, in co-operation with District organizations, to take internal action and co-operate with community groups toward the elimination of discrimination in the union, the plant, and the community.

The Eighth Constitutional Convention in 1952 gave much more detailed and comprehensive directives for action against discrimination and placed responsibilities squarely upon the International Anti-Discrimination Department.

CHANGES WITHIN THE UNION
STRUCTURAL AND FUNCTIONAL DEVELOPMENTS

One of the first developments of the new A-D program was to establish procedures whereby the policy-making officers of the Union could obtain accurate, periodic reports on the operation of the anti-discrimination policy at all levels. In 1950 a question was added to the periodic report filed by each paid field representative requiring him to indicate his A-D activities and the minorities' problems confronting the locals which he served. Such reports have become a part of the standard procedure. Careful study of the statements furnished valuable clues to those responsible for the program. The field staff in each union local in the district provided the A-D and Organization departments with a picture of the "in-plant conditions" and the "inner local situation," and community patterns surrounding the plant.

Large wall charts have been prepared which show in tabular form the progress of each local, and provide a basis for discussion of appropriate remedial measures at district conventions. In order to develop adequate channels through which to project such a program from the International level down to the individual union member, an effort has been made to organize effective local, city-wide, and district-wide A-D committees. The national A-D Department has helped such groups by preparing a descriptive manual, projects, and by contributing field assistance.

This effort met with varied results. In Kansas City, where the most intensive A-D committee attempt was made, the by-product was probably more fruitful for the long range development of a program than the immediate result. In their effort to eliminate in-plant discrimination, the A-D committees attempted to reach the rank and file through the shop steward group. This effort disclosed a weakness in the steward system and explained why the entire union program was weak. Intensive steward training programs were then instituted in which all aspects of the UPWA program were explained, including the A-D program. Closer observation by the International staff revealed that this weakness in local in-plant leadership was by no means confined to this area. As a result the education function of the Union was reoriented and expanded.

Since this experience of the Kansas City self-survey showed clearly the essential interdependence of these departments, the quality and range of co-operation between them has grown steadily. The union's Education Department has been completely reorganized and the educational functions of the A-D Department have been integrated into the educational program with growing effectiveness. In the past four years, increasing attention has been given to the development of periodic staff schools, district leadership schools, and local and district steward training schools.

Finally, the increasing co-operation between the vice presidents in charge of the A-D Department and the Organization Department and the growing joint responsibility of the staffs for the field administration and policing phase of the A-D program, provide a strong basis for the application of the union's anti-discrimination policy at the local level. By this means, too, a larger segment of the paid union staff can be deployed in implementing the A-D program. The most recent development in this direction is the addition of program coordinators to the field staff working at the district level. These include among their technical training specific skills in the handling of human relations problems. Program co-ordinators are now working in Districts 1, 3, 6, and 9. Subsequently, it is expected that such staff members will be assigned to each district. The responsibility for administering this program has been delegated by the International Executive Board jointly to the vice presidents in charge of the A-D Department and the Organization Department. The programs of the co-ordinators in the various districts are directed by the National Program Co-ordinator who is responsible to the above vice presidents.

The UPWA Co-ordinator Program was initiated in January of 1953. It represented a shift in general emphasis from training specific local leadership to carry out the essential functions of the local union to promotion of various aspects of the International union's program at the district and local levels. The feeling was that local leadership might be best built around issues pertinent to the membership. Through the co-ordinated activities of such a staff, program emphasis can be varied to meet more effectively the specific needs of each district at a given time while simultaneously contributing to the attainment of the over-all union program. The first program emphasis was on discrimination. The goal to "sweep discrimination from the union and the plant" and the very tangible results obtained since the inception of this program show the impact of this co-ordinated effort.

Between 1952 and 1955 six A-D conferences were held at the district level and two national A-D conferences were convened. Many of the inequities, such as misuse of members of minority groups by the companies and by their own union brothers and sisters, did not come to light until frank and open discussions were made possible by the district conferences.

The first National Anti-Discrimination Conference in October, 1953, was the result of a mandate from the 1952 Constitutional Convention. It directed its officers to conduct an intensive campaign against plant discrimination; this campaign was followed by a national conference. The official call issued to all locals stated the specific purpose of this conference as follows:

1. To discuss and formulate plans to completely eliminate discrimination and segregation in UPWA plants.
2. To project activities for the purpose of achieving equal rights in towns with UPWA plants and in the national community.

The intense interest of the membership in the problem of discrimination in their plants is evidenced by the fact that this conference drew a larger number of delegates than the Wage Rate and Job Standards Conference of the previous summer. Three hundred and thirteen elected delegates from locals throughout the United States and Puerto Rico and thirteen executive board members were in attendance.

During the spring of 1955, a second District Conference was held jointly by the two southern districts, 8 and 9, at Atlanta University and a second National A-D Conference met in Chicago. Both reflected the prime importance accorded the problem of minorities by the International and its determination to have the most important and influential leadership at all levels participate in its program for the elimination of discrimination and segregation within its jurisdiction. In both cases, the delegates designated to deal with basic union economic issues such as wages and contracts also attended the discussions of discrimination and women's activities. In the former case, the A-D conference was followed by the annual district (8 and 9) conventions, while in the latter, the Second National A-D Conference, the Second National Women's Activities Conference, and the Third Biennial Wage and Contract Conference were combined and integrated into a five-day meeting covering all three issues. Four-hundred and fifty delegates participated in these meetings. Consequently, the most influential leadership of the union was involved in such a way as to demonstrate realistically the inter-relations of these issues and the need for equal treatment of all minorities.

As an incentive for the achievement of the campaign goal, citations were awarded to the two districts and the seven individual local unions which had done most during the six months prior to the First National A-D Conference to eliminate segregation and discrimination from the plants. The first district prize went to District No. 1, and the second, to District No. 6. The prize for the local making the most outstanding contribution went to Local 80A (Campbell Soup Co.) Camden, New Jersey. Honorable mention citations were given six other locals. These prizes were awarded for specific actions of locals which eliminated some definite type of discrimination within a plant reported to the Anti-Discrimination Department by members of the International field staff or by other available sources. This report described detailed statements from some 39 locals in nine districts in the United States.

Outstanding accomplishments since the First National A-D Conference were recognized at an Awards Banquet during the Second National A-D Conference. Citations were presented to five locals distributed over five districts: Districts 1, 3, 6, 8 and 9, while honorable mention awards went to two district councils and four locals in Districts 3 and 4. Highest praise was accorded Local No. 347 and the persons who assisted it in a carefully executed campaign to open jobs to Negro clerical and professional workers in the "front offices" of the Armour Company. Special citations were given to some eighteen young women, white and colored, whose repeated application for clerical positions helped to prove the existence of a discriminatory pattern. Well-documented complaints were filed with the President's Committee on Government Contracts. Persistent efforts of this local on behalf of the complainants and negotiations with the President's Committee and the company resulted in the employment of Negro white-collar workers in the main office of a Chicago meat packer for the first time. Parleys are now in process to open similar opportunities in the main offices of other meat packing firms where UPWA has jurisdiction in Chicago and other major cities.

Minority Leadership Participation

Participation of minority groups in the leadership of the union at various levels and their employment on its administrative and field staffs have increased in recent years. By the spring of 1955, there were Negroes, Mexican-Americans, and women employed on the International field staff and the administrative office staff was composed of people of various races, religions, and national origins.

In the spring of 1955, one of the four officials selected by the total membership of a constitutional convention of the union was a Negro elected for his third consecutive term as vice president. Likewise, three of the nine district directors serving in the United States were Negroes, two of whom were elected by their respective district delegates at the Ninth Constitutional Convention in 1954. One of these, who directs the southwestern area (District 8), was probably the first Negro to serve as a district director of an international union in the South. The other succeeded to the leadership of District 1, the oldest and largest in the union, which includes the Chicago area.

Three of the eleven heads of administrative departments at the International level are Negroes. They are in the A-D, the Program, and the Grievance Departments. Among the seven International represent-atives, one is from the Negro and one is from the Mexican-American group, while one, a white woman, is the first of her sex to hold a job at this occupational level in the UPWA hierarchy. Of the sixty-six represent-atives, eighteen (15 male and 3 female) are Negro, four are Mexican-American, and three are white women. The International office staff of nineteen employees includes a wide variety of racial, religious, and national origin groups.

Several of the largest and most outstanding locals have Negro presidents, secretaries, or chief stewards, and two Negro women are district executive board members. Such leadership is distributed over six of the nine districts in the United States including the most extensive and oldest districts in the UPWA: Districts 1, 3, 4, 6, 7 and 9. Some 26,000 UPWA members of 15 locals are under the leadership of Negro presidents, chief stewards or financial secretaries. It seems apparent that the Negro minority is represented at all major leadership levels and is widely diffused geographically.

The Mexican-American and female leadership at the International level is less pronounced. Their local participation and leadership are probably underestimated in the data available here. It should be noted, however, that in 1954, Local No. 54 (Armour and Co.) in Fort Worth elected a Mexican-American as its first woman president.

Certain important changes in the character of services rendered to the membership have taken place since 1949. At the present time, all master contracts with the Big Four Packers—Swift, Cudahy, Armour and Wilson—contain non-discrimination clauses outlawing unfair treatment of *applicants* or *employees* in plants over which it has jurisdiction. These chains, particularly Cudahy and Armour, are in the process of eliminating segregated facilities in their plants in the South as well as in the North. Among the southern cities involved are Fort Worth, Birmingham, Atlanta, Albany, Tifton and Moultrie. While some repercussions of this desegregation process have occurred, the writer finds no evidence that they have deterred the process or that the national program, services, or stability of the International union have been adversely affected.

The union attributes much of its recent success in narrowing the wage rate spread between its northern and southern packing plants to the growing unity and objectivity of its white and colored members. During the period from 1943 to 1954, the first eleven years of its life, the differential between the common labor wage rates in the South and the metropolitan rate of the North has decreased from 25 cents to 5½ cents....

This accomplishment probably will be increasingly impressive to the membership since the packing industry is expanding "at a much more rapid rate in the South than in any other section of the country."

Between 1947, when the sugar locals were affiliated with UPWA, and 1953, the reduction in the North-South wage differential was very small, from 51 cents to 50 cents. Since that time, however, Union efforts to narrow this difference have been intensified and, coincidentally or consciously, efforts to eliminate discrimination in sugar refineries and locals, particularly in the southern district, have been accelerated. Significant internal union political developments and unprecedented changes in race relations have occurred since 1953. These will be discussed elsewhere in this chapter.

The 1954 sugar negotiations had mixed results. The American Sugar Company contract provided for a ten-cent increase in hourly wage rates plus fringe benefits estimated to cost another four cents per hour. Furthermore, through an agreement between this company and UPWA locals in its eastern and southern refineries, the North-South differential was reduced to about 38 cents per hour. As the largest of the Louisiana refineries, the American Sugar Company agreement has generally set the pattern for all other refineries in the area. However, this was not the case in these negotiations (1954). The Henderson Sugar Company of New Orleans met the ten-cent raise given by the American Sugar Company and agreed to fringe benefits costing an additional two to three cents per hour.

The remaining firms, Godchaux and Colonial, after several months of bargaining offered only five cents per hour increase and no additional fringe benefits. The locals of both of these companies went on strike on April 14, 1955, to get the ten-cent raise provision given to employees of the American Sugar refinery. The Colonial strike was settled on September 13th on basis of an agreement which provided for a ten-cent per hour raise, five cents immediately and an additional five cents beginning January 1, 1956. The Godchaux stoppage was ended in December, 1955 with a new contract granting a ten-cent raise on terms much like those at Colonial.

The 1955 contract with the customarily pattern setting American Sugar Company plant at New Orleans has resulted in a 15-cent per hour general increase in wage rates plus fringe benefits estimated at nine cents per hour effective on October 1, 1955. Three cents of the general increase is to apply toward further reducing the North-South wage differential. Since October 1, 1954 the American Sugar Company's North-South differential has been reduced by six cents and its new scale ($1.59) exceeds that of the Godchaux plant by 20 cents an hour with 19 cents more in fringe benefits, according to the UPWA Sugar Director.

The locals that withdrew from UPWA prior to the 1954 negotiations and thus bargained independently with their employers fared even worse. Two of these locals were offered a three-cent raise, refused it, struck to raise the company offer, lost their strikes, and finally were forced to accept the original company offer. The Imperial Sugar Company of Sugarland, Texas, agreed to give its 600 employees a ten-cent raise provided its three Louisiana competitors do likewise. It will be even more clearly apparent from subsequent sections that despite disruptive influences in the southern sugar locals, UPWA has persisted in its program of strengthening Negro-white unity in its rank and file in full compliance with its A-D policy as a means of developing stronger and more stable bargaining power. By refusing to hold its International Convention at any hotel or public place which segregates or denies service to any minority within its membership, UPWA has succeeded in altering the policies of hotels in several communities. These include hotel and restaurant facilities in such cities as Omaha, Denver, Waterloo, Mason City, Sioux City, Ottumwa, Fort Dodge, Des Moines, Fort Wayne, St. Louis, Selina, Kansas City, and Oklahoma City.

The impact of this action upon southern locals has been revealed in the resolution adopted at the Tenth Constitutional Convention of District 9, UPWA, which convened at Memphis, Tennessee, February 26–28, 1954. The District embraces eight southeastern states including Virginia, North Carolina, South Carolina, Florida, Georgia, Alabama, Mississippi, and Tennessee, and represents approximately 6,000 members. This resolution states "that it shall be the policy of District 9 UPWA-CIO never to hold a district convention in circumstances where they must be held under conditions of segregation on the basis of race or color." Thus, the 1955 convention was held at Atlanta University because unsegregated commercial facilities could not be found.

Within the union, segregated local membership meetings have been eliminated in the South as well as the North. In the southern districts, non-segregated banquets, parties, and picnics have occurred; in the past four years mixed banquets have been held in downtown Atlanta in connection with the District 9 Convention of UPWA.

CHANGES IN THE PLANT

The union also has moved against discrimination in the plants. The UPWA has placed primary reliance upon its collective bargaining contracts and the grievance machinery provided by them to eliminate discriminatory employment practices in the plants.

Even before the advent of the new program, the International declined to sign or service any contracts negotiated by its locals which did not contain a clause forbidding discrimination. However, the Self-Survey showed that there were weaknesses in the application of this policy. Since that time, the machinery for its enforcement has been strengthened and its importance re-emphasized to all elements of the union. As a result, compliance has improved notably. The rigorous enforcement of the above mentioned contracts with the Big Four Packers makes possible the settlement of complaints alleging discrimination through the normal grievance machinery. The union reports that such clauses are now included in 90% to 95% of all contracts signed with its locals and that the recalcitrants are confined primarily to the small independent plants.

A major part of the new A-D program has aimed at encouraging the local to use the terms of the contract as a means of eliminating discriminatory hiring and in-plant practices. The most significant and complete application occurred in the Chicago plant of Swift and Company where the union alleged that qualified Negro women were refused employment. An arbitration award required the company to hire the complainants and awarded them seniority rights and back pay from the date of the offense. An arbitration award to the union against the Rath Packing Company of Waterloo, Iowa, has opened the way for Negroes to enter the mechanical gang in that plant. They may progress from helper to apprentice to journeyman on the basis of their seniority and qualifications.

In many grievances filed by UPWA locals alleging contract violations of a discriminatory nature, the practices have been eliminated by negotiation at some stage in the standard grievance procedure. Efforts to open all-white departments and jobs to members of minority groups and to ban segregated plant facilities have brought encouraging results. By October 1951 twelve plants in Chicago, St. Louis, Kansas City, and Sioux City had discontinued separate locker rooms; food facilities of three other plants were opened to Negroes on an unsegregated basis and separate drinking foundations were eliminated at a few plants. Since this time, such efforts have continued successfully in plants located in all districts. Since 1952, increasing attention has been given to southern plants with tangible results which are discussed in more detail elsewhere; separate facilities have been eliminated in plants located in such cities as Fort Worth, Birmingham, and Baltimore.

Union-conducted investigations showed that in some plants both Negro men and women were denied employment, in others Negro women, and in still others both Negro and Mexican-American men and women were denied employment. The union also found that in certain plants minority groups were employed only in certain departments, usually the less desirable ones. For example, Negroes were generally absent from the mechanical gangs, and from the sliced bacon, canning, meat packing, and other specialized manufacturing departments. According to the union, by February, 1951, such patterns of discrimination had been eliminated from several plants through the use of the grievance machinery.

Since that time the efforts of locals and the field staff to eliminate discriminatory hiring practices have continued with a measure of success in plants in various sections of the country. Reports from all UPWA districts in the United States show that the greatest success has been achieved in the hiring of Negro women, and the discontinuance of all-white departments, and segregated plant facilities and services, including the cafeterias and locker rooms.

Understandably, such equalitarian efforts have not been without cost. To the embarrassment of the Union A-D program, all-white UPWA stockhandlers' locals have generally resisted the use of Negroes except in the labor pool. During 1953–54, the International Executive Board made strong demands upon these to discontinue their discriminatory practices. While there were other points of difference, insistence upon application of the International A-D policy was perhaps the "final straw" which resulted in the disaffiliation of four out of nine stockhandlers' locals: the stockyards at St. Joseph, Kansas City, Fort Worth, and Omaha. However, the Board has not changed its position and the first signs of change in minority practices of UPWA stockyard locals are apparent in the agreement recently concluded between Local No. 278 and the Belt Railroad and Stockyards Company of Indianapolis, signed during October, 1955. This contract provides not only for the standard non-discrimination clause embracing applicants for employment as well as employees but it also requires that job openings be posted by the company and that persons in the labor pool, to which Negroes in the past have generally been confined, be allowed to bid on these without prejudice because of race. This is the first time in the history of the Union that the latter clause has been included in a contract with a stockyard local.

The Swift local at Moultrie, Georgia withdrew shortly after being strongly censured by the Ninth Constitutional Convention in May, 1954, for obstructing the application of the International A-D policy to its plant facilities. Unquestionably, the firm insistence by the International upon compliance with this policy by the five southern sugar locals that obtained local industrial union (LIU) charters was a factor, though probably not the sole cause of their action.

SEQUENCE OF DEVELOPMENTS—IN THE UNION AND PLANT
PERIOD 1949 TO MID-1952.

The period 1949 to May 1952 (Constitutional Convention) was one of fact-finding, experimentation, and innovation. The information-collecting phase was complete and the union action program under way by the end of 1951. The union-wide promotion necessary for the success of the Self-Survey, the widespread asking of searching, probing questions of officials and members, as well as the facts themselves—some of them surprising and disturbing and others a source of pride and satisfaction—generated a ferment which prompted the forceful constructive action begun during the period. It became increasingly apparent that such action could not be successfully undertaken without making substantial and permanent commitments of the union's resources to the solution of the problems and conditions revealed. The 1949 Convention created an Education Department and the 1950 Convention started an Anti-Discrimination (A-D) Department. For the first time, a committee on problems of discrimination was established for the 1950 Convention. Since that time it has become a normal part of the convention machinery and has initiated far-reaching resolutions.

Through the close co-operation of the A-D and Education Departments and the creative experimentation of their staffs, a variety of A-D techniques were tried and tested. The frequent loan of the A-D Department's professional staff member to the Organization and Education Departments highlighted the interdependence of these hitherto distinct programs and the resulting co-operative effort led to subsequent changes. During this period the Education Department's program gained in scope and effectiveness as its emphasis was shifted in response to observed needs.

The continuous appraisal and re-appraisal and the willingness to try the unorthodox in so far as it seemed to meet the specific demands of the union at a particular time have contributed to the dynamic drive which has accelerated change and brought positive tangible results during the period since 1949 far beyond what the writer would have anticipated at the program's inception.

In short, it was a period of creative (sometimes daring) trial and error, experimentation, and study that set the stage for the more deft and still somewhat venturesome efforts of the current period which began in the summer of 1953.

The action phase of the new program, officially initiated in Kansas City on March 31, 1950, was followed by unprecedented consideration of discrimination at the Convention in May of that year. Major activity for the next two years was concentrated in Districts 1, 3, and 4. District 1 was already the most advanced in the application of the Union's non-discrimination policy. During this period, there was increased activity in other districts, notably District 6. Within the next two years greater emphasis was given to the program in the border state area (District 7) and South (Districts 8 and 9).

PERIOD MID-1952 TO 1956

The Convention of May 1952 inaugurated an all-out A-D program with the full benefit of the information from the Fisk-directed Self-Survey and from subsequent more specific UPWA-conducted inquiries which pin-pointed particular cities, plants, and locals in order of their relative urgency. At this Convention, the report of the A-D Department, including a summary of the rank and file survey findings of five cities, initiated a day-long discussion of A-D problems and culminated in the adoption of strong resolutions shaping the future A-D program. As a result of the Convention mandate to concentrate upon the immediate elimination of all discriminatory practices from the plants with a specific deadline for this achievement, this union embarked upon a course of action the end of which has not yet been reached.

Among the demands submitted during the contract negotiations with the Big Four Packers after this convention was the urgent request that the then existing non-discrimination clause be strengthened in order to more effectively handle prevalent types of discrimination. The bargaining committees representing workers in these chain plants called attention to refusal to hire women, particularly Negro and Mexican-American; exclusion from certain preferred departments and jobs, including those in mechanical gangs; and, for the first time, the demand that segregation itself in the use of facilities be eliminated from all plants in the South as well as elsewhere.

The acceptance of these demands by the Armour and Cudahy chains during October of 1952 opened the way for UPWA's decision to attack segregation itself as the crucial obstacle forestalling the eradication of discrimination of all kinds within the union's sphere of influence. All locals, North and South, were instructed to demand "immediate removal of discriminatory signs" requiring segregated use of plant facilities—locker rooms, cafeteria, etc.

Efforts of the leadership of some southern locals to implement the desegregation instructions in their plants precipitated opposition from some of their white rank and file membership and certain UPWA district officials and administrative officials. This gave the International leadership cause for some anxiety but did not induce it to compromise on the principle involved.

During the post-1952 Convention months when the above mentioned negotiations with the Big Four Packers were in progress and the accelerated tempo of the A-D program was becoming increasingly apparent, informal simultaneous charges that this union was "communist dominated and controlled" and that it was "going to merge with or be absorbed by the Amalgamated Meat Cutters and Butcher Workmen of North America (AFL)" were made to the CIO.

An investigation absolved the union of these charges on October 13, 1953. These charges were allegedly inspired by elements of UPWA leadership in the South and officials of other labor organizations in the southern area in order to forestall the UPWA's aggressive implementation of its non-discrimination policy, particularly its non-segregated aspects. Thus the vice president and secretary-treasurer charged that the director of District 9 had, during July 1953, conspired with others to prevent the implementation of the union's non-discrimination policy in Atlanta and had encouraged locals to withdraw from UPWA. Counter-charges of communistic leanings were made.

It seems likely that forthright desegregationist actions of the Armour Company in certain of its southern plants focused attention upon the basic issues involved and contributed much to their clarification and final resolution. In December 1952, segregation in the cafeterias in the Armour plants at Oklahoma City and Fort Worth was eliminated. Negro women were hired for the first time and placed in locker rooms on a non-segregated basis at the Oklahoma City plant, without incident. At Fort Worth, this precipitated a period of tension but did not stop the integration process.

In accordance with the agreement, management at Fort Worth removed discriminatory signs from its plant and decided to remove the cafeteria partition. However, rump meetings were called to demand that the signs be restored and that the partition be retained. Also, demands were made for resignations of officers supporting UPWA policy. Management complied by following Local 54's bargaining committee's request to restore the signs and leave the partition. Following this, the International president requested the call of a special meeting of the local's executive board and bargaining committee. Here he defined the UPWA position on this matter and urged quick action to secure company compliance. Within a month the cafeteria wall was removed and the signs taken down. No incidents occurred.

A few weeks after these changes, in March, 1953, the white group opposed to desegregation of facilities at the Fort Worth Armour Plant, nominated an all-white slate of officers to oppose the incumbent group which had had the responsibility for administering the above mentioned change. Despite the tension and fears engendered, the biracial group of candidates won by a significant margin. Fifty-one white members of a total local membership of about 1,400 resigned from the union in protest. By the spring of 1954 some thirty-five of these had applied for re-instatement.

A little more than a year later, the white director of District 8 who, according to International officials, did not actively and unequivocally support the union in this change, was defeated by a Negro member of this Fort Worth Armour local who had at one time been its president. This Negro director of a predominantly white, southern area was elected by the delegates from that district at the Ninth Constitutional Convention of UPWA at Sioux City, in May, 1954.

These developments alerted the International leadership to the previously submerged obstacles to its non-discrimination policy in this district as a whole. It was felt that under the district leadership in control at the time, rank and file participation in the affairs of the district was not representative and that district conventions had not recently been held as required by the union constitution. Thus, during the spring of 1953 such a convention was held and in the fall of that year the first district anti-discrimination conference met. In the course of the discussion of in-plant discrimination problems, "detailed consideration was given to the serious problems of segregation and discrimination in the sugar plants in Louisiana."

The following statement summaries some of the findings of this conference:

"The delegates described the extreme conditions which existed there (in the sugar plants of Louisiana), including not only the more common practices of separate lockers and lunch rooms, but even segregated paylines. The conference delegates decided that an especially strong program of action would be necessary in this area to wipe out the very bad attitudes and practices which our members encounter at every turn.

"As a consequence of this stronger policy, the local at the American Sugar Company plant in New Orleans succeeded in getting the segregated payline abolished, and workers now receive their pay checks according to their badge numbers without distinction as to race. There were no "incidents" from this change, as some had predicted."

Shortly thereafter, a small group of the district leadership sought permission from the National CIO to withdraw these locals from UPWA and place them under CIO-granted local industrial union (LIU) charters. The union contended that these leaders were not representative of the membership of these southern sugar locals and that "their real objection was to the enforcement of the UPWA's strong anti-discrimination policy." The UPWA and CIO together conducted a referendum in each local concerned and CIO declined to issue LIU charters to any of these locals unless a majority of their voting membership requested withdrawal from UPWA. As a result of referenda held during the first half of 1954, the largest four of the nine Louisiana sugar locals voted to remain in UPWA while five of the smaller ones disaffiliated and accepted LIU charters.

According to the present district director, those remaining in UPWA have a membership of about 3,100 while those having withdrawn number some 1,300. He states further that subsequent to his election to this office in May, 1954, two unsuccessful efforts to raid the American and the Colonial Sugar locals have been made. The first attempt was made by dissident members of these locals who had withdrawn from UPWA and were trying to establish LIUs in their plants. The second raid was attempted by the International Association of Machinists (IAM-AFL) at American and by the Southern Sugar Workers, Independent, at Colonial. In each of the first elections, the losing LIU groups polled slightly more than one-half as many votes as the UPWA locals involved, while in the second elections UPWA locals received a larger share of the total votes than in the first. On the other hand, in the other two LIU vs. UPWA elections involving Henderson and Godchaux employees, UPWA majorities were larger and no subsequent attempts were made to challenge its control.

The pattern of development in District 9 which encompasses the southeastern area (Alabama, Georgia, North Carolina, South Carolina, Virginia, Mississippi, Tennessee, and Florida) during the second period is not unlike that found in District 8 (Texas, Oklahoma, Arkansas, Louisiana, and New Mexico). As a result of negotiations between locals and the plants they represented, the Armour plant in Birmingham removed all racial signs from drinking fountains in November, 1952, while segregated locker rooms were eliminated and Negro women hired for the first time at the Atlanta Armour plant in March, 1953.

During July of 1953, the smoldering opposition to the union's desegregation efforts erupted. The vice president in charge of the anti-discrimination program and the secretary-treasurer of UPWA, who was the previous director of District 9, filed charges against the then director of this district for violation of the International's non-discrimination policy and requested that he be brought to trial under Article XIX of the constitution. It was stated that he "had been personally involved in gross violations of the union's anti-discrimination policies and has directed and permitted certain of his staff members and some local unions under his jurisdiction to engage in violations of the union's anti-discrimination policies."

The incident precipitating these charges allegedly occurred when Local 275, representing several companies in Atlanta, voted during the month of July, 1953, to hold a social affair including dinner and the showing of motion pictures at the CIO Hall on July 31, for white members only, a similar meeting to be held a week later for its Negro members at the Washington Park for Negroes. The district program co-ordinator, acting in keeping with the International discrimination policy, invited Negro members to attend the meeting in order to view some travel pictures made by him on a recent trip abroad. It is alleged that some of the Negro members were denied admission and that the district director and program co-coordinator disagreed as to the appropriateness of such action.

Discussion of the merits of this controversy is not essential for our purposes here nor does the writer feel that he has sufficient information to appraise it. Suffice it to say, that extreme friction arose between the district and International leadership; that district field personnel were split in their loyalties, some siding with the accused district director and others with the accusers; that some locals seriously considered disaffiliation though none did so at the time; that confusion and misunderstanding were for a time widespread and threatening among rank and file membership of the district; and that in some cases significant numbers of whites withdrew from their UPWA locals.

For instance, the executive board of locals 33 (Armour and Company) and 136 (an amalgamated local) in Birmingham considered disaffiliation and virtually all white members withdrew from Local 108 (Swift, Atlanta). In the latter case, the local continued to perform its functions under the leadership of the remaining Negro members. This local has successfully withstood decertification efforts led by the former local leadership which withdrew, and white members are reported to be gradually re-affiliating. During the winter of 1954, white and colored members joined forces to elect all officers to the positions which they had filled in order to hold the local together during the period of conflict. All of these officers were Negroes.

These incidents and the charges and counter-charges occurred in the midst of the informal CIO investigation and inevitably became a part of it. While recognizing the union's autonomy in determining the final disposition of the matter, this CIO committee recommended that:

"1. Without commenting on the accuracy of the charges themselves, they be disposed of by the UPWA Board on receiving (the director's) assurance of full support for the entire UPWA program against discrimination; his assurance that he will actively and aggressively implement that program in the Union's District 9, and his giving assurances that he will not engage in any campaign attempting to secure the dis-affiliation of any local unions.

"2. The staff members who have been discharged be re-instated subject to all the rules and regulations pertaining to staff members of the UPWA."

The union accepted this recommendation in interest of intra-CIO harmony and upon receiving the requested assurance reinstated the director. It made one additional provision, that a district-wide anti-discrimination conference be planned and conducted under unsegregated conditions within two months. This conference was conducted on December 5–6, 1953, in Atlanta at a Negro hotel. The two most important resolutions adopted at this meeting were a call for the elimination of all forms of segregation in the plants in which UPWA has bargaining rights by May 3, 1954, the date of the Ninth Constitutional Convention, and a call for support of the NAACP in the fight for the elimination of school segregation.

Educational efforts in this district were not confined to the equal rights phase of the UPWA program. According to the district program co-ordinator, six week-end union schools were conducted in various parts of the district in order to bring all aspects of the union's program to the membership in these areas. The curricula were worked out by the co-ordinator in co-operation with the director and other members of the staff. Negroes attended all of these schools except one and difficulties were encountered only at Moultrie, Georgia, on April 2 and 3, 1954. Here, the verbal attacks upon the instructors, the abuse, and threats, leveled against them, particularly the Negro teacher, were so violent that the procedures of the school were successfully disrupted and the staff left town. It was felt that this attack was carried out by a small organized group in the area and that it stemmed solely from their objections to the union's anti-discrimination program.

This school was to have served plants in Moultrie, Tifton, Albany, and vicinity and was to have had a bi-racial membership. As a result of this incident, the Anti-Discrimination Committee of the Ninth Constitutional Convention was instructed by the Executive Board to invite the participants to appear before it in an informal hearing prior to the Convention. After hearing both sides, the Committee recommended to the Convention that it strongly condemn the union members "whose violent opposition to our equal rights program sabotaged the school," that another school be held under the direction of District 9 within four months which white and colored members would attend without injury or intimidation and that special emphasis be placed on the anti-discrimination program in their district including a special campaign to eliminate all segregated facilities in this area by the end of 1954. These resolutions were adopted by the Convention after a spirited debate.

The day after they were adopted, the incumbent director of District 9 was defeated by the votes of the delegates from the locals in his district by a member of the District 9 field staff who promised to implement the non-discrimination policy and who had previously shown an inclination to follow it. The new District 9 director, like his counterpart, inherited some opposition to the A-D program. Before the second school demanded by the Convention could be held, the Swift local at Moultrie, Georgia, disaffiliated giving as its main reason its unwillingness to desegregate plant facilities. This local has about 500 members, one-fifth of whom are Negroes.

These dissident developments have been described in some detail not because they are typical but because they indicate some of the problems involved in applying racial practices which run counter to the prevailing customs, mores, and traditions of the community.

It is probably more worthy of comment that there are 59 locals in the southern districts, most of which are moving toward the full application of the union policy. Six locals have disaffiliated, one in District 9 and five in District 8, involving a membership of about 1,850. In both southern districts, the directors, who are alleged to have opposed the full implementation of the national A-D policy after the 1952 Convention, have been defeated by the votes of delegates from locals in their respective districts and replaced by directors who pledge themselves to follow this policy. One of these is the Negro previously mentioned as the only member of this minority elected to direct the activities of a national union in the deep South. Despite problems in the southern sugar locals which the latter inherited, under his leadership unprecedented contract gains have been obtained from some of the major southern sugar producers, and two long bitter strikes on economic issues have been concurrently conducted in Louisiana to successful conclusions. District 9 reports that every contract negotiated in the past year (1954–1955) contains the UPWA A-D clause. This covers 68 contracts, all signed since the Supreme Court decision of May 17, 1954. No small feat for a district which embraces most of the "Old South" where such clauses are definitely not the rule in union-management agreements.

The five sugar locals in District 8 which disaffiliated did not generally fare as well in their 1955 contract negotiations as the sugar locals in the area that retained their affiliation with UPWA. Former local No. 1420 at Mathews, Louisiana, struck when the company offered a three-cent per hour raise, lost its strike, and ultimately settled for the company's original offer (three cents). Former local No. 1422 of the Supreme Sugar Company, Supreme, Louisiana, accepted a three-cent per hour wage rate reduction imposed by the company. Former local No. 1474 at Raceland, Louisiana, which has about 100 members, accepted the Godchaux Sugar Company's offer of a five-cent per hour raise. The more favorable results of UPWA locals have been discussed elsewhere.

CHANGES IN THE COMMUNITY

While UPWA officially recognizes its responsibility in eliminating discriminatory practices in communities where its members live, efforts in this area have been understandably less intensive, more widely scattered, and less productive of demonstrable results than those within the union and the plants. However, its interest in this domain has been clearly shown. Both the quality and quantity of the results have increased from year to year and the union efforts have been broadened in scope since 1949. Its community action may be classified generally into three categories: protests in cases of obvious discrimination against minority groups; co-operation with and support of other agencies having as their goal the improvement of human relations, such as the NAACP, local Urban Leagues and various types of Mayors' Commissions on Human Relations; and specific UPWA initiated measures to break down discrimination and segregation in public facilities such as restaurants, hotels, theaters, and public school systems. Analysis of numerous reports of such activities from all districts reveals that, generally speaking, the earlier types of activities were mainly of the protest and co-operation variety and that these have tended to be followed by the third type as local union leadership with the help of the International has gained a higher level of sophistication in the use of specific techniques of change available to them in their particular communities.

The following description of selected community activities reported by the director of the Anti-Discrimination Department, the first group occurring during the period 1951 through the spring of 1952 and the second, from May 1952 to the summer of 1954, reveal the character of these developments and the changes during this period.

PERIOD 1951–1952

DISTRICT 1

The district has taken the initiative and led the fight to save UPWA member, Lester Heard, from extradition to Tennessee where he stands in danger of mob violence. District representatives have participated in various meetings, rallies, and demonstrations on civil rights including the NAACP rally held in Washington, D.C., in February 1952.

Acting quickly and with firm decision, the district was among the leading organizations which protested the Cicero riots and called for indictment of the mob leaders. It also took an active part in protesting the bombings in Cairo, Illinois, and the conviction of Willie McGee.

In February of this year (1952) the district set up a Mexican-American Committee and immediately dispatched a delegation to the U. S. Immigration Department protesting intimidation and arrest of Mexican workers who are under constant threat of deportation.

DISTRICT 3

In recognition of UPWA leadership, Edward Danner, UPWA field representative was appointed to serve on the Omaha Mayor's Human Relations Committee.

In Sioux City, the committees of the locals have been carrying on a campaign to stop police intimidation among the Negro people.

DISTRICT 5

An aggressive program by the stewards in the district has broadened the field of employment throughout Los Angeles area for members of minority groups.

The district has co-operated with various community organizations in the Los Angeles area protecting the rights of minority group members, securing employment through local or state agencies, and also in receiving unemployment compensation.

DISTRICT 6

The district has been active in urging its local unions to press for the enactment of anti-discrimination laws in New York and New Jersey. To carry on this work, the district is also encouraging various committees to elect Negro candidates to various offices through the counties, cities, and states.

Through these efforts of co-ordination with CIO, AFL and other organizations, there have been several appointments of Negroes to official positions. In many areas, Negroes are participating on city, county, and state ballots.

DISTRICT 7

The district conducted its first educational school in September, 1951, at the Yellow Banks Hotel, Webster, Indiana, with no discrimination or segregation. Such progress is a real accomplishment for the district and for the state of Indiana.

PERIOD 1952—SPRING 1954

DISTRICT 1

A picket line of white and Negro packinghouse workers and a mass delegation of UPWA members to the Mayor of Chicago influenced the Chicago Housing Authority to decide in favor of supporting the right (which was violently disrupted) of Negro families to live in the formerly all-white Trumbull Park Homes Project.

DISTRICT 3

The Surf Ballroom case, initiated by the district, resulted in a judgment of $400 for the plaintiff.

The Anti-Discrimination Committee of Local 46 in Waterloo, Iowa, succeeded in having a prejudiced tavern owner convicted of violating the Iowa Civil Rights Law and is now fighting for a city-wide FEPC law and the Council for Equal Job Opportunities, initiated by Omaha locals, is successfully drawing together broad community support for a similar ordinance in that city.

DISTRICT 4

A conviction for disorderly conduct, resulting from a charge brought by an anti-Negro home owner because of an interracial house meeting in Kansas City, was reversed after concentrated protest to the city police and the judge by our local unions.

John Hope II, *Equality of Opportunity: A Union Approach to Fair Employment* (Washington: Public Affairs Press, 1956). The book has an introduction by Sen. H. H. Humphrey. Selection is from p. 100 to p. 130. Notes and tables omitted.

43

"THE SCOURGE OF RACE HATRED"

by Bishops of the A. M. Church

In February 1956, the Council of Bishops of the African Methodist Church adopted this statement:

An integrated church in an integrated society is the declared policy of American Protestantism. Virtually every major denomination in the United States has hailed the Supreme Court decision on the integration of schools as a milestone in the achievement of human rights. Likewise, the Roman Catholic Church has condemned racial discrimination as "unjust and un-Christian."

In this struggle for universal acceptance of an integrated society, the Negro church plays an increasingly vital role. We have witnessed instance after instance of sacrifice, toil and even bloodshed by ordained ministers of the Gospel determined to make a reality out of the professions of Democracy....

Our people must know that all men are created equal, and that any divergence from this principle is hypocrisy, in fact, immoral. The people must likewise know that the law of the land is second only to the law of

God and that to openly flout the dictates of the highest tribunal is flirting with tragedy. . . .

We believe it to be our Christian duty to awaken a social consciousness concerning these vital issues. This represents teaching the Gospel of Christ in a practical sense. Telling our Brethren how they can live and play in peace and harmony is a task of our ministry. . . .

As followers of Christ we are opposed to violence and mob action. This latter must not be confused with mass action, a technique we must learn to employ in certain fields against those who would exploit us. Who would sell their wares to us for profit must not at the same time oppose our march to freedom.

We commend therefore the citizens of Montgomery, Alabama, who in protest against injustice have refused to lend sustenance to their oppressors. The "Spirit of Montgomery" must be applied wherever possible against individuals, corporations, local and national, who fail to stand up and be counted. . . .

May God grant us the strength and courage to fight on, never once turning backwards in our march. May the scourge of race hatred, segregation and unjust discrimination vanish forever from the face of the earth.

Ernest A. Campbell and Thomas F. Pettigrew, *Christians in Racial Crisis: A Study of Little Rock's Ministry* (Washington: Public Affairs Press, 1959), pp. 155–56.

44

TRENDS IN PATTERNS OF RACE RELATIONS IN THE SOUTH SINCE MAY 17, 1954

by John Hope II

Let us consider some of the major developments which have occurred since this important decision was rendered. One of the most revealing consequences has been the realization that there is no longer a "Solid South," that the self-interests of various elements of the South are not identical.

Nineteen states and the District of Columbia constitute the areas primarily affected by the School Segregation Decision: Alabama, Delaware, the District of Columbia, Florida, Georgia, Kansas, Louisiana, Kentucky, Maryland, Mississippi, Missouri, North Carolina, Oklahoma, South Carolina, Tennessee, Texas, Virginia, and West Virginia. No serious legal efforts have been made to circumvent it in the District of Columbia, Delaware, Kansas, Kentucky, Maryland, Missouri, Oklahoma, Texas, or West Virginia. Desegregation is taking place steadily and rather rapidly in all of these except Texas, and in that state it is proceeding moderately well in the western and central sections. Looking more closely at the twelve-state classification of the South which eliminates some of the border states, they may be traced cautiously on a continuum from desegregating, through waiting, to "hard core" or resisting states. In order of progress toward desegregation, they are Kentucky, Texas, Arkansas (desegregating); Tennessee, Florida (waiting); and North Carolina, Virginia, Alabama, Louisiana, Georgia, South Carolina, and Mississippi (officially resisting). Although the exact relative positions and classifications of these states might be debatable, and under the volatile social climate now prevailing, they may quickly change positions, this classification seems to have validity. In the first three of these (Arkansas, Kentucky, and Texas) public school desegregation has begun. In three others the state supreme courts have declared the statutes which provide for segregation of the races in the public schools to be unconstitutional. These are Florida, Tennessee, and Texas. In Tennessee, Anderson County was ordered by a Federal court to integrate its public schools by the fall of 1956; the Governor of Tennessee has refused to call a special session of the Legislature, at the request of pro-segregationist groups; and has strongly reiterated his statement that law and order would prevail in the State. The Nashville Board of Education has declared to the Federal District Court that it would desegregate its schools in compliance with the School Segregation Decision and at recent public hearing was adjudged by the Court to be "proceeding with deliberate speed" in developing its plan. It has thus been given additional time to complete its plans for integration.

The states in which most strenuous efforts have been made to devise legal methods of evading the decision, and in which such efforts appear to have the strong backing of executive and legislative officials and community support include Alabama, Georgia, Louisiana, Mississippi, and South Carolina. In recent months North Carolina and Virginia have moved into this area, and there are now fears that the progress of Texas may be slowed.

In describing the diversity of reaction to the school desegregation decisions, Dr. James M. Nabrit, Jr., makes the following statement in the current issue of *The Annals:*

Those reactions ranged all the way from open defiance of the Court and a call for its impeachment to complete acceptance and implementation of the opinion. Proposals extended from those calling for abolition of public schools and evasive tactics on the one hand to those embracing immediate integration and progressive or gradual integration on the other, and within the entire range responsible executive and legislative leaders submitted numerous propositions. Many became a part of state constitutions by amendment; others became law by legislative enactment; others became operative through executive and administrative regulations; others passed only one branch of the legislature; others languish in committees; while still others served merely as material for political speeches.

In support of this decision, the major religious Faiths of the nation, through their organizational institutions, have advocated compliance with the law of the land as interpreted by the Supreme Court. Every major Protestant denomination in the South has made public pronouncements commending the decision. The Southern Baptist Convention, in June, 1954 said in part: "We recognize the fact that this Supreme Court decision is in harmony with the Constitutional guarantee of equal freedom to all citizens and with the Christian principles of justice and love for all men." The North Georgia Conference of the Methodist Church had the following to say: "We believe our people should face the practical phases of this decision with the courage, poise and maturity of law-abiding citizens." The Presbyterian Church, U.S. (Southern) proclaimed, "That the General Assembly affirmed that enforced segregation of races is discrimination which is out of harmony with Christian theology and ethics...." In Louisiana, the Arch-Bishop of the Catholic Church has taken a strong position against segregation and against those officials who resist the integration of Parochial schools. The Parochial schools will be desegregated in the fall of 1956. In the midst of the welter of threats of interposition and nullification by State officials and politicians in the "hard core" states, the newly elected Governor of Mississippi, Mr. Coleman, has denounced as foolhardy any attempts at nullification.

Organized Labor, both CIO and AFL, was on the side of the desegregation forces before the recent merger, and its position has been strengthened by the merger. However, there is little evidence today that organized labor has definitely committed its forces in an active effort to facilitate desegregation in the South. On the contrary, there are rumblings from dissident southern locals which may force organized labor into a more active role in the coming months. Major organizing drives are planned in the South in the near future and it is likely that these activities will focus the desegregation issue more sharply within the ranks of southern workers.

Undoubtedly, one of the most important factors in the ultimate resolution of the South's race problem is the vigorous entrance of national mass media of communication into the school desegregation controversy. Truly the South's "skeleton" is "out of the closet," exposed to public view on a national and even a world scale. Despite the many protests that come from southern leadership, particularly pro-segregationists, a much more informed and sophisticated public opinion both inside and out of the South is bound to emerge. As this development takes place, we may expect calm to replace hysteria and reason to supersede emotion as the people of the South move toward the elimination of this last major geographical area of social lag in the movement toward full democracy in the United States. National magazines have had a series of articles on the Supreme Court decisions, on the Negro in American life, on school desegregation, and on the practices of racism in the South. *Life* reported on the desegregation process in Hoxie, Arkansas; *Collier's* has run two articles by Alan Paton, author of *Cry the Beloved Country,* on the Negro in the South and in the North. The *Saturday Evening Post* has carried an article by Hodding Carter, and *Life,* by William Faulkner. *Look* magazine has given an exposé of the infamous Till case and, more recently, has issued an eighteen-page report on America's greatest legal, political and emotional crisis since the Civil War, entitled "The South *vs.* the Supreme Court." The national press, particularly the New York *Times,* has systematically covered developments in the South for the American people. The importance attributed to these developments by this important newspaper is attested by a recent total coverage of the southern scene by a team of its major reporters, which appeared recently as a New York *Times* special feature. [March 13, 1956].

Television, the youngest and probably the most powerful of the mass media, played an active and subtle part in conditioning the people of the South for the acceptance of Negroes in other than their traditional roles. Motion pictures have made a similar contribution in some recent films such as "Pinky," "Intruders in the Dust," "Lost Boundaries," and "Trial." Novels dealing with racial problems of the Southern region have for some years appeared on best seller lists. More recently, technical books such as *The Negro and the Schools; Schools in Transition; The Strange Career of Jim Crow,* and others have appeared to play an important role in educating the mind of America and sensitizing its conscience.

While this diversified assortment of instruments of mass communication is probing the minds and hearts of Americans in every section of the nation and creating awareness and understanding of the problem, national intergroup relations agencies with resources and professional staffs are increasingly establishing programs in the South. This movement is still in its beginnings. Several national organizations with intergroup relations interests as well as those concerned solely with intergroup relations are now in the planning stage of committing financial and manpower resources for the specific purpose of organizing communities for the acceptance and implementation of the School Segregation Decision. These include church, labor, and minority (other than Negro) oriented agencies, and organizations whose intergroup relations operations have hitherto been confined primarily to the North. Others that have been working in the South are intensifying their efforts, re-organizing and re-vitalizing their programs to meet the post–May 17th demands. The NAACP which in keeping with the best of American tradition has successfully obtained redress of major grievances through court action is now looking to the social scientist and social engineer as it forges effective techniques for the implementation of its legally established gains. The Southern Regional Council has completely reorganized and now stands as the hub of a twelve-state network of human relations councils which are working for the extension of the previously mentioned horizontal communication between Negroes and whites as a means of resolving interracial conflict and establishing a land of true democracy in the South in which equality of opportunity will prevail without regard to race. One of its most recent developments is the establishment of a panel of highly qualified social scientists and social engineers for the purpose of assisting the state affiliates in strengthening and intensifying their programs. The American Friends Service Committee, the Anti-Defamation League of B'Nai B'Rith, the American Jewish Committee and the National Conference of Christians and Jews are increasing their activities in this area.

The Negro Community's Role in Changing Race Relations Pattern

It has become increasingly apparent since the final decree that compliance with the Decision would not be voluntary and that organized opposition groups would apply vigorous and sometimes ruthlessly violent measures to discourage Negroes from seeking enrollment in the schools nearest their homes even though now white. Such measures have also been applied to whites who appeared to favor desegregation and even to those who, while not favoring the policy, felt a responsibility for complying with the law.

Such tactics are crucial to the success of the resistance movement because the initiation of the process of desegregation in any community, in the absence of voluntary compliance by the school board, is dependent upon a petition from a parent to enter his child in a school whose pupils are now confined to the other race. Refusal of a school on the basis of race to enroll such an applicant forms the basis for suit in the Federal District Court for compliance with the Supreme Court Decision. It should be emphasized that this procedure does not depend upon mass action by Negroes though many of these cases have been based upon complaints of several parents. It seems apparent that the necessary suits for admission to schools are forthcoming. District Courts in several southern and border states now have such cases, e.g., Arkansas, Delaware, Kentucky, Louisiana, Missouri, South Carolina, Tennessee, Texas, Virginia, and perhaps others. It is too early to observe any pattern in the decisions rendered by the Federal District Courts in such cases. It is likely that the interpretation of "deliberate speed" will vary from court to court.

In several communities in the "hard core" states, particularly Mississippi and Alabama, pro-segregationist groups have applied various types of sanctions against Negroes whose names appeared on desegregation petitions and against those who attempted to qualify as voters. In general, economic pressures have been the favored weapons, including refusal to sell merchandise, refusal or cancellation of credit arrangements, and discharge from jobs. The outstanding example of this technique and its consequences is in Orangeburg, South Carolina and vicinity where severe economic measures have been directed against Negroes and counter-reprisals have been used by Negroes with masterful effectiveness. The Southern Regional Council finds eighteen published cases in which economic pressure was used during 1955. These were concentrated in the "hard core" states i.e., South Carolina, seven; Mississippi, four; Alabama, three; North Carolina, three; and Texas, one. In addition, intimidation, violence, and even murder have been employed to forestall desegregation of schools and prevent Negroes from voting. The outstanding examples of such tactics are the murder of Dr. Lee at Belzoni, Mississippi and the shooting of Gus Counts, a grocery store owner, both of whom encouraged Negroes to register and vote. The prevailing opinion seems to be that the result of the reprisal techniques has been a notable stiffening of resistance and more effective organization in the Negro community, a clarification of the fundamental issues at stake, and a grim, though not truculent, determination to "see it through" even at the greatest risk to personal and economic safety. The real prospect that by so doing their children may live under conditions approaching equality of opportunity is creating fresh incentive.

The Negro's role as petitioner has not been confined to school desegregation in the past two years. The previously mentioned Maryland Park decision of the Supreme Court broadened the scope of the School Segregation Case to apply to public park facilities. The same Federal District Court which originally ruled on this case has recently ruled in the Seashore State Park case that segregation in the Seashore Park could not be continued by leasing it to a private concern. In the area of local transportation facilities, the Court of Appeals, Fourth Circuit, in South Carolina reversed the decision of the lower court in holding the South Carolina segregation law illegal in the case of a Negro woman who sued a local bus company for damages because the driver required her to change her seat in accordance with the state segregation law.

The Montgomery bus boycott, which was not originally aimed at eliminating segregated seating but simply more courteous and satisfactory service to Negro customers within the limits of the state and city segregation laws, has now become an attack on the segregation laws *per se*. On the basis of the court precedents now in use, it is difficult to see how such segregation laws will not be ultimately vacated by the Supreme Court if not by a lower court.

The Montgomery and the Orangeburg cases have not been discussed in detail in this paper because the facts are generally known. They are significant because they have demonstrated that the Negro community can, under most adverse circumstances, organize itself for effective mass action as consumers. It has shown to business interests generally that this group can organize and withhold its purchases of goods and services from hostile or discriminatory sellers in sufficient quantity and for a sufficiently sustained period of time to curtail seriously profits if not cause large losses or ultimate failure.

Forces Uncommitted but Apparently on the Brink of Positive Action

The executive branch of the Federal Government, explicitly committed to the attainment of equality of citizenship for all of its people and confident in its major accomplishment of all but ending segregation in the Armed Forces of the nation and substantial progress in the elimination of discrimination in hiring, discharging, and up-grading of minorities employed by firms who have contracts with the Federal Government, seems poised to take some form of positive action in the desegregation controversy now raging throughout the "hard core" states of the South. In his State of the Union Message of 1956, the President said in part, "It is disturbing that in some localities allegations persist that Negro citizens are being deprived of their right to vote and are likewise being subjected to unwarranted economic pressures. I recommend that the substance of these charges be thoroughly examined. . . . " The Nashville, *Tennessean* of March 10th, 1956 reported that the President has formally requested of Congress the appointment of a bipartisan committee to investigate this charge. While it is doubtful whether Congress will grant his request at this session, the President states that in the absence of such a committee, he will take some other form of action in this direction. The Department of Justice has prepared a bill for presentation to Congress aimed at strengthening the civil rights statutes of the Federal criminal code in order to more effectively protect the Negro's personal safety and his right to vote and the safety of whites who dissent from the pro-segregationists' position. On the other side, the impact of the School Segregation Decision has forced both of our candidates for the Democratic Presidential nomination to make increasingly strong pronouncements in favor of the implementation of this decision and its irrevocable status as the law of the land. It is likely that the range of compromise and maneuverability open to the two major parties in writing their platform statements on minorities has been considerably narrowed and the positions of the ultra-conservative southern Democrats in party politics weakened to an unprecedented degree.

The United States Department of State has recognized the implication of this ruling in the successful achievement of good international relations, particularly with a newly independent and aggressive Asia and an awakening Africa. As the leader of the Free World in its intense ideological competition with the forces of communism, its area of vacillation and equivocation in matters of race has been sharply narrowed.

In his keynote address to the Twelfth Annual Institute of Race Relations at Fisk University, Dr. Charles S. Johnson, President of Fisk University, has the following to say about the cataclysmic changes which have taken place in the Free World over which the United States now exercises leadership in the brief span of one decade from 1945 to 1955:

In 1945 we were just emerging from the Second World War. Two-thirds of the peoples of the world were still living under what was regarded as the unbreakable grip of colonial and racial imperialism. . . . Between 1945 and 1955, however, the world has completely reversed itself, and all Asia has broken into our awareness with cataclysmic impact. Africa has revealed itself in the throes of a final and definitive rebellion, ranging from mau mau in Kenya to sullen passive resistance in South Africa.

Seven years after the close of the war eight of the Asian nations with a population of 600,000,000 had become independent, and on April 18, 1955, there was held in Bandung, Indonesia a conference disturbing to the whole of the western world. It was a conference of twenty-nine recently independent colored nations of Asia and Africa, representing over a billion people, more than half of the population of the world. It was not a racially truculent conference, but it was a symbol and a formal announcement of the end of western domination, and of the determination of the peoples of Asia and Africa, hereafter to determine their own destinies. They hoped by their stand to preserve the peace of the world against the West.

It is apparent as never before that in the world of the present and the foreseeable future, our pattern of minority-majority relations in the United States, and particularly those of Negro-white relations in the

South, constitute a significant factor in the maintenance of world peace and thus our survival.

In this period of turbulent and tortuous transition, the major industrial and financial interests of the nation, many of which have large installations in the South, appear to have maintained an uneasy silence in the controversy probably hoping that this storm would pass over and leave them to "business as usual." However, as the pro-segregationist resistance movement has grown and economic reprisal has emerged as a major technique of resistance, business has recognized reluctantly that it is "in the middle," beset by boycotts and counter-boycotts from which it sees no escape as long as the pro- and anti-segregationist forces remain in bitter economic combat. Gradually, the entrepreneur of the most powerful and successful modern capitalistic nation on earth is forced to choose between profits, economic growth, and industrial stability, on the one hand, and the full and long-range implications of non-compliance with the desegregation rulings on the other. During the past decade, he has discovered the "Negro market" and has learned to exploit it profitably. He had adjusted his production and distribution practices to fit the basic tenets of the prevailing white supremacy system. He does not want to lose this market so recently obtained and yet he does not wish to antagonize the large and more lucrative "white market." Thus, his salvation is in economic stability and, consequently, the school desegregation issue for him must be restated in terms of manpower and markets, economic development or capital withdrawal. Equality of treatment of workers and customers without regard to race, not simply the question of whether Negro children will be taught in the same class with whites are the terms in which he must view this Decision in his long range planning. Furthermore, the dominant industrial and financial structure is national rather than regional or local. Thus, we may expect southern businessmen increasingly to appraise the current issue in terms of profits rather than the nostalgic preservation of "a southern way of life." Most of the capital that has created the unprecedented industrial boom in the South is migrant capital from other sections of the nation which can and will flow to more profitable areas if the social terrain of the South becomes such that it cannot be profitably invested here. Again, the School Segregation Decision has significantly altered the alternatives available to entrepreneurs as it has in other areas of social life.

There is some evidence that business interests are beginning to move toward a decision as to their role in the present conflict. During the month of March of this year the specialized mass media of business and industry have invaded the South as the general national press did in previous months and significant news stories are beginning to appear in business newspapers and magazines which describe rather clearly the dilemma in which business finds itself in the South under the present conditions and repeatedly raises the question as to whether failure to settle amicably the present tensions will cut short the economic development of the South which is so gravely needed by this region and the nation as a whole. A New York financial columnist, Sylvia Porter, has contributed two syndicated articles under her column *Your Money's Worth* during the month of March. One is headed "Integration Effects on Dixie Industry" and the other, "Race Row Perils Industry in the South." The March 24th issue *Business Week* contained a long article entitled "Business in a Troubled South" while the *Wall Street Journal* on consecutive days discussed the implications of boycotts of whites against whites, whites against Negroes, and Negroes against whites. The same business daily carried an article entitled "Desegregated Jobs" on April 3rd in which it described positive accomplishments in the southern plants of the International Harvester Company. These and many other articles, closed discussion among business leaders, etc., serve to place the racial problem in focus in the business mind in a way which more clearly places before it the rational alternatives which it faces in the present and future South.

The forces described to this point are long range forces which were either actually or potentially working for integration during this period. But there are powerful and ruthless short-range forces arrayed on the opposite side.

Negative Forces Affecting Patterns of Race Relations

As mentioned previously, vigorous resistance to school desegregation has occurred in that part of the old southern agricultural economy moving eastward through Mississippi to Louisiana, Alabama, Georgia, and South Carolina, i.e., the so-called Black Belt. It is the area of once rich black soil and prosperous agriculture which includes the areas of highest Negro concentration in the South. It is the section which nurtured and developed the white supremacy doctrine and through its political dominance spread it through law, mores, customs, and traditions throughout the whole southern economy. The keystone of this political ascendancy was the political oligarchy based in part upon the maintenance of ignorance among the Negro and white masses and their systematic disfranchisement. While the once dominant cotton and tobacco economy which supports it has decreased in economic importance as compared with urban industrial interests, such political dominance over the whole South, and its high prestige in the nation's Congress as a whole has not been successfully challenged by the forces of the New South. This political domination of the total scene and its disproportionate power in the Congress of the United States relative to other regions of the nation and to the industrial South of the Piedmont and highland areas remains a formidable obstacle to the democratization of the South. However, for several years the rapid urbanization draining population from the Black Belt counties and the rapid industrialization of the South, centered primarily outside of the Black Belt, have been threatening the political power of the Black Belt politicians and the economic power of large-scale agriculture which dominates this region.

In fact, it seems quite plausible that the School Segregation Decision crystallized the struggle for control between the old agricultural South and the new industry-oriented South and that we are witnessing the death struggle of the old order and the frantic efforts of its political leadership to preserve its position of power, rather than an honest effort to keep Negro and white pupils separated on the basis of principle. Certainly, one of the most striking characteristics of this movement is the position of leadership taken by the executive and legislative representatives and Congressional representatives from the "hard core" states. It appears to be an effort to re-establish their claims in a re-solidified South in spite of the fact that the divergent self-interests of the various elements of an increasingly complex economy make this rationally impossible. The objectives of these leaders of the white supremacy system are being sought through the organization and manipulation of groups, the most important being the White Citizens Councils (WCC) which claims a membership of sixty thousand in Mississippi alone. Although these groups operate under various names from state to state, there is evidence of close coordination among them. According to the January, 1956 issue of *Southern School News*, there is a total of forty-four resistance groups, large and small, operating in fifteen states. At least a dozen of these are major movements. The Federation for Constitutional Government states that its purpose is to coordinate the work of such organizations, and it includes representatives from the major resistance groups on its Board. Among its leadership are found such well-known figures as Strom Thurmond, the late Fielding Wright, James Eastland, and Herman Talmadge. It seems apparent that this is a new manifestation of the Dixiecrat movement, fighting to maintain its political power by enlisting a large bloc of voters through appeals to racial fears and prejudices.

The movement does not appear to be a grass-root movement but one dominated by the political and economic elite of the Old South which is luring the masses of unthinking whites by playing upon their racial prejudices and antagonisms. The object of these groups seems to be to maintain their position of leadership by silencing all dissenting points of view, particularly those of white leadership. They use, directly or indirectly, the weapons of economic pressure, violence, demagogy, and public opinion formation through southern mass media organs and their positions as leading public officials and status figures in their communities. Incidents surrounding the preparation and issue of the Southern Manifesto illustrate the current intensity of these pressures.

It may be concluded that the pro-segregation forces have a powerful short-range advantage on their own grounds, but that the pro-integrationists have with them the long-run pervasive forces working within and outside the region. The advantages of the pro-segregation forces include the following: control of governmental machinery; influence on opinionmaking media and individuals; large financial sources; a mass public opinion long conditioned by rabble-rousing and appeals to race hatred; conservative white control of the economy; and economic dependence and political impotence of Negroes in those areas where they are most numerous. On the other hand, all of the major national forces—religious, cultural, economic, political and industrial, and international considerations—are moving in the direction of Integration.

Appendix

A Summary of the Extent of Public School Desegregation in the Southern and Border States during the Period 1955 to March, 1956.

No public school desegregation—Alabama, Florida, Georgia, Louisiana, Mississippi, North Carolina, South Carolina, Tennessee, and Virginia.

A summary of the extent of public schools desegregation in the remaining states follows:

ARKANSAS   Hoxie, Fayetteville, and Charleston.

DELAWARE   1,230 of 10,500 Negro students in mixed classes. Out of twenty-one school districts, twelve have some degree of integration. They are: Wilmington, Claymont, New Castle, Alfred I. du Pont, Delaware City, Conrad, Alex I. du Pont, Arden, Hockessin and Rose Hill.

KENTUCKY   Approximately 300 out of 43,361 Negro school age children are reported in mixed classes. Twenty out of 224 school districts are involved. Included are: Lexington, Floyd County, Louisville (one white in formerly Negro school and the School for Blind was integrated), Wayne County, Boone County, Knox County, Campbell County, Daviess County, Perry County, Crittenden County, Knott County, Hopkins, Pendelton, and Adair Counties. (See report of State Department of Education).

MARYLAND   4,000 Negroes out of 92,000 believed in mixed classes. Integration in eight of 23 counties plus the city of Baltimore. These counties are: Carroll County, Baltimore County, Alleghany County, Washington County, Montgomery County, Prince George County, Anne Arundel County and Cecil County.

MISSOURI   Approximately 85% of state's Negro children attending mixed schools. 135 out of 172 high school districts have Negro enrollment in formerly white schools.

OKLAHOMA   264 schools with mixed classes. Biggest influx of Negroes is in Oklahoma City. 127 Negro teachers dismissed.

TEXAS   Sixty-five of 1,800 districts desegregated. Five Negro teachers lost jobs in Karnes County. Communities in which there was desegregation include: Big Spring, Friona, San Marcos, Karnes, El Paso, Corpus Christi, San Antonio, Tahoka, and Austin.

WEST VIRGINIA Fifty out of 55 counties have started some school desegregation. Counties not desegregating are Berkeley, Grant, Hampshire, Hardy, and Jefferson. One Negro teacher assigned to 9th grade homeroom at Woodrow Wilson High School.

Phylon, second quarter, 1956, vol. 17, pp 105–18, footnotes omitted.

45

SOUTHERN VIGNETTES (1956)

by Anonymous

Two experienced white journalists went South in 1956; here are extracts from African-Americans talking to these observers:

"We talk *to* each other," Dr. Charles Johnson, mild-mannered, scholarly, wisely humorous President of Fisk University in Nashville, told us shortly before his sudden death in October, 1956: "The next step is talking *with* each other. How little we know other people! There was the elderly lady who visited the Indian Village at the World's Fair in Chicago several years ago. As she watched the exhibit there she was moved to speak a friendly word to one of these aborigines, and she asked him, 'How do you like our country?'

"Or there was the man who went to France and on a street corner in Paris he saw a black man, a fine-looking Senegalese. Being from the South, the white man went up to him and said, 'How you like it here, boy?' The African just looked at him. He asked again, 'Boy, you like it here pretty well?' This time the man just let out a great stream of Senegalese, and the American said to him, 'Look here, you've not been over here so long you've forgotten your own language, have you?'"

Or, as Bonita Valien, an especially articulate young Negro woman who is also a sociologist at Fisk University in Nashville, tells you, "What is communication? White people want to talk to, beyond or for—but never with—the Negro, and of course that pattern's disappearing. But we think Montgomery, Alabama, and fifty thousand Negroes in protest, is communication, too. The difference is that the message isn't the same; just not what was being communicated before.

"Another thing I'd like to mention is this talk about voluntary integration. 'You can't legislate this!' Well, apparently you don't segregate voluntarily, because there are laws to enforce segregation. Why not laws to enforce integration? 'How can you legislate people's attitudes?' they ask. You can't, of course, but people do change their attitudes, all the time, and you can make it logical and comfortable for them to do so."

A Negro teacher in Louisville, Kentucky, points out: "Communication is a two-way street. In the past Negroes have worked *for* white people and in the process of survival have learned how to work *on* white people, now they must also learn how to work *with* white people."

The Negro insurance man is obviously prosperous and even more obviously eager to talk with any white person who will share concern in mutual problems. "We had a case about public beach segregation here in the courts recently. And the lawyer on the other side said to me one day, 'Aren't you fellows trying to rush this thing? You've got the white man down with this Supreme Court school decision, now you're trying to start on the parks. It's like stomping in his face." That made me sort of mad. I said, 'Let's look at a little history. Let's be factual. In 1863, Lincoln signed the Emancipation Proclamation. It's nearly a hundred years later. Is that rushing? Look, the Constitution of the United States was written by all white men, didn't have a single Negro signer. The Federal Court in South Carolina and the other states in the 1954 lawsuit were all white men. The nine men on the Supreme Court of the United States are all white, not a single Negro. We're just trying to get the white people to keep their own laws. We've not made any new ones or broken any old ones!"

The elderly Negro man sits in his office and looks at you shrewdly. You know that, during a lifetime of being known as a "fighter" and a "trouble shooter," he has had to make many such evaluations of white people. After a while, he chuckles and tells you a story. "About four weeks ago I went to town just north of here to make a talk. I had a little time before my appointment, and so I went into a restaurant I knew to get a cup of coffee. It's a bootleg joint, too, and there were three white men in there. It was Sunday morning, about eleven thirty. When I came in the Negro waiter repeated my name out good and loud a couple of times and after I sat down in one of the booths, one of the white men came over to me. 'I read something you said a while back on intermarriage. I don't believe I agree with what you advocate.' 'I'm not advocating anything,' I said. 'I was asked if I believed in intermarriage and I said yes. If I was asked if I believe in sunshine, I'd say yes. I know the sun's shining. That's a fact. I know my grandfather was a white man. There's nothing you can do about it, nothing I can do about it. Maybe neither one of us like it, but two human beings are mixed in me. And there are about two million you can identify who are white and Negro. And then there are about three million more you can't identify, unless they tell you. So that's an eternal verity, like the sun shining.' Well, the man went and got another drink and came back: 'But I'm a Southerner.' I said, 'Southerner's met Southerner then. Where you from?' 'Georgia.' 'Well, I'm from Virginia, and when's Georgia been more Southern than Virginia?' He got another drink, came back and leaned on my table: 'God Himself is against intermarriage.' 'Maybe so,' I said. 'You read the twelfth book of Numbers. Moses married an Ethiopian woman. Anyway, I'm sitting here looking at you, part white and part black, just like the sun is shining. The sun's a fact and I'm a fact.'"

And there are the Negroes who talked with us earnestly against integration. "Far as I can see, do more harm than good. Just put our kids where they be hurt. Even if they wasn't any trouble from the white folk, how we gonna get as good clothes for our children? They'd stay embarrassed all the time. And the teachers would all be white. Couldn't expect them to pay as much attention to a Negro child—ours all at the foot of the class, whites all at the top, we'd just have more trouble with everything." A Negro lawyer from Mississippi tells an NAACP conference that 99 per cent of the state's Negroes believe desegregation would be impossible there at this time.

"Negroes in Mississippi are used to waiting," a young Negro man in one of the middle cities explains. "We'll wait on. We hadn't expected such a defiance against the Supreme Court of the United States—reaction and trouble, yes, but not this organizing. But the Negroes feel real sympathy for the white folks. We know this is the end of the world for many of them. And the Negroes know we're going to win, now or a little later—it's coming."

And in state after state the words are repeated until they become a regular theme song among the white Southerners: "We were getting along fine, everything would be all right—if the outsiders would just leave us alone—if the NAACP wouldn't come and stir up trouble!"

A young Negro executive in one of the state offices of the Association shakes his head at the familiar words and smiles with a sad mixture of tolerance and frustration. "When a man cuts out a cancer growing inside him he may be stirring up trouble, sure—or he may be trying to cure a worse trouble." He gets up from his desk suddenly and walks around the room, slapping the back of his hand against several of the enlarged photographs hanging there. They show some of the Negro schools in his state with dilapidated outside toilets, potbellied stoves for heat of the one-room buildings; and some of the hovels the Negro pupils call home. "Would you call this 'getting along fine'? Would you call this 'separate but equal'? Would you call going into the court to ask for some of the liberty, equality and justice we're always hearing about 'stirring up trouble'?"

He sits down again, as suddenly as he stood. "You know what a white man here said to me yesterday? Over the phone, of course. He said he guessed the South could thank God they had the NAACP instead of the Mau Maus."

Wilma Dykeman and James Stokely, *Neither Black Nor White* (New York: Rinehart, 1957), pp. 12, 24, 40, 61, 95.

46

OUR STRUGGLE (1956)

by Martin Luther King, Jr.

A comprehensive expression of Dr. King's outlook in the mid-1950s appeared in the first number of a new "movement" periodical.

The segregation of Negroes, with its inevitable discrimination, has thrived on elements of inferiority present in the masses of both white and Negro people. Through forced separation from our African culture, through slavery, poverty, and deprivation, many black men lost self-respect.

In their relations with Negroes, white people discovered that they had rejected the very center of their own ethical professions. They could not face the triumph of their lesser instincts and simultaneously have peace within. And so, to gain it, they rationalized—insisting that the unfortunate Negro, being less than human, deserved and even enjoyed second-class status.

They argued that his inferior social, economic and political position was good for him. He was incapable of advancing beyond a fixed position and would therefore be happier if encouraged not to attempt the impossible. He is subjugated by a superior people with an advanced way of life. The "master race" will be able to civilize him to a limited degree, if only he will be true to his inferior nature and stay in his place.

White men soon came to forget that the southern social culture and all its institutions had been organized to perpetuate this rationalization. They observed a caste system and quickly were conditioned to believe that its social results, which they had created, actually reflected the Negro's innate and true nature.

In time many Negroes lost faith in themselves and came to believe that perhaps they really were what they had been told they were—something less than men. So long as they were prepared to accept this role, racial peace could be maintained. It was an uneasy peace in which the Negro was forced to accept patiently injustice, insult, injury and exploitation.

Gradually the Negro masses in the South began to reevaluate themselves—a process that was to change the nature of the Negro community and the social patterns of the South. We discovered that we had never really smothered our self-respect and that we could not be at one with ourselves without asserting it. From this point on, the South's terrible peace was rapidly undermined by the Negro's new and courageous thinking and his ever-increasing readiness to organize and to act. Conflict and violence were coming to the surface as the white South desperately clung to its old patterns. The extreme tension in race relations in the South today is explained in part by the revolutionary change in the Negro's evaluation of himself, and of his destiny and by his determination to struggle for justice. *We Negroes have replaced self-pity with self-respect and self-depreciation with dignity.*

When Mrs. Rosa Parks, the quiet seamstress whose arrest precipitated the nonviolent protest in Montgomery, was asked why she had refused to move to the rear of a bus, she said: "It was a matter of dignity; I could not have faced myself and my people if I had moved."

The New Negro

Many of the Negroes who joined the protest did not expect it to succeed. When asked why, they usually gave one of three answers: "I didn't expect Negroes to stick to it," or, "I never thought we Negroes had the nerve," or, "I thought the pressure from the white folks would kill it before it got started."

In other words, our nonviolent protest in Montgomery is important because it is demonstrating to the Negro, North and South, that many of the stereotypes he has held about himself and other Negroes are not valid. Montgomery has broken the spell and is ushering in concrete manifestations of the thinking and action of the new Negro.

We know that:

WE CAN STICK TOGETHER

In Montgomery, forty-two thousand of us have refused to ride the city's segregated buses since December 5. Some walk as many as fourteen miles a day.

OUR LEADERS DO NOT HAVE TO SELL OUT

Many of us have been indicted, arrested, and "mugged." Every Monday and Thursday night we stand before the Negro population at the prayer meetings and repeat: "It is an honor to face jail for a just cause."

THREATS AND VIOLENCE DO NOT NECESSARILY INTIMIDATE THOSE WHO ARE SUFFICIENTLY AROUSED AND NONVIOLENT

The bombing of two of our homes has made us more resolute. When a handbill was circulated at a White Citizens Council meeting stating that Negroes should be "abolished" by "guns, bows and arrows, sling shots and knives," we responded with even greater determination.

OUR CHURCH IS BECOMING MILITANT

Twenty-four ministers were arrested in Montgomery. Each has said publicly that he stands prepared to be arrested again. Even upper-class Negroes who reject the "come to Jesus" gospel are now convinced that the church has no alternative but to provide the nonviolent dynamics for social change in the midst of conflict. The thirty thousand dollars used for the car pool, which transports over twenty thousand Negro workers, school children and housewives, has been raised in the churches. The churches have become the dispatch centers where the people gather to wait for rides.

WE BELIEVE IN OURSELVES

In Montgomery we walk in a new way. We hold our heads in a new way. Even the Negro reporters who converged on Montgomery have a new attitude. One tired reporter, asked at a luncheon in Birmingham to say a few words about Montgomery, stood up, thought for a moment, and uttered one sentence: "Montgomery has made me proud to be a Negro."

ECONOMICS IS PART OF OUR STRUGGLE

We are aware that Montgomery's white businessmen have tried to "talk sense" to the bus company and the city commissioners. We have observed that small Negro shops are thriving as Negroes find it inconvenient to walk downtown to the white stores. We have been getting more polite treatment in the white shops since the protest began. We have a new respect for the proper use of our dollar.

WE HAVE DISCOVERED A NEW AND POWERFUL WEAPON—NONVIOLENT RESISTANCE

Although law is an important factor in bringing about social change, there are certain conditions in which the very effort to adhere to new legal decisions creates tension and provokes violence. We had hoped to see demonstrated a method that would enable us to continue our struggle while coping with the violence it aroused. Now we see the answer: face violence if necessary, but refuse to return violence. If we respect those who oppose us, they may achieve a new understanding of the human relations involved.

WE NOW KNOW THAT THE SOUTHERN NEGRO HAS COME OF AGE, POLITI-
CALLY AND MORALLY

Montgomery has demonstrated that we will not run from the struggle, and will support the battle for equality. The attitude of many young Negroes a few years ago was reflected in the common expression, "I'd rather be a lamp post in Harlem than Governor of Alabama." Now the idea expressed in our churches, schools, pool rooms, restaurants and homes is: "Brother, stay here and fight nonviolently. 'Cause if you don't let them make you mad, you can win." The official slogan of the Montgomery Improvement Association is "Justice without Violence."

The Issues in Montgomery

The leaders of the old order in Montgomery are not prepared to negotiate a settlement. This is not because of the conditions we have set for returning to the buses. The basic question of segregation in intrastate travel is already before the courts. Meanwhile we ask only for what in Atlanta, Mobile, Charleston and most other cities of the South is considered the southern pattern. We seek the right, under segregation, to seat ourselves from the rear forward on a first come, first served basis. In addition, we ask for courtesy and the hiring of some Negro bus drivers on predominantly Negro routes.

A prominent judge of Tuscaloosa was asked if he felt there was any connection between Autherine Lucy's effort to enter the University of Alabama and the Montgomery nonviolent protest. He replied, "Autherine is just one unfortunate girl who doesn't know what she is doing, but in Montgomery it looks like all the niggers have gone crazy."

Later the judge is reported to have explained that "of course the good niggers had undoubtedly been riled up by outsiders, Communists and agitators." It is apparent that at this historic moment most of the elements of the white South are not prepared to believe that "our Negroes could of themselves act like this."

Miscalculation of the White Leaders

Because the mayor and city authorities cannot admit to themselves that we have changed, every move they have made inadvertently increased the protest and united the Negro community.

[1955]

Dec. 1   They arrested Mrs. Parks, one of the most respected Negro women in Montgomery.

Dec. 3   They attempted to intimidate the Negro population by publishing a report in the daily paper that certain Negroes were calling for a boycott of the buses. They thereby informed the thirty thousand Negro readers of the planned protest.

Dec. 5   They found Mrs. Parks guilty and fined her fourteen dollars. This action increased the number of those who joined the boycott.

Dec. 5   They arrested a Negro college student for "intimidating passengers." Actually, he was helping an elderly woman cross the street. This mistake solidified the college students' support of the protest.

Two policemen on motorcycles followed each bus on its rounds through the Negro community. This attempt at psychological coercion further increased the number of Negroes who joined the protest.

In a news telecast at 6:00 P.M., a mass meeting planned for that evening was announced. Although we had expected only five hundred people at the meeting, over five thousand attended.

Dec. 6   They began to intimidate Negro taxi drivers. This led to the setting up of a car pool and a resolution to extend indefinitely our protest, which had originally been called for one day only.

Dec. 7   They began to harass Negro motorists. This encouraged the Negro middle class to join the struggle.

Dec. 8   The lawyer for the bus company said, "We have no intention of hiring Negro drivers now or in the foreseeable future." To us this meant never. The slogan then became, "Stay off the buses until we win."

Dec. 9   The mayor invited Negro leaders to a conference, presumably for negotiation. When we arrived, we discovered that some of the men in the room were white supremacists and members of the White Citizens Council. The mayor's attitude was made clear when he said, "Comes the first rainy day and the Negroes will be back in the buses." The next day it did rain, but the Negroes did not ride the buses.

At this point over forty-two thousand Montgomery Negroes had joined the protest. After a period of uneasy quiet, elements in the white community turned to further police intimidation and to violence.

[1956]

Jan. 26   I was arrested for traveling thirty miles per hour in a twenty-five-mile zone. This arrest occurred just two hours before a mass meeting. So, we had to hold seven mass meetings to accommodate the people.

Jan. 30   My home was bombed.

Feb. 1   The home of E. D. Nixon, one of the protest leaders and former state president of the NAACP, was bombed. This brought moral and financial support from all over the state.

Feb. 22   Eighty-nine persons, including the twenty-four ministers, were arrested for participating in the nonviolent protests.

Every attempt to end the protest by intimidation, by encouraging Negroes to inform, by force and violence, further cemented the Negro community and brought sympathy for our cause from men of good will all over the world. The great appeal for the world appears to lie in the fact that we in Montgomery have adopted the method of nonviolence. In a world in which most men attempt to defend their highest values by the accumulation of weapons of destruction, it is morally refreshing to hear five thousand Negroes in Montgomery shout "Amen" and "Hallelujah" when they are exhorted to "Pray for those who oppose you," or pray "Oh Lord, give us strength of body to keep walking for freedom," and conclude each mass meeting with: "Let us pray that God shall give us strength to remain nonviolent though we may face death."

The Liberal Dilemma

And death there may be. Many white men in the South see themselves as a fearful minority in an ocean of black men. They honestly believe with one side of their minds that Negroes are depraved and disease-ridden. They look upon any effort at equality as leading to "mongrelization." They are convinced that racial equality is a Communist idea and that those who ask for it are subversive. They believe that their caste system is the highest form of social organization.

The enlightened white southerner, who for years has preached gradualism, now sees that even the slow approach finally has revolutionary implications. Placing straws on a camel's back, no matter how slowly, is dangerous. This realization has immobilized the liberals and most of the white church leaders. They have no answer for dealing with or absorbing violence. They end in begging for retreat, lest "things get out of hand and lead to violence."

Writing in *Life*, William Faulkner, Nobel prize-winning author from Mississippi, recently urged the NAACP to "stop now for a moment." That is to say, he encouraged Negroes to accept injustice, exploitation and indignity for a while longer. It is hardly a moral act to encourage others patiently to accept injustice which he himself does not endure.

In urging delay, which in this dynamic period is tantamount to retreat, Faulkner suggests that those of us who press for change now may not know that violence could break out. He says we are "dealing with a fact: the fact of emotional conditions of such fierce unanimity as to scorn the fact that it is a minority and which will go to any length and against any odds at this moment to justify and, if necessary, defend that condition and its right to it."

We southern Negroes believe that it is essential to defend the right of equality now. From this position we will not and cannot retreat. Fortunately, we are increasingly aware that we must not try to defend our position by methods that contradict the aim of brotherhood. We in Montgomery believe that the only way to press on is by adopting the philosophy and practice of nonviolent resistance.

This method permits a struggle to go on with dignity and without the need to retreat. It is a method that can absorb the violence that is inevitable in social change whenever deep-seated prejudices are challenged.

If, in pressing for justice and equality in Montgomery, we discover that those who reject equality are prepared to use violence, we must not despair, retreat or fear. Before they make this crucial decision, they must remember: whatever they do, we will not use violence in return. We hope we can act in the struggle in such a way that they will see the error of their approach and will come to respect us. Then we can all live together in peace and equality.

The basic conflict is not really over the buses. Yet we believe that, if the method we use in dealing with equality in the buses can eliminate injustice within ourselves, we shall at the same time be attacking the basis of injustice—man's hostility to man. This can only be done when we challenge the white community to re-examine its assumptions as we are now prepared to re-examine ours.

We do not wish to triumph over the white community. That would only result in transferring those now on the bottom to the top. But, if we can live up to nonviolence in thought and deed, there will emerge an interracial society based on freedom for all.

Liberation, April 1956, vol. 1, pp. 3–6; in James M. Washington, ed., *The Essential Writings and Speeches of Martin Luther King, Jr.*, (San Francisco: HarperCollins, 1991), pp. 75–81.

47

THE NAACP AND EXTREMISM (1956)

by the Editors of the Crisis

The above was the title of an editorial in the *Crisis;* it conveys a sense of the strategy and tactics of the liberation effort, as seen by the leaders of the NAACP.

Enemies of the NAACP, and even some of our best friends and well-wishers, are charging the Association with immoderate and unreasonable haste, of intransigence and extremism, not only in our procedures in public school desegregation, but in other related aspects of our fight for full citizenship. According to these critics, there is no middle group—only the White Council extremists on the one hand and the NAACP radicals on the other. Newspapers in the Deep South are filled daily with the wildest lies of hatred and fear, smears and innuendoes, unfounded assumptions and groundless charges that the Association is stirring up racial tension, is made up of Communists, etc., etc.

Actually, however, our fulminators and defamers are the real extremists, the most stubborn upholders of segregation and racial inequality to be found in the United States. Some of them, including some Congressmen, are even trying, it seems, to organize a New Confederacy, not only to fight the NAACP, but also the United States Supreme Court and all constituted authority. These are the people who are openly boasting that they will not obey the law of the land, the people who plan to keep the Federal Courts busy on "nonracial excuses" for continued segregation, the people who rant about the nine Supreme Court justices as the "nine ninnies." These are the real extremists—not the NAACP.

These white Southern extremist groups accuse the Association of being precipitous and thoughtless in action and guilty of irresponsible rabble rousing.

However, the charge currently being made (and echoed in sections outside the South) is that the Association is "forcing" the issue, "going too fast" and "pushing too hard." The Southern wail now is "go slow!"

Let us examine this "gradualism" warning to see what it means to most Southerners and what it means to Negroes and the NAACP. To most Americans the word has its simple dictionary definition of "changing or moving by degrees." To the defiant Southerner, however, the word, as he uses it, always means "never." What the Southerner wants, it seems, is a gradual improvement of the Negro's status *within* the segregated pattern. He wants the Negro to advance over on the "Negro's side" of the racial fence as a Negro but he wants no breaches made in the wall of racial separation. Even the slightest change arouses his fears and he begins to rant about "outside pressures," "gradualism," "our Negroes want segregation," and all sorts of twaddle which has not even the remotest connection with the issue under discussion.

Take the case of Autherine Juanita Lucy which provoked the mob action at the University of Alabama. Did the NAACP act precipitously in her case, since many of our friends, as well as our enemies, have accused us of pushing her entry into the University? Miss Lucy applied for admission to the University of Alabama, not under the recent United States Supreme Court rulings of May 17, 1954, and May 31, 1955, but under the Court's ruling on the admission of Negro students to southern graduate schools, a decision handed down in June 1950. It was not until two years later, in 1953, that Miss Lucy applied for admission to the University of Alabama. And she spent two years in the courts seeking admission. No court action is ever hurried or precipitous and neither Miss Lucy nor the NAACP can be accused of unreasonable haste in her case. Miss Lucy was patient. The NAACP was patient. NAACP lawyers were patient. Surely this was gradualism to suit the most technical interpretation, but what happened when the Court, on February 1, 1956, ordered Miss Lucy's admission to the University of Alabama?

The whole world knows of the rioting, the mob rule on a university campus, and the threats of lynching when she applied at the beginning of the semester in February. We ask, who were the gradualists in this case. Who were the unreasonable, precipitous groups? The incitement to mob action, the stirring up of racial ill-will, the hasty actions were all on the part of the whites, not on the part of Miss Lucy or the National Association for the Advancement of Colored People. Or let us take the case of segregated housing in the United States. The Negro ghetto, offspring of segregated housing, is one of the most flagrantly prejudiced and unconstitutional practices leveled against Negroes. Though Negroes had long been segregated in housing, it was in 1917 that Louisville, Ky., passed an ordinance to perfect housing segregation. This led to the famous case of *Buchanan vs. Warley* (1917) and the United States Supreme Court decision declaring the Louisville and all such ordinances illegal. But it was thirty-two years later before the Supreme Court outlawed the restrictive covenant in 1949. Again the NAACP and Negroes were patient, relying on the orderly processes of the courts.

Negroes worked for thirty years to be allowed to purchase Pullman accommodations in the South, to be permitted to eat in dining cars without being hidden, like lepers, behind a curtain. And the ICC ruling banning segregation of interstate passengers in rail and bus transportation and waiting rooms of stations was handed down only last fall—November 25, 1955.

Segregation, "the Southern way of life," is doomed. It is doomed legally; it is doomed morally. The Negro masses are in revolt against it. They know from bitter experience that separation always means inequality. They know that Southerners have never done anything effectual to bring them equality, that outside pressures and the courts—perfectly legal procedures—are always needed to achieve even the modest gains we have made. And these the NAACP and Negroes shall continue to use. No time is gained by settling a great question wrong. And the NAACP and Southern Negroes are resolved to settle it right—by legal and constitutional means.

Crisis, April 1956, vol. 63, pp. 226–27.

48

THUNDER IN THE SOUTH (1956)

by Abner W. Berry

A veteran African-American journalist offered a probing analysis early in 1956 of the resistance beginning to envelop and transform the nation.

The unmistakable rumblings of a new battle for democracy in the South have given rise to a number of mistaken theories as to why it is happening.

There is the theory that it is happening automatically because of some "change of heart." This view omits the basic social and historic underlying causes. There is another view which is fundamentally just as "automatic" in its assumptions, but which appears to have a more materialist basis. This view argues that the "plantation system is dying because of industrial advances." Hence, there is a sort of automatic process of the dying of the jimcrow system. Perhaps even more startling is the explanation advanced by a writer in the quarterly review, *Dissent,* a publication which says it is Socialist but "anti-Stalinist." Mr. Bob Bone, writing in the Spring edition of the magazine says:

"We are living in a period when foreign policy considerations are decisive in determining the course of domestic events. America must garrison an empire; therefore some form of permanent military conscription is inevitable.... America must staff its fighting forces with loyal personnel; therefore important concessions must be made to a disadvantaged minority group which numbers over 15,000,000. The Negro question has become a military manpower question—a matter of organizing American resources for war."

According to Bone we are witnessing a "revolution" in race relations "with the armed forces acting as the vanguard of social progress." Logically, one could conclude from this that the planning for war is "good" for the Negro people. But would Bone dare to assert that his opinion is shared by the Negro people?

Looking at another aspect of the integration drive, Bone asserts that integration is taking place "at a time when reaction has the initiative in all other political spheres." Bone therefore sees it as "paradoxical" that segregation should be receding while political repressions, he predicts, will increase.

The main and most palpable error of Bone is that he overlooks entirely the fact that Negroes throughout the country have been fighting stubbornly for years against every form of racism. To accept his thesis one would have to believe that the political reactionaries are capable of projecting contradictory programs—one for racial democracy and the other for political dictatorship. Further, we are to believe that integration is inevitable for reasons of foreign policy, and in view of the influx of industry into the South and the increased mechanization of farms in the old plantation belt.

Now it is true that Negroes are being displaced on the old plantations by the introduction of machinery. This process is forcing Negroes into the

Southern and Northern towns and cities. *But their leaving the land has not automatically done away with the racist pattern, nor has it reduced the dominance of cotton as a crop.*

Negroes moving to the cities have affected the fight for integration by exercising their political and economic power. Is not this what is happening today in the city of Montgomery? Recently I was told by a leader of the Montgomery bus boycott that the "economic squeeze" of the White Citizens Councils could not work in a city "because the role of the whites and Negroes are too closely intertwined." It is this, along with Negro migration from the farms, rather than any automatic process, which accounts for the connection between the growth of Negro city dwellers and the fight for integration. The implied decrease of cotton production is refuted by the crop reports. The Jackson (Miss.) *Daily News,* for example, headlined a story last December 9:

"Two Million Bales is State Cotton Crop For Year"

And the story astonishingly informs us:

"This year's crop, boosted by advanced farming methods, came from 1,700,000 acres, the lowest since 1871. Last year's harvested acreage totalled 1,960,000 acres."

The figures do not show that "cotton is not King." They show that the King is able to get fatter and richer on the labor of fewer subjects. The mass of sharecroppers, as a leading business weekly pointed out recently, are being turned into *day laborers.* And the remaining croppers work for both wages and "shares" farming reduced acreage. But the old feudal relationships remain the same—jimcrow, terror at the polls or even at the "threat" of Negroes appearing at the polls. The mass of displaced former farmers become new pools of labor for the run-away northern industries.

A look at a few of the recent moves shows that industries are indeed moving into the old plantation belt. The Alexander Smith Carpet Company went to Greenville, Miss., and DuPont's largest Orlon plant is located in Camden, S.C. In almost every case, whether it is the manufacture of tires, newsprint, artificial fibres or cotton textiles, the northern plant is moving closer to its basic raw material. This has tended to bolster the old plantation, although contributing to its "modernization" in every other way except socially and politically.

The industries which have come to the Black Belt have not only given added incentives to the plantations for furthering their economic development, but they have tended *to take over and strengthen the semi-feudal social relations there.* Since these relations are based, in the main, on the peculiar racist oppression of the Negro people, they have offered some measure of protection against unionization and labor solidarity in the industries. Just as the plantations had sharecropping as the major occupation for Negroes, the industries have set aside special "Negro" jobs, with the bosses assuming the same paternal relationship to Negro employees (and whites, too, for that matter) as obtained between the plantation owner and his tenants.

This is not an entirely new historical phenomenon; the Japanese capitalists were able to build an entire national economy of heavy industry without carrying through the traditional social and political reforms associated with the bourgeois revolution. There, the landowner-nobles simply built industrial establishments in the feudal domains. The peasant became worker, or worker-peasant within the same old relationships that existed before the industries grew.

But the Japanese feudal capitalists had feudal relations uncorrupted by racist trappings; the southern industrialist depends upon segregation and the super-exploitation of Negroes for his continued enjoyment of feudal privileges. He therefore makes common cause with the plantation owners on the economic, social and political fronts. In Alabama, the industrial barons of Birmingham, led by U.S. Steel and Republic Steel, have teamed up with the rulers of the Black Belt counties of the South to thwart all moves to break the stranglehold of the white supremacy politicians. The textile and tobacco interests of Virginia, North and South Carolina have done the same in relation to the old Tidewater racists. And in Georgia and Mississippi, the power monopolies and other industries share the rulership of the state with the big planters.

If industrial concentration, as such, were to lead automatically to Negro emancipation, Birmingham, Ala., should now lead the South in fulfilling the promise of the Civil War. For Birmingham is truly the industrial Capital of the South, the rival of Pittsburgh, itself. Instead, it is a company town where racism is as firmly installed in power as in any smaller Black Belt metropolis.

Moreover, the penetration of industry into the southern Black Belt establishes a political bridge between the plantation economy and its social system and northern reaction. Before the Civil War there was some acute contradiction between the aims of the slaveholders and those of the northern capitalists. The same cannot be said today of the political aims of the Black Belt racist politicians and those who represent the monopolies of industry and finance in the North today. The political expression of this unity between the "backward" South and the "progressive" industrial leaders of the "free world" is the firm alliance in Congress between the so-called "southern bloc" and the right-wing Republicans.

Sen. William E. Jenner, the Indiana Republican, stands shoulder to shoulder with James O. Eastland, of Mississippi, called by some, "Mr. Segregation," and by others, "the voice of the Republican South." Sen. Karl E. Mundt, of North Dakota, as did the late Sen. Robert A. Taft, of Ohio, is now spending most of his spare time stumping Eastland's domain, pleading for a union of southern Democrats and Mid-West reactionaries.

But more people can cross a bridge than those for whom it was built. And organized labor, as well as the independent movement of the Negro people, are coming to see that they, too, must organize nationally against the racist-conservative alliance. Thus, it can be said that the influx of industry into the South is creating the conditions for the break-up of the racist system; that industry multiplies the system's grave diggers.

There are indications that organized labor is slowly rising to the challenge. The elevation of two Negroes to AFL-CIO vice-presidencies and the strong tone adopted at the founding convention—and since—against all forms of racism, mark heightened awareness of this age-old stumbling block in the path of southern union drives. However, it depends upon the conscious and determined fight of the Negroes in the organized labor movement to remove the feudal-racist relationships which plague the South and hamper the northern workers. For it is certainly not the intention, nor the tendency, of big and little industry to weaken these racist relationships. And to hold that industrialization automatically weakens or destroys southern racism is worse than gradualism; it is a promise of "pie in the sky." It attributes to monopoly capital a liberating role which both present fact and past history refute.

The plantation system is very much alive. This is the core of the evil. In those Deep South states where the White Citizens Councils cast a pall over the hopes of democracy, it is the political representatives from the plantation areas who still dominate, as for example, James O. Eastland of Sunflower County. Such counties are represented in state legislatures far beyond their population proportions. They have been able in these legislatures to block all efforts aimed at a more equitable and democratic reapportionment. The basis of the political strength of these political racists is the absolute denial of the vote to Negro majorities and their alliance with the big industrialists in Southern cities.

Political life in the old plantation belt, and the activities of its representatives in the state and Federal government, belie assertions that we can proceed "paradoxically," as Mr. Bone writes in *Dissent,* toward broader rights for Negroes and greater McCarthy-style repressions against peace advocates, progressives and Marxists.

In Mississippi, where Negroes have not yet enjoyed any of the concessions made by the Federal government (except those on establishments of the Armed Forces), whites, as well as Negroes, are denied freedom of speech by the racist system. An Ohio Episcopal minister, the Rev. Mr. Alvin Kershaw, was denied the right to speak at the University on February 19 on the school's "Religious Emphasis Week" program, because he was termed "subversive" by the state legislature. Rev. Kershaw, it seems, had "admitted" membership in the National Association for the Advancement of Colored People. Dr. Norton King, sociology professor and chairman of his department in the university, resigned because he said he would not be allowed to discuss the "segregation question" in his sociology classes. For similar reasons Dr. William Buchanan, a government professor at Mississippi State College, turned in his resignation.

Everyone is acquainted with the public works of Sen. Eastland in the field of political repression and witch-hunting. But almost unnoticed is the quiet work on segregation being done by the chairman of the Senate Foreign Relations Committee, Sen. Walter George, the Georgia Democrat. Or that of Rep. Richards, of South Carolina, chairman of the House Foreign Relations Committee. The compulsions to liberality on the Negro question, growing out of foreign policy needs, seem not to have affected these two—and there are many others—who have as much to say about foreign relations as any other two men in Washington outside the Cabinet.

The fact is that "great progress" made so far on the "race relations front" has not gone beyond the periphery. The core of the evil remains.
And it is against this core in the plantation belt that the embattled Negroes in Montgomery, Birmingham, Columbia, S.C., Memphis, Tenn., the Mississippi Delta and points south, are directing their attack.
It was from the heart of the plantation area that the fight for unsegregated schools began—in Prince Edward County, Va., and Clarendon County, S.C. It was—and is—the Delta of Mississippi where Negroes

braved murder and armed assault for their right to cast a ballot. Emmett Louis Till is not so much a victim of blind racism, provoked by a "wolf whistle" at a white woman, as a martyr to the *plantation* axiom that a Negro's vote is worth his life. Rev. George Wesley Lee, who was murdered in Belzoni, Miss., a few months before the Till murder in August, and Lamar Smith, shot and killed in Brookhaven while working for Negro votes on August 2, 1955, testify to Negroes' determination in this direction. The battle of the Negro people for political rights—this is what terrifies the racists.

The effect of the U.S. Supreme Court ruling against segregation, and the tremendous effort at popularizing it done by the NAACP, has left its mark on the Southern Negroes. They move into battle against segregation now with the knowledge that jimcrow laws have been declared illegal. And the murder of Till has stiffened the fight. "The law is on our side," is stated alongside the old stand-by "God is on our side," wherever there is a fight.

The vigor of the Negroes' drive for enforcement of the nation's laws has spilled over into the church bodies of all denominations. In turn, the Negro movement has stimulated the churches to act, and the labor movement, turning from its old economism, is developing a program geared to the social and political demands of the Negro people.

Even in the heart of the South, the pressure of the Negroes for economic rights has influenced trade unions. This was seen in the adjustments of the Negro workers' demands in the giant Esso refinery at Baton Rouge, La.; the unexampled Negro-white solidarity displayed in the sugar strike in Louisiana; and in the prompt demand for an apology by the Alabama Rubber Workers Union when officials accused its members of having participated in a mob action directed at Miss Lucy.

Almost everywhere, except in the Federal government agencies, the Negro is finding allies in his fight to realize in life the promise of the law and the U.S. Constitution. J. Edgar Hoover is asked to do something about terror in Mississippi and he swiftly attacks Dr. T. R. M. Howard, a terror victim, for being dissatisfied with FBI negligence. President Eisenhower is content to let the courts handle the civil rights question. The Democrats are trying to look both ways: towards "party harmony" with the Southern bloc, which means maintaining the status quo, and toward the Negro voters who are insisting that the status quo is inimical to their interests.

But no one can ignore the civil rights question. The Negro movement, now sparked by, but going beyond the organizational confines of the

NAACP, has given every indication that Negroes everywhere, and especially in the South, are irrevocably committed to the fight for immediate full equality. Gradualism is out. Men cannot die gradually. Bombs do not explode gradually. Mobs do not gather gradually. And Negroes are dying.

It is the aroused mass of Negroes, irrevocably committed and united against "the southern way of life," which constitutes the main factor today in the drive for one America, one American citizenship, a nation truly indivisible with liberty and justice for all. They will not now turn back.

There are other factors, not to be overlooked or underestimated. These include the united labor movement, the re-awakened Church movement promoting the practice of brotherhood here and now on *this* earth, and the general search for an ethic dynamic enough to square the traditional American democratic tenets with American political and social reality.

Overlying this domestic process is the enormous struggle of the colonial and former colonial peoples of the world against imperialism, colonialism and racism everywhere. This world movement has placed the racists on the defensive. It has noticeably accelerated the pace of the entire democratic movement in the United States of which the Negro battle for equality is an inspiring part.

This was reflected in a statement by Rev. King to a February 14 press conference in Chicago when he described the Montgomery bus boycott as a movement of "passive resistance," adding:

"It is a part of something that is happening all over the world. The oppressed peoples are rising up. They are revolting against colonialism and imperialism and all other systems of oppressions."

Rev. King, living in the heart of the old plantation belt, said nothing about the "great progress" being made. His eyes were on the future. For the Negroes in Montgomery, as well as other plantation areas, still live under the pall of planter rule, with its naked white supremacy dictatorships and the forceful exclusion of Negroes from the mainstream of political, social and economic life.

But the road can never again be back. The door to equality is being kicked open, the road irrevocably taken. It is no corner battle, no "private quarrel" of an oppressed minority. It never was, as the keen mind of Tom Jefferson saw back in the first two decades of the nineteenth century when he called it "a firebell in the night." It was no private quarrel when the generation of Lincoln had to face it and fight it out. It is no private quarrel today. For involved in its outcome is the very existence of the democratic tradition for the entire nation. The Eastlands are enemies of the American nation, no less than of the Negro people. Their racism is the shield for that reactionary conspiracy which allies the Dixiecrats and the top Big Business agents in the Republican Party. The Negro people are turning the fire of their passion for freedom against the core of the evil: the plantation system and its suppression of democracy. Their victory can only be America's victory.

Masses and Mainstream, April 1956, pp. 7–14.

49

DESEGREGATION AND RACIAL TENSIONS (1956)

by Roy Wilkins

It is a pleasure to greet again our members and friends in the Southeast region of the NAACP, and particularly those in South Carolina.

There were some signs last summer that the traditional Southern hospitality would no longer be extended to me as executive secretary of the NAACP. Federal Judge Ashton Williams took special pains to suggest from his bench that I should not be permitted to speak again in South Carolina.

But of course he did not mean that. Judge Williams believes, like all good Americans—and certainly all federal judges—in freedom of speech. We may not like what a man has to say, but we have not yet got to the place where we bar him from speaking, as long he observes the proprieties.

Personally, I don't like what Senator James Eastland of Mississippi and Senator Strom Thurmond of South Carolina say in their speeches but I would not bar either of them from speaking. In fact it would not be exaggerating too much to say that the more such men speak, the more aid they render our cause.

Nevertheless, I *am* sorry, indeed, that my Columbia speech struck Judge Williams as such a poor one—even though it is a difficult task for an NAACP speaker to please a listener who thinks of the NAACP in the same way he thinks of the Ku Klux Klan. The NAACP, after all, has always proceeded according to the law and has always obeyed the rulings of the courts, even when we thought those rulings were unfair. This is in conspicuous contrast to the Klan which, as everyone is aware, has made its own laws, put itself up as judge and carried out its own punishments, while at the same time ignoring the U.S. Supreme Court and all the other courts.

In these respects the Klan has a resemblance to some organizations recently formed in South Carolina and elsewhere in the South, but no resemblance to the NAACP. I could agree heartily with Judge Williams if he were to declare that South Carolina would benefit if all those organizations did not exist here.

For South Carolina and the South are faced with a problem requiring sober, honest, fair, and sincere consideration.

Basic Question

Here is the big, basic question for Southerners: Shall we obey the law as to our race relations, or shall we defy the law and insist that our 1856 philosophy be the pattern for 1956? Specifically, shall we comply with the Court's opinion on public schools?

On all sides we hear that tensions between the races have increased and that conditions have worsened.

I suggest that if this is true, the underlying bedrock cause is the refusal on the part of the Southern whites to recognize the Negro as a citizen.

The millions of words that have been written and spoken on the Negro, the public schools, the Supreme Court, and the host of other items in the race relations picture have ignored completely this fundamental issue of status.

Consciously and subconsciously, Southern Whites have treated our people as wards, to be done with as they in their wisdom see fit. It comes as a great shock to them to have the highest court in the land hear, evaluate, and uphold the Negro's claims *as a citizen*.

In the southern scheme of things, Negroes were to do as they were told, regardless of their own desires, or any laws to the contrary. This is the "tradition" of which so much is now being made.

The result is that most white Southerners have come to believe, deeply, sincerely and completely, that they have a God-given right to control Negroes. They are bewildered, frustrated, angry, and defiant when this system is challenged.

Editor Thomas Waring, of the *News and Courier,* has complained to the world that the press, radio, television and national magazines are "against" the South, and that they refuse to give its spokesmen a hearing.

In its January issue, *Harper's Magazine* published an article by Mr. Waring which concerned itself principally with assertions that Negroes *as a race* are immoral, criminal, diseased and mentally retarded.

Antiquated Arguments

These "arguments" are strikingly similar to those made in slavery debates more than a hundred years ago. In the light of what has happened to the Negro and the rest of the world since 1860, the Waring contentions, even if sincerely held by scores of thousands of persons, are nonetheless invalid. Because most people once thought the world flat did not make it a fact.

The Waring article, like so much of the talk out of the South, blandly brushes aside the clear responsibility of the South itself for the present "statistics" on Negroes. People who are held to a substandard economic level, barred almost completely from your textile industry, for example, cheated year after weary year as sharecroppers, paid a pittance as domestic servants, denied hospital care, and until five years ago barred from state medical schools—still barred in South Carolina—these people are supposed to be healthy, happy, thrifty, educated, well-housed, responsible, dedicated citizens.

For eighty years Negroes have gone to school in shacks, while whites had the best the government could afford; yet they are now supposed to be the scholastic equals of whites.

Why doesn't Editor Waring compare the Negro students in Boston or Hartford or Pittsburgh or Toledo or Minneapolis with the white students in Charleston or Columbia or Spartanburg or Memphis or Atlanta?

A two-legged man can always out-run a cripple; the point is, how would he do against other two-legged men?

But even if it had any validity, the Waring thesis would astound and disgust thoughtful people inside and outside the South. For they ask: What has all this to do with *equality as a citizens under the law?*

And this is the question our opponents persistently refuse to discuss. Instead, they have chosen to chase down a hundred emotional and unrelated by-paths, some of them ridiculous in the extreme.

They have gone "hog wild and pig crazy" passing laws against the NAACP and desegregation. But on February 18, Attorney General Eugene Cook of Georgia admitted in a speech that most of the laws just passed by his legislature would be "stricken down in due course." The same holds true for what the South Carolina legislature is doing. Its members are merely exercising themselves.

The South Carolina state legislature, for example, in February, called upon the Attorney General of the United States to place the NAACP on his subversive list. Well, if the NAACP were truly a Communist-front organization we would have been on the list long ago. The Communist charge against us is a feeble lie being used throughout the South to excite the gullible and the ignorant.

Assault on NAACP

The assault upon the NAACP, of course, is only one of the methods being employed to intimidate the Negro population, create tension and by-pass the basic issue.

There are the White Citizens Councils. More than a year ago the Montgomery *Advertiser* called them "manicured Ku Klux Klans" and it is still a good description.

The Councils constitute a conspiracy to defy the Supreme Court's school ruling and maintain white supremacy. Although they repeat over and over that they do not sanction violence, their public and private statements, mass meetings, and hate literature have been creating the climate in which violence has occurred. The hoodlums have been given the green light.

The murders in Mississippi, the bombings in Montgomery, Alabama, the violence directed at Rev. M. DeLaine, the gunshots into the home of Rev. M. Hinton, our state president, in Columbia, and the disgraceful rioting at the University of Alabama, may all be traced directly to the hysterical atmosphere whipped up by the Citizens Councils and their spokesmen.

United States Senators cannot go about the country preaching lawless defiance of courts and constitutional government without sharing the responsibility for the violence that may ensue.

Governors of states who preach nullification by means of the fancy word, "interposition," are also encouraging more direct violation of law and personal rights.

At the University of Alabama under pitiful hypnosis of the whiteness cult, 1000 young white men demonstrated their superiority over Negroes by throwing eggs and rocks at one lone Negro girl.

In admiration for this 1,000-to-1 battle, a group of men in Lake City, S.C., is reported to have sent a case of eggs to the University.

This, then, is what we are offered as proper and credible debate of a constitutional question; this is the type of mentality for which Editor Waring seeks a hearing in the forums of the rest of the nation.

Violence Encouraged

But the encouragement of violence by innuendo—Senator Eastland, addressing White Councils at Montgomery, Alabama, following the University riot said: "I know you people of Alabama are not going to let the NAACP take over your schools"—is not the only sin of the Councils.

For cowardly and reprehensible economic pressures are the primary weapon of this organization. Sharecroppers, day laborers, home and farm owners, small retail business men and even domestic servants have been "squeezed" if they signed a petition or otherwise spoke up for their rights.

To appreciate the scope of the cowardice, one must remember that none of the victims threatens the power structure of the South. Negroes own no great industries publish no daily papers, sit in no legislatures, have only a fingernail hold in financial circles, are not sheriffs, sit on no court benches, and hold only a few scattered and minor political offices. Their industrial employment is limited to unskilled categories.

What threat do they pose? Are these Citizen Council members, these industrial executives, bankers, educators, editors, ministers of the gospel and other respectable white community leaders any safer or happier because some Negro family is made to face sudden disaster? Does it make a textile executive more secure to know that a Negro widow with four children over in Clarendon county is thrown off the land and has to beg bread and milk for the "sin" of assuming she is a human being?

Is this the thinking, are these the acts, which Editor Waring claims should be "understood" by the North?

Problem of South

Probably nothing illustrates the problem of the South so well as the Montgomery bus protest. And Montgomery city officials, all of whom belong to the White Citizens Councils, have met the situation in the customary southern manner. The police state has come out in the open at Montgomery. The grand jury has indicted 115 persons under a state anti-boycott law. This is the Soviet communism method. Here we have the police knocking on doors and taking men away. Here we have mass arrests. Here we have a grand jury delivering a lecture on observance of the segregation line. Precisely like the Communists. Its report said:

"Segregation laws and the NAACP attack on segregation are the primary cause of the unrest and increasing tension between whites and Negroes in Montgomery. In this state we are committed to segregation by custom and by law; we intend to maintain it.

"The settlement of differences over school attendance, public transportation and other public facilities must be made within those laws which reflect our way of life."

What the grand jury said, my friends, is: Here in Montgomery we don't care a hoot about any law except *our* law; don't get any notions about the Supreme Court or the Constitution, or the United States; this is Montgomery, Alabama, and this is what we say black people must do—or else. So 115 people, including practically all the leading ministers among Negroes, are subject to fines and jail sentences.

Understanding Negroes

Montgomery whites claim not to be able to understand "their" Negroes. Well, I'll be glad to explain. "Their" Negroes are sick and tired of segregation, of the daily insults and mistreatment and daily humiliations. It is that simple. Their cups have run over.

The grand jury to the contrary, there was no "outside interference" at Montgomery. Negro ministers there took the lead and guided their flocks toward dignity. The entire nation has been inspired by their quiet Christian courage.

If these men of God go to jail there is a good chance that thousands over the country will follow them to similar jails for similar "crimes."

The time has come for freedom. We have been patient—God knows!— but the time is here. Who can say with truth that we want to go too fast?

Ninety years is a long time to wait—no man who waits that long is going too fast.

Certainly, as far as education is concerned, there has been ample warning of the changes to be expected. A Maryland court in 1935 ordered a Negro student admitted to the law school of the University of Maryland. In 1938 the United States Supreme Court put the handwriting on the wall with its decision in the Gaines case at the University of Missouri. Now, twenty years from the Maryland signal and seventeen years from the Missouri notice they tell us we are trying to "force" something "overnight."

Moreover, up to the present, every advance has had to be fought for; almost nothing has been voluntarily given. We won what we now have; the South gave none of the major items in good will and fairness. And what do we ask when we say the time is here? We ask the acknowledgement of our status as citizens. We ask the rights and privileges and responsibilities of citizenship. We ask equality with other citizens under the law.

Desegregation Problem

The school desegregation problem can be solved if the South will begin by recognizing Negro citizenship—unreserved citizenship. This is the first requisite. From that point plans can be made for a "good faith" beginning on desegregation. Negro citizens will meet any such beginning more than half way, with understanding and good will.

Nothing stands in the way of the easing of tensions except the flat refusal of Southern Whites to make a start. Surely, Negroes cannot be expected to bargain when they are presented with nothing but a "never, never" proposition to bargain over; and when they refrain from discussion on such a basis, they surely cannot be accused fairly of creating or maintaining tension.

In 1857—99 years ago—the Supreme Court declared a Negro had no rights which a white man was bound to respect. That decision was reversed by the Civil War, yet today many whites are following the Dred Scott decision and ignoring all that has happened since. The present situation is squarely in the hands of the leaders of opinion in the South. Condemnation of the NAACP is a smokescreen. A plea for understanding based on considerations of timing is understandable; a plea for understanding based on defiance of constitutional government is a plea for anarchy and secession.

The white people of the South must face up to the basic questions of law and citizenship under law. I, for one, do not for a minute underestimate the difficulties, real or imagined, which confront them in their soul-searching. But in every question there are right and wrong sides, profitable ones and unprofitable ones, comfortable ones and uncomfortable ones, easy and difficult ones.

The choice for them is not easy, but it must be made. Our people and our Association stand ready, as always, to help them arrive at a just decision.

It is long past time to begin.

Crisis, April 1956, pp. 197–201; 254–55. This is an address delivered on February 24, 1956, before the Southeast Regional Convention, NAACP, in Charleston, S.C.

50

THE NEW NEGRO (1956)

by E. Franklin Frazier

Thirty years ago a New Negro made his appearance in the North, following closely upon the mass migrations of Negroes from the South during and following World War I. His emergence was marked by race riots in which he resisted violence with violence. On the spiritual plane, the emergence was heralded by an artistic and literary renaissance in which the Negro made a new evaluation of his experience in America.

Today a New Negro is emerging in the South. So far, no race riots have marked the event nor are there any indications—yet—that the new spirit among Southern Negroes will produce an artistic and literary renaissance. Nevertheless, there are indications all over the South that the Negro is no longer afraid to face the white man and say frankly that he wants equality and an end to segregation.

Nothing so dramatizes the difference between old and new attitudes of the Negro in the South as the contrast between the dignity and courage of Autherine Lucy and the reported attitude of her parents. According to the New York *Times,* Miss Lucy's father said, with reference to her behavior: "We raised ten head of children, nine of them still living and every one of them was taught to stay their distance from white folks, but to give them all their respect. If Autherine has changed from this, she didn't get her new ideas from home."

The boycott of buses in Montgomery, which began as a spontaneous mass movement against discrimination and segregation, has revealed how deep and how widespread is the new spirit. Despite violence and threats of violence the Negro continues his fight to exercise the right to vote. Negro college students are for the first time showing a militant spirit in regard to segregation and discrimination. The autocratic administrations of Negro colleges, especially state schools, have taught humility and acceptance of existing racial patterns; as a consequence, their graduates have been on the whole apathetic toward the race problem. Therefore, Negroes as well as the white controllers of Negro education were startled when the students at the South Carolina State College for Negroes went on strike because state officials threatened to investigate the affiliations of the faculty and student body with the National Association for the Advancement of Colored People. The leader of the students was expelled and the students went back to classes under threat from the Negro administration; they refused, nevertheless, to eat bread supplied from a bakery owned by a member of the White Citizens Council. More recently, at the State College for Negroes in Tallahassee, Florida, the students struck against the bus company after two female students were arrested for defying segregation regulations.

Whatever may have been the real feelings of Miss Lucy's father, his statement contains a significant observation—namely, that she did not acquire her new ideas at home. The new spirit of the Southern Negroes is a radical break from the traditional pattern of race relations. The old pattern had its roots in a rural society, and, just as the emergence of the New Negro in the North was due to the flight of the Negro from feudal America, so the emergence of the New Negro in the South is primarily the result of the movement of Negroes to cities.

The urbanization of southern Negroes has resulted, first, in a marked change in their occupations. At present, only about a third of the Negroes in the South gain their living from agriculture. Negro workers have not been assimilated into manufacturing, trade and service industries to the same extent as white workers; and many Negroes who have migrated to the southern cities have been forced to move a second time and seek a living outside the South. Nevertheless, because of conditions in southern agriculture, Negroes continue to move into southern cities and those who find work get a new outlook on life as industrial workers. Although Negroes are still kept, on the whole, to unskilled occupations, they receive much higher wages in industry than they did from agriculture. In 1949 the median income of urban Negro workers was twice that of Negro farmers, including owners, renters and laborers, and today the median income of urban Negroes is between three and four times that of rural Negroes. Moreover, although the median income of Negro families in southern cities is only 56 per cent that of white families, this represents an increase during the past six or seven years.

This improvement in the Negro's economic status has had several important effects upon his conception of himself and of his position in the South. He has a greater sense of security and he is in a better position to contribute money to the fight for equality in American life. This shows, for example, in the tremendous growth of NAACP membership in the South. The Negro can now buy those things—radios, televisions, newspapers and magazines—which symbolize a middle-class standard of living and are indicative of his new orientation to the world. The Negro middle class in the South has grown considerably, due largely to the increase in the number of Negro teachers and other professional and white collar workers as well as skilled workers.

The social consequences of urbanization, even more than the economic, helped to bring about profound changes in the Negro's attitude towards his place in southern society. First among these social consequences has been the improvement in his educational facilities. Undoubtedly the Supreme Court desegregation decisions were responsible for some of the recent improvements. But this development was already under way before the decisions, notably during the period of rapid industrialization of the South between 1940 and 1952 when the region's per capita income increased over 200 per cent. The improvement in Negro education was reflected in the reduction of the disparity between the per capita expenditure for the instruction of white and Negro children; in the increase in school attendance at all levels, especially at the secondary level; in the equalization of Negro and white teachers' salaries (except in Mississippi and South Carolina), and in new buildings and other facilities for Negroes.

The influence of formal education in bringing about a new spirit among southern Negroes is only one of a number of factors which have been breaking down their social and mental isolation. In the larger southern cities, relations between whites and Negroes have necessarily undergone changes. For example, in the country store or small-town bank, the Negro is generally expected to observe the "etiquette of race relations" and wait until white people are served. But in the large-city chain stores the customer, who has no status because of race, takes his turn in line. One of the reasons for the present racial tensions in regard to transportation in southern cities is that there is an attempt to maintain a caste relationship in an area of social relations that has become highly mobile and secular.

The effect of mere physical mobility upon Negro attitudes should not be overlooked. Thousands of southern Negroes, rural as well as urban, are moving about the country more than at any time in their history. They see Negroes occupying positions and enjoying rights which were undreamed of a few decades ago. Moreover, they themselves are treated with greater respect when they leave the South. This physical mobility has been increased by the military draft. But military service has done more; it has given the Negro a new conception of his role and his rights as an American citizen. This effect is heightened when the Negro serves in an "integrated" army unit. Men with military experience have often taken the lead in demanding the Negro's right to the ballot. It is perhaps not an accident that the recognized leader of the bus boycott in Montgomery, Alabama, is a minister who served in the armed forces.

Thus the appearance of a New Negro in the South is due primarily to the breakdown of the social and mental isolation in which the Negro people have lived. In a short story which appeared during the Negro renaissance in Harlem, Rudolph Fisher portrayed the astonishment of a Negro migrant from the South who could hardly believe his eyes when he saw a Negro policeman. There are few southern Negroes today who would be astonished at the sight. If they have not seen a Negro policeman in the South, they have become accustomed to seeing him on the screen or on television. Again, the increasing literacy of southern Negroes, resulting from their better education, furnishes another escape from their former mental isolation. Now they can read newspapers and magazines—especially the Negro publications, most of which are located outside the South. These publications constantly play up the Negro's fight for equality, the victories which he has won and the achievements of Negroes everywhere.

The new conception which the southern Negro is acquiring of himself and his place in American life as the result of urbanization is being fostered by the dominant forces in our changing society. Although the growth of labor unions in the South has been retarded by the racial situation, Negro workers are acquiring a new grasp of their relationship to industry through the efforts of the more progressive unions. The present battle for civil rights, which has a special meaning for southern Negroes, is giving his own battle for equality a new orientation. Moreover, southern Negroes are becoming aware of the struggle of the colored colonial peoples for self-determination and the leaders, at least, are to some extent identifying their own struggle with the larger one.

This new awareness of the social and economic forces in American life as well as in the world at large is the mark of the New Negro in the South. And the attitude of the New Negro is perhaps best expressed in the response of a Negro farmer in South Carolina who had been subjected to economic pressure: "We don't scare any more."

Nation, July 7, 1956, vol. 183, pp. 7–8. This was part of a special issue of the *Nation* entitled "Time To Kill Jim Crow."

51

A SOUTHERN NEGRO'S VIEW OF THE SOUTH (1956)

by Charles S. Johnson

The president of Fisk University was able to reach a wide readership by the latter part of 1956. This essay includes the statement issued by almost one hundred African-American educators in October 1954; a statement quite unreported then by newspapers like the *New York Times*.

It is not merely by accident or inadvertence that the viewpoint of the Negro Southerner is consistently omitted from characterizations of the "Southern point of view and way of life." It is a part of the Southern way of life to disregard it. Some writers, in order to provide a touch of realism for persons outside the South, explain that "the better-thinking elements of both races" prefer to leave things as they are, or "it is only the outsider and agitator who want to stir up things and change the social pattern of the South." But these are not Negroes themselves speaking.

A few years ago a university press editor in one of the Upper South states projected a volume that would represent the range of Negro thought on race relations, from conservative to liberal to radical opinion. The title was "What the Negro Wants." In the final result, all of the Negro writers seemed to think and want substantially the same things; the differences appeared only in the literary styles of the authors. This irritating unanimity provoked the editor to one of the most extraordinary introductions in publishing history. He censured the writers for thinking and wanting the wrong things, and advised them what they should be wanting!

The common desires of Southern Negroes reflect a viewpoint about which several generalizations can be made.

(1) The Southern Negro viewpoint is more broadly national than regional. There are very few, if any, Southern Negroes who do not want full American citizenship, even though there are undoubtedly those who, if they had it, would make no better use of it than some of their white counterparts. In philosophy, the Southern Negro identification is with the nation and not with the Southern region, which is, in spirit, separatist.

(2) The present-day Southern Negro does not share the belief of the Southern white that he is inferior as a human being, even though he may earn lower wages and have fewer years of schooling. Sixty or seventy years ago there were many who *acted* as if they believed themselves inferior, although they no longer actually believed it. What is for white Southerners most difficult to understand, in these days, is the absence of both the belief in inferiority and the simulation of this belief. More than this, there has been a measurable loss of Negro respect for the white pretenders to a superiority that can only be sustained by legal statutes and illegal violence, or the threat of it.

The apparent change in the attitude of the Southern Negro reflects the difference between the political and social structure in the South itself as of today and sixty years ago. The genteel tradition of the South has been extinguished with the displacement of the Southern gentleman and planter aristocrat in business and politics by the culturally undisciplined new generations coming into power. The genteel tradition needed no segregation laws to confirm cultural superiority and position in society.

(3) It is variously expected that Negro Southerners, as a result of their limited status in the racial system, would be bitter or hostile or patient or indifferent. They are typically none of these. If a generalized attitude can be defined, it would be something closer to forbearance. Bitterness grows out of hopelessness, and there is no sense of hopelessness in this situation however uncomfortable and menacing and humiliating it may be at times. Faith in the ultimate strength of the

democratic philosophy and code of the nation as a whole has always been stronger than the impulse to despair.

(4) The Southern Negro does not seriously expect very much change in his civil rights status through "grass roots" conversion. There has indeed been improvement in education, health, housing and welfare at this level, as an aspect of general improvement in community facilities. But in employment and wages, voting, personal security, access to cultural facilities and other requisites of democratic living, there has been very little change except that brought about by a stronger and higher authority.

It was the Federal Government that wiped out the racial differentials in Southern wages, and the Federal courts that equalized white and Negro teachers' salaries and opened the ballot box. It was the impact of national and world criticism that curbed mob violence in the South, and gave the stigma of crime to such brutal indulgences as the Emmett Till case in Mississippi; it was not the local courts or the neighbors. Few Southern whites of liberal or humane views regarding Negro civil rights want personal responsibility among their less liberal friends for advocating such. It is simpler if the mandate comes from some unchallengeable and objective authority that is stronger than the community itself.

That is why so many dark fingers are crossed in the United States today, as the compassionate high court patiently awaits local compliance with its school desegregation decrees. For all the recent, and welcome, advances in border regions, the deep South is still erupting with white citizens' councils, and the Southern state Legislatures, which are dominated by the medieval pillars of the rural "grass-roots" areas, are passing defiant and, in some instances, brazenly insulting legislation in the name of the Southern way of life.

Just what do these Southerners stand for? The stereotypes and arguments in defense of what is called the Southern way of life are put forth by Southerners of presumed high responsibility, who are, in fact, the greatest present danger to American democracy. The reasons they give for insisting on racial segregation are defined as sociological and cultural, rather than moral or ethical or even humane. No Southern white opinion, respectable or otherwise, has, in the past half century, seriously ventured a moral or ethical or humane justification of the Southern way of life.

It is true that there have been some fundamentalist attempts to torture the Holy Scriptures into a blessed condonement of inequality and inhumanity. Biblical scholars are considerably bewildered and embarrassed about the religious convictions of these mentalities.

There have been, too, attempts to "prove" that Negro students in the available Southern schools measure lower in educational achievement than white students. But Negro youth in Ohio, where there are better schools available, measured higher in the comprehensive intelligence tests for army recruits than the white youth of every state in the South except Florida, where there has been much migration from the North. With a historical one-third of the educational facilities, Negro youths have managed to do at least two-thirds as well as Southern white students on their own ground. It is a tortuous logic that would use the tragic results of inequality to establish the need of continuing it.

Equally illogical is the economic character of the Southern way of life.

The United States has lately experienced tremendous social and economic changes. There has been a shift in our economic perspective not yet fully recognized. The vast productive potential has made necessary the development of new areas of consumption and these are no longer to be found in sufficient quantity abroad. The most obvious and immediate outlet for an expanding economy is the increased purchasing power of the underdeveloped markets at home. This is impossible in a social economy, like that of the South, that artificially limits earning power through a restrictive racial system.

We cannot escape the fact that the Negro minority market alone, even when held down by unequal opportunity and limited education to one-half its potential, is equal to the total wealth of Canada or to our total foreign exports.

The Southern region, despite the inevitable currents of industrialization, continues to cling to the older patterns of its inadequate agrarian economy. Mr. Hodding Carter of Mississippi is responsible for the statement that 65 per cent of the white college graduates have to leave the region to find adequate careers.

Closely related to this plantation economy and "way of life" is the illusory role and historical philosophy of "states' rights." This is the basis of attacks upon the Supreme Court and the reckless array of state legislation confirming the ancient policies of racial inequality.

Mr. William Faulkner, the Mississippi Nobel laureate, in a second thought on this whole issue, said: "We sold our states' rights back to the Federal Government when we accepted the first cotton price support subsidy twenty years ago. Our economy is not agricultural any longer. Our economy is the Federal Government. We no longer farm in Mississippi cotton fields. We farm now in Washington corridors and Congressional committee rooms." Thus, if there has been broadening of Federal powers, it has been made necessary by the demands of the Southern states themselves.

Finally, what of the political character of the Southern way? Most of the Legislatures are dominated by rural representatives who lack the cultural sophistication of an increasingly urban and industrial age. As a result the region is anti-labor, anti-capital, anti-race, anti-liberal, anti-civil rights, anti-education, anti-intellectual, anti-technology, anti-Federal Government; it is provincial and isolationist to the core.

Political leadership has to adjust to this level of operation, and does so whenever it prizes political success above national welfare or the dominant current of human rights sweeping over the world. At the present, the preoccupation of the Southern Legislature is not with improving the health, welfare and economy of the region but with defeating "civil rights" as a national policy.

It is the tragic truth today that in the face of the world's turning away from the crass inhumanities of racial snobbery and imperial domination, we have a substantial part of an entire region asserting defiance of freedom and the laws that support it. It is a tragic pity that while the rest of the world is given new attention and respect to basic human rights, every device from subversion of law to violence is being employed to defeat the Constitution, and with such frantic desperation that no voice of stern national statesmanship dares defy, without apology and compromise, this organized retreat from freedom to tyranny and feudalism.

There has been no bold and forthright national statesmanship that would dare look at the nation as a whole and its intractable parts, and face a common destiny in the new kind of world we have today.

Even in the North, it is not yet fully recognized that the real issue is not how much education Negroes and other minorities can get in a segregated system, but how to improve the education of all American youth; not how racial minorities can be gradually and cautiously insinuated into industry and labor organizations, but how to increase and improve the total manpower potential of the nation for maintaining our productive capacity.

The issue is not how unsanitary some enforced racial slums and ghettos may have become, but how to improve the health and welfare of the nation without regard to race or sex or national origin; not how much a person thinks his property loses in value if a Negro moves into his neighborhood, but how to achieve a free market for living space for the people of the nation.

Basically, this is a struggle today not between North and South, or whites and Negroes, or between the national and international points of view. It is a struggle between those who believe in democracy and those who do not.

Of all the voices raised in this crisis, the one most ignored has been that of the southern Negro.

In October, 1954, a group of nearly 100 Negro educators and civic leaders met in Hot Springs, Ark., and drafted a statement of invitation to sober and intelligent cooperation in working out this admittedly difficult problem. Although it was issued to the national press through its central services in the Southern region, it has been one of the most ignored public invitations on record.

Since it still lies buried in limbo, it is perhaps worth quoting from it:

Good statesmanship in a democracy requires that all segments of the population participate in the implementation of the court's decision, which is of common concern. The idea is still too prevalent that the issues involved can be resolved without Negro participation. Some public officials speak as if only white Americans are involved. We are all, Negro and white, deeply and equally involved. Many Negroes can contribute sound, intelligent and statesmanlike techniques for the handling of the inevitable issues....

The court's decision makes possible a single school system with the opportunity for the people in the region to marshal their educational resources and to develop a philosophy that brings to education generally a new perspective and to the nation a new spirit. This cannot be done in a dual system of education. Let it be clearly understood that we are not pleading for Negroes alone. We are concerned about the best education that can be made available to every child in the South....

Ours is a common democracy in which the weakest and the strongest, the most privileged and the most disadvantaged, the descendants of every race and every nation, can share and happily boast that we are proud to be American. Children educated from the beginning in such a system will insure for us all a future of which we can be as proud as of the abolition of slavery and child labor, woman suffrage, equal educational opportunities for women, and the institution of the public schools themselves.

Time will prove that our fears have no foundation in fact just as has been proved by the implementation of previous court decisions. Segregation breeds fear; and when the barriers of segregation are at last removed from American life, we will wonder why we feared at all....We as Negro citizens stand ready to cooperate whole-heartedly in the progressive fulfillment of these democratic objectives.

None of this cooperation has been seriously sought or accepted. The course of events has left no alternative to Negroes but the courts. This is an unnecessary waste of ability and social statesmanship, and repudiation of a gracious and tempered gesture of goodwill aimed at helping the whole nation surmount a common problem.

The really critical problem of the present, we believe, is the confusion of the moral imperatives of this issue with the tired policy of moderation, our current middle-of-the-road philosophy. Whatever the personal sentiment, there can be no middle-of-the-road attitude toward morality or legality, if the fabric of our society is to remain inviolate. Where there is repudiation of the integrity of the Court, our ultimate constitutional authority, on one issue, there is repudiation of the integrity of the Court and the law on any or all issues. No one expects laws to reform the hearts of people, and this is not their purpose. They can, however, and do, according to the venerable Judge Learned Hand, control the disorderly, even at times at the risk of making them angry.

The issue today is human equality and national civil rights, and the touchstone is the racial segregation that prevents this human equality. Whatever our internal national differences on domestic issues, we are a total nation to the rest of the world, and no allowances can safely be made for regional defections from our basic American philosophy and practice. At stake is our survival in a world in which we are losing our allies by millions, the allies we need for military aid and support, friendship, trade and the essential raw materials for our industrial growth.

The essence of our system of government and life is voluntary cooperation in a democratic process that respects the dignity and rights of individuals. Our faith in the power of the human spirit to achieve the ends of a free society has given hope to millions of mankind over the world. We cannot default on this promise. This is our moral challenge in a national crisis.

N.Y. Times Magazine, September 23, 1956.

52

WHOSE ORDEAL? (1956)

by L. D. Reddick

Robert Penn Warren was a teacher at Vanderbilt while I was a student at Fisk. These two moderately famous universities of Nashville, Tennessee had few contacts with each other. There may have been two or three furtive friendships and an occasional individual visit or group tour, but there was no general fraternizing, no intellectual communion. Fisk had Negro students and a mixed—Negro and white—faculty; Vanderbilt had white students and a white faculty. And though I was the head of the student council and the Wranglers Club, I did not know a single fellow undergraduate at Vanderbilt.

In this light, it is understandable that we at Fisk never saw or talked with Professor Warren. We heard about him though and those others— mostly his colleagues—who banded themselves together as the "Fugitives" and published their views in a book, *I'll Take My Stand.* We felt that this collection of essays by these white Southern intellectuals was a plea for mythical ante-bellum days and a rejection of the modern world of urbanism and equalitarianism. Robert Penn Warren himself wrote the chapter on education. He argued politely that his aristocracy should study the liberal arts and that his Negroes—and perhaps poor whites—should be trained vocationally, mostly in agriculture. This was best, he concluded, for

> in the past the Southern Negro has always been a creature of the small town and farm. That is where he still chiefly belongs, by temperament and capacity; there he has less the character of a "problem" and more the status of a human being who is likely to find in agricultural and domestic pursuits the happiness that his good nature and easy ways incline him to as an ordinary function of his being.

These words were written more than 25 years ago and Mr. Warren has moved on to a notable literary career and Yale. Still, I keep hearing loud echoes from Nashville in his latest book, *Segregation: The Inner Conflict in the South.*

This is a slight volume, just 66 pages: an enlargement of an essay that appeared in *Life* magazine. Its importance is more symbolic than substantive. This is the account of Mr. Warren's return visit to the South and the passing conversations he had with Southerners on race relations. It has the intimate touch and some of the interviewees are individually drawn.

But the picture that emerges is the old familiar one that may be noticed any day in cruder colors in the extremist press of the Deep South: The mistakes of the North are emphasized; the weaknesses of the Negro underscored; and above all, there is the determination of Southern white folk, they say, that "nobody's a gonna *make* us. If we let the nigger in... we'll do so when we're good and ready!" Mr. Warren, I think, puts it explicitly, at the end of his book, in an interview that he has with himself:

Q. Are you for desegregation?

A. Yes.

Q. When will it come?

A. Not soon.

Q. When?

A. When enough people in a particular place, a particular county or state, cannot live with themselves any more. Or realize they don't have to.

This is the way it goes: Countless editors, scholars and men of letters, in and out of the South, who personally might shrink from killing an insect, give their sanction to the intransigence of the racists. Is it too much to say that there is a connection between the essays, editorials and novels of the literary neo-Confederates and the howling mob that blocks the path of little Negro children on the way to school integration?

As I see it, the main story—the fresh story—that is coming out of the South today is of the Southern Negro. What mountains of courage it must take for Negro children to walk past a cluster of hostile white adults, through a corridor of National Guardsmen, into classrooms filled with white teachers and students! And the Negro parents. No matter how they look or how they talk, theirs are *deeds* of valor. (Have we all gone so far that the heroic image is blurred out, if it is not clothed in a white skin?)

Or imagine the pressures that the bus boycotters of Montgomery and Tallahassee are enduring. At times it seems that the whole weight of the local law-making and law-enforcing structure has been brought down upon people who made a simple decision: They chose not to continue to buy a service that was not acceptable to them.

What must be the thoughts and feelings of Southern Negroes as they see the legislatures and courts stripping them of the legal aid and counsel of the NAACP? Or when they read the front page of the morning paper, playing up conflict and the activities of white citizen's councils, and the editorial page, immobilizing the North and hurling threats at Negroes and the Supreme Court? Well might the Negroes of the South cry out in anguish with the idiot of *Boris Godunov,* *"Oi, oi oi."*

There is pain, of course, deep and immeasurable but that is not the sound that we are hearing today from the Southern Negro. Rather, the mood is one of resolution; almost exhilaration, the temper of a man who has moved beyond complaint and self-pity, who has given up attempting to appease his oppressors, who at last has moved into positive action himself and will struggle—alone if necessary—until he is victorious or completely crushed. He will not permit his sentiments to be dissembled by provocation or hate. But come what may, the Southern Negro, I believe, has accepted his ordeal and has committed himself to endure it. For him, the inner conflict has eased.

New Republic, September 24, 1956. Dr. Reddick, a close associate of the Reverend Martin Luther King, Jr., was head of the history department at Alabama State College in Montgomery throughout the events of 1955–56.

53

ARE NEGROES EDUCABLE? (1956)

by Martin D. Jenkins

As part of the reactionary offensive commonly called McCarthyism and as a component of the resistance to the liberation efforts of the African-American population, a resurgence of racist propaganda appeared. Important in this was the powerful weekly *U.S. News and World Report.* Typical was its publication in September 1956 of an essay by one Frank C. J. McGurk entitled "A Scientist's Report on Race Differences" that reiterated the canard of the inferior "intelligence" of African-derived peoples and insisted that "improvement of Negroes' social and economic status does not reduce this deficiency." The president of Morgan State College in Maryland replied to this slander in the *Baltimore Sun* (September 29, 1956) after that paper had indicated agreement with McGurk.

I wish to comment on your editorial "Standards of Schooling" (September 19) with particular reference to (1) your uncritical acceptance of the conclusion of Associate Professor McGurk that an improved environment does not appear to affect intelligence-test performance, and (2) your lightly veiled conclusion that desegregation constitutes "a threat to standards in public education."

1. I believe *The Sun* to be in serious error in its ready and uncritical acceptance of Dr McGurk's conclusions. Certainly, one of the prime responsibilities of the journalist is to check the source of this data!

U.S. News & World Report, in which his article appears, is well known as a prosegregation magazine. It presents here a purported "scientist's" report on race differences which supports its prosegregation line. Yet, this "scientist" is not an authority in his field but rather a little-known psychologist of low academic rank whose published scientific work consists of one brief article in a psychological journal.

It is impossible in the space available here to present a critical review of Dr. McGurk's article. He makes the common error of placing undue confidence in the equating of the socio-economic status of the white and Negro subjects of the studies he reviews.

If one were charitable, one would attribute this to naiveté. But it is all too clear that Dr. McGurk has set out to prove a thesis. He disregards entirely the many studies which show the positive effect of an improved environment on test performance. His conclusions and sweeping generalizations would be accepted by few if any psychologists of repute. Yet the temper of the times is such that *The Sun* readily embraces them.

You state, "But Dr. McGurk disposes of that, too. Environmental conditions for the Negro population have improved tremendously, as we all know, during the last one third of a century. But this improvement is not reflected at all in the most recent studies...."

Now really, *The Sun* ought to know better. If this were true, it would mean that there are inherent biological racial differences in capacity for attainment. You are reviving here an outmoded interpretation which was rejected early in the nature-nurture controversy.

This brief quotation from your editorial includes both a questionable assumption and an error in fact. Although there has been gratifying absolute progress, actually the environmental conditions of the masses of the Negro people have not improved *tremendously* in the last third of a century. There is a real question as to whether, *relative to the general population*, they have improved more than slightly. The *average* Negro child still attends the poorest schools in his community; he is still confined to the poorest neighborhoods with the poorest cultural resources; he still may not aspire, except in a limited way, to the best and most respected jobs; he is still in the lowest economic class—in Baltimore, the income of the average Negro worker is only 52 percent of that of the average white worker; he still experiences that lack of expectation which should be the heritage of every American boy and girl; and he still lives his life encysted in a caste culture and isolated from the main current of American life.

It is axiomatic that an improvement in environment results in an improvement in test performance because all psychological measurement is based on the experience of the children tested.

On the basis of test performance (all of these are averages), whites are superior to Negroes, urban children to rural, native whites to immigrants, children of high socio-economic status to those of lower. Southern Negro children who migrate to northern communities show an increase in I.Q. and achievement as do rural children from impoverished communities who move to cities. Southern whites make lower scores than northern whites and the differential increases as the difference between the cultural level of the respective communities increases. Particularly significant is the fact that in World War I the average intelligence-test score of Negro recruits from a number of northern states was higher than that of white recruits from several southern states; and that in World War II the rejection rate of registrants due to failure to meet minimum "intelligence" standards was higher for whites in Georgia, Virginia, Alabama, South Carolina, Arkansas, Texas and North Carolina than for Negroes in New York, Illinois, Massachusetts, Michigan, Indiana and Ohio. All of these differences are clearly due to environment; to attribute them to inherent factors based on race or geographic selection would be manifestly absurd.

2. Apparently, the principal point of your editorial is that racial desegregation may constitute a "threat to standards in public education." No doubt you are entirely unaware of the subtle arrogance reflected in the way you have posed the question. Obviously, Negro children are already a part of public education. In this respect nothing is being changed by desegregation—exactly the same children are involved. So, overall, standards cannot be affected by interchanging children in the schools.

What you really seem to mean is that there may be a threat to standards in what formerly were white schools. There are a number of "threats" to standards: on any test, half of the school population falls in the lower half of the distribution—these lower-scoring children constitute a threat; the many white children who come to Baltimore from southern and rural areas constitute a threat; the bulk of the children of low socio-economic status constitute a threat. No one would suggest the setting apart of these children in order to maintain standards.

Now there is no question whatever that the *average* achievement level of Negro children is lower than that of white children in any given grade. In view of some of the things I have mentioned above, we could hardly expect otherwise. It is important to recognize, however, that these children do not constitute a discrete group. They fall within the range of the white school population and present educationally at least the same problem presented by any below-grade pupils. It is significant, too, that many Negro children are above average and that some are at the very highest level in test performance. My own studies have shown that there are Negro children who are among the brightest children in America.

The problem then is first of all an educational one. For administrators and teachers in our schools, it means treating every child on his or her merits; it means smaller classes and appropriate guidance procedures; it means the implementation of developmental and remedial procedures in terms of the needs of individual children; it may mean that under-privileged children generally will be retarded. But it does not necessarily mean a lowering of standards.

For the public it means what it should have meant all along—willingness to furnish the funds to provide an adequate education for all of our children.

But there is something more basic. What we have to do in this community and others is to provide Negro children exactly the same opportunities for development that other American children have. When we do this, we will have no problem. It is just that simple. Until we do this, we cannot expect these children and adults to measure up fully to American standards. This is what our national leadership and particularly the Supreme Court so clearly see. This is why we are having now this battle for full citizenship rights. This is why *The Sun* should be less disturbed about a threat to standards in public education and more disturbed about the racial bars to opportunity which exist in our community.

Reprinted in the *Crisis*, November 1956, pp. 535–37.

54

WHITE MAN, LISTEN! (1957)

by Richard Wright

Three years before Wright passed away in Paris, at the age of fifty-two, he published an impassioned volume whose title indicates his motivation—to make the oppressor understand that those who had been oppressed for centuries had always resisted and were now on the brink of a new crescendo of protest. Two selections follow:

In the Gold Coast the Britishers were always alarmed when the Africans went off by themselves to hold their political rallies and were constantly asking: "What did they say? What are they planning? Don't they want partnership?"

At Bandung the proud Australians were in the embarrassing position of chiding Indonesians and Indians and Africans for having excluded them from the greatest international conference that ever took place in Asia in modern times.

I've been informed by reliable international experts that in New Delhi the white ambassadors of European nations fret and fume because they do not have easy access to a tan-skinned Nehru who spent a third of his adult life in prison under white jailers.

Because I've pointed out these tendencies to recoil and self-possession on the part of Asians and Africans, some critics have sought to brand me a racist. This is a primitive reaction and is akin to accusing a messenger who brings you bad news of having created the bad news he brings.

This Asian-African recoil and withdrawal have many determinations, the most distinctive and powerful of which is to reorganize their lives in accordance with their own basic feelings. The truncated religious structure comes again to the fore and reasserts itself, much to the astonishment of Europeans. The conference of black artists and writers recently concluded in Paris by *Présence Africaine* is a vivid example of this stocktaking on the part of the elite of the black world. It is a recoil and withdrawal prompted by psychological necessity, but it is far from being a negative gesture. It is a regrouping of psychological forces for constructive action—psychological forces that have been scattered and paralyzed for centuries.

Perhaps the most graphic and lyrical of these men was W. E. B. DuBois; indeed, one might say that it was with him that the Negro complaint reached almost religious heights of expression. DuBois prays to God in public:

> *Listen to us, Thy children: our faces dark with doubt*
> *are made a mockery in Thy sanctuary. With uplifted hands*
> *we front Thy heaven, O God, crying:*
> *We beseech Thee to hear us, good Lord!*

And then, vehemently, in Old Testament style:

> *Doth not this justice of hell stink in Thy nostrils, O God?*
> *How long shall the mounting flood of innocent blood roar*
> *in Thine ears and pound in our hearts for vengeance? Pile*
> *the pale frenzy of blood-crazed brutes who do such deeds*
> *high on Thine altar, Jehovah, and burn it in hell forever*
> *and forever.*
> *Forgive us, good Lord! we know not what we say!*

Moods such as these have suffused the many books of DuBois, and where the mood is absent *per se,* we find it projected in terms of history, fiction, verse. Here we see the outright curse of the Negro migrant lifted to a hymn of bitterness; here we see the long, drawn-out moan of the blues turned into a phrase of lament; here we see the brutal cynicism of illiterate Negroes converted into irony; here we watch the jerky lines of *The Dirty Dozens* transmit themselves into the surging rhythms of free verse; here indeed we see Pushkin and Dumas turned into raging, livid demons! Poor Phyllis Wheatley would have burned to a cinder if such searing emotions had ever entered her frail body.

Following DuBois, James Weldon Johnson lifted his voice; listen to Johnson, as conservative a Negro as ever lived in America; but his eyes were riveted upon this:

> *Quick! Chain him to that oak! It will resist*
> *The fire much longer than this slender pine.*
> *Now bring the fuel! Pile it 'round him! Wait!*
> *Pile not so fast or high, or we shall lose*

The agony and terror in his face.
And now the torch! Good fuel that! The flames
Already leap head-high. Ha! hear that shriek!
And there's another! wilder than the first.
Fetch water! Water! Pour a little on
The fire lest it should burn too fast. Hold so!
Now let it slowly blaze again. See there!
He squirms! He groans! His eyes bulge wildly out,
Searching around in vain appeal for help!

Was it otherwise with other writers? No. You've seen the images of horror that a conservative like James Weldon Johnson evoked. Yet, I, coming from an entirely different social stratum, wove the same vision of horror into another pattern in a poem called "Between the World and Me":

And one morning while in the woods I suddenly stumbled
upon the thing,
Stumbled upon it in a grassy clearing guarded by scaly oaks
and elms.
And the sooty details of the scene rose, thrusting themselves
between the world and me...

There was a design of white bones slumbering forgottenly
upon a cushion of gray ashes.
There was a charred stump of a sapling pointing a blunt
finger accusingly at the sky.
There were torn tree limbs, tiny veins of burnt leaves, and
a scorched coil of greasy hemp;
A vacant shoe, an empty tie, a ripped shirt, a lonely hat,
and a pair of trousers stiff with black blood.
And upon the trampled grass were buttons, dead matches,
butt-ends of cigars and cigarettes, peanut shells, a
drained gin-flask, and a whore's lipstick;
Scattered traces of tar, restless arrays of feathers, and the
lingering smell of gasoline.
And through the morning air the sun poured yellow surprise
into the eye sockets of a stony skull...

And while I stood there my mind was frozen with a cold
pity for the life that was gone.

The ground gripped my feet and my heart was circled with
icy walls of fear—
The sun died in the sky; a night wind muttered in the grass
and fumbled with leaves in the trees; the woods poured
forth the hungry yelping of hounds; the darkness
screamed with thirsty voices; and the witnesses rose
and lived:
The dry bones stirred, rattled, lifted, melting themselves
into my bones.
The gray ashes formed flesh firm and black, entering into
my flesh.
The gin-flask passed from mouth to mouth; cigars and
cigarettes glowed, the whore smeared the lipstick red
upon her lips.
And a thousand faces swirled around me, clamoring that
my life be burned...

And then they had me, stripped me, battering my teeth
into my throat till I swallowed my own blood.
My voice was drowned in the roar of their voices and my black wet body slipped
and rolled in their hands as they bound me to the sapling.
And my skin clung to the bubbling hot tar, falling from me
in patches,
And the down and the quills of the white feathers sank
into my raw flesh, and I moaned in my agony.
Then my blood was cooled mercifully, cooled by a baptism
of gasoline.
And in a blaze of red I leaped to the sky as pain rose like
water, boiling my limbs

Panting, begging, I clutched childlike, clutched to the hot
sides of death.
Now I am dry bones and my face a stony skull staring in yellow surprise at the
sun...

Did ever in history a race of men have for so long a time the same horror before their eyes? I know that for short periods horrors like this have come to men, but they ended at last; I know that in war horror fills the minds of all, but even wars pass. The horrors that confront Negroes stay in peace and war, in winter and summer, night and day.

Richard Wright, *White Man, Listen!* (Garden City, N.Y.: Doubleday, 1957) pp. 68–69; 134–38.

55

PROGRAM OF THE SOUTHERN CHRISTIAN LEADERSHIP CONFERENCE (1957)

The monumental success of the Montgomery bus boycott movement helped induce mass civil rights struggles elsewhere, as in Mobile and Birmingham, Alabama, with the Reverend Joseph E. Lowery and the Reverend Fred L. Shuttlesworth, respectively, in the leadership and with the Reverend Charles K. Steele in Tallahassee, where a bus boycott also succeeded, and in Atlanta and Savannah—the latter led by the Reverend William Holmes Borden. It stimulated the voter drives throughout the South, such as that in Alabama led by Charles G. Gomillion.

To keep this momentum going, King, Steele, and Shuttlesworth issued a call for militant black clergymen to meet in Atlanta in January 1957. Sixty African-Americans, mostly clergymen, did meet and prepared the ground for a larger meeting of about one hundred clergymen in New Orleans in February. Here appeared the Southern Christian Leadership Conference (SCLC), with King as president and the Reverend Ralph Abernathy as treasurer.

Their public announcement in a leaflet called *This is SCLC* appeared later that year and was often reprinted somewhat revised. Here it is:

Aims and Purposes of SCLC

The Southern Christian Leadership Conference has the basic aim of achieving full citizenship rights, equality, and the integration of the Negro in all aspects of American life. SCLC is a service agency to facilitate coordinated action of local community groups within the frame of their indigenous organizations and natural leadership. SCLC activity revolves around two main focal points: the use of nonviolent philosophy as a means of creative protest; and securing the right of the ballot for every citizen.

Philosophy of SCLC

The basic tenets of Hebraic-Christian tradition, coupled with the Gandhian concept of *stayagraha*—truth force—is at the heart of SCLC's philosophy. Christian nonviolence actively resists evil in any form. It never seeks to humiliate the opponent, only to win him. Suffering is accepted without retaliation. Internal violence of the spirit is as much to be rejected as external physical violence. At the center of nonviolence is redemptive love. Creatively used, the philosophy of nonviolence can restore the broken community in America. SCLC is convinced that nonviolence is the most potent force available to an oppressed people in their struggle for freedom and dignity.

SCLC and Nonviolent Mass Direct Action

SCLC believes that the American dilemma in race relations can best and most quickly be resolved through the action of thousands of people, committed to the philosophy of nonviolence, who will physically identify themselves in a just and moral struggle. It is not enough to be intellectually dissatisfied with an evil system. The true nonviolent register presents his physical body as an instrument to defeat the system. Through nonviolent mass direct action, the evil system is creatively dramatized in order that the conscience of the community may grapple with the rightness or wrongness of the issue at hand....

SCLC and Voter-Registration

The right of the ballot is basic to the exercise of full citizenship rights. All across the South, subtle and flagrant obstacles confront the Negro when he seeks to register and vote. Poll taxes, long form questionnaires, harassment, economic reprisal, and sometimes death, meet those who dare to seek this exercise of the ballot. In areas where there is little or no attempt to block the voting attempts of the Negro, apathy generally is deeply etched upon the habits of the community. SCLC, with its specialized staff, works on both fronts: aiding local communities through every means available to secure the right to vote (e.g. filing complaints with the Civil Rights Commission) and arousing interest through voter-registration workshops to point up the importance of the ballot. Periodically, SCLC, upon invitation, conducts a voter-registration drive to enhance a community's opportunity to free itself from economic and political servitude. SCLC believes that the most important step the Negro can take is that short walk to the voting booth.

SCLC and Civil Disobedience

SCLC sees civil disobedience as a natural consequence of nonviolence when the register is confronted by unjust and immoral laws. This does not imply that SCLC advocates either anarchy or lawlessness. The Conference firmly believes that all people have a moral responsibility to obey laws that are just. It recognizes, however, that there also are unjust laws. From a purely moral point of view, an unjust law is one that is out of harmony with the moral law of the universe, or as the religionist would say, out of harmony with the Law of God. More concretely, an unjust law is one in which the minority is compelled to observe a code which is not binding on the majority. An unjust law is one in which people are required to obey a code that they had no part in making because they were denied the right to vote. In the face of such obvious inequality, where difference is made legal, the nonviolent resister has no alternative but to disobey the unjust law. In disobeying such a law, he does so peacefully, openly and nonviolently. Most important, he *willingly* accepts the penalty for breaking the law. This distinguishes SCLC's position on civil disobedience from the "uncivil disobedience" of the racist opposition in the South. In the face of laws they consider unjust, they seek to defy, evade, and circumvent the law. BUT they are *unwilling* to accept the penalty for breaking the law. The end result of their defiance is anarchy and disrespect for the law. SCLC, on the other hand believes that civil disobedience involves the highest respect for the law. He who openly disobeys a law that conscience tells him is unjust and willingly accepts the penalty is giving evidence that he so respects the law that he belongs in jail until it is changed.....

SCLC and Segregation

SCLC is firmly opposed to segregation in any form that it takes and pledges itself to work unrelentingly to rid every vestige of its scars from our nation through nonviolent means. Segregation is an evil and its presence in our nation has blighted our larger destiny as a leader in world affairs. Segregation does as much harm to the *segregator* as it does to the *segregated*. The *segregated* develops a false sense of inferiority and the *segregator* develops a false sense of superiority, both contrary to the American ideal of democracy. America must rid herself of segregation not alone because it is politically expedient, but because it is morally right!

SCLC and Constructive Program

SCLC's basic program fosters nonviolent resistance to all forms of racial injustice, including state and local laws and practices, even when this means going to jail; and imaginative, bold constructive action to end the demoralization caused by the legacy of slavery and segregation— inferior schools, slums, and second-class citizenship. Thus, the Conference works on two fronts. On the one hand it resists continuously the system of segregation which is the basic cause of flagging standards; on the other hand, it works constructively to improve the standards themselves. There MUST be a balance between attacking the causes and healing the effects of segregation.

SCLC and the Beloved Community

The ultimate aim of SCLC is to foster and create the "beloved community" in America where brotherhood is a reality. It rejects any doctrine of black supremacy for this merely substitutes one kind of tyranny for another. The Conference does not foster moving the Negro from a position of disadvantage to one of advantage for this would thereby subvert justice. SCLC works for integration. Our ultimate goal is genuine intergroup and interpersonal living—*integration*. Only through nonviolence can reconciliation and the creation of the beloved community be effected. The international focus on America and her internal problems against the dread prospect of a hot war, demand our seeking this end.

56

NONVIOLENCE AND RACIAL JUSTICE (1957)

by Martin Luther King, Jr.

The leading spokesperson of the upheaval that rocked the United States beginning in the late 1950s here explains the philosophy that motivated him:

It is commonly observed that the crisis in race relations dominates the arena of American life. This crisis has been precipitated by two factors: the determined resistance of reactionary elements in the south to the Supreme Court's momentous decision outlawing segregation in the public schools, and the radical change in the Negro's evaluation of himself. While southern legislative halls ring with open defiance through "interposition" and "nullification," while a modern version of the Ku Klux Klan has arisen in the form of "respectable" white citizens' councils, a revolutionary change has taken place in the Negro's conception of his own nature and destiny. Once he thought of himself as an inferior and patiently accepted injustice and exploitation. Those days are gone.

This new self-respect and sense of dignity on the part of the Negro undermined the south's negative peace, since the white man refused to accept the change. The tension we are witnessing in race relations today can be explained in part by this revolutionary change in the Negro's evaluation of himself and his determination to struggle and sacrifice until the walls of segregation have been finally crushed by the battering rams of justice.

The determination of Negro Americans to win freedom from every form of oppression springs from the same profound longing for freedom that motivates oppressed peoples all over the world. The rhythmic beat of deep discontent in Africa and Asia is at the bottom a quest for freedom and human dignity on the part of people who have long been victims of colonialism. The struggle for freedom on the part of oppressed people in general and of the American Negro in particular has developed slowly and is not going to end suddenly. Privileged groups rarely give up their privileges without strong resistance. But when oppressed people rise up against oppression there is no stopping point short of full freedom. Realism compels us to admit that the struggle will continue until freedom is a reality for all the oppressed peoples of the world.

Hence the basic question which confronts the world's oppressed is: How is the struggle against the forces of injustice to be waged? There are two possible answers. One is resort to the all too prevalent method of physical violence and corroding hatred. The danger of this method is its futility. Violence solves no social problems; it merely creates new and more complicated ones. Through the vistas of time a voice still cries to every potential Peter, "Put up your sword!" The shores of history are white with the bleached bones of nations and communities that failed to follow this command. If the American Negro and other victims of oppression succumb to the temptation of using violence in the struggle for justice, unborn generations will live in a desolate night of bitterness, and their chief legacy will be an endless reign of chaos.

The alternative to violence is nonviolent resistance. This method was made famous in our generation by Mohandas K. Gandhi, who used it to free India from the domination of the British empire. Five points can be made concerning nonviolence as a method in bringing about better racial conditions.

First, this is not a method for cowards; it *does* resist. The nonviolent resister is just as strongly opposed to the evil against which he protests as is the person who uses violence. His method is passive or nonaggressive in the sense that he is not physically aggressive toward his opponent. But his mind and emotions are always active, constantly seeking to persuade the opponent that he is mistaken. This method is passive physically but strongly active spiritually; it is nonaggressive physically but dynamically aggressive spiritually.

A second point is that nonviolent resistance does not seek to defeat or humiliate the opponent, but to win his friendship and understanding. The nonviolent resister must often express his protest through noncooperation or boycotts, but he realizes that noncooperation and boycotts are not ends themselves; they are merely means to awaken a sense of moral shame in the opponent. The end is redemption and reconciliation. The aftermath of nonviolence is the creation of the beloved community, while the aftermath of violence is tragic bitterness.

A third characteristic of this method is that the attack is directed against forces of evil rather than against persons who are caught in those forces. It is evil we are seeking to defeat, not the persons victimized by evil. Those of us who struggle against racial injustice must come to see that the basic tension is not between races. As I like to say to the people in Montgomery, Alabama: "The tension in this city is not between white people and Negro people. The tension is at bottom between justice and injustice, between the forces of light and the forces of darkness. And if there is a victory it will be a victory not merely for 50,000 Negroes, but a victory for justice and the forces of light. We are out to defeat injustice and not white persons who may happen to be unjust."

A fourth point that must be brought out concerning nonviolent resistance is that it avoids not only external physical violence but also internal violence of spirit. At the center of nonviolence stands the principle of love. In struggling for human dignity the oppressed people of the world must not allow themselves to become bitter or indulge in hate campaigns. To retaliate with hate and bitterness would do nothing but intensify the hate in the world. Along the way of life, someone must have sense enough and morality enough to cut off the chain of hate. This can be done only by projecting the ethics of love to the center of our lives.

In speaking of love at this point, we are not referring to some sentimental emotion. It would be nonsense to urge men to love their oppressors in an affectionate sense. "Love" in this connection means understanding good will. There are three words for love in the Greek New Testament. First, there is *eros*. In Platonic philosophy *eros* meant the yearning of the soul for the realm of the divine. It has come now to mean a sort of aesthetic or romantic love. Second, there is *philia*. It meant intimate affectionateness between friends. *Philia* denotes a sort of reciprocal love: the person loves because he is loved. When we speak of loving those who oppose us we refer to neither *eros* nor *philia;* we speak of a love which is expressed in the Greek word *agape*. *Agape* means nothing sentimental or basically affectionate; it means understanding, redeeming good will for all men, an overflowing love which seeks nothing in return. It is the love of God working in the lives of men. When we love on the *agape* level we love men not because we like them, not because their attitudes and ways appeal to us, but because God loves them. Here we rise to the position of loving the person who does the evil deed while hating the deed he does.

Finally, the method of nonviolence is based on the conviction that the universe is on the side of justice. It is this deep faith in the future that causes the nonviolent resister to accept suffering without retaliation. He knows that in his struggle for justice he has cosmic companionship. This belief that God is on the side of truth and justice comes down to us from the long tradition of our Christian faith. There is something at the very center of our faith which reminds us that Good Friday may reign for a day, but ultimately it must give way to the triumphant beat of the Easter drums. Evil may so shape events that Caesar will occupy a palace and Christ a cross, but one day that same Christ will rise up and split history into A.D. and B.C., so that even the life of Caesar must be dated by his name. So in Montgomery we can walk and never get weary, because we know that there will be a great camp meeting in the promised land of freedom and justice.

This, in brief, is the method of nonviolent resistance. It is a method that challenges all people struggling for justice and freedom. God grant that we wage the struggle with dignity and discipline. May all who suffer oppression in this world reject the self-defeating method of retaliatory violence and choose the method that seeks to redeem. Through using this method wisely and courageously we will emerge from the bleak and desolate midnight of man's inhumanity to man into the bright daybreak of freedom and justice.

Christian Century, February 6, 1957, Vol. 74, pp. 165–67.

57

THE NEGRO VOTER IN ALABAMA (1957)

by C. G. Gomillion

One of the salient characteristics of a democratic society is "Freedom of Speech." Voting is a form of speaking. In a democracy voting is considered not only a right of every responsible citizen but an obligation as well. It is an instrument which the citizen uses in his effort to contribute to the general welfare and to protect and promote his own well-being. "The ballot is the citizen's best self-help tool. It is the potent evener in a democracy. One who is without the ballot is a political dependent. Without the ballot one is politically disarmed. Voting is the most vital of the civil rights because upon it rests all of the other basic rights."

Someone has written that "A voteless people is a hopeless people." The Negro citizens of Alabama are not entirely voteless, but their per cent of the total electorate in the State is small, only about 6 per cent of those registered to vote. This 6 per cent constitutes approximately 52,000 who are registered to vote, an increase of 26,776 since 1952. In spite of this 100 per cent increase in the number registered during a period of four years, only about 1 in every 5 Negroes 21 years of age and over is registered. Negroes constitute about 30 per cent of the voting age population. Whites constitute 70 per cent of the voting age population, but they had 94 per cent of those registered to vote in 1956. Ten out of every 15 whites of voting age were registered, but only 3 out of every 15 Negroes were so registered....

Most of the counties having the lowest percentages of the Negro voting age population registered have high percentages of Negroes in their total population, or they are in the Black Belt, or both. One student of this problem has classified the Alabama Counties into four types on the basis of (1) the difficulties involved in becoming registered and (2) the per cent of those voting. The "prohibited Counties" are Bullock, Lowndes, and Wilcox; the "difficult Counties" are sixteen in number and include Dallas, Jefferson, Macon, and Montgomery in which Negro citizens have had great difficulty registering. The "moderate Counties" are fifteen in number, and include such as Houston, Lee, Madison, and Mobile. Typical of "liberal Counties" are Calhoun, Etowah, Tuscaloosa, and Walker.

In order to vote in Alabama, one is legally required to possess certain specified qualifications. One must have been a *bona fide* resident within the State for two years, within the county for one year, and within the precinct or ward in which he desires to register for a period of three months. In addition, he must have registered at the courthouse, or at some other officially designated place in the county in which he lives. The registration process requires that the applicant fill out a questionnaire consisting of twenty-one questions which were prepared by the Justices of the Alabama Supreme Court, as provided for in the Voter Qualification Amendment to the Constitution of Alabama, ratified by the electorate on December 11, 1951. In most counties the applicant himself must fill out the questionnaire but in some counties a registrar fills out the question-naire as the applicant answers the questions read to him by the registrar. In some counties, members of the Board of Registrars require applicants to answer additional oral questions and/or read and interpret selections from the Constitution of the United States. The oral questions are those which the registrars themselves formulate or select.

After the questionnaire has been filled out, and the oral questions,if any, have been answered, the applicant swears that he has answered the questions to the best of his ability, that he will "support and defend the Constitution of the United States and the Constitution of the State of Alabama," that he has not been a member of any group which advocated nor is he a member of any group which advocates the overthrow of the government of the United States or the State of Alabama by unlawful means, that he has never been convicted of any offense which would disqualify him from registering, and that he knows of nothing that would disqualify him. Before the registrar can issue a certificate of registration to the applicant, the applicant must produce "a duly registered, qualified elector" who lives in the same county and who can and will swear that he has known the applicant for a stated period of time, that the applicant has lived at a stated place for a specified number of years or months, and that he knows of no reason why the applicant should be disqualified from registering. The person who so testifies for the applicant is usually referred to as a "voucher."

After the voucher has testified, the application is ready for review and appraisal by the registrars. If the applicant has answered all questions to the satisfaction of the Board and if the Board accepts as satisfactory the sworn testimony of the voucher, the applicant is entitled to a Certificate of Registration, signed by at least two members of the Board. In some counties, the registrars review and appraise the application of the potential voter and the testimony of the voucher before the applicant leaves the place of registration, and issues the Certificate of Registration directly to the applicant. In most counties, however, the registrars review the applications after the close of the day of registration, and send the Certificates to those whom the Board qualifies.

The payment of a poll tax, except for those exempted, is a prerequisite to voting in Alabama. If the person who receives his Certificate of Registration is between the ages of 21 and 45, and is not a veteran of the Armed Forces of the United States, he must pay a poll tax of $1.50 per year in order to be eligible to vote. If he is an honorably discharged veteran of the Armed Forces of the United States, he may take his discharge paper to the office of the Probate Judge and have it recorded. If this is done, the veteran is exempted from the payment of the poll tax. If the person who receives his Certificate of Registration is over 45 years of age, he is not required to pay the poll tax.

There are many factors which contribute to the low rate of voting among Negroes in Alabama. Some do not qualify to vote because of their limited recognition and appreciation of the significance of voting. Others who are greatly dependent upon the white community for their economic well-being are afraid to manifest an interest in, or to participate in, politics. Perhaps the most important factor contributing to the low rate of voting among Negroes is the difficulty of getting a Certificate of Registration. The questionnaire which the applicant is required to fill out contains 21 questions, some of which have several parts. Those persons who do not like to fill out questionnaires postpone applying for registration, sometimes for a very long period. Those who read and/or write slowly often prevent others from appearing before the Board. In many counties, if a Negro applicant fails to answer every question, or if he makes a single mistake, the application is not approved, the applicant is not notified, and is not given an opportunity to complete or correct his application. In some counties, the registrars do not work full days. They come to work late, and/or leave work early. Occasionally only one of the registrars reports for work, and cannot work because the law requires that at least two registrars be present when applications are accepted and/or applicants certified. The registrars themselves retard the process by holding conversations with the applicants. In some counties, the registrars do not function regularly because they lack adequate supplies or equipment, or there is no room available in which they can work.

Some Boards of Registrars have resigned rather than provide opportunities for Negroes to qualify as electors. Several times within the last fifteen years Macon County has been without a functioning Board of Registrars. The last period extended from January 16, 1956 to June 3, 1957. When the State Appointing Board delays filling these vacancies, prospective voters are denied the opportunity to register. Some Boards of Registrars require Negro applicants to secure white voters to vouch for them. In many cases this is a very difficult task for some, and impossible for others. There are known instances in which a Negro applicant has appealed to at least a dozen white voters in his effort to secure a voucher. Even in cases where the Boards of Registrars permit a Negro voter to vouch for a Negro applicant, the Board will recognize and accept only a Negro voter who is known to a Board member. Often when Negro voters are permitted to vouch for Negro applicants, they are restricted by having a limited quota assigned, such as two or four applicants per month. Some applicants have filled out as many as five questionnaires before they received their Certificate of Registration.

Some of those who are registered fail to vote regularly because of placing little value upon the act, because of not wanting to pay the poll tax, because of forgetting to pay the tax, or forgetting to go to the polls on election day. Some do not vote because they believe that one vote does not matter.

Many efforts have been made by individuals and agencies in Alabama to increase the number of Negro voters. Civic and political organizations have conducted programs of civic education in an effort to aid non-voters to discover and understand the significance of political action, and the influence of politics upon other aspects of their welfare. For the voters, instruction is given in analyzing and appraising political issues, proposed legislation, the performance of public officials, and the qualifications of candidates for public office.

In various counties Negro voters have invited public officials to meet with them and to discuss matters of concern to them. Appeals have been made to public officials—local, state, and federal—to rectify discrimination and unfairness against Negro citizens. In Macon County, citizens on several occasions have appealed to the Governor and his associates on the

Appointing Board to appoint citizens to the Board of Registrars. They have also appealed to the United States Department of Justice to investigate the practice of delaying appointments to the Board, which delay deprives interested potential electors from qualifying to vote. Appeals have also been made to the citizens of the community and of the State to urge public officials to provide a Board of Registrars within the County.

In some counties Negro voters have cooperated with whites in such interracial organizations as Labor Unions, the Southern Conference Education Fund, and the Southern Regional Council in efforts to stimulate registration and voting among citizens who appear to be politically indifferent.

There is within the State the Alabama State Coordinating Committee for Registration and Voting, the major objective of which is to provide political education and to stimulate intelligent political action among Negro voters within the State. This organization has a full-time director, who visits affiliated units in many of the counties and cities within the State. Each of the nine Congressional Districts is organized and holds district meetings once per quarter. There are usually two Statewide meetings held per year. The State office through its director attempts to coordinate the political activities of Negroes throughout the State.

Although it is not known how many of the 52,000 registered Negroes voted in the 1956 presidential election, an analysis of the voting in some places in the State suggests that the Negro voters exerted some political influence. Although the 279,982 votes cast for Stevenson exceeded those cast for Eisenhower by 85,099, the latter candidate received a majority of votes in ten of the 67 counties in the State, among which were Jefferson, Macon, Mobile, and Montgomery counties. It is estimated that three-fourths of the Negro votes in Jefferson County were cast for Eisenhower. In Macon County, for the first time since Reconstruction, the Republican candidate received a majority of the votes. A conservative estimate is that approximately 90 per cent of the Negro votes in this County were given to Eisenhower. Of the 2,500 votes cast by Negroes in Montgomery, approximately 59 per cent voted for Eisenhower.

In four cities in Alabama in 1956 Negro voters were able to vote for Negro candidates. In Fairfield, a lawyer, Demetrius C. Newton and a teacher, Varnard F. Thomas competed with white candidates for positions on the city council. Neither was victorious, but each was successful enough in the first primary to participate in the run-off election. In

Huntsville, L. C. Jamar, educator and journalist, was not successful in his campaign for a position on the city council. Alex Herman and Clarence H. Montgomery in Mobile were more successful in their campaign for membership on the Mobile County Democratic Executive Committee. Both were elected. In Pritchard, Alabama the Reverend Joshua A. Barney, a clergyman-carpenter, lost in his effort to secure a position on the city council.

In order to increase the political strength and opportunities of Negro citizens in Alabama, Negro voters in increasing numbers are (1) studying the interrelation between politics and other phases of human welfare, (2) analyzing and appraising political issues, the behavior of public officials, and the records of candidates for public office, (3) stimulating unregistered citizens to qualify as electors, (4) appealing to public officials to perform their duties without unfair discrimination against any group, (5) voting for the proposed legislation and the prospective officials who will promote the general welfare, and (6) offering themselves for public office. Many of the voters are working actively in civic associations, registration clubs, voters leagues, and political parties.

Journal of Negro Education, 26 (Spring 1957): 281–86. Tables omitted. Charles Gomillion at this time was dean of students, Tuskegee Institute. In *Gomillion v. Lightfoot* (364 U.S. 339 1960), the Supreme Court rejected an effort in 1957 by Alabama to so gerrymander Tuskegee City as to eliminate effectiveness of black voters. The case was of great importance in the judicial aspect of the struggle against Jim Crow. See on this Derrick A. Bell, Jr., *Race, Racism and American Law*, 2nd ed. (Boston: Little Brown, 1980), pp. 157–61.

58

CONSIDER THE NEGRO TEACHER (1957)

by Nick Aaron Ford

The author, a teacher at Morgan State College in Baltimore, examines one of the complex results of illegalizing segregated education:

Since the Supreme Court's decision three years ago outlawing racial segregation in the public schools, much sympathy has been expended on the "victims" of the Court order. Some have said that the worst sufferers from this "monstrous" deed are white parents who from birth have known only "white superiority," who have never doubted the reality of the stereotype of Negro crap-shooters, razor-wielders, sex fiends or super-stitious clowns. We are asked to picture these parents dying a thousand deaths each morning as their children trudge off to school where a few black students may be cowering on the grounds and in the buildings.

Others may suggest that it is the white children who are most to be pitied. For are not these youngsters being forced to listen to the incorrect (or worse) language of Negro pupils, and are they not at the impression-able age when they will imitate the bad habits of Negro schoolmates—and at the same time voluntarily form close friendships with them?

There are those, too, who are sure that the Court's decision has been hardest on Negro parents—parents who have learned through bitter experiences of unemployment, economic reprisals and brutality to accept their status as "inferiors," parents who feel more at ease living in black ghettos and moving among people who have at least an understanding of their unrealized dreams, parents who live with fear as their children leave home each morning to sit in classrooms and play during recess with the sons and daughters of white supremacists.

I have also heard it said that the Negro children themselves are the real martyrs in this de-segregation struggle. Suddenly lifted from a school situation of mutual respect and cordiality where they were encouraged to join wholeheartedly in every kind of extracurricular activity, they now are thrust into an electric atmosphere; their talents are rejected everywhere outside the classroom; and, at the same time, they are expected to perform at the level of the best of their classmates. When some of them fail miserably, all of them are condemned as poor educational risks. When some of them fight back when jeered by mobs, all of them are classed as juvenile delinquents. When some of them make high grades, they are considered unrepresentative of their race. When they form little groups of their own for study or for play, they are accused of preferring segregation to integration. When they actively seek comradeship among their white fellow-students, they are charged with forcing "social equality."

And what of the white teacher? If education is problem-solving, here indeed—in the new relationships that must follow in the wake of the Court decree—is a problem to be solved. But might it not be difficult for an intelligent white teacher of social studies to read the Declaration of Independence with a straight face when he knows some children who are looking up at him would be beaten severely should they insist on the

Declaration's full and prompt implementation? It would be equally painful for such a teacher to read and interpret the Constitution of the United States to a mixed class when he knows that the parents of some of his students have been assaulted, even killed, for attempting to exercise the right to vote. Furthermore, if there is such a vast difference between the rate of learning and the quality of academic achievement of white and Negro children because of race (as a small minority of psychologists contend), must there not be an *Educational Psychology for Negroes* and a manual on *Methods of Teaching Arithmetic to Negro Children,* and how can the harassed teacher master all the new pedagogical texts necessary to make him understand how to teach the two Negro children in his class of 35 and carry on his regular class schedule at the same time?

But the individual whose dilemma concerns me most, because I know him best, is the Negro teacher. In many sections of the South, he faces the choice of swearing *opposition* to the Constitution of the United States and thereby retaining his job, or swearing *allegiance* to the Constitution and losing his job. Last summer, 17 teachers in one Southern state showed me contracts they were given which required that they sign affidavits swearing their opposition to integration in public schools and affirming their disinterest in teaching in an integrated situation. In another state, I was shown contracts for Negro teachers which were subject to cancellation or renewal at the end of each 30-day period, depending upon the conduct of the signer. Since some of the teachers had satisfactorily held their positions for as long as 20 years, it seemed obvious that "conduct" referred specifically to attitudes toward integration.

The dilemma of the Negro teacher is not due wholly to integration. Under the "separate but equal" doctrine which antedated the Supreme Court decision of May 17, 1954, other contradictions had to be endured. A former Negro colleague of mine, who had been principal of a rural high school for 11 years, was awarded the degree of Masters of Arts after many summers of study at a Western university. Upon his return from the graduating exercises, the county superintendent of education called him in to inform him that his contract would not be renewed for the next year. He was assured that his work had been eminently satisfactory, but unfortunately his M.A. degree plus his 11 years of teaching entitled him under state law to a salary higher than that of the white high school principal who had no graduate degree. And since the county authorities had no intention of paying a Negro more than a white man occupying a similar position, the only alternative was to secure another Negro principal with less training and no tenure.

But although the threat to the Negro teacher's professional security is serious, the undermining of his morale is catastrophic. Some Negroes in all occupations have resigned themselves to martyrdom. They defy all demands to compromise their principles or suppress their opinions, even though such defiance may mean hardship for themselves and their families. But the vast majority of peace-loving and law-abiding Negroes avoid the hero's lonely stand. Like their white counterparts, they will fight for their rights if they must, but they are prepared to pay for peace and comfort with outward conformity. Many will sign contracts with affidavits opposing integration; while in the silence of their souls they will shout, "Down with segregation!"

Not only is the Negro teacher's livelihood jeopardized, but his intellectual competence is questioned as well. He may attend the same graduate schools as his white colleagues and receive the same degrees based on the same requirements, but in the push toward integration he is usually referred to as an inferior teacher. Part of the very evidence which helped to destroy the "separate but equal" doctrine rests on the assumption that a school with an all-Negro faculty, even though the buildings and equipment may be superior, does not provide an education equal to that provided by an all-white faculty. Any school with an all-Negro faculty and an all-Negro student body is classified as inferior; white schools with all-white faculties are never thus classified, except on the basis of such criteria as buildings and equipment.

The fact is that in several large cities in the South, the average Negro teacher has more academic training and more tenure than his white colleague, which is not surprising since white college graduates have a far larger assortment of occupations open to them at higher salaries than do Negroes. And since the teaching profession represents for the Negro one of the highest paid white collar occupations available, once a Negro qualifies for a teaching position he generally remains until retirement—improving his status and salary by periodic attendance at summer school.

Finally, although the Negro teacher knows there is no fate more bleak than a loss of faith in the only political doctrine that guarantees freedom and equality for all, the application of this doctrine is so half-hearted in many sections that his hope drains away. He knows democracy means equal opportunities for employment based on merit alone, but he sees teaching positions go begging in the South and the North while thousands of his race with first-class teaching certificates are forced to take menial jobs in domestic service because boards of education will not even examine their applications and educational credentials. In cities which have already accepted the principal of integration, brilliant and experienced Negro teachers are passed over when promotions open up.

I dwell on the problems of the Negro teacher because it seems to me so evident that the survival of America as a free and responsible nation depends so largely on the devotion and moral integrity of our teachers. Any deprivation which encourages despair, which robs educators of their dignity, self-respect and chance for advancement robs the whole nation. Unless we are resolved to apply the teachings of our democratic tradition to teachers, what hope is there that the next generation of Americans will understand and deeply care about the decencies that make America worth saving?

New Republic, April 15, 1957, pp. 14–15.

59

WHERE'S THE HORSE
FOR A KID THAT'S BLACK?

by Langston Hughes

Under the auspices of the Authors League of America, a National Assembly of Authors and Dramatists met in New York City in May 1957. Langston Hughes used his few minutes at the podium to say:

Bruce Catton spoke today of the writer's chance to be heard. My chance to be heard, as a Negro writer, is not so great as your chance, if you are white. I once approached the Play Service of the Dramatists Guild as to the handling of some of my plays. *No,* was the answer, they would not know where to place plays about Negro life. I once sent one of my best known short stories, before it came out in book form, to one of our oldest and foremost American magazines. The story was about racial violence in the South. It came back to me with a very brief little note saying the editor did not believe his readers wished to read about such things. Another story of mine which did not concern race problems at all came back to me from one of our best known editors of anthologies of fiction with a letter praising the story but saying that he, the editor, could not tell if the characters were white or colored. Would I make them definitely Negro? Just a plain story about human beings from me was not up his alley, it seems. So before the word *man* I simply inserted *black,* and before the girl's name, the words *brownskin*—and the story was accepted. Only a mild form of racial bias. But now let us come to something more serious.

Censorship, the Black List: Negro writers, just by being black, have been on the blacklist all our lives. Do you know that there are libraries in our country that will not stock a book by a Negro writer, not even as a gift? There are towns where Negro newspapers and magazines cannot be sold—except surreptitiously. There are American magazines that have *never* published anything by Negroes. There are film studios that have never hired a Negro writer. Censorship for us begins at the color line.

As to the tangential ways in which many white writers may make a living: I've already mentioned Hollywood. Not once in a blue moon does Hollywood send for a Negro writer, no matter how famous he may be. When you go into your publishers' offices, how many colored editors, readers, or even secretaries do you see? In the book review pages of our Sunday supplements and our magazines, how often do you see a Negro reviewer's name? And if you do, 9 times out of 10 the Negro reviewer will be given a book by another Negro to review—seldom if ever, *The Sea Around Us* or *Auntie Mamie*—or *Compulsion*—and yet a reviewer of the caliber of Arna Bontemps or Anne Petry or J. Saunders Redding could review anybody's books, white or colored, interestingly. Take Lecturing: There are thousands and thousands of women's clubs and other organizations booking lecturers that have never had, and will not have, a Negro speaker—though he has written a best seller.

We have in America today about a dozen top flight, frequently published, and really good Negro writers. Do you not think it strange that of that dozen, at least half of them live abroad, far away from their people, their problems, and the sources of their material: Richard Wright—*Native Son* in Paris; Chester Himes—*The Primitives* in Paris: James Baldwin—*Giovanni's Room* in Paris. William Denby—*Beetle Creek* in Rome; Frank Yerby—of the dozen best sellers, in Southern France; and Willard Motley—*Knock On Any Door* in Mexico. Why? Because the stones thrown at Autherine Lucy at the University of Alabama are thrown at them, too. Because the shadow of Montgomery and the bombs under Rev. King's house, shadow them and shatter them, too. Because the body of little Emmett Till drowned in a Mississippi river and no one brought to justice, haunts them, too. One of the writers I've mentioned, when last I saw him before he went abroad, said to me, "I don't want my children to grow up in the shadow of Jim Crow."

And so let us end with children. And let us end with poetry—since somehow the planned poetry panel for which I was to have been a part, did not materialize. So therefore, there has been no poetry in our National Assembly. Forgive me then, if I read a poem. It's about a child—a little colored child. I imagine her as being maybe six or seven years old. She grew up in the Deep South where our color lines are still legal. Then her family moved to a Northern or Western industrial city—one of those continual migrations of Negroes looking for a better town. There in this Northern city—maybe a place like Newark, New Jersey, or Omaha, Nebraska, or Oakland, California, the little girl goes one day to a carnival, and she sees the merry-go-round going around, and she wants to ride. But being a little colored child, and remembering the South, she doesn't know if she can ride or not. And if she can ride, where? So this is what she says:

> Where is the Jim Crow section
> On this merry-go-round,
> Mister, cause I want to ride?
> Down South where I come from
> White and colored
> Can't sit side by side.
> Down South on the train
> Down South on the train
> There's a Jim Crow car.
> On the bus we're put in the back—
> But there ain't no back
> To a merry-go-round:
> Where's the horse
> For a kid that's black?

Masses and Mainstream, July 1957, vol. 10, pp. 46–48.

60

LITTLE ROCK, ARKANSAS (1957)

by Roy Wilkins

After the N.A.A.C.P. board made its position known, I took a few steps on my own. Two days before Governor Faubus was to have his day in court, I got in touch with the White House and asked the President to meet with a number of Negro leaders to consider the unrelenting persecution of Negro citizens in areas of the South. I was boiling mad. Before the voting on Title III of the 1957 Civil Rights Act the President had invited Senator Russell to the White House and listened to all that Georgian nonsense about bayonets in the South. The only bayonets I could see were those planted by a Southern governor against nine black children and the Supreme Court of the United States. Then the President had invited Governor Faubus to Newport for an audience. The leaders of the Southern resistance to the Supreme Court seemed to be welcome any time, but the President had shut his door on Negro leaders. I told him that we did not relish having our destiny debated by others while we sat in the anteroom, that we were entitled to be heard.

The next day, Sherman Adams, keeper of the President's door, telephoned me. He said the President would agree to see a delegation of less than ten leaders, "six if possible." The date set for the meeting was October 15, but over the next forty-eight hours events ran out of control in Little Rock, and I didn't get into the Oval Office until the following summer.

With Little Rock coming to a boil, Adam Clayton Powell sent me a cable inquiring about my views on the crisis. I sent him a letter, which gives a sense of how I felt at the time.

September 19, 1957

Dear Adam:

I have your wire asking for comment on Arkansas. I cannot comment in language suitable either for the stationery of the N.A.A.C.P. or the ears of a Baptist clergyman.

All unbiased observers agree that there was no incipient violence in Little Rock when the Governor called out the troops, allegedly to preserve peace and order.

It must be remembered that the school desegregation plan developed by Little Rock school officials was challenged in the courts as being too slow by N.A.A.C.P. attorneys acting for parents, but was approved twice by the Federal court. We accepted the court's ruling and prepared the people to go along with it, even though we were not satisfied.

The hysterical opponents now charge that a judge from North Dakota has come down to Arkansas and forced a plan on Little Rock without knowing anything about the local situation. Ridiculous.

We shall see by tomorrow whether the conference Governor Faubus had with President Eisenhower had any meaning or whether it was just one of those things.

I have great difficulty in speaking calmly about the role of President Eisenhower in this whole mess. He has been absolutely and thoroughly disappointing and disillusioning from beginning to end. I am willing to grant that perhaps he did not want to get into a fight on behalf of the Negro but he didn't do anything when the authority of his own Federal Government was challenged.

I have tried very hard to be fair and objective about Mr. Eisenhower. I have tried to make allowances for the pressures under which he works. I have made allowances for the need of Southern votes in Congress to pass some of the legislation necessary for the well-being of our country. Yet with all these allowances, I still believe that any President of all the people would at least have issued a strong statement on the individual cases of violence that have occurred since the desegregation opinion, even if he did not issue a statement calling for overall observance of that opinion.

I just cannot for the life of me understand how a President could have allowed the mistrust to develop that presently exists in the South.

Firm words and resolute action by him and his Administration would have rallied public opinion in 1955 when there was ample evidence that things were going badly. The white people in the South who could be called moderate were begging for some encouragement from the Chief Executive. The wobbly liberal white opinion in the North that knew what was right but hesitated was looking to Washington for a word. The President kept silent. His Administration wore kid gloves publicly and did nothing privately (that we know of) in the Roosevelt manner so that the White Citizens' Councils, the ignoramuses (and many in the North) felt that they had a green light to do as they pleased.

The situation has hardened not because the N.A.A.C.P. is insisting on obedience to the Supreme Court, but because the White House had abandoned its own Supreme Court and has abdicated leadership in a great moral crisis.

I cannot help but believe that even Calvin Coolidge would not have turned in such a performance.

Very sincerely yours,
/s/   Roy Wilkins

P.S. When Senator Russell made his "bayonet" speech on July 2, the President promptly invited him to the White House, where they chatted for 50 minutes. What was agreed upon, nobody knows, but Russell emerged seemingly reassured. On July 16, in the late afternoon, the White House released a statement on behalf of the President (he was on the golf course) saying he was demanding his full, four-point civil rights bill. At his press conference on the morning of July 17, Mr. Eisenhower calmly announced that he "did not know" about Part III of the bill, and that he "never intended" that thus and so should happen. At that moment he pulled the rug out from under Brownell and gave the signal for the elimination of Part III from the bill. His attitude encouraged further chopping of the bill, which might not have taken place if he had stood firm.

My view was not very diplomatic but I'm afraid it was accurate. President Eisenhower had done what he had done—and the chickens had come home to roost in Little Rock.

The day after I wrote to Adam, Judge Davies knocked the last legal pretense out from under Governor Faubus. "Now begins the crucifixion," the governor said dolefully. What baloney, I thought to myself. The governor was not Jesus. Defying the Supreme Court was no ministry; it was disgusting. Judge Davies enjoined Governor Faubus and the National Guard from obstructing integration at Central High School. Within three hours, the governor called off his troops. The city and state police took over through the weekend.

I knew that we had won only the easiest part of the battle. The following Monday, the nine Negro children succeeded in entering Central High School—through a side door. A mob of about 800 angry whites then surrounded the school. The police did not break up the crowd. After three hours, Daisy Bates decided to get the children out of there. When they were safe, she told President Eisenhower that they would not return until she had his word that they would be protected.

It was an inspired challenge. Mrs. Bates was a direct and independent-minded woman. No one could tell her what to do; she acted by her own light and vision. Those particular strengths of character squared well with the N.A.A.C.P.'s working strategy, which was to keep the national office out of Little Rock, leaving the leadership of the fight in the hands of state and local officers. We did not want to provide Governor Faubus with the pretext that "outside agitators" were responsible for the fight. Mrs. Bates handled things her own way. To show her contempt for the bigots, she didn't mend the broken picture window at her home or replant the scorches left on her front lawn by burning crosses. She left those scars as symbols of the disgraceful conduct of her foes. Her challenge to President Eisenhower came from the same impulse. The next day he federalized the Arkansas National Guard and ordered a group of 1,200 paratroopers from the 101st Airborne, one of the toughest units in the U.S. Army to Little Rock. I suppose he would have done what he did anyway, but Mrs. Bates certainly prodded him on his way.

I didn't expect Governor Faubus to draw in his horns, even though he had retreated. One of the more persistent misconceptions about those times is that once President Eisenhower bit the bullet and sent the troops to Little Rock everything worked itself out. The reality was far more complex. By the beginning of October, it was clear that most of the white children at Central High School were willing to make desegregation work, but the adults just wouldn't leave them alone. Once President Eisenhower withdrew the paratroopers, leaving federalized National Guardsmen in their place, life for the nine Negroes became a daily misery. A small band of white students—I don't believe there were more than thirty or forty in all among the 1,900 youngsters in the school—set itself the job of running the black youngsters out. White adults egged the young thugs on, and school officials were either too lax or too frightened to do much about the problem.

The reports I received were infuriating. The favorite target of the white kids was Minnie Jean Brown, a sixteen-year-old girl in the eleventh grade.

She was a friendly, outgoing student who wanted to major in English. She was also tall and strong, the most imposing of the nine Negro school-children. In no time the renegade white students singled her out for elimination. For weeks she was jeered, blocked from entering her classroom, kicked, threatened, kept away from her table in the cafeteria, hit with bowls of soup, bombarded with racist epithets. Until December she held her temper; then two white boys baited her beyond endurance and she spilled her cafeteria tray on them. For this retaliation, she was suspended. After some reconsideration, the school authorities readmitted her, but they exacted a promise that she would not strike back at her tormentors no matter what the provocation.

The attacks grew worse. "Any day upon entrance to school I may be welcomed with a lotion or water shower from the second floor stairway," she told us. "Walking down the hall I am insulted countless times. When I enter classrooms, I hear phrases like, 'Here comes that nigger, Minnie Jean.' I can be kicked, hit with rocks and candy, smeared with ink, souped in the cafeteria. Scores of things can and usually do happen to me in the course of a day." Finally, in February a white girl trailed Minnie Jean from the first to the third floor of Central High, calling her a "nigger bitch." Minnie Jean turned on the girl and called her "white trash." For those two words of reprisal the board of education expelled Minnie Jean for the remainder of the school term.

It was a familiar, shabby story. Rather than protect and stand by the target of racial injustice, the authorities chose to solve their "problem" by getting rid of the victim. I had seen such things happen hundreds of times. Unconscious or conscious, the motive behind such actions was to leave black people so numb with injustice that they would give up in despair.

When I looked a little more deeply into the situation, I discovered that in the months leading up to Minnie Jean's expulsion there had been no fewer than forty-two separate attacks on the Negro students at Central High. I am sure that the actual total was much higher—it was a matter of pride among the nine not to complain. Gloria Ray, one of Minnie Jean's classmates, refused even to talk to school authorities about what she had suffered until a white boy who tried to push her down the steps snarled, "I'm going to get you out of this school if I have to kill you."

The worst problem was that the National Guardsmen appeared to have orders to do nothing about these attacks except observe them. This was something more than benign neglect. Obviously, in ordering the admittance of the Negro students, the court had been thinking not merely about their physical entry to the premises of Central High but also of protecting their right to obtain an education. Just as obviously, they could not get that education if the troops on the scene did nothing about the malevolence of young white hoodlums. The default of the guard left the tiny minority of white troublemakers in charge. When Minnie Jean was expelled, the same young punks turned up with labels on their lapels reading, *One down— eight to go.*

When I told Wilber M. Brucker, Secretary of the Army, what was going on, I received only a bland assurance from one of his aides that everything possible was being done, that I had to understand that school authorities were responsible for control and discipline, and that the troops would not "usurp" that authority. Thus we were confronted with the incredible spectacle of the government of the United States placing the burden of enforcing the orders of its high courts upon the slender shoulders and young hearts of the eight teenagers who were left after Minnie Jean was expelled. That summer the N.A.A.C.P. awarded the schoolchildren and Mrs. Bates the Spingarn Medal in honor of and gratitude for what they had done.

Roy Wilkins, with Tom Mathews, *Standing Fast: An Autobiography* (New York: Penguin, 1984), pp. 250–54.

61

CHALLENGING LITTLE ROCK (1957)

Daisy Bates, publisher, with Mr. Bates, of the weekly *State Press* in Little Rock, Arkansas, was president of the Arkansas NAACP and decisive in developing the antiracist struggle in that state. In her autobiography, Mrs. Bates described the ordeal of the nine African-American children who, in 1957, challenged the Jim Crow policies dominating education in Little Rock. This account is from that autobiography:

Minnijean Brown

Minnijean Brown, sixteen years old and in the eleventh grade, was tall, attractive, and outgoing. Her manner was friendly and good-natured. She sang well, was good at sports, and liked dancing. She was the oldest of four children and lived with her parents, Mr. and Mrs. W. B. Brown.

Minnijean's feelings were quickly mirrored in her face. At school she was subjected to no greater pressure than were the other Negro pupils. However, the incidents in which she was involved were certainly more dramatic, if not spectacular.

The first of these incidents took place on October 2, 1957. Minnijean and Melba Pattillo were roughed up by several unidentified boys and girls in the corridors as they left their second class for the day. One girl deliberately ran into Minnijean, and a group of boys formed a line to block her entrance to her classroom. Then followed an incredible catalogue of violence:

Minnijean was kicked by a boy as she was going to her seat at "pep" assembly, prior to a football game.

She was threatened by a pupil who said, "I will chase you down the hall and kick all your teeth out the next time you do what you did yesterday afternoon." The boy alleged that she had made insulting gestures at him. Minnijean insisted she did not remember ever seeing him before. The boy was taken to the principal's office and reprimanded.

By the middle of December Minnijean had had enough. After repeated provocation by white pupils blocking her path as she attempted to reach a table in the cafeteria, she warned her persecutors that they might get something on their heads. On December 17, when chairs had been shoved in her way, she emptied her tray on the heads of two boys. These boys excused her, saying that she had been annoyed so frequently they "didn't blame her for getting mad." The boys were sent home to change their clothing. But Minnijean was suspended for six days because of the incident.

Soon after she returned to her classes, a pupil emptied a bowl of hot soup on Minnijean. The reason he gave was that he remembered she had earlier spilled chili on two white boys. He was suspended for three days....

One of the many unprovoked attacks was witnessed by Mrs. Brown. Toward the end of January, she was waiting for Minnijean at the Fourteenth Street exit. At about 3:30 P.M., Minnijean came out of school and saw that her mother was parked at the curb. Minnijean quickened her steps as she made her way to the car. Just before she reached her mother, a pupil, Richard Boehler, came up in back of Minnijean and gave her a vicious kick. Mrs. Brown, seeing this cruel attack on her daughter, screamed and jumped from the car. She started toward the boy but a teacher, who had also seen the incident, apprehended the boy and took him to the office of the Vice-Principal for boys. Boehler, who had been suspended from school earlier that same day, stated that he kicked Minnijean because he "was dared to." He also claimed that Minnijean had stamped on his leg in French class, but he couldn't remember the day. During the subsequent investigation, one of the soldiers reported that Boehler had previously threatened Minnijean with a knife.

Mrs. Brown attempted to file charges against Boehler, but the prosecuting attorney, J. Frank Holt, refused to issue a warrant for his arrest. He said that it was a matter for the school authorities. The school officials, in turn, did not take any action because of Boehler's suspension earlier that day. Poor Minnijean remained at home for a few days until she could sit without pain.

On February 6 Minnijean was suspended for the second time. She walked into my house that afternoon. "They did it to me again," she began. "I just lost my temper. I know it will make it harder for the other kids, but I just couldn't take it any longer."

Pacing the floor, she told me how a girl had been pestering her for days. "When I entered the building this morning," she related, "this girl followed me from the first floor to the third floor, kicking me on the back of my legs and calling me names. As we were entering our homeroom, she called out, 'black bitch.'

"I turned and screamed, 'White trash! Why don't you leave me alone? If you weren't white trash, you wouldn't bother with me!' The girl looked startled for a moment. I started for my seat. She threw her pocketbook at me and hit me on the head with it. I picked up the bag. My first impulse was to knock the devil out of her with it."

"I'm glad you were able to restrain yourself," I said.

"Yes, I am, too," she acknowledged. "I threw the bag on the floor and walked away in disgust. Then, while I was eating my lunch in the cafeteria, during first lunch period, a character walked over to the table and deliberately dumped a hot bowl of soup on me. A national guardsman came over and took us to Mr. Powell's office. He told the Vice-Principal he had dumped the soup on me because he remembered I had poured chili on some white boys."

The other Negro students later told me they had reported this same student several times to school authorities for harassing them.

The Principal, Jess W. Mathews, suspended both Minnijean and the boy. The suspension notice he sent to her parents stated:

Reinstated on probation January 13, 1958, with the agreement that she would not retaliate, verbally or physically, to any harassment but would leave the matter to the school authorities to handle.

After provocation of girl student, she called the girl "white trash" after which the girl threw her purse at Minnijean.

Upon recommendation of Superintendant of Schools Virgil Blossom, the Board of Education expelled Minnijean for the remainder of the school term.

After Minnijean's expulsion the small group of students who began tormenting the Negro children began wearing printed cards that read: "One down and eight to go." ...In the ensuing weeks and months the families of the Negro pupils were also constantly under attack from the segregationists. Gloria's mother was forced to resign her job in the Welfare Department because of a series of unpleasantnesses which followed when her fellow employees learned that her daughter was "one of the nine."

Carlotta's father was forced to seek employment out of the state because building contractors in Little Rock refused to employ him.

The strain was too much for Terrance Roberts' family and they moved to California.

Elizabeth's mother was fired from her job at the State School for the Blind where she was a teacher.

Of the original nine pupils, only five remained in Little Rock. They were: Carlotta Walls, Jefferson Thomas, Thelma Mothershed, Elizabeth Eckford, and Melba Patillo. Barred from school, they took correspondence courses offered to high school pupils by the University of Arkansas.

Daisy Bates, *The Long Shadow of Little Rock: A Memoir* (New York: David McKay, 1962), pp. 116–24; 159–60.

62

THE MEANING OF THE WASHINGTON PILGRIMAGE
(1957)

by W. E. B. Du Bois

The last Civil Rights Act passed by Congress was in 1875. Agitation for a new and more adequate bill intensified especially after World War II and particularly after the Supreme Court desegregation verdicts of 1954 and 1955. Filibustering and floundering in Congress prevented such legislation. Finally, in the fall of 1957, a Civil Rights law was enacted. Part of the pressure producing this was a march on Washington in May 1957; Du Bois's comments on this follow:

It was no easy matter for American Negroes to bring 27,000 representatives to Washington to protest against lawlessness and discrimination. The meeting might have become an hysterical and bitter demonstration, which the police—if not the army—would have been only too ready to suppress. On the other hand the meeting might have been so calm and moderate as to be meaningless. This the paid Red-baiters tried to ensure. The result lay between these extremes. The feeling of tremendous self-repression pulsed in the air and was held in check by long-imposed religious custom. The music and the shouting were not there in a throng which could have sung like the thunder of cataracts and groaned with memories that few peoples could match. It was wise that all this emotion was held in check, but it passes understanding how, on the other hand, the President of the United States could sit silent through this meeting and "never say a mumblin' word!"

But these pilgrims expressed themselves, not only in thousands of personal and group conferences, but in some clear words of the speakers. The clearest advice to the persons present was: "Register and Vote!" If to those present and listening this advice meant nothing more than it has since 1876, it had little significance. But it must have meant more; it had to mean more.

The American people as a mass have little faith in voting. It is seldom that more than half of the eligible voters go to the polls. Few voters expect or try to better conditions, secure more equitable laws or higher type of officials by elections. A letter to a congressman may help, if he ever sees it; but a ballot? Who trusts it, whether it is cast for the Republican or Democratic party, or for a "Third Party" which "endorses" either?

But the advice at the Washington Pilgrimage to register and vote touched a new note. It did not refer to the great parties. Every person who listened knew that right there in Washington, looking on and listening in, lay the whole power and the vast machinery of government. The Republicans cannot return to power without the Negro vote; the Democrats cannot assume power without it. Congress was in session and over the way sat the Supreme Court. Was the Pilgrimage appealing to these repositories of power? No. These folk were thinking of Montgomery, Ala., where recently a boycott of house servants and low-paid laborers was able to rid them partially of petty discrimination in their transportation to work, based on race and color.

The boycott did not keep a good many of them from losing their jobs; from lower wages; from illegal arrest and, above all, from the deliberate refusal of officials to stop mob violence or even attempted murder against black folks and their leaders. These leaders in Washington told them to register and vote in Montgomery, and in a thousand counties, cities and towns in Mississippi, Louisiana, Georgia, Florida and South Carolina, where local government has sunk to bribery, cheating, mob violence and anarchy under local dictators like "Senator" Eastland, chairman of the Senate Committee on the "Judiciary."

If the Pilgrims and their people will follow this advice, and if the U.S. government will make democratic government—which it recommends to Hungary—possible in the rural South, the government of that section of the U.S. will be revolutionized. That is why the white South and its new industry will never allow eligible Negroes this right to vote, if they can help it. That is why President Eisenhower's advice to the States to assume more power of taxation and administration will never be implemented so long as the two great parties can rule the nation from Washington in defiance of democratic procedures. If the people take back control of local government, freedom and democracy will rule the nation as they once did until the Slave Power seized control of the Federal Government.

Of course, for the localities and their voters to seize and hold government, they must be free to vote; they must know the facts as to laws, officials and elections; they must have the whole undergrowth of rank weed and noisome swamp cleansed from the local governments of the southern South. There must be public schools run by each community: there must be a free local press and lectures from all over the land and the world to teach Mississippi what civilization is and may be.

And then must come Social Reform; and it can start right in the Negro Church where the boycott started.

National Guardian, July 8, 1957.

63

ELIZABETH ECKFORD GOES TO SCHOOL (1957)

by Daisy Bates

A dramatic moment in Little Rock is recounted by its main director:

Dr. Benjamin Fine was then education editor of *The New York Times*. He had years before won for his newspaper a Pulitzer prize. He was among the first reporters on the scene to cover the Little Rock story.

A few days after the National Guard blocked the Negro children's entrance to the school, Ben showed up at my house. He paced the floor nervously, rubbing his hands together as he talked.

"Daisy, they spat in my face. They called me a 'dirty Jew.' I've been a marked man ever since the day Elizabeth tried to enter Central. I never told you what happened that day. I tried not to think about it. Maybe I was ashamed to admit to you or to myself that white men and women could be so beastly cruel.

"I was standing in front of the school that day. Suddenly there was a shout—"They're here! The niggers are coming!" I saw a sweet little girl who looked about fifteen, walking alone. She tried several times to pass through the guards. The last time she tried, they put their bayonets in front of her. When they did this, she became panicky. For a moment she just stood there trembling. Then she seemed to calm down and started walking toward the bus stop with the mob baying at her heels like a pack of hounds. The women were shouting, 'Get her! Lynch her!' The men were yelling, 'Go home, you bastard of a black bitch!' She finally made it to the bus stop and sat down on the bench. I sat down beside her and said, 'I'm a reporter from *The New York Times*, may I have your name?' She just sat there, her head down. Tears were streaming down her cheeks from under her sun glasses. Daisy, I don't know what made me put my arm around her, lifting her chin, saying, 'Don't let them see you cry.' Maybe she reminded me of my fifteen-year-old daughter, Jill.

"There must have been five hundred around us by this time. I vaguely remember someone hollering, 'Get a rope and drag her over to this tree.'

Suddenly I saw a white-haired, kind-faced woman fighting her way through the mob. She looked at Elizabeth, and then screamed at the mob, 'Leave this child alone! Why are you tormenting her? Six months from now, you will hang your heads in shame.' The mob shouted, 'Another nigger-lover. Get out of here!' The woman, who I found out later was Mrs. Grace Lorch, the wife of Dr. Lee Lorch, professor at Philander Smith College, turned to me and said, 'We have to do something. Let's try to get a cab.'

"We took Elizabeth across the street to the drugstore. I remained on the sidewalk with Elizabeth while Mrs. Lorch tried to enter the drugstore to call a cab. But the hoodlums slammed the door in her face and wouldn't let her in. She pleaded with them to call a cab for the child. They closed in on her saying, 'Get out of here, you bitch!' Just then the city bus came. Mrs. Lorch and Elizabeth got on. Elizabeth must have been in a state of shock. She never uttered a word. When the bus pulled away, the mob closed in around me. 'We saw you put your arm around that little bitch. Now it's your turn.' A drab, middle-aged woman said viciously, 'Grab him and kick him in the balls!' A girl I had seen hustling in one of the local bars screamed, 'A dirty New York Jew! Get him!' A man asked me, 'Are you a Jew?' I said, 'Yes.' He then said to the mob, 'Let him be! We'll take care of him later.'

"The irony of it all, Daisy, is that during all this time the national guardsmen made no effort to protect Elizabeth or to help me. Instead, they threatened to have me arrested—for inciting to riot."

Elizabeth, whose dignity and control in the face of jeering mobsters had been filmed by television cameras and recorded in pictures flashed to newspapers over the world, had overnight become a national heroine. During the next few days newspaper reporters besieged her home, wanting to talk to her. The first day that her parents agreed she might come out of seclusion, she came to my house where the reporters awaited her. Elizabeth was very quiet, speaking only when spoken to. I took her to my bedroom to talk before I let the reporters see her. I asked how she felt now. Suddenly all her pent-up emotion flared.

"Why am I here?" she said, turning blazing eyes on me. "Why are you so interested in my welfare now? You didn't care enough to notify me of the change of plans—"

I walked over and reached out to her. Before she turned her back on me,

I saw tears gathering in her eyes. My heart was breaking for this young girl who stood there trying to stifle her sobs. How could I explain that frantic early morning when at three o'clock my mind had gone on strike?

In the ensuing weeks Elizabeth took part in all the activities of the time—press conferences, attendance at court, studying with professors at nearby Philander Smith College. She was present, that is, but never really a part of things. The hurt had been too deep.

On the two nights she stayed at my home I was awakened by the screams in her sleep, as she relived in her dreams the terrifying mob scenes at Central. The only times Elizabeth showed real excitement were when Thurgood Marshall met the children and explained the meaning of what had happened in court. As he talked, she would listen raptly, a faint smile on her face. It was obvious he was her hero.

Little by little Elizabeth came out of her shell. Up to now she had never talked about what happened to her at Central. Once when we were alone in the downstairs recreation room of my house, I asked her simply, "Elizabeth, do you think you can talk about it now?"

She remained quiet for a long time. Then she began to speak.

"You remember the day we were to go in, we met Superintendent Blossom at the school board office. He told us what the mob might say and do but he never told us we wouldn't have any protection. He told our parents not to come because he wouldn't be able to protect the children if they did.

"That night I was so excited I couldn't sleep. The next morning I was about the first one up. While I was pressing my black and white dress—I had made it to wear on the first day of school—my little brother turned on the TV set. They started telling about a large crowd gathered at the school. The man on TV said he wondered if we were going to show up that morning. Mother called from the kitchen, where she was fixing breakfast, 'Turn that TV off!' She was so upset and worried. I wanted to comfort her, so I said, 'Mother, don't worry.'

"Dad was walking back and forth, from room to room, with a sad expression. He was chewing on his pipe and he had a cigar in his hand, but he didn't light either one. It would have been funny, only he was so nervous.

"Before I left home Mother called us into the living-room. She said we should have a word of prayer. Then I caught the bus and got off a block from the school. I saw a large crowd of people standing across the street from the soldiers guarding Central. As I walked on, the crowd suddenly got very quiet. Superintendent Blossom had told us to enter by the front door. I looked at all the people and thought, 'Maybe I will be safer if I walk down the block to the front entrance behind the guards.'

"At the corner I tried to pass through the long line of guards around the school so as to enter the grounds behind them. One of the guards pointed across the street. So I pointed in the same direction and asked whether he meant for me to cross the street and walk down. He nodded 'yes.' So, I walked across the street conscious of the crowd that stood there, but they moved away from me.

"For a moment all I could hear was the shuffling of their feet. Then someone shouted, 'Here she comes, get ready!' I moved away from the crowd on the sidewalk and into the street. If the mob came at me I could then cross back over so the guards could protect me.

"The crowd moved in closer and then began to follow me, calling me names. I still wasn't afraid. Just a little bit nervous. Then my knees started to shake all of a sudden and I wondered whether I could make it to the center entrance a block away. It was the longest block I ever walked in my whole life.

"Even so, I still wasn't too scared because all the time I kept thinking that the guards would protect me.

"When I got right in front of the school, I went up to a guard again. But this time he just looked straight ahead and didn't move to let me pass him. I didn't know what to do. Then I looked and saw that the path leading to the front entrance was a little further ahead. So I walked until I was right in front of the path to the front door.

"I stood looking at the school—it looked so big! Just then the guards let some white students go through.

"The crowd was quiet. I guess they were waiting to see what was going to happen. When I was able to steady my knees, I walked up to the guard who had let the white students in. He too didn't move. When I tried to squeeze past him, he raised his bayonet and then the other guards closed in and they raised their bayonets.

"They glared at me with a mean look and I was very frightened and didn't know what to do. I turned around and the crowd came toward me.

"They moved closer and closer. Somebody started yelling, 'Lynch her! Lynch her!'

"I tried to see a friendly face somewhere in the mob—someone who maybe would help. I looked into the face of an old woman and it seemed a kind face, but when I looked at her again, she spat on me.

"They came closer, shouting, 'No nigger bitch is going to get in our school. Get out of here!'

"I turned back to the guards but their faces told me I wouldn't get help from them. Then I looked down the block and saw a bench at the bus stop. I thought, 'If I can only get there I will be safe.' I don't know why the bench seemed a safe place to me, but I started walking toward it. I tried to close my mind to what they were shouting, and kept saying to myself, 'If I can only make it to the bench I will be safe.'

"When I finally got there, I don't think I could have gone another step. I sat down and the mob crowded up and began shouting all over again. Someone hollered, 'Drag her over to this tree! Let's take care of the nigger.' Just then a white man sat down beside me, put his arm around me and patted my shoulder. He raised my chin and said, 'Don't let them see you cry.'

"Then, a white lady—she was very nice—she came over to me on the bench. She spoke to me but I don't remember now what she said. She put me on the bus and sat next to me. She asked me my name and tried to talk to me but I don't think I answered. I can't remember much about the bus ride, but the next thing I remember I was standing in front of the School for the Blind, where Mother works.

"I thought, 'Maybe she isn't here. But she has to be here!' So I ran upstairs, and I think some teachers tried to talk to me, but I kept running until I reached Mother's classroom.

"Mother was standing at the window with her head bowed, but she must have sensed I was there because she turned around. She looked as if she had been crying, and I wanted to tell her I was all right. But I couldn't speak. She put her arms around me and I cried."

Daisy Bates, *The Long Shadow of Little Rock* (New York: David McKay, 1966), pp. 69–76.

64

THE AFRICAN-AMERICAN PRESS
AND MONTGOMERY

by Several Newspapers

A recent unpublished doctoral dissertation provides a bird's-eye view of the manner in which the African-American press treated the Montgomery events.

Of the boycotters, the *State Press* declared that:

They have set out to do one thing only—and that one thing is to walk or perhaps ride a neighbor's car. By doing this, they have cost the bus company some three thousand dollars a day, it is said...Arrest and formal charges have failed to halt them. If it were possible for all appeals to be lost, the boycotters would still be the winners. They have captured popular appeal and the public will underwrite their expense. There are few movements in our time which have been so generally approved. Whatever else may happen the Negroes of Montgomery have a new dignity throughout the world.

Similarly inspired by the Montgomery story, the *Louisiana Weekly* was jubilant that ministers of their city, New Orleans, had taken a stand with the boycotters and had agreed to help financially. When the boycott was over, the *Weekly* again endorsed the boycotters and indicated that it considered Martin Luther King to be a great man.

The Tennessee *Memphis Tri-State Defender* also commended King and others for getting involved. This kind of leadership, it declared, was what was needed all over the South.

The *Atlanta Daily World* featured articles about the boycott on its front page beginning as early as December 18, 1955. However, it took no editorial position until February of 1956 when it lauded Dr. King and his cause.

The *Birmingham World*, however, took a more forthright position as early as December 13, 1955 when it described Mrs. Rosa Parks as an outstanding woman and warned that as long as the segregation law remained as it was, no blacks would be able to ride the bus in peace. Entitled, "Blockade to Fairness," the *Birmingham World's* article differed in content from an article bearing the same title and published on the same day in its maternal counterpart, the *Atlanta Daily World*.

Both Sarah Fleming and Rosa Parks were the subject of the *Atlanta Daily World's* "Blockade to Fairness." The *Daily World* reported that "a woman" in Montgomery was accused of failing to obey a bus driver and of violating the segregation law (presumably Rosa Parks). In suggesting that litigation be instituted to do away with the law which gave the bus drivers the right to police, it appeared to express a preference for legal action instead of a boycott. It pointed to the case of Sarah Fleming who had filed suit in the U.S. Court of Appeals for the 4th circuit. The U.S. Court of Appeals held on July 15, 1955 that the Supreme Court decision in the school cases should also apply to segregation of city buses....

It was not until February of 1956 that the *Miami Times* carried an opinion of the boycotts on its editorial pages. When it did, it commended the spirit of the boycott in Montgomery and vowed to keep it under close scrutiny.

Jubilant over the fact that the boycott was initiated by local Alabamians, the *Dallas Express* quipped, "who would have thought that Negroes in Alabama would boycott." This is living proof, it argued, of "a new day." As King became nationally known, the *Express* editor wrote, "although whites see Martin Luther King as a bumptious Negro, we need to train more to be like him because all he is asking for is his rights."

There was no significant opinion expressed on the boycott in the editorial pages of the *Norfolk Journal and Guide*. However, the paper did comment on September 6, 1958 when the boycott was ending in order to emphasize King's call for no violence. The *Baltimore-Richmond Afro-American* was less timid on the issue. It made clear its support as early as December 17, 1955. Without mentioning the names of the leaders of the boycott, it predicted that if the boycott could hold out for two weeks, that would be long enough.... After pledging its support of the boycott in several editorials, the *Afro-American* admonished its readers:

> The bus boycott in Montgomery is the most important happening in Alabama this year. Passengers said, It's my dime, my feet and from now on, I am walking...Organize your community, choose your leaders and follow their directions. Firmly in good temper and within the law, press for the rights of a U.S. citizen and accept no compromise. Register and vote and where that is temporarily impossible invoke passive resistance.

Late in May 1956, Florida A & M students staged a bus protest in Tallahassee. Although Carrie Patterson and Wilhelmenia Jakes, the initiators of the boycott, were acquitted of all charges, the boycott continued. The city made every attempt at a partial solution. For example, blacks were told that they could sit anywhere, except a three-seat bench in front, which would be reserved for whites. This proposal was rejected and the boycott continued until two black drivers were hired and all other demands were met. By June 8 of 1956, blacks in the city of Miami were considering a boycott of city buses. Blacks in the city of Atlanta toyed with the idea in January of 1957. Although Atlanta blacks did not resort to a boycott, they did pressure city officials to obey the law. Birmingham too sought an end to bus discrimination but met tremendous opposition and delay even after the segregation laws had been ruled unconstitutional.

On the other hand, many cities repealed their bus segregation laws after witnessing the gradual dismantling of segregation laws by the courts and the economic "strangle hold" around the neck of the Montgomery Bus Company. An editorial taken from the *Southern Patriot* and reprinted in the *Arkansas State Press* revealed the following actions that had occurred in southern communities by the summer of 1956:

It may have been a false dawn when the press spread the word that the U.S. Supreme Court in ruling on a Columbia, S.C. case, had outlawed segregation in interstate travel. But lots of places in the South saw the light.

In Richmond, Norfolk and Portsmouth, Va.; in Knoxville, Chattanooga and Nashville, Tenn.; in Hot Springs and Little Rock, Arkansas, the city bus lines dropped seating restrictions . . . and the process went smoothly. The Nashville line is accepting applicants from Negroes for drivers' jobs.

The Montgomery, Alabama City lines, which have suffered immense financial loss during the six-months boycott, tried to institute an integration order. But city officials obtained an injunction against the move from a state judge. On June 5, a federal court ruled 2–1 that segregation in city bus lines was unconstitutional. The ruling will be appealed. Ironically in north Alabama the transit buses in Florence started operating in an integrated basis without meeting interference from any source. And the line's manager declared that things are going better than before.

Thus, the custom of maintaining segregated local buses was gradually eradicated in many Southern cities. The battle, however, was not over because interstate buses and the facilities inside bus stations remained segregated. . . .

Benjamin F. Clark, *"The Editorial Reaction of Selected Black Newspapers to the Civil Rights Movement"* (Ph.D. Dissertation, Howard Univ., 1989), pp. 116–25.

65

LITTLE ROCK, ARKANSAS (1957)

by Several Youngsters

After near civil war and with scores of soldiers to ensure security, nine African-American children were able to attend Central High School in Little Rock, Arkansas, in the fall of 1957. Some of the youngsters of that school, black and white, were interviewed. Here is the account, as introduced by Anthony Lewis:

The self-control of one of the Negro children did finally crack. Minnijean Brown, sixteen years old, was unable to go on enduring the segregationist students' taunts—and worse—without replying in kind. She was suspended briefly in December and then again in February for getting into a fray. Persons in the North then got up a fund to send Minnijean to a private school in New York, the New Lincoln School, and she graduated from there the following year. Before she left Central High, Minnijean participated in a remarkable interview conducted for the National Broadcasting Company by a Norwegian correspondent, Mrs. Jorunn Ricketts. Five other Central students were on the program: three white girls— Sammy Dean Parker, Kay Bacon and Robin Woods—one white boy, Joseph Fox, and one Negro boy, Ernest Green. These excerpts from the transcript were printed in the *Times* on October 14, 1957:

MRS. RICKETTS: Do you think it is possible to start working this out on a more sensible basis than violent demonstration?

SAMMY: No, I don't because the South has always been against racial mixing and I think they will fight this thing to the end.... We fight for our freedom— that's one thing. And we don't have any freedom any more.

ERNEST: Sammy, you said that you don't have freedom. I wonder what do you mean by it—that you don't have freedom? You are guaranteed your freedoms in the Bill of Rights and your Constitution. You have the freedom of speech—I noticed that has been exercised a whole lot in Little Rock. The freedom of petition, the freedom of religion and the other freedoms are guaranteed to you. As far as freedom, I think that if anybody should kick about freedoms, it should be us. Because I think we have been given a pretty bad side on this thing as far as freedoms.

SAMMY: Do you call those troops freedom? I don't. And I also do not call free when you are being escorted into the school every morning.

ERNEST: You say why did the troops come here? It is because our government— our state government—went against the federal law.... Our country is set up so that we have forty-eight states and no one state has the ability to overrule our nation's government. I thought that was what our country was built around. I mean, that is why we fight. We fought in World War II together—the fellows that I know died in World War II, they died in the Korean War. I mean, why should my friends get out there and die for a cause called "democracy" when I can't exercise my rights—tell me that.

ROBIN: I agree with Ernest.

JOE: Well, Sammy, I don't know what freedom has been taken away from you because the truth there—I know as a senior myself—the troops haven't kept me from going to my classes or participating in any school activity. I mean, they're there just to keep order in case—I might use the term "hotheads"—get riled up. But I think as long as—if parents would just stay out of it and let the children of the school at Central High figure it out for themselves, I think it would be a whole lot better. I think the students are mature enough to figure it out for themselves.... As far as I'm concerned, I'll lay the whole blame of this trouble in Governor Faubus's lap.

SAMMY: I think we knew before this ever started that some day we were going to have to integrate the schools. And I think that our Governor was trying to protect all of us when he called out the National Guard—and he was trying to prepare us, I think.

ERNEST:... Well, I have to disagree... I know a student that's over there with us, Elizabeth, and that young lady, she walked two blocks, I guess—as you all know—and the mob was behind her. Did the troops break up the mob?

ROBIN:... And when Elizabeth had to walk down in front of the school I was there and I saw that. And may I say, I was very ashamed—I felt like crying—because she was so brave when she did that. And we just weren't behaving ourselves—just jeering her. I think if we had had any sort of decency, we wouldn't have acted that way. But I think if everybody would just obey the Golden Rule—do unto others as you would have others do unto you—might be the solution. How would you like to have to... walk down the street with everybody yelling behind you like they yelled behind Elizabeth?

MRS. RICKETTS: Sammy, why do these children not want to go to school with Negroes?

SAMMY: Well, I think it is mostly race mixing.

MRS. RICKETTS: Race mixing? What do you mean?

SAMMY: Well, marrying each other.

MINNIJEAN: Hold your hand up. I'm brown, you are white. What's the difference? We are all of the same thoughts. You're thinking about your boy—he's going to the Navy. I'm thinking about mine—he's in the Air Force. We think about the same thing.

SAMMY: I'll have to agree with you.

ERNEST: Well, getting back to this intermarriage and all that. I don't know [where] people get all that. Why do I want to go to school? To marry with someone? I mean, school's not a marriage bureau.... I'm going there for an education. Really, if I'm going there to socialize, I don't need to be going to school. I can stand out on the corner and socialize, as far as that.

MINNIJEAN: Kay, Joe and Robin—Do you know anything about me, or is it just that your mother has told you about Negroes?...

MRS. RICKETTS:... Have you ever really made an effort to try to find out what they're like?

KAY: Not until today.

SAMMY: Not until today.

MRS. RICKETTS: And what do you think about it after today?

KAY: Well, you know that my parents and a lot of the other students and their parents think that the Negroes aren't equal to us. But—I don't know. It seems like they are to me.

SAMMY: These people are—we'll have to admit that.

ERNEST: I think like we're doing today, discussing our different views... if the people of Little Rock... would get together I believe they would find out a different story—and try to discuss the thing instead of getting out in the street and kicking people around and calling names—and all that sort of thing. If... people got together it would be smoothed over.

KAY: I think that if... our friends had been getting in this discussion today, I think that maybe some of them—not all of them—in time would change their mind. But probably some of them would change their mind today.

SAMMY: I know now that it isn't as bad as I thought it was—after we got together and discussed it.

KAY: [Sammy and I] We both came down here today with our minds set on it [that] we weren't going to change our mind that we were fully against integration. But I know now that we're going to change our mind.

MRS. RICKETTS: What do your parents say to that?

KAY: I think I'm going to have a long talk with my parents.

Anthony Lewis, *Portrait of a Decade: The Second American Revolution* (New York: Random House, 1964), pp. 63–66.

66

THE CIVIL RIGHTS BILL OF 1957

by Charles H. Thompson

The 1957 Civil Rights Act was very weak. The editor of the *Journal of Negro Education* thus evaluated it:

On September 9, 1957, it was announced that President Eisenhower had just signed the Civil Rights Bill which had been passed by the Congress some weeks previously. The announcement reiterated the conclusions voiced by a number of people immediately after the Congress had passed the Bill, that it was a "historic" document—being the first Civil Rights Bill passed by the Congress since 1875. Time can only disclose how "historic" this act was. Recent events, however, suggest that its significance was more psychological than practical in meeting the real problems of civil rights for Negroes.

The Civil Rights Bill as finally passed and signed by the President was a considerably different document from the one originally passed by the House. The current bill still provides for a bipartisan commission to be appointed by the President and confirmed by the Senate, and makes provision for the creation of a Civil Rights Division in the Department of Justice under the specific supervision of an assistant attorney general. Unlike the original bill, however, it is confined exclusively to the protection of the right to vote. Title III, which dealt with other aspects of civil rights, was eliminated in its entirety. In fact, the original measure was so drastically amended by the Senate that question was raised on the part of its proponents as to whether it would be better to carry the fight over to the next session of Congress and try to obtain a better bill, or whether it would be better strategy to accept the current bill, rather than no bill at all.

As is now known the latter alternative prevailed. The rationalization underlying this move varied, but can be summarized briefly under two heads. First, there were those who urged acceptance of the bill because, while it was not satisfactory, it seemed to them to represent a first step, and it was thought to be wiser to accept what could be got now and work for amendments later. It is reported that the NAACP represented this point of view. Second, there were those who conceded that the Bill had fallen below original expectations, but that it still provided so much more than Negroes had that it would be a decided gain. It was reported that this was the view of the Eisenhower administration.

Despite its limitations, this Act has been designated by some people as "historic," and primarily, it seems, because it is the first piece of civil rights legislation to come out of the Congress in 82 years. Whether this fact is sufficient to warrant the characterization of "historic," of course, is open to question. In fact, it is even debatable whether the provisions of the Act itself are of such outstanding significance as to add sufficient weight to the characterization to justify it without serious question.

Whether this Act should be characterized as "historic" or not, several observations should be noted. First, it would be very misleading to assume, as a number of the proponents of this Act have assumed, that if Negroes are assured the right to vote in all areas of this country, they can thereby secure for themselves all or even most of the civil rights to which they are entitled. While the untrammelled right of Negroes to vote would be very helpful in any effort to obtain and maintain their civil rights, events past and present indicate that it is not a decisive factor, and, in view of the Negro's minority status, could not be decisive.

What is even more important, however, is the fact that some of the most crucial civil rights of Negroes are outside of the area which possession of the ballot could be expected to protect; for example, the right to be free from discrimination in employment, or more recently, to be free from economic and other reprisals. The most serious and critical disadvantage which Negroes suffer at present is economic, and much, if not most, of it is due to race. For example, in 1949 the median income of Negro families in the District of Columbia was only 64 percent of the median income of white families; but according to a recent survey, for 1956, it was found that the gap instead of closing had widened, so that the median income of Negro families was only 59 percent of the median income of white families. The elimination of Title III from the current bill makes it practically impossible to do anything realistic about this situation.

It should be emphasized that those who insist that the current bill is only a first step in the direction of securing civil rights for Negroes are undoubtedly correct. It is our hope that they will make every effort to see that this step is immediately followed by others which will more realistically meet the Negro's civil rights problem.

Journal of Negro Education 26: (Fall 1957) 433–34.

67

ON VOTING

by an Anonymous African-American

Sometime in the 1950s in Florida at a voting league rally, an unidentified person said:

There's one thing the Negro has that the white man wants but can't get unless you give it to him. That's your vote. He can take your home, your family, your possessions, even your life, and often nothing can be done about it. But the law prohibits him from going into the voting booth with you. He can offer you a million dollars for your vote, but he can't get it unless you give it to him.

Hugh D. Price, *The Negro and Southern Politics* (New York: New York University Press, 1957), p. 112.

68

THE NEW HEAVEN AND THE NEW EARTH

by Howard Thurman

The Reverend Dr. Thurman, dean, Marsh Chapel, Boston University, was one of the most provocative among Afro-American intellectuals in the post–World War II era. Here is an address he gave November 12, 1957, at Virginia Union University; the occasion commemorated the 125th anniversary of the American Baptist Home Mission Society.

In reflecting upon the interpretation of certain aspects of the American Negroes' encounter with higher education, one fact stood out clearly in my mind. I could never find, see, or talk with any college-trained Negro who was not discouraged. Why? Because the response to the impact of higher education was one of frustration. And frustration is what a man experiences when he is unable to achieve the thing which he seeks to achieve. This frustration, in turn, becomes tragedy when a man is convinced that he is unable to achieve something because of some weakness in himself. Or again, frustration becomes tragedy when it finds expression in terms of compromise. In other words, a man may decide that the thing which he seeks has no reality for him at the level of his living. Therefore, of necessity, he must scale down his desires and dreams so that they will come within the reach of possibility.

This is very illuminating if we look at it carefully and apply it to what is happening in higher education with us. Many times in the past, we shifted vocational aspirations for the things we really wanted to do because in our society those goals were unachievable. When I was in college, for instance, there were certain vocational goals you just didn't have. They were unrealistic despite the fact that they were like fires kindled in you as a result of your exposure to what was involved in higher education. You scaled your demands down so that they would come within reach of being achieved by one located in society as you are located. Then there was another way that we dealt with frustration. We looked at our environment and sought to operate on our environment in order to bring within our reach the goals which we have envisioned for ourselves.

It is important to point out that something also happened to higher education when it sought to communicate and to bring the full impact of its insight and resources to the minds of American Negroes. Higher education had to make an adjustment. This adjustment caused it to become a practitioner of the cult of inequality. It did not deliberately set out to be an apostle of inequality, but in its adjustment to these new demands, it began compromising in various ways. One of the things that evolved was a distinction between higher education generally and Negro higher education, in particular. For a long time, for instance, Howard University's Medical School was a Class A Negro medical school. What kind of medical school is that—Class A, Negro?

Changes were wrought which made the medical school just Class A, period. But this was one of the ways in which higher education became a handmaiden of the cult of inequality. Such an emphasis invaded the curricular offering. When I was an undergraduate at Morehouse College, I wanted to study philosophy. My mind was full of questions that only this kind of discipline would help me understand. The curriculum provided for no such offering. There was logic for a half year and a wonderful course in ethics, so called, which gave the president the opportunity to become acquainted intimately with the seniors and to expose them to his working philosophy, but it didn't teach you anything about ethics as a discipline. This was not an accident, and in this regard, Morehouse was not unique. For if students are exposed to the creative process which causes them to raise profound questions about meanings and to seek answers, they may go on to raise questions about the structure of the institution which made it possible for them to get their college education. In other words, the total issue involving the segregated schools in our society would have to be dealt with.

There was another element that was present in the dynamics of this situation. It was the ethical imperative growing out of the Christian commitment which established the missionary schools. These schools were segregated, of necessity, but within the ethical imperative, no category existed for the segregated schools within the missionary movement. The missionaries themselves were faced with the same problem which faced higher education. How can you put at the disposal of the students the full and boundless insight of the Christian ethic and the moral imperative which it carries, and at the same time, not become a handmaiden of the cult of inequality? Some kind of adjustment had to be made. How could the problem be counteracted so as to produce students who were emotionally healthy?

One of the first steps was to find teachers who had points of view that could not quite be contained within a segregated structure. Among them were people who had a profound sense of mission in their work and were well trained. Such persons quietly withered as they found themselves working in a "foreign country," and unable to identify either with the Negroes to whom they ministered or with the white persons who lived in the cities in which the institutions were located. How to do effective work under such circumstances was the crucial issue.

One solution was to accept segregation without raising any question beyond the fact. The profound immorality of segregation is that it limits the area of the magnetic field of ethical and moral responsibility. To make clear my meaning: When I was a boy in Florida, I joined the church at the age of 12. I believed in the Kingdom of God. I was an active worker in the church and had reasonable intelligence. But it did not ever cross even the periphery of my awareness that I should recognize any moral responsibility to any of the white people in Daytona, Florida. They were not within the area of my ethical awareness. They were ethically out of bounds. What was true for me was true for any young white boy who may have belonged to the First Baptist Church, uptown. This is the immorality of segregation. He was not within the area of my ethical awareness; I was not in the area of his ethical awareness.

I remember vividly one day when I was raking leaves in Mrs. Blochard's yard as a part of my work in the afternoon after school, I had a traumatic experience with her little daughter. As fast as I raked the leaves into a pile, she would go through the pile picking out beautiful colored leaves and show them to me or put them in another pile. This meant that I had to do my work over and over again. Finally I said to her, "If you don't stop, I will tell your mother and she will make you go in the house." Her reaction: She reached into her little pinafore, found a straight pin, came over, and stuck me with it. I reacted to the pain; whereupon she said, "Why did you do that? You can't feel." This is the graphic and monumental godless iniquity of segregation.

It posed a crucial problem for all who came under the aegis of the profound missionary commitment to find a way to broaden the area of ethical awareness. They were handicapped in doing it because they themselves were rootless and were working on a frontier far removed from the congregation in the North which gave to them a sense of belonging.

There belongs also in this picture another important element. Gradually young Negro teachers educated for the most part in the North came into the schools. They were educated at Amherst, or Williams, or Mt. Holyoke, or some other Eastern institution. They had had the experience of education in an entirely different kind of environment. When those of us who had never been in the kind of environment in which they had studied came into contact with them, the ceiling of our own hopes was raised in a new way. They talked about things that were utterly foreign to our way of life and thought. I remember the first time I heard one of these men talk about his experience in being elected to Phi Beta Kappa. They tended to be very exacting and were unwilling to accept extenuating circumstances as justification for poor work and bad preparation. They did not seem to be willing to take into account the kind of distorted personalities that segregation had produced in us. What the white missionary had pointed to us as possibilities for us tended not to seem real because they were people from another world, a world that did not know segregation. When young Negro teachers began saying these same things to us, the possibilities of higher education extended now beyond the limited boundaries of self-service.

The problem that now posed itself was, can you operate within a context of segregation in a manner that will release the mind for a creative attack on the fact of segregation. If I may speak personally again, it was at this point that my understanding of Booker T. Washington was a source of great inspiration to me. It seemed to me that what Mr. Washington said in his life and work was this: You must make your hands commit to memory skills with raw materials so that they will be able to create something that has a utility value in the open market. The thing you create can be exchanged for economic goods, thus guaranteeing the economic stability of your life and enabling you to free your mind to brood effectively and creatively over the problems inherent in segregated living.

When this concept is applied at the level of higher education, then the service motive is structured in a new way. It goes something like this. If you can acquire certain professional skills so that you can administer to certain needs of your own community, within the segregated community, then you will be able to establish economic security within this closed circuit. Hence, for a long time, the professional ceiling was established around the ministry, medicine, dentistry, and teaching. The law and social work came later. It was a simple step to broaden this concept so that the professional intent would include any person whose needs you could meet without regard to whether that person was located within or without the so called segregated world. . . .

While all these things were taking place, something else was happening on the broad stage of American and world life. The operation of the forces about which Dr. Cobb has just spoken is a case in point. Forces that from one point of view seemed blind and mindless were undermining all established patterns and structures of subjection all over the world. In a sense these were climaxed during the second world war.

Twenty-two years ago when I was in India, as I sat in a train compartment in Calcutta, a little Indian porter staggered into the compartment with a trunk on his head and two heavy pieces of luggage in his hands. He put them down and then with great effort established them securely in the luggage rack. A British colonel was waiting. When the porter finished, the colonel gave him a coin. He looked at the coin, and then looked into the face of the colonel, and tossed the coin back so that it struck the colonel on the nose. Immediately the colonel struck the Indian across the shoulders with his bamboo stick. The Indian snatched the stick from his hand, broke it on his bony knees, and threw it out of the train window. The train started moving and the porter jumped out of the train and ran along side pouring out expletives which I could not understand but I could feel. All the way to his destination, the colonel kept muttering to himself; the only thing that I could hear was a repetition of the phrase, "it's time for me to retire and leave this blank country." The force of revolution was at work.

When the Atlantic Charter was informally "formalized," and the concept of the four freedoms made manifest, the people of India wanted to know whether in the Prime Minister's judgment, these applied to India. As I remember it, the expressed or implied reply was a negative one. Mr. Roosevelt, however, had to say that it applied to everybody. Now why did he have to say this? The Allied Nations were faced with a new kind of enemy, the enemy who could not be opposed by the enthusiasm which was built around a slogan like "Save The World For Democracy." The enemy this time had a hard core of purpose around which everything was oriented. The word "fascism" became the symbol of a faith. It defined man in concrete terms. It declared what was to be the nature of the new order which it would bring into being. Everything was spelled out in detail. This left no live option for the democracies. They had to match this, idea for idea, fact for fact. They could not meet psychologically or philosophically a concrete definition of fascism with broad generalizations about the meaning of democracy. This demand created for the democracies a very real problem. The degree to which they spelled out the meaning of democracy in clear cut working definitions, to that degree did they create unrest within the democracy, for now people who felt that they were denied democratic practice within the countries themselves could have this denial defined in the light of definitions created by the necessity to combat fascism. The rest of the story is recent history.

The irony is that the Christian community has so often been less articulate in this regard than the state. Its members have the spiritually humiliating experience of seeing the secular forces take positions which they were unable to match even in the name of their ethical imperative. Long after the formal abolishing of segregation in the armed forces, the Christian Church remained segregated. This is what I mean.

Finally, the combination of all of these forces and many others which time will not permit me to enumerate creates a situation in which the impact of higher education on the Negro can issue in courage, enthusiasm, and hope, rather than frustration. For the forces that are at work in the environment, making for community, are at last beginning to work in him, causing him to be able to make more and more an unconditional response to the fruits of learning. To make an unconditional response to the impact of truth and to follow that truth wherever it leads, transcending all barriers and all contexts—it is into this new earth that the American Negro is catapulted in his encounter with higher education....

Journal of Negro Education 27 (Spring 1958): 115–119; published in part.

69

SEGREGATION IN HIGHER EDUCATION:
A CRITICAL SUMMARY (1958)

by Preston Valian

Though segregation at the college and professional level had been ruled against by the Supreme Court several years before the *Brown* decision of 1954, even there progress was quite partial. Here is a summary view of the matter published late in 1958.

Despite the rather clear mandate of the Supreme Court with respect to desegregation of tax-supported colleges, there is a wide range of variations in compliance among the states. Seven states and the District of Columbia have acted to remove all racial admission barriers in their tax-supported colleges. Since the Supreme Court decision did not affect private or church-affiliated colleges, some private colleges still remain segregated in these seven states. The situation in these seven states is as follows:

1. *Arkansas*: Seven formerly white public colleges are open to Negro students at both graduate and undergraduate levels. The one Negro state-supported college has not reported any enrollment of white students. Two private colleges have been desegregated. Philander Smith (predominantly Negro) has had white students, and College of the Ozarks has admitted Negro students.

2. *Delaware*: The two public colleges—the University of Delaware (formerly all-white) and Delaware State College (formerly all-Negro) have been desegregated. Two private schools—Goldey Beacom School of Business and Wesley Junior College—remain segregated.

3. *District of Columbia*: Wilson Teachers College (white) and Miner Teachers College (Negro) were merged to form the District of Columbia Teachers College. At present 65 per cent of the students are Negroes. All other colleges have been desegregated.

4. *Kentucky*: Thirty-one of the state's 40 colleges, including all 9 of its tax-supported colleges are desegregated. There are approximately 600 Negro students attending formerly all-white colleges and approximately 50 white students enrolled at Kentucky State College (formerly all-Negro).

5. *Maryland*: All public colleges have been desegregated in practice or in principle. Four formerly Negro public colleges have been desegregated but only one—Morgan State College—has enrolled white students. Eighteen private colleges have been desegregated.

6. *Missouri*: All 15 of the state supported colleges and universities have been desegregated and Negroes are enrolled at 10. Lincoln University (formerly all-Negro) has a large white enrollment.

7. *Oklahoma*: All 18 of Oklahoma's state supported colleges and universities and practically all of its private and independent colleges accept students without reference to race.

8. *West Virginia*: All 10 of the state's public colleges and universities eliminated racial restrictions in 1954.
   Five of the 7 private colleges have been desegregated.

In addition to the seven states named above which have desegregated all state-supported colleges, the following five states have partially desegregated their state-supported colleges:

1. *Louisiana*: Four of 7 formerly all-white public colleges have accepted Negroes.
   Four of 10 formerly all-white private colleges have accepted Negroes. Xavier University (predominantly Negro) has enrolled white students.
2. *North Carolina*: Six of the 12 formerly all-white public colleges have accepted Negroes, while one of the 5 Negro state colleges has enrolled white students.
3. *Tennessee*: The University of Tennessee has admitted Negroes only to selected graduate and professional levels. Five formerly all-white state teachers colleges have been desegregated. Tennessee A & I State University (for Negroes) had white students in 1956.

   Among the formerly all-white private colleges and universities, Vanderbilt, Peabody, the University of the South (Sewanee), and Madison will admit Negroes within some limitations, while Scarritt, Maryville and Tusculum will admit Negro students without any special restrictions. All 6 of the private Negro colleges will admit white students and four (Fisk, Meharry, Knoxville and Morristown) have white students enrolled.
4. *Texas*: Of 47 white public colleges, 27 have been desegregated. The University of Texas is open at all academic levels. Eighteen formerly all-white private colleges have been desegregated in practice or in principle, but the larger white private colleges remain segregated except for special graduate or professional courses.

   Thirty-five formerly all-white colleges reported an enrollment of 750 Negro students and 65,000 white students.
5. *Virginia*: Four of the 10 formerly all-white public colleges have approximately 90 Negroes on their campuses.

Five private colleges have been desegregated.

The following five states have not desegregated any tax-supported colleges:

1. *Alabama*: Technically, the University of Alabama is still desegregated as a result of the Arthurine Lucy case, but there have been no further applicants. Spring Hill College, a Jesuit school in Mobile, has accepted Negro students since 1951. Talladega College, a predominantly Negro college, has enrolled white students in recent years.
2. *Florida*: No desegregation in any public college, although under court order to desegregate University of Florida in September. One predominantly white Catholic college, Barry College, is reported to be willing to accept students without regard to race.

3. *Georgia*: All public colleges are segregated. One private college—Columbia Theological Seminary (Presbyterian)—accepts both Negro and white students.
4. *Mississippi*: All public colleges are segregated. One Catholic college for the training of priests is desegregated.
5. *South Carolina*: No public college has been desegregated. Allen University, a Negro college, has a white student in attendance.

In summary, of approximately 200 tax-supported formerly all-white colleges and universities in the 17 states and the District of Columbia, well over half, distributed in 12 states and the District of Columbia, will now accept Negro students. In addition, there is an undetermined but significant number of formerly all-white private and church-affiliated colleges which will now accept students without regard to race. It is worth noting that at least one of these desegregated private colleges is to be found in each of the 17 states. These private colleges are for the most part church-affiliated schools, and all the major religious denominations are represented among their sponsors.

Some General Observations

The following general observations appear to be relevant to the process of desegregation of higher education in the 17 formerly segregated-school states:

1. One of the unanticipated consequences of college desegregation has been a focusing of attention on the rôle and function of the Negro public colleges. In general this has resulted in measures to strengthen these institutions. In the District of Columbia and the seven states which have accepted college desegregation as good public policy, consideration has been directed to the place of the former Negro colleges in a desegregated educational system. In many of these seven states, the early feeling that one or more of the Negro public education facilities should be abandoned has been replaced by efforts to make these institutions more efficient and more functional. In West Virginia, for example, the land-grant functions of West Virginia State College have been transferred to the University of West Virginia, while in Kentucky, the University of Kentucky and Kentucky State College are jointly conducting cooperative extension courses for the Greater Frankfort area.
2. It is perhaps no longer surprising to note that the students in the white colleges are often far ahead of the governing boards and administrators in their acceptance of desegregation. During recent years, the University of Miami Student Senate, the graduate students of Emory University, the

students of Emory University's School of Religion, the student paper at Furman University, the students at Texas Technological College, have voted for or spoken out for desegregation. None of these schools is desegregated.

3. The resistance to college desegregation has resulted in some instances in serious violations of academic freedom, interference with internal administration of some colleges on the part of public officials, heavy faculty turnover, and, in at least one instance, a refusal by one college (Clemson) of a $350,000.00 grant for nuclear research.

4. If desegregation is defined as the process of bringing Negro and white students into the same schools by the removal of racially restrictive admission barriers, and integration is defined as the participation of Negro and white students in extra-curricular and school related activities, as well as classroom activities, it becomes apparent that we are dealing largely with desegregation and not integration in this Yearbook. In Arkansas, for example, Negro women students do not stay in the dormitories of the University of Arkansas, and at the University of Texas, Negroes are not permitted on varsity intercollegiate athletic teams. *The Daily Texan*, University of Texas campus newspaper, surveyed the situation of 173 Negroes attending class among 16,000 white students and concluded that "desegregation is not enough." It called for the "integration of all university dormitories within the next few years," removal of restrictions on Negro athletes participating in Southwest Conference competition, and elimination of discriminatory practices in campus organizations.

5. It is interesting but hardly surprising to note that the question of faculty desegregation does not yet receive serious consideration and is far more advanced in the predominantly Negro schools than in the newly desegregated formerly white schools. [James A.] Hedrick found that in a study of 348 white graduate students in four Southern universities in 1954 that 48 per cent stated that they would be willing to accept Negroes as teachers of their classes, and in two of the institutions the percentages were 70 per cent and 51 per cent.

6. A final observation is warranted on the future of the Negro college and this suggests the presumptuous rôle of prophet. It does not require prophesy, however, to interpret the action of the Southern Association of Colleges and Secondary Schools when last December, after investigating sixty-three Negro colleges, it admitted only 18 to membership. This step, in itself, appears to presage the beginning of the end of the Negro college in the traditional sense. Colleges with predominantly Negro student bodies will remain in the future, but they must be prepared to meet and surpass the educational standards set for other American colleges and universities. The Negro college has the potential to make a special contribution to the South and to the Nation because while it is located in the South, it is much less

hampered in its approach to many Southern problems than are those institutions whose energies are divided and whose objectives are confused by allegiance to regional habits which are inconsistent with national principles. The Negro College has the potential to demonstrate to the South and to the Nation what a really unsegregated institution, in spirit as well as in fact, can be. But only by accepting the coming of desegregation and integration as a challenge to achieve and to maintain the highest educational standards can the Negro college hope to fulfill its opportunity to serve as an example of democratic education.

Journal of Negro Education, 27 (Summer 1958): 373–80; published in part. Footnotes omitted. The author was chairman, Department of Social Science, Fisk University.

70

"WITH ALL DELIBERATE SPEED" (1958)

by Charles H. Thompson

An unprecedented feature of the *Brown* decisions of 1954 and 1955 was that they affirmed that implementation was *not* to be immediate but rather was to be accomplished sometime in the future "with all deliberate speed." This invited delay and new litigation, which the racists certainly provided. One case of relevance was decided in the summer of 1958; the Court reiterated that segregation in public schools was illegal. Nevertheless, it remained true that "all deliberate speed" still did not mean *now*. At best, it meant what Dr. Thompson's last paragraph in the following commentary suggested.

In a decision which is second in importance only to that in the *Brown* case, where the United States Supreme Court originally ruled that racial segregation in public education was illegal, the Court ruled again on the question on August 12, 1958, and handed down its detailed opinion on September 29, 1958.... The immediate issue decided here was whether objection to implementation of the Court's ruling, even by mob violence, was sufficient grounds for delaying implementation of the desegregation decree. But the basic issue was whether the Court really meant what it said when it ordered that desegregation should be implemented "with all deliberate speed."

The Court has answered this basic question unanimously and unequivocally in the affirmative. And this, in the face of the most demagogic vilification that this high body has received in the past 75 years; despite the notorious lack of either moral or political leadership on the part of the Chief Executive; and despite the fact that three new justices have been added to the Court since the original decision. The Court ruled unequivocally: "The constitutional rights of respondents are not to be sacrificed or yielded to the violence and disorder which have followed upon the actions of the Governor and Legislature.... [L]aw and order are not to be preserved by depriving the Negro children of their constitutional rights."

As suggested, this decision is second only to the original opinion in the *Brown* case. It was the opinion of many persons on both sides that if the Court had upheld the *Lemley* decision, it would have been tantamount to a reversal of the original decision and would have been an open invitation to all of the other states involved to attempt to frustrate the implementation of the *Brown* decision merely by a show of force. And the implementation of the desegregation decree would have been set back at least 50 years.

The Court's opinion encompassed an issue which went beyond the immediate case, but which undoubtedly would be the next subject of litigation. In fact, as the court was delivering its opinion on September 29, 1958, the Court of Appeals for the Eighth District was in the process of issuing a temporary order restraining the School Board in Little Rock from leasing public school property to a private corporation for the purpose of running segregated schools. Anticipating this development which had been announced by the Governor of Arkansas, the Court again observed unequivocally: "...the prohibitions of the Fourteenth Amendment extend to all action of the State denying equal protection of the laws, whatever the agency of the State taking the action, or whatever the guise in which it is taken. In short, the constitutional rights of children not to be discriminated against in school admission on grounds of race or color declared by this Court in the *Brown* case can neither be nullified openly and directly by state legislators or state executive or judicial officers, nor nullified indirectly by them through evasive schemes for segregation whether attempted "ingeniously or ingenuously.""

Obviously, more for the purposes of education of the public than as a rebuttal, the Court addressed itself to the demagogic contention of a number of Southern politicians that Supreme Court decisions were not the law of the land, that the responsibility for and the control of public education were vested exclusively in the State, and that the Court had no authority in the premises. The Court noted that for 155 years beginning with Chief Justice Marshall in 1803, reaffirmed by Chief Justice Taney in 1859, and by Chief Justice Hughes in 1932, it was the province and duty of the Court to say what the law is, and that every state legislator or officer was bound by his oath to support it.

As to public education, the Court observed. "It is, of course, quite true that the responsibility for public education is primarily the concern of the States, but it is equally true that such responsibilities, like all other state activity, must be exercised consistently with federal constitutional requirements as they apply to state action. The Constitution created a government dedicated to equal justice under law. The Fourteenth Amendment embodied and emphasized that ideal. *State support of segregated schools through any arrangement, management, funds, or property cannot be squared with the Amendment's command that no State shall deny to any person within its jurisdiction the equal protection of the laws.* (Emphasis added.) The right of a student not to be segregated on racial grounds in schools so maintained is indeed so fundamental and pervasive that it is embraced in the concept of due process of law."

What the next steps of the segregationists will be are not exactly clear. One thing is certain, however; namely that the phrase, "with all deliberate speed" does not mean turning back the clock, or even stopping it.

Journal of Negro Education 27 (Fall 1958): 437–38.

71

AGAIN, ON AFRICAN-AMERICAN "INTELLIGENCE"
(1958)

by Horace Mann Bond

The resurgence of "scientific racism" accompanied the White Citizens' Councils and the KKK and the assorted murderers who sought to maintain the Bourbon society. One instance of this has already been noted. Another—far from the last—appeared from a somewhat more distinguished source in 1958 and got this response by the dean, School of Education, Atlanta University.

Never before has the literature of psychology witnessed so determined an effort to establish, as a fact, the proposition that there are "native differences between Negroes and whites as determined by intelligence tests." Dr. Audrey M. Shuey, Chairman of the Department of Psychology in the Randolph-Macon College for Women, at Lynchburg, Virginia, has examined 288 studies of Negro intelligence tests and other criteria of educational and intellectual attainment. The documents examined included 35 monographs, or sections of books; 135 articles; 47 published reviews, "interpretations, criticisms, or comments;" 62 were unpublished master's theses, many from the newly established graduate schools for Negroes in the South; and 9 doctoral theses.*

By the interesting device of discarding all "interpretations, criticisms, comments," and even conclusions in individual studies, and taking the statistical tables reporting differential scores as the only, bona-fide, "results," Dr. Shuey arrives at what she calls a "remarkable consistency in test results, whether they pertain to school or pre-school children, to high school or college students, to drafts of World War I or World War II, to the gifted or the mentally deficient, to the delinquent or criminal." This "remarkable consistency" becomes the foundation of her concluding inferences, that "point to the presence of some native differences between Negroes and whites as determined by intelligence tests."

Some of the most ardent advocates of racial equality, who have provided the majority of the studies used by Dr. Shuey in this amazing *tour de force*, must feel, after reading Dr. Shuey's book, that it is a wise scholar, indeed, who can recognize his own brain-child after it has undergone the deft, assiduous surgery of this author's excisions. "One should," Dr. Shuey says blithely in her introductory chapter, "in every case distinguish the *results* from the comments or conclusions of the authors or those of the reviewers." An example is the exhumation of Howard W. Odum's 1913 Philadelphia study of 300 Negro children, that reported 21% of white children advanced one or more years above their chronological ages, while only 5% of the Negro children were so advanced. Odum is quoted as stating, in his conclusions, that "Environment alone seems sufficient to account for majority of results." But for Dr. Shuey's purposes, only the statistical figure of "racial" difference matters. Odum's "comment" may lightly be brushed aside, as "relatively subjective and...not necessarily accurate."

Similarly, Dr. Shuey brushes aside Carl C. Brigham's famous recantation, in 1930, of his previous (1923) conclusion, that Negro inferiority was

*A review of Audrey M Shuey, *The Testing of Negro Intelligence*. Foreword by Henry E. Garrett. Lynchburg, VA.; J. P. Bell and Co., 1958.

indicated by tests administered to World War I draftees. In this case Brigham's first interpretations are accepted because they are consistent with the "results," i.e., the statistical tables. His reconsideration is rejected also on the testimony of Dr. Henry E. Garrett (Dr. Shuey's mentor and contributor of the *Foreword* to the book), that Brigham did not know what he was saying in 1930. "Environmentalists" whose studies contribute grist to Dr. Shuey's mill include this reviewer, whose 1926 study of Oklahoma Negro teachers is reported as part of the total pattern of "remarkable consistency;" studies by Clark Foreman, with whom this reviewer collaborated; and even such staunch equalitarians as William C. Bagley and Otto Klineberg. Besides this reviewer, Negro students who are made, through Dr. Shuey's curious form of assessing "evidence," to appear as heralds of their own native inferiority, include A. S. Beckham, Ambrose Caliver, H. G. Canady, R. P. Daniel, Allison Davis, R. K. Davenport, T. E. Davis, Charles S. Johnson, Howard H. Long, Martin D. Jenkins, and many others.

Suffice it here to say, that this method carries the classic concept of the scientific method in the physical sciences, and animal experimentation, to an application to research carried out under other philosophies of causation, in a degree that neither Niels Bohr nor W. Heisenberg would now find acceptable in interpreting research in physics. Dr. Shuey's unique determination, and method, provoke interest in her career, and in the motives that prompted this work of infinite, indefatigable labor. She is a native of Rockford, Illinois, born in 1900, who took her doctorate at Columbia University in 1931. An instructor in New York University from 1929–1934, she has been in the faculty of the Randolph-Macon Woman's College since that time, enjoying rapid promotions to her present position as Chairman of the Department of Psychology.

While the present volume is her *magnum opus*, eleven previous articles are listed in the *Educational Index* and *Psychological Abstracts*. It is important to note that Dr. Shuey began her research as a student of animal learning; the method and predispositions of the classic animal experimenter, and geneticist, are apparent in her present review of the literature involving one aspect of human learning. Her first published article dealt with "Some experiments with kittens on the simple alternation problem." Three of her articles have had Jewish subjects; one, on the defect of color-blindness among Jewish students, and two on the intelligence of Jewish students. Her conclusions were that the oft-heralded superiority in intelligence of the Jewish student, when compared to native-born American Protestant whites, was a myth. It was shortly after the publication of the latter article that Dr. Shuey left her post as Instructor at New York University to assume her duties at Randolph-Macon.

Dr. Shuey's only previous publication in the field of "racial psychology" appears to have been one in which she described the "results" of "matching" 33 pairs of white and Negro co-eds at New York University, the "results" showing the inferiority of the Negroes.

Before undertaking this review, the writer consulted several of the authorities on the art and science of book-reviewing. He discovered that it was his duty to his readers, to ask, "What seems to have been the author's purpose in writing this book?"

It is not a difficult question to answer, although Dr. Shuey never clearly indicates what her purpose was. She does deplore what she regards as defects in existing text-books in General Psychology, in the treatment of Negro-white differences. She states that "Negro-white differences are likely to be dealt with summarily," that "there is a considerable unanimity among the authors in the treatment of the problem of Negro intelligence," that there are "equivocal headings" that lean toward environmental explanations of Negro-white differences. She notes an apparent favoritism on the part of the text-book authors, in quoting only a few studies of racial differences, such as those based on World War I comparisons, Klineberg's studies of *Selective Migration*, and Martin D. Jenkins' study of *Superior Negro Children*. She finds that existing literature holds "the concept of race itself to be indefinite (or confused) and consider it hazardous for psychologists to base conclusions on insecure anthropological foundations." She feels strongly that a new and more comprehensive treatment of the subject is needed: she says of current works,

In accounting for the stated or inferred differences in test scores achieved by Negroes and whites, all of the authors have taken a common point of view represented by such statements as: intelligence tests presuppose a common cultural and educational background which does not exist; no test is completely free from a cultural bias; test gains can be expected from improved environment; and socio-economic differences in the United States vitiate differences in intelligence test scores.

Additionally, "existing books stress the variability within groups; and the majority of the authors consider the racial results to be inconclusive." Finally, "they appear to favor the environmental interpretation, generally giving it the last word."

As these deficiencies in existing textbooks constitute the outline of Dr. Shuey's book, and her conclusions neatly disagree with what she says the majority of psychologists believe, her one explanation as to why she wrote the book seems slightly more than disingenuous: "...it may be that there are students who would desire a more comprehensive survey of the field of Negro intelligence. It is for the last group, of course, that this book is written."

One could take the enormous amount of time required to carry on the detailed examination of the numerous sources here reviewed, only if one were gripped by a sense of enormous importance of the task. It is clear that Dr. Shuey wrote this book for the reasons that any author (including the present reviewer) has ever written a book. One writes a book of this sort because one has a mighty impulsion to do so. Dr. Shuey believes that the fact of racial differences is enormously important, that the inferiority of the Negro is likewise a fact of tremendous importance, and she has written a book to reveal her impulsion and to set forth the views she thinks neglected in existing sources of information. This reviewer is informed, that the book is being widely circularized in such a battleground of "integration," as Florida; there is a further ascription of this free circulation to such organizations as the White Citizens' Councils.

The polemic *Foreword* contributed by Dr. Garrett sets the tone of the book. He states that "...a number of well meaning but often insufficiently informed writers have taken the position that racial differences ought not to be found; or, if found, should immediately be explained away as being somehow immoral or reprehensible."

Is this true? This reviewer is unfamiliar with any scholars in the field who have taken the position imputed to "some" by Dr. Garrett.

This reviewer, however, has taken, since his first publication, in 1924, of an article, "Intelligence Tests and Propaganda" (*The Crisis*, June, 1924), the stand that the results of intelligence tests could better be explained by environmental, than genetic, causations. He has also maintained the view, that a great many efforts to attach genetic explanations to intelligence test results were obviously, and not "somehow," "immoral *and* reprehensible." Note that we do not here impute either quality, personally, either to Dr. Garrett, nor to Dr. Shuey; we believe them to be utterly sincere, "well meaning *and* insufficiently informed," laboring under a great impulsion whose nature they themselves do not consciously understand.

In this we are more charitable than Dr. Garrett, who does impute dishonesty to those who disagree with his own interpretation of intelligence test scores, and those of Dr. Shuey's. In that deliciously defensive style long familiar to students of sub-liminal racial attitudes and prejudices ("Some of my best friends are Jews," or "I had a Negro mammy myself,") he adds: "I welcome every *honest* effort to aid Negroes in improving their status as American citizens, *but* I do not believe that it is necessary to 'prove' that no racial differences exist, nor to conceal and gloss them over, if found, in order to justify a fair policy toward Negroes." And, in another revealing non-sequitur, "The *honest* psychologist, like any true scientist, has no preconceived racial bias."

Methinks the gentleman protests too much.

Dr. Shuey's minutiae of test "results" is too detailed to permit references, in this review, to a number—indeed, 288—of specific references quoted. One specific question is, why did Dr. Shuey refer five times to one master's thesis from Fisk University—that of T. E. Davis—and refer only once, and then incidentally, to Kenneth Eell's now classic field study of *Intelligence and Cultural Differences* in Rockford, Illinois—her native city?

After all, Dr. Shuey's ground rules reduce the "evidence," and the area of controversy, to the "results." Dr. Shuey has defined as "results"; i.e., the frequency tables reporting scores and I.Q.'s. Indeed, one wonders why the author did not content herself merely with statistical tables. This reviewer, and, I believe, almost every psychologist in the Nation, would have cheerfully agreed with Dr. Shuey's final contention, that almost anywhere in the United States, an "intelligence test" given to unselected groups of Negroes and whites, would show superior scores for the white subjects. The writer would conclude that this simply means that everywhere in the United States, the American Negro is a subordinated, underprivileged social caste; while Dr. Shuey takes these "results" to mean that the Negro is innately inferior in intelligence, to white persons. So far as "Negro Intelligence" is concerned, the book adds nothing to our knowledge of the field.

Two general questions can, and need, to be asked. Both have to do with the general principle of "honesty" gratuitously raised by Dr. Garrett's *Foreword*.

Much of the apparent, overwhelming weight of Dr. Shuey's "evidence" comes from her practise of comparing the attainment of Negro students with national norms, in studies quoted by her that deal only with Negro subjects. For example, note her citation of a study made by this reviewer in 1926, of Oklahoma Negro teachers. It was manifestly impossible, in 1926, and perhaps today, for a Negro researcher to administer tests to Oklahoma white teachers. I was, perforce, obliged to use national norms as a basis for comparison. Obviously, had I been able to test Oklahoma white teachers, the differences between my two local samples would have been far less, and perhaps even non-existent, as compared to the differences that show up when my Negro results are set against the national norm background.

In no less than 178 cases, Dr. Shuey compared reported results of tests administered to Negro children, in all Negro researches, with national norms. Most of these instances were in the South, and the studies were carried on by Negroes who, manifestly, would have found it impossible to test white subjects in the same neighborhood.

Is this the work of an "honest" psychologist, Dr. Garrett?

The second general question this reviewer must raise, is perhaps an impertinence when addressed to a feminine, feline psychologist. It is the question of the consistency with which Dr. Shuey's "results" and "inferences" may be applied to other material reported by her, but not discussed in her text.

My question arises from the fact that for many years it has been noted that white Southerners invariably score below white Northerners on intelligence tests. Loyal as I am to my native section, and to my environmentalistic, social-inheritance predispositions, I have stoutly resisted the animadversions of my white Yankee acquaintances, who would like to explain this set of facts on the theory that Southern white persons are the descendants of the degenerate portion of the American Anglo-Saxon heritage. Say I: "Southern whites *do* score below Northern whites; but this is due to the circumstances of historic and contemporary educational, cultural, and social disadvantages, to which residents of the section have been immemorially exposed, as compared to Northern whites."

Perhaps unwittingly (although we Southerners can never really trust these Yankees in our midst!), Dr. Shuey's material is so extensive that it provides the most damaging evidence ever assembled, to document this damnable Yankee insinuation. Her own "results," that must inevitably lead to the conclusion that there are "some native differences between Northern and Southern whites, as determined by intelligence tests," are set forth in Table I, below.* As will be seen, at every point, and in each study quoted, the Northern whites score above Southern whites.

In short: Dr. Shuey, is it true what they say about Dixie?

*The table is omitted–ed.

Journal of Negro Education 27 (Fall 1958) 519–23. The "scientific racism" literature reached a climax in the 1961 publication (by Public Affairs Press in Washington) of Carleton Putnam's *Race and Reason: A Yankee View*, a book officially embraced by Mississippi and Louisiana. In December 1961 the American Anthropological Association felt obliged to adopt—unanimously—a resolution "reaffirming the fact that there is no scientifically established evidence to justify the exclusion of any race from the rights guaranteed by the Constitution of the United States....All races possess the abilities needed to participate fully in the democratic way of life and in modern technological civilization." See James Graham Cook, *The Segregationists* (New York: Appleton-Century-Crofts, 1962), pp. 351–356.

72

THE TIME IS NOW (1958)

by Paul Robeson

The shameless hounding and persecution of Paul Robeson—involving relentless activity by J. Edgar Hoover's FBI—is better understood when one examines Robeson's own views, ideas, and words. This opportunity is available in his book *Here I Stand*; it could find no "reputable" publisher in the 1950s, and so Othello Publishers was created. (Lloyd L. Brown, whose work has appeared elsewhere, was decisive in this.) The book went unreviewed and unnoticed by the dominant media of the time. Parts of chapters 4 and 5 are reprinted; their prophetic quality as to the developments in the ensuing years will be clear to an attentive reader:

As I see it, the challenge which today confronts the Negro people in the United States can be stated in two propositions:

1. Freedom can be ours, here and now: the long-sought goal of full citizenship under the Constitution is now within our reach.
2. We have the power to achieve that goal: what we ourselves do will be decisive.

These two ideas are strongly denied or seriously doubted by many in our land, and the denial and doubt are demonstrated both by action and inaction in the crisis of our time. Let me begin by discussing the first proposition.

Those who are openly our enemies—the avowed upholders of the myth of White Supremacy—have bluntly stated their position on the matter: Not now and not ever shall the Jim Crow system be abolished. "*Let me make this clear,*" declared Eastland, the foremost spokesman for this group, in a Senate speech ten days after the Supreme Court outlawed school segregation, "*the South will retain segregation.*" And the strength of this viewpoint was shown when a hundred other Senators and Representatives from the South signed a manifesto in which they denounced the Court's decision and pledged that they would resist enforcement. The whole world has seen how these defiant words have become defiant deeds.

Others, who claim to be our friends, insist that the immediate enforcement of our lawful rights is not possible. We must wait, we are told, until the hearts of those who persecute us have softened—until Jim Crow dies of old age. This idea is called "Gradualism." It is said to be a practical and constructive way to achieve the blessings of democracy for colored Americans. But the idea itself is but another form of race discrimination: in no other area of our society are lawbreakers granted an indefinite time to comply with the provisions of law. There is nothing in the 14th and 15th Amendments, the legal guarantees of our full citizenship rights, which says that the Constitution is to be enforced "gradually" where Negroes are concerned....

The viewpoint that progress must be slow is rooted in the idea that democratic rights, as far as Negroes are concerned, are not inalienable and self-evident as they are for white Americans. Any improvement of our status as second-class citizens is seen as a matter of charity and tolerance. The Negro must rely upon the good will of those in places of power and hope that friendly persuasion can somehow and some day make blind prejudice see the light.

This view is dominant in the upper levels of government and society throughout the land. It is easy for folks on the top to take a calm philosophical view and to tell those who bear the burden to restrain themselves and wait for justice to come. And, Lord knows, my people have been patient and long-suffering: they have a quality of human goodness, of tenderness and generosity that few others have. As the New York *Times* put it: "When one regards the violent history of nationalism and racism in the rest of the world, one must be thankful for the astonishing gentleness and good humor of the Negroes in the United States."

But patience can wear out—and if the patience of some of us wore out before that of others, it doesn't matter today. The plain fact is that a great many Negroes are thinking in terms of *now*, and I maintain and shall seek to prove that the goal of equal-rights-now can be achieved.

It has been said, and largely forgotten, that by the year 1963, the centennial of the Emancipation Proclamation, full freedom should be won. Well, I believe that still. The year of 1963 can indeed celebrate the winning of full citizenship rights, in fact and not only on paper, for every Negro in every city, county and state in this land. In 1963 a Negro statesman from Mississippi can be sitting in the Senate seat now disgraced by Eastland, just as the Negro Senator Hiram Revels once replaced the traitor Jeff Davis in that same office. I say that Jim Crow— and "Gradualism" along with it—can be buried so deep it can never rise again, and that this can be done now, in our own time!

Is this but a dream, a fantasy that "can't happen here"? For an answer let us look with our eyes wide open at the world around us: let us look to the reality of our day, the *changed situation* which indicates that the time is ripe, that the opportunity is here.

The changed situation is this: *Developments at home and abroad have made it imperative that democratic rights be granted to the Negro people without further delay*. A century has passed since Frederick Douglass pointed out that "The relations subsisting between the white and black people of this country is the central question of the age," and a half century since Dr. Du Bois proclaimed that "The problem of the twentieth century is the problem of the Color Line." Today we see that the prophetic truth of those statements has grown a thousandfold, and that the time has come when the question of the age and the problem of the century must be resolved.

It is obvious today that the issue of Negro rights is a central question in our national life. A typical comment is that of the editors of *Look* magazine who see in this issue "America's greatest legal, political and emotional crisis since the Civil War"; and typical, too, is the opinion of the New York *Times* that "a social revolution with profound implications for domestic accord and world leadership confronts this country today." But in all of the discussion of this question which fills the press and the air waves and which resounds from platform, pulpit and conference table, little light is shed on the basic factors that are involved.

It is not merely a matter of "domestic accord" that is involved in our national crisis. The fact is that constitutional government in the United States cannot be maintained if Negroes are restricted to second-class citizenship. President Eisenhower, against his will and inclination, was compelled to recognize that the very structure of our government was imperiled by the defiance of Faubus in Little Rock; and for the first time since Reconstruction days Federal troops were moved in to uphold the Constitution. But the Administration and the dominant group it represents has not as yet been compelled to recognize an even more fundamental question: democracy cannot survive in a racist America. When a government spokesman appeals to the White Supremacists "to remember America as well as their prejudices," he reflects the persistent blindness of those who still hope to eat their cake and have it, too.

I say that it is utterly false to maintain, as so many do, that the crux of the issue is personal prejudice. In a baseball game, a umpire's decision may be based upon some prejudice *in his mind*, but a state law that makes it a crime for Negroes to play baseball with whites is a statute *on the books*. The Jim Crow laws and practices which deny equal rights to millions of Negroes in the South—and not only in the South!—are not private emotions and personal sentiments: they are a system of legal and extralegal *force* which violates and nullifies the Constitution of the United States.

We know that this condition has prevailed for many years, and it might be asked at this point: Why can't it go on like this for years to come? What compelling factor in our national life calls for a change at this time?

The answer is: The interests of the overwhelming majority of the American people demand that the Negro question be solved. It is not simply a matter of justice for a minority: what is at stake is a necessity for all. Just as in Lincoln's time the basic interests of the American majority make it necessary to strike down the system of Negro enslavement, so today those interests make it necessary to abolish the system of Negro second-class citizenship.

Increasingly it is becoming clear that the main roadblock to social progress in our country—for labor, for education, for public health and welfare—is that very group which stubbornly opposes equal rights for Negroes. The 100 Congressional signers of the Southern manifesto against desegregation are not only the foes of the Negro minority: they are a powerful reactionary force against the people as a whole. Holding office by virtue of Negro disfranchisement and reelected term after term by the

votes of a handful of whites, these lawless Dixiecrats are lawmakers for
the entire nation. The White Supremacy they espouse does not elevate the
white workers in industry or the poor white farmers, and they have helped
promote and maintain the economic process that has drained off most of
the wealth from Southern resources and has made that section much
poorer than the rest of the country.

The upholders of "states' rights" against the Negro's rights are at the
same time supporters of the so-called "right-to-work" laws against the
rights of the trade unions. The reactionary laws which have undermined
the gains of Roosevelt's New Deal—the anti-labor Taft-Hartley Act, the
anti-foreign-born Walter-McCarran Act, the thought-control Smith Act—
all were strongly backed by the Dixiecrats in Congress. Until their
political power is broken, there can be no real social or economic progress
for the common people anywhere, North or South. Indeed, it is clear that
not only will there be no progress, but there will be further retrogression
unless this political cancer is removed from public life.

The attention of the nation is focused now on the words and deeds of
those who are resisting the Supreme Court's decision that segregated
schools are unlawful. The national conscience, which has for so long
tolerated segregation as a "local custom," cannot and will not permit the
defenders of Jim Crow to substitute mob violence and anarchy for
constitutional government. The conflict today pertains mainly to the
schools, but the signers of the Southern manifesto were not wrong when
they saw the Court's decision as a threat to the "habits, customs, traditions
and way of life" of White Supremacy. If the evil doctrine of "separate but
equal" was struck down in reference to public schools, how can it be
lawful in any other area of public life?

The die has been cast: segregation must go. The White Citizens
Councils may foment mob resistance, and Southern senators and governors may rant and rave against a new Reconstruction, and the President
may try to look the other way—but the vast majority of Americans, the
indifferent and lukewarm as well as the most progressive, are not going to
give up their democratic heritage in order to deny that heritage to fellow
citizens who are colored.

We know, of course, that the democratic-minded majority is slow to
move, and that the poison of race prejudice has deeply corroded the whole
of our national life. The make-up of the Federal government is not too
different from the state governments in the South: it, too, is a white man's
government. Not a single Negro is a member of the powerful Senate and

there are only three among the 435 members of the House of Representatives. Legislation in behalf of civil rights could not be defeated or emasculated by the Dixiecrats without the support of Congressmen from other parts of the country....

That other factor—relentless, powerful, compelling—is the pressure of world opinion against racism in the United States. This pressure is widely recognized in our national life, and both the pressure and our recognition of it are constantly growing. The case of Emmett Till, lynched in Mississippi, and of Autherine Lucy, barred from the University of Alabama, aroused a storm of condemnation from beyond our borders; and the story of Little Rock—in words and pictures—shook the world. Indeed, the pressure of world opinion was itself an important factor in the very decision of the Supreme Court which evoked the defiance of the Arkansas governor. In his argument in support of school desegregation, the Attorney General of the United States reminded the high tribunal that "The existence of race discrimination against minority groups in the United States has an adverse effect upon our relations with other countries."...

What, then, has brought about the persistent and growing pressure from all parts of the world on this issue? One cause is the shattering experience of World War II—the untold havoc and horror committed by Nazis in their drive to win domination for their so-called Master Race. Millions were slain and millions more suffered disaster. The world has learned the terrible lesson of Hitler: racism, backed by the power and technology of a modern industrial state, is a monster that must never be unleashed again. What difference is there between the Master Race idea of Hitler and the White Supremacy creed of Eastland? Who can convince the European peoples that the burning cross of the white-robed Klan is different from the swastika of the Brownshirts? America, of course, is not a fascist nation, but the deep-rooted racism here and its violent outbursts arouse the worst fears of those who survived the holocaust of Hitlerism.

Those who tell the world that racism in American life is merely a fading hangover from the past, and that it is largely limited to one section of our country, cannot explain away the infamous Walter-McCarran Immigration Act passed by Congress since the war. No decree of Nazi Germany was more fully racist than this American law which is, in the words of Senator Lehman, "based on the same discredited racial theories from which Adolf Hitler developed the infamous Nuremberg Laws." Look how our immigration quotas are allotted: from Ireland's 3 million people, 17,000 may come to our country each year; but from India, with her 400 millions, the quote is—100! Usually we Negroes do not think much about immigration laws because we've been here for centuries, but in our midst there are many from the West Indies, and their talents and vitality have been important to our communities far beyond their numbers. Under the Walter-McCarran law, with all of its provisions to reduce "non-Nordic" immigration, the number of Negroes who can come from the Caribbean or anywhere else has been drastically cut down.

After the defeat of Hitlerism, the nations came together in a worldwide organization; and our country, which had not belonged to the old League of Nations, became a leading force in the United Nations. Founded in San Francisco and making its headquarters in New York, the U.N. brought the eyes of the world upon the United States. From the outset, Negro leaders of vision saw in the new organization a new opportunity to win backing for their people's democratic demands. Shortly before he was ousted from his leading post in the National Association for the Advancement of Colored People (which he had helped to found), Dr. Du Bois addressed an appeal for Negro rights to the U.N. In that historic document, he pointed out that racism in America was now an international problem. He wrote:

A discrimination practiced in the United States against her own citizens and to a large extent in contravention of her own laws, cannot be persisted in without infringing upon the rights of the peoples of the world....This question, then, which is without doubt primarily an internal and national question, becomes inevitably an international question, and will in the future become more and more international as the nations draw together.

That is exactly what has come to pass, and those in our midst who were too blind to see that truth ten years ago can read it today in the headlines of the world. The U.N. itself reflects the great changes that have come about "as the nations draw together." Today there are twenty-nine nations in the Asian-African bloc in the U.N., and as the roll call of the General Assembly is taken we hear the names of new nations that are members now—among them African nations like Ghana and Sudan and others. Like a great barometer the U.N. registers the changing climate of the world as the wave of colonial liberation sweeps onward....

It is high time for Negro leadership to take a new look at the world beyond our borders and to stop parroting the fearful wails of Washington officialdom that Asia and Africa may be "lost to the Free World." No doubt there are some folks who stand to lose a great deal as the colonial peoples take over their own lands and resources, but what in the world do Negro Americans have to lose over there? *Our* problem is how to get some of that freedom and dignity that other colored folks are getting these days. What we have to be concerned about is what we can *get*, and not be worrying our heads about what the Big White Folks might *lose!* . . .

Yes, the peoples of the free colored nations are our natural friends: their growing strength is also ours. When the Ambassador from India is Jim Crowed in Texas, and when the Finance Minister of Ghana is Jim Crowed in Delaware, they and their people feel exactly as we do. Diplomatic apologies are made to them, but they know that the President and the Secretary of State make no apology or restitution to the 16 millions of us who daily undergo the indignities of race discrimination, nor to the millions of others—the American Indians, the Mexican-Americans, the Puerto Ricans and people of Asian descent—who are insulted and outraged in this "Land of the Free." And so it is that the colored peoples, two-thirds of all mankind, are shouting that the Walls of Jericho must come tumbling down. . . .

The Power of Negro Action

"How long, O Lord, how long?"—that ancient cry of the oppressed is often voiced these days in editorials in the Negro newspapers whose pages are filled with word-and-picture reports of outrages against our people. A photograph of a Negro being kicked by a white mobster brings the vicious blow crashing against the breast of the reader, and there are all the other horrible pictures—burning cross, beaten minister, bombed school, threatened children, mutilated man, imprisoned mother, barricaded family—which show what is going on.

How long? The answer is *As long as we permit it.* I say that Negro action can be decisive. I say that we ourselves have the power to end the terror and to win for ourselves peace and security throughout the land. The recognition of this fact will bring new vigor, boldness and determination in planning our program of action and new militancy in winning its goals.

The denials and doubts about this idea—the second part of the challenge which confronts us today—are even more evident than those I noted in regard to the first. The diehard racists who shout "Never!" to equal rights, and the gradualists who mumble "Not now," are quite convinced that the Negro is powerless to bring about a different decision.

Unfortunately, it is also true that to a large extent the Negro people do not know their own strength and do not see how they can achieve the goals they so urgently desire. The basis for this widespread view is obvious. We are a minority, a tenth of the population of our country. In all the terms in which power is reckoned in America—economic wealth, political office, social privilege—we are in a weak position; and from this the conclusion is drawn that the Negro can do little or nothing to compel a change.

It must be seen, however, that this is not a case of a minority pitting itself against a majority. If it were, if we wanted to gain something for ourselves by taking it away from the more powerful majority, the effort would plainly be hopeless. But that is not the case with our demand. Affirming that we are indeed created equal, we seek the equal rights to which we are entitled under the law. The granting of our demand would not lessen the democratic rights of the white people; on the contrary, it would enormously strengthen the base of democracy for all Americans. We ask for nothing that is not ours by right, and herein lies the great moral power of our demand. It is the admitted *rightness* of our claim which has earned for us the moral support of the majority of white Americans.

The granting of our demand for first-class citizenship, on a par with all others, would not in itself put us in a position of equality. Oppression has kept us on the bottom rungs of the ladder, and even with the removal of all barriers we will still have a long way to climb in order to catch up with the general standard of living. But the equal *place* to which we aspire cannot be reached without the equal *rights* we demand, and so the winning of those rights is not a maximum fulfillment but a minimum necessity and we cannot settle for less. Our viewpoint on this matter is not a minority opinion in our country. Though the most rabid champions of "white superiority" are unwilling to test their belief by giving the Negro an equal opportunity, I believe that most white Americans are fair-minded enough to concede that we should be given that chance.

The moral support of the American majority is largely passive today, but what must be recognized—and here we see the decisive power of Negro action—is this:

Wherever and whenever we, the Negro people, claim our lawful rights with all of the earnestness, dignity and determination that we can demonstrate, the moral support of the American people will become an active force on our side.

The most important part of the Little Rock story was not what Governor Faubus and the local mobs did, nor was it what President

Eisenhower was moved to do: the important thing was that nine Negro youngsters, backed by their parents, the Negro community and its leadership, resolved to claim their right to attend Central High School. The magnificent courage and dignity these young people displayed in making that claim won the admiration of the American public. Their *action* did more to win the sympathy and support of democratic-minded white people than all the speeches about "tolerance" that have ever been made....

I have pointed to the sources of strength that exist at home and abroad. What power do we ourselves have?

We have the power of numbers, the power of organization, and the power of spirit. Let me explain what I mean.

Sixteen million people are a force to be reckoned with, and indeed there are many nations in the U.N. whose numbers are less. No longer can it be said that the Negro question is a sectional matter: the continuing exodus from the South has spread the Negro community to all parts of the land and has concentrated large numbers in places which are economically and politically the most important in the nation. In recent years much has been written about the strategic position of Negro voters in such pivotal states as New York, Ohio, Pennsylvania, Michigan, Illinois and California, but generally it can be said that the power of our numbers is not seen or acted upon. Let us consider this concept in connection with something that is apparent to all.

Very often these days we see photographs in the newspapers and magazines of a Negro family—the husband, wife, their children— huddled together in their newly purchased or rented home, while outside hundreds of Negro-haters have gathered to throw stones, to howl filthy abuse, to threaten murder and arson; and there may or may not be some policemen at the scene. But something is missing from this picture that ought to be there, and its absence gives rise to a nagging question that cannot be stilled: *Where are the other Negroes?* Where are the hundreds and thousands of other Negroes in that town who ought to be there protecting their own? The *power of numbers* that is missing from the scene would change the whole picture as nothing else could. It is one thing to terrorize a helpless few, but the forces of race hate that brazenly whoop and holler when the odds are a thousand to one are infinitely less bold when the odds are otherwise.

I am not suggesting, of course, that the Negro people should take law enforcement into their own hands. But we have the right and, above all, we have the duty, to bring the strength and support of our entire community to defend the lives and property of each individual family. Indeed, the law itself will move a hundred times quicker whenever it is apparent that the power of our numbers has been called forth. The time has come for the great Negro communities throughout the land—Chicago, Detroit, New York, Birmingham and all the rest—to demonstrate that they will no longer tolerate mob violence against one of their own. In listing the inalienable rights of man, Thomas Jefferson put *life* before *liberty, and the pursuit of happiness*; and it must be clear that for Negro Americans today the issue of *personal security* must be put first, and resolved first, before all other matters are attended to. When the Negro is told that he must "stay in his place," there is always the implicit threat that unless he does so mob violence will be used against him. Hence, as I see it, nothing is more important than to establish the fact that we will no longer suffer the use of mobs against us. Let the Negro people of but a single city respond in an all-out manner at the first sign of a mob—in mass demonstrations, by going on strike, by organizing boycotts—and the lesson will be taught in one bold stroke to people everywhere.

It was an excellent idea to call for a Prayer Pilgrimage for Freedom to assemble in Washington on May 17, 1957, the third anniversary of the Supreme Court decision, and the thousands who gathered there were inspired with a sense of solidarity and were deeply stirred by the speeches that were made. In terms of dignity and discipline the gathering was a matter for great pride. But there was at the same time a sense of disappointment at the size of the rally which did not, as a national mobilization, truly reflect the power of our numbers. Various charges were later made in the press, and heatedly denied, that important elements of leadership had "dragged their feet" in the preparation, but no constructive purpose would be served by going into those arguments here. The point I wish to make is this: When we call for such a mobilization again (and it ought to be done before another three years pass), we must go all-out to rally not tens of thousands but hundreds of thousands in a demonstration that will show we really mean business. And we should do more than listen to speeches and then go quietly home. Our spokesmen should go to the White House and to Congress and, backed by the massed power of our people, present our demands for action. Then they should come back to the assembled people to tell them what "the man" said, so that the people can decide whether they are satisfied or not and what to do about it.

The time for pussyfooting is long gone. If someone or other fears that some politician might be "embarrassed" by being confronted by such a delegation, or is concerned lest such action seem too bold—well, let that timid soul just step aside, for there are many in our ranks who will readily go in to "talk turkey" with any or all of the top men in government. We must get it into our heads—and into every leader's head—that we are not asking "favors" of the Big White Folks when, for example, we insist that the full power of the Executive be used to protect the right of Negroes to register and vote in the South. And when we really turn out for such a demand the answer can only be yes.

The *power of organization*, through which the power of numbers is expressed, is another great strength of the Negro people. Few other areas of American life are as intensively organized as is the Negro community. Some people say that we have far too many organizations—too many different churches and denominations, too many fraternal societies, clubs and associations—but that is what we have and there is no use deploring it. What is important is to recognize a meaningful fact which is so often denied: Negroes can and do band together and they have accomplished remarkable works through their collective efforts. "The trouble with our folks"—how often you have heard it (or perhaps said it yourself)—"is that we just won't get together"; but the plain truth is that we just about do more joining and affiliating than anybody else. "Our folks are just not ready to make financial sacrifices for a good cause," we hear, and yet we see that all over the country congregations of a few hundred poor people contribute and collect thousands of dollars year in and year out for the purposes that inspire them.

The Negro communities *are* organized and that condition is not made less significant by the fact that our people have formed a great number of organizations to meet their needs and desires. Organizations like the N.A.A.C.P., which has won many splendid victories in the courts for our rights and has done much other notable work, deserve a much greater membership and financial support than is now the case. Yet it is clear that to exert fully our power of organization we must bring together, for united action, all of the many organizations which now encompass the masses of our people. The great struggle and victory in Montgomery, Alabama, against Jim Crow buses proved beyond all doubt that the various existing organizations of the Negro community can be effectively united for a common purpose. Of course the factor of leadership, which I shall discuss later in this chapter, is a key point, but what I wish to emphasize here is that the *organizational base* for successful struggle exists in all other communities no less than in Montgomery. And who, in the face of the brilliant organization of every practical detail that was devised and carried through by our people in Montgomery, can still assert that Negroes do not have the capacity for effective collective action? What other mass movement in our country was better planned and carried out?

The central role that was played in Montgomery by the churches and their pastors highlights the fact that the Negro church, which has played such a notable part in our history, is still the strongest base of our power of organization. This is true not only because of the large numbers who comprise the congregations, but because our churches are, in the main, independent *Negro* organizations. The churches and other groups of similar independent character—fraternal orders, women's clubs, and so forth—will increasingly take the lead because they are closer to the Negro rank-and-file, more responsive to their needs, and less subject to control by forces outside the Negro community.

Here let me point to a large group among this rank-and-file which is potentially the most powerful and effective force in our community—the two million Negro men and women who are members of organized labor. We are a working people and the pay-envelope of the Negro worker is the measure of our general welfare and progress. Government statistics on average earnings show that for every dollar that the white worker is paid the Negro worker gets only 53 cents; and that the average Negro family has a yearly income of $2,410 compared with an average of $4,339 per year for white families. Here, on the basic bread-and-butter level, is a crucial front in our fight for equality and here the Negro trade unionists are the main force to lead the way.

It must be seen, too, that in relation to our general struggle for civil rights the Negro trade unionists occupy a key position. They comprise a large part of the membership of our community organizations and at the same time they are the largest section of our people belonging to interracial organizations. Hence the Negro trade union members are a strategic link, a living connection with the great masses of the common people of America who are our natural allies in the struggle for democracy and whose active support must be won for our side in this critical hour.

To our men and women of organized labor I would say: A twofold challenge confronts you. The Negro trade unionists must increasingly exert their influence in every aspect of our people's community life. No church, no fraternal, civic or social organization in our communities must be permitted to continue without the benefit of the knowledge and experience that you have gained through your struggles in the great American labor movement. You are called upon to provide the spirit, the determination, the organizational skill, the firm steel of unyielding militancy to the age-old strivings of our people for equality and freedom.

Secondly, on your shoulders there is the responsibility to rally the strength of the whole trade union movement, white and black, to the battle for liberation of our people. Though you are still largely unrepresented in the top levels of labor leadership, you must use your power of numbers to see to it that the leadership of the A.F.L.-C.I.O., which has shown much concern for the so-called "crusade for freedom" abroad, shall not continue to be silent and unmoving in our crusade for freedom *at home*. You must rally your white fellow workers to support full equality for Negro workers; for their right to work at any job; to receive equal pay for equal work; for an end to Jim Crow unions; for the election of qualified Negroes to positions of union leadership; for fair employment practices in every industry; for trade union educational programs to eliminate the notions of "white superiority" which the employers use to poison the minds of the white workers in order to pit them against you.

I have watched and participated in your militant struggles everywhere I have been these past years—in Chicago with the packinghouse workers; with the auto workers of Detroit; the seamen and longshoremen of the West Coast; the tobacco workers of North Carolina; the miners of Pittsburgh and West Virginia; the steel workers of Illinois, Pennsylvania, Indiana and Ohio; the furriers, clerks and garment workers of New York and Philadelphia; with workers in numerous other places throughout the land—and I feel sure that you will meet the challenge which confronts you today.

To all groups in Negro life I would say that the key to set into motion our power of organization is the concept of *coordinated action*, the bringing together of the many organizations which exist in order to plan to carry out the common struggle. We know full well that it is not easy to do this. We are divided in many ways—in politics, in religious affiliations, in economic and social classes; and in addition to these group rivalries there are the obstacles of personal ambitions and jealousies of various leaders. But as I move among our people these days, from New York to California, I sense a growing impatience with petty ways of thinking and doing things. I see a rising resentment against control of our affairs by white people, regardless of whether that domination is expressed by the blunt orders of political bosses or more discreetly by the "advice" of white liberals which must be heeded or else. There is a rapidly growing awareness that despite all of our differences it is necessary that we become unified, and I think that the force of that idea will overcome all barriers. Coordinated action will not, of course, come all at once: it will develop in the grass-roots and spread from community to community. And the building of that unity is a task which each of us can undertake wherever we are.

A unified people requires a unified leadership, and let me make very clear what I mean by that. Recently the distinguished Negro journalist Carl T. Rowan, who had published in *Ebony* magazine an interview with me, was himself interviewed about that subject on a radio network program where he said: "It's Robeson's contention that the Negro people will never be free in this country until they speak more or less as one voice, and, very obviously, Robeson feels that one voice should be something close to his voice."

Actually, that is *not* how I feel, and I would not want Mr. Rowan or anyone else to misunderstand my view of this matter. The one voice in which we should speak must be the expression of our entire people on the central issue which is all-important to every Negro—our right to be free and equal. On many other issues there are great differences among us, and hence it is not possible for any one person, or any group of people, to presume to speak for us all.

Far from making any such claim for myself, what I am advocating is in fact the opposite idea! I advocate unity based upon our common viewpoint as Negroes, a nonpartisan unity, a unity in which we subordinate all that divides us, a unity which excludes no one, a unity in which no faction or group is permitted to impose its particular outlook on others. A unified leadership of a unified movement means that people of *all* political views—conservatives, liberals, and radicals—must be represented therein. Let there be but one requirement made without exception: that Negro leadership, and every man and woman in that leadership, place the interests of our people, and the struggle for those interests, above all else.

There is a need—an urgent need—for a national conference of Negro leadership, not of a handful but a broad representative gathering of leadership from all parts of the country, from all walks of life, from every viewpoint, to work out a *common program of action* for Negro Americans in the crisis of our times. Such a program does not exist today and without it we are a ship without a rudder; we can only flounder around on a day-to-day basis, trying to meet developments with patchwork solutions. We must chart a course to be followed in the stormy days that are here and in the greater storms that are on the way, a course that heads full square for freedom.

The *power of spirit* that our people have is intangible, but it is a great force that must be unleashed in the struggles of today. A spirit of steadfast determination, exaltation in the face of trials—it is the very soul of our people that has been formed through all the long and weary years of our march toward freedom. It is the deathless spirit of the great ones who have led our people in the past—Douglass, Tubman and all the others—and of the millions who kept "a-inching along." That spirit lives in our people's songs—in the sublime grandeur of "Deep River," in the driving power of "Jacob's Ladder," in the militancy of "Joshua Fit the Battle of Jericho," and in the poignant beauty of all our spirituals.

It lives in every Negro mother who wants her child "to grow up and be somebody," as it lives in our common people everywhere who daily meet insult and outrage with quiet courage and optimism. It is that spirit which gives that "something extra" to our athletes, to our artists, to all who meet the challenge of public performance. It is the spirit of little James Gordon of Clay, Kentucky, who, when asked by a reporter why he wanted to go to school with white children replied: "Why shouldn't I?" and it is the spirit of all the other little ones in the South who have walked like mighty heroes through menacing mobs to go to school. It is the spirit of the elderly woman of Montgomery who explained her part in the bus boycott by saying: "When I rode in the Jim Crow buses my body was riding but my soul was walking, but now when my body is walking my soul is riding!"

Yes, that power of the spirit is the pride and glory of my people, and there is no human quality in all of America that can surpass it. It is a force only for good: there is no hatefulness about it. It exalts the finest things of life—justice and equality, human dignity and fulfillment. It is of the earth, deeply rooted, and it reaches up to the highest skies and mankind's noblest aspirations. It is time for this spirit to be evoked and exemplified in all we do, for it is a force mightier than all our enemies and will triumph over all their evil ways.

For Negro action to be decisive—given the favorable opportunity which I have outlined in the previous chapter and the sources of strength indicated above—still another factor is needed: *effective Negro leadership*. In discussing this subject I shall not engage in any personalities, nor is it my intention either to praise or blame the individuals who today occupy top positions in our ranks. Such critical appraisal must, of course, be made of their leaders by the Negro people, and so I would like here to discuss not this or that person but rather the *principles* of the question, the standards for judgment, the character of leadership that is called for today.

The term "leadership" has been used to express many different concepts, and many of these meanings have nothing to do with what I am concerned with here. Individuals attain prominence for a wide variety of reasons, and often people who have climbed up higher on the ladder are called leaders though they make it plain that their sole interest is personal advancement and the more elevated they are above all other Negroes the better they like it. Then, too, it has been traditional for the dominant group of whites, in local communities and on a national scale as well, to designate certain individuals as "Negro leaders," regardless of how the Negro people feel about it; and the idea is that Negro leadership is something that white folks can bestow as a favor or take away as punishment.

The concept that I am talking about has nothing to do with the matters of headline prominence, personal achievement, or popularity with the powers-that-be. I am concerned, rather, with Negro leadership in the struggle for Negro rights. This includes those who are directly in charge of the organizations established for such purpose, and many others as well—the leaders of Negro churches, fraternal and civic organizations, elected representatives in government, trade union officials, and others whose action or inaction directly affects our common cause.

The primary quality that Negro leadership must possess, as I see it, *is a single-minded dedication to their people's welfare.* Any individual Negro, like any other person, may have many varied interests in life, but for the true leader all else must be subordinated to the interests of those whom he is leading. If today it can be said that the Negro people of the United States are lagging behind the progress being made by colored peoples in other lands, one basic cause for it has been that all too often Negro leadership here has lacked the selfless passion for their people's welfare that has characterized the leaders of the colonial liberation movements. Among us there is a general recognition—and a grudging acceptance—of the fact that some of our leaders are not only unwilling to make sacrifices but they must see some gain for themselves in whatever they do. A few crumbs for a few is too often hailed as "progress for the race." To live in freedom one must be prepared to die to achieve it, and while few if any of us are ever called upon to make that supreme sacrifice, no one can ignore the fact that in a difficult struggle those who are in the forefront may suffer cruel blows. He who is not prepared to face the trials of battle will never lead to a triumph. This spirit of dedication, as I have indicated, is abundantly present in the ranks of our people but progress will be slow until it is much more manifest in the character of leadership.

Dedication to the Negro People's welfare is one side of a coin: the other side is *independence*. Effective Negro leadership must rely upon and be responsive to no other control than the will of their people. We have allies—important allies—among our white fellow-citizens, and we must ever seek to draw them closer to us and to gain many more. But the Negro people's movement must be led by *Negroes,* not only in terms of title and position but in reality. Good advice is good no matter what the source and help is needed and appreciated from wherever it comes, but Negro action cannot be decisive if the advisers and helpers hold the guiding reins. For no matter how well-meaning other groups may be, the fact is our interests are secondary at best with them.

Today such outside controls are a factor in reducing the independence and effectiveness of Negro leadership. I do not have in mind the dwindling group of Uncle Toms who shamelessly serve even an Eastland; happily, they are no longer of much significance. I have in mind, rather, those practices of Negro leadership that are based upon the idea that it is white power rather than Negro power that must be relied upon. This concept has been traditional since Booker T. Washington, and it has been adhered to by many who otherwise reject all notions of white supremacy.

In Booker Washington's day it was the ruling white man of the South whose sympathy was considered indispensable; today it is the liberal section of the dominant group in the North whose goodwill is said to be the hope for Negro progress. It is clear that many Negro leaders act or desist from acting because they base themselves on this idea. Rejecting the concept that "white is right" they embrace its essence by conceding that "might is right." To the extent that this idea is prevalent in its midst, Negro leadership lacks the quality of independence without which it cannot be effective.

Dedication and independence—these are the urgent needs. Other qualities of leadership exist in abundance: we have many highly trained men and women, experienced in law, in politics, in civic affairs; we have spokesmen of great eloquence, talented organizers, skilled negotiators. If I have stressed those qualities which are most needed on the national level, it is not from any lack of appreciation for much that is admirable. On the local level, especially, there are many examples of dedicated and independent leadership. Indeed, the effective use of Negro power—of numbers, of organization, of spirit—in Montgomery was the result of Negro leadership of the highest caliber. And the whole nation has witnessed the heroic dedication of many other leaders in the South, who, at the risk of their lives and all they hold dear, are leading their people's struggles. There are many from our ranks who ought to be elevated to national leadership because by their deeds they have fully demonstrated their right to be there.

We should broaden our conception of leadership and see to it that all sections of Negro life are represented on the highest levels. There must be room at the top for people from down below. I'm talking about the majority of our folks who work in factory and field: they bring with them that down-to-earth view which is the highest vision, and they can hammer and plow in more ways than one. Yes, we need more of them in the leadership, and we need them in a hurry.

We need more of our women in the higher ranks, too, and who should know better than the children of Harriet Tubman, Sojourner Truth and Mary Church Terrell that our womenfolk have often led the way. Negro womanhood today is giving us many inspiring examples of steadfast devotion, cool courage under fire, and brilliant generalship in our people's struggles; and here is a major source for new strength and militancy in Negro leadership on every level.

But if there are those who ought to be raised to the top, there are some others already there who should be retired. I have noted, in another connection, that the Negro people are patient and long-suffering— sometimes to a fault. The fault is often expressed by permitting unworthy leaders to get away with almost anything. It is as if once a man rises to leadership, his responsibility to his people is no longer binding upon him.

But, in these critical days, we ought to become a little less tolerant, a little more demanding that all Negro leaders "do right."

There are others, honest men beyond all doubt and sincerely concerned with their people's welfare, who seem to feel that it is the duty of a leader to discourage Negro mass action. They think that best results can be achieved by quiet negotiations they carry on. And so when something happens that arouses the masses of people, and when the people gather in righteous anger to demand that militant actions be started, such men believe it their duty to cool things off.

We saw this happen not long ago when from coast to coast there was a great upsurge of the people caused by the brutal lynching of young Emmett Till. At one of the mass protest meetings that was held, I heard one of our most important leaders address the gathering in words to this effect: "You are angry today, but you are not going to do anything about it. I know that you won't do anything. You clamor for a march on Mississippi but none of you will go. So let's stop talking about marching. Just pay a dollar to our organization and leave the rest to your leaders. If you want to do something yourself, let each of you go to your district Democratic leader and talk to him about it."

Well, what would a congregation think of their pastor if the best he could do was to tell them: "You are all a bunch of sinners, and nothing can make you do right. There is no good in you and I know it. So, brothers and sisters, just put your contributions on the collection plate, go home and leave your salvation to me."

No, a leader should encourage, not discourage; he should rally the people, not disperse them. A wet blanket can never be the banner of freedom.

Of course there must be negotiations made in behalf of our rights, but unless the negotiators are backed by an aroused and militant people, their earnest pleas will be of little avail. For Negro action to be effective—to be decisive, as I think it can be—it must be *mass* action. The power of the ballot can be useful only if the masses of voters are united on a common program; obviously, if half the Negro people vote one way and the other half the opposite way, not much can be achieved. The individual votes are cast and counted, but the group power is cast away and discounted.

Mass action—in political life and elsewhere—is Negro power in motion; and it is the way to win.

An urgent task which faces us today is an all-out struggle to defeat the efforts of the White Supremacists to suppress the N.A.A.C.P. in the South. As in South Africa, where the notorious "Suppression of Communism Act" is used to attack the liberation movement, the enemies of Negro freedom in our country have accused the N.A.A.C.P. of being a "subversive conspiracy" and the organization has been outlawed in Louisiana, Texas and Alabama, and legally restricted in Georgia, Virginia, South Carolina and Mississippi. City ordinances, as in Little Rock, are also used for this purpose.

The indifference with which various other organizations viewed the suppression in 1955 of the Council on African Affairs, which was falsely labeled a "Communist front," should not be repeated now by any group in the case of the N.A.A.C.P. The Red-baiting charges against that organization are utterly untrue, as the makers of such charges know full well; and those elements in Negro leadership who have in the past resorted to Red-baiting as a "smart" tactic should realize that such methods serve no one but our people's worst enemies.

Throughout the South—Little Rock, Montgomery and elsewhere—the state and local leaders of the N.A.A.C.P. have set a heroic and inspiring example for Negro leadership everywhere. All of us—the Negro people of the entire country—must rally now to sustain and defend them.

In presenting these ideas on the power of Negro action, the sources of that power, and the character of leadership necessary to direct that power most effectively, I offer them for consideration and debate at this time when the challenge of events calls for clarity of vision and unity of action. No one, obviously, has all the answers, and the charting of our course must be done collectively. There must be a spirit of give and take, and clashing viewpoints must find a common ground. Partisan interests must be subordinated to Negro interests—by each of us. Somehow we must find the way to set aside all that divides us and come together, Negroes all. Our unity will strengthen our friends and win many more to our side; and our unity will weaken our foes who already can see the handwriting on the wall.

To be free—to walk the good American earth as equal citizens, to live without fear, to enjoy the fruits of our toil, to give our children every opportunity in life—that dream which we have held so long in our hearts is today the destiny that we hold in our hands.

As an appendix to this volume by Robeson, a note was printed on the history of the Council of African Affairs by W. Alphaeus Hunton, its executive secretary.

The work of the Council on African Affairs, Paul Robeson stated publicly on more than one occasion, was the one organizational interest among many with which he was identified that was closest to his heart. He was instrumental in the establishment of the Council in 1937 and for eighteen years, until its dissolution in 1955, was intimately associated with its activities, serving most of that time as the organization's chairman. His unswerving devotion to the cause of African freedom, his world-encompassing vision, and his powerful voice and big human spirit were of inestimable importance in forwarding the Council's efforts toward rallying Americans, black and white, in support of Africa's liberation from imperialist bondage.

One reflection of the Africans' recognition and appreciation of his great service was the selection of Paul Robeson as one of the three recipients— together with Kwame Nkrumah, now Prime Minister of free Ghana, and Nnamdi Azikiwe, Prime Minister of Eastern Nigeria—of the award of "Champion of African Freedom," bestowed by the National Church of Nigeria at ceremonies attended by 5,000 at Aba, Nigeria, on January 29, 1950.

The Council on African Affairs for many years stood alone as the one organization in the United States devoting full-time attention to the problems and struggles of the peoples of Africa.

No detailed account of the council's work can be given here, but it may be helpful to say something briefly about its major functions. Its prime objective was to provide a sound basis of accurate information so that the American people might play their proper part in the struggle for African freedom. To that end, the Council serviced the press with African news and background information; provided speakers, films, and exhibit materials wherever requested; published a monthly bulletin of information and comment on African developments; circulated numerous pamphlets and factual reports; and maintained an extensive African library and research facilities.

Though the dissemination of information was central in its work, the Council was not content to function simply as an information agency. It sought to translate knowledge into action. From 1944, when the shape of postwar African policy was under consideration, to 1955 and Bandung, the Council organized assemblies ranging from conferences of community leaders to a Madison Square Garden rally for the purpose of hammering out, and enlisting public support for programs of action in the interest of the African people's welfare and freedom.

Beginning with the founding conference of the United Nations in San Francisco the Council maintained a close watch on the activities and policies of the world organization pertaining to Africa and colonial countries in general. It brought to public attention and helped generate protests against the pro-imperialist and compromising stand of the United States delegation on such issues as trusteeship and colonial independence, the status of South West Africa, the question of Italy's former colonies in Africa, and the tyranny of racist rule in the Union of South Africa. "The knowledge that we have friends at the other end of the Atlantic is comforting and inspiring in our struggle for freedom from want and heartless exploitation," a Nigerian trade union leader wrote the Council's officers.

Another facet of the Council's work, an area of activity in which its influence was perhaps most effective and widespread, pertained to campaigns to provide direct assistance for Africans in emergency situations. The significance of one of these campaigns has been described by Dr. Z. K. Matthews, a distinguished educator and a leader of the African National Congress in South Africa, and one of the 156 men and women placed on trial there for "treason" in 1957 when the Strijdom regime launched an all-out assault on the vanguard of the forces striving for democratic rights.

Writing from South Africa in 1953, Dr. Matthews said of the Council, "Africans in this country have benefited directly from its practical interest in their affairs. As far back as 1945 when a severe drought struck the Eastern Cape Province of the Union of South Africa, hundreds of Africans...had cause to be thankful that such a body as the Council on African Affairs was in existence....The Council made available financial aid and food supplies of various kinds collected in America to be forwarded to the area for distribution among the needy. Many African children, women and older people in the area concerned owed their lives to the assistance given by the Council."

It was in relation to their campaign that the late Senator Harley M. Kilgore in 1946 declared: "The Council on African Affairs deserves the wholehearted support of every American for its great fight to secure freedom and full democratic rights for the oppressed and starving South Africans and other colonial peoples....Every American who supports the

Council's drive to aid the starving South Africans will be striking a solid blow for world freedom."

But two years later came the official branding of the Council as "subversive" and the descent of the McCarthyite blanket of fear and suspicion smothering all free democratic expression. Nevertheless, despite heavy obstacles, the work went on and further campaigns were organized to provide financial aid to help defray the expenses of the Union charged with conspiring with the Mau Mau, and to provide for the support of the dependents of the thousands of men and women jailed in South Africa during the Campaign of Defiance of Unjust Laws.

There was also the work of the African Aid Committee, headed by Dr. W. E. B. Du Bois, who was elected as Vice Chairman of the Council in 1949. Among this Committee's accomplishments was the collection and forwarding of funds to aid the families of 26 miners shot down during a strike in the coal pits of Enugu, Nigeria.

Such, in brief, were the main features of the work of the Council on African Affairs. Though the organization was ultimately forced to suspend its activities, what it achieved could not be undone. Today, with Africa's millions demonstrating their determination to manage their own affairs for their own benefit, there is growing realization of the folly of continuing to give European or American economic and strategic objectives in the continent priority over African self-determination and emancipation.

Paul Robeson, *Here I Stand*, (New York: Othello Associates, 1958,), pp. 82–116, in part. Reprinted Boston: Becason Press, 1971 with introductions by Lloyd L. Brown and Sterling Stuckey.

73

A WHITE CITIZEN COUNCIL MEMBER AND CHARLES GOMILLION: AN EXCHANGE (1959)

Charles G. Gomillion (b. 1900) was for many years associated with Tuskegee Institute, holding positions as dean of the School of Education, dean of Students, and dean of the College of Arts and Sciences. Gomillion was president of the Tuskegee Civic Association from 1941 to 1945 and from 1951 to 1968. He led a successful boycott against racist white business establishments in Tuskegee in the early 1950s. His historic action prevented gerrymandering (*Gomillion* v. *Light-foot*, 1960). The following exchange with a member of the White Citizens Council occurred early in 1959.

Thoughts of a White Citizen Council Member

To Charles Gomillion:

Who I am is unimportant. The important thing is that I'm a southerner from Lake Charles, Louisiana, and I have a few things to say to you. I have just finished reading an article in a Coronet magazine labeled *The Integration Fight is Killing Tuskegee*.

You and your ideals make me sick. You and the rest of the colored race had it made before you started all this integration crap. I belong to a branch of the White Citizens Council here in Lake Charles, La. I just want you and the rest of your friends to know that we will never integrate! We will stop integration if it takes bloodshed!

A few years ago I knew several negro boys my age. We were fairly good friends. Now, I would not speak to them because of what their race is trying to pull. Now I hate all niggers.

Its people like you who are leading the rest of the negro's down the wrong trail.

I do not think of myself as better than a negro. But I believe that if I want segregation and the majority of the people in the south want segregation we should be able to have it. In fact, we are going to have it!

I believe in the negro having everything that I have, just as long as he stays on his side of the fence.

I don't want to see intermarriage between a colored man and white women. It may happen up in yankee land but it won't happen here.

In short, Gomillion, you and your associates are fighting a losing battle. And I assure you there (are) many like I who are ready to fight anywhere, any sort of way for segregation. And as far as the Supreme Court is concerned they can go to hell! If they want another civil war they will sure as hell get it.

If you don't like it in the south why not move to the north. Those damn Yankees love niggers. Don't they?

The letter above was not dated, was not signed, and did not carry a street address. The envelope was postmarked "Lake Charles, La., Feb. 26, 1959 6:30 P.M." It was addressed to "Charles G. Gomillion, Tuskegee Institute, Tuskegee, Alabama."

Reply

March 7, 1959

The Southerner
Member of a Branch of a White Citizens Council
Lake Charles, Louisiana
Author of the letter to Charles G. Gomillion,
  Tuskegee Institute, Tuskegee, Alabama;
  Postmarked February 26, 1959

Dear Sir:

Thank you for the very informative letter which you sent me. It happens that I was not at home when it was delivered. Please pardon my delay in responding. Some of the delay is due to my uncertainty as to whom or where to send the reply. I regret that in your effort to enlighten me you neglected to identify yourself by name or address. This failure makes it impossible for me to send you a personal and private reply, which I should like to do. Since this is not possible, I think that it is courteous that I endeavor to have it published, in the hope that you will discover that your effort was not in vain.

I regret that you underestimate your importance. Who you are *is* important. Your behavior affects many persons, even me. Because you are important, and because my well-being, directly or indirectly, is affected by your conception of yourself and of your relation to others, I hope that you will consider how important you are.

You are more than "a southerner from Lake Charles, Louisiana"; you are *an American*, I presume, and one who has probably read the Declaration of Independence, and the Constitution of the United States of America. It is quite likely, also, that you have pledged allegiance to the Flag of the United States, our Homeland. I am inclined to believe that at some time in the past you have professed to believe in the concept of democracy, the principle of equality of opportunity. I am inclined to believe, further, that basically you are a "good American," because you have chosen (1) to inform me of your affiliation, and of your intention, (2) to warn me of impending danger, and (3) to advise me as to what I should do. For this I am grateful.

Congratulations on your reading *CORONET*, which magazine

frequently contains important articles. Unfortunately, however, the title of the article which you read, "The Integration Fight is Killing Tuskegee," is misleading. If Tuskegee is being killed, it is not being killed by the "integration fight." If it is being killed, might it not be by short-sighted, narrowminded, and undemocratic public officials and citizens who deprive some American citizens of civil rights and opportunities by refusing to register them, and by gerrymandering a city? Those in favor of integration did not reduce the size of the city, nor did they propose to abolish a county. They do not seek to destroy the integrity and the prestige of an historic municipality; they try to build its resources, enhance its prestige, and make it a model for democratic living and progress.

By this time, I hope that you have recovered from your illness. I regret that you were made "sick" by me and my ideals. Whenever I am responsible for the illness of anyone, I am unhappy.

I am sorry that you have decided not to speak to the Negroes whom you have known "because of what their race is trying to pull." Is it fair to them? Have *they* mistreated you? Have you asked them whether or not they are in favor of what you think "their race is trying to pull"? I regret even more your development of the capacity to "hate." Hatred is both expensive and dangerous. It takes time and effort to hate. And when one is hating, he cannot be loving. When he is acting on hatred, he cannot be engaged in noble efforts. Persons who hate are unhappy persons. Many of them are afraid, and fear is dangerous. Many persons who are afraid find it difficult to resist the temptation to engage in vice or crime. Love is much more satisfying, and honorable, than hatred. Please examine your present emotional content, and see if you might not want to talk with your one-time "fairly good" Negro friends. If you listen to them, and objectively examine their civic status and opportunities, you might discover in them something which you admire. If you discover in them nothing which elicits your respect, you would rise to the challenge if you would decide to meet and work with them in an effort to help them become worthy of your respect, and possibly of your love. If you do not think of yourself "as better than a negro," then you can afford to do this.

I am glad that you believe "in the negro having everything I have." If by "everything" you mean the civic status and opportunities to which you have access, that is exactly what Negroes are working for. When you are willing for "the negro" to have everything you have "just as long as he stays on his side of the fence," you write as if you and he are not in the same field. You and he are living in the United States of America one nation, indivisible. Where is the fence that divides? How can the Negro stay on "his side of the fence" if he does not see any fence, and if the Federal Government does not recognize the existence of any fence?

There are many implications which can be drawn from your statement that you "don't want to see intermarriage between a colored man and white women." Polygyny is not legal in the United States. Do you mean to imply that there is the possibility that two or more white women might become the wives of a colored man? Or do you mean to imply that intermarriage between a white man and a colored woman would meet with your approval? Or that you are not interested in what the white woman might think about the extra-marital relations of the white man and the colored woman? Since no man is able to marry a woman if she says "No," do you imply that there are some white women who could not, or would not say "no"? Does your statement suggest that there are some white women whose judgment you do not trust? In the United States, is not legal marriage between healthy persons considered more honorable, and more in keeping with the moral code of our culture, than illegal extra-marital relations?

You err when you say that my associates and I are "fighting." We are not "fighting." We are simply working hard to be good, productive Americans. We are trying diligently to get the same kind of education you and your associates want so that we may be able to make contributions to the culture which are comparable to those which you and your associates make. We do not want to fight; we want to learn and earn. We do not want to shed blood; we want to maintain the peace. We regret that you threaten to shed blood.

It happens that I cannot answer your question as to whether or not "damn Yankees love niggers." I have never asked anyone I know whether or not he loved me. Those whom I know seem to love justice, fair play, the Golden Rule, and recognize and respect the rights of their fellow Americans. I do know that they have allowed me many more opportunities to develop my mind and my cultural interests and competencies than have Southern white Confederates.

As for leaving the South, I am not interested. I was born in the South, and attended the public elementary school in my native state, South Carolina. Although the educational opportunities in the county in which I lived were grossly inferior to those provided for white youth, as reported by white citizens, I did have the opportunity to read the Declaration of Independence, and the Constitution of the United States, and I believed what I read. I believed that I was a full citizen of this Nation, and that this was a land of opportunity, where the law-abiding and the industrious could prosper. I believed, also, that it was the duty of every American citizen to contribute constructively to the development of his Fatherland. I have spent my past years studying the arts of peace, not the science of war. Professionally, I have sought to enlighten and heal the minds of youth and men, not to poison them. My mission is to shed light, not blood, and I hope that I may be permitted to shed it in the South before the more martial-minded shed blood. Because I believe firmly that those who live by the sword shall perish by the sword. I am not now prepared "to fight anywhere, any sort of way." I am a worker, not a fighter.

As sincere as I think you are, I hope that the United States Supreme Court will not take your suggestion to "go to hell." To "go to hell" would be cowardly. There is too much work yet to be done in America. The Supreme Court in some of its recent decisions has been merely trying to implement the American value of equality of opportunity, and to rectify the unfortunate decision of the 1896 Court. The present Court now knows that if Western Civilization is to survive, it will need contributions from citizens who have developed themselves to the optimum, and this can be done only when opportunities are unrestricted. We can either work cooperatively and honorably, and try to compete successfully with undemocratic opponents, or we can waste our resources, efforts, and time, and wait for subjugation. What is your choice?

I hope that if you have read this letter you will accept it in the spirit in which it is written. It is not my desire to offend. I do not threaten you. I am sorry that you hate me. I do not hate you. This might not be of any value to you, but it makes me feel good. I can sleep at night, and I can study and work during the day. I do not have to plan courses of action designed to shed blood. I am a student, eager to learn, and would appreciate an opportunity to meet and confer with you. Those who really know me say that I am gentle, kind, and generous. I invite you and your associates to meet with my associates and me in friendly fellowship. You might discover that we are good Americans. If you observe that we are un-American, you could have us arrested and imprisoned. *Don't kill us! Don't shed our blood!* Let the constituted legal authorities do that.

Very truly yours,

Charles G. Gomillion
Box 31
Tuskegee Institute, Alabama

This is published in *Clinical Sociology Review* (1988): 27–32; the *Review* is edited by Jan E. Fritz of California State University, San Bernardino, to whom the editor is indebted.

74

YOUTH MARCH FOR INTEGRATED EDUCATION (1959)

by Several Authors

As the decade of the 1950s approached its end, it became clear that the Supreme Court's call, in 1955, for integrated education to proceed with "all deliberate speed," evoked much deliberation and little speed.

A result was the intensification of massive demonstrations urging swift and positive action. A notable example was the Youth March for Integrated Education. On April 18, 1959, about 26,000 students—white and African-American—came to Washington to demand an end to segregated public education. They bore with them 250,000 signatures to a nationwide petition for this purpose. The sponsorship was very impressive. A. Philip Randolph was the decisive personality in this effort.

Printed below are several documents: (a) the statement in the House, by Rep. Charles C. Diggs, Jr., of Michigan, dealing with this event; (b) the call for the March from the organizers; (c) the remarks made at the Lincoln memorial on April 18 by Roy Wilkins; (d) the speech by Martin Luther King, Jr., (e) the statement by the youth delegation to the White House culminating the effort:

[a]

REPRESENTATIVE DIGGS'S STATEMENT

Mr. DIGGS. Mr. Speaker, in the CONGRESSIONAL RECORD of April 20, 1959, beginning on page 6352 under the heading "Washington Window," there appear comments and several newspaper articles referring to the April 18, 1959, youth march on Washington for integrated schools. Inserted in the RECORD by the gentleman from Georgia [Mr. FORRESTER], these materials are used in an attempt by implication to link the youth march with Communist Party movement. I should like to set the RECORD straight on this piece of slander.

The 1959 youth march was very fully and objectively covered by Washington and other daily newspapers around the country. It involved nearly 26,000 white and Negro students from all parts of the Nation and outstanding, substantial, national personalities, both white and Negro, from the fields of Government, labor, religion, entertainment, and other interests. It was definitely a large action and, in that respect, indication of the growing demand on behalf of school integration and the enforcement of all constitutionally guaranteed civil rights. A delegation of these youth from the march was received at the White House by Deputy Assistant to the President Gerald D. Morgan, and Presidential Aide E. Frederick Morrow.

By including, among the newspaper clippings in this April 20 discourse, an article published in the Communist Party's Sunday Worker on the subject of the youth march, an attempt is made to infer a connection between the two. Of course, the Communist press would comment upon this march. It, too, is the press and reports on events of national interest. Of course, the Communist Party, through its press, would imply sympathy toward a cause that is humanitarian or just, however feigned its sympathy as a means to its own end. This is the Communist Party tactic—the avowing of itself as the savior for mankind's every just cause. Why else, as a Nation, are we concerned about its attempts to identify with India's, Africa's, China's, the world's needs, its unrelenting efforts to win alignments through expressions of sympathy and profferings of economic, technological, and even military assistance to nations in need? Who denies that there is hunger and disease and slavery and economic oppression and deprivation of human rights in the world and that these are the causes of which communism, on the one hand, is saying, "I am the way to overcome them," and democracy, on the other hand, is saying, "No, I am the way"?

It is ironic that with those who have some vested interest in the continuation of segregation between the races and oppression of the rights of Negro citizens, anything having to do with the democratic ideals of justice, equality, liberty, and opportunity between and for all men must somehow be linked up with communism. It is more ironic that this inference and charge should come from such groups when the truth is it is this group's very position on race relations and civil rights which is the boon to communism. During my 5 years in Congress, I have observed all kinds of positions on questions of race relations and civil rights. There are those of my colleagues, who while not in favor of integration, at least command respect for their human reasonableness in the level and character of their opposing fight. On the other hand, there is that small band of vitriolic and demagogic diehards whose approach to these issues is so completely divorced of reason and at such an animalistic level that while they defeat their own efforts to sell their blind hatred and bigotry to thinking people, they nevertheless make fodder for the Communist cause. The use of inference as a tactic for hurling vitriolic unreasoned charges is not subtle and does not escape attention and the evaluation it deserves.

Congressional Record, May 20, 1959, vol. 105, p. 8694.

[b]

WHY WE MARCH: THE CALL

It is of some interest that in its penultimate paragraph, this call quotes—without quotation marks and without credit—the words of Dr. Du Bois written in 1906. They are italicized below.

On April 18, thousands of American young people will march in the Nation's Capital in the largest demonstration of youth in our history. They will come from all parts of the country, by bus, plane, train, and car, and will represent all faiths. In Washington, they will be joined together in a great union of protest and action—the youth march for integrated schools.

We March for Real Democracy—Now

For over a century, the American Negro has been brutally and undemocratically denied the rights guaranteed to all citizens by our Constitution. The traditional rights of free speech, of suffrage, of due process, of equal protection under the law have been withheld from millions of Americans. And today, a minority of southern racist leaders is endangering our free educational system. This minority is threatening to close public schools, leaving thousands of our young people stranded, barred from the benefits of sound education.

Is this the way of real democracy?

We march to protest the century-long mistreatment of Negro citizens. They have waited long enough. We march to demand real democracy—now.

We March in Defense of the Supreme Court

Because of its recent decisions in behalf of equal educational opportunities for the Negro, the Supreme Court has been subjected to a battery of vicious attacks. Dangerous attempts have been launched to curb the power of the judicial branch of Government, which has moved courageously to defend the rights of Negroes. We protest against these attacks and call upon the executive and legislative branches to back up the Supreme Court in its reflection of the will of the majority.

We March for Civil Rights Legislation

Once again, Congress is being presented with an alternative: either to strengthen American democracy or to retreat before the campaign of the Dixiecrats. The procivil rights majority in Congress, greatly reinforced by the November elections, will have the opportunity to pass the Douglas-Celler-Javits-Powell bill, which goes a long way in helping the Negro and other minorities to achieve equality in all areas of life.

But time and time again, Congress has compromised the will of the people. We march to protest minority rule in Congress, and to demand the passage of the Douglas bill. We march to demand an immediate end to the spectacle of Congressional double-dealing that encourages resistance to the law and deforms the democratic process.

Civil rights legislation is long overdue. We march for just laws—now.

We March for Executive Action

We march to confront the President directly with the conviction of young people that he must use all of his powers to bring about the speedy integration of the schools. Specifically, we call upon him to speak out morally for the Supreme Court decision of May 17, 1954, and to use his influence to destroy the disease of segregation.

We March as Part of Our Democratic Duty

When the wheels of government are slow in expanding our democracy (less than 500 students have been integrated in the deep South), when they get bogged down in compromises and maneuvers, we have the moral obligation in a democratic society to register our protest—through action. The essence of democratic government is the participation of the people themselves. Our failure to move against undemocratic practices leaves the field open to forces hostile to democracy.

Throughout our history, dramatic action by deeply concerned people has served to awaken the whole nation to its sense of duty. The power of the democratic idea symbolized by a vast march of sincere, earnest, disciplined, and dedicated people will influence those who have not yet taken a clear stand. Such a demonstration presses forward the cause of democracy and social progress in the courts, legislature, and all areas of American life.

Thus, American young people march not only to demonstrate solidarity with their embattled fellow students of the South, but for the deepening and reinforcing of our democracy. *We demand for every American every single right guaranteed by the Constitution, political, civil, and social and until we get these rights, we will never cease to protest and assail the ears of America.* We will continue to march, to petition, to demonstrate, and to persuade. It is our responsibility to do so.

We march on April 18 for the total victory of equal rights for all. We can no longer endure compromises and delays. We want a program for speedy integration—and we won't take no for an answer.

Come to Washington on April 18.

YOUTH MARCH FOR INTEGRATED SCHOOLS

CONGRESSIONAL RECORD, AS CITED, P. 8695. THE SENTENCE ITALICIZED BY THE EDITOR IS TAKEN—WITHOUT ACKNOWLEDGMENT—FROM THE NIAGARA ADDRESS OF 1906, WRITTEN BY DR. DU BOIS—SEE MY *DOCUMENTARY HISTORY,* VOL. 1, P. 907.

[C]

ROY WILKINS'S SPEECH

It is most fitting and proper that the youth of this Nation should make their feelings known in plain fashion on the issue of desegregation in the public schools.

Education has always been a matter of deep concern to young people and their parents and in the age in which the uses of machines have climbed to a new high level, when electronics, engineering, chemistry, and the atom have sent our world forward at unprecedented speed, education is more necessary than ever.

Literally, one must be trained in order to live. The day is long past when what you don't know won't hurt you. Ignorance and lack of skill not only will hurt, but may well destroy.

But the world's mechanical and scientific progress has made more necessary than ever before an adequate education in human relations. The whole world is instantly aware of the revolt in far-off Tibet, where once news from that country might have taken weeks to reach Washington. The Prime Minister of Great Britain can be in Moscow on Sunday and in Washington or Ottawa on Tuesday. An African leader is jailed in Nyasaland, and a Japanese prince married in Tokyo. The stories are in our newspapers and the pictures on our television screens within hours, often minutes. The story of the Montgomery bus protest is on the front pages of papers in Stockholm, Rome, and New Delhi as soon as it is printed in Chicago.

In this kind of a world, it is silly to talk about segregating people because of their color, because they wear robes or veils, because they speak French or Swahili, because they are Buddhists or Moslems, or Presbyterians, or because their spiritual leaders are called ministers or priests or rabbis.

Yet, here in the greatest country in the world, in the country which has grown great in the minds and hearts of mankind everywhere because it has been built on the guarantee of equality and individual liberty, we are engaged in degrading debate on whether American children, regardless of race, shall be educated together in our public schools.

Our highest court has held that they shall be so educated in accordance with the equal protection clause of the 14th amendment to our Constitution. It has said plainly that racial segregation in public schools is unconstitutional and denies to Negro children equality of opportunity in education.

But instead of complying with the Court's opinion and taking advantage of the leeway it had allowed local communities in planning to make beginnings in good faith, several of the States and many localities have refused to obey the ruling. They are defying the Court and tearing up the Constitution.

This resistance is the plan of adults, not of young people. Many of the leaders of the resistance have lived their lives, or are so far along that they cannot, or will not, change. Their world is behind them. They don't understand India any more than Kipling did. They don't know—and don't care—about the differences between Vietnam and Ghana, or between Ecuador and Ethiopia. What is Kenya and where is Leopoldville?

What kinds of people live in these places? What are their colors, their religions, their eating habits? Our segregationists cry, who cares—what do they have to do with the United States?

So, living in their world of yesterday, they fight the uprooting of segregation and inequality which they nurtured in the land of the free. Yesterday it did not matter much to the rest of the world what the Governor of Arkansas did to 9 Negro children, or to 9,000. Today it matters a great deal. When Alabama sentenced a Negro man to death for the robbery of $1.95 the mail flooded into U.S. embassies in every part of the world and mounted to such a volume as to cause the Secretary of State to communicate, formally and officially, with the Governor of Alabama. The Jimmie Wilson case damaged the image of America in the eyes of the world—and the image of America in these delicate and dangerous days must be the concern of every citizen.

It is your concern because this is the world in which you will have to grow up and serve. This is the world in which you will choose a career, marry, rear children, govern and be governed. It is a world in which education will be a tool without which men cannot live and function or know happiness, satisfaction and peace.

For education will give us the knowledge of each other, the mutual respect and dedication to the ideal of liberty and equality which will keep us all free. It has been the fashion to talk in terms of the damage which segregation has done to the Negro children, and to forget the corrosive injury it has done to white youngsters. No more revealing or tragic story has come out of the desegregation campaign than that from the small town of Clay, Ky., where a white girl of 14 declared: "I'd rather grow up to be an idiot than to go to a school with a nigger in it." The segregated system made this girl a useless citizen for the world of 1970 by the time she had barely reached her teens.

That is why it is not merely silly to talk about maintaining segregation in public education; it is well-nigh suicidal. It could lose us the struggle for the hearts of men, be it cold or hot.

So you are here to say by your presence and in your resolutions that you want integrated schools for all American children. You have every right to say this to your Government and to all among the citizenry who will listen. No one has a better right, for in so speaking, you are demanding only that the high pronouncements and glorious traditions of this beloved bastion of freedom be vindicated, and that we be about the business of building the kind of world in which your generation can preserve freedom.

Congressional Record, as cited, p. 8696.

[d]

MARTIN LUTHER KING, JR.'S SPEECH

As I stand here and look out upon the thousands of Negro faces and the thousands of white faces, intermingled like the waters of a river, I see only one face—the face of the future.

Yes, as I gaze upon this great historic assembly, this unprecedented gathering of young people, I cannot help thinking—that a hundred years from now the historians will be calling this not the "beat" generation, but the generation of integration.

The fact that thousands of you came here to Washington and that thousands more signed your petition proves that this generation will not take "No" for an answer—will not take double talk for an answer—will not take gradualism for an answer. It proves that the only answer you will settle for is—total desegregation and total equality—now.

I know of no words eloquent enough to express the deep meaning, the great power, and the unconquerable spirit back of this inspiringly original, uniquely American march of young people. Nothing like it has ever happened in the history of our Nation. Nothing, that is, except the last youth march. What this march demonstrates to me, above all else, is that you young people, through your own experience, have somehow discovered the central fact of American life—that the extension of democracy for all Americans depends upon complete integration of Negro Americans.

By coming here you have shown yourselves to be highly alert, highly responsible young citizens. And very soon the area of your responsibility will increase, for you will begin to exercise your greatest privilege as an American—the right to vote. Of course, you will have no difficulty exercising this privilege if you are white.

But I wonder if you can understand what it feels like to be a Negro, living in the South, where, by attempting to exercise this right, you may be taking your life in your hands.

The denial of the vote not only deprives the Negro of his constitutional rights—but what is even worse—it degrades him as a human being. And yet, even this degradation, which is only one of many humiliations of everyday life, is losing its ability to degrade. For the southern Negro is learning to transform his degradation into resistance. Nonviolent resistance. And by so doing he is not only achieving his dignity as a human being, he is helping to advance democracy in the South. This is why my colleagues and I in the Southern Leadership Conference are giving our major attention to the campaign to increase the registration of Negro voters in the South to 3 million. Do you realize what would happen in this country if we were to gain 3 million southern Negro votes? We could change the composition of Congress. We could have a Congress far more responsive to the voters' will. We could have all schools integrated—north and south. A new era would open to all Americans. Thus, the Negro, in his struggle to secure his own rights is destined to enlarge democracy for all people, in both a political and a social sense.

Indeed in your great movement to organize a march for integrated schools you have actually accomplished much more. You have awakened on hundreds of campuses throughout the land a new spirit of social inquiry to the benefit of all Americans.

This is really a noble cause. As June approaches, with its graduation ceremonies and speeches, a thought suggests itself. You will hear much about careers, security, and prosperity. I will leave the discussion of such matters to your deans, your principals, and your valedictorians. But I do have a graduation thought to pass along to you. Whatever career you may choose for yourself—doctor, lawyer, teacher—let me propose an avocation to be pursued along with it. Become a dedicated fighter for civil rights. Make it a central part of your life.

It will make you a better doctor, a better lawyer, a better teacher. It will enrich your spirit as nothing else possibly can. It will give you that rare sense of nobility that can only spring from love and selflessly helping your fellow man. Make a career of humanity. Commit yourself to the noble struggle for equal rights. You will make a greater person of yourself, a greater Nation of your country, and a finer world to live in.

Congressional Record, as cited, pp. 8696–97.

[e]

PRESIDENTIAL DELEGATION STATEMENT

Four African-American young people—three female, ranging from seventeen to twenty-six years of age—were seen by a president's assistant for fifteen minutes. He told them President Eisenhower was vacationing in Georgia and shared their concerns. They left at his office this statement:

In the light of the considerations which we discuss below, we respectfully urge that you give consideration to the following proposals, which we feel would enable the Federal Government to place its weight behind the movement for the integration of the schools:

1. The Chief Executive should make an explicit moral as well as legal commitment of the full resources of the Federal Government to the objective of achieving orderly, effective, and speedy integration of the schools.

2. The Chief Executive should place his weight behind the passage of a truly effective civil rights bill in the present session of Congress. As far as school integration is concerned, we believe that the Douglas-Javits-Celler bill is by far the most comprehensive and effective piece of legislation before Congress. It deserves, we feel, the full support of the administration.

The Douglas-Javits-Celler bill is an historic and statesmanlike proposal. It empowers the Federal Government to move into the center of the school picture and to undertake, on a nationwide basis, careful and constructive planning of the Nation's march toward integration. It provides the expert counseling, the financial aid, and the legal authority necessary to achieve this end.

The several admirable features of the bills introduced on behalf of the administration likewise merit vigorous support, especially those adding to the protection of the right to vote.

3. The Chief Executive should call a White House conference of youth and

student leaders, chosen from national and regional organizations, both North and South, to discuss ways in which youth may participate in the implementation of the Supreme Court decision.

4. The Chief Executive should intervene in the case of Asbury Howard, Jr., the 18-year-old Negro youth from Bessemer, Ala., who has been sentenced to the chain gang for 1 year for coming to the defense of his father when the latter was attacked by a mob. Cases such as this must be brought to the attention of the Nation and of the State authorities if a wrong is to be redressed and justice done.

We make these recommendations in the light of the following urgent considerations:

1. Nearly 5 years have elapsed since the Supreme Court ruled that in the field of education "separate but equal" has no place. But today only some 800 of 2,890 biracial school districts in Southern and border States have begun desegregation even on a token basis. In five States, there has been no desegregation in public education. In the past 3 years, the number of districts instituting new desegregation plans has shrunk to a mere handful.

2. This situation is not acceptable to the youth and the students of the United States. For us, the youth, the question of school integration is the central moral issue of our time. Not only are the rights of minorities at stake; American democracy itself, and the supremacy of our Government, the very survival of the Constitution, are at issue.

We must point out that American youth have made strong and repeated affirmation of their support for the Supreme Court decision and the integration of the schools. Among the most recent demonstrations of this are the following:

(a) In August 1957, when the delegates of over 300 student governments, representing over 1 million students, expressed their belief at the U.S. National Student Association's 10th National Student Congress, that—

Segregation in education by race is incompatible with human equality. It is now also unconstitutional. In the face of ethical concepts, legal requirements, and global ramifications, there can be no justification for delay in the implementation of the Supreme Court decision.

(b) At the National Student Conference of the YMCA and YWCA held last December at the University of Illinois;

(c) At the 1958 convention of the National Federation of Catholic College Students held in San Francisco;

(d) At the 11th National Student Congress last August when delegates from 50 southern campuses expressed their desire for the abolition of segregation;

(e) At the 1958 youth march in Washington, when 10,000 students expressed their moral support for integration.

The petition campaign and youth march for integrated schools, with its 20,000-member march, its quarter of a million signatures, and its nationwide support, has won more support among the young people than any other national campaign or issue in the past 15 years.

3. Concern over the integration of the U.S. schools is not limited to this country. The delegates from the 75 national unions of students outside the Communist bloc, meeting in Lima, Peru, at the International Student Conference this spring, condemned the continued practice of racial segregation in our country. Similar grave concern was expressed at the World Assembly of Youth held in New Delhi last summer.

4. As young Americans, we appreciate the difficulties confronting those who work to implement integration of the schools. We commend the efforts of the courts, the Civil Rights Commission, and members of the administration such as Attorney General Rogers and Secretary Flemming on behalf of integration. Yet, if massive resistance has been defeated in Virginia, it is very much alive in South Carolina, Georgia, Alabama, Mississippi, Louisiana. The leaders of the Deep South do not seek time to accommodate to integration, but to block it altogether. They do not wish to discuss compliance with the law but ways to evade it.

5. The crisis that centers around the integration of the schools is a national question. It affects school systems and national minorities in all parts of our land. It must, we feel, have the fullest attention of the Federal Government if a solution is to be reached, if the Nation is to have the leadership for progress, for the creation of a truer, fuller democracy that it so deeply needs.

Congressional Record, as cited, pp. 8697–98.

75

ON THE THIRD WORLD AND ITS CHALLENGE TO THE GREAT POWERS (1959)

by Mordecai W. Johnson

The Reverend Dr. Johnson, at this time president emeritus of Howard University, spoke before a plenary session of the Atlantic Congress in London on June 6, 1959. The editor has sought to convey the speech's essence in the above title.

Your Lordship, Mr. President, distinguished members of the NATO Congress: I am glad beyond measure to be here and to speak to you on behalf of the Fourth Committee, which has to do with the relationship between the NATO countries, the Atlantic community, and the under-developed peoples.

I suppose one of the reasons why you have been so kindly constrained to invite me is because I am one of those under-developed peoples (Laughter) and you would like to hear about the world from the way it looks down under. I am indeed from among the under-developed peoples; I am the child of a slave. My father was a slave for twenty-five years before the emancipation; my mother was born in slavery; I have lived practically all my life on the territory of former slave States, so when you hear me talk you are dealing with the real under-developed thing.

Yet I have early in my life come into contact with what I conceive to be the noblest and best element in the Western World, namely those Christian educational missionaries who founded the first colleges and universities for Negroes. I am today working in a university founded by them on the basis of principles which are precious to the Western World, for when these men founded Howard University they put it on the cornerstone of the inherent dignity and immeasurable possibilities of the human individual as such, and they enrolled slaves and the children of slaves with their own sons and daughters without hesitation and without fear, being confident that on that campus they would be able to bring them all to maturity, to responsibility and democratic and Christian creativity. I am indebted to those men for the development of my powers, for teaching me how to live freely from the deepest inclinations of my being, and for giving me the power to give my life away freely for causes that I love. So you are not only listening to the child of a slave who can give you authentic words from down under. You give heed at this moment to one who knows the deepest and purest traditions of the Western World, who loves those traditions, who reveres the men who handed them to him, and who loves the community of peoples out of whom they have come.

Now I am very tired. It has been a struggle for me to be able to stay here, but I have a message for you; I have had it in my heart for a long time. But when a man is tired he may speak poorly, when he finds merely that his words are inadequate to say well what he wants to say. Please keep in mind that I speak with the highest esteem for the members of the Atlantic Community, and that whatever I say is intended, as my father used to say when he preached, to stir up your pure minds in order that the cause that is precious to you may come to victory on the highest level.

As I read all the papers that have come into my section, I find that they are all certain that the second phase of the war between the Atlantic Community and the Soviet Union has already begun, and that is the economic phase. I have always looked upon the economic purposes of the

Soviet Union as their primary purposes, so that in my humble judgment we are just now beginning to confront the central and most powerful purposes of the Soviet Union and her allies. In my humble opinion there is no appraisal of what is going to come to us better than can be found in the twenty-fifth chapter of Matthew, in which it says "And at midnight there was a cry made, 'The bridegroom is at hand. Go ye out to meet him'." I have a feeling that the bridegroom of our Western civilization is at hand, and that we are now at the parting of the ways; that when we meet this economic offensive we are going to meet the most powerful opposition of ideas, the most vigorously intelligent handling of the economic and spiritual factors of life in a revolutionary way that any group of people in the world has faced, and we are going either to adjust ourselves to meet that onslaught of idea-power and economic organizational power with a vigorous readjustment of our lives, or we are going down and possibly lose any power to control the trend of history for years to come. But if we do meet it boldly, realizing from the beginning that it will involve the use of all of our powers to the maximum extent, we may be able to pursue a course of action which will not only lead to victory but which will lift our democratic life to a higher level of functioning than we have ever known before, and give us a radiant power over the lives and affections of men around this world, such as we have not had in five hundred years.

Now if this is going to happen to us, I think we need to do two things that are somewhat uncongenial to us. We have to go back and make a re-estimate of our enemy, and we have got to acquire some humility in the appraisal of ourselves. Up to this time we have been looking at the military side of our enemy, his totalitarian organization and his aggressive subversion, and we have been filled with disgust and fear, and we have been facing him primarily with military organization, cohesive and powerful economic organization. We have rather paid little or no attention to the central focus of what he is about in this world. Now we have got to look at that central focus, and if we are wise I think we will not allow our emotions of revulsion to prevent us from appraising him on the level represented by his highest and most intelligent and pure-hearted devotee. It is a great mistake to appraise any movement like the movement represented by the Soviet Union and the Chinese People by continually listing of their faults. God has never yet been able to choose a faultless movement for the projection of His powerful purposes. One pure-hearted man at the head of a thousand men, fifty percent of whom are full of faults, is able by the inspiration of his purity of heart, his moral power, to keep them in cohesive union, to bring to their assistance forces that are primarily selfish in character, and to bring about a change in human affairs that could not be calculated beforehand.

We must try to take a look at the Soviet Union through the eyes of their purest, most devoted and honourable men. When you do that you will see that at the central part of the Communist movement there is a simple and great faith. It is a faith that, with the scientific and technical intelligence which we have at our disposal in the modern world, if we put it in the hands of the right man, the struggle for existence in this world could be overcome in a world-wide way and that poverty, squalor, ignorance, disease and early death could be conquered and the foundation laid for a great society in which culture would be available to all human beings.

These men believe this with a passion that is not exceeded by any movement in the world except early Christianity. They are all responding to it every day and every hour with an enthusiasm which is nothing short of remarkable. On the ground of Russia and the Chinese soil they are making achievements of one kind or another which have astonished us, and they are preaching it now around the world with an evangelistic enthusiasm that is immense. This message that they have is very fittingly addressed to the under-developed peoples of the world of whom there are one billion, two hundred million, all of whom have a scale of living which is under a hundred dollars per capita per year, all of whom are living in a primarily agricultural civilization, and a very poor type of agriculture at that, all of whom are living in countries in which there is very little industry to supplement agriculture, all of whom are impoverished in the field of scientific and technical intelligence, and to most of whom it makes no difference how much money you would give them, they would have no governmental personnel prepared to make a wise and well coordinated use of scientific and technical plans and projections.

The Soviet Union is saying to these people, "Here we come to you from among those who, like yourself, have suffered. We have come not to make you strong and powerful so that you could dominate, exploit and humiliate your fellows, we have come to show you how to treble and quadruple your agricultural production, to supplement your agriculture with the industries which we will show you how to establish, to lend you scientific and technical personnel, to sit down and talk with you about plans for the further development of your country, to lend you money at rates so low that you will see in an unequivocally clear manner that we are not trying to make a profit on you, and we are prepared to devote ourselves to this task for months and years solely because we believe that there is in you the power to conquer the struggle for existence in your country, and we want to have the joy of seeing you do that."

If we do not see that in them we shall have no power to deal with them because it is there. It is there. In pursuit of that purpose they are prepared to enter into a pure-hearted relationship with the people of Asia and Africa. Now, what do I mean by that? In spite of the fact that they do not have any metaphysics akin to our religion, they have something that is very important, they have radical, universal ethics in their relationship to the black and brown and yellow peoples of the world. They have said in their literature—do not misunderstand this—"We take our position quite contrary to the Second International. We are not out to organize the white working people in the world. We are out to organize the working people of the world, and we say it to all of our workers everywhere, in Africa, in Asia and in the homelands of the colonial powers. 'Make solidarity with workers. Pay no attention to their national origin. We want to unite the workers of the world for a great society in which the struggle for existence is conquered and all are led to a new freedom on the basis of that conquest.'"

Now they stand on a territory that constitutes one-fourth of the landed areas of this world. They have one-third of the population of this world, and they have now established themselves in a place where they know that we no longer have the military power to dislodge them. 800,000,000 of these 1,000,000,000 (1 billion 200 million) people that are under-developed are on the border of the Soviet Union and of China, so close that they have to cross no water to reach them, they can also touch their hands any time of day, and they can speak to them without a long-distance telephone.

But all these 800 million people are black and brown and yellow Asiatics who in times past have suffered at the hands of the peoples whom we represent, and who have some fear of us. They look at what the Soviet Union and the Chinese people have done by their faith, with admiration, and they are proud to believe that if they could have the right kind of relationship with any group of people in this world they themselves could do that.

We are up against an immense antagonist. How many of these people does he have to win? Why, if he won India alone he would all but tip the scales of the majority population of the human race, and in a few months after that might turn the tables on us and put us in the minority of the world. We are up against a great antagonist with a great passion, with an immense achievement as a result of that passion, and with a profound faith that he is getting ready to turn the corner which leads to our graveyard. No, which leads to the graveyard and to the grave which we are digging for ourselves. He believes that.

Now let us take a look at ourselves. I said the next thing we have got to do is to acquire some humility in the appraisal of ourselves. We are going to enter this contest with a great handicap. We speak of ourselves in a highly complimentary fashion as the free peoples of the world. Indeed we are, and the one who is speaking knows how true that is, for in our domestic institutions we are the freest and most flexibly organized people in the world. We are most sensitive to the will of the people, and we have developed parliamentary institutions which are precious to the whole of the human race and which we rightly want to preserve. But it takes a great man like Toynbee to tell us that in the relationship with the people of Asia and Africa this is not so of us; that for 500 years we have been aggressors against them, we have attacked and conquered nearly all of them, we have exploited their natural resources in a manner which they consider to have been unjust, and we have often segregated and humiliated them on the land of their fathers and in the presence of the graves of their mothers. They remember these things, and in this hour when they are called upon to choose between us and the Soviet Union there is in their hearts a fear of us which they cannot easily eradicate.

In the second place we are still wounded, we are divided in our minds today by moral habits which have descended from the colonial system which we have not yet been able to overcome. We present an equivocal picture in what we are doing now. The under-developed peoples of the world have only to look at Africa to see how divided our minds are. On the one hand we see the noble British one by one freeing their peoples from the colonial yoke, freeing them deliberately, supporting them in their freedom, and inviting them in their freedom to come back to your mother country which is now for you no longer an empire but a commonwealth. Every now and then we see the noble French rise with a passionate gesture and say to their peoples, "Are we holding you? Then be free," and then under their breath they say in prayer, "But do come back. We want you to be with us." The other day we saw a declaration from the Belgians saying, "This pathway of freedom is what we intend to pursue. Our plans are in the making and will be ready." But you look at Africa, it is magnificent to see that some 70 million of the peoples have been freed under these circumstances by members of this organization. But there are 110 millions of Africans who are neither free nor under mandate, still dominated politically, still having their natural resources exploited, not for their good but for the good of those who exploit. We see on the shores of Africa instances of the most deliberate and cruel segregation on the land of their fathers and in the presence of the graves of their mothers. Nobody can look at Africa without knowing that we are divided in our minds and that we have not yet been able to summon either the political power or the moral power to overcome that division. Though the God of our fathers has vetoed the colonial system and closed the open gates of the world against it, we are still reluctant to turn it loose, and we may yet shame ourselves by admitting one more venture to reopen those gates.

May I say to you again, we have as yet been able to put no great world-encircling concept in the place of the colonial system to which we have been devoted for some 500 years and which is now fallen. What greater idea do we have now of a world encircling nature that we can offer these under-developed peoples of Asia and Africa, of which they can be members as we, in which they can be respected just as we, they can move freely out of their own spontaneous enthusiasm just as we? I suggest to you that we do not yet have one. There are no great words coming from us today regarding that city that hath foundations that was made for the whole human race of one blood; and because we do not have it we are in some difficulty in approaching these Asiatics and Africans.

I have sat often in these meetings when we talk about what we want to do for them economically, and I have sat for a whole hour and heard us talk tactics, heard us talk self-interest, heard us saying that we must do these things in order to protect ourselves without one world of pure-hearted love for these people, without one single intimation that we are moved by a sense of obligation to do these things for them because it is a great thing to be in a position to create freedom in this world.

When those early white men came to the place where I was to be educated they came to ask nothing, nothing. They looked at me when my trousers were not pressed, and my face was not clean, and said, "Mr. Johnson, will you read?" They knew I was no mister but they knew what I could be, and they came there for only one purpose, for the joy that was set before them in making a man out of me and turning me loose in the world. I tell you that one of the great, great differences in our preparations is that we seem to have lost the power to speak to these Asiatics and Africans that way; and so our program of economic helpfulness is an adjunct and a servant of our military activities. We talk about it that way in our congresses and parliaments. We say to our people, "Why are we asking you for 3 billion dollars, why? Because we have got to have it to defend ourselves, to take care of our self-interest." If we ask for a little more money in addition to that, attached hereto, we say, "Of course, we cannot give all of our money for that purpose, we have got to have a benevolent margin which we give away simply because they need it." I will tell you that up until this date the greater portion of all that we are now devoting to the people of Africa and Asia in the field of economic help, even as an adjunct and accessory to the military, is in the field of benevolence that is not beyond condescension. There is as yet no substantial sum of money, and no substantial program developed for them purely out of the motive to make them free from the struggle of existence and to give them a chance to be men.

Let me say again—I told you you must watch me and bear with me—only those who love greatly can talk this way. I say to you that as I look at this great economic program it seems to me to be on the periphery of our interest, almost an afterthought, it has never sat in the chair directly in front of us and grasped the central focus of our hearts. We have a great military program, which represents the greatest power of provision planning and coordination that we are capable of. In the Marshall Plan and other great projects we have had great programs of development protective of and stimulative of each other, which is one cause for admiration among men. But our program of economic helpfulness is a puny vein and comes into our minds as an after-thought, never having received prolonged thought from us, prolonged affection, and robust attention. Moreover—I am trying to be hard, and my purpose is, as my father used to say, to stir up your pure minds—that program is dependent today too largely upon little droplets of annual appropriations which expire on June 30th, and which no sensible and thoughtful man with great purpose in his heart can make any plans about. I am at a university, and no sooner do I get my appropriation for 1960 than they call me in immediately for 1961 and maybe 1962, and it is awfully hard to plan money in that short range. Sometimes we get money for professors at the end of one year and we cannot use it because it is too late to use it. And yet we are trying to build up the economy of nearly half the human race from little droplets of annual appropriations which expire on June 30th and which permit no planning and give no index that we have any purpose to devote ourselves to this objective in an unequivocal manner beyond one year.

Again, there is no central organization in existence of our making which plans to use and to co-ordinate all the economic powers that we have for this purpose and to see to it that they work. I tell you, Ladies and Gentlemen, we are going into the fight of a determinative lifetime and we are not prepared. We are not prepared. We are not morally prepared. We are not purely prepared in our hearts in their orientation towards the thing that we want to do for these people. We are not committing ourselves to any long-range purpose when we know that it may take years and years to develop the economies of these people. We have no great central organization for talking with them, for listening to their ideas or exchanging ideas with them, for approach in cooperation with them, for applying a fit measure to them.

It is hard for me to say these things to those that I love, but it is so, and it points to a weakness so great that God Himself, who loves you, must weep when He looks at it for fear that, walking so boldly and in such a self-congratulatory manner into the battle of your life-time, you may fail and ruin the thing that He has loved you for from the foundation of the world.

Now if the Chairman will bear with me for a minute, I will say swiftly what I think we have got to do. The first thing we have got to do is not economic, it is religious. The first step that we must take is to put the colonial system behind us in our minds and renew our allegiance to the Christian world-view, regarding the nature of human nature and the possibilities of human nature and the possibilities of a free human society in this world, based on these considerations. The British know what I mean; you great Frenchmen, who pioneered the Illumination, know what I mean; you great Germans, who have meditated upon Socialism long before the idea was born among the Russians, you know what I mean. I mean the thing that Abraham Lincoln meant when he said, "Government of the people, for the people and by the people, dedicated to the proposition that all men are created equal, all men." And he said, "I have never had a political idea in my life that was not based upon this great proposition, and when I read that proposition I not only see the slaves set free but I see the last tyranny lifted from the back of the last man."

The world is in front of our eyes, with just a few hours away from the children of any people on earth. Our missionaries and our scientists tell us that every child in this world who is normal shares with us the essential dignity and higher possibilities of human life that are immeasurable. Now look this world in the face. We are either going to dedicate ourselves to serve that world, on the conviction that all men are created equal, or else we are going to turn our faces away and morally die and deserve to die because, having seen the God that we have seen and turned our faces away, it is better that we had not been born.

The next thing we have got to do, and we shall need the help of God to do it and the help of each other, we have got to give our consent to the veto on the colonial system and turn all the strength of these Atlantic powers to the liquidation of the remaining remnants of the colonial system in Africa. We have got to listen to the cries of these 110 million black Africans who are crying out against political domination, economic exploitation, segregation and humiliation, as if we were listening to the words of our own children, and we have got to say to them, as we have never said, "I tell you, my son, this is Britain that hears you, this is France that hears you, this is Belgium that hears you, this is Portugal that hears you, this is Germany that hears you, this is your Uncle Samuel that hears you, and I'm coming and I am going to do what you want to be done, so help me God, as if I were performing a great act of expiation before God and making a demonstration before the whole world of the purity of my purposes toward you." We have got that to do, and if we think that it is at all possible for us to influence the people of Asia in the way that we need to influence them without doing this, we mistake human nature and the order of this universe.

In the third place we must accept the moral responsibility towards the people of Asia that is indissolubly connected with the enormous scientific and technical knowledge, organizational resources and constructive powers that we have, and we have got to go to them with a pure heart and say, "We have come to you not to offer you aid for the sake of your military helpfulness, not to hand you economic assistance as people put a halter on a bag of oats before a mule's mouth in order that, while you are eating the oats, we may lead you along the pathway to take up a load which otherwise, of your own free will, you would not take, but to offer men this program purely in order that they may be free in the same sense that we are free, in order that they may conquer the struggle for existence in their territory in the way that we are conquering it, and in order that they may be members with us of that great society which we have in our hearts and which we intend shall cover this world."

We ought in the next place to take this whole business out of the range of benevolence, put it before us not as an accessory to our military program but as the greatest of all programs in itself—listen to me—for which the military program, as big as it is, is only a fence-building and protecting operation, to handle the program in the central focus of our being, to accept it as an obligation not to be done with our cigar money nor with our chewing-gum money nor our cigarette money but to be done, if necessary, with our very blood, because we cannot live in our hearts and see them suffer impoverishment the way they suffer and hold what we have and eat the bread of peace. We must cease to think about little benevolent annual drops of money. We are no mere jugglers of money. We are the greatest producers of scientific and technical intelligence in the world, of the most diversified scientific and technical intelligence; we know more about the multiplication of agricultural products than any group of human beings in the world. We know more about building up great dairy herds and pure milk supplies than any group of people in the world. We know more about lending money, borrowing money, the effective use of money. We know more about trade, and all these things that have to do with the building up of a great economic order.

This thing that I am talking about calls upon us to use all of these things in a co-ordinated fashion to an end which we determine to do or die if we do not do it. If we will do that, we have got to have an organization to do it with. I do not know enough to tell you what organization to use. I can tell you what kind it has got to be. It has got to be akin to this great military organization that spoke to us this morning; it has got to be led by minds that understand economic procedures through and through; it has got to be as diversified as the populations of the earth to which we go; it has got to be a planning organization that can send a team of men into any country and help them in a few days, to discover the natural resources there, the soil there, the possibilities of development there, and come back with a program that they have talked over with the people; and men who after they have got that program know what scientists and technicians to choose, what administrative organizers to choose, and send them there and keep them there until the work is done.

I see we have used up nearly all my time, and I have got to quit reluctantly. This is going to cost you something. It may cost us as much as one-tenth of all the productive power of the western world. It may even come to the place where it costs us the necessity to recoil from our high standard of living substantially in order that the money thus sacrificed may be put into this program—pulling back our standard of living in order that we may lift up the standard of life all over this world, and deserve the gratitude of the men who are looking to us for leadership. I tell you that this is the program for which we were born in the world. It is as if God were standing before us today saying to you, "My sons, this is what I brought you into the world for. Don't be afraid. Go on and do it for me. Nothing that you suffer will be too great. I'll give you the power to bear it, and I will make your name loved and respected and honoured all over this world." If we do it, we will entirely transform the relations that have existed between us and the peoples of Africa and Asia for nearly five hundred years. We will give them hope such as they have never had in all these years, and they will know that it came from us because we loved them. It will infuse our democratic institutions with a new and radiant life and put them upon a higher level than they have ever been in all their lifetime, and it will place us in a position where we can look at the Communists and say to them, "Krushchev, you miscalculated. You thought that we were morally incapable of this, and therefore you had to deceive us. Now let us sit down and talk. What you say you want to do for this world, can't you see that I am doing it? Why can we not do it together? What you say you want to do for the world and you say you cannot do without totalitarian power, do you not see I am doing it with freedom and flexibility and listening to the wish of the people? Turn away from your methods, my son. Come with your brethren in the Christian world who are your brothers indeed, and let us do these things together."

Now you will forgive me, will you not, for taking the Chairman's time, but I had a message for you that was so big that a stone would have burst unless it got it out of its system. Hear me now, for even in these times men like you ought to listen to a stone.

Roy L. Hill, ed., *Rhetoric of Racial Revolt* (Denver: Golden Bell Press, 1964), pp. 245–57; published in full.

76

THE TACTIC OF NON-VIOLENCE AND ITS QUESTIONING (1959)

by Robert F. Williams and Martin Luther King, Jr.

The documents following the 1954 and 1955 *Brown* decisions have shown how little actual desegregation was accomplished in ensuing years. The disappointment was intensified because the decisions evoked great hope and an almost naive belief that Jim Crow was mortally wounded, if not dead.

In fact, beginning in 1952, eleven southern states had adopted various types of legislation aimed at preventing or limiting desegregation. These ranged from abolishing public schools to grants for private education to laws requiring that teachers instruct students of one race only. Thus, as 1957 ended, Alabama, Florida, Georgia, Louisiana, Mississippi, North Carolina, South Carolina, and Texas had *no* pupils in desegregated situations and others had minor proportions in such generally token schools.

Furthermore, not only was there noncompliance with and defiance of the law; there also was, in the late fifties, a report jointly issued by the American Friends Service Committee, the National Council of Churches of Christ, and the Southern Regional Council—quoting a page summary in the *New York Times* (June 15, 1959)—that: "Law and order have deteriorated in the South since the Supreme Court's outlawing of school segregation." The report, noted the *Times*, "pointed to killings, bombings and mob action since 1955"; indeed, there had been "530 specific cases of violence, reprisal and intimidation."

This situation helped provoke expressions questioning or rejecting the non-violence outlook associated with Dr. King. An early expression of this significant development was the challenge offered by Robert F. Williams. An exchange between Williams and King follows:

[a]

CAN NEGROES AFFORD TO BE PACIFISTS?

by Robert F. Williams

Robert Williams and Mabel Williams published a militant paper, the *Crusader*, in Monroe, North Carolina. Robert Williams had been president of the Union County branch of the NAACP. His suspension therefrom because of his views received nationwide attention. Here he explains his position:

In 1954 I was an enlisted man in the United States Marine Corps. As a Negro in an integrated unit that was overwhelmingly white, I shall never forget the evening we were lounging in the recreation room watching television as a news bulletin flashed on the screen. This was the historic Supreme Court decision that segregation in the public schools is unconstitutional. Because of the interracial atmosphere, there was no vocal comment. There was for a while complete silence. I never knew how the Southern white boys felt about this bulletin. Perhaps I never will, but as for myself, my inner emotions must have been approximate to the Negro slaves' when they first heard about the Emancipation Proclamation. Elation took hold of me so strongly that I found it very difficult to refrain from yielding to an urge of jubilation. I learned later that night that other Negroes in my outfit had felt the same surge of elation.

On this momentous night of May 17, 1954, I felt that at last the government was willing to assert itself on behalf of first-class citizenship, even for Negroes. I experienced a sense of loyalty that I had never felt before. I was sure that this was the beginning of a new era of American democracy. At last I felt that I was a part of America and that I belonged. That was what I had always wanted, even as a child.

I returned to civilian life in 1955 and the hope I had for Negro liberation faltered. I had returned to a South that was determined to stay the hand of progress at all costs. Acts of violence and words and deeds of hate and spite rose from every quarter. An attitude prevailed that Negroes had a court decree from the "Communist inspired court," but the local racist had the means to initiate the old law of the social jungle called Dixie. Since the first Negro slaves arrived in America, the white supremacists have relied upon violence as the potent weapon of intimidation to deprive Negroes of their rights. The Southerner is not prone to easy change; therefore the same tactics that proved so successful against Negroes through the years are still being employed today. There is open defiance to law and order throughout the South today. Governor Faubus and the Little Rock campaign was a shining example of the Southern racists' respect for the law of the land and constituted authority.

The State of Virginia is in open defiance of federal authority. States like my native state of North Carolina are submitting to token integration and openly boasting that this is the solution to circumvention of the Supreme Court decisions. The officials of this state brazenly slap themselves on the back for being successful in depriving great numbers of their colored citizens of the rights of first-class citizenship. Yes, after having such great short-lived hope, I have become disillusioned about the prospect of a just, democratic-minded government motivated by politicians with high moral standards enforcing the Fourteenth Amendment without the pressure of expediency.

News Blackout

Since my release from the Marine Corps I could cite many cases of unprovoked violence that have been visited upon my people. Some, like the Emmett Till case, the Asbury Howard case and the Mack Parker incident, have been widely publicized. There are many many many more, occurring daily in the South that never come to the light of the press because of a news blackout sponsored by local racist officials.

Laws serve to deter crime and to protect the weak from the strong in civilized society. When there is a breakdown of law and the right of equal protection by constituted authority, where is the force of deterrent? It is the nature of people to respect law when it is just and strong. Only highly civilized and moral individuals respect the rights of others. The low-mentality bigots of the South have shown a wanton disregard for the well-being and rights of their fellowmen of color, but there is one thing that even the most savage beast respects, and that is force. Soft, polished words whispered into the ears of a brute make him all the more confused and rebellious against a society that is more than he can understand or feel secure in. The Southern brute respects only force. Nonviolence is a very potent weapon when the opponent is civilized, but nonviolence is no match or repellent for a sadist. I have great respect for the pacifist, that is, for the pure pacifist. I think a pure pacifist is one who resents violence against nations as well as individuals and is courageous enough to speak out against jingoistic governments (including his own) without an air of self-righteousness and pious moral individuality. I am not a pacifist and I am sure that I may safely say that most of my people are not. Passive resistance is a powerful weapon in gaining concessions from oppressors, but I venture to say that if Mack Parker had had an automatic shotgun at his disposal, he could have served as a great deterrent against lynching.

"Turn-the-Other-Cheekism"

Rev. Martin Luther King is a great and successful leader of our race. The Montgomery bus boycott was a great victory for American democracy. However, most people have confused the issues facing the race. In Montgomery the issue was a matter of struggle for human dignity. Nonviolence is made to order for that type of conflict. While praising the actions of those courageous Negroes who participated in the Montgomery affair, we must not allow the complete aspects of the Negro struggle throughout the South to be taken out of their proper perspective. In a great many localities in the South Negroes are faced with the necessity of combating savage violence. The struggle is for mere existence. The Negro is in a position of begging for life. There is no lawful deterrent against those who would do him violence. An open declaration of nonviolence, or turn-the-other-cheekism is an invitation that the white racist brutes will certainly honor by brutal attack on cringing, submissive Negroes. It is time for the Negro in the South to reappraise his method of dealing with his ruthless oppressor.

In 1957 the Klan moved into Monroe and Union County. In the beginning we did not notice them much. Their numbers steadily increased to the point wherein the local press reported as many as seventy-five hundred racists massed at one rally. They became so brazen that mile-long motorcades started invading the Negro community. These hooded thugs fired pistols from car windows, screamed, and incessantly blew their automobile horns. On one occasion they caught a Negro woman on the street and tried to force her to dance for them at gun point. She escaped into the night, screaming and hysterical. They forced a Negro merchant to close down his business on direct orders from the Klan. Drivers of cars tried to run Negroes down when seen walking on the streets at night. Negro women were struck with missiles thrown from passing vehicles. Lawlessness was rampant. A Negro doctor was framed to jail on a charge of performing an abortion on a white woman. This doctor, who was vice-president of the N.A.A.C.P., was placed in a lonely cell in the basement of a jail, although men prisoners are usually confined upstairs. A crowd of white men started congregating around the jail. It is common knowledge that a lynching was averted. We have had the usual threats of the Klan here, but instead of cowing, we organized an armed guard and set up a defense force around the doctor's house. On one occasion, we had to exchange gunfire with the Klan. Each time the Klan came on a raid they were led by police cars. We appealed to the President of the United States to have the Justice Department investigate the police. We appealed to Governor Luther Hodges. All our appeals to constituted law were in vain. Governor Hodges, in an underhanded way, defended the Klan. He publicly made a statement, to the press, that I had exaggerated Klan activity in Union County—despite the fact that they were operating openly and had gone so far as to build a Klan clubhouse and advertise meetings in the local press and on the radio.

Cringing Negro Ministers

A group of nonviolent ministers met the city Board of Aldermen and pleaded with them to restrict the Klan from the colored community. The city fathers advised these cringing, begging Negro ministers that the Klan had constitutional rights to meet and organize in the same way as the

N.A.A.C.P. Not having been infected by turn-the-other-cheekism, a group of Negroes who showed a willingness to fight caused the city officials to deprive the Klan of its constitutional rights after local papers told of dangerous incidents between Klansmen and armed Negroes. Klan motorcades have been legally banned from the City of Monroe.

The possibility of tragedy's striking both sides of the tracks has caused a mutual desire to have a peaceful coexistence. The fact that any racial brutality may cause white blood to flow as well as Negro is lessening the racial tension. The white bigots are sparing Negroes from brutal attack, not because of a new sense of morality, but because Negroes have adopted a policy of meeting violence with violence.

The Screams of the Innocent

I think there is enough latitude in the struggle for Negro liberation for the acceptance of diverse tactics and philosophies. There is need for pacifists and nonpacifists. I think each freedom fighter must unselfishly contribute what he has to offer. I have been a soldier and a Marine. I have been trained in the way of violence. I have been trained to defend myself. Self-defense to a Marine is a reflex action. People like Rev. Martin Luther King have been trained for the pulpit. I think they would be as out of place in a conflict that demanded real violent action as I would in a pulpit praying for an indifferent God to come down from Heaven and rescue a screaming Mack Parker or Emmett Till from an ungodly howling mob. I believe if we are going to pray, we ought to pass the ammunition while we pray. If we are too pious to kill in our own self-defense, how can we have the heart to ask a Holy God to come down to this violent fray and smite down our enemies?

As a race, we have been praying for three hundred years. The N.A.A.C.P. boasts that it has fought against lynching for fifty years. A fifty-year fight without victory is not impressive to me. An unwritten anti-lynch law was initiated overnight in Monroe. It is strange that so-called Negro leaders have never stopped to think why a simple thing like an anti-lynch law in a supposedly democratic nation is next to impossible to get passed. Surely every citizen in a republic is entitled not to be lynched. To seek an anti-lynch law in the present situation is to seek charity. Individuals and governments are more inclined to do things that promote the general welfare and well-being of the populace. A prejudiced government and a prejudiced people are not going to throw a shield of protection around the very people in the South on whom they vent pent-up hatreds as scapegoats. When white people in the South start needing such a law, we will not even have to wait fifty days to get it.

Stop Lynching with Violence

On May 5, 1959, while president of the Union County branch of the National Association for the Advancement of Colored People, I made a statement to the United Press International after a trial wherein a white man was supposed to have been tried for kicking a Negro maid down a flight of stairs in a local white hotel. In spite of the fact that there was an eyewitness, the defendant failed to show up for his trial, and was completely exonerated. Another case in the same court involved a white man who had come to a pregnant Negro mother's home and attempted to rape her. In recorder's court the only defense offered for the defendant was that "he's not guilty. He was just drunk and having a little fun." Despite the fact that this pregnant Negro mother was brutally beaten and driven from her home because she refused to submit, and a white woman neighbor testified that the woman had come to her house excited, her clothes torn, her feet bare, and begging her for assistance, the court was unmoved. The defendant's wife was allowed to sit with him throughout the trial, and his attorney asked the jury if they thought this white man would leave "this beautiful white woman, the flower of life for this Negro woman." Some of the jurymen laughed and the defendant went free. This great miscarriage of justice left me sick inside, and I said then what I say now. I believe that Negroes must be willing to defend themselves, their women, their children and their homes. They must be willing to die and to kill in repelling their assailants. There is no Fourteenth Amendment, no equal protection under the law. Negroes *must* protect themselves, it is obvious that the federal government will not put an end to lynching; therefore it becomes necessary for us to stop lynching with violence. We must defend ourselves. Even though I made it known that I spoke as an individual American citizen, I was suspended by the N.A.A.C.P. for advocating violence. The N.A.A.C.P. was so fearful of the consequence of this statement that I heard about my suspension over the radio before I got an official notice. The radio announcer tried to give local Negroes the impression that the N.A.A.C.P. advocated turn-the-other-cheekism. The thing that struck me most was not the suspension, but the number of letters and telegrams I received from Negroes all over America who showed a readiness to fight. The Negro on the street who suffers most is beginning to break out of the harness of the nonviolent race preachers. The fact that the N.A.A.C.P. had to issue a statement saying, "The N.A.A.C.P. has never condoned mob violence but it firmly supports the right of Negroes individually and collectively to defend their person, their homes and their property from attack" is a strong indication of the sentiment among the masses of Negroes. How can an individual defend his person and property from attack without meeting violence with violence? What the N.A.A.C.P. is advocating now is no more than I had advocated in the first place. I could never advocate that Negroes attack white people indiscriminately. Our branch of the N.A.A.C.P. in Union County is an interracial branch.

King Cashes in on War

It is obvious that the Negro leadership is caught in a terrible dilemma. It is trying to appease both white liberals who want to see Negro liberation given to us in eye-dropper doses and the Negro masses, who are growing impatient and restive under brutal oppression. There is a new Negro coming into manhood on the American scene and an indifferent government must take cognizance of this fact. The Negro is becoming more militant, and pacifism will never be accepted wholeheartedly by the masses of Negroes so long as violence is rampant in Dixie. Even Negroes like King who profess to be pacifists are not pure pacifists and at times speak proudly of the Negro's role of violence in this violent nation's wars. In a speech at the N.A.A.C.P. convention, he said, "In spite of all of our oppression, we have never turned to a foreign ideology to solve our problems. Communism has never invaded our ranks. And now we are simply saying we want our freedom, we have stood with you in every crisis. For you, America, our sons died in the trenches of France, in the foxholes of Germany, on the beachheads of Italy and on the islands of Japan. And now, America, we are simply asking you to guarantee our freedom." King may not be willing to partake in expeditions of violence, but he has no compunction about cashing in on the spoils of war. There are too many Negro leaders who are afraid to talk violence against the violent racist and are too weak-kneed to protest the warmongering of the atom-crazed politicians of Washington.

Some Negro leaders have cautioned me that if Negroes fight back, the racist will have cause to exterminate the race. How asinine can one get?

This government is in no position to allow mass violence to erupt, let alone allow twenty million Negroes to be exterminated. I am not half so worried about being exterminated as I am about my children's growing up under oppression and being mentally twisted out of human proportions.

We live in perilous times in America, and especially in the South. Segregation is an expensive commodity, but liberty and democracy too, have their price. So often the purchase check of democracy must be signed in blood. Someone must be willing to pay the price, despite the scoffs from the Uncle Toms. I am told that patience is commendable and that we must never tire of waiting, yet it is instilled at an early age that men who violently and swiftly rise to oppose tyranny are virtuous examples to emulate. I have been taught by my government to fight, and if I find it necessary I shall do just that. All Negroes must learn to fight back, for nowhere in the annals of history does the record show a people delivered from bondage by patience alone.

Liberation, September 1959, pp. 4–7.

[b]

THE SOCIAL ORGANIZATION OF NON-VIOLENCE

by Martin Luther King, Jr.

Note here Dr. King's concluding sentences where he enunciates his abhorrence of war and of its advocacy as well as his denunciation of nuclear weaponry. This was to be a growing feature of his ensuing activity.

Paradoxically, the struggle for civil rights has reached a stage of profound crisis, although its outward aspect is distinctly less turbulent and victories of token integration have been won in the hard-resistance areas of Virginia and Arkansas.

The crisis has its origin in a decision rendered by the Supreme Court more than a year ago, which upheld the pupil placement law. Though little noticed then, this decision fundamentally weakened the historic 1954 ruling of the Court. It is imperceptibly becoming the basis of a *de facto* compromise between the powerful contending forces.

The 1954 decision required for effective implementation resolute Federal action supported by mass action to undergird all necessary changes. It is obvious that Federal action by the legislative and executive branches was half-hearted and inadequate. The activity of Negro forces, while heroic in some instances, and impressive in other sporadic situations, lacked consistency and militancy sufficient to fill the void left by government default. The segregationists were swift to seize these advantages, and unrestrained by moral or social conscience, defied the law boldly and brazenly.

The net effect of this social equation has led to the present situation, which is without clear-cut victory for either side. Token integration is a developing pattern. This type of integration is merely an affirmation of a principle without the substance of change.

It is, like the Supreme Court decision, a pronouncement of justice, but by itself does not insure that the millions of Negro children will be educated in conditions of equality. This is not to say that it is without value. It has substantial importance. However, it fundamentally changes the outlook of the whole movement, for it raises the prospect of long, slow change without a predictable end. As we have seen in Northern cities, token integration has become a pattern in many communities and remained frozen, even though environmental attitudes are substantially less hostile to full integration than in the South.

This then is the danger. Full integration can easily become a distant or mythical goal—major integration may be long postponed, and in the quest for social calm a compromise firmly implanted in which the real goals are merely token integration for a long period to come.

The Negro was the tragic victim of another compromise in 1877, when his full equality was bargained away by the Federal Government and a condition somewhat above slave status but short of genuine citizenship became his social and political existence for nearly a century.

There is reason to believe that the Negro of 1959 will not accept supinely any such compromises in the contemporary struggle for integration. His struggle will continue, but the obstacles will determine its specific nature. It is axiomatic in social life that the imposition of frustrations leads to two kinds of reactions. One is the development of a wholesome social organization to resist with effective, firm measures any efforts to impede progress. The other is a confused, anger-motivated drive to strike back violently, to inflict damage. Primarily, it seeks to cause injury to retaliate for wrongful suffering. Secondarily, it seeks real progress. It is punitive—not radical or constructive.

The current calls for violence have their roots in this latter tendency. Here one must be clear that there are three different views on the subject of violence. One is the approach of pure nonviolence, which cannot readily or easily attract large masses, for it requires extraordinary discipline and courage. The second is violence exercised in self-defense, which all societies from the most primitive to the most cultured and civilized, accept as moral and legal. The principle of self-defense, even involving weapons and bloodshed, has never been condemned, even by Gandhi, who sanctioned it for those unable to master pure nonviolence. The third is the advocacy of violence as a tool of advancement, organized as in warfare, deliberately and consciously. To this tendency many Negroes are being tempted today. There are incalculable perils in this approach. It is not the danger or sacrifice of physical being which is primary, though it cannot be contemplated without a sense of deep concern for human life. The greatest danger is that it will fail to attract Negroes to a real collective struggle, and will confuse the large uncommitted middle group, which as yet has not supported either side. Further, it will mislead Negroes into the belief that this is the only path and place them as a minority in a position where they confront a far larger adversary than it is possible to defeat in this form of combat. When the Negro uses force in self-defense he does not forfeit support—he may even win it, by the courage and self-respect it reflects. When he seeks to initiate violence he provokes questions about the necessity for it, and inevitably is blamed for its consequences. It is unfortunately true that however the Negro acts, his struggle will not be free of violence initiated by his enemies, and he will need ample courage and willingness to sacrifice to defeat this manifestation of violence. But if he seeks it and organizes it, he cannot win. Does this leave the Negro without a positive method to advance? Mr. Robert Williams would have us believe that there is no collective and practical alternative. He argues that we must be cringing and submissive or take up arms. To so place the issue distorts the whole problem. There are other meaningful alternatives.

The Negro people can organize socially to initiate many forms of struggle which can drive their enemies back without resort to futile and harmful violence. In the history of the movement for racial advancement, many creative forms have been developed—the mass boycott, sitdown protests and strikes, sit-ins—refusal to pay fines and bail for unjust arrests—mass marches—mass meetings—prayer pilgrimages, etc. Indeed, in Mr. Williams' own community of Monroe, North Carolina, a striking example of collective community action won a significant victory without use of arms or threats of violence. When the police incarcerated a Negro doctor unjustly, the aroused people of Monroe marched to the police station, crowded into its halls and corridors, and refused to leave until their colleague was released. Unable to arrest everyone, the authorities released the doctor and neither side attempted to unleash violence. This experience was related by the doctor who was the intended victim.

There is more power in socially organized masses on the march than there is in guns in the hands of a few desperate men. Our enemies would prefer to deal with a small armed group rather than with a huge, unarmed but resolute mass of people. However, it is necessary that the mass-action method be persistent and unyielding. Gandhi said the Indian people must "never let them rest," referring to the British. He urged them to keep protesting daily and weekly, in a variety of ways. This method inspired and organized the Indian masses and disorganized and demobilized the British. It educates its myriad participants, socially and morally. All history teaches us that like a turbulent ocean beating great cliffs into fragments of rock, the determined movement of people incessantly demanding their rights always disintegrates the old order.

It is this form of struggle—non-cooperation with evil through mass actions—"never letting them rest"—which offers the more effective road for those who have been tempted and goaded to violence. It needs the bold and the brave because it is not free of danger. It faces the vicious and evil enemies squarely. It requires dedicated people, because it is a backbreaking task to arouse, to organize, and to educate tens of thousands for disciplined, sustained action. From this form of struggle more emerges that is permanent and damaging to the enemy than from a few acts of organized violence.

Our present urgent necessity is to cease our internal fighting and turn outward to the enemy, using every form of mass action yet known—create new forms—and resolve never to let them rest. This is the social lever which will force open the door to freedom. Our powerful weapons are the voices, the feet, and the bodies of dedicated, united people, moving without rest toward a just goal. Greater tyrants than Southern segregationists have been subdued and defeated by this form of struggle. We have not yet used it, and it would be tragic if we spurn it because we have failed to perceive its dynamic strength and power.

To set the record straight on any implications that I am inconsistent in my struggle against war and too weak-kneed to protest nuclear war, may I state that repeatedly, in public addresses and in my writings, I have unequivocally declared my hatred for this most colossal of all evils and I have condemned any organizer of war, regardless of his rank and nationality. I have signed numerous statements with other Americans condemning nuclear testing and have authorized publication of my name in advertisements appearing in the largest circulation newspapers in the country, without concern that it was then "unpopular" to so speak out.

Liberation October 1959; see Robert F. Williams, *Negroes Without Guns* (New York: Marzani and Munsell, 1962), pp. 11–15. See Don Shoemaker, ed., *With All Deliberate Speed* (New York: Harper and Bros., 1957), especially tables on pp. 225–26. For analysis, see Albert Blaustein and C. C. Ferguson, *Desegregation and the Law* (New Brunswick, N.J.: Rutgers University Press, 1957).

POSTSCRIPT

Rarely has history's periodization seemed so logical as in this instance, with the 1960s looming. That decade marks an intensification of the black liberation effort, a growth of nationalism, and yet the persistence of black-white unity.

The final volume of this documentation of the history of the African-American people, now being prepared, will end with the killing of Martin Luther King, Jr. The person symbolizing that people's striving may be murdered, but its essence—seeking "freedom over me"—is immortal.

Index

503

Free Catalog!
Books of African-American Interest
From Carol Publishing Group

Thank you for buying this book!

Carol Publishing Group proudly publishes dozens of books of African-American interest. From history to contemporary issues facing Black Americans and popular culture, these books take a compelling look at the African-American experience.

Selected titles include: • **The African Cookbook: Menus and Recipes From Eleven African Countries and the Island of Zanzibar** • **African Names: Names From the African Continent for Children and Adults** • **Afro-American History: The Modern Era** • **The Autobiography of Jack Johnson: In the Ring, and Out** • **Black Hollywood: The Black Performer in Motion Pictures, Volumes One & Two** • **Black is the Color of My TV Tube** • **The Black 100: A Ranking of the Most Influential African-Americans, Past and Present** • **Black Robes, White Justice: Why Our Legal System Doesn't Work for Blacks** • **Break It Down: The Inside Story From the New Leaders of Rap** • **Call Her Miss Ross: The Unauthorized Biography of Diana Ross** • **Caroling Dusk: An Anthology of Verse by Black Poets** • **Clotel: Or, the President's Daughter** • **A Documentary History of the Negro People in the United States, Volumes One through Six** • **Good Morning Revolution: Selected Poetry and Prose of Langston Hughes** • **Harriet Tubman: The Moses of Her People** • **Introduction to African Civilizations** • **Langston Hughes: Before and Beyond Harlem** • **Life & Times of Frederick Douglass** • **Lyrics of Lowly Life: The Poetry of Paul Laurence Dunbar** • **Man, God and Civilization** • **Michael Jackson: The Magic and the Madness** • **Muhammad Ali: A View From the Corner** • **Negro in the South** • **The Negro Novelist: 1940-1950** • **Negrophobia: An Urban Parable** • **Negro Slave Songs in the United States** • **Paul Robeson Speaks: Writings, Speeches and Interviews 1918-1974** • **Prisoners of Our Past: A Critical Look at Self-Defeating Attitudes Within the Black Community** • **Racism and Psychiatry** • **Repeal of the Blues: How Black Entertainers Influenced Civil Rights** • **Thurgood Marshall: Warrior at the Bar, Rebel on the Bench** • **To Be Free: A Volume of Studies in Afro-American History** • **Up From Slavery** • **The Way it Was in the South: The Black Experience in Georgia** • **What Color Is Your God?: Black Consciousness and the Christian Faith** • **The Whole World in His Hands: A Pictorial Biography of Paul Robeson** • **Why Black People Tend to Shout: Cold Facts and Wry Views from a Black Man's World** • **Work, Sister, Work: How Black Women Can Get Ahead in the Workplace** • **Zulu Fireside Tales**

Ask for these African-American Interest books at your bookstore. Or for a free descriptive brochure, call 1-800-447-BOOK or send your name and address to Carol Publishing Group, 120 Enterprise Ave., Dept. 1431, Secaucus, NJ 07094.